Felix Schürmann
The Grey Undercurrent

Felix Schürmann

The Grey Undercurrent

Whalers and Littoral Societies at the Deep
Beaches of Africa (1770–1920)

Translated by
Joe Paul Kroll

DE GRUYTER
OLDENBOURG

First published in German © Campus Verlag GmbH, Felix Schürmann, Der graue Unterstrom. Walfänger und Küstengesellschaften an den tiefen Stränden Afrikas (1770–1920), Frankfurt am Main 2017.

The translation of this work was funded by Geisteswissenschaften International – Translation Funding for Work in the Humanities and Social Sciences from Germany, a joint initiative of the Fritz Thyssen Foundation, the German Federal Foreign Office, the collecting society VG WORT and the Börsenverein des Deutschen Buchhandels (German Publishers & Booksellers Association).

Despite careful production of our books, sometimes mistakes happen. Unfortunately, the funding information for the translation was not included in the original publication. This has been corrected. We apologize for the mistake.

ISBN 978-3-11-162173-9
e-ISBN (PDF) 978-3-11-075991-4
e-ISBN (EPUB) 978-3-11-076007-1

Library of Congress Control Number: 2022948716

Bibliographic information published by the Deutsche Nationalbibliothek
The Deutsche Nationalbibliothek lists this publication in the Deutsche Nationalbibliografie; detailed bibliographic data are available on the internet at http://dnb.dnb.de.

© 2024 Walter de Gruyter GmbH, Berlin/Boston
This volume is text- and page-identical with the hardback published in 2023.
Cover image: Clifford Warren Ashley, Whaler and Bumboats at Brava (1907), New Bedford Whaling Museum, Catalog No. 2013.43. The painting shows a bustling harbor scene at Brava, Cape Verde Islands, with local vendors plying their trades alongside an anchored whale ship.
Typesetting: Integra Software Services Pvt. Ltd.

www.degruyter.com

Acknowledgments to the First edition

The present study, shortened here for publication, was accepted by the Faculty of Philosophy and History of Goethe University Frankfurt in 2015 as a dissertation for the degree of Doctor of Philosophy. In the approximately five years during which it came into being, so many people offered support, inspiration and encouragement that it is barely possible to name them all. My gratitude is due above all to the unflagging patience and good will of my doctoral adviser Andreas Fahrmeir, who was always willing to offer expert advice even at short notice. I am no less thankful to Benjamin Steiner, who, over the course of many conversations, never failed to provide me with advice and criticism, all the while urging me to press ahead.

The research centre "Normative Orders" at Goethe University Frankfurt generously funded the writing of this study with a research scholarship and by offering many other kinds of support, not least that of productive research environment. My research was also supported by the Association of Friends and Benefactors of Goethe University and by the German Historical Institute in Washington, DC. The long final stages of completing the manuscript were made possible by a scholarship from the Leibniz Institute of European History in Mainz. The LOEWE research cluster "Animals – Humans – Society" at the University of Kassel offered an inspiring and friendly setting in which to complete this study in addition to enabling its original publication. My thanks go to Andreas Eckert, Sebastian Conrad and Margit Pernau for adopting the German edition of this book as part of the *Globalgeschichte* series, published by Campus Verlag. I am also grateful to the "International History" working group in the Association of German Historians (VHD) and to Goethe University Frankfurt for the awarding prizes to this study.

Many other people had a part to play in bringing this project to fruition. I would very much like to thank Helmut Bley, Kirsten Rüther and Inga-Dorothee Rost for awakening my interest in African history; Brigitte Reinwald for encouraging me to pursue this subject; Parfait Bokohonsi, Ulrike Hamann, Tina Kramer, Ronja Metzger, Stefanie Michels and Esther Ries for an ongoing discussion of our projects that was never less than stimulating; Bernhard Gißibl for "grey"; Judith Lund for sharing her research data and the late Klaus Barthelmeß for sharing his contacts; Laura Peireira, Ben Simons and many more librarians and archivists for their helpfulness; Nancy Cole for helping me find my way around Massachusetts; Hartmut Bergenthum and the librarians working with the DFG special collection on sub-Saharan Africa at Frankfurt University Library for the exemplary speed and skill with which they kept me supplied with reading matter; Geert Castryck, Philippe Kersting, Gabriel Klaeger, Winfried Speitkamp, Glen Thompson, Constantin Wagner, Annika Wellmann and Stephanie Zehnle for the opportunity to present and discuss parts of this study in conferences, colloquiums and workshops;

Daniel Hausmann, for always finding something in need of improvement; Simon Benecken for reading through parts of the manuscript even though he had no time to do so; Caroline Authaler for urging me towards greater clarity; Pablo Rodriguez for helping me with Spanish texts; Pedro Marcelinho for showing me Cape Verde; Antje Schürmann for moral support and the use of her hard drive; Johanna Wurz for applying the final polish; and Dale Chatwin, Dag Henrichsen, Frances Ruley Karttunen, Helmut Kersten, Jill Kinahan, Daniel Lange, Susan Lebo, Ana Roque, Gunter von Schumann and Abdul Sheriff for a wealth of useful hints and information.

My special thanks go to my parents, Bettina and Klaus Schürmann, who have consistently supported me with love, patience and trust as I followed my path. It is to them I dedicate this book.

Frankfurt, February 2017
Felix Schürmann

Acknowledgments to the English edition

This book is the English translation of *Der graue Unterstrom: Walfänger und Küstengesellschaften an den tiefen Stränden Afrikas, 1770–1920*, published by Campus (Frankfurt am Main) in 2017. I have added a few additional references to secondary literature that has come out after 2017, but apart from that left the original text with only minor changes. Publishing an English translation for a broader international audience would not have been possible without the help of many people and institutions. It is a great pleasure for me to thank Joe Paul Kroll for producing an excellent translation with immense care for detail. The generous prize "Geisteswissenschaften international", jointly awarded by the Fritz Thyssen Foundation, the VG Wort, the Börsenverein des Deutschen Buchhandels (German Publishers and Booksellers Association), and the German Federal Foreign Office, made the translation possible. Annette Prassel at Campus provided valuable assistance in the funding process. During the editorial process I could rely on the support of Josefa Cassimo and Dominic Keyßner. Finally, I thank the editors at De Gruyter, Jana Fritsche and Rabea Rittgerodt, for kindly accepting the book for their program and supporting me during different stages of the publishing process.

Frankfurt, October 2022
Felix Schürmann

Contents

Introduction: Outward bound — 3

Passages I: Hunting whales off the coast of Africa — 38

1 From whaling ground to trading port: Walvis Bay, 1780–1860 — 65

2 Discord magnified: Delagoa Bay, 1780–1845 — 117

Passages II: Experiencing the world aboard a whaler — 156

3 A stabilising flow of goods: Saint Augustin, Madagascar, 1830–1860 — 211

4 Provisioning as a power resource: Mutsamudu, Anjouan, 1835–1890 — 239

5 Promise and endeavour: Port Louis, Mauritius, 1789–1878 — 279

Passages III: Going ashore — 324

6 Under the sign of abolition: Cabinda, 1850–1855 — 362

7 The emergence of a west African whaling community: San Antonio, Annobón, 1825–1950 — 399

8 Whaleships into migration vehicles: Furna, Brava, 1770–1920 — 443

Conclusion: Homeward bound — 503

Archival Sources — 509

Published Sources — 519

References — 529

Vessels Index — 557

Places Index — 563

Introduction: Outward bound

Soon after nightfall on 19 August 1727 four men attacked Charles Rambouillet, an officer of the venerable First Regiment of Foot Guards who was out walking in one of London's wealthiest districts. Having taken his wallet, watch, cane, hat and a ring, and leaving him badly hurt, Rambouillet's assailants vanished unrecognised into the night.[1] Rambouillet's mugging was one of a string of crimes encouraged by the fact that London was among Europe's darkest cities. One resident, the writer Daniel Defoe, complained in 1729 that "London, that used to be the most safe and peaceful city in the universe, is now become a scene of rapine and danger". Defoe demanded that the streets of London be brightly illuminated at night in order to make life in the city after dusk as safe as it was after dawn.[2]

At the time of Defoe's death in 1731 the state of London's street lights had barely improved, with no more than approximately one thousand municipal lights in the whole city. Though London – alongside Ayutthaya, Edo, Constantinople and Paris – was one of the world's largest cities, in a sense it comprised two completely different places – "one by day and another by night", as the historian Eric Dolin put it.[3] Yet by the early 1740s – when Charles Rambouillet, having survived his ordeal, was looking forward to retirement – London was considered probably the best illuminated cities in the world. In the space of only a few years the authorities had erected no fewer than five thousand oil lamps, to which were added another ten thousand in the 1760s and 1770s. By 1780, the Oxford Road alone could boast more street lamps than all of Paris, where street lighting had begun a hundred years earlier. Illuminating London brought about a marked decline in nocturnal crime and set an example for the country as a whole, with thousands of street lamps put up in Birmingham, Hull and elsewhere.[4]

England's streets were at first illuminated chiefly by rapeseed oil. In the latter part of the eighteenth century, however, whale oil and spermaceti became the fuels of choice instead. Whale oil, which was obtained from the blubber of

---

1 *The London Gazette*, 22.08.1727, 8.
2 Defoe, *Second Thoughts are Best*, 10.
3 Dolin, *Leviathan*, 105.
4 Beer, "The Early History of London Street-Lighting", 322f.; Falkus, "The Early Development of the British Gas Industry", 218f; Falkus, "Lighting in the Dark Ages of English Economic History", 248f.; Graham, "The Migrations of the Nantucket Whale Fishery", 179–181; Notes and Queries, 12; O'Dea, *The Social History of Lighting*, 97; Schivelbusch, "The Policing of Street Lighting", 62f.; Stackpole, *Whales & Destiny*, 18f.

https://doi.org/10.1515/9783110759914-001

whales, burned more brightly than rapeseed oil and came with the added benefit of not producing soot. Spermaceti, a waxy liquid found in the "case" (forehead) and "junk" (the "melon" or nose) of the sperm whale, was considered a particularly valuable fuel and could be used in lamps as well as being turned into candles.[5] In order to encourage production of whale oil – few British vessels were fitted out for whaling in the early eighteenth century – the government doubled its bounty on whalers from twenty to forty shillings per ton in 1750.[6]

Combined with increasing demand, this measure caused a precipitate rise in British whaling from 1753 onwards. Yet demand continued to exceed supply, as Britain's nascent manufacturing industry required whale oil as a lubricant and detergent. At this time most of Britain's whale oil was imported from the North American colonies, especially from Massachusetts, where whalers specialised in the particularly valuable oil of the sperm whale. "The purest sperm oil lubricated the finest machines of the industrial revolution, illuminated the nation's lighthouses and along with spermaceti candles lit the interiors of factories and the better houses", notes the historian Dale Chatwin with regard to the economic significance of sperm whale products.[7] In 1754 the New England colonies exported some 4,000 tuns of whale oil to London alone, rising to 5,000 tuns in 1763 and 8,000 tuns in 1771.[8] Unlike their British counterparts, Massachusetts whalers set sail not for the seas between the Atlantic and Arctic oceans but rather southwards, where whaling vessels had hitherto barely ventured. Charting the hunting grounds of the central and south Atlantic Ocean marked the beginning of the ascent of America's whaling industry, which was to remain the largest in the world for more than a century.

***

As the first London streets went up in lights, in May 1739 slavers in Anomabu, an entrepôt on the coast of modern Ghana, loaded eighty-seven human beings onto the *Charming Susanna*, which had sailed from Rhode Island. Among them was Broteer Furro, a boy from the hinterland barely ten years old for whom the ship's steward, Robertson Mumford, had paid an intermediary four gallons of rum and a piece of cloth. In so doing, Mumford had taken advantage of an ancient

---

[5] Falkus, "Lighting in the Dark Ages of English Economic History", 254, 266; Graham, "The Migrations of the Nantucket Whale Fishery", 180f.; Hohman, *The American Whaleman*, 4.
[6] Jackson, *The British Whaling Trade*, 55f.
[7] Chatwin, "A Trade so Uncontrollably Uncertain", 35.
[8] Francis, *A History of World Whaling*, 55; Graham, "The Migrations of the Nantucket Whale Fishery", 184; Jackson, *The British Whaling Trade*, 55–59, 91.

privilege allowing seamen to run their own little sidelines in the course of trading voyages. These transactions were known as "ventures", and "Venture" was the name Mumford gave to young Broteer Furro, whom he brought to the coast of Connecticut as his domestic servant in August 1739.[9]

Venture was sold on several times in his adult life. Although his work as a slave was by definition unpaid, he undertook other jobs and was able to save enough to buy – as only very few slaves in the American colonies could at the time – his freedom from his master in 1765. Venture adopted the surname Smith and moved to Long Island, where he earned enough money to buy the freedom of his wife and three children. For several years he cut timber by day and caught fish by night, occasionally also finding time to sell watermelons to seamen.[10]

In 1770 Venture signed aboard a whaler. Aware of the growing demand for whale oil, the last of his owners, Oliver Smith, a merchant and shipbuilder from Stonington, Connecticut had put together a crew of some twenty African and Native American workers and arranged for their hire by a Nantucket shipowner, William Rotch, who fitted out whaling vessels for Atlantic voyages.[11] "After being out seven months", Venture Smith later recalled, "the vessel returned, laden with four hundred barrels of oil."[12] This was a very rich haul indeed by the standards of time, and with his share, in addition to the money saved up from his previous jobs, Smith was able not only to buy his family out of slavery, but also to purchase a plot of land in Stonington. Venture's eldest son Solomon also shipped out on a whaler in 1773. Yet this voyage, unlike his father's, brought only misfortune to the family when Solomon died of scurvy.[13]

***

On 30 September 1791 two ships left the port of Nantucket, an island south of Cape Cod and not far from Venture Smith's property on the coast of Connecticut. The *Asia* and the *Alliance* were headed for the Indian Ocean, where they were to explore new whaling and sealing grounds. These, it was hoped, would contribute to reviving Nantucket's economy, which depended heavily on whale oil and related products and had suffered greatly as a result of the American

---

9 Saint/Krimsky, *Making Freedom*, 9–28; "Voyage 36067, Charming Susanna (1739)". Voyages: The Trans-Atlantic Slave Trade Database (2009), accessed. September 15, 2022, http://www.slavevoyages.org. On these sidelines pursued by ordinary seamen see Rediker, *Between the Devil and the Deep Blue Sea*, 130–132.
10 Saint/Krimsky, *Making Freedom*, 29–76.
11 Ibid., 138; Vickers, "Maritime Labor in Colonial Massachusetts", 300.
12 Quoted in Saint/Krimsky, *Making Freedom*, 138.
13 Ibid., *Making Freedom*, 74f.

war of independence (1775–1783). After stops at the Canary Islands, the Cape Verde Islands and Trinidade the two vessels reached the Cape of Good Hope in January 1792. In order to make essential repairs and to take on board water, timber and cattle, they put to anchor for days at a time first at Cape Town and then at Saldanha Bay, continuing their eastward journey in February. The *Alliance* and the *Asia* crisscrossed the Indian Ocean for several months using a copy of the chart drawn up by James Cook on his third voyage and finally reached Australia. However, they caught only few whales along the way. After putting in at Port Louis in Mauritius, where merchants told the crew about the annual migration of humpback whales along the coast of Madagascar, the two vessels set sail for that island's north-eastern shore. There, in August they discovered a rich hunting ground for humpback whales off the island of Sainte-Marie. The *Asia* and the *Alliance* were probably the first whaling vessels to reach that part of the Indian Ocean.[14]

Early in the morning of 29 August – the crew had just spent the night trying out the carcass of a humpback whale caught the day before – the *Alliance* was approached by canoe. Fifteen men clambered over the gunwales, one of whom, "an exceeding old Gentleman with a long beard" according to the ship's log, introduced himself as a representative of the "king" of Sainte-Marie. Though the seamen marvelled at the men's peculiar dress and curiously platted hair, they accorded no great significance to this visit, such deputations from local potentates and merchants being fairly commonplace occurrences on board whalers in coastal waters. Bartlett Coffin, master of the *Alliance*, agreed to receive the king the next day, whereupon the visitors left the ship.[15]

The following morning the crew were storing away their recent batch of whale oil in the ship's hold when they saw five large canoes heading straight for the *Asia* and the *Alliance*. On hearing shell trumpets sound from the canoes and musket shots from the island, the officers of the two ships lost no time in responding. One of them recalled reading in the journals of Captain Cook that "the Blowing of the Shell never was known to denote peace".[16] Bartlett Coffin gave the order to cut and run. Meanwhile Elijah Coffin, his counterpart in command of the *Asia*, had begun to hoist up the anchor before realising that time was running out and likewise ordering the rope to be cut. Though the ships had lain virtually becalmed for several days, the wind now picked up and filled the

---

14 Dickson, "The Cruise of the Nantucket Ships 'Asia' and 'Alliance'", 9–11; Stackpole, *The Sea-Hunters*, 194–198.
15 Pinkham, *The Log Book of the Good Ship Alliance of Nantucket Captain Bartlett Coffin*, 29. & 30.08.1792.
16 Ibid., 30.08.1792.

sails. "We were wonderfully favoured [. . .] and delivered from the Land", Andrew Pinkham, the first mate of the *Alliance*, noted in his ship's log.[17] The attackers were only a musket shot away by the time the *Asia* too picked up speed. "We run for our Lives" was what that ship's second mate, Sylvanus Crosby, entered into the log.[18]

***

There is no direct connection between the three stories sketched out above. And yet there is a point at which their strands meet, and that is the history of whaling. The expansion of street lighting in London and other European cities was decisive in causing whaling to grow from a branch of fishing to an economic sector in its own right. Venture Smith and his son Solomon are only two among the many thousands of men from all walks of life who tried to get ahead by engaging in the whale hunt. This is true even of the attackers of Sainte-Marie, which was a notorious hive of pirates in the eighteenth century: they had reason to believe that the *Asia* and the *Aliance* would themselves make good catches. Taken together, what these vignettes show is that the business of whaling was consequential beyond the seas and beyond the societies directly involved in processing or consuming its products. The pursuit of many species to the brink of extinction was not the only legacy of whaling. It has shaped the experience of countless people upon whose lives it touched in manifold and often surprising ways – at sea and on land, in great ports and on small islands, in the Sea of Okhotsk and in the Great Australian Bight.

It is this conception of whaling as a mobile practice, global in scope and with far-reaching, often incidental consequences, that this study seeks to make its own. As their expeditions began to reach out into all oceans from the mid-eighteenth century onwards, European and North American whalers created a network of hunting grounds, communication routes, entrepôts and supply chains that spanned the globe – a novel spatial system created and daily animated and elaborated by seamen in pursuit of whales. At the peak of this age of whaling in the mid-nineteenth century, approximately 900 whalers, crewed by some 20,000 seamen, were plying the oceans.[19] In order to sustain themselves during their voyages, which often lasted several years at a time, crews visited whatever islands and ports on the mainland coasts lay along the trail of their prey. Along these imagined tracks of whales, determined by the ocean's currents, there

---

17 Pinkham, *The Log Book of the Good Ship Alliance of Nantucket Captain Bartlett Coffin*, 29. & 30.08.1792.
18 Log ASIA, 1791–1794, 30.08.1792.
19 Hohman, *The American Whaleman*, 5f., 41f.

grew relations of exchange and communication which left traces both on board ship and on dry land.

For the depth of these traces and the intensity of these relations to be determined, it is necessary first to delimit the scope of observation. The point made by the historian Kären Wigen with regard to the basic challenge of writing maritime history applies with particular force to whaling: "Since seafaring humans are caught up in truly global webs, even a colossal fragment like the Pacific Ocean is not big enough to contain most oceanic themes."[20] The scope of observation within which I shall assess the consequences of the stopovers made by whalers is a topography spanning two oceans and encompassing locations on the eastern and western coasts of Africa and on the continent's offshore islands.

There are two principal factors in determining the choice of Africa as a reference space within which to situate the scope of observation. The first is concerned with the exigencies of scholarship: unlike in the case of the Pacific or North Atlantic Oceans, barely any research has yet been undertaken into the social and cultural history of whalers and their activities in the seas around Africa. Second, defining the subject in these terms can help contribute to a better understanding of Africa's historic links with the maritime worlds of the Atlantic and Indian Oceans. Research into these links tends focus on the grand narratives of European expansion and Atlantic slavery, of colonialism and imperialism. It is no doubt justified and indeed necessary to pay particular attention to these connections, not least because they explain marginalisations of Africa that continue to this day. Yet the thorough examination of colonialism and slavery has itself engendered powerful paradigms which sometimes seem to predispose historical inquiry to assume the ubiquity of power differentials. To assume, however, that any contact between African littoral societies and vessels coming from Europe or America must of necessity have been predetermined by inequalities of power and by subjugation in terms of an ineluctable Western hegemony would be ahistorical and misleading.[21] Moreover, such a narrow view of the past leaves Africans themselves with no chance of appearing as empowered historical actors[22] in their own right, conceiving of them

---

20 Wigen, "Introduction", 2.
21 Auböck, "Afrika südlich der Sahara", 75f.; Bayart, "Postcolonial Studies", 70f.; Juneja, "Debatte zum Postkolonialismus aus Anlass des Sammelbandes 'Jenseits des Eurozentrismus'- von Sebastian Conrad und Shalini Randeria", 90–93; Schwartz, "Introduction", 6.
22 I follow Alf Lüdtke in taking "actors" to refer to people or groups who "are in equal measure objects of and subjects of the world and of history." Unlike such terms as "subject" or "agent", the figure of the actor implies neither an autonomous nature nor a functional dependence on the part of those to whom it is applied. Actors "use and interpret such instructions as

instead only as passive victims. The people who sailed to Africa, meanwhile, appear as mere agents of an imperial project and an essentialised "West". Amid such simplifications, what is unexpected and ambiguous, paradox and contradictory, disparate and idiosyncratic is all too easily ignored. One possible reason for the persistence of this problem in historical research on Africa may be that historians impose a strict sequential and causal order on their narratives with a view to defusing the clichéd perception of a notoriously chaotic continent. As the historian and political scientist Achille Mbembe has observed in this context, "Research on Africa has hardly stood out for its attempts to integrate nonlinear phenomena into its analyses."[23]

Consequences direct and incidental

As Umberto Eco remarked, "the history of Pacific exploration is the history of people forever discovering lands they were not looking for."[24] This observation may be generalised to denote a trait common to previous eras: historical actors acted intentionally, but history, as Jürgen Habermas has noted, seldom conforms to the motives of those who set out to make it, "for the historical context is not exhausted by the mutual intentions of human beings."[25] History, as Wolfgang Reinhard has put it, "tends to emerge dialectically from unintended side-effects" rather than in direct consequence of its actors' intentions.[26] The encounters between whalemen and littoral societies in Africa provide vivid illustrations of this trait of history. Whalers set out in pursuit of whales. Their aim was not to influence life along the African littoral, let alone to reshape it. But that is what they sometimes ended up doing, and that is the story to be told in this book.

A glance at whalers' logbooks will often show the first few pages placed under the heading "Outward bound", meaning the first stage of a vessel's

---

incentives in a situational and personal manner. In their appropriations they produce something of their own, they evince self-will. Actors act, they take action – not only as they please, but as mere puppets, either. They explore and use opportunities and scopes for action, but they can create them too. [. . .] Historic actors do not find themselves on an open field; they cannot do just anything. But even when following mere routines or directives, they are active and produce their own version of events, and hence also their everyday reality." (Lüdtke, "Alltagsgeschichte, Mikro-Historie, historische Anthropologie", 635, 642).

23 Mbembe, *On the Postcolony*, 17.
24 Eco, *Inventing the Enemy*, 206.
25 Habermas, *On the Logic of the Social Sciences*, 35.
26 Reinhard, "Kolonialgeschichtliche Probleme und kolonialhistorische Konzepte", 87.

journey on leaving its home port. To be "Outward bound" meant to embark upon a time of uncertainty. Not only were the men henceforth constantly exposed to potentially lethal forces of nature, as was anyone taking to the high seas. Whalers had to confront the added uncertainty of being unable to predict the route or the duration of their voyage with any degree of accuracy. Seamen in a well-run merchantman could reach a reasonably good estimate of the time till their return. In a whaling vessel, however, they were left with no choice but to count the days in ascending sequence if they wanted to measure the temporal dimension of the voyage they were experiencing. In the log of the *Globe* from New Bedford, Massachusetts, for instance, the seaman John Coguin recorded the "951st" day, adding: "May God bring the voyage to a speedy termination."[27] The uncertainty inaugurated by being "Outward bound" tended to be perceived a greater on board a whaler than it was on a merchantman or a fishing vessel on the high seas. Yet the uncertainty of being outward bound was not only temporal in nature, but also eminently spatial. For whaling crews, it invariably meant sailing into unfamiliar waters and to confront new challenges – unpredictable encounters and unexpected events as well as experiences apt to collide with previously unquestioned notions.

I have tried to introduce a similarly explorative element into this book, into the questions it asks and into the search for answers. What were the consequences, both direct and incidental, of whalers' visits to the African coast and its offshore islands? This question deliberately leaves open what kind of effect is to be identified, since these effects differed widely depending on local conditions. After all, in some places whalers were the only or indeed the first vessels to visit the coast regularly, and the arrival of seamen from afar would have played out very differently here than in places that had long been established nodal points in maritime networks of exchange and communication before being integrated into the system of provisioning whalers. No less different than local conditions were the dynamic effects arising from interactions between seamen and local populations. I shall reframe the question asked in each chapter depending on what aspects of life changed most markedly in consequence of contact with whalers, sometimes foregrounding economic and sometimes social or political aspects.

Two further questions supplement those concerning the direct and incidental consequences felt on the African littoral: first, what did it mean for seamen in whaling vessels to come into contact with people on the coast of Africa? This question asks us to consider not only coastal settlements but also the vessels

---

27 Log GLOBE, 1869–1872, 12.10.1871.

themselves as arenas in which history plays out. To answer it, it is necessary not only to consider these contacts as events in coastal areas of Africa, but also to embed them in a social, cultural and quotidian history of whaling. And finally: what were the effects of whaling on the maritime routes of trade and communication around the African continent? The thought behind this last question is whether interaction between whalers and littoral societies was able lastingly to integrate what had previously been a relatively isolated place into networks of exchange in the Atlantic or Indian Oceans. This, in turn, raises the question of how historical spaces emerge and are perpetuated, that is, whether spatial links created by vessels and their crews dwindled in tandem with whaling or whether they survived its decline.

The overarching purpose of this question is to contrast commonplace and all too often dichotomous notions of African societies' maritime external relations in the eighteenth and nineteenth centuries with a largely forgotten phenomenon of exchange and communication that resists being forced into paradigmatic patterns of interpretation and cannot be explained simply in terms of grand narratives, for instance that of European expansion. The questions of representations and discourses emphasised (sometimes excessively) particularly by historians working in the field of postcolonial studies are not at the centre of this study. This is an exploration of history that is interested above all in action and in the social praxis of actors. The people whose practices and expressions helped contributed towards the reality of these situations continue to play a rather marginal role in history as it is written. These people were Africans whose everyday lives were not spent waiting to be colonised as if for a preordained fate – which is why I find "precolonial" to be an inappropriate category[28] – and seamen who had to assert themselves with regard to their surroundings from a subordinate class position.

A past that is not yet history

Encounters and relations between whalers and African littoral societies are events of a past whose sign-bearing remnants have so far scarcely been placed in meaningful contexts. In other words, the *res gestae* have not yet produced a *narration rerum gestarum*; the past awaits its representation as history – unlike

---

28 For a critique of the concept of "precoloniality" see Ahmad, "The Politics of Literary Postcoloniality", 18, McClintock, "The Angel of Progress", 85 and Reid, "Past and Presentism", 135f.

in the case of Australia and Oceania, for which some histories of such encounters and relations already exist.[29]

The lack of such a research tradition in the African case is probably due not least to the fact that the wide-ranging network of relations woven around the continent by whalers includes a multitude of different arenas and actors – a multitude which eludes the clearly defined frames of observations through which historians prefer to view the objects of their study. A part may also be played by the tendency of many historians to consider whaling in terms of national history, as part of (say) British or American economic and social history rather than as a phenomenon of global entanglements. Yet some studies by historians of the United States, of Africa and of whaling do indeed discuss contacts between vessels' crews and littoral societies at least as an incidental and a few cases even as their principal aspect, albeit with reference only to a single coastal settlement. Only one study exists that foregrounds such contact, an unpublished dissertation on "American Whalers and Africa" submitted in 1967 by Carl Norman Haywood of Boston University. In the following, I shall summarize the findings of Haywood's study and other relevant scholarship in order to reach a point from which the past may be recast as history.

To date Haywood's study is the only monograph to give a systematic account of the activities of whalers in the seas around Africa.[30] It was written as part of the research pursued at Boston University's African Studies Center on the American role in the so-called "legitimate trade" which replaced the Atlantic Slave trade in the nineteenth century. Its emphasis is accordingly on economic and social history: Haywood enquires into the nature and scope of the trade in which the crews of American whalers engaged in the course of the stops made for provisioning along the African coast and into the social side-effects of these activities. Based on logbooks, some seamen's diaries and the records of a number of American consulates, he examines events in nine locations on the western, southern and eastern coasts of Africa, mainly between 1800 and 1875. He concludes that the seamen were purposeful "businessmen" whose strategies for action were guided chiefly by principles of economic opportunity.[31]

---

[29] See esp. Carr, "In the Wake of John Kanaka"; Chappell, "Beyond the Beach"; Gray, "Trading Contacts in the Bismarck Archipelago during the Whaling Era"; Mrantz, *Whaling Days in Old Hawaii*; Richards, *Pakehas around Porirua before 1840*; Richards, *Whaling and Sealing at the Chatham Islands*; Russell, *Roving Mariners*; see also Webb, *On the Northwest*.

[30] Haywood, "American Whalers and Africa"; see also Haywood, "American Contacts with Africa".

[31] Haywood, "American Whalers and Africa", 132.

Haywood was the first historian to incorporate the records of whalers themselves into historical research on Africa. In doing so, he opened up a corpus of sources that had previously gone unnoticed in this context but which has scarcely been used again since. His study yielded a variety of new insights, for instance concerning the ports at which whalers called repeatedly and the temporal dimensions in which they were frequented. For the present study, Haywood's research serves as an important reference and raises questions which I shall continue to pursue from chapter to chapter. The fact that these questions remain open is due in large part to the fact that Haywood himself was able only to give merest outlines of answers; his thesis is simply too short to give due consideration to specific circumstances in all the relevant locales. Africa's southern and eastern coasts are dealt with in fifty pages, the western coast merits another fifty-six, half of which are devoted to the Azores, which scarcely qualify as offshore islands and whose historic ties with Africa are negligible. The few pages Haywood devotes to each section of the coast consequently offer not enough space for an appraisal of the impact of proven contacts on historical processes in a given place. One reason for this lack is that historical research on Africa was in its infancy at the time Haywood was working and hence there were very few publications on littoral societies in Africa on which he might have drawn.

Aside from Haywood's dissertation, research at Boston University in the 1960s yielded several other studies in which the activities of American whalers in the seas around Africa form at least a secondary aspect. Alan Booth, in a dissertation on the influence of American actors on the history of South Africa in the eighteenth and nineteenth centuries completed in 1964, also discussed the operations of whalers in the bays of southern Africa. Booth calls attention to the political dimensions of these activities and emphasises how whalers undermined the claims of colonial powers by ignoring their efforts to regulate the movement of vessels in the coastal waters they sought to control.[32]

In addition, in 1965 two other Boston historians, Norman Bennett and George Brooks, edited a sourcebook of documents by a variety of American actors who visited the African coast in the nineteenth century. Besides texts written by merchants and consuls, the collection contains excerpts from the logbooks of whaling vessels recording landfalls in the eastern Indian Ocean, for instance on the coast of Madagascar and the island of Anjouan.[33] The historians Peter Duignan

---

[32] Booth, "Americans in South Africa" (published as Booth, *The United States Experience in South Africa*); see also Booth, "American Whalers in South African Waters".
[33] Bennet/Brooks, *New England Merchants in Africa*, esp. 185–188.

and Lewis Gann of Stanford University summarised the key findings of their Boston colleagues in their synthetic account of historic relations between the United States and Africa.[34]

These works aside, research on historic whaling operations off the African coast has been limited to a few essays dealing with particular locations and chiefly addressing questions of environmental history and marine ecology, with a particular interest in the number of whales killed and the effect this had on marine ecosystems. The visits of seamen and their doings on land, by contrast, are barely considered at all.[35] Other essays identify the temporal and spatial foci of whaling operations in particular waters, but again have little (if anything) to say about contacts with littoral societies.[36]

For its part, historical research on Africa has paid scant attention to whaling. It receives no mention in the standard overviews of African history.[37] The archaeologist Jill Kinahan is alone in having drawn upon the records of whalers for an empirical study. In her dissertation on Walvis Bay on the coast of what is now Namibia she supplements her archaeological method with a historiographical discussion of written sources by seamen, including some whalers' logbooks, excerpts of which are reproduced.[38] Taking together these sources and her own finds of harpoon fragments, such exchange objects as glass beads, and whale bones, Kinahan concludes that the local ǂAonîn population maintained regular trading links with the whalers who began to frequent the bay in the late eighteenth century and that they incorporated the exchange objects they acquired from seamen into existing trading relations with actors further inland. Apart from Kinahan, a few scholars do mention the activities of whalers as a factor in their research on individual littoral societies, without however themselves drawing upon seamen's records. I shall discuss the findings and claims of this research in the chapters on the relevant locales.

---

34 Duignan/Gann, *The United States and Africa*, 59f.
35 Best/Ross, Catches of Right Whales from Shore-Based Establishments in Southern Africa; Best, "The Presence of Right Whales in Summer on the West Coast of South Africa"; Griffiths et al., "Impacts of Human Activities on Marine Animal Life in the Benguela".
36 Dekker/De Jong, "Whaling Expeditions of the West India Company to Walvis Bay"; Richards/Du Pasquier, "Bay Whaling off Southern Africa".
37 See e.g. Eckert/Grau/Sonderegger, *Afrika 1500–1900*; Fage/Tordoff, *A History of Africa*; Falola, *African History Before 1885*; Harding, *Geschichte Afrikas im 19. und 20. Jahrhundert*; Iliffe, *Africans*; Shillington, *History of Africa*; Thornton, *Africa and Africans in the Making of the Atlantic World*.
38 Kinahan, *Cattle for Beads*; see also Kinahan, "The Impenetrable Shield".

Records of vessels and beaches

What documents can offer insights into contacts between whalers and African littoral societies? Research into the history both of ordinary seamen and of Africa in the eighteenth and nineteenth centuries faces the shared difficulty of what historians agree is a paucity of sources. Crews and most African societies alike favoured the spoken over the written word. But the fact that historical actors should have failed to leave behind records of a kind convenient to posterity is a problem faced not only by research concerned with subaltern or non-European actors.[39] The past can only ever be observed in the form of mediations which those who study it must consider fraught with difficulties. It is mediated first by historical actors themselves, who leave traces only to the extent and in the manner they were able to do so within the societal force fields surrounding them.[40] Second, it is mediated by the archive, which filters, shapes and transforms what may be known and said about the past.[41] And third, it is mediated by the paradigms, perspectives and positions of those asking questions of the past from their vantage point in the present.[42] These mediations – rather than incomplete documentation, which is inevitable – pose challenges to any attempt at representing something of the past as history. Yet the present study faces a particular challenge in the heterogeneity of the sources on which it must draw in order to answer the questions it has set itself.

∗∗∗

As Karl Schlögel has noted: "Each mode of movement comes with its specific way of seeing the world, its particular prerogatives, and probably also its historic locus, its periods of waxing and waning significance. Each engenders its specific genre and its specific rhetoric – its modes of writing, reporting, depicting, and categorizing – and each has its own aids and sources of information."[43] The source of information where whaling is concerned is the logbook. These texts offer crucial insights into the movements of vessels and the places visited by seamen – and how often, with what frequency and in what periods they did so. Approximately 5,000 logbooks from the era of American-style pelagic

---

39 McNeill, "Comment on Miller", 30; Northrup, *Africa's Discovery of Europe*, x.
40 See e.g. Ginzburg, *The Cheese and the Worms*, 126.
41 See esp. Foucault, *The Archaeology of Knowledge*.
42 See e.g. Dening, "A Poetic for Histories", 353, 359.
43 Karl Schlögel, *In Space We Read Time*, 216.

whaling are preserved, most of them from American vessels. Scarcely any are preserved from vessels of other nations that plied the southern oceans in search of whales.[44]

Short of reading them all, there is no way of ascertaining how many of the preserved logbooks record voyages to the seas surrounding the African continent. Although such important repositories as the New Bedford Whaling Museum and the Nantucket Historical Association have largely catalogued their holdings of logbooks with regard to the whaling grounds visited, other major collections – for instance those of the New Bedford Free Public Library and the Providence Public Library – have been indexed but incompletely and imprecisely. Since whalers' journeys usually lasted several years and spanned several oceans, operating in different whaling grounds, a vessel might, for instance, visit the coast of Angola even if its stated destination upon sailing had been the South Pacific. At its outset a vessel's voyage was uncertain both spatially and temporally, that is to say, its duration was as doubtful as its ultimate destination. In order to identify relevant logbooks, then, I not only followed the archival indexes and the scholarly literature on whaling, but also relied on the snowball effect: logbooks usually record any encounter with another vessel, thereby pointing to other whalers operating in the same waters whose logbooks may also have been preserved. The database of all known *American Offshore Whaling Voyages*, compiled by Judith Lund and others, has proved an invaluable aid in verifying the sometimes incomplete and imprecise information contained in the logbooks.[45]

New England whalers began keeping logbooks in the eighteenth century as their voyages extended into more distant waters. These logs followed the record-keeping practices developed by British mariners in the latter part of the sixteenth

---

44 Of some 15,000 sailings from North American ports during this era, approximately 4,750 logbooks are preserved, compared to a ratio of a mere 250 books for 5,000 sailings from ports in other countries. British vessels, which made around 2,700 voyages and hence had the second largest share of whaling in the southern oceans, have left a mere 35 logs and comparatively few records of other kinds. The logbooks known to historians are preserved in over eighty archives, in addition to which there are likely to be hundreds of logbooks in private hands, out of reach to historians. (Busch, *Whaling Will Never Do for Me*, 19; Forster, "The Cruise of the Whaler Gipsy", 111; Jones, "The British Southern Whale and Seal Fisheries", 22, 28; Malloy, "Journals and Logbooks", 220–222; Shearman, *Whaling Logbooks and Journals*; Wray/Martin, "Historical Whaling Records from the Western Indian Ocean", 213).

45 Lund et al., *American Offshore Whaling Voyages*; on the database see also Schürmann, "Neue Hilfsmittel zur amerikanischen Walfanggeschichte", 256f.

century and largely unchanged since. A logbook provided shipowners[46] with a chronological account of a voyage. As a rule, it was a kind of diary whose daily entries were divided into three "parts": noon to 8 p.m. (*first part*), 8 p.m. to 4 a.m. (*second part*) and 4 a.m. to noon (*third part*). The ship's log was usually kept by its first mate, a duty formalised in law in the United States. As the captain's deputy, the first mate was considered a trustworthy leader while being of sufficient standing in his own right to describe a voyage in terms not dictated by the captain.[47]

There were, however, numerous exceptions to this rule. For instance, the logbook of the barque *Reaper* of Salem, Massachusetts was kept by her master, Benjamin Neal from 1837 to 1839, while that of the barque *Emerald*, also of Salem, was from 1838 to 1840 entrusted to the cooper Henry Nichols. In some British whalers, the log was kept by the ship's surgeon, who was considered the ablest writer aboard.[48] It was by no means a rarity for another officer, the captain himself or a seaman of lesser rank to take on the task. The author might also change in the course of a voyage, for instance if the original logkeeper deserted or was discharged.[49] Entries usually kept track of wind and weather conditions, of the vessel's tack, speed and position, of its landfalls and encounters with other vessels, of seamen's absences – and of course of whales. Occurrences on board or during shore leave tend mostly to figure in logbooks when they might have financial or legal consequences – deaths, floggings, desertions or strikes, for instance.[50]

During landfalls, the logbook would usually record the crew's activities, including any trade they engaged in and the sums involved, and any other notable occurrences. Some authors included detailed description of coastal settlements in their logs and added poems, sketches or personal remarks of their own. Most logbooks, however, are kept brief and to the point, recording only that section of events considered necessary by the author to meet the documentary purpose of

---

46 An American whaling vessel would usually belong to a group of investors, of whom the captain himself was often one. Most shareholders would spread the investments across several vessels in order to minimise their risk.
47 Miller, *And the Whale is Ours*, 8; Sherman, *The Voice of the Whaleman*, 26–28, 33f.
48 Forster, "The Cruise of the Whaler Gipsy", 110; Log EMERALD, 1838–1840; Log REAPER, 1837–1839. Unless otherwise indicated, the vessels mentioned in this study were all whalers.
49 A case in point was the *Falcon* of New Bedford, whose log was kept by its first mate, John Commerford, who was discharged by Captain Harty while in port at Jamestown. (Log FALCON, 1887–1890, 29.09.1888).
50 On the value of logbooks as sources see Gray, "Light Aits from the South"; Sherman, "The Nature, Possibilities and Limitations of Whaling Logbook Data", 35–39; Sherman, *The Voice of the Whaleman*, 35, 46–71.

this functional type of text – "a monotonous sameness and almost universal carelessness for detail", according to the Australian historian Greg Dening.[51] Even such serious events as the violent death of a seaman might merit no more than the briefest of notes in some logbooks.

In January 1809 Charles Gardner, master of the *Argo* of London, recorded an attempted mutiny. The seaman John Morgan had cut himself in the leg in the course of dismembering a sperm whale; the wound subsequently became infected. Since his injury left Morgan unable to work, Captain Gardner denied him the ration of grog to which the *Argo*'s crew were usually entitled. This upset Morgan to the point of raising his hand against the captain, who had him put in irons.[52] Did this incident really constitute a mutiny, which the American historian Jesse Lemisch has defined as "the captain's name for what we have come to call a 'strike'"?[53] Lemisch's remark points to a difficulty which is fundamental in dealing with logbooks: what a ship's log records or ignores, what it glosses over or exaggerates, what it makes up or conceals was usually up to the first mate or captain. Being in charge of the vessel, it would have been in their interest to record a strike as an attempted mutiny rather than a legitimate protest, a seaman's severe injury as self-inflicted or damage to the vessel as resulting from a storm rather than a navigational error. For the log was usually the only official record of a voyage, and as such it was central to any subsequent legal proceedings. It constituted, to quote Dening once more, a journey's "public history". Since sources that would allow us to compare this public history against alternative, private histories are hard to come by, discrepancies are often hard to spot, even though the books themselves may sometimes reveal inconsistencies. For instance, entries in logbooks will sometimes mention seamen whom one would not expect to find on board according to the crew lists.[54] In appraising logbooks, Dening suggests paying particular attention to allusions and phrases pregnant with meaning, to subtexts and ambiguities which suggest that something extraordinary may be hidden under the veneer of seeming normality:

> Every officer read the log in a knowing way for the meaning in and behind the words, for what was not said at all, for the system in its preservation. Every officer knew, because they were practiced in it, what sort of public history a log might be, and how different it was to other more private histories. Indeed for the scandal they wanted to reveal, for the

---

51 Dening, *Islands and Beaches*, 244.
52 Log ARGO, 1808–1811, 22.01.1809.
53 Lemisch, *Jack Tar in the Streets*, 406.
54 See e.g. McCormick, *Two New Bedford Whalemen*, 75.

intrigue of being an insider to another past, they made other private histories, in letters or journals tucked away from official scrutiny.[55]

The authors of logbooks were seldom good writers. Punctuation marks tend to be omitted, capitalisation is often erratic and spelling sometimes phonetic. In order to convey this writing and the thought behind it with the greatest possible degree of immediacy, I have made corrections to the passages quoted here only in such cases when, for instance, missing punctuation might leave the meaning unclear. What these quotations also illustrate is that only very few logbooks can claim poetic qualities. As Stuart Sherman, who in 1965 produced the definitive study of logs from the era of American-style pelagic whaling, has remarked, "The monotony of a logbook simply reflects the monotony with which the one day followed another. Whalemen faced hardship and danger so often that even the logbook entries describing them were casual and off-hand."[56]

***

In the case of the whalemen, the records Dening describes as "private histories" can be grouped into four genres: diaries, travelogues, memoirs and letters. Such personal testimonies often provide more detailed accounts of encounters during landfalls and the situations arising from them than logbooks do, and they offer insights into individual seamen's experiences and emotional responses. Whereas logbooks are naturally concerned with the mundane events of everyday life at sea, such testimonies often concentrate on the extraordinary, for instance on gruelling struggles with whales, violent storms or conflicts on board.[57] Yet these texts too do not offer direct access to the experiences of their authors, who in the act of writing could not but situate themselves within discourses. Although they are less formalised than logbooks, as textual genres diaries, travelogues, memoirs and letters obey specific conventions and bear the stamp of the system of cultural reference within which they were produced. Unlike many other eighteenth- and nineteenth-century European or North American actors to have left written testimonies of their experiences in Africa, however, the whalemen did not come in pursuit of a paternalist agenda. While this does not in itself make their records more objective, truthful or open-minded than those of missionaries or colonial officials, they clearly come without the burden of an imperial project.

"Every intelligent officer of a vessel which makes long voyages has his journals and memoranda", remarks Gurdon Allyn, master of a succession of whalers

---

55 Dening, *The Death of William Gooch*, 7.
56 Sherman, *The Voice of the Whaleman*, 35.
57 Creighton, *Rites & Passages*, 14.

and sealers, in the preface to his memoirs.[58] Yet the fact that many seafarers – and especially higher-ranking ones – should have kept records of their time at sea does not mean that published texts or those preserved in archives are equally representative of the social group of the men who went whaling. Lemisch has pointed out that the seamen who leave testimonies of themselves tend largely to be the successful ones, those who rose to become officers or went on to do well for themselves on land.[59] Moreover, the self-testimonials we have from whalers are nearly all by white men. As the American historian Margaret Creighton has observed with regard to this relatively privileged position, "None of these white American diarists can be trusted to provide a detached, anthropological view of the beliefs and behaviors of men of different races and nationalities."[60]

It is in the travelogue that we find the clearest evidence of the power of conventional forms to shape narratives. Records of sea voyages are an ancient part of literature, with famous examples including Homer's epic account of the travels of Odysseus and the book of Jonah, which forms part of both the Christian Old Testament and the Jewish Tanakh. Over the centuries conventions of narrative structure and recurring themes have emerged in writing about sea voyages, and their persistence can be observed in nineteenth-century seamen's accounts of their whaling experiences. Broadly speaking, these texts fall into four categories. The first is the disaster narrative, which centres on such an event as a shipwreck or mutiny; the second is the exotic narrative, where the emphasis is on encounters with strange people in faraway places; the third is the reform narrative, which offers an indictment of living and working conditions aboard ship and calls for improvements; and the fourth is the conversion narrative, in which the narrator finds in the Christian faith a remedy for the iniquities of his life at sea.[61]

Until the mid-nineteenth century, an ordinary seaman was no more likely to publish a book than was a North American trapper or a Saxon coachman. In the rare cases of a manuscript by a whaleman finding both a publisher and audience, the texts tended to conform to the type of the disaster narrative, telling of such shocking events as the sinking of the *Essex*, rammed by a sperm whale in 1820, or the bloody mutiny on the *Globe* in 1824.[62] Beginning in 1840,

---

58 Allyn, *The Old Sailor's Story*, preface.
59 Lemisch, *Jack Tar in the Streets*, 376.
60 Creighton, "Fraternity in the American Forecastle", 533.
61 Foulke, "Voyage Narratives", 462; Lefkowicz, "Whaling Narratives", 469.
62 See esp. Chase, *Narrative of the Most Extraordinary and Distressing Shipwreck of the Whale-Ship Essex*; Comstock, *The Life of Samuel Comstock, the Terrible Whaleman*; Holden, *A Narrative of the Shipwreck, Captivity and Sufferings of Horace Holden and Benj. H. Nute*; Lay/Hussey, *A Narrative of the Mutiny, on Board the Ship Globe, of Nantucket, in the Pacific Ocean*.

however, seamen's chances of having their writings published took a marked upturn when Richard Henry Dana Jr. of Massachusetts published a memoir of his years as a seaman aboard a merchantman.[63] Dana's account of the brutality of everyday shipboard life and the draconian punishments meted out to seamen sparked the reading public's interest in a new kind of tale of life at sea, one that was naturalistic and social-realist in the style of the "reform narrative" described above.

Such was the success of Dana's *Two Years Before the Mast* that American publishers began to take a stronger interest in the writings of seamen, particularly those occupying lower rungs of a vessel's hierarchy. This led to the publication of reform narratives by whalemen too, some of which were clearly inspired by Dana's book. Conversion narratives began to appear around the same time. They are closely related to reform narratives in their focus on the hardships of life at sea, but the solution they offer is not so much political – for instance, a ban on flogging – as religious, a turn towards the Christian faith.[64] But the popularity of seamen's accounts of their experiences was not limited to tales of reform and conversion. The 1840s also saw growing interest in exotic yarns that owed less to Dana than to romantic tales of the sea, a new "Sea Adventure Fiction" following such examples as the novels of James Fennimore Cooper. Since their voyages often took them to the remotest parts of the world and offered ample romance and adventure, seamen in general and whalers in particular were in a good position to capitalise on the public appetite for exotica.[65]

A further factor in the increasing popularity of texts by ordinary seamen was the enlarged standing, beginning in the 1830s, of the US Navy as the embodiment of the nation. A series of conflicts involving American naval forces between 1798 and 1815 as well as an increased awareness of the economic importance of maritime trade led to a widespread interest in and sympathy for seamen, in whose trials and tribulations many Americans saw a reflection of their own national spirit and struggle.

Sailors' writing was affected by the emergence of a market for it. Some authors began their shipboard journals with subsequent publication in mind, one example being John Ross Browne, who had already published several pieces both of journalism and of fiction before signing aboard the barque *Bruce* of

---

63 Dana, *Two Years Before the Mast*.
64 See e.g. Browne, *Etchings of a Whaling Cruise*; Nordhoff, *Whaling and Fishing*; Olmsted, *Incidents of a Whaling Voyage*.
65 See e.g. Hazen, *Five Years Before the Mast*, and for sea adventure fiction in general the analysis by Cohen, *The Novel and the Sea*, chapter 3.

Fairhaven, and on whose account of his voyage I shall be drawing in several of the following chapters.[66] In order to meet the supposed expectations of readers, texts might be altered (sometimes repeatedly) by both authors and publishers, who made cuts or added information from encyclopaedias.[67] This editing process might also entail exaggeration, the subsequent embellishment of anecdotes or the wholesale invention of incidents. Since few journeys are documented by multiple sources – for instance, both a logbook and a travelogue – individual statements are often impossible to verify.[68]

In publishing their accounts, seamen pursued a variety of aims which may have overlapped and which are often hard to distinguish in retrospect. Whereas some authors hoped above all for literary fame, others were driven above all by financial motives, by a desire to give the public an understanding of everyday life aboard ship, or simply to make sense of their experiences at sea.

Closely related to the travelogue is the textual genre of the seaman's memoir. Unlike travelogues, such accounts tell not of one or several voyages, but of their author's entire life – or at least a large part of it. Although many of these texts can be assigned to one of the four kinds of travelogue discussed above,[69] memoirs continued to be published in the late nineteenth and early twentieth centuries and thus at a time when the American whaling industry had entered its long decline. The literary marketplace too was different from what it had been in 1840s and 1850s. Many of the memoirs to be published in the early twentieth century took their bearings from the newer formats of the dime novel or pulp magazine, which were huge commercial successes in the United States and Europe.[70] These late memoirs in particular seem to be written in the awareness that whaling under sail on the high seas is about to fade into memory and treat it as a subject of reminiscence.

Memoirs and travelogues alike were usually based on diaries. Some seamen kept diaries above all as personal mementoes, as a means of coping with day-to-day existence and committing their experiences to memory. Others hoped one day

---

66 Browne, *Etchings of a Whaling Cruise*, *2f., *11, *25. All names of persons and vessels are altered or anonymised in Browne's account; the fact that his vessel was the barque *Bruce* of New Bedford under the command of Captain Silas P. Alden can be deduced from his posthumously published correspondence. (Browne, *J. Ross Browne*, 9f., 17f.) On Browne see also Gilje, *Liberty on the Waterfront*, 66f.
67 See e.g. the editorial remarks in Ely, *There She Blows*, xxxii, 71; Haley, *Whale Hunt*, 17f.; Robbins, *The Gam*.
68 See e.g. Schürmann, "Review of Thomas W. Smith".
69 For an example of a memoir following the pattern of a conversion narrative see Smith, *A Narrative of the Life, Travels and Sufferings of Thomas W. Smith*.
70 See e.g. Barker, *Thrilling Adventures of the Whaler Alcyone*.

to leave their diaries to relations, friends or loved ones. Others yet planned from the outset to publish a travelogue or memoir on the basis of their diary. In any case, diaries usually remained in private hands and are far less often found in archives than logbooks, In some cases, the author's relations or heirs repurposed the volumes as scrapbooks, pasting in newspaper cuttings or postcards and thereby rendering them useless for research – a fate also suffered by some of the logbooks that were kept in private hands. Nonetheless Margaret Creighton was able to find nearly two hundred diaries or diary-like records in American archives.[71]

A comparable study of British whaling has yet to be produced. However, the generally poor availability of sources for British whaling suggests that diaries too are likely to be far fewer than in the United States, where the industry was more important. Even at its peak in the 1820s British whaling scarcely accounted for more than one per cent of the merchant fleet's overall tonnage. Since British shipowners responded to changes in the market quite swiftly by switching to other fields, fewer shipping companies ended up specialising in whaling than was the case in North America. And unlike in New England, no economic areas organised around whaling and no specialised ports emerged in the British Isles. London was the centre of British whaling in the southern seas, but even there it was easy to miss the few whalers among the mass of vessels docking in the Thames. Public interest in the activities of whalers and their memoirs and travelogues was much greater in North America than it was in Britain. This marginal role played by British whaling is reflected in the availability of sources, with far fewer diaries and logbooks preserved and systematically collected.[72]

One of the most striking features of many diaries is their resemblance to logbooks. Such was certain seamen's adherence to the form that in some cases the two types of record seem indistinguishable. Accordingly, an item catalogued as a "journal" in the archive may turn out to be the draft of a ship's log. This practice marks the relevant diaries as part of a strategy of professional advancement, for in keeping a log a seaman proved his ability to perform an officer's task.[73] Even diaries that follow the form of the logbook less closely frequently (though by no means always) contain less of their authors' feelings, moods and personal opinions than might be expected in texts of this kind. The author's emotional response to the events he describes often is not spelt out but left to the imagination.

---

71 Creighton, *Rites & Passages*, 7; Lefkowicz, "Whaling Narratives", 468f.; Miller, *And the Whale is Ours*, 13; Sherman, *The Voice of the Whaleman*, 39, 43.
72 Chatwin, "A Trade so Uncontrollably Uncertain", 4–11.
73 Creighton, *Rites & Passages*, 12; Sherman, *The Voice of the Whaleman*, 42.

Any attempt at an explanation must take into account the fact that aside from the quarters of the captain and the first mate there were no private spaces aboard a whaling vessel. As Dening has noted, "Sailors make history out of their experience in total institutions and know what sort of impersonal language gives them privacy and what sort of personal language exposes them."[74] No seaman below the rank of first mate could expect to keep his diary away from other crew. For instance, during the voyage of the barque *Emigrant* from 1844 to 1847, Captain James Shearman found letters and diaries in which a seaman, Ben Ely, criticised his regime in no uncertain terms. In revenge, the furious captain read other seamen passages concerning them, sometimes of a highly personal nature, exposing Ely to the hostility of the men of whom he had written so candidly.[75]

On board whaling vessels, diaries were kept by seamen of different rank, age and social background. I have already noted that the testimonies that have been preserved do not accurately reflect the composition of vessels' crews. A remarkable point with regard to diaries is that wives who accompanied captains on their voyages left quite a few such records to posterity, of which at least fifty-two are known. What makes these texts remarkable among the written records of whaling vessels is that they were written by individuals who were not themselves involved in whaling. Their observations are often more detailed than those found in the notes of seamen while being written from a position of relative social isolation. Some of these texts by captain's wives have been published since the 1930s.[76]

Letters are relative rarities in the archives of whaling, making up a mere eight per cent of the corpus of self-testimonials identified by Creighton.[77] Although seamen aboard whaling vessels did indeed write countless letters, very few them have found their way into the archives. In evaluating these sources, my previous remarks on diaries apply, including the possible reticence auf authors who had to reckon with letters falling into the wrong hands. Captain Weeden of the *Ceres*, for instance, once banned his men from sending letters from Honolulu because he had been made aware of the criticism they contained of his running of the vessel.[78]

***

---

74 Dening, "A Poetic for Histories", 357.
75 Ely, *There She Blows*, 66f.
76 Alexander, "Women at Sea", 483; Bolster, "To Feel Like a Man", 1185; Busch, *Whaling Will Never Do for Me*, 136; Creighton, *Rites & Passages*, 7f.; Sherman, *The Voice of the Whaleman*, 43.
77 Creighton, *Rites & Passages*, 209.
78 Ibid., 100f.

Among the sources able to offer an outside perspective on contacts between whalers and littoral societies are the records kept by American consulates in many African ports or nearby islands. Their job brought consuls into contact with whalers in several ways. They recorded the arrival and departure of vessels sailing under their country's flag, sent their foreign ministry reports of commercial and other activities taking place in their respective districts, and were the place to turn for seamen who had been discharged from or left behind by their vessels, or who wanted to alert the authorities to abuse by captains and officers. Yet shipmasters were also regular visitors to consulates, for instance to ask for help in settling conflicts on board or to obtain certification of storm damage to the vessel that would indemnify them against claims by its owners.[79]

Beginning in the 1790s the Department of State redoubled its efforts to build a network of consulates – not least on account of an early distrust of diplomatic missions, which American politicians distrusted as supposed hotbeds of intrigue and scheming. American foreign policy at the time thought of itself chiefly as supporting foreign trade, which had a significant part to play in the country's economic growth. This was the task of consulates rather than embassies or legations.[80] In the eighteenth and nineteenth centuries twenty American consulates were established along the African coast and on its offshore islands.[81] The records I draw upon here are those of the consulates which had the most dealings with whalers, namely those at Luanda, Lourenço Marques, Port Louis and Santiago.

Of particular value to this study are the shipping records kept by each consulate, albeit not consistently for the duration of its existence. Moreover, some records have been lost or destroyed in wars or natural disasters. Other consular papers are of lesser interest for the purposes of this study, being mostly records of everyday consular business: correspondence with local authorities, acknowledgements of State Department circulars, the issuing and notarising of various documents to

---

79 Booth, *The United States Experience in South Africa*, 136; Sherman, *The Voice of the Whaleman*, 57, 61.
80 De Santis/Heinrichs, "United States of America: The Department of State and American Foreign Policy".
81 1796 in Algiers (Algeria), 1797 in Tangier (Morocco), 1799 in Cape Town (South Africa) and in Tripoli (Libya), 1818 in Santiago (Cape Verde), 1832 in Alexandria (Egypt), 1834 in Zanzibar, 1836 in Jamestown (St Helena), 1855 in Port Louis (Mauritius), 1856 in Monrovia (Liberia), 1858 in Freetown (Sierra Leone), 1860 in Tananarive (Madagascar), 1864 in Luanda (Angola), 1867 in Mahé (Seychelles), 1869 in Dakar (Senegal), 1883 in Accra (Ghana), 1887 in Lourenço Marques (Mozambique) and 1890 in Addis Ababa (Ethiopia) and in Saint-Denis (La Réunion). In many cases, the exact date of a consulate's establishment is hard to establish since there may have been American merchants charged with consular tasks before an official consul was installed.

American citizens and – again and again – conflicts on board American vessels including strikes, desertions and discharges.[82] By and large, these incidents had no great impact on interactions with African littoral societies.

Newspaper articles offer another potential source of information on contacts between whalers and littoral societies. A significant part of the readership of daily or weekly general-interest newspapers published in New England whaling ports – such as the *New-Bedford Mercury* or the *Columbian Courier* – would have been involved in whaling either directly or indirectly, in the latter case for instance as relatives of whalemen or as workers in sectors processing whale-derived products. Newspapers provided these readers with a steady flow of news from parts of the world frequented by American whalers. Returning seamen, mostly captains or officers, provided newspaper editors with accounts of vessels' whereabouts and particularly good catches, or of such notable events as shipwrecks, mutinies or pirate attacks.[83] Even items of specifically nautical interest found their way into newspapers from time to time, such as a newly discovered reef off the coast of Mozambique or good anchorages for whalers off the eastern coast of Madagascar.[84] Newspapers would sometimes also print quite detailed reports on individual places, including Cape Town, Mauritius, Zanzibar or the Cape Verde Islands.[85] The information came not only from seamen but also from American consulates or merchants.

The most important source corpus for the present study consists of records produced by seamen; a systematic survey of all potentially relevant print publications would exceed its remit. But in order to broaden the base of information particularly with regard to the early days of American whaling on the high seas, I have consulted four newspapers published in New Bedford, namely the *Columbian Courier*, the *New-Bedford Daily Mercury*, *The Medley* and the *New Bedford Mercury*. By contrast, I shall refer only occasionally to the *Whalemen's Shipping List*, a trade publication likewise appearing in New Bedford, which – unlike the other papers cited – has not yet been indexed. In order to supplement seamen's records, I have looked for references to whaling in the Port Louis *Mercantile Record*, which carried regular reports on shipping in the port.

---

82 Busch, *Whaling Will Never Do for Me*, 62.
83 Currie, *Thar She Blows*, 60; Sherman, *The Voice of the Whaleman*, 70.
84 See e.g. "Capt. Oscar . . ." *New-Bedford Mercury*, 07.08.1835, 3; "Passandana Bay." *New-Bedford Mercury*, 02.02.1838, 2.
85 See e.g. "Cape of Good Hope – Hottentots, &c." *New-Bedford Mercury*, 28.07.1820, 1; "Capt. Brock . . ." *New-Bedford Mercury*, 30.05.1834, 2; "Recollections of St. Helena." *New-Bedford Mercury*, 20.03.1835, 4; Browne, "Sketches of the Arabs", 4.

In the chapters on each "beach", I have consulted additional sources to flesh out the already mentioned material and to incorporate other voices and perspectives. Depending on the locale, these might include records of explorers, missionaries, merchants, naval officers or other observers of the relations discussed here.

Beaches and passages

The seaman Charles Nordhoff saw his first whaling ground in the mid-nineteenth century from the deck of a New Bedford whaler. "I was looking for some peculiarity in the color of the water, the strength of the breeze, or the quality of the atmosphere, to distinguish this from the other parts of the ocean", he recalled that moment in a later travelogue. But in fact, the sea in the Mozambique Channel turned out to be "as deeply blue, the breezes as gentle, and the air as hazy as it generally is in those portions of the tropics."[86]

As the ocean's inscrutable surface conceals its mysterious inhabitants from the eyes of their pursuers, so it also hides its mysterious past from the curious gaze of posterity. "Where are your monuments?" Derek Walcott asks the sea in his poem "The Sea Is History". The poet, born in Saint Lucia, gives the answer himself: "The sea has locked them up."[87] Only when explored in an appropriate fashion will the sea yield up its secrets – the life and the past beneath its surface. Maritime history is a peculiar form of history that is shaped by peculiar actors and obeys peculiar logics. In the following, I shall discuss the methodological and conceptual assumptions underlying my discussion of maritime history and the choice of terminology they entail.

***

"Today the seas no longer divide countries and continents as once they did; it is they which connect the peoples and weave together their destinies." This remark, which sounds like an observation on twentieth-century globalisation, was in fact made in 1833 by Carl Ritter, a geographer and member of the Berlin Royal Academy of Sciences. Ritter also took this opportunity to discuss ships, arguing that they had become "means of weaving together", having "imparted a soul" to the oceans which had previously rolled about in a "will-less" fashion.

---

86 Nordhoff, *Whaling and Fishing*, 90f.
87 Walcott, *Selected Poems*, 137.

It was shipping, according to Ritter, which has so deeply transformed the spatial relations between "lands, continents and islands".[88]

Although they are nearly two hundred years old, Ritter's thoughts about the connective dimension of the sea and its consequences for spatial relations at the global level seem more relevant than ever. We find historians repeatedly making very similar points at conferences and in publications.[89] Considered as a phenomenon of ever denser connectivity, a history of links forged across borders, maritime history is a field that has enjoyed considerable popularity and has been the subject of conceptual debates among historians for some years now. The contacts between whalers and African littoral societies also fall under this heading.

Under the impression of the discourse of globalisation, postcolonial critiques and other intellectual currents, historians have developed or recast a whole range of approaches and concepts – or borrowed them from other disciplines – in order better to emphasise the particular dynamics and reciprocal forces at work in such phenomena of cross-border interaction as cultural transfers, processes of hybridisation or acts of translation. Besides this emphasis on reciprocity, such approaches as transnational history, *histoire croisee*, histories of transfer or entangled histories share an understanding of historical spaces that goes beyond viewing them as containers in the manner long customary in historical studies.[90] Such ideas have also been discussed in other branches of the humanities and social sciences, where theoretical and conceptual approaches have proliferated to the point of being impossible to oversee.[91]

Some researches that have followed such approaches have been criticised for not turning their critical attitude towards the prefigurative assumptions of a national historiography based on an assumption of spatial containers back on themselves and not inquiring into their blind spots and short cuts. Historians, the criticism goes, were slow to examine such popular images as "network", "current", "globality" and other terminological fashions of the digital age and to ask how they contributed to constituting objects of scholarly interest as well as

---

88 Ritter, "Über das historische Element in der geographischen Wissenschaft", 55. Unless otherwise indicated, all translations in this book from sources not originally in English are the author's own.
89 See e.g. Hoerder, "Crossing the Waters", 12; Klein/Mackenthun, "Das Meer als kulturelle Kontaktzone", 2f.
90 On the programmatic claims of these approaches see esp. Randeria, "Geteilte Geschichte und verwobene Moderne"; Subrahmanyam, "Connected Histories"; Werner/Zimmermann, "Vergleich, Transfer, Verflechtung".
91 Günzel, *Raum: Ein interdisziplinäres Handbuch*.

illuminating them. To this end, Frederick Cooper has cautioned historians against projecting ideas of global connectivity based on experiences of the present and anticipations of the future onto the past. This was liable to produce totalising and misleading paradigms in which important distinctions and discontinuities were distorted and obscured.[92]

In the present study I approach this problem by adopting a mode of observation that is itself adaptable and movable, one that explores history and its spatial dimensionality from the perspective of its actors' mobile practices. This kind of history might be described, to borrow a term from the ethnographer James Clifford, as a "history of locations and a location of history".[93] Its polylocal field of inquiry detaches history from its genealogical rootedness in space. The individual components of this field of examination may be thought of, to use a term established in cultural studies by Mary Louise Pratt, as consisting of contact zones. In places where people of different cultural and social formations entered into relationships, exchange between them was apt to generate dynamics of their own by which the systems of rules and ways of life predominant in such places might become sundered, wholly or in part, from those of neighbouring areas.[94] In coastal areas, however, such processes were subject to a particular condition: the coastline separating land and sea became a contact zone only when vessels anchored there. Their dual aspect as borders and liminal spaces, as both limiting and expanding spheres of movement and action, made coastal spaces contact zones of a particular type – a type which Dening calls a "beach".

Dening takes the term "beach" to denote less a particular topographical or geological feature than a space on which contacts and interactions exist in tension, in which dynamic becoming need not lead to static being. "A liminal space in which each moment is steeped in the twofold past of each side of the beach."[95] Unlike the "frontiers" familiar from the history of settler colonialism, beaches did not necessarily entail the overpowering and supersession of one side by another. Beaches, according to Dening, "have to be crossed both by those who came first and those who come after." This makes them a permanently "double-edged space, in-between; an exit space that is also an entry space; a space where

---

92 Cooper, "Was nützt der Begriff der Globalisierung?", 139, 150f., 159; Luutz, "Vom 'Containerraum' zur 'entgrenzten' Welt".
93 Clifford, Routes, 31. See also George Marcus's concept of *multi-sided ethnography*: Marcus, "Ethnography in/of the World System".
94 Pratt, *Imperial Eyes*, 4, 6f.
95 Dening, "Tiefe Zeiten, tiefe Räume", 17.

edginess rules."⁹⁶ As a characteristic feature of beaches as transitional and in-between spaces Dening cites the importance of intermediaries, the decisive influence on the dynamic of encounters exerted by such figures as interpreters and pilots, beachcombers and middlemen, and all manner of intermediaries and boundary characters.⁹⁷ One reason I pick up on Dening's figuration of the beach in this study is that the image it evokes points directly to a key aspect of the contacts discussed here. In order to cut on down on expenses, whalers preferred docking in remote coastal settlements and islands than in major ports with the latest equipment and infrastructure. Accordingly, the spatial environment in which whalemen came into contact with littoral societies was less markedly pre-structured by quays and jetties, bars, brothels and other waterfront buildings than the environments in which merchant seamen would often make landfall. This means that the manner in which seamen moved onshore was prefigured, perhaps less strongly but certainly in different way.

Another metaphor for the in-between that I use here is that of the "passage". The word broadly denotes the action of moving through or across one space to reach another or, in the sense of a passage*way*, the conduit through which such a movement is made. Numerous scholars and writers have been fascinated by the metaphor of the passage, among them Walter Benjamin, who was guided by the idea that "passages" – his example being the *passages* or "arcades" of nineteenth-century Paris – had "no outside – like the dream."⁹⁸ Benjamin had intended to use the word in the title of his unfinished *opus magnum*, which today is considered a key inspiration for non-linear forms of writing history.⁹⁹ Yet the word "passage" also occurs in relation to whaling. To be "on passage" meant to be sailing between stages on a journey, whereas "outward bound" marked the first leg of a voyage on leaving one's home port and "homeward bound" the last leg back there.

It was usually on passage, between legs of their voyages, that whalers encountered littoral societies in Africa. Their principal objectives were moving targets on the open seas. This peculiarity is at the root of a distinctive trait of the whalers movements: the specific regularity of their patterns. For vessels carrying cargo or passengers, the sea represented a space to be bridged, a transitional or

---

96 Dening, *Beach Crossings*, 13, 16. Similar thoughts on coastal areas as fluid borders can be found in the work of scholars working in other fields, not least in that of Jacques Derrida, on whom see Feldbusch, *Zwischen Land und Meer*, 18f.
97 Dening, *Beach Crossings*, 18; idem, *Islands and Beaches*, 31–34.
98 Benjamin, *The Arcades Project*, 406. The German title is *Das Passagen-Werk*.
99 For a discussion of Benjamin's work in this context see Jenkins/Munslow, *The Nature of History Reader*, 135.

transit space which separated – or, if we follow Ritter, connected – two coastal ports. Whalers, on the other hand, found their "destinations" at sea and below its surface; from their perspective, coastal settlements were the transitional spaces and landfalls mere interludes. To stop at beaches, in bays and in ports meant interrupting their real business. And while companies engaged in cargo and passenger shipping were naturally keen to reduce time spent at sea by using ever faster vessels, the owners of whalers invested in ever larger vessels, in tenders and supply chains in order to extend the time spent at sea and thereby to increase returns. This peculiarity of whalers strikes me as noteworthy because it left its mark on the situations in which crews encountered African littoral societies. Unlike settlers, missionaries, colonial officials, merchants and many another actor landing on African beaches in vessels from Europe and North American whalers on passage did not seek to influence local conditions and to remake them according to their own agenda. And since the appearance of whales and hence the route and duration of a voyage could not be reliably predicted, it was far from clear at the time of sailing what places a whaler would visit over the course of the next few months. The unpredictable movements of whales thus made for a certain unpredictability of contact situations.

Sailors encountered the inhabitants of African coastal areas not only on beaches, but also when they came aboard their vessels as merchants, pilots, envoys or prostitutes. Yet the group who most often joined vessels from the beaches consisted of seamen who signed aboard along the way. What was still a rare occurrence in the eighteenth century – for instance, to replace men who has deserted or been killed during a long voyage – became a commonplace practice in the nineteenth. American whalers in particular would often hire parts of their crew on passage. As their operations extended further afield and went on for longer, whalers had ample opportunity to take on board unskilled men who would accept lower pay and prove less refractory than American seamen. Most jobs aboard ship could be learnt quickly enough.[100]

The rules and ranks by which shipboard life was hierarchically structured to some extent levelled differences between crew members of different backgrounds. By linking everyday action and experience to sharply delineated positions of status, the vessel was in many respects a de-individualising site of barracks-style socialisation, comparable to a prison or labour camp.[101] And yet from the perspective of social and cultural history it was an exceptionally

---

100 Gillis, "Islands in the Making of an Atlantic Oceania", 31.
101 Dening, *Islands and Beaches*, 159. The sociologist Heinrich Popitz uses the term "barracks-style socialisation" (*kasernierte Vergesellschaftung*) to denote "processes of socialisation under conditions prohibiting those involved from simply dispersing. Conflicts can thus not be

dynamic site. Because seamen had constantly to deal with different cultural and social practices among their changing crew, the historian David Chappell has called ships travelling or "periplean frontiers".[102]

Such a view of whaling vessels as dynamic and open-ended socio-cultural structures reveals their resemblance to beaches. Seamen were moulded by the societies into which they were socialized and in which they learnt to make certain categorial assumptions. Yet ships' crews, far from being replicas in miniature of such societies, were specific communities shaped at sea and governed by their own specific rules. Nor could a littoral society be taken to stand *pars pro toto* for its respective hinterland, less still for an entire continent such as Africa. For centuries littoral societies in various parts of the Atlantic world had had more in common with each other than with societies further inland. The same phenomenon has been observed with regard to the Indian Ocean and the Mediterranean.[103]

Encounters between whalers and African littoral societies thus were not encounters between representative of "the West" on the one hand and "Africa" on the other. Such blanket ascriptions played a far smaller part in shaping these encounters than situational factors which were constantly renegotiated and recast by the actors involved.[104] We may follow the anthropologist Marshall Sahlins in adding that this process of negotiating and casting always develops a dynamic of its own, one "which meaningfully defines the persons and the objects that are parties to it." "Nothing guarantees", as Sahlins emphasises, "that the situations encountered in practice will stereotypically follow from the cultural categories by which the circumstances are interpreted and acted upon."[105] It would thus be misleading to discuss contacts between whalers and African littoral societies simply in terms of an inside/outside dichotomy. Both vessels and beaches as the locations in which this history was played out and seamen and littoral societies and its actors ought therefore to be taken as categories providing orientation and making phenomena describable, not as sealed-off containers.

The history of contacts between seamen and littoral societies is a history of entanglements inasmuch as relations of exchange and communications as they

---

resolved by separating, quitting, resigning, divorcing, leaving, moving. Our society's typical avoidance behaviour is foreclosed." (Popitz, *Prozesse der Machtbildung*, 6).
102 Chappell, "Beyond the Beach", 1–9.
103 Gillis, "Islands in the Making of an Atlantic Oceania", 30; McPherson, *The Indian Ocean*, 122f.
104 On this idea see Pesek, "Die Kunst des Reisens", 67, 98.
105 Sahlins, *Historical Metaphors and Mythical Realities*, 35.

existed on beaches and on board vessels might be the points from which grew relations capable of outlasting short-lived contact situations. Regular visits to a beach by whalers might for instance lead to durable trade links or to migrations of people. Unlike studies of entanglement which focus on the macro level – examining such systems as knowledge or law, such processes as globalisation or modernisation, such entities as states or societies – I take a historical and anthropological approach to examining such entangled practices on beaches and on board vessels.[106]

Because this story of entanglements is not a story of the entanglement of great strands of structural-historical processes, we might prefer to think of it as a history of entanglements "from below", although I do not use that term in the full sense given to it by E. P. Thompson and other exponents of new labour history. What the term stands for here is principally a level of observation, one that foregrounds the "little people" – "Those on whom the forces of the world press most hardly", as Greg Dening has put it.[107] We know that such actors have left comparatively few texts of their own. Yet, as Alf Lüdtke has pointed out, "experiences and actions are more than texts".[108] Although the subaltern may not always – to borrow Gayatri Spivak's phrase – be able to speak,[109] we nonetheless find subalterns to have been actors and indeed travellers whose actions and travels we can observe in a variety of ways. As the historian Rhys Isaac has remarked, "In the documents surviving from the past, the social historian can everywhere find traces – occasionally vivid glimpses – of *people doing things*."[110] According to Isaac, actions are to be considered as statements and their meanings unlocked accordingly. What meanings can we unlock by observing the actions of seamen and coastal inhabitants?

Africa's deep beaches

Research which deals with a large area of observation but which seeks to avoid falling into the traps of homogenisation and generalisation must not lose sight of

---

106 For a notion of "entanglement" that takes on such overarching interpretations see Shalini Randeria's manifesto for "entangled histories", which she describes as an attempt "to reconceptualise past and present relations between Western and non-Western societies." (Randeria, "Geteilte Geschichte und verwobene Moderne", 87).
107 Dening, *Beach Crossings*, 12.
108 Lüdtke, *Herrschaft als soziale Praxis*, 17.
109 Spivak, *Can the Subaltern Speak?*
110 Isaac, *The Transformation of Virginia*, 324.

the particular – all the more so since the African beaches examined in this study pose questions different from those of the histories of colonialism and slavery which have been so influential in shaping historically informed research on Africa more generally. We may accordingly think of these beaches as *deep* beaches, not least because the events and processes discussed here reach further into the past than the late-nineteenth- and twentieth-century phenomena which have come to form the increasingly narrow focus of scholarly interest in African history since the 1980s.[111] In an attempt to do justice to different social, economic, political and cultural conditions, I have structures this study according to a spatial principle, with each chapter constituting a microhistorical examination of relations between whalers and a littoral society on a particular beach. The consequences of these relations are assessed against the background of specific local circumstances. Accordingly, the chapters need not be read in order, but can each stand alone as case studies in their own right.

This does not, however, mean that the chapters are arranged in an altogether arbitrary fashion. Their sequence follows the vessels to the beaches in accordance with the main phases of whaling in the seas around Africa. The first two chapters look at beaches on which whalers landed as they began to pursue southern right whales in the bays of southern Africa, Walvis Bay and Delagoa Bay. The next three chapters focus on island locations which whalers incorporated into their topography in the course hunting sperm whales in the western Indian Ocean: Saint Augustin in Madagascar, Mutsamudo in Anjouan (Comoro Islands) and Port Louis in Mauritius. There follow two chapters on beaches on the west coast of Africa much frequented by whalers as they began to hunt humpback whales in the mid-nineteenth century, Cabinda and Annobón. The final chapter is devoted to an island port frequented by whalers throughout the era of American-style pelagic whaling, the Cape Verdean island of Brava.

This choice of beaches does not comprise all the ports on the African coast where whalers might have been expected to land. Their visits to Madagascar were not limited to Saint Augustin, nor was Cabinda the only port they frequented in Angola. From time to time whalers might also drop anchor in coastal areas that fall outside the scope of this study altogether, for instance Socotra off the Horn of Africa.[112] I have chosen to limit myself to what I consider to be the most important elements of a topography of whaling in the African context because a complete account of all ports of call would have extended this study's scope so far as to render impossible a discussion of specific conditions at

---

111 Reid, "Past and Presentism".
112 See e.g. Log HERCULES II, 1834–1836, 19.12.1834–08.01.1835.

each beach. Represented in this selection are all relevant areas of the African coast and the sea surrounding it and all the main phases of whaling there – but not all beaches that might have been visited in every coastal area.

Since they concern beaches that were indeed among whalers' principal landfalls, three of my omissions require further justification. First, unlike Haywood, I do not discuss the Azores, for these islands, important though they were as a staging post in the Atlantic, have barely any historical connections to Africa.[113] Second, no study is made of the South African Ports of Cape Town, Simon's Town and Port Elizabeth. Their infrastructure was such that whalers indeed called there frequently, although skippers tried to avoid them on account of comparatively steep charges for provisions and a high risk of desertion on the part of disgruntled seamen.[114] Since, however, whalers made up only a small part of the mass of vessels to dock in South African ports in any given year, they seem to me not have made a mark there as distinctive actors. Third, and for the same reason, there is no account here of Zanzibar, a busy global port where traffic was so heavy as to make whalers a negligible presence.

✳✳✳

I have already remarked upon the fact that African actors encountered seamen not only on the beaches but also on the vessels themselves, and that the crews of whaling vessels formed distinct communities in their own right. If, then, we are to come to an appropriate understanding of the contacts under discussion here, we must consider conditions not only on the beaches, but also aboard the vessels. I have added three chapters to this study in order to do so. The first examines when and why whalers came to the seas around Africa, where in these waters their operations were concentrated and how the age of American-style pelagic whaling ended there. The second asks how seamen experienced their voyages aboard whalers and what experiences set them apart from other actors who landed on African beaches in vessels in the eighteenth and nineteenth centuries. The third enquires into the typical patterns of action displayed by seamen on shore leave and how a whaler putting into port conditioned the specific circumstances of these actions.

These chapters on vessels do not fit seamlessly into this study's overall structure, which is organised around African beaches. They address circumstances which imprinted themselves on contacts between seamen and littoral societies from the earliest days of American-style pelagic whaling until its end,

---

113 Vieira, "The Fortunate of the Fortunates", 233f.
114 Booth, *The United States Experience in South Africa*, 28f., 39f., 209.

and their range, both spatial and temporal, extends further than that of the chapters discussing particular beaches. Yet these chapters too need not be read in order. They relate to the chapters on the beaches as the whalers' passages relate to their landfalls: as transitions, as legs of a voyage, as periods of in-between that are yet too significant to be thought of as merely bridging a gap. I therefore call these chapters "Passages" and insert them between the blocks of chapters on beaches outlined above.

This way of structuring the book is guided not only by the intention of allowing for a thorough examination of specific conditions aboard the vessels and on the various beaches. It is also an attempt to confront a fundamental challenge in the representation of history. Past times are no less rich in layers, voices and meanings than the present, yet because its form pushes it towards homogenisation and the ironing out of ambiguities, the classical mode of narrating history causally and sequentially is barely capable of doing justice to this contradictory plurality.[115] "The words with which I evoke the past are a mixture of [. . .] voices that began to speak in my head, sometimes in the first person, sometimes in the second, sometimes in the third", the historian Robert Rosenstone has said of his work, adding: "For years I attempted to smooth the narrative and turn them into one coherent, unified voice, but when I tried to do so, they stopped speaking."[116] By highlighting relations between whalers and African littoral societies in a series of self-contained case studies rather than blending them into a narrative synthesis or an overarching "grand" interpretation, I try to preserve something of the many-voiced character of the past, its surprising juxtaposition of phenomena and at least the possibility of there being altogether different but no less plausible stories to tell.

Yet an account that is polylocal by design will struggle to produce a narrative that is truly multiperspectival, giving equal weight to the voices of all actors. Like any historical narrative, this study too must remain incomplete and open to improvement. Its intention is hence to invite rather than foreclose further investigation. I have already said that I was unable to consider all places that whalers might have visited in Africa. Moreover, since my approach largely follows the perceptions of the seamen, I cannot give an authoritative view of the effects of whalers' landfalls beyond the beaches, in the interior, whether in terms of information flows or the subsequent circulation of exchange goods. For the same reason, I can only suggest an answer to the question of whether African societies retain a memory of whalers transmitted in oral traditions or

---

115 Lüdtke, "Alltagsgeschichte, Mikro-Historie, historische Anthropologie", 645f.; Medick, "Mikro-Historie", 48.
116 Rosenstone, *The Man Who Swam Into History*, xiii.

other cultural practices by pointing to the available ethnographic literature on some of the beaches concerned. And since whaling vessels were masculine worlds and the African actors of whom the whalers tell in their sources were likewise overwhelmingly male, women's voices are not represented here in a manner that would reflect their importance in African littoral societies.

Passages I: Hunting whales off the coast of Africa

Into what waters surrounding the African continent were whalemen in pursuit of their quarry? In the eighteenth and nineteenth centuries whalers generally shifted their areas of operation in wave-like movements. A group of American historians of whaling has summarised this phenomenon as follows: "Expansion reflects exploration and discovery of new concentrations of catchable, commercially valuable whales, whereas contraction reflects the exhaustion and abandonment of those areas of whale concentration and the declining demand for whale oil."[1] Unlike the "regular" fishing industry, the low reproduction rate of its prey meant that commercial whaling was constantly forced to find new hunting grounds in order to maintain or increase its profits.[2] Sometimes these whaling grounds were liable to shift so quickly as to surprise even the seamen themselves. "It happens that parts of the sea which were years ago famous cruising grounds, are now entirely deserted, while every year new grounds are discovered", remarked Charles Nordhoff as he sailed the Indian Ocean aboard a New Bedford whaler in the mid-nineteenth century.[3] Aside from the dynamic of whaling grounds being opened up or closed down, which was inherent in the nature of the enterprise, the areas for which captains would set sail or which they preferred to avoid were also subject to such external factors as naval conflicts, fluctuating demand for whale products or such whims of nature as oceanic currents and winds. Drawing an analogy with the gold rush, the historian Daniel Francis compared whaling captains to "prospectors restlessly searching for the big strike", who "moved from one hunting ground to another, swiftly killing off the animals in one place, then passing on to the next."[4]

---

[1] Smith et al., "Spatial and Seasonal Distribution of American Whaling and Whales in the Age of Sail", 8.
[2] The distinction made in English between *whaling* and *fishing* recognises not only a biological difference in the quarry, but also the different ways in which it is pursued. Fish are caught, whales are hunted – they are tracked, stalked and slain. The seamen involved were aware of this peculiarity of whaling, as is evident in the following remark by Ben Ely, who was a seaman in the barque *Emigrant* from 1844 to 1847: "The danger and anxiety attending the capture of a whale, are very similar to those risks and solicitudes which huntsmen will encounter in pursuit of game." (Ely, *There She Blows*, 48) In his novel *The Hunter and the Whale* (1967), the South African writer Laurens van der Post drew a poetic comparison between whaling and hunting elephants.
[3] Nordhoff, *Whaling and Fishing*, 92f.
[4] Francis, *A History of World Whaling*, 149.

The crucial determining factor in the whalers' movements was of course the migrations of the whales themselves. In the age of American-style pelagic whaling, whalers in the southern oceans hunted chiefly sperm whales (*Physeter macrocephalus*), southern right whales (*Eubalaena australis*) and humpback whales (*Megaptera novaeangliae*) – species known for long annual migrations.[5] Of these species, sperm whales could be hunted with the least seasonal variation, their diet – squid, octopus and fish – being less subject to seasonal fluctuation than that of the baleen whales, which fed chiefly on krill and plankton. Although sperm whales too migrate between feeding and mating grounds, their movements are subject to more complex patterns, depending on age and sex, than those of southern right or humpback whales, and thus were as difficult for whalers to predict as the weather: sperm whales might turn up in any reasonably warm sea, but could not reliably be found in any particular location (Fig. 1).[6]

Unlike sperm whales, southern right and humpback whales move in steady rhythms between the polar seas, which offer them a wealth of food in summer, and warmer coastal waters, where they mate and give birth in winter. Southern right whales start leaving the Antarctic Ocean in May and head north up to a

---

[5] On whale migrations see Stern, "Migration and Movement Patterns". As by-catch or for practice, whalers would also hunt pilot whales (known to seamen as "blackfish"), bottlenose dolphins ("cowfish") and other small cetaceans. Blue whales, fin whales, sei whales and other species found in the seas around Africa, on the other hand, were too fast, dived too deep or sank too suddenly when dead to be feasibly chased by rowing boats. "Sometimes these finbacks are very large and go through the water with great speed, but none of the whalers bother with them", the harpooner Robert Ferguson, sailing off the coast of Madagascar in the New Bedford barque *Kathleen* in 1882, observed in his diary (Ferguson, *Harpooner*, 111; for a description of a successful attempt by American whalers to capture and kill a blue whale see Eldridge, *Lewis William Eldridge's Whaling Voyage*, 11f.). The phrase "American-style pelagic whaling" is derived from the periodisation proposed by Randall R. Reeves and Tim D. Smith, who distinguish it from earlier and later periods by three characteristic traits. American-style pelagic whaling pursued above all sperm and right whales, doing so in whaling expeditions lasting several years and spanning the globe. It was dominated by the United States, which made up eighty per cent of the industry and contributed the overwhelming portion of capital, labour and expertise. Although they were earlier inventions, such technological features as the use of whaleboats operating from mother ships and onboard tryworks became the norm in this era. (Reeves/Smith, "A Taxonomy of World Whaling", 90f.; for a similar periodisation see Davis/Gallman, "American Whaling, 1820–1990", 56f.)

[6] Weir, "A Review of Cetacean Occurrence in West African Waters from the Gulf of Guinea to Angola", 11; Whitehead, "Sperm Whale". In the Atlantic, sperm whales occurred mostly south of the equator between February and April, whereas they could be found year-round in the Indian Ocean, but especially between March and June. (Smith et al., "Spatial and Seasonal Distribution of American Whaling and Whales in the Age of Sail", 7).

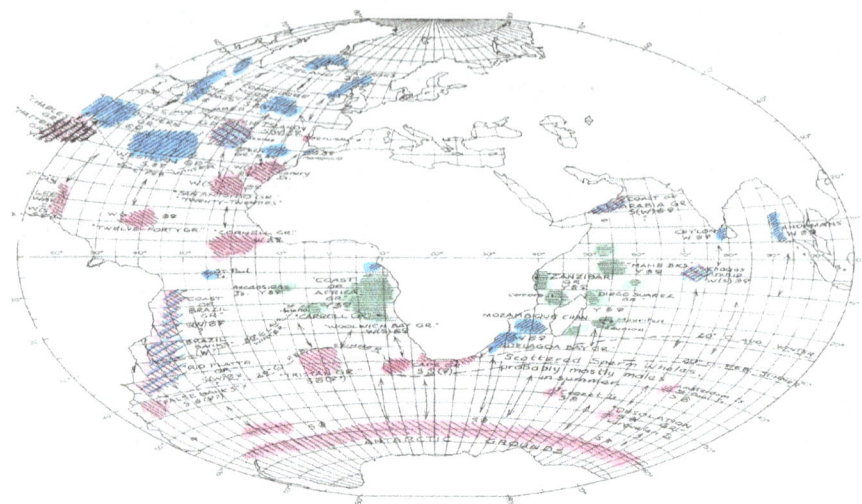

Fig. 1: Sperm whaling grounds in the Atlantic and Indian Oceans. This map is based on statistics of sperm whaling from the eighteenth to the twentieth century. It was drawn in 1959 by the American marine biologist Raymond Gilmore and revised in 2008 by the Australian zoologist John Bannister. For each whaling ground, it indicates the primary season (S = summer, W = winter, Y = year-round) and the sex of the whales killed.
Smith et al., "Spatial and Seasonal Distribution of American Whaling and Whales in the Age of Sail".

latitude of approximately 15°S, that is, up to about the northern tip of Madagascar or the coast of Angola. ("Never known of a Right Whale's crossing the Line", noted Charles Smith, first mate of the New Bedford barque *Sunbeam*, in 1904.[7]) Humpback whales, on the other hand, do cross the "line", i.e. the equator. Their regular return to the same coastal waters made the animals an easy prey for whalers, who also took advantage of overlapping populations of southern right and humpback whales in certain locations. Yet this also meant that stocks in areas of intense whaling activity were liable after a few years to decline so far as to force whalers to look elsewhere. Generally speaking, these different migratory patterns meant that whaling activity was more concentrated for shorter periods in southern right and humpback whaling grounds than those where sperm whales were hunted.

In the following, I shall consider the exploitation of whale stocks in the seas around Africa in the light of the overall development of American-style pelagic whaling. What emerges are four sub-types of whaling, each of which was

---

7 Ashley, *The Yankee Whaler*, 9.

carried on for a few decades in various waters off the coast of Africa: the Atlantic sperm whale hunt, the hunt for southern right whales in the bays of southern Africa, sperm whaling hunt in the western Indian Ocean and the hunt for humpback whales off the eastern and western coasts of Africa.

The bay of whales

Europeans became aware of the presence of whales off the western coast of Africa in the course of Portuguese and Hispanic explorations of the Atlantic. Vasco da Gama, for instance, observed many whales on his way to the coast of what is now South Africa, and his brother Paulo nearly lost his life in the attempt to kill a few of them. A few years later Duarte Pacheco Pereira told of a bay full of whales on the coast of south-western Africa, to which he gave the gave the name "Angra de balea" (Bay of the Whale or Bay of Whales), which, in the Dutch-English form "Walvis Bay", it retains to this day. Beginning in around 1610, vessels sailed from the Netherlands and France to the Cape of Good Hope in pursuit of fur seals. Their voyages, along with those of the East Indiamen who began plying the routes between Europe and Asia in the sixteenth century, yielded further knowledge about whales in the waters surrounding Africa. They also confirmed the account of Marco Polo, who had written of whales in the Indian Ocean in the thirteenth century. Such observations can be traced back further still, with classical accounts of Alexander the Great's Persian campaign telling of whales in the northern Indian Ocean.[8]

In Europe, the commercial interest in exploiting whales goes back to at least the eleventh century, when Basque fishermen began to hunt northern right whales in order to bring their flesh, bones, tongues and baleen to market. In the course of the high and late Middle Ages Basque vessels penetrated further into the North Atlantic as the market for their produce extended ever further into the European interior. Beginning in the early 1600s vessels from England, the Netherlands, Denmark, Hamburg, Altona and Bremen were outfitted for whaling according to the

---

[8] Barros, "Extracts from 'Da Asia'", 166f.; Ellis, "Whaling, Aboriginal", 1227f.; Griffiths et al., "Impacts of Human Activities on Marine Animal Life in the Benguela", 313; Pereira, *Esmeraldo de Situ Orbis*, 88; Ravenstein, *A Journal of the First Voyage of Vasco da Gama*, 4, 6; Richards/ Du Pasquier, "Bay Whaling off Southern Africa", 231f. The Arab explorer al-Mas'udi wrote of whales in the Indian Ocean as early as the tenth century, but his writings were not known in Europe till the nineteenth century (Pearce, *Zanzibar*, 133). Another sixteenth-century reference to whales in the Indian Ocean is to be found in Barbosa, *A Description of the Coasts of East Africa and Malabar in the Beginning of the Sixteenth Century*, 165f.

Basque model – equipped, that is, with rowing boats, harpoons and lances. Commercial interested shifted to the oil into which the whales' blubber was rendered and which was used as lamp oil, as a lubricant or to make soap. Whalers from such ports as Amsterdam, Hull or Bayonne hunted chiefly bowhead and other right whales in the north Atlantic and particularly in the bays of the Svalbard archipelago (Spitsbergen). The whales of the South Seas[9] remained, for the time being, beyond their reach. Seamen still had to bring any whales they killed ashore in order to try out the oil from the blubber before decomposition set in. Long voyages into distant seas and tropical climes could barely seem a viable option in these circumstances. For their part, the European colonial bases than began to spring up along the African coast in the fifteenth century did not engage in whaling – unlike in the case of Brazil, for instance, where the Portuguese authorities established shore whaling industry after the Basque model in Recôncavo de Bahia around the year 1602.[10] Before the age of American-style pelagic whaling dawned in the mid-eighteenth century, the only short-lived attempt to exploit whale stocks off the African coast was made by Dutch whalers.

Dutch vessels dominated European whaling in the seventeenth century. They had discovered rich hunting grounds for bowhead whales in sub-arctic waters, and the English Civil War had set back the efforts of their likeliest competitors. As the century progressed, however, and French, British, Hamburg and Danish vessels began to join the competition for dwindling stocks, Dutch whalers began to explore new whaling grounds further afield.[11] They identified promising waters off Table Bay at the Cape of Good Hope, where the Dutch East India Company had established a victualling station in 1652. But the hunts for southern right whales that set out from the station were poorly organized and unprofitable, and operations ceased in 1693.[12]

In its search for new commercial opportunities and hoping to build on the experience gathered in trading along the west coast of Africa, the Dutch West India Company branched out into whaling in the early 1700s. In 1726 it sent the whaler *Acredam* to the bay which Pereira had called "Angra de baleia" and

---

9 In the context of whaling, the term "South Seas" is used to refer not to the south Pacific, but more generally to any waters south of the sub-Arctic islands which lay at the centre of the earlier northern whaling ground. In British law, the "south seas" were defined as the seas south of the British Isles. (Chatwin, "A Trade so Uncontrollably Uncertain", 2).
10 Alden, "Yankee Sperm Whalers in Brazilian Waters", 269f.; Barthelmeß, "Auf Walfang", 14–19; Carreira, *The People of the Cape Verde Islands*, 42f.; Ellis, "Whaling, Aboriginal", 231–234.
11 Schokkenbroek, *Trying-out*, 35f.
12 Barthelmeß, "Auf Walfang", 24; Booth, *The United States Experience in South Africa*, 34f.; Griffiths et al., "Impacts of Human Activities on Marine Animal Life in the Benguela", 308f.

which the Dutch now named "Walvisbaai". The two-year expedition was, however, a failure. The haul of baleen fell below the company's expectations – no attempt was made to transport blubber over thousands of miles – and neither the captain nor the first mate survived the voyage. Before the *Acredam* had even returned the company dispatched a second vessel, the *Sonnesteijn*, to the bay. The *Sonnesteijn* fared better, with Captain Metselaar recording no fewer than sixty whales killed as well as returning with four elephant tusks he had acquired on the coast. In 1729 the company sent a third vessel, the *Vrijheijt*, to the bay. But she never reached her destination, being forced to turn around off the coast of modern-day Gabon by a conflict between captain and crew. The larger part of the crew fell ill with scurvy on the homeward journey, and both the captain and his successor as well as the harpooner perished. A second voyage to Walvis Bay by the *Sonnesteijn* in 1731 also ended in disaster. She failed to hunt down any whales, but was so heavily damaged along the way that the company was forced to break her up upon return. In view of these costly failures, the company gave up its involvement in whaling, and no European whaler ventured into the south Atlantic for the next forty years.[13]

The growth of Atlantic sperm whaling

In 1688 Edward Randolph, a colonial official, reported back to London that the "New Plimouth Colony have great profit by whale killing" and that, moreover, "I believe it will be one of our best returns."[14] As Randolph's report shows, demand for whale oil had led to the emergence of commercial whaling not only in Europe. In the 1630s fishermen in the Massachusetts Bay Colony, Plymouth Colony and other British possessions in North American began to hunt northern right whales, pilot whales and, if they came within view of the shore, humpback whales. These activities developed into a minor but profitable part of the colonial fishing industry centred on the island of Nantucket, which was conveniently situated close to the whales' migration routes. Around 1700 fishermen began to move from shore whaling to expeditions onto the open sea. There they encountered sperm whales, whose oil burned brighter in lamps than that of baleen whales and whose spermaceti – the wax obtained from the sperm whale's skull and nose – could be turned into candles commanding a high price. In

---

13 Dekker/De Jong, "Whaling Expeditions of the West India Company to Walvis Bay", 50–61; den Heijer, *Goud, Ivoor en Slaven*, 101–104.
14 Quoted in Jenkins, *A History of the Whale Fisheries*, 224.

view of growing demand for sperm oil and spermaceti in both the colonies and in Great Britain – where the Rococo fashion for corsets and panniers also revived the market for whalebone – Nantucket vessels began to explore new whaling grounds off Newfoundland, in the Davis Strait and off Nova Scotia.[15]

Between 1715 and 1750 the Nantucket whaling fleet grew from six to approximately sixty vessels, while whale oil became one of New England's principal exports. As whaling expeditions ranged further afield and lasted longer, in the mid-1700s shipowners began to use two-masted schooners in place of single-masted sloops and to equip them with onboard tryworks for the boiling out of whale oil and with highly manoeuvrable rowing boats. Since whales could now be fully processed aboard ship, expeditions to distant seas lasting months or even years became viable. They turned out to be distinctly more efficient and profitable than whaling operations limited to the nearby north Atlantic. The historian Daniel Vickers has estimated that the Nantucket whalers doubled there productivity between 1715 and 1775. A constant demand for whale products was ensured above all by the nascent industries of England, which used whale oil to cleanse wool and as a lubricant. American whalers now began to explore ever new hunting grounds in a rapid process of expansion that would soon take their vessels to the coast of Africa.[16]

In the 1740s and 1750s Britain's wars against Spain and France continued to curtail the range of whalers in the Atlantic. By the 1760s and 1770s, however, American whalers were able to explore the habitats of sperm whales unhindered, following the equatorial currents south and eastwards. Only few firsthand sources relating to these voyages survive, but such early chroniclers of whaling as Thomas Beale, Alexander Starbuck and Obed Macy – the latter drawing not least on oral traditions from Nantucket – at least offer an outline of the gradual expansion of whaling grounds. It appears that the vessels would sail along the coast of North America into the Caribbean Sea before turning east, exploring first the Gulf of Guinea and then the area around the Azores

---

15 Barthelmeß, "Auf Walfang", 24–26; Dolin, *Leviathan*, 46–62, 71–73, 90–94, 101–107; Hilt, "Contracts, Risk Taking and Diversification in the American Whaling Industry", 17f., 20; Simons, "Christopher Hussey Blown Out (Up) to Sea", 9; Sorge-English, "9 Doz and 11 Best Cutt Bone", 20, 24; Spence, *Harpooned*, 36f.; Stackpole, *The Sea-Hunters*, 15–29; Starbuck, *History of the American Whale Fishery*, 4–36, 41, 168; Warrin, *So Ends This Day*, 67.

16 Dolin, *Leviathan*, 94, 101f., 107f., 119f.; Spence, *Harpooned*, 43; Starbuck, *History of the American Whale Fishery*, 21f., 169–171; Starbuck, *The History of Nantucket*, 376f.; Vickers, "Maritime Labor in Colonial Massachusetts", 268. One factor in the comparatively large efforts made by Nantucket seamen to develop sperm whaling may have been the emphasis given by the Quakers, who had become the largest Christian denomination in the island in the eighteenth century, to light and illumination.

(known to the seamen as "Western Islands"). According to Macy, whalers first set sail from Nantucket – whose fleet had by then grown to nearly one hundred vessels – for the Gulf of Guinea in 1763. One vessel is recorded as returning from there with three hundred barrels in 1768, a respectable yield for the time.[17] Another area much visited in these years was the Cape Verde Islands, some 600 kilometres off the coast of modern Senegal. Not only could sperm whales be found here in all seasons, but whalemen could also rely on familiar infrastructure for their provisions, New England merchantmen having already for some years been in the habit of calling on the islands for victualling and to trade in salt.[18]

Among the first whalers to have sailed from North American ports with the "Coast of Africa" as their express destination and of which we know by name are the schooner *Yarmouth* (1772) and the sloop *Bellisle* (1773) from New Bedford and, from Nantucket, the brigs *Polly* (1774) and *Pembroke* (1775) and the sloop *Rochester* (1774).[19] Nantucket whalers at the time distinguished between voyages to "Guinea" and those to the "Coast of Africa". The former probably referred to the section of coastline between modern Guinea and Cameroon, where seamen might come ashore for drinking water; the latter would accordingly have denoted the lower Guinean coastal waters between Cameroon and Angola. Starbuck records that in 1773 a fleet of at least fourteen whalers set sail for the "Coast of Africa".[20] In the same year the Newport brig *Leviathan* discovered a rich sperm whaling ground off the coast of South America which subsequently became known as the "Brazil Banks" and from which whalers began to penetrate ever further into the south Atlantic. Southern right whales could be reliably taken in the estuary of the River Plate, and by 1775 New England merchants were dispatching a fleet of fifteen vessels to the Falkland Islands.[21] At the outbreak of the American war of independence in the same year the New England Whaling fleet had grown to at least 350 vessels manned by some 4,700 seamen. At least 121 of

---

17 Mc Devitt, "The House of Rotch", 113f.; Macy, *The History of Nantucket*, 54; Sanderson, *Follow the Whale*, 212; Stackpole, *The Sea-Hunters*, 33–35, 51f.
18 Alden, "Yankee Sperm Whalers in Brazilian Waters", 277; Townsend, "Where the Nineteenth Century Whaler Made His Catch", 177.
19 Job Almy & Amos Samson. Whaling contract between Job Almy, John Burden and Samson Amos. 24.08.1773. Rhode Island Historical Society, MSS 9001-A.; Log POLLEY, 1774–1775; Lund et al., *American Offshore Whaling Voyages*, 471, 488, 650; Stackpole, *The Sea-Hunters*, 69; Starbuck, *The History of Nantucket*, 484.
20 Stackpole, *The Sea-Hunters*, 53, 68; Starbuck, *History of the American Whale Fishery*, 56.
21 Alden, "Yankee Sperm Whalers in Brazilian Waters", 276–279; Mc Devitt, "The House of Rotch", 207–212, 604; Stackpole, *The Sea-Hunters*, 55; Starbuck, *History of the American Whale Fishery*, 176.

these vessels sailed to the south Atlantic, eighty-five of them from Nantucket alone.[22]

European whalers did not participate in the south Atlantic sperm whale hunt until war broke out in the American colonies. The lesson learnt from the Dutch West Indian Company's costly failure in Walvis Bay was that exploring new whaling grounds was a riskier investment than sticking to familiar waters. European shipowners continued to prefer sending their vessels to the established whaling grounds on the border between the Arctic and the Atlantic Ocean. Notwithstanding the setback incurred by British whaling as a consequence of the Seven Years' War (1756–63) with France over supremacy in the north Atlantic, British vessels, which had benefited from subsidies and tax breaks since 1733, gradually replaced the Dutch as the principal whaling nation in these seas in the later seventeenth century.[23] The emergence of an independently operating whaling industry in North America was thus likely to raise eyebrows in Britain, which had reason to fear a threat to its own hard-won predominance. To keep the new competition in check, the British authorities in 1765 began to impose regulatory measures aimed at keeping American vessels away from north Atlantic whaling grounds in particular. The indirect effect of these measures was to concentrate American whaling operations in the south Atlantic and to gather a unique wealth of sperm whaling expertise in Nantucket. Since the British Isles at this time were importing approximately four times the quantity of whale oil from New England that British whalers themselves were able to provide, the mother country was in danger of growing economically dependent on its own colonies for an important commodity.[24] Edmund Burke raised this issue in a speech in parliament in 1775, drawing attention to the key importance of the New England whaling industry and to the fact that the Americans were already casting their harpoons "on the coast of Africa".[25] For their part, New Englanders were well aware of the importance of their whaling industry, with whale oil accounting for more than half of direct exports to Britain in the years preceding the war.[26]

---

22 Mc Devitt, "The House of Rotch", 187f.; Starbuck, *History of the American Whale Fishery*, 57.
23 Dolin, *Leviathan*, 102–104, 124f.; Francis, *A History of World Whaling*, 54f.; Jackson, *The British Whaling Trade*, 54–69; Mc Devitt, "The House of Rotch", 192, 559f.; Spence, *Harpooned*, 45, 49–51.
24 Dolin, *Leviathan*, 125–127; Francis, *A History of World Whaling*, 61f.; Graham, "The Migrations of the Nantucket Whale Fishery", 182f.; Starbuck, *History of the American Whale Fishery*, 44–50.
25 Burke, *The Writings and Speeches of Edmund Burke*, vol. III, 117.
26 Mc Devitt, "The House of Rotch", 115.

Southern right whales in the bays of southern Africa

The American war of independence (1775–83) brought ruin to the New England whaling industry. The Royal Navy destroyed approximately eighty-five per cent of the colonies' whaling fleet, requisitioned British whalers as troopships and impressed countless seamen on both sides of the Atlantic into naval service. Although it claimed a neutral stance, Nantucket alone saw more than one thousand of its seamen captured or killed and lost nearly all of its by now 150 vessels. Meanwhile the Continental Congress imposed a ban on the export of whale products to Britain, causing imports to London to collapse from 4,000 tonnes in 1775 to a mere fifty-two tonnes in 1776. With American competition laid low, Britain took advantage of the situation by imposing heavy import duties on foreign whale products while increasing subsidies to British whalers as well as offering bounties of £100 to £500 those of its vessels bringing home the richest haul from the south Atlantic whaling grounds. At least seventy-six British whalers sailed for the south Atlantic during the war, nearly all of them with crews recruited or impressed from New England. These vessels also reached the coast of West Africa, where, for instance, the *Slacombe* of Liverpool bagged five sperm whales in 1781. For American whalers, these British policies spelt the loss of their most important market. London alone imported several thousand tons of whale oil annually and spent more than £300,000 on lighting its streets – more than any other city in the world. Since conditions in New England had made whaling unprofitable, hundreds of skippers, seamen and shipowners specialising in sperm whaling left Nantucket and set up diaspora communities elsewhere on the north Atlantic seaboard, with Dartmouth (now part of Halifax, Nova Scotia) and Milford Haven in Wales as notable examples. Many other seamen signed on aboard British vessels. The largest and economically most influential group of exiles left New England in 1786, when William Rotch, probably the most powerful shipowner in American whaling, sailed for Dunkirk with a fleet of first six and ultimately a total of forty-four vessels and one hundred and fifty seamen. The French government supported these exiles with generous subsidies and other privileges in an attempt to revive its own whaling industry, which had lain dormant since 1766. Although Dunkirk did indeed soon become a major whaling port and the New England whaling industry gradually recovered once the war had ended, it was above all British vessels which explored new whaling grounds in the south Atlantic in this period. Yields from British expeditions into the south Atlantic first exceeded those obtained in the north in 1789, and the years around 1790 were among the most productive of what was known as Britain's "southern whale fishery". In 1793 the British fleet of "southern whalers" comprised ninety-three vessels with some 1,800 crew. Nearly all these vessels as well as most French ones at this time were skippered by American exiles.[27]

In 1789 the *Emilia* became the first whaler to round Cape Horn, thereby ushering in the age of sperm whaling in the Pacific, which was to become the principal ground for American-style pelagic whaling in the nineteenth century. The *Britannia* and the *William and Ann* reached the coast of Australia in 1791. All three vessels were owned by London company of Samuel Enderby & Sons, which since the War of American Independence had pursued the strategy of manning whalers with captains, officers and harpooners who had emigrated from Nantucket and to send them to waters in which British merchantmen had reported whale sightings. The first American whalers to reach Australia were the *Asia* and the *Alliance*, both of Nantucket. On their way to the Australian whaling grounds British and American whalers also explored the waters of the western Indian Ocean, particularly around Madagascar. In 1800 the London *Kingston* became the first whaler known to have sailed for Madagascar as her primary destination.[28]

Many vessels from Dunkirk and Dartmouth continued in this period to concentrate on the south Atlantic, while extending their whaling grounds to the east of the Cape of Good Hope. Besides the Gulf of Guinea, which was the destination above all of Dartmouth whalers, their operations now began to centre on Walvis Bay and Delagoa Bay, now Maputo Bay on the coast of Mozambique. Here whalers found anchorage in sheltered inlets and could intercept southern right whales on their migrations from their feeding grounds in the Antarctic Ocean to the more northerly seas in which they would mate and calve. Although their oil was considered less valuable than that of sperm whales, southern rights,

---

27 Alden, "Yankee Sperm Whalers in Brazilian Waters", 284; Chatwin, "A Trade so Uncontrollably Uncertain", 25f.; Clayton, "Nantucket Whalers in Milford Haven, Wales", 5–7; Dolin, *Leviathan*, 156, 163f.; Du Pasquier, "Catch History of French Right Whaling Mainly in the South Atlantic", 270; Francis, *A History of World Whaling*, 62f., 69–73; Graham, "The Migrations of the Nantucket Whale Fishery", 183–194; Jackson, *The British Whaling Trade*, 66–68, 93–95; Basil Lubbock. *British Whalers, 18th Century*. Manuscript, 1935. Caird Library, National Maritime Museum, LUB/38/2; Mc Devitt, "The House of Rotch", 222f., 240–250, 279–289, 292–312, 343–350, 608; Spence, *Harpooned*, 55, 57, 61f., 66–68; Stackpole, *The Sea-Hunters*, 142f.; Stackpole, *Whales & Destiny*, 115, 187; Starbuck, *History of the American Whale Fishery*, 58–81, 139, 153; Starbuck, *The History of Nantucket*, 383.
28 Chatwin, "A Trade so Uncontrollably Uncertain", 2, 27; Dickson, "The Cruise of the Nantucket Ships Asia and Alliance", 9–11; Jackson, *The British Whaling Trade*, 92, 98–106; Spence, *Harpooned*, 57f., 63–66; Stackpole, *Whales & Destiny*, 15–17, 123–131; Wray/Martin, "Historical Whaling Records from the Western Indian Ocean", 213.

besides offering a source of baleen, were also a fairly easy quarry. Averaging half a kilometre to four kilometres an hour, they are comparatively slow swimmers and because of their high fat content float when dead. Southern right whales follow the cold Benguela Current along the coast of western Africa up to the estuary of the Cunene river, which marks the border between Angola and Namibia, and sometimes even as far as modern Gabon. Besides Walvis Bay, a reliable whaling ground for southern rights was Baía dos Tigres, an island off the southern coast of what is now Angola. On the east coast of Africa, the whales penetrate far into the Mozambique Channel, which separates Madagascar from the African continent.[29]

Whalers began to frequent Walvis Bay and Delagoa Bay in about 1785, largely from July to September. They would also occasionally set sail for the Bight of Sofala, which is close to the provincial capital of Beira in modern Mozambique. The hunt for southern right whales also extended into certain bay on the coast of the Cape Colony, notably Table Bay, False Bay, Saldanha Bay and St. Helena Bay. Yet Walvis Bay remained the most visited whaling ground for southern rights, probably not least because it was less dangerous sailing for European and North American vessels than the coast of Mozambique. According to the historian Alan Booth, Walvis Bay "was about as popular as the Brazil Banks [. . .] both grounds attracted more American whalers than any other place in the world."[30] At least half of Nantucket's whaling fleet, which once more numbered some thirty vessels, visited Walvis Bay in this period. Most British southern whalers, too – approximately twenty-five vessels – could also be found plying the waters off south-western Africa around 1790. Walvis Bay alone was visited by twenty to thirty vessels per year in the mid-1790s.[31] Under the impression of this development, in 1789 Cape Colony merchants began to set up their own whaling stations in the territory, from which single-masted sloops

---

29 Brito/Picanço/Carvalho, "Small Cetaceans off São Tomé (São Tomé and Príncipe, Gulf of Guinea, West Africa)", 3f.; Carvalho et al., "Temporal Patterns of Population Structure of Humpback Whales in West Coast of Africa (B Stock)"; Bruton, *The Essential Guide to Whales*, 23; Francis, *A History of World Whaling*, 71; Mc Devitt, "The House of Rotch", 361, 606f.; Spence, *Harpooned*, 62; Stackpole, *The Sea-Hunters*, 110; Stackpole, *Whales & Destiny*, 162; Townsend, "Where the Nineteenth Century Whaler Made His Catch", 177; Weir, "Occurrence and Distribution of Cetaceans off Northern Angola, 2004/05", 228–231; Weir, "A Review of Cetacean Occurrence in West African Waters from the Gulf of Guinea to Angola", 5–7.
30 Booth, "American Whalers in South African Waters", 278f.
31 Ibid., 278f.; Jackson, *The British Whaling Trade*, 108f.; Richards/Du Pasquier, "Bay Whaling off Southern Africa", 232–234; Smith, "The Struggle for Control of Southern Moçambique", 210–217; Stackpole, *The Sea-Hunters*, 164f.; Wray/Martin, "Historical Whaling Records from the Western Indian Ocean", 215f.

hunted (mostly) southern right whales in coastal waters. Although these operations continued throughout the nineteenth century, they remained a marginal aspect of the colonial fishing industry, in which no more than a few vessels ever engaged at one time.[32]

***

"Sunday last arrived in this port, from Woolwichbay, the ship Judith, of Dunkirk", *The Medley* newspaper of New Bedford reported in August 1793.[33] What may at first seem an unremarkable event was in fact anything but, for vessels of William Rotch's Dunkirk fleet were not in the habit of sailing for New England ports. The background to this visit was explained to reporters by Paul Ray, the ship's master: *Judith* had left Dunkirk in the summer of 1792 and with about ten other whalers had successfully pursued southern right whales in Walvis Bay. At the season's peak, in June 1793, the British ship *Liverpool* appeared in the bay, soon revealing itself to be not a whaler but a privateer. Armed with twenty guns, the *Liverpool* first captured *Phebe*, another Dunkirk ship, before going on to attack *Judith*. Captain Ray wasted no time in ordering the anchor to be cut and making a run for safety.[34]

Such incidents also occurred in Delagoa Bay and other whaling grounds in 1793. To shipowners, they were harbingers of the crisis into which the wars between revolutionary France and its European rivals would plunge whaling throughout the next two decades.[35] The whalemen of Dunkirk and Dartmouth found themselves out in a disadvantageous situation by the war. Some émigré seamen and shipowners, William Rotch among them, returned to New England. British whaling was much weakened by periodic impressments of its crews by the Royal Navy. The strength of the southern whaling fleet fluctuated during period, from ninety-three vessels in 1793 to twenty-five in 1797, up to ninety-nine in 1804 and down again to forty-eight by 1814. No fewer than four British

---

[32] Barthelmeß, "Auf Walfang", 24; Best/Ross, "Catches of Right Whales from Shore-Based Establishments in Southern Africa", 276–285; Booth, "American Whalers in South African Waters", 281; Booth, *The United States Experience in South Africa*, 35f., 38; Ellis, *Men and Whales*, 306; Griffiths et al., "Impacts of Human Activities on Marine Animal Life in the Benguela", 308f.; Richards/Du Pasquier, "Bay Whaling off Southern Africa", 235.
[33] "Ship News." *The Medley or Newbedford Marine Journal*, 23.08.1793, 3.
[34] Ibid., 3.
[35] "Newbedford Marine Journal." *The Medley or Newbedford Marine Journal*, 27.01.1794, 3; Pinkham, *The Log Book of the Good Ship Alliance of Nantucket Captain Bartlett Coffin*, 11.–13.09.1793; Richards/Du Pasquier, "Bay Whaling off Southern Africa", 244f.; Stackpole, *The Sea-Hunters*, 171–176; Stackpole, *Whales & Destiny*, 229f.

whalers were lost to Dutch attacks off the Cape of Good Hope in 1804 alone.[36] Such incidents were among the reasons why, beginning in 1798, the British whaling fleet moved the larger part of its operations to the eastern Indian Ocean, where new whaling grounds were exploited off Timor, Australia and New Zealand.[37]

Since the competing naval powers gave little consideration to vessels sailing under neutral flags, the war in Europe also adversely affected American whaling. Time and time again the Royal Navy stopped American vessels in order to arrest British deserters (actual or supposed) among their crews. France and Britain imposed naval blockades on one another, and each impounded merchandise destined for the respective enemy found aboard American vessels. The undeclared "Quasi-War" (1798–1790) between France and the United States added to the risks faced by American whalers. In response to continuing attacks on American vessels, in 1807 President Jefferson signed into law the Embargo Act, in consequence of which the United States was virtually cut off from overseas trade – and US shipping brought to the brink of collapse. More than thirty thousand seamen were out of work and whaling largely ceased. From the American perspective, the worst in a succession of conflicts to affect its whaling industry in the age of Atlantic revolutions was the War of 1812 (1812–1814), in which the British navy blockaded America's eastern seaboard and destroyed nearly its entire whaling fleet. For her part, the American frigate *Essex* dealt a severe blow to British whaling by single-handedly destroying twelve vessels, amounting to half of Britain's whaling fleet in the Pacific.[38]

Sperm whaling off Africa's eastern coast

The American whaling industry soon recovered following the peace treaties of Geneva and Paris, signed in 1814. It took only a few years for the fleet to outgrow

---

36 Chatwin, "A Trade so Uncontrollably Uncertain", 27, 29; Mc Devitt, "The House of Rotch", 375–385; Spence, Harpooned, 66, 70; Stackpole, *Whales & Destiny*, 270.
37 Richards/Du Pasquier, "Bay Whaling off Southern Africa", 246.
38 Chatwin, "A Trade so Uncontrollably Uncertain", 27; Dening, *Islands and Beaches*, 26f.; Francis, *A History of World Whaling*, 77; Gassert/Häberlein/Wala, *Kleine Geschichte der USA*, 175–178, 181, 209–213, 219; Jackson, *The British Whaling Trade*, 112f.; Jones, "The British Southern Whale and Seal Fisheries", 22; Kugler, "The Penetration of the Pacific by American Whalemen in the 19th Century", 23; Mc Devitt, "The House of Rotch", 418–427, 448–452; Starbuck, *History of the American Whale Fishery*, 91–95. Nantucket lost more than eighty per cent of its whalers (93 of 116 vessels) in the War of 1812.

its pre-1812 strength. Demand was driven not only by the reopening of the British market, but also by the fact that more and more lighthouses and trains were now illuminated by sperm whale oil. New England shipowners outfitted ever larger vessels for whaling, from an average displacement of 280 tonnes in 1820 to approximately 400 in in 1840. The draughts of these vessels were now often too deep to negotiate the sandbanks off Nantucket harbour. New whaling fleets of varying size now grew up in ports from Sag Harbor in the south to Boston in the north, the most important of them based at Fairhaven, New London and Sag Harbor, but above all at New Bedford on the southern coast of Massachusetts. Between 1820 and 1880 New Bedford accounted for half of all American whaling produce and became the country's richest city. By contrast, Britain's southern whaling, which had also grown after 1814 and reached an all-time peak in 1820 with 137 vessels, went into a steady decline after 1840 (Tab. 1). A number of reasons for this decline may be cited, among them the lower productivity of British whalers compared to their American counterparts, the phasing out of whale oil in favour of gas lighting begun in 1814, the gradual withdrawal of state subsidies between 1821 and 1824, the complete opening of the British market to whale produce imported from Australia (1823) and the United States (1843), and the fact that the losses incurred in the War of 1812 led many investors to shy away from whaling as a risky business. But every year until the late 1830s between 78 and 123 British whalers continued to sail for the southern seas. However, they scarcely competed directly with American vessels, instead concentrating on waters little frequented by them off Timor and the Moluccas. At the same time British whalers were shifting the larger part of their activities to sub-Arctic waters. However, pack ice claimed several vessels while overhunting repeatedly made for poor catches. By 1843 the British whaling industry had lost eighty-two vessels in the north and fallen irrecoverably behind the American competition. Only fourteen whalers sailed from British ports in 1849, many of them old and dilapidated. An attempt

Tab. 1: British whalers in the southern oceans, annual average 1800–1846 (summarised by decades).

1800–1810	72
1810–1820	64
1820–1830	90
1830–1840	94
1840–1846	54

Source: Enderby, *Proposal*, 10.

made that year by British shipowners to revive the "southern whale fishery" soon had to be abandoned for lack of capital. Samuel Enderby & Sons of London, the oldest and formerly the leading company in the business, folded in the mid-1850s.

Aided by Jeremiah Winslow, an American shipowner, in 1816 France began to turn Le Havre into a centre of whaling, sending subsidised vessels mainly to the south Atlantic and the Pacific. In 1836 some German shipowners began to send whalers to the Pacific, especially from Bremen. Set against the development of whaling in the United States, however – in 1833 alone, 392 whalers with crews totalling some 10,000 sailed from American ports, with an estimated 70,000 people depending on whaling for their livelihoods, directly or indirectly – the few dozen French and German whalers were something of a sideshow. It was American vessels too that took the lead in exploring new whaling grounds in these decades. Once the *Globe* of Nantucket had identified a rich sperm whaling ground in the central Pacific, American whalers gradually extended their range across the ocean's entirety.[39]

This boom in sperm whaling in the Pacific had consequences for the seas around Africa. An estimated one in four vessels sailing to or from the Pacific whaling sounds chose a route through the Indian Ocean, with British whalers more likely to do so than American. Along the way, many of them would linger in the area of Madagascar to hunt sperm whales there. In 1823 the *Swan*, which belonged to Enderby of London, became the first vessel expressly to sail for the waters around the Seychelles. Five years later Nantucket whalers went hunting for sperm whales in the coastal waters of Zanzibar. In the western Indian Ocean, sperm whales were particularly prevalent in the "Zanzibar Ground" between Zanzibar and the Comoros, in the "Mahé Bank" north of the island of that name in the Seychelles, and to lesser degree in the "Fortune Banks" of the coral island of Coëtivy in the south of the Seychelles. Sperm whales were also to be found in the Mozambique Channel and off the southern and north-eastern coasts of Madagascar, especially from May to July. The Saya de Malha Bank, a vast undersea plateau to the south-east of the Seychelles, was another ground

---

39 Busch, *Whaling Will Never Do for Me*, 3; Chatterton, *Whalers and Whaling*, 148; Chatwin, "A Trade so Uncontrollably Uncertain", 28–32, 115; Davis/Gallman, "American Whaling, 1820–1990", 56–59, 62; Davis/Gallman/Hutchins, "The Decline of U.S. Whaling", 569f.; Du Pasquier, "Catch History of French Right Whaling Mainly in the South Atlantic", 271; Francis, *A History of World Whaling*, 78f., 125–135; Hilt, "Contracts, Risk Taking and Diversification in the American Whaling Industry", 70f.; Hohman, *The American Whaleman*, 5, 9; Jackson, *The British Whaling Trade*, 117–130, 136–142; Jones, "The British Southern Whale and Seal Fisheries", 23–25; Lindgren, "Let Us Idealize Old Types of Manhood", 166f.; Oesau, *Die deutsche Südseefischerei auf Wale im 19. Jahrhundert*, 16f., 57f., 77f., 128f.; Spence, *Harpooned*, 83f., 93, 96, 99, 123; Starbuck, *History of the American Whale Fishery*, 95f.; Williams, "The Whale Fishery", 105.

in which sperm whales could be hunted between February and July. They could be found year-round, but particularly from August to December, in the Mascarene Basin around the islands of Mauritius and La Réunion. In the 1850s whalers began to extend their range northwards into the Arabian Sea, hunting sperm whales chiefly off points in the south-east of the Arabian Peninsula, notably Ra's Fartak, Mirbat and the Khuriya Muriya Islands.[40]

Its many sperm whaling grounds were not the only point in favour of the Indian Ocean as far as whalers were concerned. Unlike the Pacific, it had – at least in parts – already been well surveyed in nautical charts and almanacs, and unlike the seas of the sub-Arctic, it presented no natural obstacle to whalers operating there throughout the year. The Indian Ocean presented good opportunities for victualling, for instance the island of Anjouan in the Comoros, but also ports with a well-developed infrastructure of repair docks, hospitals, consulates and a supply of spare parts. Port Louis in Mauritius is a prominent example. Whalers were able to take advantage of the Indian monsoon by heading for waters off the African coast before the onset of the winter monsoon and then following the trade winds towards the Seychelles, crossing various whaling grounds along the way.[41]

However, the Agulhas Current and other strong currents made navigation in the western Indian Ocean a comparatively tricky business. The infrastructure of the East India trade, moreover, and that of Port Louis in particular, was expensive to use as well as confronting mariners with time-consuming red tape. What is more, a myth circulated among whalers throughout the nineteenth century according to which the sperm whales of the Indian Ocean were warier than those found elsewhere, making it longer and harder work for a vessel to fill its casks with oil. "The slightest noise causes them to disappear with marvelous celerity", the seaman Charles Nordhoff noted in in the mid-nineteenth century.[42] Yet the greatest problem posed by the Indian Ocean was its lack of truly reliable hunting grounds, forcing whalers into lengthy spells of costly inactivity. Nordhoff's own vessel, for example, crisscrossed a sperm whaling ground off Madagascar for a fortnight without so much as a glimpse of a whale.[43] In the logbook of the *Arab* of Fairhaven, sailing in the western Indian Ocean in

---

40 Beale, *The Natural History of the Sperm Whale*, 151f.; Chatwin, "A Trade so Uncontrollably Uncertain", 2, 89f.; Kugler, "The Penetration of the Pacific by American Whalemen in the 19th Century", 24; Macy, *The History of Nantucket*, 224f.; Starbuck, *History of the American Whale Fishery*, 97f.; Wray/Martin, "Historical Whaling Records from the Western Indian Ocean", 218–224.
41 Wray/Martin, "Historical Whaling Records from the Western Indian Ocean", 214, 219.
42 Nordhoff, *Whaling and Fishing*, 161f.; Wray/Martin, "Historical Whaling Records from the Western Indian Ocean", 214, 226.
43 Nordhoff, *Whaling and Fishing*, 98.

1851, Captain Samuel Braley resorted to a Nantucket nursery rhyme to describe the sperm whales' unpredictable ways: "Now you see it; now you don't / Perhaps you will; perhaps you won't."[44]

Humpbacking off the eastern and western coasts of Africa

"The humpback whale is the most dangerous creature to handle that can be found in the water", observed John Williams, who sailed the Indian Ocean as an ordinary seaman in the early 1840s, of humpback whales, explaining that "We seldom go out of a scrape with one without several holes being stove in our boats."[45] Although their oil was considered valuable, whalers tended to pursue humpback whales when their attempts to catch sperm whales had been in vain. The log kept by the Salem bark *Emerald* of its voyage from 1838 to 1840 offers a vivid example of how seamen not only consistently ignored humpback whales, but would even abandon the chase in their boats when they came to the belated realisation that what they had in their sights was a humpback.[46] While seamen were aware that humpback whales would regularly return to particular locations, they found the hunt to be difficult as well as dangerous. The humpback, as Nordhoff noted, "is exceedingly hard to kill, runs to windward at great speed on being struck, and generally sinks when killed."[47] Another of Nordhoff's observations in the Indian Ocean around 1850, however, in retrospect reads like a portent of the whaling industry's looming crisis: "Sperm whales are now much scarcer than in years past."[48]

By 1846 the American whaling fleet had grown to its largest size ever, with 735 vessels and approximately 18,000 seamen. And for each whaleman, there were estimated to be another six persons on shore who depended on the whaling industry for their livelihood. The single largest whaling port at this time was New Bedford, which accounted for around 200 of these vessels, more than the combined whaling fleets of all European nations. The New Bedford fleet grew by another 129 vessels by 1857. British southern whalers had by this time

---

44 Log ARAB, 1849–1852, 15.05.1851.
45 Williams, *The Adventures of a Seventeen-year-old Lad and the Fortunes He Might Have Won*, 43.
46 Log EMERALD, 1838–1840, 29.07., 04.08. & 12.09.1838, 19.07., 21.–31.07., 03.08., 13.08. & 15.–16.08.1839.
47 Nordhoff, *Whaling and Fishing*, 175f.
48 Ibid., 161f.

virtually disappeared, with a mere nine of them sailing in 1843.[49] Yet American whalers continued to explore new hunting grounds. In 1843 the New Bedford whalers *Hercules* and *Janus* became the first to catch bowhead whales off the Kamchatka peninsula in eastern Russia; in 1848 the *Superior* of Sag Harbor became the first whaler to sail through the Bering Strait, finding rich stocks of bowhead whales in the western Arctic; in 1851 grey whales began to be hunted off the coast of California; and finally, in 1854 the first whalers reached Point Barrow on the northern coast of Alaska.[50] The US government increasingly came to view the country's thriving whaling industry as a matter of national interest, to be supported by such measures as oceanographic expeditions and the compilation of whaling statistics (Fig. 2). A survey produced by the Senate in 1850 placed whaling in thirteenth place among the nation's industries, its significance comparable to that of mining. In the state of Massachusetts, it even ranked third, surpassed only by the shoe and garment industries.[51]

Yet the intensive hunting of the 1840s soon brought about a noticeable decline in sperm and southern right whale populations. Whalers had to undertake ever longer journeys to meet their targets, and after their 1846 peak, the number of American whalers declined for the first time since the War of 1812. From 1848 onwards the industry also began to lose both labour and investors to the American west, where the Californian gold rush had just set in. In the 1850s more and more voyages made a loss.[52] Against this backdrop, turning to the previously little-hunted humpback whale was a move by the whaling industry at least to delay the coming slump. It was encouraged by technological innovation that made humpback whales easier to catch. In 1848 Lewis Temple, an

---

49 Creighton, *Rites & Passages*, 36; Francis, *A History of World Whaling*, 78f., 91; Hohman, *The American Whaleman*, 5f., 42, 45; Stone, "Whalers and Missionaries at Herschel Island", 102.
50 Busch, *Whaling Will Never Do for Me*, 3; Dolin, *Leviathan*, 227–229; Spence, *Harpooned*, 107, 113, 117–119.
51 Creighton, *Rites & Passages*, 6; Davis/Gallman, "American Whaling, 1820–1990", 59; Hilt, "Contracts, Risk Taking and Diversification in the American Whaling Industry", 67f.; Hohman, *The American Whaleman*, 4; Kugler, "The Penetration of the Pacific by American Whalemen in the 19th Century", 25.
52 Francis, *A History of World Whaling*, 103; Spence, *Harpooned*, 113, 117; Starbuck, *History of the American Whale Fishery*, 112; Starbuck, *The History of Nantucket*, 341. The role of the depletion of whale stocks in the declining productivity of the American whaling industry remains subject to debate. Set against the population figures before whaling began, as estimated by environmental historians, the losses to whaling before the early twentieth century would have been so low overall as to suggest that overfishing was not the problem. However, certain areas which were the site of particularly intensive whaling activity may well have already witnessed a marked decline in populations in the nineteenth century. On this discussion see esp. Davis/Gallman/Hutchins, "The Decline of U.S. Whaling".

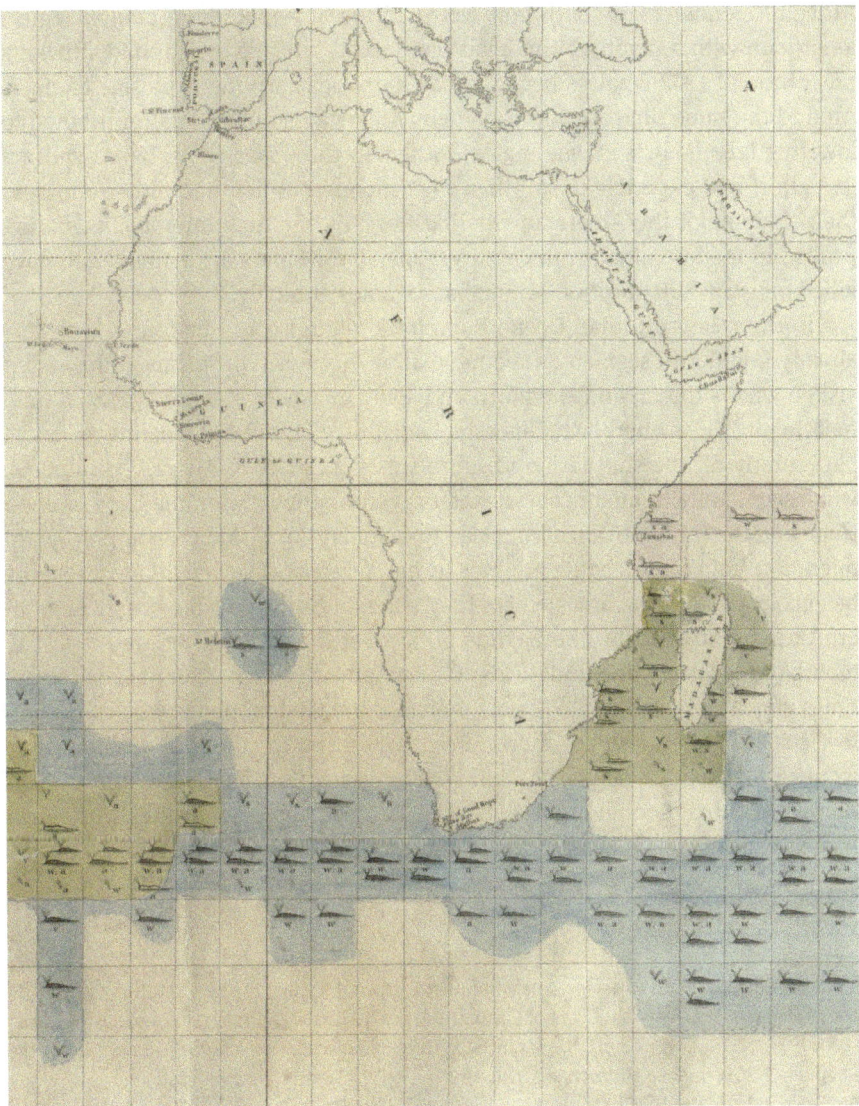

Fig. 2: Whaling grounds around the African continent in the mid-nineteenth century; detail of a map produced in support of the American whaling industry. It was drawn in 1851 by the oceanographer Matthew Maury and based on whaler's logs of the 1840s.
Map image courtesy of the Norman B. Leventhal Map Center at the Boston Public Library.

African American blacksmith from New Bedford, invented the "Temple toggle", a harpoon with a pivoting iron head that locked in place once it had struck its prey; around 1852 whalers began to use harpoons carrying explosive charges. Around the same time advances made by American shipbuilders contributed to lowering labour costs in whaling, with the new three-masted barques requiring less effort and expertise to sail than the schooners which had hitherto formed the backbone of the American whaling fleet. By the time humpback whaling peaked in the late nineteenth century, American whalers are estimated to have killed between 500 and 1,000 humpback whales annually.[53]

In the western Indian Ocean humpback whales could be found in waters already familiar to seamen as sperm whaling grounds. For instance, they often visited waters directly off the north and south coasts of Madagascar from June to October.[54] Elsewhere, whalers established new humpback whaling grounds, particularly off the southern and south-western coasts of Africa.[55] Humpback whales generally frequent coastal waters everywhere between the Cape of Good Hope and the Gulf of Guinea from May to October, the period of their northward migration from their feeding grounds in the Antarctic. They could most reliably be encountered in the areas where they mate and calve: off the coasts of modern Gabon and Angola, the islands of São Tomé and Príncipe, and near the mouth of the Congo, the underwater Congo Canyon, where sperm whales sometimes may also be found.[56] Whalers preferred to take humpback whales in shallow coastal waters, where there was little escape for them and where they would not sink too deep once killed. The gases that formed within a dead humpback whale sooner or later float the carcass. Whalemen would thus attach buoys to the whales they had caught and wait until they resurfaced.[57]

---

[53] Best/Allison, "Catch History, Seasonal and Temporal Trends in the Migrations of Humpback Whales along the West Coast of Southern Africa", 1; Davis/Gallman, "American Whaling, 1820–1990", 59f.; Griffiths et al., "Impacts of Human Activities on Marine Animal Life in the Benguela", 309; Spence, *Harpooned*, 115.

[54] See e.g. Log WILLIAM LEE, 1850–1851, August 1850.

[55] Spence, *Harpooned*, 114f.; Wray/Martin, "Historical Whaling Records from the Western Indian Ocean", 217, 228.

[56] Brito/Picanço/Carvalho, "Small Cetaceans off São Tomé (São Tomé and Príncipe, Gulf of Guinea, West Africa)", 3f.; Carvalho et al., "Temporal Patterns of Population Structure of Humpback Whales in West Coast of Africa (B Stock)"; van Waerebeek/Ofori-Danson/Debrah, "The Cetaceans of Ghana, a Validated Faunal Checklist"; Weir, "Occurrence and Distribution of Cetaceans off Northern Angola, 2004/05", 228–231; Weir, "A Review of Cetacean Occurrence in West African Waters from the Gulf of Guinea to Angola", 10f.

[57] Nordhoff, *Whaling and Fishing*, 175f.

In the 1840s increased commercial interest in humpback whales brought the hunt to waters which had hitherto scarcely attracted of whalers at all. From the island of St Helena in the south Atlantic many vessels would head due east to the Baía dos Tigres on the coast of modern Angola before slowly working their way northwards, often keeping the coast in view throughout. Seamen often advanced only by boat, leaving the mother ship at anchor for days on end. By this process, known to whalers as "humpbacking", they gradually reached the Gulf of Guinea, often stopping for provisions at the island of Annobón and thence heading straight back to St Helena. For its part, St Helena was more than a victualling station, but also allowed whale oil to be loaded onto merchantmen that would ensure its onward transit and allow the whalers themselves to spend more time working the whaling grounds, as well as relieving them of the unloved task of traversing the "doldrums", the often windless area around the equator. To whalers, this triangular route between St Helena, the Baía dos Tigres and Annobón offered an added advantage in that sperm whales might sometimes be bagged along the way.[58]

"Making money with a vengeance"

"All the oil sent in by us last fall said to be still on the wharf unsold, waiting better prices", was what Horace Palmer learnt when, in March 1880, his ship met another whaler in the south Atlantic. By this time Palmer had spent two years cruising in the Atlantic as an ordinary seaman in the barque *Wanderer* of New Bedford, during which time his ship had also visited the humpback whaling grounds off south-western Africa. Although the *Wanderer* had made a decent enough haul – 1150 barrels of oil – the general picture drawn in Palmer's diary is unremittingly bleak: "I don't think there is a single person in the ship, from 2nd mate down, that has a cent coming to him. This is making money with a vengeance." Many formerly profitable vessels that the *Wanderer* encountered now were running up repair bills in excess of their profits from whale oil and baleen. St Helena witnessed an increase in cases of captains being forced to give up their vessels because the cost of essential refits outweighed the anticipated returns of the voyage. Palmer noted that "It is now expected that certainly

---

[58] Weir, "A Review of Cetacean Occurrence in West African Waters from the Gulf of Guinea to Angola", 10–12. For an account of the "doldrums" siehe Whitecar, *Four Years Aboard the Whaleship*, 376.

three and possibly four whalers will leave their hulks for fire wood at St. Helena this spring."[59]

Palmers observations offer vivid testimony to the decline of American-style pelagic whaling. Its first indication had been the diminishing returns from sperm whaling, and it took a nosedive with the beginning of modern petroleum extraction in 1859. The most direct blow, however, came in the form the American Civil War (1861–1865), in which ninety whalers were lost to attacks by Confederate warships and privateers. Another forty-six whalers, the so called "Stone Fleet", were requisitioned by the Union, filled with rocks and sunk in the entrances to the ports of Charleston and Savannah in an attempt to cut off supplies to the Confederacy. All in all the war nearly halved the American whaling fleet, reducing it from 514 to 263 vessels. It also created new opportunities for investors, many of whom were reluctant, once the war had ended, to plough their money once more into the uncertain business that was whaling.[60]

Once the transcontinental railway was completed in 1869 most of the shipowners who had remained in the business moved their whalers from Massachusetts to San Francisco, from where they sailed mostly to hunt bowhead whales in the sub-Arctic north Pacific and the Arctic Ocean proper. Baleen, unlike whale oil, was still a valuable commodity. However, entire fleets were lost in the pack ice off Alaska in both 1871 and 1876 – forty-three vessels in all, the greatest peacetime shipping disaster of the nineteenth century. In 1877 the American whaling fleet still numbered 163 vessels, a figure which had gone down to 124 by 1886. Forty-six of these vessels still plied the Atlantic, most of them old and in poor repair, which would explain Palmer's previously cited remarks about the condition of the fleet.[61] Its size continued to decline, to ninety-seven vessels in 1890, forty-eight in 1900 and a mere thirty-two at the outbreak of the First World War.[62] In August 1924 the *Wanderer*, in which Palmer had sailed forty-four years earlier to hunt humpback whales off the coast of Angola, left New Bedford once more for the south Atlantic. Her first port of call was to be the Cape Verdean island of Brava, were additional men were to be hired. But

---

59 All quotations from Palmer, *The Diary of a Foremast Hand on the First Voyage of the Bark Wanderer – Whaler of New Bedford, 1878–1880*, 35f.
60 Francis, *A History of World Whaling*, 152–155; Kugler, "The Penetration of the Pacific by American Whalemen in the 19th Century", 26; Spence, *Harpooned*, 119; Starbuck, *History of the American Whale Fishery*, 100–103. For a summary of reasons for the decline of American whaling see Basberg, "Two Hegemonies – Two Technological Regimes", 9–16.
61 Clark, "The American Whale-Fishery", 321f.; Francis, *A History of World Whaling*, 155–160; Kugler, "The Penetration of the Pacific by American Whalemen in the 19th Century", 26; Starbuck, *History of the American Whale Fishery*, 103–109.
62 Dolin, *Leviathan*, 362.

after only one day at sea her anchor rope broke in a storm. The crew took to the boats while the *Wanderer* drifted inexorably towards the rocky coast, finally being wrecked off Cape Cod.[63] The *Wanderer* was the last vessel to go whaling from an American port. Her loss marked the end not only of what was once an important sector of the country's economy but also of American-style pelagic whaling as such.[64]

In line with this general trend, the number of American whalers in African waters also declined after the outbreak of the outbreak of the Civil War. Worn-out two-masters in particular continued to ply the waters off south-western Africa and St Helena. Yet by the mid-1880s, when just about fifty vessels still sailed for the Atlantic, very few ever made it as far as the Indian Ocean anymore. "The Indian Ocean was once an important right-whaling ground, but it is now practically abandoned", the journal *Science* noted in 1887.[65] The appearance of whalers on the coast of Africa after 1900 was a rarity: between 1905 and 1907 the brig *Sullivan* of Norwich was operating off Angola, among other places, while the barque *Josephine* of New Bedford was cruising in the Indian Ocean.[66] That vessels should have been outfitted for whaling at all during this period was due to the continuing demand for baleen or "whalebone". As Charles Smith, first mate of the *Sunbeam*, put it pithily in August 1904, "Right Whale oil ain't worth beans; you hunt him for bones."[67] Rococo fashions had long gone out of style, but baleen continued to be traded as a relatively cheap by-product of whaling, useful in the manufacture such items as hats, umbrellas, fishing rods or riding crops. Unlike whale oil and spermaceti, which came increasingly to be replaced by petroleum and its derivatives, the demand for baleen did not decline as the nineteenth century progressed. in fact, in increased, especially when, after about 1870, women's clothing in late Victorian Britain once more took on a "courtly" aspect and whalebone corsets and bustles in particular came into fashion. In the United States, a pound of baleen sold for 41 cents in 1855 and $5.80 in 1904 – more than ever before or since – while the price of sperm whale oil fell from $1.53 per gallon in 1860 to 53 cents in 1910. As corsets fell out fashion, however, and as plastics, spring steel and other materials

---

63 "Last of the Whalers Wrecked in Storm." *New York Times*, 27.08.1924, 7; Halter, *Between Race and Ethnicity*, 141f.
64 While the *Wanderer* was the last whaler to sail from an American port, the last to return was the schooner *John R. Manta*, which reached its home port of New Bedford in August 1925.
65 Clark, "The American Whale-Fishery", 321f.
66 Log JOSEPHINE, 1905–1907; Log SULLIVAN, 1905–1907.
67 Ashley, *The Yankee Whaler*, 9.

emerged as substitutes for baleen, demand began to decline in 1907 and collapsed within a few years.[68]

In sum, the dynamic of exploration and exploitation outlined here can be broken down into four main phases of whaling in the seas around Africa. The first marks the spatial expansion of sperm whaling in the 1760s and 1770s, when hundreds of vessels from New England sailed for the central and south Atlantic, many of them for the Gulf of Guinea and the Cape Verde Islands. In the second, beginning in the mid-1780s, European and American whalers exploited populations of southern right whales in the bays of southern Africa, particularly in Walvis Bay and Delagoa Bay. The third phase began in the 1820s, when the western Indian Ocean became the focus of sperm whaling, which was dominated by American vessels. In the fourth, American whalers in the 1840s began systematically to exploit humpback whale stocks off the south-western coast of Africa. Each phase lasted between twenty and fifty years, with the often sudden rush to exploit a particular whale ground being easier to pinpoint in time than its end, which usually came as a slow petering out of whaling activity.

The movements of the whales ultimately guided those of their pursuers (Fig. 3). Finding and chasing whales drew whalers away from the well-trodden paths of merchant shipping and created a distinctive transoceanic structure of its own. The movements of whalers were more than just links in the chain running from the capture of whales to their subsequent processing and sale onshore. The sea itself was the centre and the goal of these movements, and in that respect whaling, though it was probably the most far-ranging of practices involved in the exploitation of natural resources,[69] differed from the other economic processes that contributed to the emergence of a global economy in the eighteenth and nineteenth centuries, which often went hand in hand with territorial expansion.

The shipwreck of the *Wanderer* in 1924 marked the end of American-style pelagic whaling. Much photographed, the vessel became the icon of a vanished era. One such photograph shows a group of seamen who escaped the wreck against the background of the *Wanderer*'s hulk (Fig. 4). Several of the crew came from the Cape Verde Islands. The photograph stands not only for the demise of American whaling, but also for the key role which African labour had played in its lifetime. Yet the loss of the *Wanderer* did not spell the end of whaling in the seas around

---

68 Barthelmeß, "Auf Walfang", 7; Clark, "The American Whale-Fishery", 322; Davis/Gallman, "American Whaling, 1820–1990", 61; Dolin, *Leviathan*, 356f., 361f.; Francis, *A History of World Whaling*, 147.
69 Reeves/Smith, "A Taxonomy of World Whaling", 82.

"Making money with a vengeance" — 63

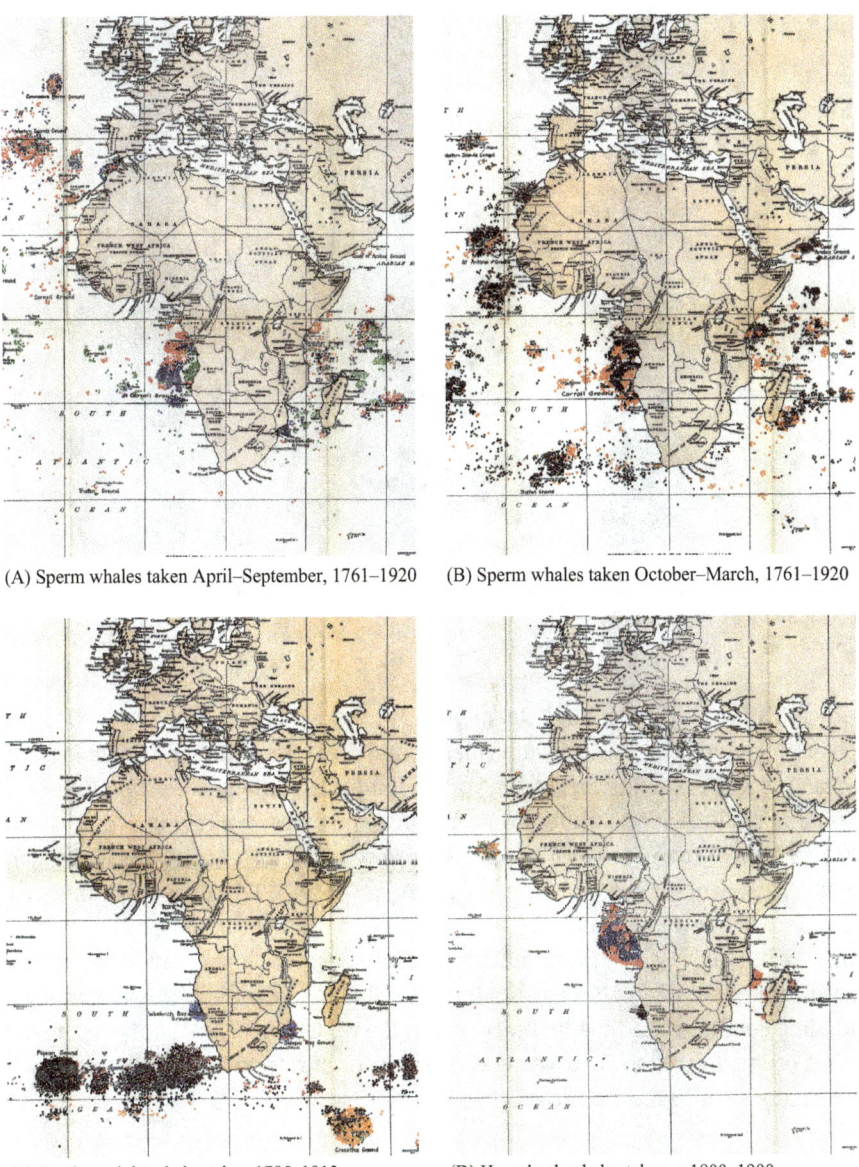

(A) Sperm whales taken April–September, 1761–1920
(B) Sperm whales taken October–March, 1761–1920
(C) Southern right whales taken 1785–1913
(D) Humpback whales taken. c.1800–1900

Fig. 3: Spatial distribution of whaling in the seas around Africa, 1761–1920. Excerpts from four world maps prepared in 1935 by the American zoologist Charles Haskins Townsend and based on over 50,000 references in the logbooks of American whalers. Each dot marks a vessel's position on a day when one or more whales were taken.
Courtesy of the Wildlife Conservation Society Canada.

Fig. 4: Seamen on the coast of Cuttyhunk Island with the wreck of the *Wanderer* in the background, 26 August 1924.
Courtesy of the New Bedford Whaling Museum.

Africa. In 1905 steel-clad and steam-powered vessels armed with explosive harpoons began to head for the south Atlantic and the western Indian Ocean. Most of these vessels were Norwegian, but other European nations were involved too. Whaling stations soon sprung up in European colonies, notably in South Africa (from 1908), Portuguese West Africa (1909), Portuguese East Africa (1910), German South West Africa (1912) and French Equatorial Africa (1912), from which this new kind of whaling vessel sailed in pursuit of sperm, humpback and southern right whales, but above all of the various rorqual species, which previously had barely been hunted at all.[70] Although its intensity fluctuated widely, Norwegian-style whaling continued into the 1970s. However, the vessels involved hardly ever made stops or landfalls, and their voyages therefore do not form part of the history of interactions which this book seeks to trace.

---

70 Best/Ross, "Catches of Right Whales from Shore-Based Establishments in Southern Africa", 285–287; Ellis, *Men and Whales*, 305–316; Griffiths et al., "Impacts of Human Activities on Marine Animal Life in the Benguela", 309f.; Tønnessen/Johnsen, *The History of Modern Whaling*, 208f., 214, 313–316.

1 From whaling ground to trading port: Walvis Bay, 1780–1860

In January 1845 William Carroll, the American consul in St Helena, had a remarkable discovery to report to the Department of State in Washington. On Possession Island, a rocky islet off the coast of what is now Namibia, seamen had discovered the corpses of two Americans – corpses which, covered as they were in the solidified excrement of seabirds, were supposed to have suffered but little decomposition: "They [. . .] looked as fresh as if they had not been interred more than a fortnight", one newspaper reported, citing a letter written by Carroll in evidence.[1] The plaques found attached to the corpses identified them as those of Charles Church, died aged 21 in December 1791 aboard the *Atlantic* of Nantucket, and Daniel Smith, died in December 1832 aboard the schooner *Betsey* of New London, aged 32. Both had perished in whaling vessels and appear to have been deposited upon the island for want of earth in which to bury them on the rocky shore. The crew that discovered finally gave them a proper funeral.[2]

At the time of their discovery the Possession Island corpses were already relics of (largely) bygone age. Most of the American whalers who visited the south-western coast of Africa did so in the years between the end of the American War of Independence (1783) and the outbreak of the Quasi-War with France (1798) and had limited their operations almost exclusively to Walvis Bay. Two Dutch vessels had already set sail for this coastline in pursuit of whales in the early eighteenth century, but where exactly they hunted and whether they met anybody ashore is unknown.[3] Although it is sometimes claimed that American vessels had called at the coast of modern Namibia as early as the 1760s and 1770s, there are no sources to confirm this.[4]

---

[1] *Whalemen's Shipping List*, 18.03.1845. In 1844 workers on Ichaboe, another rocky island off the south-western coast of Africa, had discovered the bodies of two seamen, one of whom inscriptions revealed to have been deposited in 1689 by a Dutch vessel, the other in 1791 by an American whaler. Both were said to have been well preserved beneath several feet of guano. The hair of one was exhibited as a curiosity in New Bedford some years later. ("Extraordinary Exhumation on the Coast of Africa." *New-Bedford Mercury*, 24.05.1844, 2; "A Mummy from Ichaboe." *New-Bedford Mercury*, 28.02.1845, 4; Liesegang, "Die Guanogewinnung auf den Inseln und an der Küste Südwestafrikas", 39; Warrin, *So Ends This Day*, 137; Watson, "The Guano Islands of Southwestern Africa", 634).
[2] *Whalemen's Shipping List*, 18.03.1845.
[3] See the chapter "Passages I" in this book.
[4] This claim can be found e.g. in Booth, *The United States Experience in South Africa*, 34, 61; Gruntkowski/Henschel, "!Nara in Topnaar History", 41; Lau, *Southern and Central Namibia in*

In this chapter, I shall begin by retracing the shifting fortunes of whaling in Walvis Bay and describing some aspects of its geography. Drawing on the findings of archaeological and ethnographic research, I shall then draw an outline of the littoral societies that mariners would have encountered in Walvis Bay before examining interactions between these groups and their consequences. Finally, I shall discuss the most important consequence of whaling for Walvis Bay, its emergence as a trading port with connections far afield.

Black whaling

When did the first whaler drop anchor off the coast of modern Namibia? Since eighteenth-century whaling is far less well documented than its nineteenth-century counterpart, it is impossible to give an exact answer. Some scholars suppose New England whalers to have visited Walvis Bay as early as the 1760s,[5] but they do so without reliable evidence. What is certain is only that in the late 1780s Walvis Bay became, alongside the Brazil Banks, the whaling ground for which American whalers most frequently set sail and from which they returned with the most impressive hauls.[6] The first whaler identifiable by name to have set sail for the coast of what is now Namibia was the *Sandwich* of London, which operated there in 1785 and 1786.[7] In 1789 eleven vessels from Nantucket alone sailed for Walvis Bay; one of them, the *Ranger*, returned home with 1150 barrels of oil, thereby becoming the first whaler in history to exceed a yield of 1000 barrels in a single season. This spectacular success opened up good career prospects for the seamen involved, no fewer than nine of whom went on to become captains, and brought Walvis Bay to the attention of British as well as American whalers.[8] After all, the hunt for southern right whales – known to seamen as "black whaling" on account of the whales' blue-black colouring – at the time was the mainstay of

---

Jonker Afrikaner's Time, 94; Stackpole, *The Sea-Hunters*, 53, 165; Vigne, "The Hard Road to Colonization" and Wallace, *History of Namibia*, 56. Booth cites Obed Macy's *History of Nantucket*, but Macy merely claims that American whalers had operated off the Guinea Coast from 1763. (Macy, *The History of Nantucket*, 54)

5 Cooper, "American Corporate Investments in Namibia", 23.
6 Booth, "American Whalers in South African Waters", 278; Booth, *The United States Experience in South Africa*, 34.
7 Kinahan, "The Historical Archaeology of Nineteenth Century Fisheries at Sandwich Harbour on the Namib Coast", 5.
8 Stackpole, *Whales & Destiny*, 315–317.

British whaling in the south Atlantic.[9] Around 1790 half the Nantucket fleet, most of the British southern whalers and a good many of William Rotch's Dunkirk-based vessels would regularly visit Walvis Bay.[10]

"Whales & Seals frequent all along", noted Captain Thomas Boulden Thompson, commander of HMS *Nautilus*, which was exploring the Namib Coast on behalf of the British Admiralty.[11] These waters are among Africa's most productive ecosystems. The continental shelf is rich in nutrients and home to an extraordinary variety of plant and animal life, and the upwelling of the oxygen-rich Benguela Current brings swarms of fish to the coast. The fish in turn attract countless seals and seabirds, while the Benguela Current also supports a rich plankton life that provides food for baleen whales.[12] Southern right whales in particular swim far into Walvis Bay, mating and calving there from May to September. Humpback and fin whales also follow the current to the south-western coast of Africa as part of their annual migrations, but seldom enter the bay itself.[13]

"January 28th, Friday. Roused by a whale", Carl Hugo Hahn noted in his diary in 1853, as the coaster *Prince Edward*, aboard which the missionary was sailing from Cape Town, neared Walvis Bay. "He amused himself by frolicking about our ship for the better part of an hour."[14] Not only their curiosity, which would sometimes make them approach vessels, made southern rights easy prey for whalers; they also kept close to the coast and were slow swimmers. Their carcasses were rich in fat and floated on the surface, and they rarely displayed defensive behaviour of the kind dangerous to whalers chasing them in open boats. Though a wounded southern right might sometimes try to strike its pursuers a blow with its flukes, experienced harpooners knew that a prick to the whale's sensitive nose

---

[9] Sperm whale oil, the chief product of American whaling, accounted for only twenty-two per cent of British whale produce in 1788. (Jackson, *The British Whaling Trade*, 114)
[10] Booth, "American Whalers in South African Waters", 278f.; Booth, *The United States Experience in South Africa*, 37f.; Du Pasquier, "Catch History of French Right Whaling Mainly in the South Atlantic", 270f.; Du Pasquier, *Les Baleiniers Français de Louis XVI à Napoléon*, 148; Stackpole, *The Sea-Hunters*, 165. Most of the American whalers frequenting Walvis Bay came from Nantucket. Vessels from New Bedford, which at the time rivalled Nantucket for dominance of American pelagic whaling, only began to head for Walvis Bay in the 1790s, the first on record being the *Eliza* under Captain Benjamin Coleman in 1794. (Duignan/Gann, *The United States and Africa*, 59; Stackpole, *Whales & Destiny*, 316f.)
[11] Quoted in Kinahan, "The Impenetrable Shield", 39.
[12] Sittert/Crawford, "Historical Reconstruction of Guano Production on the Namibian Islands", 13; Walker, "African Fisheries", 656.
[13] On humpback whales off Walvis Bay see e.g. Log NORTH AMERICA, 1797–1799, 03.– 04.06.1799. On fin whales in Walvis Bay see e.g. Log OCEAN ROVER, 1859–1862, 08. & 12.01.1860.
[14] Hahn, *Carl Hugo Hahn Tagebücher*, 643.

would soon put an end to such dangerous resistance.[15] Compared to sperm whales southern rights were a safe quarry indeed, and such cases as that of a boat belonging to the *North America* of Nantucket, which was smashed by a southern right whale in Walvis Bay in June 1799,[16] were notable for their rarity.

Whalers usually spent several weeks and often months "black whaling" in Walvis Bay. The *Ann* of Dunkirk, for instance, which arrived there in May 1792, stayed for ten weeks, taking both southern right and sperm whales.[17] The British whaler *London* remained from June to September 1793, the *Boston Packet* of Nantucket from late May to mid-July 1795 and the *North America* of Nantucket from early June to mid-August 1799.[18] The longest stay of a whaler in Walvis Bay on record is that of the *Union* of New Bedford, which was anchored there from early April to mid-August 1796.[19]

Ships would usually anchor in the middle of the bay. As soon as the men descried a whale's blow, they manned the boats. Since whalers in Walvis Bay anchored in close proximity to one another, rivalry between crews was not uncommon and boats would often fight over a particular whale.[20] A further complication was added by the frequent fog, which not only made difficult work for the lookout, but also meant that retrieving whales that had been killed was something of an art.[21] Since wounded whales attempted to flee the bay, boats often had to follow them onto the open sea. Yet the mother ship remained in place, acting meanwhile as a floating factory in which whales' oil was tried out and their baleen removed.[22] Both these tasks were extremely hard work. Each southern right whale contained up to a ton of baleen, keratin plates which whalemen had to prise out of the carcass's mouth and cleanse by hand. Moreover, the blubber of southern right whales might yield twice as much oil as that of a sperm whale of the same size – up to 30,000 litres in a fully grown whale. Flensing and trying out accordingly were extremely laborious operations, and a single whale could take more than a week to process.[23]

***

---

15 Hohman, *The American Whaleman*, 180f.
16 Log NORTH AMERICA, 1797–1799, 19.06.1799.
17 Stackpole, *Whales & Destiny*, 316f.; Log ANN, 1791–1792, 20.05.1792.
18 Choyce, *The Log of a Jack Tar*, 4f.; Log BOSTON PACKET, 1794–1795, 28.05.– 12.07.1795; Log NORTH AMERICA, 1797–1799, 07.06.–15.08.1799.
19 Log UNION, 1796, 08.04.–14.08.1796.
20 See e.g. Log PLATO, 1833–1834, 10.–18.08.1834.
21 Log NORTH AMERICA, 1797–1799, 11.07.1799.
22 Booth, *The United States Experience in South Africa*, 36.
23 Hohman, *The American Whaleman*, 180f. On the processing of whales see the chapter "Passages II" in this book.

The war between revolutionary France and its European opponents reached Walvis Bay in June 1793, when a British privateer, the *Liverpool*, attacked whalers sailing under the French flag and captured one, the *Phebe*. Meanwhile, the *Trois Amis* only narrowly escaped a British warship at the head of the bay.[24] Since the warring naval powers were not above interfering with neutral shipping, the Napoleonic wars made life hard for whalers of all nations. Walvis Bay nevertheless remained a much-frequented whaling ground, at least in the early years of the war. Even in 1795 Thomas Alexander, who was exploring the seas off south-western Africa as master of the frigate HMS *Star*, could still report that whalers considered Walvis Bay "the best bay for that fishing along the coast."[25] Only in 1798, when the United States began naval action against France in the undeclared "Quasi-War", do records show a distinct drop in the number of whalers there. Whalers resumed regular operations in Walvis Bay as soon as the Treaty of Mortefontaine ended hostilities in 1800. When the *Leviathan* of London arrived there in June of that year, she found seven other whaleships already at anchor.[26] Yet the European powers were still at war with one another and the situation remained dangerous.[27]

The outbreak of the 1812 war seems to have put a temporary stop to all whaling activity off the south-west African coast, but the peace treaties of Geneva and Paris, concluded in 1814, reopened the sea lanes to Walvis Bay, and whaling appears to have resumed there by 1815. In that year the missionary Johann Hinrich Schmelen encountered the whaler *Prince Town* of London in Angra Pequeña, a bay 200 nautical miles to the south, he was told by her captain "that this was not a proper place where they use to cast anchor but about one weeks journey farther to the north were in generally more ships met together [sic]."[28] But British whalers too had since the 1790 shifted their sights to sperm whales and hence to new whaling grounds in the Pacific and the Indian Ocean, and Walvis Bay never recovered its pre-eminence.[29]

A noticeable decline in stocks of southern right whales may also have contributed to whalers' visits to Walvis Bay becoming less frequent. On this point, however, the sources give contradictory information. In July and August 1843

---

24 Du Pasquier, *Les Baleiniers Français de Louis XVI à Napoléon*, 84; "Ship News." *The Medley or Newbedford Marine Journal*, 20.09.1793, 3.
25 Quoted in Kinahan, *By Command of their Lordships*, 39.
26 Log LEVIATHAN, 1800–1801, 23.07.1801.
27 See the chapter "Passages I" in this book.
28 Schmelen, *Journal from the Year 1815*, 26.05.1815, School of Oriental and African Studies, CWM/LMS/South Africa Journals/Box 2.
29 Haywood, "American Whalers and Africa", 83.

the schooner *Franklin* of New London claimed to find no whales in Walvis Bay, whilst missionaries in November 1846 observed it to be so full of southern rights that they would sometimes collide with vessels.[30] The missionary Friedrich Wilhelm Kolbe, who spent several months in the area, in March 1848 wrote that "In the past there must have been many whales around Walvis Bay, but nowadays they are said to be most rare."[31] Yet the British explorer Francis Galton remembered a large herd of whales virtually ploughing the sea when, in August 1850, he was approaching Walvis Bay by sea, and another explorer, James Chapman, also observed numerous whales there.[32] Whatever may explain such discrepancies, the fact remains that whalers continued to take southern right whales in Walvis Bay in large numbers into the 1830s, but after about 1840 went there only sporadically.[33] The reduced number of vessels and the shortness of their sojourns – now only a few days or weeks at a time – suggests that after 1814 Walvis Bay served above all as a last resort for whalers who had had no luck hunting sperm whales and now had to make do with the oil of southern right whales, which was less profitable.

While whaling in Walvis Bay went into a slow decline, traffic in Angra Pequeña increased in the 1830s, when British and American vessels opened up the seas around the bay for seal hunting.[34] Some sealers were not content to seek their prey on the bay's rocky offshore islands and also pursued a side-line in whaling. No fewer than seven such vessels in search of both whales and

---

30 Allyn, *The Old Sailor's Story*, 59; Mossolow, *Die Geschichte von Rooibank-Scheppmannsdorf*, 5. In 1822 the missionary James Archbell also reported from Walvis Bay of the danger posed to shipping by its abundance of whales. See Vigne, "James Archbell's 'Beschrijving der Walvischbaai en omliggende plaatsen aan de westkust van Africa' in 1823", 32.
31 Kolbe, excerpt from a letter dated 10.03.1848, Archiv- und Museumsstiftung Wuppertal, Schriftarchiv, Archiv der Rheinischen Mission, RMG 2.585 (Beiträge zur Geschichte der Stationen), C/i 6. 1.
32 Chapman, *Travels in the Interior of South Africa*, vol. 1, 176; Galton, *The Narrative of an Explorer in Tropical South Africa*, 14f.
33 Griffiths et al., "Impacts of Human Activities on Marine Animal Life in the Benguela", 309.
34 Between approximately 1790 and 1825 numerous British and American vessels had sailed for the Falkland Islands, South Georgia and the South Shetland Islands to hunt seals. (Busch, "Cape Verdeans in the American Whaling and Sealing Industry", 104f.) They would seem to have turned to the rocky islands off the coast of Namibia only once they had brought seal populations between Cape Horn and the Antarctic to the brink of extinction. On sealing in these rocky islands see e.g. Allyn, *The Old Sailor's Story*, 30. (Allyn visited the Namib Coast as captain of the sealer *Spark*.)

seals were anchored in Angra Pequeña in June 1835 alone.[35] Some vessels were still looking for whales in Walvis Bay at this time, including, in April 1836, the *Commodore Perry* of New London and the *Pocahontas* of Portsmouth.[36] The French government also took an interest in sealing and whaling, dispatching the corvettes *la Circé* (1834) and *l'Héroïne* (1835) to the south-west African coast to gather information on these operations and to underscore France's claim to participation in them. However, this expedition seems not to have resulted in any French whalers sailing for Walvis Bay.[37]

As interest in humpback whales increased in the mid-1800s and drew whalers to the coast of Angola in great numbers, traffic around Walvis Bay grew busier once more. Though humpbacks were rarer visitors to the bay than southern rights, they did pass it regularly on the way to their mating grounds between May and October. Some whalers would hence cruise on an area of sea known as the Carroll Ground in the hope of intercepting humpback and, if they were lucky, sperm whales too.[38] Although some vessels hunted humpback whales in the bay itself – for instance, the *Commodore Perry* of New London in 1837[39] – far more preferred the Angolan coast. Only few of these vessels ever called at Walvis Bay, and seldom for more than a few days at a time.[40] The last vessel recorded as having come to the bay in the hunt for humpbacks was the

---

35 Allyn, *The Old Sailor's Story*, 45. In Angra Pequeña whalers sometimes had only to lower their boats in order to take the humpback whales that gathered in the bay itself. Some whalers found Angra Pequeña to be distinctly more profitable than Walvis Bay (Log PLATO, 1833–1834, 27.06.–01.08.1834). The difficulty, however, lay in securing whales once they had been caught, for their carcasses soon sank and were liable to be eaten by sharks. Another problem with this particular bay was its extreme lack of drinking water. On these difficulties see e.g. Log HERCULES II, 1834–1836, 23.–25.04., 08.05., 16.–21.05. and 07.07.1836.
36 Alexander, *An Expedition of Discovery into the Interior of Africa*, vol. 2, 90, 92f.
37 Layrle, "Bericht des Schiffsleutnants Layrle über den Walfang im südlichen Atlantischen Ozean", 136f.; "Secours donnés bâtiments de l'état aux navires baleiniers du commerce." *Annales Maritimes et Coloniales* 20.2 (1835), 189–191. In the mid-1830s between 32 and 34 whalers sailed from France – chiefly from Le Havre – for the south seas. (Du Pasquier, "Catch History of French Right Whaling Mainly in the South Atlantic", 271)
38 Log BERTHA, 1878–1881, 20.01.1881. In 1859 the vessels operating in the seas off Walvis Bay included the brig *Pavillon* of Holmes Hole, the barque *Keoka* of Westport and the *Hannawah* of Greenport (Log PAVILION, 1858–1860, 10.–15.02.1859) For an example of an exceptionally good catch in the immediate vicinity of Walvis Bay see Log STEPHANIA, 1847–1850, June & July 1850.
39 Alexander, *An Expedition of Discovery into the Interior of Africa*, vol. 2, 90f., 94.
40 See e.g. Log KATHLEEN, 1852–1855, March & April 1854; Log STEPHANIA, 1847–1850, 24.–29.06.1850.

barque *Sunbeam* of New Bedford (Fig. 5), which anchored there for five days in January 1884.[41]

Yet it is impossible to give an exact quantitative measure of the development of whaling in Walvis Bay. Activity was at its most intense at a time from which few logbooks and other documents by seamen are preserved, and when few other actors who might have left written sources resided in the bay of visited it.[42] For the 1785–1805 period the historians Rhys Richards and Thierry Du Pasquier have identified a total of 186 individual whaleships that came to Walvis Bay from the United States, Great Britain and France. According to their findings, whaling

Fig. 5: The *Sunbeam* of New Bedford, photographed in 1904 in the north Atlantic. In 1884 she became probably the last whaler ever to enter Walvis Bay under sail. Alongside full-rigged ships, barques such as this were the type most commonly used in nineteenth-century American pelagic whaling.
Image courtesy of the New Bedford Whaling Museum, item number 1974.3.1.18.

---

41 Log SUNBEAM, 1882–1886, 29.01.1884.
42 Haywood, "American Whalers and Africa", 81.

in Walvis Bay peaked from 1792 to 1796, when between twenty-five and twenty-eight vessels anchored there annually.[43] Records of individually identifiable vessels. however, give only a minimum figure whose relation to the actual number of whalers present at any given time is hard to determine. For instance, James Choyce, a seaman who arrived in Walvis Bay in June 1793 aboard the British whaler *London*, claims to have observed some forty vessels operating there at the same time,[44] while the *Union* of New Bedford, which sailed from Walvis Bay in August 1796, according to its log left behind "30 Sail of Ships in ye Bay".[45] Such figures tally with those of the historian Alan Booth, who has estimated that Walvis Bay was visited each season by approximately fifteen vessels from Nantucket, over a dozen from Britain and a significant portion of William Rotch's forty-four vessels.[46]

The number of vessels appears to have declined slightly with the outbreak of the Napoleonic Wars. Whereas it had been between twenty and thirty from 1793 to 1798,[47] for the years 1798 to 1805 Richards and Du Pasquier arrive at figures ranging from three (1800) to fifteen (1801) whalers annually.[48] The sparse records available for the following years provide no grounds for supposing that these figures increased again before the War of 1812.[49] For one and a half years of the war, no visits at all by whalers to Walvis Bay are recorded, and in no year of the subsequent decades are more than seven vessels (in 1834[50]) confirmed to have operated there. Only in 1862 does whaling in the bay seem to have spiked one last time, when twelve vessels anchored there according to Booth.[51] Afterwards whaling in Walvis Bay was for all purposes dead, with not a single whaler recorded until the *Sunbeam* called early in 1884 (see above).

---

43 Richards/Du Pasquier, "Bay Whaling off Southern Africa", 233.
44 Choyce, *The Log of a Jack Tar*, 4.
45 Log UNION, 1796, 14.08.1796.
46 Booth, *The United States Experience in South Africa*, 34; Booth, "American Whalers in South African Waters", 278.
47 Booth, *The United States Experience in South Africa*, 34; Booth, "American Whalers in South African Waters", 278.
48 Richards/Du Pasquier, "Bay Whaling off Southern Africa", 233.
49 Starbuck, *History of the American Whale Fishery*, 210–213. The last whaleship recorded in Walvis Bay before the outbreak of the War of 1812 was the *Hope* of Nantucket; see Starbuck, *History of the American Whale Fishery*, 212f.
50 On whaling in 1834 see Log PLATO, 1833–1834, 8.–18.08.1834, and Allyn, *The Old Sailor's Story*, 43.
51 Booth, "American Whalers in South African Waters", 281.

The desert behind the fog

"We are lost On the Cost of Africa, it has ben fogy all day", reads the log of the barque *Kathleen* of New Bedford for 10 March 1854.[52] Dense fog had already surrounded the vessel for days on the way to Walvis Bay, making it impossible for Captain Allen even to use the sextant. Only by sounding the depths and listening to the waves breaking on the shore were the seamen able to estimate their distance from the coast. In this, the *Kathleen* was luckier than many other vessels (and indeed some whales), which were seized by the treacherous currents off the south-western coast of Africa and washed ashore on the sand of the Namib Desert. Even today numerous wrecks testify to the dangers that made a section of this coastline notorious as the "Skeleton Coast". When the fog lifted and the coast finally came into view on 12 March, the *Kathleen* found herself four nautical miles off Walvis Bay.[53] In other cases the outline of the coast could be discerned amid the fog until the vessel had come within a few dozen metres of it, and some ran aground, for instance the *Stephania* of New Bedford in June 1850.[54]

"It is the most Desolate place that I ever saw", was the somewhat disheartened impression recorded in the log when the *Kathleen*'s first boat put in at Walvis Bay, "their is nothing ashore but sand."[55] A desert is usually defined by precipitation below 250 millimetres per year; the average along the 800 nautical miles of the coast of modern Namibia is 15 millimetres, making it the most arid area in sub-Saharan Africa. Rainfall in Walvis Bay itself is less than 10 millimetres.[56] It is one of the driest inhabited places on earth. The sand dunes begin at the shore and extend between 130 and 200 kilometres inland. "Nothing is to be seen of the serounding Country but sand hills", remarked Edward Gardner, who visited the bay in 1803 as master of an American whaler.[57] The missionary Carl Hugo Hahn, who travelled overland to Walvis Bay in 1844, recorded this in his diary: "To your left we had the arid and infertile mountains of sand, to our

---

52 Log KATHLEEN, 1852–1855, 10.03.1854.
53 Ibid., 12.03.1854.
54 Log STEPHANIA, 1847–1850, 22.–26.06.1850.
55 Log KATHLEEN, 1852–1855, 12.03.1854.
56 Ito, "Changes in the Distribution of the !Nara Plant That Affect the Life of the Topnaar People in the Lower Kuiseb River", 67; see also the precipitation map in Erkkilä/Siiskonen, *Forestry in Namibia*, 21. The *Kingston* of London, which arrived in Walvis Bay in May 1801, was also unable to determine its position for several days on account of dense fog (Log KINGSTON, 1800–1801, 21.–23.05.1801).
57 Quoted in Kinahan, "The Impenetrable Shield", 50.

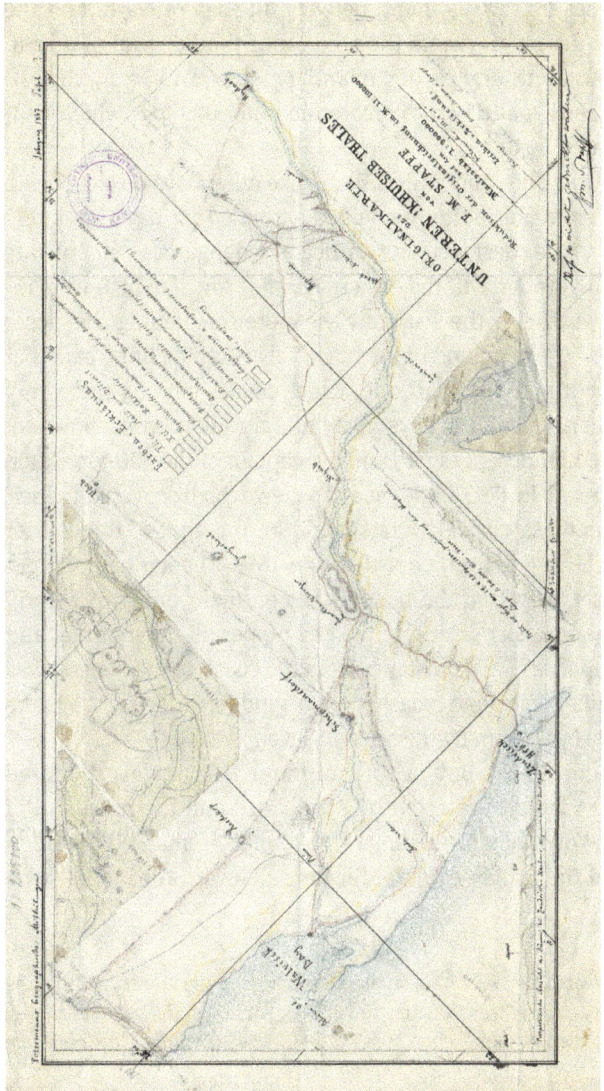

Fig. 6: This map of Walvis Bay and the adjacent area of the !Kuiseb valley, hand-drawn after sketches by Friedrich Moritz Stapff, was supposed to be published in the geographical journal "Petermanns Geographische Mitteilungen" in 1887. As Stapff was dissatisfied with this draft (see his comment "Darf so nicht gedruckt werden"/"May not be printed like this" on the lower right), it was fundamentally revised and supplement with further details before publication (as "Originalkarte des unteren !Khuiseb Thales." 69 × 41 cm, 1:100.000. *Dr. A. Petermann's Mitteilungen aus Justus Perthes' Geographischer Anstalt* 33 [1887]: 224/T11).
Courtesy of the Gotha Research Library at University of Erfurt, SPK 40 29 B [01, 547$112201555].

right the immeasurable ocean."⁵⁸ It is there, between the sea of water and the sea of sand, that the hot desert air meets the cold air of the Benguela Current. This air is cooled by the Antarctic and carried inland by the prevailing southwesterly winds, where it condenses at dawn to create the notorious fog, which usually dissipates in the midday heat.⁵⁹

But the fog did not always lift, and Walvis Bay – like other bays on the Namib Coast, including Angra Penqueña – often remained shrouded for days on end.⁶⁰ Although the approaches to the coast were not particularly dangerous – at any rate compared with the whaling grounds off the eastern coast of Africa, which were infamous for their stormy weather – the sea grew the more threatening the closer vessels came to the shore. "The headland of the bay [. . .] is nothing but a sand-bar covered almost entirely by the sea at high tide, which makes landing there very dangerous, for the weather is nearly always misty and a rapid current flows towards the North", observed François Renier Duminy, captain of the 500-ton Dutch frigate *Meermin*, in Walvis Bay in 1793.⁶¹ One vessel's crew who discovered to their cost just how treacherous these coastal waters could be was that of the coaster *Flora* as it approached Walvis Bay from Cape Town in 1859. The fog had still not dissipated when the vessel arrived at the head of bay on the evening of 1 April. Captain Legros decided not to risk docking in the bay proper till the morning and meanwhile to wait at a supposedly safe distance from the coast, but the vessel was nonetheless caught in a tidal wave and smashed on a sandbank. Before dawn the *Flora* had been completely broken up by the sea and seven lives were lost.⁶²

If a vessel made it into Walvis Bay in spite of these vicissitudes, it offered safe anchorage in shallow water, protected by sandbanks and the headland of Pelican Point (Fig. 6). "You lay in it as in a mill pond", remarked Boulden Thompson in 1786.⁶³ And the British explorer Sir James Edward Alexander, who

---

58 Hahn, *Carl Hugo Hahn Tagebücher*, 149. For a similar description of the landscape from the pen of a missionary see Kolbe, excerpt from a letter, 10.03.1848, Archiv- und Museumsstiftung Wuppertal, Schriftarchiv, Archiv der Rheinischen Mission, RMG 2.585 (*Beiträge zur Geschichte der Stationen*), C/i 6. 1f.
59 Carson, *Geheimnisse des Meeres*, 204; Ito, "Changes in the Distribution of the !Nara Plant That Affect the Life of the Topnaar People in the Lower Kuiseb River", 67; Schultze, *Aus Namaland und Kalahari*, 60.
60 See e.g. Log HERCULES II, 1834–1836, 13.–19.05.1836.
61 Duminy, *Duminy-dagboeke*, 281.
62 Chapman, *Travels in the Interior of South Africa*, vol. 1, 190f.; Hahn, *The Letters of Emma Sarah Hahn*, 213–215; Hahn, *Carl Hugo Hahn Tagebücher*, 1139–1141.
63 Quoted in Kinahan, "The Impenetrable Shield", 44. In 1788 the crew of the *Sea Horse* of Gloucester observed a part of this headland suddenly disappear in six feet of water. (Starbuck, *History of the American Whale Fishery*, 182f.)

visited Walvis Bay in 1837, observed that "It is a very safe bay, the holding ground is good, nothing can hurt a vessel anchored behind Pelican Point."[64] As for the local population, it could survive only because the !Kuiseb river brings fresh water to the area from the Khomas Highland some 200 kilometres away. Yet the !Kuiseb is an ephemeral river, carrying water only twice a year for a few days at a time following the rains in the Khomas Plateau, which only about every ten years are plentiful enough for the river to reach its mouth in the southern part of Walvis Bay, briefly turning it into an oasis. The rest of the time "it vanishes into the sands", as the Johann Hinrich Schmelen put it in 1824.[65] But even when the !Kuiseb is fully absorbed by its riverbed it nonetheless forms a reserve of groundwater reachable by plants with deep roots and human beings with wells.[66] The most reliable source of fresh water for crews was a bay approximately thirty nautical miles to the south, surrounded by dunes and known as Sandwich Harbour – probably named after the whaler *Sandwich* of London, which plied the waters of the Namib Coast in the mid-1780s.[67] However, the dunes made it difficult to bring cattle to the beach from inland and seamen accordingly had little opportunity for trading.[68]

Between seas of sand and water

Like the entire coast of modern Namibia, Walvis Bay played no part in Atlantic shipping when whaling began there. The first vessel to sail into the bay is

---

[64] Alexander, *An Expedition of Discovery into the Interior of Africa*, vol. 2, 100; see also the appraisal of anchorages in the bay in Owen, *Narrative of Voyages to Explore the Shores of Africa, Arabia, and Madagascar*, vol. 2, 135.
[65] Schmelen, "Kurzer Bericht Schmelens über seine Reise nach der Walfischbai", 222. On the ecology of the !Kuiseb-Region see Botelle/Kowalski, *Changing Resource Use in Namibia's Lower Kuiseb Valley*, 13–15.
[66] In the age of whaling the !Kuiseb river still had two tributaries in the immediate vicinity of Walvis Bay, only one of which is still in existence. (Kinahan, "Human and Domestic Animal Tracks in an Archaeological Lagoon Deposit on the Coast of Namibia", 95)
[67] Budack, "The ǂAonîn or Topnaar of the Lower !Kuiseb Valley and the Sea", 12; Een, *Memories of Several Years in South-western Africa*, 27; Galton, *The Narrative of an Explorer in Tropical South Africa*, 15; Kinahan, "The Historical Archaeology of Nineteenth Century Fisheries at Sandwich Harbour on the Namib Coast", 1, 4f.; Kinahan, *Pastoral Nomads of the Central Namib Desert*, 99. Sandwich Harbour was known to the local population as as "Anixab".
[68] Sydow, "Contributions to the History and Protohistory of the Topnaar Strandloper Settlement at the Kuiseb River Mouth near Walvis Bay", 73. For a description of Sandwich Harbour see Kinahan, *Cattle for Beads*, 25, 39. The warship HMS *Grecian* took a total of 25 tons of fresh water onboard at Sandwich Harbour in January 1852. (Kinahan, *By Command of their Lordships*, 76, 95f.)

commonly supposed to have been the caravel *São Cristóvão*, under the command of the Portuguese navigator Bartolomeu Dias, which anchored here in 1487. Two other Portuguese expeditions, under Diogo Cão and Duarte Pacheco Pereira passed Walvis Bay in the 1480s and 1490s respectively, the latter giving it the name it has retained, in one form or another, to this day: *Angra de balea* or "whale bay".[69] The East Indiamen of the sixteenth and seventeenth centuries saw no reason to call at Walvis Bay, though some of them were certainly shipwrecked off the Namib Coast and survivors may have made it to the shore.[70] Even the victualling station founded by the Dutch East India Company at the Cape of Good Hope in 1670 left Walvis Bay largely unaffected. Although the company had sent the *Grundel* (1670) and the *Boode* (1677) to explore the coastline, they found neither the reserves of copper they had hoped for nor any other trading opportunities to speak of, and the company left off any further exploration of the area. The research expedition which brought the frigate *La Vénus* to the Namib Coast in 1733 likewise did not give rise to any colonial projects on the part of the French.[71]

Perhaps the history of Walvis Bay would have taken a different course had Thomas Boulden Thompson not missed the mouth of the Orange River in April 1786. Boulden Thompson, who was only twenty at the time, was captain of HMS *Nautilus* on an expedition to ascertain the suitability of the south-western coast of Africa for a penal colony on behalf of the British government. The settlement of tens of thousands of convicts would have required a reliable source of water, which Boulden Thompson hoped to find in the Orange River, now the border between Namibia and South Africa.[72] But the *Nautilus* sailed past its mouth without spotting it amid the flat and sandy coast, proceeding for nearly a thousand nautical miles up the Namib Coast "without seeing a tree, or procuring a drop of fresh

---

[69] Pereira, *Esmeraldo de Situ Orbis*, 88; Wilken/Fox, *The History of the Port and Settlement of Walvis Bay*, 1f. Dias had initially called it "Golfo de Santa Maria da Conceição", but that name soon fell into oblivion. Variants encountered in whalers' logs include "Walwich Bay", "Walweck Bay", "Walwick Bay", "Walfish Bay", "Whale Bay" or even "Woolwich Bay". To the local population it was known as "!Gomen-||gams". (Budack, "The ǂAonîn or Topnaar of the Lower ! Kuiseb Valley and the Sea", 3)

[70] Kienetz, "The Key Role of the Orlam Migrations in the Early Europeanization of South-West Africa", 556; Schumann, "Schiffe und ihre Mannschaften vor Namibias Küste", 104f., 109. Shipwrecks between Walvis Bay and Angra Pequeña include that of the Dutch merchantman *Vlissingen* in early 1747 (Werz, *The "Vlissingen"*).

[71] Gewald, "Untapped Sources", 420; Hartmann, "Early Dutch-Namibian Encounters", 11–13; Wilken/Fox, *The History of the Port and Settlement of Walvis Bay*, 2.

[72] Christopher, "From the 'Ballad-Singing Monkey' to the 'Cunning Savages'", 762; Christopher, *A Merciless Place*, 323–328; Kinahan, "The Impenetrable Shield", 25.

water", as Boulden Thompson noted despondently.[73] In his report to his superiors he concluded that the area was wholly unsuitable for the projected penal colony, which instead was founded two years later in Australia.[74]

∗∗∗

The fog that brought so many vessels to grief on the Namib Coast gave sustenance to a plant unique to this area, the !nara (*Acanthosicyos horridus*). In addition to the groundwater it obtains through its roots, which reach into soil up to a depth of forty metres, this melon thrives on the moisture provided by the fog.[75] Its green fruits are an important source of nutrition for the inhabitants of the Walvis Bay and its hinterland, and according to archaeological findings has been so for at least 2000 years.[76] Even the earliest written sources regarding Walvis Bay and Sandwich Harbour, for instance the log of the *Boode* (1677), mention the !nara and how it is gathered and processed.[77]

Such was the importance accorded to the fruit by the inhabitants of Walvis Bay that among the Nama societies, who live as hunters and herders in the south of modern Namibia, they were known as the *!Naranin* or "people of the !nara". This epithet, which can be traced at least as far back as the nineteenth century, conveys something of the disdain felt by the herdsman for the gatherer and was never adopted by the people thus designated. They called themselves ǂAonîn, which derives from the Khoekhoegowab word ǂáob or ǂáos, which can mean "tip" or "top" as well as "peak" or "end point". Accordingly, there are many ways in which the name ǂAonîn might be translated: as "people on top" (of the Nama), as "people of the peak" (of a hill or dune), as "people of the end" (of the mainland) or as "people of the edge" (of the territory inhabited by the Nama).[78]

---

73 Quoted in Christopher, "From the 'Ballad-Singing Monkey' to the 'Cunning Savages'", 761.
74 Ibid., 761–763; Pybus, *Epic Journeys of Freedom*, 98f.; Vigne, "The Hard Road to Colonization".
75 Ito, "Changes in the Distribution of the !Nara Plant That Affect the Life of the Topnaar People in the Lower Kuiseb River", 68.
76 Kinahan, *Pastoral Nomads of the Central Namib Desert*, 96, 115, 151f.; Sandelowsky, "Mirabib", 222, 226, 270, 274f.
77 "Tagebuch des Schiffes Boode", 51. The !nara is also of key importance to the fauna of the Namib Desert as part of the diet of animals including mice, beetles, jackals, oryxes and springboks. (Ito, "Changes in the Distribution of the !Nara Plant That Affect the Life of the Topnaar People in the Lower Kuiseb River", 68)
78 Budack, "The ǂAonîn or Topnaar of the Lower !Kuiseb Valley and the Sea", 1f.; Budack, "A Harvesting People on the South Atlantic Coast", 1; Dentlinger, *The !Nara Plant in the Topnaar Hottentot Culture of Namibia*, 6; Een, *Memories of Several Years in Southwestern* Africa, 31; Hoernlé, "The Social Organization of the Nama Hottentots of South-West Africa", 6; van Damme/van den Eynden, "Topnaar or Hottentot?", 217; Köhler, "Die Topnaar-Hottentotten am unteren Kuiseb", 99f. Alternative but less common spellings of "ǂAonîn" are "ǂAunin" and

What is uncertain is whether the people whose tools, whistles, grinders, pottery, fireplaces and other relicts have been found in archaeological digs in the Walvis Bay were in fact direct ancestors of the nineteenth-century ǂAonîn.[79] The missionary Christian Baumann, who worked among the ǂAonîn from 1878 to 1883, records that "according to the old ones" they had come to Walvis Bay only in the 1820s, having left a coastal area some 300 nautical miles to the north in the late eighteenth century.[80] The anthropologist Winifred Hoernlé was also told in 1912 by the descendants of local chieftains that the ǂAonîn had "originally" lived in the region of what is now Namibia's north-western frontier and had, following their migration to the Walvis Bay area, absorbed a local Nama population into their own social structures.[81]

Evidence for far-ranging movements of ǂAonîn along the coast may be found in the fact that even in the extreme north-west of Namibia many places have old names in Khoekhoegowab, the language of the Nama. Since there were no Khoekhoegowab-speaking societies in the interior, these names can most probably be traced back to the ǂAonîn.[82] It is, however, doubtful whether these movements really took the form of a single migration or trek from the north to Walvis Bay around 1800, for the oldest descriptions of the population of Walvis Bay, dating from the seventeenth century, agree with more recent (eighteenth- and nineteenth-century) accounts in many details, notably with regard to clothing, jewellery, language or the use of the !nara.[83] Rather than a single communal migration, it strikes me as more plausible – not least with regard to Oswin Köhler's ethnographic findings – to suppose that groups of ǂAonîn covered large distances along the coast and in so doing encountered other societies, including the Damara or

---

"ǂOunin". The Cape Dutch name for the ǂAonîn, "Topnaar", follows their self-description in translating "ǂáob" or "ǂáos" as "top", which means much the same in Dutch as it does in English. (Budack, "A Harvesting People on the South Atlantic Coast", 1; Köhler, "Die Topnaar-Hottentotten am unteren Kuiseb", 99f.)

79 Kinahan, *Cattle for Beads*, 43; Sandelowsky, "Mirabib", 222, 226, 270, 274f. See also Gruntkowski/Henschel, "!Nara in Topnaar History", 39.
80 Köhler, "Die Topnaar-Hottentotten am unteren Kuiseb", 105; Mossolow, *Die Geschichte von Rooibank-Scheppmannsdorf*, 2.
81 Hoernlé, "The Social Organization of the Nama Hottentots of South-West Africa", 12.
82 Köhler, "Die Topnaar-Hottentotten am unteren Kuiseb", 106.
83 Budack, "The ǂAonîn or Topnaar of the Lower !Kuiseb Valley and the Sea", 5f., Vigne, "The Hard Road to Colonization". The observations made in 1786 by Boulden Thompson and fifty years later by Jean-Baptiste Cécille, captain of the French corvette *l'Héroïne*, are strikingly similar. See e.g. the descriptions of clothing and jewellery by Boulden Thompson (in Kinahan, "The Impenetrable Shield", 40) and Cécille ("Bericht des Kommandanten Cécille über die Fahrt der Korvette l'Héroïne", 140).

the Herero.[84] The continuities across the supposed watershed of 1800 or thereabouts suggested by the written sources make the immigration of a major new group to the area seem unlikely, and hence I shall use the name ǂAonîn for the population of Walvis bay in pre-1800 contexts too.

But where exactly were the ǂAonîn living when the first whalers sailed into Walvis Bay in the 1780s? The records left by early visitors concur with the archaeological evidence in suggesting that the ǂAonîn had settled not on the beach itself, but several kilometres inland.[85] Furthermore, abandoned dwellings found close to the bay by such visitors as Boulden Thompson in 1786 or Alexander in 1837 indicate that the ǂAonîn were in the habit of moving between habitations.[86] They probably did so as part of seasonal changes in their subsistence patterns. From December to March, when the !Kuiseb Congo river brought water from the Khomas Plateau to the coast, the ǂAonîn set about the !nara harvest, combing through the hinterland of Walvis Bay and cutting the fruits, each weighing up to one kiliogramme, from their thorny vines. The melons were gathered in nets made of reeds and animal sinew and carried back to the dwellings, where they were peeled and cooked in clay pots with milk or water to produce ǂgoa-garibeb, a kind of gruel that could be eaten straight away or formed into cakes preserved by drying and burying.[87] It is also likely that particular kinship groups (!hao-!nas) claimed ownership of certain !nara bushes.[88]

When their reserves of !nara were close to being exhausted the ǂAonîn shifted their economic activities to the beach (Fig. 7). In the lagoons of Walvis Bay the men used wooden spears and oryx horns to hunt fish, especially rays,

---

84 Köhler, "Die Topnaar-Hottentotten am unteren Kuiseb", 105–107.
85 Budack, "The ǂAonîn or Topnaar of the Lower !Kuiseb Valley and the Sea", 36.
86 Alexander, *An Expedition of Discovery into the Interior of Africa*, vol. 2, 77; Kinahan, "The Impenetrable Shield", 43.
87 Alexander, *An Expedition of Discovery into the Interior of Africa*, vol. 2, 72; Andersson, *Lake Ngami*, 21f.; Budack, "The ǂAonîn or Topnaar of the Lower !Kuiseb Valley and the Sea", 8, 14; Hahn, *Carl Hugo Hahn Tagebücher*, 150f.; Kolbe, excerpt from a letter, 10.03.1848, Archiv- und Museumsstiftung Wuppertal, Schriftarchiv, Archiv der Rheinischen Mission, RMG 2.585 (*Beiträge zur Geschichte der Stationen*), C/i 6. 2f.; Mossolow, *Die Geschichte von Rooibank-Scheppmannsdorf*, 8. On the processing of !nara in the twentieth century see Moritz, *Die Nara, das Brot in der Wüste*, 11.
88 This is may be inferred, for instance, from an observation by the missionary Friedrich Wilhelm Kolbe, who in March 1848 wrote of the ǂAonîn that "Each family has its own nara garden in the field." (Kolbe, excerpt from a letter, 10.03.1848, Archiv- und Museumsstiftung Wuppertal, Schriftarchiv, Archiv der Rheinischen Mission, RMG 2.585, C/i 6. 2f.) See also Chapman, *Travels in the Interior of South Africa*, vol. 1, 175, Köhler, "Die Topnaar-Hottentotten am unteren Kuiseb", 113 and on ownership of !nara bushes in the twentieth century Widlok, *Dealing with Institutional Changes in Property Regimes*, 4.

Fig. 7: ǂAonîn on the beach at Walvis Bay. This painting (originally in colour) by Thomas Baines depicts a group engaged in spear fishing.
Source: Wallis, *Fortune My Foe*, 48.

salmon, sand sharks and ariid catfish. Among the rocks at the northern end of the bay they could catch mackerel and blennies (of the family *clinidae*, *klipvisse* in Afrikaans) with their bare hands. Dolphins and porpoises might also be taken as the tide receded. Also hunted were seals, turtles – which can no longer be found in the bay – and, using dogs as well as bows and arrows, penguins, pelicans and other seabirds, which also provided eggs.[89]

---

[89] Budack, "The ǂAonîn or Topnaar of the Lower !Kuiseb Valley and the Sea", 12, 15–23, 27–31; Cécille, "Bericht des Kommandanten Cécille über die Fahrt der Korvette l'Héroïne", 141; Goodridge, *Narrative of a Voyage to the South Seas*, 34; Kinahan, "The Impenetrable Shield", 40; Kinahan, *Pastoral Nomads of the Central Namib Desert*, 110; Kolbe, excerpt from a letter, 10.03.1848, Archiv- und Museumsstiftung Wuppertal, Schriftarchiv, Archiv der Rheinischen Mission, RMG 2.585 (*Beiträge zur Geschichte der Stationen*), C/i 6. 1; Morrell, *A Narrative of Four Voyages*, 299; Mossolow, *Die Geschichte von Rooibank-Scheppmannsdorf*, 9; "Tagebuch des Schiffes Boode", 51. Edmund Gardner, who came to Walvis Bay as captain of an American whaleship in 1803, observed countless dogs there ("twenty dogs to each person"; quoted in Kinahan, "The Impenetrable Shield", 50). Among the ǂAonîn fishing was the preserve of the

The ǂAonîn who greeted Boulden Thompson in April 1786 led him approximately four miles south of the bay to a dune valley in which tamarisks grew. There he found around twenty huts with eighty-five inhabitants, most of them men.[90] Thomas Alexander, who landed in Walvis Bay in 1795 as captain of the frigate HMS *Star*, also mentions a village some five miles away.[91] And in 1836 we find Cécile writing of an ǂAonîn settlement approximately five miles south of the bay and inhabited by around one hundred people in eighteen or twenty huts.[92] All these accounts probably refer to a settlement identified by the archaeologist John Kinahan as ǂKhîsa-||gubus. Its proximity to a comparatively reliable source of water appears to have led the ǂAonîn to choose ǂKhîsa-||gubus as the location of what was long their principal settlement. Using bent branches and sometimes also the ribs and vertebrae of whales they built some two dozen dome-like huts here.[93] Aside from ǂKhîsa-||gubus, they also used other, often temporary settlements in the vicinity of the !Kuiseb.[94] In March 1845 the missionary Heinrich Scheppmann observed six to eight families living in each of several settlements "sprinkled among the sand mounds".[95]

How many people, then, actually lived in Walvis Bay and its environs? Various estimates made between 1786 and 1853 put the figure at somewhere between one hundred and one thousand individuals, but they do not provide an adequate basis on which to draw conclusions regarding possible changes in population size. How these estimates were arrived at is unclear, and in any case outside observers would hardly have been able to form a comprehensive picture of the settlements spread across the dunes. Moreover, some estimates refer only to ǂKhîsa-||gubus (Tab. 2).

***

"They wear iron rings on their arms and legs and corals around their necks", the missionary Friedrich Wilhelm Kolbe observed of the ǂAonîn's apparel in 1848. "Young and old wear earrings and every breast is decorated with a polished bone with which they eat the narafruit and which looks exactly like a [bookbinder's]

---

men, the presence of women being considered – as on board whalers – to bode ill for the hunt. (Budack, "The ǂAonîn or Topnaar of the Lower !Kuiseb Valley and the Sea", 21)
90 Kinahan, "The Impenetrable Shield", 39f., 58.
91 Kinahan, *By Command of their Lordships*, 39.
92 Cécille, "Bericht des Kommandanten Cécille über die Fahrt der Korvette l'Héroïne", 140.
93 Kinahan, *Pastoral Nomads of the Central Namib Desert*, 102f., 107; see also Kinahan, Cattle for Beads, 33–35. Another visitor to ǂKhîsa-||gubus was Benjamin Morrell, master of the sealer *Antarctic* of New York, in 1828. (Morrell, *A Narrative of Four Voyages*, 298)
94 Köhler, "Die Topnaar-Hottentotten am unteren Kuiseb", 102.
95 Scheppmann, "Von der Kapstadt nach der Walfischbai", 238.

bone folder."⁹⁶ The appearance of the ǂAonîn reflected their subsistence patterns. Besides harvesting !nara and fishing, they gathered corals and seashells from which they fashioned necklaces and other items of jewellery.⁹⁷ They also collected ostrich eggs, kept sheep and goats, and hunted game and penguins, using the pelts to make capes and hats.⁹⁸ Contrary, then, to what the missionary Heinrich Schepmann supposed in 1845, the ǂAonîn by no means relied entirely on the !nara for their subsistence.⁹⁹ Like many societies forced to make the best of the hostile conditions imposed by an arid environment, the ǂAonîn too resorted to a combination of strategies.¹⁰⁰ This seems also to have included trade with societies in the interior: shells and Dutch copper coins have been found that testify to links extending from the coast far into the hinterland.¹⁰¹ The ǂAonîn also began to use gourds no later than the 1780s. Since gourds do not grow anywhere in the territory of modern Namibia, they must have been imported from a considerable distance, possibly from Angola.¹⁰² The discovery on the coast of copper beads, which probably found their way there from the Khomas Plateau, likewise point to trading links with the interior.¹⁰³

Fish killed by the regular sulphur (hydrogen sulphide) eruptions¹⁰⁴ and red tides¹⁰⁵ frequently washed up on the shores of Walvis Bay – as occasionally did

---

96 Kolbe, excerpt from a letter, 10.03.1848, Archiv- und Museumsstiftung Wuppertal, Schriftarchiv, Archiv der Rheinischen Mission, RMG 2.585 (*Beiträge zur Geschichte der Stationen*), C/i 6. 2.
97 Budack, "The ǂAonîn or Topnaar of the Lower !Kuiseb Valley and the Sea", 34; Choyce, *The Log of a Jack Tar*, 4; Goodridge, *Narrative of a Voyage to the South Seas*, 34. On the dress and jewellery of the ǂAonîn see also Alexander, *An Expedition of Discovery into the Interior of Africa*, vol. 2, 79.
98 Alexander, *An Expedition of Discovery into the Interior of Africa*, vol. 2, 84; Cécille, "Bericht des Kommandanten Cécille über die Fahrt der Korvette l'Héroïne", 140f.; Choyce, *The Log of a Jack Tar*, 4; Kinahan, *Pastoral Nomads of the Central Namib Desert*, 88; Morrell, *A Narrative of Four Voyages*, 298; Owen, *Narrative of Voyages to Explore the Shores of Africa, Arabia, and Madagascar*, vol. 2, 135.
99 Scheppmann, "Von der Kapstadt nach der Walfischbai", 238.
100 Widlok, *Dealing with Institutional Changes in Property Regimes*, 14. On the combination of different forms of production in the territory of modern Namibia generally see Henrichsen, *Herrschaft und Alltag im vorkolonialen Zentralnamibia*, 61–65.
101 Budack, "The ǂAonîn or Topnaar of the Lower !Kuiseb Valley and the Sea", 13; Sydow, "Contributions to the History and Protohistory of the Topnaar Strandloper Settlement at the Kuiseb River Mouth near Walvis Bay", 76.
102 Kinahan, "The Impenetrable Shield", 43.
103 Kinahan, *Cattle for Beads*, 43–45, 50.
104 Andersson, *Lake Ngami*, 249f.; Budack, "The ǂAonîn or Topnaar of the Lower !Kuiseb Valley and the Sea", 15, 37; Liesegang, "Die Guanogewinnung auf den Inseln und an der Küste Südwestafrikas", 37f.; Schultze, *Aus Namaland und Kalahari*, 54f.
105 Wyatt, "Morrell's Seals", 4.

whales. "The beach is covered in whale skeletons", the missionary Carl Hugo Hahn noted in his diary in February 1844.[106] What proportion of these carcases washed up as a result of whaling rather than for other reasons is impossible to ascertain in retrospect. What is certain is that the inhabitants of Walvis Bay knew and made use of whales before the first whalers came across the Atlantic in the late eighteenth century. As early as 1677 the crew of the *Boode* observed that the bones of southern right whales were used in building huts in Sandwich Harbour,[107] and rock paintings of whales in the interior, estimated to be about 500 years old, indicate an awareness of beached whales far from the coast.[108]

Linguistic and ethnographic studies undertaken in the twentieth century have revealed how the ǂAonîn used a far more fine-grained vocabulary to classify different kinds of whales than other groups of Nama who also spoke Khoekhoegowab. Whales (/hoëgu) fell into two principle categories, "whales with mouths full of grass" (/gãxa-am-!na-/hoëgu) and "whales with mouths full of teeth" (//gūxa-am-!na-/hoëgu). Within this dichotomy, which approximates the taxonomic division of whales into baleen whales and toothed whales, the ǂAonîn further distinguished between individual species, including southern right whales (ǂkhárab), humpback whales (khū//āb), sperm whales (gai-//gūxa-am-!na-/hoëgu), blue whales (gai-/hoëgu) and fin whales (/hai-/hoëgu). Killer whales or orcas, by contrast, they considered to be not whales, but "great dolphins" (gai-ǂgurubeb).[109]

But the ǂAonîn found more in the sea than just food. From brown algae, Cymothoidae eggs and yolks from the eggs of plough-nosed chimaeras they prepared medicinal powders and ointments.[110] Citing the tales of the elders as evidence, the anthropologist Kuno Budack claims that the beaching of a whale was considered an occasion for celebration by the ǂAonîn, who preserved the meat of southern right whales, humpback whales and fin whales by burying it the sand or by cutting it into strips and drying them in the sun. This meat they would boil or roast as needed, sometimes also eating it raw. On the other hand, the ǂAonîn supposedly avoided the flesh of sperm whales and orcas, believing it to be indigestible. The oil they applied to the skin in order to protect it from

---

106 Hahn, *Carl Hugo Hahn Tagebücher*, 148.
107 "Tagebuch des Schiffes Boode", 51. Societies elsewhere on the Namib Coast and on the western coast of modern South Africa probably made use of beached whales for thousands of years. (Griffiths et al., "Impacts of Human Activities on Marine Animal Life in the Benguela", 305f.; Noli/Avery, "Stone Circles in the Cape Fria Area", 61; Smith/Kinahan, "The Invisible Whale", 89f.) Inhabitants of the Namib Coast were still using whale bones in construction in the early twentieth century. (Schultze, *Aus Namaland und Kalahari*, 19)
108 Barthelmeß, "Auf Walfang", 9.
109 Budack, "The ǂAonîn or Topnaar of the Lower !Kuiseb Valley and the Sea", 23–25.
110 Ibid., 21, 38.

sun and salt water. A song of praise chanted by the fishermen on the beach exhorted the "flesh-rich water" (among other things) to "Give me the whale!"[111]

Tab. 2: Estimates of the population of Walvis Bay.

1786[a]	85 (in ǂKhîsa-ǁgubus)
1820[b]	500
1828[c]	250 (in ǂKhîsa-ǁgubus)
1836[d]	100 (in ǂKhîsa-ǁgubus)
1837[e]	several hundred
1844[f]	600–750
1853[g]	1,000

Sources: [a]Kinahan, *Impenetrable Shield* 40; [b]Goodridge 32; [c]Morrell 298; [d]Cécille 140; [e]Alexander, *An Expedition of Discovery into the Interior of Africa*, vol. II, 100; [f]Hahn, *Tagebücher* 150; [g]Hahn, *Tagebücher* 652.

***

"A good deal of livestock" was one thing the missionary Johann Hinrich Schmelen observed among the ǂAonîn in 1824.[112] By contrast, a later missionary, Friedrich Wilhelm Kolbe, in 1848 wrote of their "quite particular poverty", explaining that "Whereas the other Nama tribes still own livestock, which supports them, those here have nothing but the narafruit."[113] That missionary sources of the 1840s in particular should describe the ǂAonîn as impoverished gatherers of !nara[114] is due to a change of rule that occurred in the bay in the whaling era. By the time the first mission station set up in the vicinity of the bay in 1845, the ǂAonîn had largely lost their herds of sheep, goats and cattle.[115] They had fallen prey to attacks by the Oorlam Afrikaners, a group that around 1796 had migrated from the northern frontier lands of the Cape Colony to the territory of modern Namibia,

---

111 Budack, "The ǂAonîn or Topnaar of the Lower !Kuiseb Valley and the Sea", 25–27, 37f.
112 Schmelen, "Kurzer Bericht Schmelens über seine Reise nach der Walfischbai", 222.
113 Kolbe, excerpt from a letter, 10.03.1848, Archiv- und Museumsstiftung Wuppertal, Schriftarchiv, Archiv der Rheinischen Mission, RMG 2.585 (*Beiträge zur Geschichte der Stationen*), C/i 6. 2f.
114 See also Scheppmann, "Von der Kapstadt nach der Walfischbai", 238 and Tindall, *The Journal of Joseph Tindall*, 32, 40. In 1850 the explorers Andersson and Galton also observed considerable poverty among the ǂAonîn. (Andersson, *Lake Ngami*, 18, 23f.; Galton, *The Narrative of an Explorer in Tropical South Africa*, 183)
115 Hahn, *Carl Hugo Hahn Tagebücher*, 150; Scheppmann, "Von der Kapstadt nach der Walfischbai", 238.

where it established a form of economy based on armed robbery, carried out by mounted *komandos*. In 1823 some 300 Oorlam Afrikaners under the leadership of Jonker Afrikaner moved into the Khomas Plateau and forged a military alliance with the Kai‖khaun, which allowed to intensify their livestock rustling.[116] When James Edward Alexander arrived in Walvis Bay in 1837, the ǂAonîn had apparently already begun to suffer raids from the interior.[117] Over the following years the Oorlam Afrkaners brought the area under their permanent rule. In early 1845 the missionary Johannes Rath remarked that "nobody among the people was permitted to buy or sell before Jonker's arrival."[118] When Jonker Afrikaner and his large entourage did arrive in the bay on 4 March, numerous rifles and two small cannons were fired in his honour.[119]

The ǂAonîn's subjugation by the Oorlam Afrikaners will be revisited in due course. This is the place merely for a brief note on power relations in Walvis Bay before the 1840s, of which we know from only two sources. The first is the account by James Archbell, a British missionary who arrived in Walvis Bay in 1821 with his wife and an interpreter in to establish its suitability for a station of the London Missionary society. Archbell describes the ǂAonîn as a society centred on a single ruler: "They have their own king and although power was given to him voluntarily, authority appears to be with an aristocracy. When the king decides something, his lords will often oppose the carrying out of the plan."[120] The second source is the report by a British explorer, the aforementioned James Edward Alexander, who in 1837 met a ruler to whom he refers as "Quasip" and whom historical and ethnographic research has since identified as KaXab. According to Alexander, KaXab was aged approximately forty-five, wore a fur cape and was accompanied by an older man, evidently his adviser.[121] Although Archbell's and Alexander's observations are too brief and imprecise to allow for an analysis of ǂAonîn political organisation, the picture they both draw of a ruler whose power is moderated by the influence of other functionaries does suggest a resemblance to other Nama societies. These societies were organised as

---

116 Henrichsen, *Herrschaft und Alltag im vorkolonialen Zentralnamibia*, 75–83; Wallace, *History of Namibia*, 59–68. The Kai‖khaun – who appear in contemporary sources as the "Red Nation" (*Roode Nasie* or *Rote Nation*) – are considered the largest of the nineteenth-century Nama chieftaincies. (Lau, *Carl Hugo Hahn 1837–1860: A Missionary in Nama- and Damaraland – Register and Indexes*, 1262)
117 Alexander, *An Expedition of Discovery into the Interior of Africa*, vol. 2, 74f.
118 Rath, "Aus dem Tagebuch Raths", 228.
119 Scheppmann, "Von der Kapstadt nach der Walfischbai", 238.
120 Quoted in Vigne, "James Archbell's 'Beschrijving der Walvischbaai en omliggende plaatsen aan de westkust van Africa' in 1823", 33.
121 Alexander, *An Expedition of Discovery into the Interior of Africa*, vol. 2, 107f.

associations of several clans (*!Hau!Nati!*) to form chiefdoms (*!Haos*), each of which was headed by a *kaptein*, whose power was limited by other functionaries – judges, for instance.¹²²

From his anthropological fieldwork among the ǂAonîn, Budack concludes that they must have split into two groups in the early 1800s: while the larger part under the leadership of KaXab, consisting of 250 to 300 individuals, remained at the coast, a smaller group under ||NeiXab followed the !Kuiseb Congo river into the interior, settling some twenty-five kilometres from the coast at |Awa-!haos, the northern bank of a bend in the river where ana trees (*Faidherbia albida*) grew. The ǂAonîn who remained at the beach subsequently called themselves *Hurínin* or "people of the sea" and subsisted on fish and !nara, while the other group called itself *!Khuisenin* or "people of the !Kuiseb" and kept sheep, cattle and goats in the riverbed.¹²³ Since, however, archaeological evidence has shown the coastal ǂAonîn also to have kept livestock, Jill and John Kinahan have questioned Budack's conclusions. The argue that, rather than being units of political organisation, the terms *Hurínin* and *!Khuisenin* were indicators of social status. According to this understanding, the *Hurínin* were impoverished ǂAonîn who owned no livestock and were thus comparatively strongly dependent on the sea, whereas the *!Khuisenin* were herdsmen and were able (or compelled) to settle near the pastures in the interior.¹²⁴

People of the edge and people of the sea

How did ǂAonîn encounter whalers? The most detailed account of such a situation is from the pen of Edmund Gardner, who arrived in Walvis Bay in 1803 as master of an unidentified American whaler. He met a man and two women on the beach and tried – with no apparent success – to make himself understood in sign language. For their part, the ǂAonîn talked at the seamen with a similar lack of results. Communication succeeded only when "Some one made a noise like the lowing of cattle, when the young woman repeated the sound, and then laid her head on her hand shuting her eyes imitating sleep, then pointing and following

---

122 Dedering, *Hate the Old and Follow the New*, 31f., 34.
123 Budack, "The ǂAonîn or Topnaar of the Lower !Kuiseb Valley and the Sea", 3, 7, 12; Budack, "A Harvesting People on the South Atlantic Coast", 2; Mossolow, *Die Geschichte von Rooibank-Scheppmannsdorf*, 2. On KaXab and ||NeiXab see also Köhler, "Die Topnaar-Hottentotten am unteren Kuiseb", 108.
124 Kinahan, *Cattle for Beads*, 3f., 12; Kinahan, *Pastoral Nomads of the Central Namib Desert*, 118, 121; Kinahan in Wallace, *History of Namibia*, 37.

the sun 'till down, then going through the sleeping sign, and when the sun arose the third day, the Bullocks, Sheep, and Goats would be there." Gardner appears to have understood the woman's gesticulations correctly, for three days later a group of ǂAonîn arrived, driving cattle, sheep and goats to the beach. Gardner and the captains of the other whalers anchored in the bay obtained nearly all these animals in exchange for tobacco and ironware.[125]

What is striking about this encounter as described by Gardner is that the ǂAonîn soon understood what the captain was after even though neither party was able to make itself understood in words. Clearly the exchange of cattle for tobacco and iron had already become so established a practice over the years that it took only a few gestures and sounds to initiate an established pattern of interaction and settle business to both sides' satisfaction. The deal made with Gardner displays several typical patterns of communication and interaction in the contacts between ǂAonîn and ship's crews or *hurinigu*, "people of the sea".[126] This begins with the objects traded: aside from souvenirs – Gurdon Alleyn, master of the *Betsey* of New London, recalled acquiring ostrich feathers and eggs in 1836[127] – all the seamen ever bought was livestock. In his memoirs, the seaman James Choyce writes that during the four months' stay of the British whaler *London* in 1793 "we often went on shore to trade with the Hottentots for goats and small bullocks."[128] The point here is not that the seamen might not have been interested in other goods for barter, but that there was simply nothing else they wanted to be had. This included the two most important supplies in need of regular replenishment, drinking water and firewood. With no prospect of obtaining either, some whalers did not even bother to put in at Walvis Bay, for instance the *Ann* of Dunkirk, which lay at anchor there from May to July 1792.[129]

***

---

125 Quoted in Kinahan, "The Impenetrable Shield", 50.
126 The term *hurinigu* is derived from *hurib*, the Khoekhoegowab term for the sea. (Köhler, "Die Topnaar-Hottentotten am unteren Kuiseb", 100)
127 Allyn, *The Old Sailor's Story*, 46. Seamen from the British sealer *Princess of Wales* also took ivory on board in Walvis Bay in 1820. (Goodridge, *Narrative of a Voyage to the South Seas*, 32f.) In November 1825 men of the research vessel HMS *Leven* acquired antelope horns as ostrich feathers as souvenirs of Walvis Bay. (Owen, *Narrative of Voyages to Explore the Shores of Africa, Arabia, and Madagascar*, vol. 2, 136) The collection of Cold Spring Harbor Whaling Museum in Long Island, New York contains an ostrich egg decorated with a landscape drawing which, while undated, may have come from the coast of modern Namibia.
128 Choyce, *The Log of a Jack Tar*, 4.
129 Log ANN, 1791–1792, 19.05.–23.07.1792.

"The water which is dug close to the sea is potable but bad", Carl Hugo Hahn noted in his diary in February 1844.[130] Other visitors found it to be simply undrinkable. For instance, in 1837 the crew of the *Commodore Perry* of New London judged it too brackish and took no water on board at all.[131] The main problem was that while fresh water could be reached further upstream by digging in the bed of !Kuiseb Congo river, when it reached the shore it became mixed with seawater in the mudbanks that fringe the littoral.[132] Unlike the ǂAonîn, who know where to find reliable waterholes in the dry riverbed, the seamen lacked familiarity with the terrain, while the waterholes they found close to the beach were unreliable and salty. "After considerable labour in digging, we could procure nothing but salt water", recalled Charles Goodridge, a seaman who came to Walvis Bay in the sealer *Princess of Wales* of London.[133] Yet anyone approaching Walvis Bay overland – that is, through the desert – like Hahn might well appreciate such brackish water as better than nothing. Sometimes ǂAonîn would provide small quantities of better water in bowls made of ostrich eggs,[134] but this was scarcely enough for crews looking to replenish their reserves of drinking water for weeks or months.[135] All that seamen could find in abundance in Walvis Bay was fish, which at least added variety to an otherwise monotonous diet.[136]

The only firewood to be found in the bay was driftwood, which was either washed up on the beach by the tides[137] or carried towards the bay from the hinterland by the !Kuiseb – "trees brought down by the floods in the river", as James Edward Alexander observed in 1837.[138] The tamarisks, camel thorns and ana trees that grew in the dry riverbed and here and there in the dunes were clearly insufficient fuel to keep the trypots of dozens of vessels boiling for years on end.

---

130 Hahn, *Carl Hugo Hahn Tagebücher*, 148.
131 Alexander, *An Expedition of Discovery into the Interior of Africa*, vol. 2, 89.
132 Kinahan, *Pastoral Nomads of the Central Namib Desert*, 87, 99.
133 Goodridge, *Narrative of a Voyage to the South Seas*, 33.
134 Ibid.
135 In September 1793 the British whaler *London* headed for St Helena – a distance of over one thousand nautical miles – in order to take on fresh water after a stay of four months in Walvis Bay. (Choyce, *The Log of a Jack Tar*, 4)
136 Goodridge, *Narrative of a Voyage to the South Seas*, 33f.; Log STEPHANIA, 1847–1850, 26.–28.06. & 15.07.1850.
137 Kinahan, "The Impenetrable Shield", 44, 57; Owen, *Narrative of Voyages to Explore the Shores of Africa, Arabia, and Madagascar*, vol. 2, 135; Reenen, "Tagebuch über die Fahrt des Schiffes 'Meermin'", 199.
138 Alexander, *An Expedition of Discovery into the Interior of Africa*, vol. 2, 91.

During the nine weeks his vessel lay at anchor in Walvis Bay in 1799 Charles Gardner, master of the *North America* of Nantucket, bought at least six head of cattle and as many sheep.[139] Charles Griffin, master of the *Franklin* of Sag Harbor, acquired two oxen in Walvis Bay in 1839.[140] And Captain Bourne of the *Stephania* of New Bedford bartered for two oxen and nine goats in June and July 1850.[141] However, such figures for livestock acquired by barter are too rarely preserved to give a reliable indication of the quantitative scope of this trade and any change it may have undergone in the era of whaling in the bay.[142] Yet the sources do reveal certain of its quantitative aspects. In May 1786 Boulden Thompson of HMS *Nautilus* was surprised that to find that while the ǂAonîn ate meat and wore hides, their herds were nowhere to be seen – even though he had walked "2 or 3 miles" from the shore to find them.[143] Home Riggs Popham, who accompanied Boulden Thompson in the capacity of surveyor, likewise found that "They had plenty of Cattle but woud [sic] not suffer us to see where they kept them." "I beleive [sic]", he concluded, that they "drove them further inland on our arrival."[144] The crew ultimately succeeded in buying a calf and a young heifer, but even then the ǂAonîn refused to let the seamen see their herds.[145] In 1803 Charles Gardner had to wait three days for the ǂAonîn to drive their sheep, goats and cattle to the back through the dunes – and no more of them than they ended up selling to the whalemen.[146] James Edward Alexander also noted that it took a good deal of negotiation to get the ǂAonîn to bring a few sheep and goats to the beach: "They have flocks and herds, though we saw few of them."[147]

Two possible answers to the question of why the ǂAonîn should have been so keen to keep their herds out of sight of visiting seamen come to mind. For one thing, concealing their livestock offered the strategic advantage of guarding against cattle rustling as well as suggesting scarcity and hence strengthening their own bargaining position. A second answer is suggested by the archaeological research of Jill and John Kinahan. The ǂAonîn's chief pasturage was apparently located in Khaeros, a small watering hole in the !Kuiseb riverbed some

---

139 Log NORTH AMERICA, 1797–1799, 15.06., 28.06. & 14.07.1799.
140 Kinahan, *Cattle for Beads*, 17.
141 Log STEPHANIA, 1847–1850, 22.–24.06. & 16.07.1850.
142 Haywood, "American Whalers and Africa", 82.
143 Kinahan, "The Impenetrable Shield", 40, 44, 57.
144 Quoted in ibid., 58.
145 Ibid., 40, 44, 57.
146 Gardner, quoted in ibid., 50.
147 Alexander, *An Expedition of Discovery into the Interior of Africa*, vol. 2, 100.

25 kilometres east of ǂKhîsa-ǁgubus. Khaeros was probably the centre from which the ǂAonîn moved their herds in seasonal rhythms between the various watering holes in the dry riverbed and the sparse pasturages amid the dunes, where their animals fed on leaves of the trees and shrubs.[148] In view of the logistical effort involved in driving livestock to the beach for several days through high sands, it must have seemed downright impracticable to take the seamen through the same dunes to the pastures first.

What did the ǂAonîn ask of the *hurinigu* in return for their animals? Charles Gardner, in the encounter related above, mentions only iron and tobacco, stating that the latter commodity "was of more value to them than anything offered".[149] Already in 1677 the crew of the *Boode* had found that the inhabitants of Sandwich harbour "take much pleasure" in tobacco.[150] It was also bartered in Walvis Bay by Popham of the *Nautilus* (1786) and Pienaar of the *Meermin* (1793).[151] William Fitzwilliam Owen, who arrived in Walvis bay in November 1825 at the helm of the sloop HMS *Leven*, which was mapping the coast of Africa, records that the ǂAonîn had "vociferously" demanded tobacco.[152] Cécille in June 1836 acquired one adult goat and three kids for less than a pound of tobacco. "They are all greedy for tobacco", he wrote of the ǂAonîn. "The men will sell their weapons and their goats for the sake of a few inches; the women cast all shame aside and open themselves to the curiosity of strangers for even less."[153] About a year later Alexander recorded that the going price for a sheep in Walvis Bay was "two or three sticks" of tobacco.[154] The ǂAonîn seem to have set great store by tobacco smoking. "Tobacco is their idol", the missionary Friedrich Wilhelm Kolbe noted in a letter of 1848: "He among them who has much tobacco is considered the

---

148 Kinahan et al., "The Occurence and Dating of Elephant Tracks in the Silt Deposits of the Lower !Khuiseb River", 40f.; Kinahan, "Human and Domestic Animal Tracks in an Archaeological Lagoon Deposit on the Coast of Namibia", 94; Kinahan, *Pastoral Nomads of the Central Namib Desert*, 117; Köhler, "Die Topnaar-Hottentotten am unteren Kuiseb", 104.
149 Quoted in Kinahan, "The Impenetrable Shield", 50.
150 "Tagebuch des Schiffes Boode", 51.
151 Duminy, *Duminy-dagboeke*, 287–289; Kinahan, "The Impenetrable Shield", 57; Reenen, "Tagebuch über die Fahrt des Schiffes 'Meermin'", 198f. On the use of tobacco in barter in Walvis Bay see also Goodridge, *Narrative of a Voyage to the South Seas*, 32.
152 Owen, *Narrative of Voyages to Explore the Shores of Africa, Arabia, and Madagascar*, vol. 2, 136.
153 Cécille, "Bericht des Kommandanten Cécille über die Fahrt der Korvette l'Héroïne", 140.
154 Alexander, *An Expedition of Discovery into the Interior of Africa*, vol. 2, 84.

richest and happiest man upon earth."[155] The importance accorded to tobacco by the ǂAonîn may also have been due to its ability to suppress hunger pangs when food was scarce.[156]

Besides tobacco, the ǂAonîn seem above all to have been interested in beads. "From [. . .] the beads of glass & copper I found amongst them I am convinced they have had some intercourse with Europeans", noted Boulden Thompson in May 1786, observing that the ǂAonîn wore beads in their hair as well as carrying them about with in receptacles of bone and ivory.[157] Since they could obtain iron and cooper beads from the interior, in their dealings with seamen they had their sights on glass beads in particular.[158] "They are mad on tobacco and blue beads", Captain Duminy of the *Meermin* noted in 1793.[159] In ǂKhîsa-ǁgubus alone Jill Kinahan unearthed more than 1,700 eighteenth- and nineteenth-century glass beads that must have arrived with ships' crews.[160] Since copper beads had an important part to play in trade between the coast and the hinterland, we may assume that the ǂAonîn invested glass beads with value too and that they were far from being the worthless baubles as which they might have appeared to seamen.[161] Bolden Thompson and Choyce also mention the ǂAonîn showing a strong interest in the buttons on seamen's clothing.[162] Items less frequently cited as being accepted in barter are iron rods, brandy, knives, cutlery and bread.[163]

Encounters between ǂAonîn and seamen usually took place on the beach, though skippers would sometimes receive men from the shore on board their vessels, such instances including François Duminy of the *Meermin* in 1793, Benjamin Morrell of the *Antarctic* in 1828 and Jean-Baptiste Cécille of *l'Héroïne* in 1836.[164] Of his landfall, Boulden Thompson records that four ǂAonîn rubbed

---

155 Kolbe, excerpt from a letter, 10.03.1848, Archiv- und Museumsstiftung Wuppertal, Schriftarchiv, Archiv der Rheinischen Mission, RMG 2.585 (*Beiträge zur Geschichte der Stationen*), C/i 6. 4.
156 Dedering, *Hate the Old and Follow the New*, 107.
157 Kinahan, "The Impenetrable Shield", 40.
158 Kinahan, *Pastoral Nomads of the Central Namib Desert*, 120.
159 Duminy, *Duminy-dagboeke*, 290.
160 Kinahan, *Cattle for Beads*, 69.
161 Ibid., 43–45, 50; Kinahan in Wallace, *History of Namibia*, 37.
162 Choyce, *The Log of a Jack Tar*, 4; Kinahan, "The Impenetrable Shield", 43.
163 Alexander, *An Expedition of Discovery into the Interior of Africa*, vol. 2, 96; Booth, *The United States Experience in South Africa*, 39; Cécille, "Bericht des Kommandanten Cécille über die Fahrt der Korvette l'Héroïne", 140; Choyce, *The Log of a Jack Tar*, 4; Goodridge, *Narrative of a Voyage to the South Seas*, 32f.; Kinahan, "The Impenetrable Shield", 43, 57.
164 Cécille, "Bericht des Kommandanten Cécille über die Fahrt der Korvette l'Héroïne", 140; Duminy, *Duminy-dagboeke*, 292; Morrell, *A Narrative of Four Voyages*, 298.

grease on the faces and chests of him and his men in what seems to have been a gesture of welcome.[165] Other descriptions of comparable encounters, however, make no mention of such a practice.

The sources do not indicate whether seamen in Walvis Bay dealt directly with the owners of the livestock they were looking to buy, with middlemen or with political leaders such as KaXab or ||NeiXab – and in any case it would have far from obvious to the seamen themselves. What is certain is that no runaway seamen appeared there as advisors or middlemen, for unlike in most ports along the African coast, hardly anyone ever deserted his vessel in Walvis Bay. Though the dunes of the Namib might have offered hideouts, it also offered poor chances to anyone of surviving until his vessel had sailed. What was more, during the heyday of whaling, vessels usually returned straight home from Walvis Bay, further reducing incentives to desert.[166]

Only once a few merchants and missionaries began to settle in Walvis Bay in the 1840s do we hear of seamen occasionally leaving their vessels behind with or without their captain's leave. Francis Galton, who explored the territory of modern Namibia from 1850 to 1851, estimated there to be "five or six runaway sailors" living there, usually around mission stations.[167] One of them was Hans Larsen, a Dane who arrived in Walvis Bay in 1843 and who around 1850 joined another seaman, the Englishman John Allen, in establishing a cattle ranch in Otjimbingwe, some 180 kilometres in the interior.[168] In most such cases it is unknown whether the men arrived in whalers or in the guano vessels and coasters that began to ply the Namib Coast in the 1840s. Only of James Sherman, who lived as a merchant in Walvis Bay in the 1840s, do we know for certain that he had run away from an American whaleship.[169] Another recorded desertion is that of Philip Stanck, who in January 1884 absconded from the barque *Sunbeam* to an unknown fate.[170] Before the 1840s any seaman remaining in Walvis Bay is unlikely to have done so voluntarily. Pieces of wreckage, clothing and skeletons discovered in the hinterland of the coast suggest that shipwrecked seamen would sometimes try in vain to make their way through the desert.[171] In April 1796 the crew

---

165 Kinahan, "The Impenetrable Shield", 39, 57.
166 On desertion see the chapter "Passages III".
167 Galton, *The Narrative of an Explorer in Tropical South Africa*, 68.
168 Ibid., 57, 81; Metzkes, *Otjimbingwe*, 32; Tabler, *Pioneers of South West Africa and Ngamiland*, 3, 67. In 1852 Larsen and Allen travelled to Australia via Cape Town in search of gold.
169 Hahn, *Carl Hugo Hahn Tagebücher*, 373.
170 Log SUNBEAM, 1882–1886, 28.01.1884.
171 Schumann, "Schiffe und ihre Mannschaften vor Namibias Küste", 106f. In June 1850 the crew of the *Stephania* of New Bedford found a number of objects originating from vessels in Walvis Bay and took them on board. (Log STEPHANIA, 1847–1850, 16.07.1850)

of the *Union* buried Adam Miller in the bay, their black steward who had died on board.[172] An advertisement printed in 1803 in the New Bedford *Columbian Courier* announces the death of one Captain Benjamin Swivt of Nantucket in Walvis Bay, but without stating a cause.[173]

***

James Edward Alexander's unease mounted as his expedition approached Walvis Bay in April 1837. "We had many stories among the people of the wild men who lived by the sea at the mouth of the Kuisip, of their killing white sailors", he later recalled.[174] His fears seemed to be confirmed by the discovery in the south of the bay of half-buried human skeletons. One local woman told Alexander through his interpreter that these were indeed the remains of a seaman. In one incident, seamen had been caught abusing women in the bay, whereupon ǂAonîn had attacked a boat at the beach and killed the captain. In a second incident, ǂAonîn had killed several seamen in a dispute over a beached whale.[175]

"Stories" of the kind referred to by Alexander seem to have circulated widely. Charles Goodridge, who sailed from London to Walvis Bay in the sealer *Princess of Wales* in 1820, expected to find savage cannibals there.[176] Her crew hence would only go ashore armed – an insistence found in the records of other vessels too.[177] The ǂAonîn, for their part, would sometimes also carry spears when approaching seamen on the beach, putting them aside only when the encounter proved friendly.[178] In fact, such deadly confrontations as those described by Alexander were the exception in encounters between seamen and ǂAonîn, with two other cases documented. The first is that of the *Meermin*, a Dutch frigate whose crew was fishing in the bay in February 1793 when it was attacked by some sixty ǂAonîn armed with spears. The attackers seem to have been after the *Meermin*'s fishing nets and were repelled with warning shots from the crew.[179] The second case concerns the schooner *Hope* of Salem, which ran aground near Walvis Bay on 14 May 1804. Her crew made it ashore but on 20 May became involved in a

---

172 Log UNION, 1796–1796, 11.04.1796.
173 "DIED At Walwich Bay . . .". *Columbian Courier, or Weekly Miscellany*, 02.12.1803, 3. The name "Swivt" may have referred to Captain Swift of the *Union* of New Bedford. (Lund et al., *American Offshore Whaling Voyages*)
174 Alexander, *An Expedition of Discovery into the Interior of Africa*, vol. 2, 65.
175 Ibid., 79f.
176 Goodridge, *Narrative of a Voyage to the South Seas*, 32.
177 Choyce, *The Log of a Jack Tar*, 4; Log KATHLEEN, 1852–1855, 12.03.1854.
178 Goodridge, *Narrative of a Voyage to the South Seas*, 32.
179 Duminy, *Duminy-dagboeke*, 297f.; Reenen, "Tagebuch über die Fahrt des Schiffes 'Meermin'", 201.

dispute with ǂAonîn which appears to have escalated. Only two seamen survived the ensuing struggle, both badly wounded, and were lucky to be rescued by a British whaler that sailed into Walvis Bay the next day.¹⁸⁰ There is no reason, however, to suppose that such violent altercations were commonplace events – not least because barter and exchange in Walvis Bay continued over decades and must therefore have been carried on in a manner that both parties found to be workable and to some extent satisfactory.¹⁸¹ Even Goodridge's fears were ultimately dispelled: although both parties were armed on their first encounter, before long the ǂAonîn laid down their spears and began to sing and dance, with the seamen sharing in the merriment.¹⁸²

Some of the records quoted above raise the question of sexual relations between seamen and women in Walvis Bay, and specifically whether seamen forced women into such relations. The evidence does not point to a clear-cut answer. It is striking, for instance, that among the eighty-five ǂAonîn that Boulden Thompson encountered in ǂKhîsa-‖gubus in May 1786 only eight appear to have been adult women, six of whom he thought to be aged at least fifty.¹⁸³ Cécille reports that "women and children and a few men took flight in horror" when he visited an ǂAonîn settlement with a handful of seamen in June 1836.¹⁸⁴ It may perhaps be inferred from these observations that the ǂAonîn sought to conceal their women from seamen and that they had been taught to do so by the experience of abuse.¹⁸⁵ This conclusion seems to be borne by Galton's remark on the ǂAonîn he encountered in Walvis Bay in 1850: "They were well enough acquainted with sailors; [. . .] they had been savagely ill-used more than once."¹⁸⁶

More direct indications of sexual contact and abuse can be found in the writings of missionaries of the 1840s and 50s. Of the conduct of seamen in Walvis Bay, Carl Hugo Hahn had this to say in 1844: "The horrors of fornication visited by this rude class of men [. . .] upon women both married and unmarried defy description; I for one dare not commit to paper what the men themselves have

---

180 Theal, *History of South Africa*, 110f. The wreck of the *Hope* was depicted on a South West African stamp in 1987.
181 Of Angra Pequeña, the merchant Charles John Andersson reports that whaling crews tried to steal livestock by intimidating its owners or making them drunk. (Andersson, *The Okavango River*, 334) No such accounts exist for Walvis Bay.
182 Goodridge, *Narrative of a Voyage to the South Seas*, 32.
183 Kinahan, "The Impenetrable Shield", 40.
184 Cécille, "Bericht des Kommandanten Cécille über die Fahrt der Korvette l'Héroïne", 140.
185 One scholar to draw such an inference is Kinahan (*Cattle for Beads*, 93).
186 Galton, *The Narrative of an Explorer in Tropical South Africa*, 16.

told us."[187] Heinrich Scheppmann had similarly unpleasant things to report in a letter of March 1845. When vessels sailed into the bay, he recounts, "the godless sailors go to [the ǂAonîn women] and get up to their abominations", adding that seamen had tried "to give one woman brandy in order to seduce her".[188] Jan Bam, another missionary, made similar observations in Sandwich Harbour 1853.[189]

While telling in themselves, what is less clear about these accounts by missionaries is their connection with whaling. By the 1840s and 50s only few whalers still called at Walvis Bay, and where the hints given by missionaries can be traced, they lead to seamen in coasters or guano vessels.[190] Against this backdrop, the historian Randolph Vigne's conclusion that Walvis Bay had always been "a haven for sailors' lust" and that ǂAonîn women had prostituted themselves[191] appears as a somewhat dramatic reading unsupported by the historical record. This might also be said of Wolfgang Hartmann's reading of a trading conflict between the crew of the *Boode* and the inhabitants of Sandwich Harbor in the spring of 1677 as testifying to previous encounters with seamen, including those in "American and British whaling boats with their groups of sexually voracious men."[192] This is pure speculation, not least because American and British whalers only arrived in the area a century after the *Boode*.

∗∗∗

Following the !Kuiseb from the interior to Walvis Bay in April 1837, Alexander met two ǂAonîn. He records what they told his interpreter as follows: "They said that it was now the commencement of the mist rains at Walvisch Bay, when the ships arrive to catch whales; that no ships had been there for a long time, but that they now expected them every day."[193] On his arrival at the beach, Alexander found the jawbones of whales evidently set up as a signal to vessels, to help them locate the bay on the flat and sandy shoreline.[194] Alexander's account indicated not only that the ǂAonîn were able, by the mid-1830s, to predict the

---

187 Hahn, *Carl Hugo Hahn Tagebücher*, 151.
188 Scheppmann, "Von der Kapstadt nach der Walfischbai", 238.
189 Mossolow, *Die Geschichte von Rooibank-Scheppmannsdorf*, 9.
190 In December 1860 the British explorer James Chapman was told by fishermen that seamen in Sandwich Harbour had lured several ǂAonîn aboard with brandy and tobacco before abducting them. (Chapman, *Travels in the Interior of South Africa*, vol. 1, 214)
191 Vigne, "The Hard Road to Colonization".
192 Hartmann, "Early Dutch-Namibian Encounters", 13.
193 Alexander, *An Expedition of Discovery into the Interior of Africa*, vol. 2, 73.
194 Ibid., 84. Even in good visibility the sandy headland of Pelican Point was could barely be distinguished from the sand dunes in the interior, making the entrance in the bay hard to spot. (Kinahan, *Cattle for Beads*, 14; Kinahan, *By Command of their Lordships*, 82)

beginning of the whaling season with some accuracy – the American whaleships *Pocahontas* and *Commodore Perry* did indeed arrive only a few days later – but also that this event was eagerly anticipated. Already in 1825 Captain Owen of HMS *Leven* had found whale ribs planted in the sandy beach in the manner of signals.[195]

An observation made by Lieutenant Layrle, who arrived at the Namib Coast in 1835 aboard *l'Héroïne*, bears out this reading of Alexander's account. "In almost every bay along the coast" Layrle reported seeing "roving Hottentots, impelled to establish themselves on the beaches by the hope of doing barter with the whalers."[196] It seems that the inhabitants of the coast factored the whaling season into their annual migrations and moved to the beaches when it began. In the case of Walvis Bay, archaeological research has given weight to this hypothesis: Only in the latter part of the eighteenth century do the ǂAonîn appear to have congregated in ǂKhîsa-ǁgubus, having previously lived in smaller settlements among the dunes to the north of the !Kuiseb Congo river. More than 2,000 glass beads have been unearthed in ǂKhîsa-ǁgubus, suggesting that its inhabitants must have maintained close contact with visiting seamen.[197] Another point in favour of a connection between the development of ǂKhîsa-ǁgubus and the fortunes of whaling in Walvis Bay is the fact that its population went into steady decline when whalers all but ceased to call in the mid-nineteenth century.[198]

"The whole shore is strewn with a great many carcasses of all possible shapes and sizes for a distance of three miles to the South of the bay [. . .]. The English must have carried on whaling here for several years", deduced Captain Duminy of the *Meermin* in February 1793.[199] His observation suggests that it was not the chance of trading with the whalers that brought the ǂAonîn to the beaches. As James Edward Alexander recalled, "The bay people catch and eat [. . .] the carcases of whales, killed by the crews of whaling ships, afford them savoury repasts in the months of May, June, July, and August, or during the time the whalers are about the bay."[200] To the ǂAonîn, whaling in the bay opened up a new source of food, for carcasses of flensed whales washed up on the beach

---

195 Owen, *Narrative of Voyages to Explore the Shores of Africa, Arabia, and Madagascar*, vol. 2, 135.
196 Layrle, "Bericht des Schiffsleutnants Layrle über den Walfang im südlichen Atlantischen Ozean", 137.
197 Kinahan, "Human and Domestic Animal Tracks in an Archaeological Lagoon Deposit on the Coast of Namibia", 94; Kinahan et al., "The Occurrence and Dating of Elephant Tracks in the Silt Deposits of the Lower !Khuiseb River", 40f.
198 Kinahan, *Pastoral Nomads of the Central Namib Desert*, 114f.
199 Duminy, *Duminy-dagboeke*, 297.
200 Alexander, *An Expedition of Discovery into the Interior of Africa*, vol. 2, 84.

with the tides. "Ships are taking Whales and fresh carcasses drive on shore", Charles Gardner observed in 1803, adding that the ǂAonîn would eat even spoilt whale meat.[201] As early as 1793 James Choyce, whose vessel, the whaler *London*, lay in Walvis Bay from June to September, noticed that "They subsist chiefly on the carcasses of the whales that are killed by the ships and are turned adrift after the blubber is taken off. They seem to like it best when it has been lying some days on the beach, and is getting tender and smells pretty strong, then they relish it as sweet as I would a beefsteak after a long voyage."[202] And Sebastian van Reenen, a Dutch explorer who visited Walvis Bay in the same year, observed that "the beach was covered with the bones of northern right whales that had been taken by the English and Americans."[203] William Fitzwilliam Owen found Pelican Point to be virtually strewn with whale remains in 1825.[204] It has already been pointed out that the ǂAonîn made use of beached whales even before whaling began in the area, but the availability of whale meat obviously increased with the advent of the whaleships. Layrle too observed in 1835 that "the flesh of the whales, be it never so spoilt", was a "savoury treat" to the coastal population.[205]

A linguistic observation points to another consequence of whaling in Walvis Bay: *Rapūns*, the ǂAonîn term for their barbed spears, is not a genuinely Khoekhoegowab word, but probably derived from the English "harpoon".[206] This in turn suggests that the ǂAonîn began to fashion such spears after observing the harpoons used by whalers, and hence that whaling introduced a technological innovation to Walvis Bay.[207] Whether and to what extent their encounters with ships' crews further influenced ǂAonîn culture, for instance with regard to their ideas of the supernatural, is unclear. Johann Hinrich Schmelen in 1815 and James Edward Alexander in 1837 both record conversations in the south of modern Namibia which suggest that vessels had been absorbed into the cosmology of the Nama and Khoisan population. Two "bushmen" told Schmelen that the dead crossed over to the other side of the water where the devil awaited them. In this

---

201 Quoted in Kinahan, "The Impenetrable Shield", 50.
202 Choyce, *The Log of a Jack Tar*, 4.
203 Reenen, "Tagebuch über die Fahrt des Schiffes 'Meermin'", 199.
204 Owen, *Narrative of Voyages to Explore the Shores of Africa, Arabia, and Madagascar*, vol. 2, S. 135.
205 Layrle, "Bericht des Schiffsleutnants Layrle über den Walfang im südlichen Atlantischen Ozean", 137. Charles Goodridge, a seaman in the *Princess of Wales*, had already observed something similar in 1820. (Goodridge, *Narrative of a Voyage to the South Seas*, 33) See also Booth, *The United States Experience in South Africa*, 36.
206 Budack, "The ǂAonîn or Topnaar of the Lower !Kuiseb Valley and the Sea", 19.
207 As archaeological research by Jill Kinahan (*Cattle for Beads*, 16) has shown, whalers' harpoons could occasionally be found washed up on the beaches of Walvis Bay.

account, the vessels were the devil's vehicles and the seamen his minions.[208] Alexander's interlocutors declared that a white ship's captain was able to control the course of the sun.[209] The existing sources, however, are silent on whether the ǂAonîn too held such ideas and whether they influenced their dealings with ships' crews.

A claim can be found in some historical scholarship on south-western Africa to the effect that whalers had erected onshore tryworks or temporary accommodation for the men employed there.[210] This notion can be traced to the missionary Heinrich Vedder, who in his account of the "old South West Africa", published in 1934, states that American whalers had set up "small establishments" in Walvis Bay.[211] Only one source exits to support this claim, and Vedder does not name it: in February 1793 seamen in the *Meermin* discovered, in a valley to the north of the bay, "five old shacks" which they supposed to have been the work of whalers.[212] But it is most unlikely that they should indeed have been used for processing whales. For one thing, the shacks were situated in a valley some distance from the beach. What is more, whalers at the time used onboard tryworks, solidly encased in brick, and would have had no need to process whales onshore – nor would doing so have been at all practicable. Such onshore processing plants might, on the other hand, have made sense for sealers,[213] but they hardly operated in Walvis Bay, finding better hunting on the rocky islands off Angra Pequeña. Jill Kinahan is thus surely right in dismissing Vedder's claim that there had been tryworks in Walvis Bay as misleading.[214]

Whaling not only left traces in Walvis Bay itself but led to imperial rivalries over control of the south-west African coast, albeit with no direct impact on the ǂAonîn for the time being. Walvis Bay became known as a rich whaling ground at a time when European colonial empires were undergoing significant

---

208 Schmelen, Journal from the Year 1815, School of Oriental and African Studies, CWM/LMS/South Africa Journals/Box 2, 23.05.1815.
209 Alexander, *An Expedition of Discovery into the Interior of Africa*, vol. 1, 168.
210 E.g. in Krüger, *Kriegsbewältigung und Geschichtsbewusstsein*, 30.
211 Vedder, *Das alte Südwestafrika*, 15.
212 Reenen, "Tagebuch über die Fahrt des Schiffes 'Meermin'", 201.
213 For an account of sealing in the Kerguelen Islands, in the course of which seamen erected shacks and tryworks on land see Nordhoff, *Whaling and Fishing*, 196f.
214 Kinahan, "Heinrich Vedder's Sources for his Account of the Exploration of the Namib Coast", 37f. For a fundamental critique of Vedder's work see also Henrichsen, *Herrschaft und Alltag im vorkolonialen Zentralnamibia*, 302–304, Lau, "Thank God the Germans Came", Gockel, *Mission und Apartheid*, 3–61. Workers from guano vessels built a dwelling on the rocky island of Hollamsbird near Angra Pequeña in the mid-nineteenth century. (Watson, "The Guano Islands of Southwestern Africa", 641)

rearrangement. In 1783 Britain was forced to accept American independence, while in 1784 the Dutch had to give up a large part of their trading monopoly in the East Indies. Meanwhile France and Spain managed to extend their holdings, and Portugal renewed its claim to great power status by entering into an alliance with Russia. Having no importance for either the slave or the East India trade, the coast of modern Namibia had previously not had a part to play in these imperial designs. Only amid the tensions of the 1780s, when Britain's predictable efforts to compensate for the loss of its American colonies threatened to trigger a chain reaction of imperial conflicts, could even a whaling ground become the object of colonial ambitions.[215]

Against this backdrop, the voyage of HMS *Nautilus*, which called at Walvis Bay in 1786, could not but disconcert the Dutch authorities in Cape Town. In order to pre-empt British designs on Walvis Bay, the Dutch East India Company sent the frigate *Meermin* there in January 1793. On 26 February her captain, François Duminy – who before sailing had found out what he could about the coast from whalers and sealers – claimed Walvis Bay for the Netherlands.[216] Scarcely half a year later, however, it turned out that the Company was unable or unwilling to back up its nominal claim. Om 9 June the British privateer *Liverpool* entered Walvis Bay and captured two French, *Judith* and *Phebe*.[217] Following the French invasion of the Netherlands in 1795 British forces conquered the Cape Colony in an effort to prevent French control of the sea lanes between Europe and Asia. In order to extend British rule over the bays on the coast of modern Namibia claimed by the Dutch, the commander of the British fleet at the Cape in 1786 sent the *Star* – a frigate captured from the Dutch – up the coast. In Walvis Bay her captain, Thomas Alexander, had the Union Jack raised and three salvoes fired in honour if the occasion. For directions to Walvis Bay, he had relied on the captains of the *Friendship* and the *Triumph*, two British whalers he had encountered in Angra Pequeña.[218]

---

215 On the significance of whaling for British imperial strategies in the late eighteenth century see Mackay, *In the Wake of Cook*, 37–52.
216 Duminy, *Duminy-dagboeke*, 296f.; Gewald, "Untapped Sources", 425; Hartmann, "Early Dutch-Namibian Encounters", 17–19; Theal, *History of South Africa under the Administration of the Dutch East India Company*, 252–254; Wilken/Fox, *The History of the Port and Settlement of Walvis Bay*, 2f.
217 "Ship News." *The Medley or Newbedford Marine Journal*, 23.08.1793, 3; "Ship News." *The Medley or Newbedford Marine Journal*, 20.09.1793, 3.
218 Booth, *The United States Experience in South Africa*, 39; Kinahan, *By Command of their Lordships*, 27–32, 34–36; Kinahan, *Cattle for Beads*, 15f.; Wilken/Fox, *The History of the Port and Settlement of Walvis Bay*, 3f., 65. On her return to Cape Town the *Star* was renamed HMS *Hope*, the name by which the vessel is usually known in historical scholarship.

Since neither the Dutch nor the British act of taking possession conformed to the standards of international law, they went unrecognised by the other colonial powers. American whalers anyhow made a point of ignoring such claims to exclusive use, following southern right whales wherever they might be found – even into bays on the coast of the Cape Colony, whose administration was trying to set up whaling stations of its own. Without ever having attempted to enforce it on the ground, Britain officially retracted its claim to Walvis Bay at the Congress of Vienna in 1815.[219]

Whaling in the bay once more became a subject for colonial politics around 1830. Much as in the case of Delagoa Bay, the colonial administration at the Cape was concerned that American whalers were flouting British import bans by trading in guns and ammunition along the south-west coast of Africa and were even planning to establish an American colony. Their suspicions were further raised when Benjamin Morrell, an American sealer and explorer, proposed the foundation of an American colony in southern Africa in a much-read travelogue.[220] Already in 1828 the German missionary Johann Hinrich Schmelen had argued that whalers were contributing to the destabilisation of the Cape Colony's northern frontier: "If we cannot close off the coast on this side, so that the whale fishermen cease selling gunpowder there, then I believe that little good will be done here in the future."[221] These fears, however, did not produce a response in terms of colonial policy.

Komandos, merchants and missionaries

Jean-Baptiste Cécile, master of *l'Héroïne*, records that "On 1 June a large American brig, Helenmar of Portsmouth, dropped anchor at Angra." Unlike the other American vessels that he had encountered across along Africa's south-western coast, the *Helenmar* was not a whaler. "The captain", Cécille explains, "had been told that at Angra, two bottles of gunpowder would buy a three-hundred-pound ox and a poor flintlock two, that the Namaqua usually brought herds of twenty or twenty-five head to the bay for the use of the whalers."[222] Not only at Angra Pequeña did the barter in which the whalers engaged give rise to the idea that a profitable trade in cattle might be carried on. It was equally suggestive with

---

219 Berat, "Genocide", 168; Berat, "Walvis Bay and the Decolonization of International Law", 27f.; Haywood, "American Whalers and Africa", 85.
220 Booth, *The United States Experience in South Africa*, 137.
221 Quoted in Lau, *Southern and Central Namibia in Jonker Afrikaner's Time*, 28.
222 Cécille, "Bericht des Kommandanten Cécille über die Fahrt der Korvette l'Héroïne", 138.

regard to Walvis Bay. As James Edward Alexander mused in the account of his expedition, published in 1838, "It might be worth while to ship cattle from Walvisch Bay to St. Helena."[223] In retrospect this proposal stands for the beginnings of a process that succeeded the era of whaling in Walvis Bay from the mid-1840s onwards: its transformation into a trading port. This process was neither initiated by the ǂAonîn, nor did they profit from it. It was driven by three other groups who, each for reasons of their own, pursued a single goal: to use Walvis Bay as a connecting point between the interior and wider trading networks, particularly with Cape Town.

The first of these groups were the Oorlam Afrikaners, who brought Walvis Bay under their control between 1837 and 1845. They subjugated the ǂAonîn, forcing them to herd that cattle that Jonker Afrikaner had stolen.[224] In this period, Oorlam Afrikaner *komandos* constantly raided Herero and Damara pastures, capturing large herds of cattle which they traded with Cape Colony merchants, receiving especially guns, ox-carts and horses in exchange. Other Oorlam groups as well as Nama from the south of modern Namibia soon adopted this practice and formed *komandos* of their own. In 1840 the Oorlam Afrikaners founded the settlement of Windhoek in the only passage through the highlands of central Namibia. From this base, they consolidated their dominance by entering into military alliances with influential Herero *ovahona*[225] and forcing other groups, including the ǂAonîn, into vassalage.[226] By the time the missionary Johannes Rath arrived in Walvis Bay in early 1845, the local potentate to be reckoned with probably was no longer KaXab but Jonker Afrikaner.[227]

The founding of Walvis Bay seems also to have altered the strategic significance accorded to the place by the Oorlam Afrikaners. In 1843 Jonker Afrikaner ordered a road to be built between Windhoek and Walvis Bay, which was to enable the transport of goods by ox-cart and to bolster the supremacy of the Oorlam Afrikaners, who would control the haulage trade and charge tolls.[228] "I must

---

223 Alexander, *An Expedition of Discovery into the Interior of Africa*, vol. 2, 100.
224 Lau, *Southern and Central Namibia in Jonker Afrikaner's Time*, 53.
225 The Otjiherero term *ovahona* (singular *omuhuna*) is best rendered as "chief" (or, in German, *Machthaber*, lit. "power-haver"), since it implies both political power and economic power (measured in wealth of herds) as well as being associated with cultural and religious power. (Gewald, *Herero Heroes*, 15f.; Henrichsen, *Herrschaft und Alltag im vorkolonialen Zentralnamibia*, 14f.)
226 Henrichsen, *Herrschaft und Alltag im vorkolonialen Zentralnamibia*, 75–81; Lau, "Conflict and Power in Nineteenth-Century Namibia", 34; Tindall, *The Journal of Joseph Tindall*, 71.
227 Rath, "Aus dem Tagebuch Raths", 228.
228 Kleinschmidt, "Kleinschmidts Aufzeichnungen über Kl. Windhuk und die Damaras", 166; Wilmsen, *Land Filled with Flies*, 105f.

confess", noted Hahn in 1844, "that even in the [Cape] Colony I have never perceived such a work. It defies belief how people with the meanest tools – or indeed, with none at all – have achieved such a thing. Great boulders have been dug up and other smashed to pieces with rocks, trees and shrubs cleared etc. This road, some twenty-five to thirty feet wide, is to be the highway to Walvis Bay."[229] Once the road was completed, Jonker Afrikaner tightened his grip on the bay, going there in person in mid-1846 and suggesting that KaXab – who had only recently orchestrated a raid on ||NeiXab's herds in |Awa-!haos – might be well advised to remove with his people to the Swakop valley to the north. KaXab took the hint, probably also because the cattle herds driven to the coast by the Oorlam Afrikaners were encroaching on the scarce supplies of water and grazing in the !Kuiseb valley and making it impossible for the ǂAonîn's to carry on their own livestock husbandry there.[230] In the following years the ǂAonîn were riven by dissension and secession. By the time Friedrich Wilhelm Kolbe arrived in the coastal region early in 1848 KaXab appears to have lost his leadership to a younger successor, whom Kolbe describes as living in the Swakop valley with his followers and having been baptised "Friedrich" by earlier missionaries.[231]

When in 1850 rivalries began to escalate between various groups of *komandos* in the interior and an alliance of Nama groups under the leadership of the Kai||khaun attacked the Oorlam Afrikaners, the ǂAonîn lacked a unified stance. Some 300 of them joined the Oorlam Afrikaners in 1851 and 1852,[232] while the ǂAonîn of |Awa-!haos made common cause with ||Oaseb, *kaptein* of the Kai||khaun, attacking the Oorlam Afrikaners with over 400 men between Rehoboth and Windhoek. Other ǂAonîn remained on the coast, while others still fled to the Kaokoveld, an arid area on the northern frontier of modern Namibia. In re-

---

229 Hahn, *Carl Hugo Hahn Tagebücher*, 144.
230 Kolbe, excerpt from a letter, 10.03.1848, Archiv- und Museumsstiftung Wuppertal, Schriftarchiv, Archiv der Rheinischen Mission, RMG 2.585 (*Beiträge zur Geschichte der Stationen*), C/i 6. 3f.; Köhler, "Die Topnaar-Hottentotten am unteren Kuiseb", 109; Lau, *Southern and Central Namibia in Jonker Afrikaner's Time*, 55; Mossolow, *Die Geschichte von Rooibank-Scheppmannsdorf*, 4. In the mid-1840s ǂAonîn settlements in the Swakop valley included !Hei-||gamxab and ||Hunudas. (Köhler, "Die Topnaar-Hottentotten am unteren Kuiseb", 102.)
231 Kolbe, excerpt from a letter, 10.03.1848, Archiv- und Museumsstiftung Wuppertal, Schriftarchiv, Archiv der Rheinischen Mission, RMG 2.585 (*Beiträge zur Geschichte der Stationen*), C/i 6. 3f.
232 Hahn, *Carl Hugo Hahn Tagebücher*, 512; Köhler, "Die Topnaar-Hottentotten am unteren Kuiseb", 102f.; Mossolow, *Die Geschichte von Rooibank-Scheppmannsdorf*, 7f.

lation for having allied themselves to the Kai‖khaun, the ǂAonîn of |Awa-!haos were attacked by an Oorlam Afrikaner *komando* in May 1854.²³³

The second group keen to establish Walvis Bay as an entrepôt were merchants from the Cape Colony. One attraction was the prospect of acquiring cattle stolen by the Oorlam Afrikaners, but commercial interest was initially sparked above all by the guano deposits in Namibian waters. This merits a brief explanation. Off the coast of Namibia, particularly in the waters near Angra Pequeña, are situated rocky islands which are home to colonies of seabirds. The lack of rain in these parts means that the birds' excrement is not washed away into the sea, but instead forms a solid brownish substance known as guano. Over the course of centuries, guano can accumulate to a thickness of several metres, such deposits being found particularly on Ichaboe Island, but also on those of Possession, Mercury or Hollamsbird.²³⁴ These islands were known to whalers and sealers, who would occasionally land there to collect eggs.²³⁵

As guano's fertilising properties became widely known in Europe in the 1840s, British merchants dispatched vessels to explore locations known from written records of maritime expeditions to possess guano deposits. It was from Morrell's travelogue that one such merchant, John Rae, learnt of the reserves of Guano on Ichaeboe. In the greatest secrecy he sent the brig *Ann* of Bristol to the coast of south-western Africa in March 1843. Her first task was to establish the island's exact location, and since it was only about 400 metres long by 200 metres wide, her efforts long remained unsuccessful. Captain Parr had given up the search when, near Cape Town, he met an American whaler whose master was able to give him exact directions to Ichaboe. The *Ann*'s crew landed there and used pickaxes to collect a holdful of guano, landing it at Bristol in July.²³⁶

The return of the *Ann* set off a veritable scramble for guano, with British vessels in particular hastily sailing for the coast of south-western Africa. The guano of the Cape gannet (*Morus capensis*) was considered especially valuable for its high phosphate content, and was to be found in deposits up to twenty metres thick. Within two years, the islands were visited by an estimated 350

---

233 Hoernlé, "The Social Organization of the Nama Hottentots of South-West Africa", 11f.; Köhler, "Die Topnaar-Hottentotten am unteren Kuiseb", 110; Lau, *Southern and Central Namibia in Jonker Afrikaner's Time*, 115f., 122; Mossolow, *Die Geschichte von Rooibank-Scheppmannsdorf*, 9.
234 Liesegang, "Die Guanogewinnung auf den Inseln und an der Küste Südwestafrikas", 36; Watson, "The Guano Islands of Southwestern Africa", 631. For a contemporary description of Possession Island see Haywood, "American Whalers and Africa", 147.
235 See e.g. Allyn, *The Old Sailor's Story*, 30.
236 Sittert/Crawford, "Historical Reconstruction of Guano Production on the Namibian Islands", 13; Watson, "The Guano Islands of Southwestern Africa", 633–635.

vessels, arriving with some 6,000 workers and mining over 330,000 tons of guano. In October 1844 alone some 300 British and five American vessels were anchored off Ichaboe. Having, by early 1845, removed most of the guano from these rocky islands, British and then Cape Colony merchants continued guano mining at a lower intensity over the following decades, exporting their produce to Mauritius, where fertiliser was needed in the cultivation of sugar cane. In order to protect this trade against rival powers, Britain annexed twelve of these islands in 1861.[237]

Although Walvis Bay was not in the immediate vicinity of the islands, some guano vessels did call there in order stock up on meat, for instance the *Brookline* of New London in December 1844.[238] At one point between January and March 1845 nine guano vessels were anchored in Walvis Bay.[239] It seemed a hopeful enough business prospect for James Morris, a British merchant from Cape Town, to make his way overland to Walvis Bay with his wife and two sons in mid-1844. Morris's plan was to act as a middleman, not only selling sheep and cattle from the interior to visiting vessels, but also to export them to St Helena, as proposed by James Edward Alexander. Having lived there himself – and for some of that time at Longwood House, Napoleon's former residence – Morris was familiar with local conditions and prices. One head of cattle acquired from the Oorlam Afrikaners in exchange for goods worth approximately £1 10s to £2 11s would command a price of £15 in Jamestown, the port and capital of St Helena.[240] A few

---

[237] "Guano in the Island of Ichaboe." *New-Bedford Mercury*, 27.09.1844, 4; "Interesting to Agriculturalists." *New-Bedford Mercury*, 13.09.1844, 3: Allyn, *The Old Sailor's Story*, 59–61; Gewald, "Untapped Sources", 431; Kienetz, "The Key Role of the Orlam Migrations in the Early Europeanization of South-West Africa", 557f.; Kinahan, "The Historical Archaeology of Nineteenth Century Fisheries at Sandwich Harbour on the Namib Coast", 5; Liesegang, "Die Guanogewinnung auf den Inseln und an der Küste Südwestafrikas", 35f., 38; Schultze, *Aus Namaland und Kalahari*, 27f.; Sittert/Crawford, "Historical Reconstruction of Guano Production on the Namibian Islands", 13f. William Thomas, master of the *Forrester*, a British merchantman, visited Ichaboe at the peak of guano mining in January 1845 and provided a detailed record of activities there in her log, which also contain sketches of Ichaboe and a poem about the island: Log FORRESTER, 1844–1845, 07.–12.01.1845.

[238] Allyn, *The Old Sailor's Story*, 63; see also Wilmsen, *Land Filled with Flies*, 89.

[239] Scheppmann, "Von der Kapstadt nach der Walfischbai", 238.

[240] Hahn, *The Letters of Emma Sarah Hahn*, 427; Kolbe, excerpt from a letter, 10.03.1848, Archiv- und Museumsstiftung Wuppertal, Schriftarchiv, Archiv der Rheinischen Mission, RMG 2.585 (*Beiträge zur Geschichte der Stationen*), C/i 6. 7f.; Lau, *Southern and Central Namibia in Jonker Afrikaner's Time*, 95; Mossolow, *Die Geschichte von Rooibank-Scheppmannsdorf*, 1; Tabler, *Pioneers of South West Africa and Ngamiland*, 78. Morris seems not to have made Walvis Bay his permanent home and continued to own an estate in St Helena. (Hatfield, *Saint Helena and the Cape of Good Hope*, 129–133)

weeks after Morris another merchant, Peter Dixon, arrived in Walvis Bay with his wife and four children – and in the company of Jonker Afrikaner and forty of his men. The Oorlam Afrikaners not only welcomed their settlement, but had actively encouraged it by allowing missionaries to spread an invitation among Cape Colony merchants.[241]

Morris and Dixon erected a small storehouse on the beach at Walvis Bay (Fig. 8) and two wooden houses at Sandfontein, a watering place not far from ǂKhîsa-ǁgubus.[242] They were joined there in 1845 by William Latham, an Englishman who was employed as a fisherman by Morris and Dixon.[243] Another building went up on the north side of the bay, about an hour's walk from the storehouse, in August 1846. Its builder was a merchant by the name of Greyburn, who had hoped to make it the terminus of a direct connection by sea to Cape Town. This shed measured approximately 5.5 metres long by 3.5 metres wide and was erected directly on the shore on a foundation of seaweed and sand.[244] In 1845 Morris and Dixon began to sell cattle to ships' crews – including those of whalers – as well as organizing cattle treks overland to Cape Town. The business was a success, but Dixon had to leave the coast for the sake of his health in 1846 and for a while was replaced by Thomas Lawton. It was a vessel of Lawton's, the *Susan*, which was to carry cattle to St Helena, but the trade fell short of the scale that been agreed with the island's administration, causing the partnership of Morris, Dixon and Lawton to collapse in 1850. In the same year James Morris handed over his business to Thomas Morris, his nephew.[245]

The venture of Morris, Dixon and Lawton brought Walvis Bay to the attention of other businessmen such as Aaron de Pass, who set up a fishing establishment (Fig. 9) there in 1851. A merchant and shipowner who had emigrated from Britain

---

241 Tabler, *Pioneers of South West Africa and Ngamiland*, 29.
242 Kinahan, *Cattle for Beads*, 70; Tabler, *Pioneers of South West Africa and Ngamiland*, 29, 78; Tindall, *The Journal of Joseph Tindall*, 71. Morris and Dixon's venture was supported by Wesleyan Methodist Missionary Society, of which both were members. (Henrichsen, *Herrschaft und Alltag im vorkolonialen Zentralnamibia*, 83)
243 Hahn, *The Letters of Emma Sarah Hahn*, 423.
244 Andersson, Lake Ngami, 17f.; Kolbe, excerpt from a letter, 10.03.1848, Archiv- und Museumsstiftung Wuppertal, Schriftarchiv, Archiv der Rheinischen Mission, RMG 2.585 (*Beiträge zur Geschichte der Stationen*), C/i 6. 4; Mossolow, *Die Geschichte von Rooibank-Scheppmannsdorf*, 1.
245 Andersson, *Lake Ngami*, 14f.; Galton, *The Narrative of an Explorer in Tropical South Africa*, 8; Hahn, *The Letters of Emma Sarah Hahn*, 427; Henrichsen, *Herrschaft und Alltag im vorkolonialen Zentralnamibia*, 83f.; Tabler, *Pioneers of South West Africa and Ngamiland*, 29f., 67f., 78. Another vessel sometimes used by Morris and Dixon to carry cattle to St Helena was the *Foam*; see Kolbe, excerpt from a letter, 10.03.1848, Archiv- und Museumsstiftung Wuppertal, Schriftarchiv, Archiv der Rheinischen Mission, RMG 2.585 (*Beiträge zur Geschichte der Stationen*), C/i 6. 6.

to the Cape Colony in 1846, de Pass had originally planned to take a share of the livestock trade before deciding instead to export fish. The business was in the charge of John Spence, his local agent, and soon up to forty workers – mostly from Cape Town, though some were impoverished ǂAonîn – were employed in catching and processing fish in both Walvis Bay and Sandwich Harbour. They produced salted fish – mostly shark, galjoen and snook – as well as shark liver oil, which were packed in barrels and sent to Cape Town and Mauritius in de Pass's own vessels. These vessels, which included the *Elbana* and the *Seabird*, were the first to call on Walvis Bay on something approaching a regular schedule.[246] From 1853 to 1860, de Pass's annual exports from Sandwich Harbour ranged from 51 to 213 tons per year.[247] The fish laid out to dry in Walvis Bay, however, tended to be contaminated with sand and thus commanded lower prices. Nonetheless, another Cape Town fisheries entrepreneur, Barry Munnik, arrived in Walvis Bay in 1858, exporting his produce largely to Mauritius.[248] To obtain a convenient warehouse and shelter for its workers, the company of De Pass and Spence deliberately beached an iron barque, the *Eagle*, in Sandwich harbour, where its wreck can still be seen.[249]

Livestock traders and fisheries entrepreneurs were soon followed by other commercially-minded actors, including copper prospectors, big game hunters, mineworkers, and exporters of ostrich feathers and animal hides. Their stories have been well told by such historians as Dag Henrichsen and Brigitte Lau; the need not be recapitulated here.[250] For present purposes, the decisive point is that it was the livestock trade set up by ǂAonîn and whalers that brought

---

246 Hahn, *The Letters of Emma Sarah Hahn*, 427; Henrichsen, *Herrschaft und Alltag im vorkolonialen Zentralnamibia*, 21; Kinahan, *Cattle for Beads*, 40, 48; Kinahan, "The Historical Archaeology of Nineteenth Century Fisheries at Sandwich Harbour on the Namib Coast", 7f.; Köhler, "Die Topnaar-Hottentotten am unteren Kuiseb", 102, 113; Mossolow, *Die Geschichte von Rooibank-Scheppmannsdorf*, 12; Wilken/Fox, *The History of the Port and Settlement of Walvis Bay*, 127.
247 Kinahan, "The Historical Archaeology of Nineteenth Century Fisheries at Sandwich Harbour on the Namib Coast", 9.
248 Chapman, *Travels in the Interior of South Africa*, vol. 1, 191, 214; Hahn, *The Letters of Emma Sarah Hahn*, 427; Wilken/Fox, *The History of the Port and Settlement of Walvis Bay*, 56–58.
249 Kinahan, "The Historical Archaeology of Nineteenth Century Fisheries at Sandwich Harbour on the Namib Coast", 8, 10; Schumann, "Schiffe und ihre Mannschaften vor Namibias Küste", 102.
250 Henrichsen, *Herrschaft und Alltag im vorkolonialen Zentralnamibia*, 84–91, 128–157; 327–329; Lau, *Southern and Central Namibia in Jonker Afrikaner's Time*, 91; Mossolow, *Die Geschichte von Rooibank-Scheppmannsdorf*, 11f.; Wallace, *History of Namibia*, 64–68. For a list of companies in the fish trade in Walvis Bay and Sandwich Harbour in the 1860s and 1870s see

Fig. 8: The storehouse built by Morris and Dixon in 1861. Like Fig. 7, this painting (originally in colour) is by Thomas Baines.
Source: Wallis, *Fortune My Foe*, 112.

Walvis Bay to the attention of merchants in the first place. Although the connection between whaling and commerce was thus largely indirect, certain direct links can be identified. For instance, Charles John Andersson, a Swedish explorer and later a merchant, sought advice from British whaling captains before setting out for south-western Africa in 1850.[251]

The third group to develop an interest in regular connections by sea between Walvis Bay and Cape Town likewise did so under the impression of whaling, and this was the missionaries. The idea of sending mail and supplies to mission stations inland via Walvis Bay and thereby cutting down on costs for overland transport had already occurred to the Methodist London Missionary Society, which had missions in the north of the Cape Colony, around 1820. One of its missionaries, Barnabas Shaw, had been told by a whaling captain of the cattle on sale to ships' crews in Walvis Bay. In 1821 Shaw sent a young missionary, James Archbell, and his wife to Walvis Bay by sea. With the help of Jacob Link, an interpreter, Archbell was to establish whether conditions were suitable for posting a missionary there. Although (or perhaps because) Archbell was

---

Kinahan, "The Historical Archaeology of Nineteenth Century Fisheries at Sandwich Harbour on the Namib Coast", 8.
251 Andersson, *Lake Ngami*, 2.

effusive in his praise of Walvis Bay and emphatic in recommending the establishment of a mission there,[252] the Society took the precaution of sending another missionary, Johann Hinrich Schmelen, overland in 1824 to investigate matters further.[253]

Schmelen followed the course of the !Kuiseb and soon came upon the "port, which every year is visited by the whale catchers [. . .], who spend March to September catching those leviathans here."[254] Schmelen too concluded that the Society would do well to establish a station in Walvis Bay: "There [. . .] the missionaries can obtain what they require; the whale catchers will be glad to bring them clothes and other items in return for fresh meat."[255] The society might also set up a trade between the ǂAonîn and St Helena: "This would cover the expense of running the mission."[256] Yet contrary to the advice of both Schmelen and Archbell, the London Missionary Society pursued the idea of founding a station in Walvis Bay no further.

The *Rheinische Missionsgesellschaft*, by contrast, which in 1842 began to extend the sphere of its activities from the Cape Colony into the territory of modern Namibia, from the outset decided to keep its missionaries supplied by sea.[257] In a fair wind, a coaster might sail from Cape Town to Walvis Bay in about a week, whereas an ox-cart would take at least three months to reach Otjikango, the mission's first station in the interior.[258] The first two missionaries in Otjikango, Carl Hugo Hahn and Franz Heinrich Kleinschmidt, travelled the bay early in 1844 to assess its suitability for a station. Walvis Bay itself they found to be unsuitable on account of its lack of drinking water, but |Awa-!haos might offer a viable alternative,[259] offering the additional advantage, in Hahn's view, of "the natives, the female sex in particular, being less exposed to the harmful influence of the sailors."[260] Any missionary serving here in the future

---

252 Dedering, *Hate the Old and Follow the New*, 114; Vigne, "James Archbell's 'Beschrijving der Walvischbaai en omliggende plaatsen aan de westkust van Africa' in 1823", 29f.
253 Trüper, *The Invisible Woman*, 56, 100f.
254 Schmelen, "Kurzer Bericht Schmelens über seine Reise nach der Walfischbai", 222.
255 Ibid., 222.
256 Schmelen, "Kurzer Bericht Schmelens über seine Reise nach der Walfischbai", 222.
257 See e.g. Hahn, *The Letters of Emma Sarah Hahn*, 75, 97, 104.
258 Andersson, *Lake Ngami*, 13; Hahn, *The Letters of Emma Sarah Hahn*, 69f., 108; Mossolow, "Franz Heinrich Kleinschmidt", 39; Mossolow, *Die Geschichte von Rooibank-Scheppmannsdorf*, 2, 6.
259 Hahn, *Carl Hugo Hahn Tagebücher*, 150.
260 Ibid., 151.

Fig. 9: Trading post in Walvis Bay in the 1860s. The brigantine in the foreground is likely to be a Cape Town coaster.
Source: Chapman, *Travels in the Interior of South Africa*, vol. 2, 329.

ought nonetheless to put in regular appearances at the beach "that the coarse mariners too might share in his blessings."[261]

This task fell to Heinrich Scheppmann, who arrived in Walvis Bay from Cape Town aboard the *Regent Packet* in the company of another missionary, Johannes Rath, in January 1845. While Rath travelled on into the interior, the twenty-six-year old Scheppmann stayed behind to found a mission at |Awa-!haos. He did so with the approval of ||NeiXab, but to the displeasure of James Morris, who may well have perceived a threat to his sales of liquor to the ǂAonîn and the Oorlam Afrikaners.[262] Scheppmann began by building a small house, which over the next few years was to be joined by three more: one for Dixon, one for ||NeiXab and one for Ian Stewardson, a merchant who went on to marry one of Morris's

---

261 Hahn, *Carl Hugo Hahn Tagebücher*, 150.
262 Mossolow, *Die Geschichte von Rooibank-Scheppmannsdorf*, 1–5; Scheppmann, "Von Rehoboth nach der Walfischbai", 240. The station was originally to be named "Keetmansdorf" after the Society's principal, Johannes Keetman. The name no more caught on outside the Society than did that of Scheppmannsdorf, which was given to |Awa-!haos by the missionaries in 1847. (Hahn, *Carl Hugo Hahn Tagebücher*, 129; Mossolow, *Die Geschichte von Rooibank-Scheppmannsdorf*, 5) Traders and other European actors usually referred to it as "Rooibank". On Kleinschmidt see Mossolow, "Franz Heinrich Kleinschmidt".

daughters. Scheppmann succumbed to a fever in August 1847 and in December was replaced by Jan Bam, a brother-in-law of Schmelen's from Cape Town who planted a garden at |Awa-!haos and built a thatched church, which he consecrated in 1849.[263] What the settlement's founders seem not to have realised was that the !Kuiseb Congo river could sometimes flood.[264] They learnt this to their cost in January 1852, when rains over the Khomas Plateau turned the !Kuiseb into a raging torrent that washed away the church as well as the houses of Bam and Dixon, leaving only Stewardson's house and a small storehouse belonging to the mission undamaged.[265]

In spite of this setback, the *Rheinische Missionsgesellschaft* did not abandon | Awa-!haos. It acquired Greyburn's house – he would appear to have given up his business in Walvis Bay – and in February 1854 Jan Bam completed a new house for himself and his family.[266] Roughly every two years the society would charter a coaster in Cape Town in order to deliver mail and supplies such as timber or clothing to its mission stations in territory of modern Namibia. These vessels – including the *Emma*, the *Foam* and Aaron de Pass's schooner *Prince Edward* – took about a week to reach Walvis Bay or Sandwich Harbour with their cargo. Bam arranged for onward transport by ox-cart to |Awa-!haos, which took about eight hours. In |Awa-!haos, Bam and his helpers sorted and packed the supplies destined for each mission station in the interior, where they could be expected to arrive about three weeks later. If everything went smoothly, then, a parcel sent from Cape Town would take at least four weeks to reach Otjimbingwe, which the society had made the centre of its activities in 1849 on account of its better connection with Walvis Bay.[267] Frequent delays notwithstanding, this system of transport proved for more effective overall than that of the London Missionary

---

263 Hahn, *Carl Hugo Hahn Tagebücher*, 365, 380; Lau, *Carl Hugo Hahn 1837–1860: A Missionary in Nama- and Damaraland – Register and Indexes*, 1244; Mossolow, *Die Geschichte von Rooibank-Scheppmannsdorf*, 5f.
264 Ito, "Changes in the Distribution of the !Nara Plant That Affect the Life of the Topnaar People in the Lower Kuiseb River", 72, 74.
265 Andersson, *Lake Ngami*, 270; Mossolow, *Die Geschichte von Rooibank-Scheppmannsdorf*, 7.
266 Mossolow, *Die Geschichte von Rooibank-Scheppmannsdorf*, 8.
267 Galton, *The Narrative of an Explorer in Tropical South Africa*, 22; Kolbe, excerpt from a letter, 10.03.1848, Archiv- und Museumsstiftung Wuppertal, Schriftarchiv, Archiv der Rheinischen Mission, RMG 2.585 (*Beiträge zur Geschichte der Stationen*), C/i 6. 6; Mossolow, *Die Geschichte von Rooibank-Scheppmannsdorf*, 6f.; Tabler, *Pioneers of South West Africa and Ngamiland*, 10. On the coaster *Prince Edward* see Hahn, *Carl Hugo Hahn Tagebücher*, 640–644.

Society. In May 1856 Jan Bam died of a fever, like Scheppmann before him.[268] His successor was Friedrich Simon, who took up his post in 1859 and ran the station till 1868.[269] During this period the *Rheinische Missionsgesellschaft* added to its infrastructure in the bay, erecting a warehouse on the beach in early 1864.[270] There is no need to trace the further development of missionary activity in Walvis Bay here. Suffice it to be remembered that its stimulus was provided by whalers, whose activities suggested to Barnabas Shaw in 1821 that a station in the bay might advance the Christianisation of the interior.

The fateful death of John Iverson

From March 1867 to February 1869 the schooner *Gertrude Howes* of Norwich, Connecticut could be found plying the south Atlantic, catching sharks and carrying freight. Every few weeks she would call at Walvis Bay, where her crew – aside from the usual fishing – took on board ivory, cattle, sheep and sometimes passengers. These she conveyed now to St Helena, now to Moçâmedes and now to Cape Town, where she in turn took on cargos of guns, lead, gunpowder, coffee, tea and passengers destined for Walvis Bay.[271]

Early in the evening of 22 May 1868 the *Gertrude Howes* put into Walvis Bay for the sixth time in eleven months. This visit, however, was destined to take a course different from her previous ones. On 23 May her log records a "fight with the natives", with no indication given of its cause. For all its briefness, the log does note that this fight took place around 10 p.m., that is to say, in complete darkness. Hostilities continued on the following day, and John Iverson, a Danish merchant, was killed. Iverson had come to southern Africa as a seaman in 1862 and since then had been employed by Hahn, among others. Following his death several Europeans living in Walvis Bay sought refuge aboard the *Gertrude Howes*, among them one Mr Hartley, a hunter who would seem to have settled in the territory of modern Namibia in 1863, and the aforementioned merchant

---

268 Chapman, *Travels in the Interior of South Africa*, vol. 1, 176; Mossolow, *Die Geschichte von Rooibank-Scheppmannsdorf*, 10.
269 Lau, *Carl Hugo Hahn 1837–1860: A Missionary in Nama- and Damaraland – Register and Indexes*, 1252.
270 Hahn, *The Letters of Emma Sarah Hahn*, 78, 271, 273; Moritz, *Die Nara, das Brot in der Wüste*, 33.
271 Log GERTRUDE HOWES, 1867–1869. Seamen from an American warship searched the *Gertrude Howes* while she was docked at Moçâmedes in July 1868 and confiscated various items, a fact suggestive of her use in smuggling.

Ian Stewardson. The latter came on board with his family, while Hartley was accompanied by several of his African servants. The refugees reported that they had been robbed and their lives threatened. On the night of 24 May the second mate went on land with six men to bury Iverson; on 30 May the *Gertrude Howes* weighed anchor, reaching Baía dos Tigres in Angola, where the refugees disembarked, on 4 June.[272]

In retrospect, the death of John Iverson appears as a particularly consequential link in a chain of violent conflicts that shook what is now Namibia in the 1860s. In 1863 the Herero *ovahona* Zeraua and Maharero rose in revolt against the Oorlam Afrikaners and their allies. Most of the missionaries and merchants in the are supported the Herero, providing them with arms and ammunition.[273] The raid on Walvis Bay and the murder of Iverson, which were the work of an Oorlam Afrikaner *komando*,[274] must accordingly be understood as both a warning to and an act of retaliation against the Europeans who sided against the Oorlam Afrikaners.

What makes Iverson's death stand out amidst the suffering that this fighting brought to the region is its indirect role in the colonisation of Walvis Bay. In June 1868 more than a dozen missionaries, merchants and hunters signed a letter to the governor of the Cape Colony demanding that political measures be taken. Should they no longer be able to visit Walvis Bay in safety – a widespread fear since Iverson was killed[275] – the hunters and merchants saw their livelihoods in jeopardy, since the port served as the principal conduit for their wares.[276] No less dependent on Walvis Bay was the *Rheinische Missionsgesellschaft* with its system of transport and supply. The leaders of the mission thus approached not only the government of the Cape Colony but also that of Prussia with a request to protect its area of operation in south-western Africa.[277]

---

272 Log GERTRUDE HOWES, 1867–1869, 22.05.–04.06.1868; Tabler, *Pioneers of South West Africa and Ngamiland*, 54, 101f. On Iverson see Andersson, *Trade and Politics in Central Namibia*, 166f., 171f.; Couzens, "Robert Grendon", 60; Hahn, *The Letters of Emma Sarah Hahn*, 290, 295, 310.
273 Gewald, *Herero Heroes*, 22; Lau, *Southern and Central Namibia in Jonker Afrikaner's Time*, 119–140; Pool, *Samuel Maharero*, 16f., 24f.
274 Köhler, "Die Topnaar-Hottentotten am unteren Kuiseb", 111; Stals in Palgrave, *The Commissions of W. C. Palgrave*, xv.
275 In February 1871 the missionary Emma Hahn wrote from Otjombingwe that trade and shipping were still feeling the effect of Iverson's killing. (Hahn, *The Letters of Emma Sarah Hahn*, 328)
276 Stals in Palgrave, *The Commissions of W. C. Palgrave*, xv.
277 Hahn, *The Letters of Emma Sarah Hahn*, 323, 328; Henrichsen, *Herrschaft und Alltag im vorkolonialen Zentralnamibia*, 218; Loth, *Die christliche Mission in Südwestafrika*, 25.

The pressure brought to bear by merchants and missionaries was an important factor in the Cape government's decision to examine the risks and possible benefits of an intervention.[278] To this end, it dispatched William Coates Palgrave to the area as special commissioner. Palgrave had himself been a trader and elephant hunter in modern Namibia and Botswana in the 1860s, and it was probably on account of his support for the Maharero that he was assaulted and robbed by a Booi *komando* in Walvis Bay in 1868. He was also a signatory to the petition asking the Cape government to intervene.[279] The records of the ensuing negotiations between Palgrave and local chiefs have since been published and carefully analysed by historians.[280] Their outcome was the annexation of Walvis Bay by the Cape Colony in March 1878. The new government set about developing the port and its infrastructure, building warehouses, hiring dock workers – most of them ǂAonîn – and appointing customs and immigration officers.[281] Walvis Bay thus ultimately became an exclave of South Africa, retaining that status until it was handed over to a recently independent Namibia in 1994.

"Up to the middle of the nineteenth century the South West African coast harboured a virtually unspoilt native life", the archaeologist Wolfgang Sydow wrote in 1973.[282] Although the events described in this chapter form only an incomplete record of events on the beach at Walvis Bay, they do show that it was far from being cut off from the world, with several hundred whaleships entering the bay from the 1780s to the mid-nineteenth century. Since whalers for decades remained the only actors to make regular visits to Walvis Bay, their presence had a stronger impact there than in many of the other places examined in this study.

Trade between seamen and ǂAonîn opened up the beach which had hitherto limited the world as experienced by the "people of the edge", turning it into a liminal space through which passed people, animals and things.[283] The

---

278 On the other motives of the Cape government see Henrichsen, *Herrschaft und Alltag im vorkolonialen Zentralnamibia*, 247; Schürmann, "Land zu Territorium", 144–147; Stals in Palgrave, *The Commissions of W. C. Palgrave*, ix–xi, xviii–xxi.
279 Stals in Palgrave, *The Commissions of W. C. Palgrave*, xiii, xvii; Tabler, *Pioneers of South West Africa and Ngamiland*, 83–86.
280 Henrichsen, *Herrschaft und Alltag im vorkolonialen Zentralnamibia*, 247–256; Schürmann, "Land zu Territorium", 147–154; Wallace, *History of Namibia*, 106–108.
281 Henrichsen, *Herrschaft und Alltag im vorkolonialen Zentralnamibia*, 22.
282 Sydow, "Contributions to the History and Protohistory of the Topnaar Strandloper Settlement at the Kuiseb River Mouth near Walvis Bay", 73.
283 This may be the place to note that the American writer Joseph C. Hart made Walvis Bay one of the locations for his novel *Miriam Coffin* (1834), which contains the first portrayal of

fact that the ǂAonîn would regularly drive their cattle to the shore with the beginning of the whaling season in the bay indicates that the vessels' presence led to an increasingly seaward orientation of commercial strategies which also affected the hinterland. Beginning in the 1840s trading also began to attract the attention of other actors, producing what may well be the profoundest effect whaling had on Walvis Bay and engendering both connection and integration. The Oorlam Afrikaners of the interior, a handful of Cape Colony merchants and a missionary society from Rhenish Prussia contributed to turning Walvis Bay into a commercial port and integrating it permanently into maritime networks of trade and communication. Before striking out on their own, both merchants and missionaries as well as the explorers who came to Walvis Bay in the early and mid-nineteenth century relied on actors involved in whaling for information regarding the Namib Coast. Whalers are always in the background where the history of Walvis Bay and its exploration is concerned. Their knowledge of navigating the bay and their experiences trading with the ǂAonîn formed the foundation that allowed other actors to gain a foothold there. It was whalers too who showed the first guano vessels the way to the rocky offshore islands. Walvis Bay had played no part in Atlantic navigation before the 1780s. The fact that it is now the most important port between Cape Town and Lobito is due ultimately to whaling, the incidental effects of which continue to be felt long after its decline.

To the extent that Walvis Bay became transformed from a marginal to a liminal space, the "people of the edge" found themselves deprived of their own room to manoeuvre. With the herds driven from the interior to the coast depleting precious resources of water and grazing, and with the Oorlam Afrikaners attempting to exert control over events in the bay, the ǂAonîn were faced with choice of submitting or leaving. The decline of their social structure observed by missionaries in the 1840s and 50s is due above all to this development.

ǂAonîn in fiction (S. 226–228): Joseph C. Hart. *Miriam Coffin: Or, the Whale-Fisherman; a Tale*. New York: G. & C. & H. Carvill, 1834.

2 Discord magnified: Delagoa Bay, 1780–1845

We all of us detest this Mozambique:
We hate its coast and channel, isle and creek;
And any other station fain would seek.

Charles Pelham Mulvany, the surgeon of HMS *Gorgon*, was in no mood for fond farewells when he composed his verses "On Leaving Mozambique" in April 1863.[1] For more than two years the steam frigate had been patrolling the Mozambique Channel as part of a mission to obstruct the slave trade. Though this mission took the *Gorgon* to the Somali Coast, to Zanzibar, the Seychelles and Anjouan, there was nowhere in these waters that her crew feared quite like it feared the coast of Mozambique.

Cursing it day by day, and week by week,
Altho' we're serious men, not apt to speak
Strong language; but we do curse Mozambique –
Curse it with pale lip and with hollow cheek.

Time and again the seamen had returned from shore leave with fevers and dysentery. "The fever [. . .] is sharp and prostrating", remarked William Cope Devereux, a clerk in the *Gorgon* and himself a sufferer. Anyone who had withstood the first bout of fever was prone to regular relapses.[2] The symptoms of what seamen called "Delagoa fever" suggest that it would now be diagnosed as malaria, which was widespread on the coast of south-eastern Africa. It was and remains a swamp country full with many lakes, lagoons and rivers, and Lieutenant Frederick Barnard of the Royal Navy, who visited the region in 1843, recalled that barely a seaman could spend so much as a night there without contracting the fever.[3] But crews weakened by tropical disease were not the only problem faced by such officers as Barnard, Devereux and Mulvaney.

For want of fresh provisions worn and weak;
Because we can't get anything to eke
Perpetual "salt junk" and "bubble and squeak" –
Or squeak without the "bubble," which is leek
Or onions, and don't grow in Mozambique.

---

[1] Devereux, *A Cruise in the "Gorgon"*, 262f.
[2] Ibid., 259.
[3] Barnard, *A Three Years' Cruise in the Mozambique Channel*, 53f.

The further south the *Gorgon* progressed along the east African coast, the fewer became suitable anchorages in bays or other places where provisions might be taken on board. Meanwhile the swell kept growing heavier and the seas rougher under the influence of the south-east trade winds. Some vessels went to their doom here, whalers among them – the *Junius* of New Bedford, lost in 1851, being one example.[4] Mulvaney was no doubt speaking for most of the seamen in the *Gorgon* in giving voice to hope that she might soon be heading for Cape Town – "after hard lines at hateful Mozambique."[5]

The coastal waters of south-eastern Africa would have appeared all the more hazardous for lack of reliable charts, which began to be produced only in the nineteenth century. The East India companies of the various European states had set up their victualling stations in the Indian Ocean largely on islands, while leaving the mainland coast comparatively unexplored. Against this backdrop, the ship's surgeon James Prior, who sailed these seas in 1812 in the frigate HMS *Nisus*, complained that "The obscurity, in which the whole eastern coast is involved, is not only a blot upon our knowledge, but literally a blank in geography."[6] In 1798 the British merchant William White had already found to his cost that "The charts I have seen of it are very incorrect."[7] Instead of exact charts, captains long had to rely on handbooks or "Sailing Directions" for their bearings.

The place recommended in such works as the best anchorage on the south-eastern seaboard of Africa lay some one thousand miles to the north-east of Cape Town. This was a harbour carved out of the coast by the Indian Ocean and known to seamen as "Delagoa Bay", a name derived from the Portuguese *Baía da Lagoa* or "lagoon bay".[8] It was described as perfectly safe – from a navigational perspective. However, the handbooks left no doubt that this judgement was not to applied to the shore. The *Oriental Navigator* of 1801, for instance,

---

[4] Hohman, *The American Whaleman*, 195.

[5] Devereux, *A Cruise in the "Gorgon"*, 263.

[6] Prior, *Voyage Along the Eastern Coast of Africa*, v.

[7] White, *Journal of a Voyage Performed in the Lion Extra Indiaman*, 21f. White's vessel, the East Indiaman *Lion*, already damaged by a five-day storm, hit a sandbank in Delagoa Bay and lost her rudder. The masters of the six whalers anchored in the bay at the time offered to help with repairs, but the *Lion* had ultimately to be abandoned. Along with her crew, White was forced to spend several weeks in the bay, recording many observations which were published two years later and offer a valuable source for the history of Delagoa Bay. One such observation is that the local population used the bones of whales as chairs. (White, *Journal of a Voyage Performed in the Lion Extra Indiaman*, 34).

[8] Huddart, *The Oriental Navigator*, 78. The bay has been known as *Baía de Maputo* since Mozambique became independent in 1975.

alerted seamen to the presence of "elephants, tigers, leopards, and wild boars" in the bay,[9] while the *Oriental Commerce* in 1813 added a warning against the local population, some of whom were malicious and treacherous, and all cunning as well as charging exorbitant prices for provisions.[10] Yet the handbook also offered advice as to whom shipmasters could turn to if they found themselves in Delagoa Bay, for it was "much frequented by South Sea whalers, as the bay abounds in whales."[11]

An intersection of waterways

Seen from the sea and with the eyes of a ship's crew, Delagoa Bay must certainly have looked like the best anchorage far and wide – at least as far, that as, as the Ilha de Moçambique, more than 800 nautical miles north. It is spacious – forty-five kilometres across at its widest – and sheltered from the open sea by the Machangulo peninsula. Yet at seventeen kilometres, its entrance is more than wide enough to allow vessels to avoid the sandbar, provided that captains did not make the mistake of trying to enter by narrow channel separating the peninsula from the island of Inhaca.[12] Vessels could anchor both in the middle of the bay and in the estuaries of the rivers that enter the sea in the bay.[13] One of these estuaries, that of the Espírito Santo, itself forms a bay some two and half miles wide and known to whalers – whose favourite anchorage it was[14] – as "Cow Bay", perhaps after the Portuguese *cão* (dog).[15] The safest shelter from the heavy storms that regularly battered Delagoa Bay was to be found in this river, which offered deep enough anchorage even miles upstream.[16]

---

9 Huddart, The Oriental Navigator, 79f.
10 Milburn, *Oriental Commerce*, 56. A similar view of the local prices is recorded in White, *Journal of a Voyage Performed in the Lion Extra Indiaman*, 31.
11 Milburn, *Oriental Commerce*, 56.
12 Barnard, *A Three Years' Cruise in the Mozambique Channel*, 248f.; Boteler, *Narrative of a Voyage of Discovery to Africa and Arabia*, vol. 1, 20f.; Owen, "The Bay of Delagoa", 466; Smith, "The Struggle for Control of Southern Moçambique", 2f. Inhaca was known to English-speaking seamen by a variety of names including *(Cape) St Mary, Cape Colatto* and *Port Melville*.
13 Smith, "The Struggle for Control of Southern Moçambique", 2.
14 Owen, "The Bay of Delagoa", 467.
15 Smith, *A Narrative of the Life, Travels, and Sufferings of Thomas W. Smith*, 170 n. 16.
16 Milburn, *Oriental Commerce*, 56; Newitt, *A History of Mozambique*, 153. For an account of a heavy storm in the bay in 1823 see Boteler, *Narrative of a Voyage of Discovery to Africa and Arabia*, vol. 1, 193.

Besides the storms, the greatest danger to navigation was posed by shallows which might take mariners unawares. Among the whalers shipwrecked here were the *Good Intent* of London and the *South Carolina* of Dunkirk (1791), the *Eliza* of Boston and the *New Hope* of London (1794), the *Sarah* of London and the *Martha* of New Bedford (1831).[17]

Seen from the shore and with the eyes of African societies, Delagoa Bay offered no less attractive a prospect. The southern part of modern Mozambique – i.e. the portion south of the river Save – is a lowland country, largely sandy and covered in dense scrub. Its porous soils, irregular rainfall and proneness to drought were impediments to arable farming, while animal husbandry was discouraged by the ubiquitous tsetse fly, the main vector of sleeping sickness in humans and animals. Compared to the areas bordering it to the north, west and south, southern Mozambique has hence always been quite sparsely populated. The principal exceptions are centred on lagoons and rivers, which offer fertile soils and a comparatively reliable water supply even in dry periods – and it was around Delagoa Bay that most such settlements could be found.[18]

The Lebombo Mountains rise fifty kilometres west of the bay, and the rain that falls there feeds various major and minor rivers that discharge into the Indian Ocean via Delagoa Bay. No fewer than eight of these rivers and their tributaries close to the bay are navigable, and people who settled there could engage not only in agriculture and livestock rearing, but also in fishing and commerce with societies upstream, far in the interior, which could be reached by boat. The ecology of the bay also supported a considerable game population and hence offered good hunting.[19]

Of these rivers, the three principal ones are the Nkromati, which enters Delagoa Bay at its northern end, the Maputo in the south, and the Espírito Santo (now the Matola Congo river or Rio Matola), whose estuary is located roughly halfway along the eastern bank of the bay. It was the Espírito Santo which was most suitable for commercial traffic to the interior, being unusually deep and itself having two navigable tributaries. The Nkomati allowed access even further

---

17 Jones, *Ships Employed in the South Seas Trade*, 14, 21; *New-Bedford Daily Mercury*, 21.11.1831, 3; Richards/Du Pasquier, "Bay Whaling off Southern Africa", 242f., 245; Smith, *A Narrative of the Life, Travels, and Sufferings of Thomas W. Smith*, 161–166.
18 Harries, "Labour Migration from the Delagoa Bay Hinterland to South Africa", 66; Newitt, *A History of Mozambique*, 148; Smith, "The Indian Ocean Zone", 208; Smith, "The Struggle for Control of Southern Moçambique", 4; Young, "Fertility and Famine", 67.
19 Alpers, "State, Merchant Capital, and Gender Relations in Southern Mozambique to the End of the Nineteenth Century", 27; Newitt, *A History of Mozambique*, 148.

inland, albeit only by smaller boats, and was also the most easily navigable river in the Delagoa Bay area.[20]

The waterways that intersected in Delagoa Bay not only brought together people from the interior and seamen coming from the Mozambique Channel, but also attracted an annual colony of whales. Each winter southern right whales migrate north from the Antarctic in order to mate and calve in the deep bay. Whalers had grown aware of this pattern in the late eighteenth century and subsequently made regular visits to Delagoa Bay themselves, at times forming the largest group of vessels there. In this chapter, I shall begin by outlining the phases through which whaling passed in the bay before discussing the social, political and economic conditions structuring the lives of the local population. I will then go on to examine forms of encounter and interaction between that population and the whalers, highlighting their most important outcomes in conclusion.

"Great numbers of that valuable fish"

We find Portuguese seamen reporting sightings of whales in the Mozambique channel as early as the sixteenth century.[21] As in the case of Walvis Bay, whaling began no later than the 1780s, though it is equally impossible in each case to be say with any degree of certainty when the first whaleship sailed into the bay. The first vessels that can be identified by name were active there in June 1788, three years later than their counterparts in Walvis Bay. These were the *Canton* and the *Pénélope*, two vessels belonging to William Rotch, who had moved across the

---

20 Huddart, *The Oriental Navigator*, 78f.; Jackson Haight, *European Powers and South-East Africa*, 187; Smith, "The Struggle for Control of Southern Moçambique", 4f. The rivers of Delagoa Bay appear under various names and in different spellings; I have generally decided in favour of the versions most frequently encountered. The Nkomati was also known as the *Manhissa*, *Manice* or (among British seamen) *King George River*; the Matola as the *Matolla* and the Tembe as the *Katembe* or *Mahong*. British seamen commonly referred to the Espírito Santo as the *English River* or *Dundas River*, sometimes also the *Lourenço Marques River*, while the names *Mafumo River* and *Manica* are also attested. The bay itself also went by different name in the sources, for which colonial rivalries between Portugal and Great Britain offer at least a partial explanation. Particularly in the early nineteenth century the Portuguese would use the name *Lourenço Marques* for the entire bay, thereby underscoring their claim to the bay at large rather than just the Portuguese fort and its environs. The British insistence on the name *Delagoa Bay* implies a refusal to accept the Portuguese claim. A clear reference to this dispute can be bound in Owen, "The Bay of Delagoa", 465.
21 "Extractos da Relação do Naufragio da nao 'Santiago'", 331; Santos, "Ethopia oriental", 138.

Atlantic from New England to Dunkirk and whose fleet at the time operated mostly in the bays of southern Africa.[22] Other vessels from Dunkirk soon followed and were joined in 1791 by the *Alliance*, probably the first Nantucket whaler to reach Delagoa Bay.[23] 1791 is also the year of the first recorded visit by British whalers, with the *Good Intent* and the *William* of London as well as the *Joseph* of Bristol sailing to Delagoa Bay to hunt southern right whales.[24] British whaling in the area, however, is harder to quantify than the operations of French or American vessels. From 1786 to 1798 the British authorities levied a tariff on whaling in the seas to the north-east of the Cape Colony, which captains would often seek to avoid by being vague about their destinations.[25]

Whaling in Delagoa Bay peaked in the 1790s. At least twenty-five whalers are known to have been active there in 1793, more than in any year before or since. At this time Rotch had his entire fleet sail for Delagoa Bay, and it was certainly among the principal destinations to which British owners sent their vessels.[26] At the height of the season a dozen vessels might be operating in the bay at one time,[27] among them such comparatively large ones as William Rotch's full-rigged *Edward*. So many Nantucket seamen were working aboard these vessels that neighbours might find themselves once again face to face some seven thousand nautical miles from home – as the crow flies, that is, and further still by sea. "There was a great many of our towns people", Captain Pinkham entered into the *Alliance*'s log in 1 June 1793, adding: "some [. . .] informed me that my friends were well in health."[28] Many whalers – probably a large majority – spent an entire whaling season in Delagoa Bay, arriving there at more or less the same time as the southern rights and leaving when, in September or early October, the surviving whales headed back for the Antarctic Ocean.[29]

Whalers at times made up the largest proportion of vessels in the bay. About thirty Portuguese merchantmen and a few more from other countries are

---

22 Du Pasquier, *Les Baleiniers Français de Louis XVI à Napoléon*, 151, 186f.
23 Richards/Du Pasquier, "Bay Whaling off Southern Africa", 242f.; Starbuck, *History of the American Whale Fishery*, 186f.
24 Jones, *Ships Employed in the South Seas Trade*, 14.
25 Richards/Du Pasquier, "Bay Whaling off Southern Africa", 246.
26 Booth, *The United States Experience in South Africa*, 37f.; Chatwin, "A Trade so Uncontrollably Uncertain", 26; Jackson, *The British Whaling Trade*, 114.
27 Pinkham, *The Log Book of the Good Ship Alliance of Nantucket Captain Bartlett Coffin*, 01.07.1793.
28 Ibid.
29 See the observations on the arrival and departure of various whaleships in Pinkham, *The Log Book of the Good Ship Alliance of Nantucket Captain Bartlett Coffin*, 01.07.–10.06.1793.

known to have sailed into Delagoa Bay,[30] during which time at least seventy-five visits by whalers are recorded. Since relatively few logs and other relevant sources are preserved from these early days of whaling, the actual figure may well be higher still.[31]

To begin the whale hunt, a captain would anchor his vessel either in the middle of the bay, giving the crew as large as possible an area of water to scan for a whale's blow, or in the Espírito Santo estuary. Any whales they espied were approached by boat and, if taken, returned to the moored vessel, meaning that the vessel itself often moved little during its stay in Delagoa Bay.[32] For the crews, however, this meant hard work at the oars. "At 12 o'clock at night we got on board after rowing 19 hours against wind and the tide", records the diary of one seaman, John Bartlett of the *William Penn* of Nantucket, in 1793.[33] The southern right whales' comparatively thick layer of blubber meant that each specimen took several days to process, during which time a column of black smoke could be seen rising from the trypots.[34] Whalers who came to Delagoa Bay for repairs rather than to hunt or to take on provisions might also drop anchor in the eastern part of the bay, taking advantage of the shelter from wind and rain afforded by the Machangulo peninsula.[35]

It was during this early boom in whaling, on 2 September 1793, that a sixteen-gun brig sailed into Delagoa Bay. She was sailing under the Dutch flag and began to fire on the French whalers at anchor there. This was the first their captains heard of the war between revolutionary France and much of Europe. The *William Penn*, the *Port de Paix* and the *Greyhound* were taken unopposed, while the *Benjamin* of Dunkirk got away: by showing the Dutch raiders an obsolete set of papers, Captain Hussey was able to persuade them that his was an American, not a French vessel. Having made his escape, Hussey thought it wise to return not to Dunkirk but to New Bedford, where the *Benjamin* arrived in January 1794. The *Dauphin* of Lorient got away by the same ruse. Other French whalers the Dutch had to let go for want of men to crew the taken vessels.[36]

---

30 Smith, "The Struggle for Control of Southern Moçambique", 236.
31 Haywood, "American Whalers and Africa", 81.
32 Booth, *The United States Experience in South Africa*, 36; Richards/Du Pasquier, "Bay Whaling off Southern Africa", 243.
33 Quoted in Richards/Du Pasquier, "Bay Whaling off Southern Africa", 244.
34 Hohman, *The American Whaleman*, 180f.
35 Smith, *A Narrative of the Life, Travels, and Sufferings of Thomas W. Smith*, 161.
36 "Newbedford Marine Journal." *The Medley or Newbedford Marine Journal*, 27.01.1794, 3; Richards/Du Pasquier, "Bay Whaling off Southern Africa", 245; Stackpole, *The Sea-Hunters*, 173.

At the outbreak of the revolutionary wars intensive hunting seems not yet to have brought about a marked decline in the numbers of southern right whales in Delagoa Bay. They were "very numerous" that season, the British merchant William White remarked in 1798,[37] and in 1812 Captain Prior of HMS *Nisus* could still observe "great numbers of that valuable fish" in the Mozambique Channel and in Delagoa Bay.[38] So good was the hunting that whalers continued to sail for Delagoa Bay from British and American ports, albeit fewer than before the war. The risk, after all, was considerable. For instance, in 1796 the French privateer *Modeste* attacked British whalers in the bay, capturing one, the *Princess* of London.[39] In September 1803 a French whaler, the *Cyrus* of Dunkirk, was captured by a British frigate, HMS *Scorpion*.[40] In no year of the war are more than ten visits by whalers to Delagoa Bay recorded. At the peak of the season in mid-1798, for instance, six whalers were moored there, one half of them British, the other American.[41] William Rotch's vessels, including the *Maria*, continued to sail for the bay. Such, however, are the gaps in the historical record – in ships' logs and other sources – that all the figures cited here are minimum numbers, representing only documented visits by individually identifiable whaleships.[42]

As in the other bays of southern Africa, whaling in Delagoa Bay never quite returned to its pre-war scale. This falling-off would seem not to have been for lack of southern right whales. "The whole of the Mosambique channel", the British merchant Nathaniel Isaacs observed in 1831, "is a fine whaling position; the black whale being numerous".[43] Yet as far as the southern seas were concerned, the whaling industry's interest shifted above all to sperm whales and later also to humpbacks. Whaling in Delagoa Bay did, however, undergo a temporary revival from the early 1830s to the early 1840s, with increased activity from British and especially from American vessels. In June 1831 Isaacs found nine whalers in Delagoa Bay, eight of them American, one British.[44] Contemporary reports suggest intense competition between vessels, which may indicate that stock of southern right whales had by now palpably declined. Some crews would now drop their boats by night in order to begin the hunt as the day

---

37 White, *Journal of a Voyage Performed in the Lion Extra Indiaman*, 22.
38 Prior, *Voyage Along the Eastern Coast of Africa*, 24, 30.
39 Du Pasquier, *Les Baleiniers Français de Louis XVI à Napoléon*, 84, 89; Jones, *Ships Employed in the South Seas Trade*, 22. For a reference to another French attack on whalers in Delagoa Bay in 1799 see Jackson Haight, *European Powers and South-East Africa*, 122f.
40 Du Pasquier, *Les Baleiniers Français de Louis XVI à Napoléon*, 112, 192f.
41 White, *Journal of a Voyage Performed in the Lion Extra Indiaman*, 16.
42 Haywood, "American Whalers and Africa", 81.
43 Isaacs, *Travels and Adventures in Eastern Africa*, vol. 2, 334.
44 Ibid., 340, 344.

broke. Seamen were forced to comb the seas for whales for days on end, rowing dozens of miles in the process.⁴⁵ But captains of different whaleships might also agree to cooperate, letting their boats jointly patrol the bay to maximise the area covered and dividing the spoils.⁴⁶

By now most whalers, if they came to Delagoa Bay at all, would not spend the entire season there, leaving instead after a month or two to hunt sperm whales in the Mozambique Channel and elsewhere.⁴⁷ Southern right whales, which had been one of the whaling industry's main sources of profit forty years early, were now at most an incidental prize in the hunt for sperm whales. In 1843, the last year of the of the decade or in which southern right whaling picked up, at least five whaleships entered Delagoa Bay, all of them American. Such visits, however, were henceforth to be extreme rarities, with no more than one whaler per decade until the era of American-style pelagic whaling ended.

Ivory's middlemen

Unlike in the case of Walvis Bay, the population of Delagoa Bay had been familiar with vessels and their crews long before the arrival of the first whalers. Fragments of Chinese porcelain and celadon from the Song (960–1279) and Ming (1368–1644) dynasties found in the area suggest that the coast of Mozambique was already part of Indian Ocean trading networks by that time.⁴⁸ It seems, however, that the Persian and Arab traders who held these networks together never visited Delagoa Bay themselves. Besides its aforementioned navigational hazards, there was the additional problem that the monsoon winds would not carry a dhow coming from the Arabian Peninsula far enough south to reach Delagoa Bay. Merchants would instead sail for Sofala, Inhambane or the mouth of the river Save, from where their goods would have reached Delagoa Bay overland.⁴⁹

The beach of Delagoa Bay probably became a liminal space only after Vasco da Gama had landed on the coast of what is now Mozambique in 1498,

---

45 Dickson in Pinkham, *The Log Book of the Good Ship Alliance of Nantucket Captain Bartlett Coffin*, 95; Log ANN MARIA, 1835–1837, 20.06.–31.07.1836; Smith, *A Narrative of the Life, Travels, and Sufferings of Thomas W. Smith*, 161, 166.
46 Log GEORGIA, 1832–1833, 06.07.–28.08.1832; Log ISRAEL, 1841–1842, 26.05.– 30.07.1842.
47 Log GEORGIA, 1832–1833, 06.07.–28.08.1832; Log ANN MARIA, 1835–1837, 20.06.–31.07.1836; Log ARAB, 1838–1840, 23.08.–08.09.1839; Log ISRAEL, 1841–1842, 26.05.–30.07.1842.
48 Duffey, "China's Contact with Southern Africa", 32f., 35.
49 Newitt, *A History of Mozambique*, 25, 147, 151; Smith, "The Struggle for Control of Southern Moçambique", 1f.

on his first voyage to India. Portuguese East Indiamen soon became regular visitors to the area and are known to have entered Delagoa Bay no later than 1542. In 1544 Lourenço Marques, after whom the Portuguese would later name their settlement in the bay, explored the lower reaches of the Espírito Santo. At this time a vessel from the Portuguese "factory" or trading post on the Ilha de Moçambique would visit Delagoa Bay on average once a year (and later more often) to purchase ivory. Most of these merchant vessels would anchor in the bay for several months at a time, and not infrequently for half a year. They usually moored off Inhaca or at the sandy island of Xefina, which lay close to the mainland in the north of the bay, and crews would set up camp on these islands for the duration of their stay. Besides vessels that had come to Delagoa Bay on purpose, arrivals might also include survivors of shipwrecked East Indiamen who had found their way there in lifeboats or overland. Merchant vessels of other European countries may also have been occasional visitors as early as the 1590s. Ashore, seamen encountered people who bred cattle and used sewn boats or *luzios* for fishing and who had formed a multitude of small settlements along kinship lines, which had joined to form states or state-like entities.[50]

Historical and ethnographic scholarship generally considers the population of Delagoa Bay and its environs to belong to the Tsonga people, divided by linguistic and cultural criteria from the Tonga in the north, the Venda and Sotho in the west, and the Nguni in the south. But although the population denominated as Tsonga had a good deal in common in terms of both their culture and their social organization, they shared neither a state nor a language, instead speaking a variety of languages and dialects. In fact, they probably did not even think of themselves as Tsonga. The language spoken in Delagoa Bay and its environs was Ronga, which took a variety of forms. This branch of the Tsonga people is accordingly referred to as the Ronga by scholars including Alan Smith, whose research on the history of the area underpins this section. Although the Ronga did not form a political unity, a number of small sovereign states had formed on the shores of Delagoa Bay. These states would appear – the historical record is fragmentary – by and large to have lasted from the sixteenth to the early nineteenth century (Fig. 10), though there were also cases of

---

[50] Do Couto, "Narrative of the Shipwreck of the Great Ship 'São Thomé'", 82f.; Henriksen, *Mozambique*, 21, 48; Newitt, *A History of Mozambique*, 25, 114f., 149f., 153; Smith, "The Struggle for Control of Southern Moçambique", 35f., 38f. On shipwrecked seamen in Delagoa Bay see e.g. Almada, "Treatise of the Misfortune that befell the Great Ship 'São João Baptista'", 247–251, Brito, "The Wreck of the Galleon 'São João' on the Coast of Natal in the Year 1552", 100; do Couto, "Narrative of the Shipwreck of the Great Ship 'São Thomé'", 81–91 and Lavanha, "Shipwreck of the Great Ship 'Santo Alberto'", 179–185.

secession or of the absorption of one state into another. Characteristic features of these states were the importance of kinship in their internal organisation – which is why some historians have called them *lineage states*[51] – and the comparatively strong position of a single ruler. Rulership was repeatedly contested in bitterly fought succession disputes which might plunge particular states into several years of turmoil. The largest and most influential of the Ronga states, none which is likely ever to have numbered more than 25,000 inhabitants, were situated in the south of Delagoa Bay, where Inhaca controlled the area to the east of the Maputo river and Tembe that on its western shore. The other sections of the coastline and access to the rivers were also divided between the Ronga states. Magaia controlled the lower part of the Nkomati Congo river, Tembe the lower; Mfumo ruled over the estuary of the Espírito Santo, while its hinterland was Matoll territory. No state over succeeded in bringing the entire bay under its control. Portuguese ivory traders would thus travel along the various sections of coastline and riverfront by boat in order to make contact with a variety of trading partners. For their part, the Ronga states began to compete for shares in the lucrative ivory trade. This may be why the Portuguese long held off establishing a trading post in the bay: to do so would have indicated preferential treatment of one state and incurred the jealousy of the others.[52]

Most of the ivory sold by the Ronga to the Portuguese did not originate in the immediate surroundings of Delagoa Bay but was sourced in the hinterland, from areas one hundred kilometres or more distant. These supply chains, which were revived by commerce with the Portuguese and which by and large followed the course of rivers, allowed Ronga rulers to supply buyers in the bay not only with ivory, but also with hippopotamus teeth, rhinoceros horns and hooves, copper, ambergris, honey, butter and other foods – and with slaves, most whom are likely to have been prisoners of war. In exchange, the Portuguese brought beads and cloth garments as well as iron parts in small quantities. Trade did not always

---

[51] Liesegang, "Mozambique: Nineteenth Century, Early", 1032; Liesegang, "Nguni Migrations between Delagoa Bay and the Zambezi", 317.
[52] Alpers, "State, Merchant Capital, and Gender Relations in Southern Mozambique to the End of the Nineteenth Century", 25, 27f., 32; Henriksen, *Mozambique*, 48–50; Liesegang, "Beiträge zur Geschichte des Reiches des Gaza Nguni im südlichen Moçambique", 16f.; Liesegang, "Dingane's Attack on Lourenço Marques in 1833", 568; Newitt, *A History of Mozambique*, 150f., 153f.; Owen, "The Bay of Delagoa", 469, 473; Smith, "The Peoples of Southern Mozambique", 566, 569, 572; Smith, "The Struggle for Control of Southern Moçambique", 8f., 18f., 27–33. All proper names mentioned here occur in various spellings throughout the scholarly literature. The Tsonga are sometimes referred to as *Thonga*, the Ronga as *Rhonga* or *Rjonga*, Tembe as *Temby* and Inhaca as *Nyaka*.

go smoothly. There were violent clashes between Ronga and Portuguese as well as frequent warfare between Ronga states.[53]

It was Tembe that seems to have profited the most from its function as middleman in the trade between the Portuguese and societies in the hinterland, rising to eminence as the most powerful state of Delagoa Bay from the 1620s onwards. At the time Tembe covered some fifty kilometres of coast as far as the Lebombo Mountains. Neighbouring Inhaca was larger still, extending to Santa Lucia, some 250 kilometres south of the bay. In both states the development of Delagoa Bay into an important entrepôt meant an increase in their rulers' powers, and in both states this also meant an amplification of internal political rivalries. Such conflicts brought about to the secession of a new state, Machavane, in the early seventeenth century.[54]

The first Portuguese settlers arrived in what is now Mozambique in 1629. Much like European feudal lords, they were to rule over large estates or *prazos* as semi-autonomous statelets in so doing consolidate Portuguese influence in the area. *Prazos* were formed in the fertile Zambezi basin, but not in Delagoa Bay, which the Portuguese government found to be unpromising in that regard. But this change in Portugal's colonial policy made itself felt there indirectly: since Portuguese commercial shipping now concentrated on the sections of coastline in the north with access to the *prazos*, the number of vessels visiting Delagoa Bay declined sharply in the mid-seventeenth century. Several years might now elapse between the departure of on merchantman and the arrival of the next.[55]

Shipping in Delagoa Bay did undergo a brief revival in the 1680s and 90s, when British vessels in the service of the East India Company made regular visits – up to five in a single year – to purchase ivory and ambergris. Dutch East Indiamen also occasionally visited Delagoa Bay during this time. What is more, the first vessel from North America, a Massachusetts slaver, arrived there in 1680. But by 1700 traffic in Delagoa Bay was once more in decline, due perhaps to increasing piracy in the western Indian Ocean.[56]

---

53 Henriksen, *Mozambique*, 48f.; Newitt, *A History of Mozambique*, 154f.; Smith, "The Struggle for Control of Southern Moçambique", 33, 37f., 154. For an account of the rhinoceros hunt in Delagoa Bay see Boteler, *Narrative of a Voyage of Discovery to Africa and Arabia*, vol. 1, 84–86.
54 Henriksen, *Mozambique*, 49; Newitt, *A History of Mozambique*, 154f.; Smith, "The Struggle for Control of Southern Moçambique", 32f.
55 Newitt, *A History of Mozambique*, 114f., 155. For the history of the *prazos* see esp. Isaacman, *Mozambique: The Africanization of a European Institution*; Isaacman/Isaacman, *The Tradition of Resistance in Mozambique*; Newitt, "The Portuguese on the Zambezi"; Vail/White, *Capitalism and Colonialism in Mozambique*.
56 Duignan/Gann, *The United States and Africa*, 66; Jackson Haight, *European Powers and South-East Africa*, 89; Newitt, *A History of Mozambique*, 156f.; Smith, "The Struggle for Control

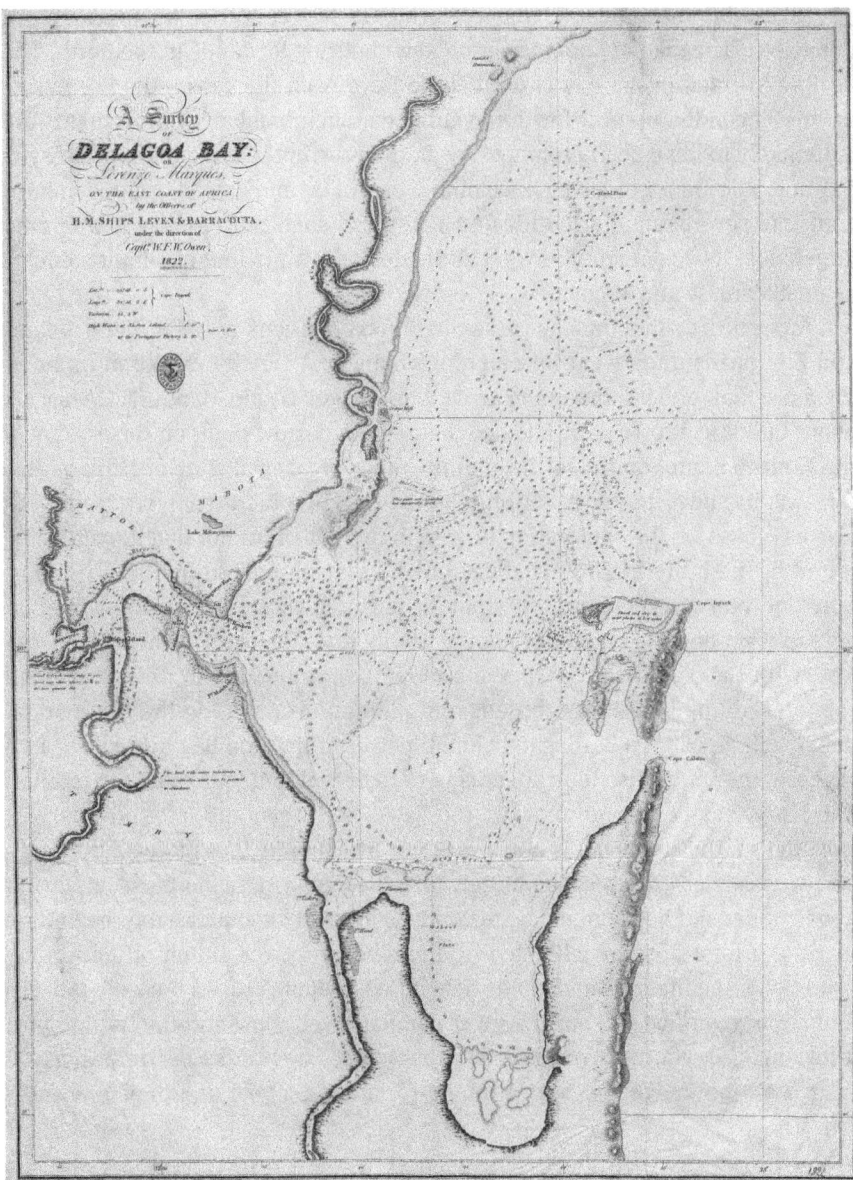

Fig. 10: Delagoa Bay on a British Admiralty Chart of 1822 (William Fitzwilliam Owen et al. *A Survey of Delagoa Bay or Lorenzo Marques on the East Coast of Africa.* London: Hydrographic Office of the Admirality, 1822).
Courtesy of the Gotha Research Library at University of Erfurt, SPK 40 30.a B [01,01].

In the late seventeenth and early eighteenth centuries some groups of Ronga left Delagoa Bay, migrating the neighbouring lowlands in the north. The decline in trade in the bay is unlikely to have been the cause, the Ronga not having depended upon it for the livelihoods. Such breakaway movements are more likely to have been prompted by an increase in the population of Delagoa Bay and a desire for independence on the part of certain kinship groups. Inhaca split into several smaller entities as a result of such processes, while Mfumo largely lost its sovereignty as a result its defeat in wars fought simultaneously against Manisse and Magaia.[57]

Around the same time as these migrations relations between Ronga states and Europeans underwent far-reaching changes. A Dutch expedition numbering more than one hundred men arrived in Delagoa Bay in March 1721. They set about building a fort – Fort Lijdzaamheid – at a narrow point on the estuary of the Espírito Santo, on the territory of the much-weakened state of Mfumo. This fort was intended to serve not only as the hub of a lucrative ivory trade, but also as a base for the exploration of gold mines which, rumor had it, were to be found in the hinterland. Fort Lijdzaamheid was plundered by British pirates only one year after its foundation, and the Dutch continued to suffer the ravages of fever and the attendant high mortality rates for years to come. Nonetheless, with the assistance of women and children from Mfumo, they expanded the fort, adding buildings, gardens and plantations, creating the first permanent trading post of a European colonial power in Delagoa Bay. Unlike the Portuguese, the Dutch also took advantage of their foothold to explore the interior. The ivory they bought up reached the bay – both then and later on – largely from the south, from what is now the South African province of KwaZulu-Natal, and was carried through Tembe territory. Besides ivory, the most important goods traded at Lijdzaamheid were copper, tin, gold dust, aloes and, beginning in 1724, a total of some 280 slaves. Since, however, the Dutch offered in exchange not the firearms and beads demanded by Ronga rulers but only tobacco and poor-quality beads, business was comparatively slow and the trading post a loss-making venture. To make matters worse, war broke out in early 1726 among all the Ronga states, continuing for around a year and impeding trade

---

of Southern Moçambique", 39, 45; van der Stell, "Extracts from a Despatch from Commander Simon van der Stell and Council to the Chamber of XVII", 44f.
57 Newitt, *A History of Mozambique*, 156, 257; Smith, "The Struggle for Control of Southern Moçambique", 28, 33f.

between the firt and the interior. In December 1730 the Dutch decided to cut their losses, abandoning Lijdzaamheid and leaving Delagoa Bay.[58]

Meanwhile political tensions gave rise to civil war in Tembe. It was won by Nwangobe, a chief who went on to subjugate the neighbouring states of Machavane and Inhaca, and who for a while controlled the entire southern shore of Delagoa Bay. Upon Nwangobe's death in the early or mid-1760s, however, Tembe suffered the same fate as Inhaca before it, being weakened by succession struggles and the formation of breakaway states, Maputo among them. In a parallel development Matoll, which had prevailed in conflicts with Magaia and Mfumo, began to gain influence from about 1729 onwards. This led, around 1750, to the secession from Magaia of a new state, Mabota. These events unfolded in parallel with a renewed interest in the bay on the part of British, Portuguese and Dutch (or Cape Colony) merchants. Between the 1750s and the 1770s the largest profits were made by the British, who took advantage of price differences within their vast empire. From Bombay and Surat they brought coarse fabrics and cheat beads and bracelets to Delagoa Bay. They also sold firearms to Ronga rulers, which neither Portuguese nor Dutch had hitherto dared to do. These goods were distributed from a semi-permanent trading post as well as by means of at least a dozen boats that could reach the interior, especially via the Espírito Santo. Such was the British presence on the Espírito Santo that it became known as the "English River", a name by which many whalers would refer to it in later years.[59]

Previously something of a backwater, Delagoa Bay now emerged as one of the leading commercial centres of south-eastern Africa. The flow of goods in the area had gradually moved towards the coast, drawing it ever more closely into trading networks in the interior and establishing the caravan – sometimes with hundreds of carriers – as the standard form of transport. Overland, the Ronga states acquired goods both for barter – ivory, copper or gold – and for

---

58 Eldredge, "Sources of Conflict in Southern Africa", 6f.; Hoppe, *Portugiesisch-Ostafrika in der Zeit des Marquês de Pombal*, 166; Jackson Haight, *European Powers and South-East Africa*, 187, 189; Newitt, *A History of Mozambique*, 157f.; Shell, "The Twinning of Maputo and Cape Town", 180–184; Smith, "The Struggle for Control of Southern Moçambique", 316; Smith, "The Trade of Delagoa Bay as a Factor in Nguni Politics", 173, 176. The most detailed account of the Dutch fort is to be found in Smith, "The Struggle for Control of Southern Moçambique", 44–113.
59 Alpers, "State, Merchant Capital, and Gender Relations in Southern Mozambique to the End of the Nineteenth Century", 32; Hoppe, *Portugiesisch-Ostafrika in der Zeit des Marquês de Pombal*, 169; Huddart, *The Oriental Navigator*, 78f.; Jackson Haight, *European Powers and South-East Africa*, 189, 137; Newitt, *A History of Mozambique*, 159; Smith, "The Struggle for Control of Southern Moçambique", 154–165, 169–176; Smith, "The Trade of Delagoa Bay as a Factor in Nguni Politics", 173.

their own use, such as hatchets, hoes, bracelets and anklets, and assegais. Items acquired from European merchant vessels – cloth garments, brass objects or glass beads – travelled by the same long-distance trade routes over mountains and far into the interior, reaching parts of modern South Africa, Zimbabwe and Botswana. For many societies in southern Africa, Delagoa Bay was the first and most important connecting point between the flow of goods in the interior on the one hand and at sea on the other.[60]

Times of crisis, times of change

Four developments in particular meant that the whaling era was a time of profound change in Delagoa Bay and its hinterland. First, a permanent European presence was established in 1777 and with it a new political and economic force in the region. Second, several groups of Nguni and Zulu, beginning in 1821, raided the area and gradually subjugated the Ronga states, which lost parts of their sovereignty and were reduced to the status of tributaries. Third, the bay's hinterland was stricken with famine and drought, first in the 1790s and again from 1817 to 1831, with negative effects on long-distance trade. Fourth and finally, the increase in the slave trade on the Indian Ocean seaboard was also felt in Delagoa Bay by the 1820s and 30s.

The first of these developments began with a storehouse and a gun emplacement erected in 1777 on the south bank of the Espírito Santo, on Mfumo territory, by the Austrian *Ostindische Compagnie*. At the head of its 150 men stood William Bolts, a disgraced merchant formerly of the East India Company whose venture had been generously funded by the Archduchess of Austria. The high prices Bolts was willing to pay for ivory brought about a rapid increase in trade and raised prices for British vessels too. Bolts's plan to expand the station into a colony on the model of the Cape Colony, however, aroused the suspicions of the Portuguese authorities, which saw a threat to their own colonial designs on the area and sent a task force to seize the station in 1781. Henceforth claiming a monopoly on trade in Delagoa Bay, the victorious Portuguese added buildings and fortifications, garrisoned the station and christened it "Lourenço Marques". It was now officially a *Présidio*, an outpost of the Portuguese empire, with a governor reporting to the governor-general on the Ilha de Moçambique, the administrative

---

60 Newitt, *A History of Mozambique*, 148; Smith, "The Struggle for Control of Southern Moçambique", 313, 322, 324, 326; Smith, "The Trade of Delagoa Bay as a Factor in Nguni Politics", 179; Young, "Fertility and Famine", 71.

centre of Portuguese colonial activity in eastern Africa. Vessels sailing under other flags were now forbidden from entering the bay even against payment of a toll. This last policy, however, was a failure, with the Portuguese unable permanently to keep out British, Dutch and French merchantmen – and whalers. To make matters worse for Portugal, the garrison mutinied in April 1790 and the fort was raided several times by French corsairs, the first in 1792. One such attack, in 1796, was made all the worse by the fort's slaves joining forces with the French raiders. The Portuguese found themselves compelled to abandon Lourenço Marques for a while and to withdraw to the interior, but the French soon left and the fort was retaken without a shot being fired. Around this time in the north of Delagoa Bay, the state of Moamba, which was expanding from the interior to the coast, gradually brought Matoll, Mabota and Magaia under its rule. For the first time a single power was now in control of the bay's northern shore, and in 1814 Portugal allied itself with Moamba in order secure its own position. The Portuguese commercial interest was strengthened by the opening, in Lourenço Marques, of a factory of the newly-established *Companhia do Comercio de Lourenço Marques e de Inhambane*. This company, the property of Vicente Tomas dos Santos, a slaver and sea-captain, was awarded the monopoly over the ivory trade in Delagoa Bay. This meant that any ivory entering the bay and its environs was to be bought up by the company, placing it in direct competition with the existing Lourenço Marques factory and its governor. Both the fort and the company, however, depended on trade with the Ronga for their own provisions. These were obtained by the Portuguese – soldiers, merchants, colonial officials together with their servants, some of them enslaved, several dozen persons all in all – in a marketplace, where bracelets, beads and cottons were bartered for maize, millet, cattle, poultry and vegetables. Among the inhabitants of the station we may also number the up to 400 Africans who settled in its immediate vicinity. While the Portuguese maintained mostly friendly relations with Moamba, Maputo, Matoll and (probably) Magaia, there were repeated armed skirmishes with Tembe, Mavota and Matola, one of which claimed the life of the governor, Miguel Lupi de Cardinas, in early 1824.[61] Incidentally, news of this

---

61 Alpers, "State, Merchant Capital, and Gender Relations in Southern Mozambique to the End of the Nineteenth Century", 43; Boteler, *Narrative of a Voyage of Discovery to Africa and Arabia*, vol. 2, 189–191; Eldredge, "Sources of Conflict in Southern Africa", 3; Fynn, *The Diary of Henry Francis Fynn*, 39; Hoppe, *Portugiesisch-Ostafrika in der Zeit des Marquês de Pombal*, 113, 170–174; Jackson Haight, *European Powers and South-East Africa*, 113, 122f., 189–191; Liesegang, "Beiträge zur Geschichte des Reiches des Gaza Nguni im südlichen Moçambique", 11, 14, 37; Liesegang, "Dingane's Attack on Lourenço Marques in 1833", 567–569; Liesegang, "Mozambique: Nineteenth Century, Early", 1032; Milburn, *Oriental Commerce*, 56; Newitt, "Drought in Mozambique", 27, 29; Newitt, *A History of Mozambique*, 159, 248, 290; Smith, "The Struggle for Control of Southern Moçambique", 156, 166–227, 281, 283; Smith, "The Trade of Delagoa Bay as a Factor

incident reached the British authorities in Cape Town by means of a whaler, most probably the British vessel *Nereid*, then at anchor in Delagoa Bay.[62]

As a result of the liberal revolution in Portugal, the authorities in Delagoa Bay relaxed the ban on foreign vessels, which were now permitted to anchor and trade in the bay on certain conditions: their papers were to be deposited at the customs house, armed Portuguese guards were to be stationed on board and mooring fees charged according to the length of stay. Moreover, a duty of twenty-five per cent was levied on all goods exported from Delagoa Bay by foreign vessels.[63] Only towards the end of the nineteenth century, however, did Portugal provide Lourenço Marques with landing stages and other elements of port infrastructure.[64]

The second of these key developments took Delagoa Bay by surprise when, on 5 July 1821, some 8,000 armed men invaded from the south – that, any rate, being the estimate of Caetano Matoso, the governor of Lourenço Marques. Skirmishes between Ronga states, Maputo in particular, and their southern neighbours are known already to have occurred in the eighteenth century, but there was a new quality to the events of 1821. With a degree of brutality previously unknown in these parts – even in wartime – the raiders attacked Tembe, Matoll, Moamba and finally the Portuguese fort itself, taking cattle herds and provisions as well as copper, beads, bracelets and necklaces. This raid marked the beginning of incursions by groups of Nguni from northern Natal into the territory of what is now Mozambique. Their northward migrations were accompanied by raids on the societies they encountered along the way and the founding of new states of their own, leading to further migrations in their turn and setting off a chain of political convulsions that would bring profound changes to life in south-eastern Africa, including Delagoa Bay.[65]

The interpretation of these events, which have gone in history as *Mfecane*, has since the 1980s been one of the most controversial topics among historians of southern Africa. At stake is relative weight of political, economic, military and

---

in Nguni Politics", 174. On the social meaning of bracelets and other annular jewellery among the Ronga see White, *Journal of a Voyage Performed in the Lion Extra Indiaman*, 28f.

62 Lys, "Letter from W. H. Lys, Esqre., to P. G. Brin, Esqre", 41.

63 Jackson Haight, *European Powers and South-East Africa*, 193, 296; Newitt, "Drought in Mozambique", 22, 28.

64 For an account of Lourenço Marques in June 1831 see Isaacs, *Travels and Adventures in Eastern Africa*, vol. 2, 340–343; for a description of the port and its infrastructure in the late nineteenth century see e.g. Bovill, *Natives under the Transvaal Flag*, 65f.

65 Liesegang, "Beiträge zur Geschichte des Reiches des Gaza Nguni im südlichen Moçambique", 237f.; Liesegang, "Nguni Migrations between Delagoa Bay and the Zambezi", 319, 321–323; Smith, "The Struggle for Control of Southern Moçambique", 244, 246–248, 250–255.

ecological factors in triggering these upheavals and influencing their course. There are various summaries of the key arguments and outcomes of these debates, but the most instructive, to my mind, is that by Elizabeth Eldrege.[66] With this in mind, I shall refrain from recapitulating the general course of events, restricting myself instead to the aspects relevant to Delagoa Bay.

Between 1821 and 1824 three or four groups of Nguni, fleeing the expanding Zulu state in the south, arrived in the area of Delagoa Bay. The looting described above occurred in the first of these migrations, that of a part of the Ndwandwe who had been driven by Zulus out of what is now KwaZulu-Natal. Zwangendaba, their leader, settled near Delagoa Bay for several years, extracting tribute from Ronga states including Tembe. Another group of Ndwandwe under the leadership of Soshangane followed in 1822, settling along the upper reaches of the Tembe river. The other groups of Nguni passed through the environs of the bay without taking up residence for long. Skirmishes and lootings, however, occurred until 1824. "If the invaded remained in their huts, they seldom experienced other ill usage than the loss of their bullocks, arms, and ornaments", was what a British naval officer, Thomas Boteler, heard in Delagoa Bay in 1822. He added, however, that "but the slightest resistance was punished with death; the hut was burned down, and every thing in it most wantonly broken and destroyed."[67] For the Ronga states, these incursions spelt economic ruin, political destabilization and the disruption of trading relations with the interior. By paying tribute, Ronga rulers were able at least to avert the collapse of their states, which Nguni pressure had brought about in other parts of southeastern Africa. Under pressure from continual Zulu attacks from the south and from drought (on which more below), both Soshangane and Zwangendaba continued to move northwards between 1824 and 1828.[68]

Once the Ndwandwe warlords had left, the Ronga states in the southern part of Delagoa Bay came under the influence of the Zulus, who since 1818 had greatly expanded their territory in modern Natal. The bordering states of Tembe and Maputo as well as the Portuguese settlement of Lourenço Marques seem to

---

[66] Eldredge, "Sources of Conflict in Southern Africa".
[67] Boteler, *Narrative of a Voyage of Discovery to Africa and Arabia*, vol. 1, 48.
[68] Isaacman, *Mozambique: The Africanization of a European Institution*, 122; Liesegang, "Beiträge zur Geschichte des Reiches des Gaza Nguni im südlichen Moçambique", 38, 51; Liesegang, "Dingane's Attack on Lourenço Marques in 1833", 569f.; Liesegang, *Mozambique: Nguni/Ngoni Incursions*, 1034; Liesegang, "Nguni Migrations between Delagoa Bay and the Zambezi", 319, 321–323; Newitt, "Drought in Mozambique", 26f.; Smith, "The Indian Ocean Zone", 235–237; Smith, "The Struggle for Control of Southern Moçambique", 250–260, 275; Young, "Fertility and Famine", 72.

have been able to preserve their autonomy only by paying tribute, notably in the form of game, to the Zulu ruler Dingane. For his part, Dingane gained permanent access to Delagoa Bay, where the Zulus traded a large proportion of the ivory they had captured for muskets and ammunition.[69] This development proceeded in parallel with a long-term reshaping of trading patterns in the hinterland. A new port sprang up some 450 kilometres to the south in the form of Port Natal, a British establishment that eroded the status of Delagoa Bay as the hub of long-distance commerce in south-eastern Africa. Societies in the interior were no able to trade ivory and other goods in Port Natal, thereby reducing Delagoa Bay's catchment area.[70]

This was the constellation amid which the Portuguese under Governor Dionísio Antonio Ribeiro sought to strengthen their influence in Delagoa Bay. Between December 1830 and July 1832 they attacked Magaia, Mavota and Matola.[71] This, however, brought the Portuguese into conflict with Dingane who, as well as being dissatisfied with Ribeiro's tribute payments, found his power threatened. A Zulu force attacked Lourenço Marques in July 1833 and burned down several outlying huts in what was clearly a warning shot from Dingane. Another attack followed in September. This time, the Zulus and the Ronga states looted the fort itself. Ribeiro, who had initially escaped to the island of Xefina, was captured by the Zulus in early October and executed without further ado on Dingane's orders. A year later the Zulus defeated Matoll, which had hitherto resisted Dinagne's overlordship. The Zulus continued to exercise indirect rule over the southern portion of Delagoa Bay until the late 1870s. Its northern environs, by contrast, from the late 1830s onwards came under the increasing influence of Gaza, a Nguni state which had emerged in the north, and of the neighbouring Swazi to the west.[72]

The third main change in the whaling era, the coming of drought and famine, affected Delagoa Bay largely indirectly. Irregular but natural fluctuations of water temperature in the Pacific, known as *El Niño*, have repeatedly caused long and unpredictable dry spells in south-eastern Africa. One such dry period is known to have occurred between 1794 and 1802, another lasted from around

---

69 Ballard, "Trade, Tribute and Migrant Labour", 103f.; Clarence-Smith, *The Third Portuguese Empire*, 34f.; Liesegang, "Dingane's Attack on Lourenço Marques in 1833", 570–572.
70 Clarence-Smith, *The Third Portuguese Empire*, 36; Liesegang, "Beiträge zur Geschichte des Reiches des Gaza Nguni im südlichen Moçambique", 52; Newitt, *A History of Mozambique*, 292f.
71 Liesegang, "Dingane's Attack on Lourenço Marques in 1833", 572f.
72 Clarence-Smith, *The Third Portuguese Empire*, 36; Henriksen, *Mozambique*, 76; Liesegang, "Dingane's Attack on Lourenço Marques in 1833", 573–578; Liesegang, "Mozambique: Nineteenth Century, Early", 1033; Newitt, *A History of Mozambique*, 293; Smith, "The Struggle for Control of Southern Moçambique", 291, 296–298, 302f.

1817 to 1831. The consequences of these dry periods varied from region to region. By laying in stores and increased hunting, some societies were able to prevent a *mahlatule* or drought turning into a *shangwa* or famine; those who failed to do so were forced to leave their settlement areas. Their migrations triggered conflicts over grazing and arable land, which sometimes escalated into wars and caused mass movements of displaced people.[73] The area's many rivers, its good fishing and hunting, and its comparatively fertile soils meant that the population of Delagoa Bay suffered less from these dry periods than did societies in other parts of south-eastern Africa. Only in the 1820s do we hear of food shortages, of a severe *shangwa* in the interior, which also affected trade in the bay itself: the famine and the upheavals connected with it caused some of the commercial networks by which goods reached Delagoa Bay to collapse.[74]

The fourth and last of the major transformations was the expansion of the slave trade, which came as a new phenomenon to the population of Delagoa Bay. While some merchantmen that moored in the bay or sailed up the Espírito Santo (Fig. 11) since the seventeenth century had bought slaves, the volume of trade was very small, only ever affecting a few people. Vessels in search of slaves usually went elsewhere.[75] For centuries and across era commercial relations between the Ronga and crews of merchant vessels were centred above all on ivory.

Before around 1800 the slave trade had played a relatively minor role, not only in Delagoa Bay but on Africa's entire eastern seaboard. The *Trans-Atlantic Slave Trade Database* gives a total of 38,531 slaves embarked at the coast of Mozambique during the eighteenth century, and a total of 174,442 for the nineteenth century. However, the database assigns only 19 voyages by slave vessels to "Lourenco Marques" and only 3 to "Delagoa". A total of 487 voyages are assigned to "Mozambique", and it remains unclear to what extent these vessels frequented Delagoa Bay.[76] It seems that the slave trade on the coast of what is now Mozambique grew rapidly from the beginning of the nineteenth century and reached its peak in the 1820s and 1830s.[77] Historians have identified four principal reasons for this surge. First, the booming production of sugar cane in

---

[73] Liesegang, "Mozambique: Nineteenth Century, Early", 1033; Newitt, "Drought in Mozambique", 18f.; Newitt, *A History of Mozambique*, 160.
[74] Newitt, "Drought in Mozambique", 20, 23f., 29; Smith, "The Struggle for Control of Southern Moçambique", 260.
[75] Smith, "The Struggle for Control of Southern Moçambique", 206, 344.
[76] Slave Voyages: The Trans-Atlantic Slave Trade Database, accessed September 15, 2022, https://www.slavevoyages.org/.
[77] Newitt, "Drought in Mozambique", 15.

Fig. 11: Two men in battle dress shown on the northern bank of the Espírito Santo in 1798. In the middle distance, the illustrator can be seen emphasising the breadth and navigability of the river, allowing entire squadrons of vessels to reach the interior.
Source: White, *Journal of a Voyage Performed in the Lion Extra Indiaman*.

Brazil, Cuba and above all Mauritius increased demand for enslaved workers. Second, British naval operations against the slave trade on the western coast of Africa redirected it towards the east. This was accompanied, third, by increasingly aggressive tactics on the part of slave traders, who now began to undertake expeditions of their own into the interior in search of slaves. Fourth and finally, the violent upheavals outlined above produced a wealth of prisoners of war to be sold on by their captors.[78]

All these developments left traces in Delagoa Bay, though the slave trade did not really pick up until about 1810. It peaked in the 1820s, after the British had signed an agreement with the Malagasy ruler Radama I to end the export of slaves from that island. Slavers in the pay of French planters in Mauritius now turned elsewhere, including to Delagoa Bay. The ensuing conflicts between a number of Ronga states were probably driven by the prospect of taking prisoners and selling them into slavery. It may also be the case that some of those

---

[78] Newitt, "Drought in Mozambique", 31; Newitt, *A History of Mozambique*, 293; Smith, "The Struggle for Control of Southern Moçambique", 350–352.

worst affected by war and famine would have sold themselves into slavery in an attempt to escape the acute threats facing them in Delagoa Bay. Slaves from Mozambique commanded high prices in Mauritius, where the planters considered them to be particularly strong and effective workers. Besides Portuguese slave vessels, Delagoa Bay was much frequented by their Brazilian counterparts. They were able to operate freely there because Portugal, jealous of its colonial claims, denied British anti-slavery patrols entrance to Delagoa Bay – unlike most other ports under Portuguese control, in which the Royal Navy had been allowed to conduct operations against the slave trade in accordance with a treaty agreed between the two nations in 1817.[79] When a British merchant, Henry Francis Fynn, visited Delagoa Bay in mid-1823, he was shown some eighty slaves lying in chains as they awaited buyers in the fort of Lourenço Marques. They appeared to be, as Fynn recorded in his diary, "the principal objects for sale" there.[80] This booming business came to an end in 1830, when Portugal finally bowed to British pressure and outlawed the slave trade.[81]

The picture drawn here of a dramatic increase in the slave trade in Delagoa Bay requires some perspective. Unlike many other African societies, the Ronga did not usually take many prisoners in the course of their campaigns. Since they would not sell members of their own states into slavery, demand for slaves in Delagoa Bay consistently outstripped supply. What is more, commercial networks in and around the bay remained centred largely on ivory, and unlike the ivory trade, that in slaved was a strictly local phenomenon. No slaves were brought to Delagoa Bay by long-distance trade routes.[82]

The lack of sources makes the volume of the slave trade in Delago Bay hard to quantify. One thing we do know is that between 1826 and 1828, at the peak of the trade, at least twelve French slave vessels sailed into the bay, each of which would have been able to take on board some 230 slaves.[83] The number of Brazilian vessels seems to have been much lower, with only eight slavers recorded as having sailed into Rio de Janeiro from Delagoa Bay between 1811 and 1830. More than ten times that number arrived from Quelimane alone during the

---

79 Boteler, *Narrative of a Voyage of Discovery to Africa and Arabia*, vol. 2, 301; Graham, *Great Britain in the Indian Ocean*, 113; Jackson Haight, *European Powers and South-East Africa*, 260; Owen, *Narrative of Voyages to Explore the Shores of Africa, Arabia, and Madagascar*, vol. 2, 218; Smith, "The Struggle for Control of Southern Moçambique", 278, 350–352; Teelock, "From Mozambique to Le Morne Brabant Mountain", 279f.
80 Fynn, *The Diary of Henry Francis Fynn*, 39f.
81 Jackson Haight, *European Powers and South-East Africa*, 234; Liesegang, "Dingane's Attack on Lourenço Marques in 1833", 573.
82 Smith, "The Struggle for Control of Southern Moçambique", 344–346.
83 Ibid., 352.

same period.[84] Up to ten thousand people a year were sold into slavery in Quelimane, whereas the trade in Delagoa Bay was clearly on a much smaller scale.[85] Although human trafficking was for a time a profitable enterprise there too, and although the consequences for its victims were no less dreadful, Delagoa Bay was never one of the centres of the slave trade in south-eastern Africa.

Brisk trade – but little desire to go ashore

The slave and ivory trades in Delagoa Bay coincided with the era of whaling there – both temporally and spatially. Whalers would sometimes observe slave vessels and their activities. William Whitten, for instance, sailing along the coast of Mozambique in the *Eureka* of Edgartown in June 1858, noted in his diary that his vessel had "Signald a Spannish slaver".[86] In 1836 the American consul in Cape Town suggested that such information might be gathered and used in combatting the slave trade.[87] The proposal was not, however, adopted by the US Navy. For their part, slave traders would sometimes disguise their vessels as whalers in an attempt to avoid being visited by patrolling vessels of the Royal Navy.[88]

Henry Fynn, the British merchant, complained in 1823 that even forty miles upstream of the Espírito Santo chiefs, through their numerous encounters with whalers and merchantmen, had themselves become seasoned traders able to exploit competition between vessels for their own ends.[89] Some whalers did indeed sail up the Espírito Santo like merchant vessels, while others remained in the bay and sent boats ashore to take on provisions.[90] As elsewhere on the coasts of both eastern and western Africa, visiting vessels would also be approached by local traders in their boats. These *luzios* measured around four metres in length, could transport up to twenty persons and could be propelled

---

[84] Florentino, "Slave Trade between Mozambique and the Port of Rio de Janeiro", 71.
[85] Newitt, "Drought in Mozambique", 15.
[86] Whitten, Journal EUREKA, 1857–1861, 23.06.1858.
[87] "From Cape Town." *New-Bedford Mercury*, 13.05.1836, 1.
[88] Barnard, *A Three Years' Cruise in the Mozambique Channel*, 58f.; Reilly, "Slavers in Disguise".
[89] Fynn, *The Diary of Henry Francis Fynn*, 41.
[90] Log ANN MARIA, 1835–1837, 17.07.1836; Log GEORGIA, 1832–1833, 12.08.1832; Log ISRAEL, 1841–1842, 26.05.–30.07.1842.

either with oars or by means of a sail woven from reeds. Some even had a cabin on deck.[91] But much business was concluded ashore. William White, who visited Delagoa Bay as a merchant in 1798, assumed that his local counterparts were trading on their own account.[92] Foreign trade, however, like such other important sectors of the economy as agriculture or hunting, were subject to the ultimate control of the Ronga rulers, who would also dispatch specialised groups of hunters, the *Maphisa*, to acquire such tradable goods as ivory or hippopotamus teeth.[93] Commercial dealings with seamen are also likely to have been subject to state approval.

What did this mean for trade "on the ground", in actual commercial situations? The most palpable expression of state control was the presence of officials who kept an eye on the sea and reported the arrival of vessels. When a boatful of seamen landed ashore, the local ruler or his deputy, usually dressed in a European military uniform, would proceed to a purpose-built residence close to the beach. Several dozen persons from the bay would then escort to seamen to this residence, where gifts were exchanged – for instance, brandy and a few items of clothing for a cow. Only once this ceremony had been completed would the ruler permit the seamen to engage in commerce. Yet in this they were not entirely free, for at no point did the official supervisor – whose title some Europeans translated as "king of the water" – leave their side. It was he who arranged for the delivery of the desired supplies, acted as mediator and interpreter in business transactions, and came on board ship when goods were handed over.[94]

Masters of whaling vessels thus had little opportunity to act on their principle of saving money by cutting out the middlemen and dealing directly with farmers. Delagoa Bay was nonetheless considered a comparatively cheap place to buy food. In their commercial strategies, Ronga rulers were more concerned with other goods, for which high prices might be charged.[95] A cow could be

---

91 Boteler, *Narrative of a Voyage of Discovery to Africa and Arabia*, vol. 1, 24–26; Fynn, *The Diary of Henry Francis Fynn*, 41; Log CHARLES COLGATE, 1863–1865, 15. & 16.05.1866; Newitt, *A History of Mozambique*, 7; White, *Journal of a Voyage Performed in the Lion Extra Indiaman*, 31f., 51.
92 White, *Journal of a Voyage Performed in the Lion Extra Indiaman*, 48f.
93 Alpers, "State, Merchant Capital, and Gender Relations in Southern Mozambique to the End of the Nineteenth Century", 37f.
94 Milburn, *Oriental Commerce*, 57; White, *Journal of a Voyage Performed in the Lion Extra Indiaman*, 25, 44f., 50. For a description of such an official by the name Shannuahguahvah, known to seamen as "English Bill", see Boteler, *Narrative of a Voyage of Discovery to Africa and Arabia*, vol. 1, 38–40, 92 and Owen, "The Bay of Delagoa", 471f.
95 Milburn, *Oriental Commerce*, 56f.

bought for one or two lengths of linen or even for a small amount of gunpowder; an iron hoop or two brass buttons would buy a chicken.[96] Sheep, goats, yams, manioc, wheat, honey, lemons, bananas, peanuts, sweet potatoes, pineapples, water melons and much else were to be found in the Ronga states, and their fishermen caught carp, mullets, eels and other fish as well as turtles and seashells that seamen might buy. In return, they sought beads and cloths, but above all garments, rings, copper wire, pipes and tobacco, as well as wigs, shoes and stockings.[97] Cloth garments were clearly something of a status symbol among the Ronga. "They wear European clothes whenever they can obtain them", observed one British naval officer, William Fitzwilliam Owen, who visited Delagoa Bay in the early 1820s. According to Owen, whalers mostly brought woollen fabrics.[98] While provisions became more expensive in the whaling era,[99] whalers seem to have found prices acceptable overall.

As already mentioned, the whalers' bartering at least partly coincided with the *mahlatule*, the severe famine in the interior. Tembe was one state that continued to sell food and cattle to ships' crews during this period. Food shortages were so dire that the local population resorted to supplementing its diet with the flensed carcasses of southern rights left behind by whalers. Eating rotting meat, however, caused disease to spread among a weakened population.[100]

In exchange for their goods, the Ronga asked above all for beads, brass and ironware, and cotton fabrics, ideally of a coarse weave and dyed blue.[101] Bracelets and anklets in particular were important markers of wealth and status in Delagoa Bay; chiefs and their wives might wear a dozen or more at a time (Fig. 12).[102] Whalers would also barter soap, metal crockery, guns and ammunition, and – as they did everywhere – tobacco, known to the Ronga as *follay*.[103]

---

96 Milburn, *Oriental Commerce*, 57; White, *Journal of a Voyage Performed in the Lion Extra Indiaman*, 48, 69; Williams, *The Adventures of a Seventeen-year-old Lad and the Fortunes He Might Have Won*, 36f.
97 White, *Journal of a Voyage Performed in the Lion Extra Indiaman*, 48f., 51–53; Williams, *The Adventures of a Seventeen-year-old Lad and the Fortunes He Might Have Won*, 36f.
98 Owen, "The Bay of Delagoa", 468, 470.
99 Huddart, *The Oriental Navigator*, 79f.; Isaacs, *Travels and Adventures in Eastern Africa*, vol. 2, 346; Milburn, *Oriental Commerce*, 57; White, *Journal of a Voyage Performed in the Lion Extra Indiaman*, 23.
100 Newitt, *A History of Mozambique*, 160; Smith, "The Trade of Delagoa Bay as a Factor in Nguni Politics", 214f.; White, *Journal of a Voyage Performed in the Lion Extra Indiaman*, 35.
101 Milburn, *Oriental Commerce*, 56f.
102 Smith, "The Struggle for Control of Southern Moçambique", 335.
103 Booth, *The United States Experience in South Africa*, 39; White, *Journal of a Voyage Performed in the Lion Extra Indiaman*, 68.

The trade in guns and ammunition was viewed with suspicion by Portugal and Great Britain, the main colonial powers in south-eastern Africa, with Britain taking it as an occasion for strategic calculations which had far-reaching consequences and of which there will be more to say in due course.

Generally speaking, trade with whalers seems to have played a not insignificant part in the Ronga economy. After all, vessels would usually be anchored in the bay for months on end and take on provisions from ashore several times during their stay.[104] Yet even in the whaling era commerce in Delagoa Bay remained focused on ivory, which was imported mostly from Zulu-controlled areas in the south. The routes along which it was transported usually passed through Maputo territory to Lourenço Marques, where it was bought up by the Portuguese and put in storage awaiting the arrival of a merchant vessel from Malabar or the Ilha de Moçambique.[105] Two other trade routes connected Delagoa Bay with eastern Transvaal. In order to acquire such goods for resale as ivory, ostrich feathers, iron and copper – or for their own use, such as hoes – traders from Delagoa Bay would travel westwards as far as the edge of the Kalahari desert. This was made worth their while by price difference which allowed them, for example, to sell guns acquired by barter in Lourenço Marques for much higher prices in the interior.[106]

Delagoa Bay's role as a centre of trade offered whalers opportunities to do good business on the side. For instance, in mid-1831 the master of the brig *Sarah* of London bought several hundred hippopotamus teeth – no doubt with a view to sell them at a profit further along in his journey.[107] Such dealings, however, were in grave breach of the trade monopoly claimed by the Portuguese. To be successful on a large scale, they had to be carried on behind the back of the governor of Lourenço Marques, whom whalers usually did not go out of their way to meet. Only few captains ever saw fit to present themselves at the fort when sailing past on the Espírito Santo.[108]

---

104 Booth, "American Whalers in South African Waters", 282.
105 Milburn, *Oriental Commerce*, 56f.; Smith, "The Struggle for Control of Southern Moçambique", 268. For a detailed account of a (failed) ivory transaction in Inhaca in mid-1831 see Isaacs, *Travels and Adventures in Eastern Africa*, vol. 2, 346–349.
106 Harries, "Labour Migration from the Delagoa Bay Hinterland to South Africa", 69.
107 Smith, *A Narrative of the Life, Travels, and Sufferings of Thomas W. Smith*, 161. While Smith does not name his vessel, it follows from the travelogue of Nathaniel Isaacs, a British merchant who came to Delagoa Bay in 1831 and heard from Daniel McKenzie, master of the *Pacific* of New Bedford, that the British whaler in question must have been the *Sarah*. (Isaacs, *Travels and Adventures in Eastern Africa*, vol. 2, 344).
108 Pinkham, *The Log Book of the Good Ship Alliance of Nantucket Captain Bartlett Coffin*, 23.09.1793.

Fig. 12: Three inhabitants of Delagoa Bay on the southern bank of the Espírito Santo in 1798. The bracelets, beads and cloth garments emphasised by the artist were long the most sought-after wares traded in Delagoa Bay.
Source: White, *Journal of a Voyage Performed in the Lion Extra Indiaman.*

Whalers would often visit the estuaries of the Espírito Santo or other rivers in order to obtain firewood and drinking water.[109] In spite of the many large rivers that emptied into the bay, drinking water was often hard to come by,[110] for the brackish water of the estuaries was still too salty to be potable. The *Oriental Navigator* of 1801 hence advised shipmasters to look out for a mountain rising on the south bank of Nkomati some five nautical miles upstream. There, they were told, "you will find three openings, the middle of which is a fresh water river; going up this river 4 or 5 leagues you may fill your calks with very good water."[111] On the Maputo and the Espírito Santo too whalers would travel several miles upstream to fill their casks with drinking water.[112] In order to guard against shallows, vessels were always preceded by two boats.[113] Once the

---

[109] See e.g. Log GEORGIA, 1832–1833, 10.08.1832.
[110] Emmerton, "A Visit to Eastern Africa", 258; White, *Journal of a Voyage Performed in the Lion Extra Indiaman*, 68.
[111] Huddart, *The Oriental Navigator*, 79.
[112] Smith, *A Narrative of the Life, Travels, and Sufferings of Thomas W. Smith*, 166.
[113] Huddart, *The Oriental Navigator*, 79.

captain had greeted the local ruler with due ceremony, there appear to have been no charges to pay for wood and water.

Captains would sometimes hire local men for such heavy work as cutting wood, but especially for the finding, chasing, killing and processing of southern right whales. "Shipped 3 natives", recorded the logbook of the *Israel* of New Bedford for 9 June 1842, about fortnight after its arrival in Delagoa Bay.[114] Local men were already looking for work aboard visiting vessels in 1798, when were hear of their receiving "a handful of sugar" per day for "unloading [a vessel's] cargo".[115] William Fitzwilliam Owen observed in the early 1820s that "many of the natives" would accept a small wage paid in clothes or tobacco to work aboard British and American whalers.[116] For one thing, these men supported crews in their everyday tasks.[117] "They worked well, were respectful in their behaviour", was Thomas Boteler's opinion of the men who worked aboard his ship in 1822.[118] But their local knowledge also made them useful as pilots, interpreters and general go-betweens, helping skippers to find their way around an area that was challenging both geographically and politically. Mariners could hire experienced specialists for such tasks in Delagoa Bay. "The English language is understood and spoken by many of the Delagoa men, and by some few remarkably well", observed Boteler, who had come to chart the bay alongside Owen.[119] For his part, Owen noted that one of his go-betweens spoke English "after the manner of the Seamen of the Whale Ships from whom he had learnt it."[120] Writing in his diary in 1823, the merchant Henry Francis Fynn similarly observed that "Among the natives of Delagoa there were many who could speak English."[121] One of them, known as Jacky, who went to work aboard the *Sarah* in June 1831, not only spoke English, but had also visited Europe.[122]

Unlike in some of the other places visited in this book, it seems that members of the local population in Delagoa Bay were only ever taken on board as seasonal workers, not as regular members of the crew. As "seasoners", they

---

114 Log ISRAEL, 1841–1842, 09.06.1842.
115 White, *Journal of a Voyage Performed in the Lion Extra Indiaman*, 32f.
116 Owen, "The Bay of Delagoa", 475; see also Boteler, *Narrative of a Voyage of Discovery to Africa and Arabia*, vol. 1, 29, 133f.
117 Liesegang, "Beiträge zur Geschichte des Reiches des Gaza Nguni im südlichen Moçambique", 14.
118 Boteler, *Narrative of a Voyage of Discovery to Africa and Arabia*, vol. 1, 134.
119 Ibid., 29.
120 Owen, "The Bay of Delagoa", 471.
121 Fynn, *The Diary of Henry Francis Fynn*, 42.
122 Smith, *A Narrative of the Life, Travels, and Sufferings of Thomas W. Smith*, 162; see also White, *Journal of a Voyage Performed in the Lion Extra Indiaman*, 59.

would return to the shore when whalers left at the season's end. Although William White claims to have heard talk in the bay of seasoners being kept on boards against their will and being sold as slaves at Cape Town,[123] no sources exist to confirm this. The files of the New Bedford customs authorities record only two seamen as having come from "Mozambique", of whom one, Manuwl Vele, sailed in the barque *Stafford* in 1865, the other, Nitorine Constantine, in the schooner *Lottie E. Cook* in 1884.[124] In addition to seasonal workers, vessels may also have been visited by women who offered their services as prostitutes. That, at any rate, is what White's reference to a few women "who come on ship-board" would seem to suggest, all the more so because White took these women to be outcasts whose conduct was at odds with the conventional forms of sexual relations he had encountered in Delagoa Bay.[125] Boteler too mentions women who were introduced to the seamen as *queens*, came aboard virtually naked, and dances, sang and smoked.[126] Owen refers to prostitution in the fort of Lourenço Marques, from where women may also have been sent aboard vessels.[127]

One striking feature of whaling operations in Delagoa Bay is the absence of something we would usually expect: in all oceans, on all coasts, seamen taking shore leave is a typical occurrence accompanying the presence of a whaler moored nearby. In Delagoa Bay, however, references to seamen going on shore leave are a rarity. They would go ashore to obtain food, water and fuel, but seem otherwise to have avoided the coast as best they could. But why?

Fear of disease was surely one important factor. The coast of south-eastern Africa had a fearsome reputation among seamen for infectious diseases, particularly the eponymous "Delagoa fever", to which the remarks by seamen from HMS *Gorgon* cited at the beginning of this chapter testify. In 1831 a seaman aboard the *Sarah* of London died only four days after going ashore; the captain and several men were killed by the fever two days later.[128] Such was his fear of disease that Tom Gardner, the cook of the *Alliance* of Nantucket, resorted to a desperate measure in June 1793, having himself buried up to the neck in sand on the beach of Delagoa Bay. Although reputed among seamen at the time to be something of a panacea, it seems not to have worked for Gardner, who reported to the surgeon of the Portuguese garrison at Lourenço Marques a week

---

123 White, *Journal of a Voyage Performed in the Lion Extra Indiaman*, 47.
124 Lund et al., *Whaling Crew List Database*.
125 White, *Journal of a Voyage Performed in the Lion Extra Indiaman*, 29f.
126 Boteler, *Narrative of a Voyage of Discovery to Africa and Arabia*, vol. 1, 26–28.
127 Owen, "The Bay of Delagoa", 478.
128 Smith, *A Narrative of the Life, Travels, and Sufferings of Thomas W. Smith*, 161f.

later. The governor, however, strictly refused to have his physician treat the American.[129]

Other perils awaiting seamen in Delagoa Bay included the hippopotamuses and crocodiles lurking on the riverbanks. Only few mariners ever considered their presence an invitation to go hunting, although Luther Little, master of the *Israel* of New Bedford, was an exception, taking his officers for a shoot in 1842.[130] But even more than savage beasts, seamen feared savage men: stories and rumours told of bloodthirsty attackers out to murder unsuspecting foreigners, and no doubt it was with such stories in mind that the crew of the *Alliance* in 1793 refused to be ashore after dark. "We were apprehensive that the Natives would come upon us and Spear us, as they had been known to one European before belonging to a ship here", records her log.[131] William White was told in 1798 that one whaler's carpenter had been killed by spears while on shore leave.[132] And the *Oriental Navigator* of 1801 issued a clear warning against the local population: "You must be continually upon your guard, the nations being in general a thievish and trayterous [sic] race; and the European traders, who have trusted to their good faith, have always been deceived and plundered."[133] The crew of the *Sarah*, which sailed into Delagoa Bay in 1831, even suspected a portion of the coastline to be inhabited by cannibals.[134]

As ill luck would have it, it was the *Sarah*'s crew which was forced by unforeseen circumstances to spend several weeks ashore. Around 9 June a heavy storm battered Delagoa Bay for three days, tearing the barque *Bramin* of New Bedford from her moorings and washing both the *Sarah* and the *Martha*, also of New Bedford, ashore in the northern part of the bay. Several men, engaged at the time in chasing southern rights, perished in the attempt to land their boats amid the heavy swell. The survivors decided to a erect a large tent close to the wrecks. One of the seamen involved, Thomas Smith, recalled in his memoirs that they were at all times surrounded by up to three hundred men armed with spears and clubs, who seemed to poised to attack and rob them at any moment. The seamen asked the local chief to put up a guard to protect them from any

---

129 Pinkham, *The Log Book of the Good Ship Alliance of Nantucket Captain Bartlett Coffin*, 07., 08. & 15.07.1793.
130 Log ISRAEL, 1841–1842, 26.05.–30.07. 1842. Elsewhere on the coast of modern Mozambique, the seaman Charles Nordhoff and several other men killed a hippopotamus in 1850. (Nordhoff, *Whaling and Fishing*, 152).
131 Pinkham, *The Log Book of the Good Ship Alliance of Nantucket Captain Bartlett Coffin*, 29.07.1793.
132 White, *Journal of a Voyage Performed in the Lion Extra Indiaman*, 31.
133 Huddart, *The Oriental Navigator*, 79.
134 Smith, *A Narrative of the Life, Travels, and Sufferings of Thomas W. Smith*, 162.

such depredations, and although their request was granted, this did not prevent the tent as well as the wrecks from being looted. The men thereupon decided to fortify themselves inside the wreck of the *Martha*, which had suffered fairly little damage, until another whaler, the *Pacific* of New Bedford, came to their rescue in August.[135]

In all those weeks of waiting, however, the dreaded assault on life and limb never came. The intruders appear to have been interested in the wrecks and the tent only for any material spoils they might find there. Seamen's fears of bloodthirsty savages or even cannibals would seem to have been based on rumour, exaggeration and seamen's yarns. Only two cases of crews being attacked by locals in Delagoa Bay are recorded. In the first, in October 1822, members of a British geographical expedition were attacked by some one hundred men armed with spears. The team, which was surveying the Tembe river at the time, was able to repel the attackers.[136] The second case is that of HMS *Nemesis*, which in mid-1840 anchored in one of the estuaries in order to repair damage suffered in a storm. After a while she was met by seamen from the *Colonel Crockett* of Newburgh. The merchantman, they said, had run aground in May while trying to sail upstream. Her crew had decided to follow the river back to the coast and in so doing had been attacked by men with spears, who had killed their captain, Orlando Austin, with the intention of roasting and eating him. Four other seamen died of Malaria. Not until February 1841 did a vessel – a whaler, the *George* of Stonington – arrive in Delagoa Bay that would take the men back to New England, where their return was heralded in such newspapers as the *New-Bedford Mercury*, the *New London Gazette* or the *Newburgh Journal*.[137]

The dangers, real or imagined, of Delagoa Bay meant that desertion was far less frequent an occurrence there than it was in other ports visited by whalers. Again, there are only a few cases on record. In spring 1833 six men from the *Hercules II* of New Bedford went absent without leave.[138] Another seaman went

---

135 Isaacs, *Travels and Adventures in Eastern Africa*, vol. 2, 343f.; *New-Bedford Daily Mercury*, 21.11.1831, 3; Smith, *A Narrative of the Life, Travels, and Sufferings of Thomas W. Smith*, 163–166. A similar incident had already occurred in 1794, when a Boston whaler – probably the *Eliza* under Captain Charles Swain – lay for months in Delagoa Bay with a damaged rudder. On the banks of a river, her crew finally found a shipwreck that was several years old but whose rudder was intact and suitable for repairing their own damaged vessel. ("Newbedford." *The Medley or Newbedford Marine Journal*, 02.01.1795, 3).
136 Boteler, *Narrative of a Voyage of Discovery to Africa and Arabia*, vol. 1, 69–73.
137 "Loss of an American Vessel and Murder of the Captain." *New-Bedford Mercury*, 05.03.1841, 1; "The Newburgh Journal . . ." *New-Bedford Mercury*, 12.03.1841, 2; "The New London Gazette . . ." *New-Bedford Mercury*, 05.03.1841, 2.
138 *New-Bedford Mercury*, 20.09.1833, 2.

missing from the *Israel* of New Bedford in 1842; he soon turned out to have taken refuge in another whaler anchored in the bay, the *Ann Maria* of New London.[139] Ten years earlier, the *Ann Marie* had already taken on a disaffected seaman in Delagoa Bay, the third mate of the *Georgia* of New London, who had, however, been discharged rather than having deserted.[140] Another whaler in the early 1840s is known to have hired two seamen who had previously absconded in Delagoa Bay.[141] In addition to these documented cases, Boteler tells of two seamen who had been left behind by a British whaler in the early 1820s.[142] Another reason why few seamen with a mind to leave their vessels did so in Delagoa Bay was the lack, until the end of the nineteenth century, of consulates, leaving them with little chance of obtaining support or even a passage home.

Colonial policy and its tensions

Although seamen in Delagoa Bay tended not to remain ashore any longer than absolutely necessary, the effects of their visits extended beyond the immediate contact situations. They did so most clearly in the sphere of the political. The beginnings of whaling in Delagoa Bay in the 1780s coincided with Portugal's efforts effectively to enforce the monopoly on trade it claimed there and to deny mooring rights to merchant vessels from other countries. Unlike the British government, which was loath to risk conflict with the Portuguese over Delagoa Bay, whalers had no regard for such claims. For instance, when in 1793 the governor ordered whalers to cease their activities and leave Delagoa Bay, not one captain obeyed. In fact, only a few days later days, the captains went in person to the Portuguese fort in order to trade, and it seems that there was nothing the governor could do about it.[143]

For their part, such coastal states as Tembe or Matoll saw no reason to forgo trade with whalers out of consideration for Portuguese interests. Meanwhile the governor shied away from intervening for fear of further antagonising the Ronga rulers, on whose good will he depended both for the ivory trade and the provisioning of his own station. The Portuguese thus restricted themselves

---

139 Log ISRAEL, 1841–1842, 26.05.–30.07.1842.
140 Log GEORGIA, 1832–1833, 06.07.–28.08.1832.
141 Williams, *The Adventures of a Seventeen-year-old Lad and the Fortunes He Might Have Won*, 38–40.
142 Boteler, *Narrative of a Voyage of Discovery to Africa and Arabia*, vol. 2, 193f.
143 Richards/Du Pasquier, "Bay Whaling off Southern Africa", 244.

to keeping a wary eye on the whalers' business and dealings and ensuring that under no circumstances did ivory change hands.[144] In so doing, they had to accept that the whalers' brisk trading exposed Portugal's inability to enforce its own claims and to sanction infractions – a problem that troubled Portuguese policymakers for many years.[145] Records left by seamen themselves show that they were well aware of the limited influence exerted by the Portuguese.[146]

While the Portuguese at first assumed only a passive role vis-à-vis the whalers, a fierce rivalry over trade with seamen soon emerged between the Ronga states. Especially Tembe and Matoll, which had still been at war with one another in the mid-1780s, now tried to steer seamen into their own respective territory and to keep them out of their rival's.[147] As soon it dawned on the Portuguese officials in Lourenço Marques that provisioning vessels might be profitable, they too wanted a share of the business and would sometimes sell livestock to the mariners. It seems likely, however, that they did so on their own account rather than on that of their government. Many of them, after all, were *degredados*, criminals sentenced to work in the colonies and who were notoriously badly paid – mostly in the form of fabrics, which they were able to use in barter.[148]

Another political consequence of whaling in Delagoa Bay merits particular attention, not being observable in this form in other whaling grounds in African waters: whaling became a factor in colonial rivalries. This phenomenon was first apparent in the 1790s, when more and more American whalers and merchantmen sailed past the Cape of Good Hope into the Indian Ocean. British policymakers worried that the United States might follow the example of the European colonial powers and try to establish a base of its own there, and in 1796 one Captain Benjamin Scott did indeed propose the foundation of such a colony to the president.[149] In order to underscore Britain's claim to bays of southern Africa and their rich whale stocks, the Admiralty in the same year sent warship to call at St Helena Bay, Angra Pequeña, Spenser's Bay and Walvis Bay.[150] Delagoa Bay was not on the itinerary, no doubt out of respect for

---

[144] Smith, "The Struggle for Control of Southern Moçambique", 210.
[145] Ibid., 225.
[146] Smith, *A Narrative of the Life, Travels, and Sufferings of Thomas W. Smith*, 166.
[147] Smith, "The Struggle for Control of Southern Moçambique", 217; White, *Journal of a Voyage Performed in the Lion Extra Indiaman*, 42.
[148] Boteler, *Narrative of a Voyage of Discovery to Africa and Arabia*, vol. 1, 31; Graham, *Great Britain in the Indian Ocean*, 110; Smith, "The Struggle for Control of Southern Moçambique", 211, 263.
[149] Duignan/Gann, *The United States and Africa*, 69f.
[150] Booth, *The United States Experience in South Africa*, 39.

Portuguese sensibilities. Britain nonetheless pondered an annexation of Delagoa Bay in the near future to keep American whalers out. Such proposals found their way into the American press, where they were greeted with indignation.[151]

After several years of relative calm, British suspicions concerning American colonial ambitions on the south-eastern coast of Africa were once again raised by the violent upheavals of the 1820s. At the height of these conflicts in 1824 John Philip, superintendent of the London Missionary Society for Southern Africa, warned that the Americans might use Delagoa Bay to send firearms and munitions to Natal and even incite the local population to wage war against the British. Britain, in Philip's opinion, would do well to establish a colonial presence of its own in Delagoa Bay, not least because it was "the best station for whale fishing on the whole coast".[152]

Since the British administration in the Cape Colony had little to go on beyond missionary reports of American activities on the south-eastern coast of Africa, several politicians and diplomats as well as officials in the Foreign Office took Philip's call very seriously. Commodore Joseph Nourse, the commander-in-chief of the Cape of Good Hope station, was himself pressing for an annexation of Delagoa Bay, if only to prevent the French from getting there first. It was thus quite in accordance with Nourse's wishes that William Fitzwilliam Owen, who was supposed to be charting the coast of south-eastern Africa, took matters into his own hands. He negotiated an agreement with the rulers of Tembe and Maputo, both of which were threatened by Nguni aggression, for a British protectorate over Delagoa Bay. Owen also raised the Union Jack there, much to the annoyance of the Portuguese, who themselves now set about concluding agreements with Tembe, Maputo and other Ronga states, raised their own flag throughout Delagoa Bay and built additional fortifications. Neither the government in London nor the colonial administration in Cape Town, however, was pleased with Owen's gambit. The agreements he had made were declared invalid, and Nourse was expressly forbidden to pursue any further initiatives in Delagoa Bay without official approval.[153]

---

151 Stackpole, *The Sea-Hunters*, 175.
152 Philip, *Letter from the Reverend Dr. Philip to P. G. Brink, Esqre*; on the contextualisation and interpretation of this source see Coupland, *East Africa and its Invaders*, 373; Jackson Haight, *European Powers and South-East Africa*, 206f.; Uys, *In the Era of Shepstone*, 9.
153 Bixler, "Anglo-Portuguese Rivalry for Delagoa Bay", 426f.; Boteler, *Narrative of a Voyage of Discovery to Africa and Arabia*, vol. 2, 192f.; Coupland, *East Africa and its Invaders*, 228f., 240; Graham, *Great Britain in the Indian Ocean*, 114f.; Henriksen, *Mozambique*, 92; Owen, "The Bay of Delagoa", 472f.; Smith, "The Struggle for Control of Southern Moçambique", 262–276, 284f. On Owen and his mission see also Coupland, *East Africa and its Invaders*, 217–270 and Jackson Haight, *European Powers and South-East Africa*, 174–176, 192–198.

Britain continued to take a cautious approach to Delagoa Bay until December 1834, when a new war erupted with the Xhosa on the eastern frontier of the Cape Colony. The fact that the US Navy was at that time setting up an East India squadron of its own (a delegation from Zanzibar would later, in 1840, travel to New York) and that American merchants and missionaries were an increasing presence south-eastern Africa revived British suspicions of American designs. In mid-1835 Vice-Admiral Sir Patrick Campbell, commander-in-chief of the Cape station at the time, reported that "the Americans intended to form a settlement somewhere in the neighborhood of Delagoa Bay" and that "an American frigate and two store-ships were expected for this purpose this year."[154] A rumour circulating among British merchants at the Cape had it that entire squadrons of American vessels were bound for Delagoa Bay with a view to annexing it and gaining a monopoly on the ivory trade in south-eastern Africa. British settlers and merchants – as well as the Cape Colony's governor, Benjamin d'Urban – urged the government in London to pre-empt any American move to that effect. In order to gain a realistic picture of what was going on, the Admiralty ordered its vessels to comb the Mozambique Channel section by section. The result was as suspected by some of the less impressionable British officials as well as Palmerston, the foreign secretary: the Americans were clearly not engaged in any colonial enterprise in south-eastern Africa.[155]

Although rumour of American colonial ambitions had been refuted, the British government remained fearful of the north-eastern portion of modern South Africa falling into the hands of a rival power if Britain failed to take possession of it first. Enemy vessels, it was feared, might use Delagoa Bay or Port Natal to block shipping lanes to and from India. In the event, a new colony was founded not by any European power but by the Boers, who proclaimed the Natalia Republic in 1839. Its boundaries were to be the Mtamvuna Congo river in the south and the Ronga states in the north, to which the Boers made no claim. British missionaries once again urged an annexation of Delagoa Bay. The government of the Cape Colony, however, refused either to do so or to recognize the new Boer state. Instead, British troops invaded the Natalia Republic in 1843, annexing it as the Colony of Natal. This put a stop to discussion of a British takeover of Delagoa Bay, for with Port Natal Britain now possessed a port of own on Africa's south-eastern coast.[156]

---

154 Quoted in Coupland, *East Africa and its Invaders*, 374.
155 Booth, *The United States Experience in South Africa*, 136–140; Coupland, *East Africa and its Invaders*, 376, 472; Duignan/Gann, *The United States and Africa*, 70f.; Jackson Haight, *European Powers and South-East Africa*, 247; Uys, *In the Era of Shepstone*, 9.
156 Bird, *The Annals of Natal*, vol. 1, 617; Galbraith, *Reluctant Empire*, 195f.; Uys, *In the Era of Shepstone*, 9f.

But how closely was American whaling in Delagoa Bay really linked to Britain's colonial policy that ultimately led to the annexation of Natal? The American historians Alan Booth, Peter Duignan and Lewis Gann have argued that the prospect of an American colony in southern Africa, raised not least by the whalers and the trade they engaged in, significantly influenced British colonial thinking and decision-making into the early 1840s.[157] In this light, the annexation of Natal might indeed appear, among other things, as an indirect response to the activities of American whalers in Delagoa Bay. Against this interpretation, however, Carl N. Haywood has argued what strikes me as the more plausible given the connections outlined above. If British policy is considered not only in terms of a few documents left by policymakers but rather in the wider context of imperial strategies and interdependences, it emerges that Britain was concerned above all with preventing the establishment of an independent Boer state and in doing so was motivated not least by economic interests. Preventing American colonial designs, on the other hand, was no longer a decisive factor by the early 1840s.[158]

One final consequence of whaling in Delagoa Bay must also be understood in its relation to colonial and economic rivalries. Under the impression of American and British whaling operations, the Portuguese decided to exploit the southern right population in Delagoa Bay themselves. They made their first attempt in 1805, when the governor of Lourenço Marques persuaded four Nantucket whalemen to stay behind and build a whaling station, from which boats were to hunt whales for processing on shore. The timing seemed favourable for such a project, with the naval war in the western Indian Ocean meaning that fewer European and American whalers came to the area than before 1790. Nevertheless, it was a failure. All four Americans had succumbed to disease by 1810, and the Portuguese, lacking the requisite skills, gave up on coastal whaling for the time being.[159]

The fact that they were able neither to keep whalers from other countries out of Delagoa Bay nor to set up a viable whaling operation of their own presented

---

157 Booth, *The United States Experience in South Africa*, 141f.; Duignan/Gann, *The United States and Africa*, 71.
158 Galbraith, *Reluctant Empire*, 195f.; Haywood, "American Whalers and Africa", 83–85. Proposals for the annexation of Delagoa Bay resurfaced in the Cape Colony around 1870, when the British government recruited thousands of workers from southern Mozambique for the Cape's plantations and gold mines. Taking possession of Delagoa Bay would have made it easier to transport these workers by sea, but the idea was soon abandoned. (Harries, "Labour Migration from the Delagoa Bay Hinterland to South Africa", 62; Young, "Fertility and Famine", 73).
159 Starbuck, *History of the American Whale Fishery*, 85.

the Portuguese authorities with a vexing problem. In 1817, after years of planning, they once more decided to set up a whaling station of their own. The man they hired to do so was a merchant by the name of Caldas, who had come to Delagoa Bay from Rio de Janeiro. In his preparations, however, Caldas made a fatal error: he failed to obtain the consent of the ruler of Tempe, an omission made worse by the fact that the ruler's relations with the Portuguese were highly strained at the time. Work had barely begun when a Tembe force attacked and destroyed the construction site, killing Caldas and his men after a brief struggle.[160]

In spite of this disaster, the Portuguese made their third attempt in the following year. Again, they brought in American seamen for the purpose, this time African-Americans who came from New England with their tools. Little is known of the scope, duration and other details of their activities. Based on Portuguese sources, Eldredge concludes that this whaling station must indeed have been completed.[161] Since, however, the records contain no remarks on Portuguese whaling operations in Delagoa Bay, any shore station they succeeded in building seems unlikely to have been operational for long.

In sum, the case of Delagoa Bay allows us to observe how a new kind of coastal trading, based on the victualling of whalers, emerged in a time of grave and far-reaching change in which the Ronga states found their stability and integrity as well as their commercial relations under threat. The scope and significance of this new trade in relation to other economic activity is impossible to establish for lack of sources. Although conflict appears to have erupted between Ronga states over access to trade with whalers, their commercial strategy continued to be centred on ivory, according only lesser importance to dealing in food and livestock as well as in slaves. The economic as well as the cultural and social effects of whaling were less pronounced in Delagoa Bay, where littoral societies had been communicating and interacting with ships' crews on and off for nearly three hundred years before the arrival of the first whalers, than in many comparable places. Seamen, for their part, fearing tropical diseases and hostile "natives", did not as a rule spend more time ashore than absolutely necessary. The most immediate effects of whaling in Delagoa Bay were felt by those of its inhabitants who worked aboard the visiting vessels and joined in the hunt for southern right whales.

The most consequential effects of whaling in Delagoa Bay were of an indirect kind, particularly its ramifications for colonial policy. By blithely trading

---

160 Owen, "The Bay of Delagoa", 471; Smith, "The Struggle for Control of Southern Moçambique", 225f.
161 Eldredge, "Sources of Conflict in Southern Africa", 8.

with the Ronga for provisions, the whalers exposed Portugal – which was trying to establish itself as the sole colonial power in the area, claiming a monopoly on trade and trying to keep out foreign vessels – as a paper tiger. This was not lost on Portugal's European rivals, which in turn was troubling to its colonial policymakers. Against this backdrop, Portugal's failed attempts to establish its own southern right whaling and thereby to keep other whalers out of Delagoa Bay appear rather as a bid to resolve this political difficulty than an economically driven project to extract more value from Lourenço Marques.

In the British Cape Colony too there were voices that found the presence of American whalers in Delagoa Bay to be a political problem. Over the course of four decades British policymakers, missionaries, military commanders and merchants repeatedly suspected the large presence of American whalers in Delagoa Bay to be a prelude to the establishment of a US colony there, or at any rate to contribute to the Cape Colony's destabilisation by means of firearms sold to Britain's current or potential enemies. Although such fears ultimately proved groundless and cannot be said to have decisively influenced policy decisions in Cape Town or London, they were remarkably durable and for a while shared by many important figures.

Passages II: Experiencing the world aboard a whaler

Unlike many other actors who arrived on African beaches from European and North American ports, whalers did not come to change the societies they encountered. A seaman to whom such a voyage was part of his everyday working life was unlikely to feel the same paternalistic motivation as a missionary or a colonial policymaker. But who were the men who travelled to the African coast in whaleships and what biographical experience might have shaped their conduct?

Of the diverse visitors to Pacific islands in the eighteenth and nineteenth centuries, Greg Denning has remarked that "They might land naked on an empty beach, but in their minds, their languages, their relationships they bring a world with them."[1] In case of whalers, the world they brought with them was shaped decisively – though not exclusively – by the experience of a life lived aboard ships. One mid-nineteenth century captain calculated that "In fifteen years of my whaling life, I have spent just seventeen months at home", observing that "I have never been present at a birth or death in my family. I can never expect more than two or three letters from home in the course of a thirty-six or forty-eight months cruise".[2] Benjamin Worth of Nantucket was a whaler for forty-one years, only seven of which he spent on land; in the case of George Gardner, also of Nantucket, it was four years and eight months on land in thirty-seven years of whaling. These skippers may be the exception, but even whalemen who did not reach the rank of captain might spend many years at sea: eighteen years in the case of Ebenezer Hunt of New Bedford, less a mere twenty-three months ashore. Most seamen, however, spent a smaller proportion of their lives on board ship.[3] Any yet whaling was not just one episode among many in a man's life. As Smith Leek noted in his diary while sailing aboard the *Delta* of Greenport in the south Atlantic in 1837, "The ship is the sailors home".[4] Life and work at sea inscribed itself into men's consciousness and into their bodies. Its specific conditions and inner logics imprinted themselves on whalemen in such a way as to make them recognisable as a distinctive group of actors in the maritime worlds of their day.

Discussing these influences in this chapter, I shall concentrate above all on aspects of social history that help understand situations of conflict. Less weight

---

[1] Dening, *Islands and Beaches*, 32.
[2] Nordhoff, *Whaling and Fishing*, 77.
[3] Bolster, *Black Jacks*, 163; Hohman, *The American Whaleman*, 84; Macy, *The History of Nantucket*, 220f.
[4] Leek, Journal DELTA, 1836–1838, 06.01.1837.

is given here to cultural history, the decisive influence of seamen's manners and mores on contact situations being discussed in the chapter "Passages III: Going Ashore". Given the lack of sources and scholarship on British whaling described at the outset, references here (unless otherwise indicated) are to American vessels, mostly in the nineteenth-century heyday of American whaling.[5] Following such scholars of maritime social history as Marcus Rediker and Paul Gilje, I work on the assumption that seamen were actors with minds of their own who participated in shaping conditions around them with strategies of their own. At the same time, I share the assumption of such scholars of maritime cultural history as Greg Denning and Scott Ashley that vessels were not just vehicles conveying people and things across the sea, taken as a transit space. Instead, vessels themselves constituted socio-cultural spaces and as such were arenas of communication and interaction that changed the people who moved within then.

Coming aboard and fitting in

Who signed on aboard a whaler and why? Distorted ideas of the intentions of men going to sea in the eighteenth and nineteenth centuries continue to circulate. On the one hand, popular adventure novels of the type represented by James Fenimore Cooper have perpetuated a romanticised notion of swashbuckling young men drawn to a life at sea by a longing for faraway places and a desire to prove their manhood. This image has found its way into historical scholarship, notably the works of Samuel Eliot Morison.[6] At the other extreme, we find the idea of the seaman as a victim of structural violence and oppression, "impressed" into service against his will by direct or indirect force. This image

---

5 Much has been written about life and work aboard whalers, particularly American ones – by eyewitnesses in the nineteenth century and historians in the twentieth. This study is not the place in which to discuss this history in all its aspects or to reconstruct scholarly debates in their entirety. The most significant studies of American whaling and its social and cultural history are Elmo P. Hohman's *The American Whaleman*, which focuses on social and labour history, Briton C. Busch's *Whaling Will Never Do for Me*, which emphasises relations of power and resistance, and Margaret Creighton's *Rites & Passages*, which foregrounds cultural history. *Thar She Blows* by Stephen Currie offers a concise overview for a non-specialist readership.
6 Of the crews of seventeenth-century New England whalers, for instance, Morison (*The Maritime History of Massachusetts*, 15) writes that they had consisted mostly of young men eager for travel and adventure. Other important studies whose view of maritime history skews somewhat towards the romantic include Chapelle, *The History of American Sailing Ships* and Wallace, *Wooden Ships and Iron Men*.

too has been enshrined in literature – *The Death Ship* (1926) by B. Traven is something of a *locus classicus* – and has recognisably influenced such historians as Jesse Lemisch.[7] Instead of favouring either of these all too straightforward interpretations, recent scholarship has analysed the practice of signing on aboard a shop as a complex in which structural factors interacted with a variety of individual motivations.

Among the most important structural factors in the North American context was rural-to-urban migration, which began in New England in the mid-eighteenth century and continued into the mid-nineteenth century. As the population grew, farmland was divided over successive generations into ever smaller plots, insufficient for feeding a family. The descendants of these farmers thus found themselves compelled to look for work in ports and cities, a migration facilitated by the rapid expansion of roads, railways and canals. Between 1820 and 1860 the population of New England towns by the sea or on the banks of a lake or river increased by 800 per cent.[8]

In the eighteenth century this group of mostly very young white men with no experience of the sea did not yet play a significant role in whaling, where seamen were recruited largely through personal networks – friends, acquaintances, relations and the people they might recommend.[9] As the industry and its need for labour grew after 1814, however, shipowners discovered a hitherto untapped source in "farm boys tired of feeding chickens and milking cows"[10] and targeted their recruitment efforts accordingly.[11] Novices could be engaged more cheaply than experienced seamen and were easily persuaded that whaling, as a New Bedford agent put it to a prospective hire, was "the finest business in the world".[12] Such recruiting agents or "boarding masters" first appeared on the coast in the 1770s and gradually found their way inland, charged by shipowners specifically with signing up "farm boys", whose lack of worldly wisdom they would often exploit by making exaggerated claims and false promises.[13]

---

[7] A late-eighteenth-century American seaman, according to Lemisch, "will tell you that he hates the sight of blue water, he hates his ship, his officers, and his messmates – and he despises himself." (Lemisch, "Jack Tar in the Streets", 377) On the topos of the tormented mariner in Traven's *The Death Ship* see Heimerdinger, *Der Seemann*, 232–238.
[8] Creighton, *Rites & Passages*, 49.
[9] Gilje, *Liberty on the Waterfront*, 16, 19.
[10] Sherman, *The Voice of the Whaleman*, 36.
[11] For a seaman explaining his motivation in these terms see Beane, *From Forecastle to Cabin*, 5.
[12] Browne, *Etchings of a Whaling Cruise*, 11.
[13] Creighton, *Rites & Passages*, 43; Hohman, *The American Whaleman*, 241; Vickers, "Maritime Labor in Colonial Massachusetts", 300. For accounts of such recruitment practices as

According to a rough estimate, about half the men hired by American shipowners to crew their whalers were tyros who had never gone to sea before and who had to learn on the job.[14] Not all of them were white "farm boys". Until the end of the eighteenth century many men belonging to such indigenous groups as the Wampanoag or the Nauset worked aboard American whalers, even forming the bulk of the crew on some vessels. Their presence sharply declined, however, as a result of resettlement, displacement and epidemic diseases between the American Revolution and around 1800. In the same period, shipowners began recruiting black seamen. One by one, the northern states banned slavery between 1777 and 1804, bringing up the number of nominally free African Americans from a few thousand to some 200,000. Their numbers were augmented by an estimated 40,000 escaped slaves from the south. Like the Native American before them, black Americans often found work to land hard to come by and thus signed on aboard ships in numbers out of proportion to their share of the overall population.[15]

Particularly in the New England whaling ports, whose Quaker traditions imbued them with a staunch opposition to slavery, shipowners and their agents tended not to worry whether a new hire was black or even a fugitive slave. Around 1780 an estimated one in four crew members aboard Nantucket whalers was of Native or African American origin, and around 1800 one in three was black. The black population of Nantucket and New Bedford doubled in the 1830s, after which the proportion of African Americans in whaling crews declined to about one in six by the late 1850s, an estimated total of 2,900 persons.[16]

What the men who signed on aboard whalers might have had in mind when doing so varied widely. Some were following in their father's or brother's

---

seen through eyes of seamen see Ely, *There She Blows*, 16, Whitecar, *Four Years Aboard the Whaleship*, 18 and Williams, *The Adventures of a Seventeen-year-old Lad and the Fortunes He Might Have Won*, 31.

14 Creighton, *Rites & Passages*, 42; Francis, *A History of World Whaling*, 94f. Trained seamen were sometimes turned away by recruitment agencies. See e.g. Nordhoff, *Whaling and Fishing*, 19.

15 Bolster, "To Feel Like a Man", 1174; Gassert/Häberlein/Wala, *Kleine Geschichte der USA*, 168, 239; Hohman, *The American Whaleman*, 50f.; Vickers, "Maritime Labor in Colonial Massachusetts", 147–192, 283f. Independence from Britain meant that the United States was no longer subject to the Navigation Act, according to which at least three quarters of a vessel's crew must be subjects of the British Crown.

16 Bolster, "To Feel Like a Man", 1173f., 1190; Dolin, *Leviathan*, 123; Farr, "A Slow Boat to Nowhere", 15–162, 164–166; Hohman, *The American Whaleman*, 51; Putney, "Black Merchant Seamen of Newport", 164f. The proportion of black seamen is impossible to establish exactly because they were not classified as such in crew lists. On the methodical difficulties of a quantitative approach see Farr, "A Slow Boat to Nowhere", 164.

footsteps, others wanted to get as far away from home as possible. Some hoped to free themselves from bourgeois society and its strictures, others wanted to prove their courage and discipline to win that society's approval. Motivations tended to be closely linked to positions in society. Young white men from rural areas in particular hoped that as whalers, they would go on exciting journeys and see exotic places.[17] In whaling ports such as Nantucket, working aboard a ship was held in social esteem; even sons of wealthy families might be raised to think of captaining or owning a whaleship as respectable careers. Black people, many of whom lived in precarious circumstances, found the prospect of room and board for months or years on end to be enticing in itself. Many hoped to earn enough in the course of a voyage to set up households and feed families of their own.[18]

Aboard the *Milwood*, which sailed for the Indian Ocean from New Bedford in June 1842, two men met who shared a motive irrespective of their different social backgrounds. John Thompson had escaped from a plantation in Maryland and had signed on as a steward to avoid a wave of arrests of fugitive slaves. The other man, who went by the name of Smith, was on the run from the police.[19] For many, the prospect of putting a considerable distance between oneself and one's pursuers on land was a strong motivation for undertaking a long journey aboard a whaler.[20] Another motive was the chance of participating in an uncommonly profitable journey, a chance – small but certainly real – even for common seamen to earn riches. This group of fortune-hunters, however, was fickle by nature: the gold rushes in California (1848) and Australia (1851) directed their attentions elsewhere and had a noticeable impact on the labour market in the whaling industry.[21]

All in all, the American whaling industry was never short of men prepared to work aboard its vessels. Cases of recruitment by force – a practice banned in New England anyhow – hence were notable for their rarity. As long as recruiting agents were able to take their pick of men, their key criteria were height,

---

17 Hohman, *The American Whaleman*, 52f., 242f.
18 Bolster, "To Feel Like a Man", 1189; Hohman, *The American Whaleman*, 49f.
19 Thompson, *The Life of John Thompson*, 119f.
20 Recruiting agents would sometimes expressly target fugitives. Browne quotes the agent with whom he signed on as having said: "A whaler is a place of refuge for the distressed and persecuted, a school for the dissipated, an asylum for the needy!" (Browne, *Etchings of a Whaling Cruise*, 11).
21 Bolster, "To Feel Like a Man", 1183; Creighton, *Rites & Passages*, 47f., 52–55; Currie, *Thar She Blows*, 13f. Employment opportunities for blacks in the northern United States in the nineteenth century were de facto limited to poorly paid jobs in a handful of sectors. (Farr, "A Slow Boat to Nowhere", 164).

strength and health. However, when more and more young men began to go west in the mid-1840s, a higher proportion of vacancies was filled by vagrants, fugitives and other outsiders for whom employment was hard to find.²²

A more challenging task was manning the higher ranks aboard ship. A voyage's success depended in large part on the skills and experience of the captain, his officers and the harpooner. Among the experienced hands who had already been one or several voyages there were ambitious seamen who may have hoped to rise through the ranks and well as those who simply had no alternative. In order to find suitable candidates for key positions such as that of harpooner, shipowners would sometimes ask for references or arrange for interviews.²³ Much less is known about recruiting practices in the British whaling industry. Like its American counterpart, it appears also to have attracted young men from the country – for instance James Choyce, who signed on aboard the *London* in 1793, aged sixteen, "seeing no better prospect than to follow the plough all the days of my life" in his rural home.²⁴ Unlike in the United States, British shipmasters were authorised to choose their own officers, which meant that captains and their preferred officers could often be hired only as a group, leaving shipowners less leeway in assembling a crew.²⁵

Whatever else their intentions may have been, seamen were united in their desire to make money. Unlike in merchant shipping, their pay was calculated as a share or "lay" of the earnings of a voyage, a percentage agreed upon when signing on. The greater part of the profits went to shipowners, however, and only about thirty per cent to the crew. The key by which this share was apportioned depended on a variety of factors; what is observable, however, is that it changed to advantage of the lower ranks as the nineteenth century progressed. In mid century, the lower ranks could expect together to receive between nine and fifteen per cent of profits, while the captain and his officers shared twelve to twenty-four per cent. Taken individually, this could mean that a captain signed on for one fifteenth of a voyage's profits, a first mate for one twenty-fourth, an lower-ranking officer for one fortieth or one seventieth and a harpooner for one ninetieth. A common seaman would receive no more than 1/150th and usually less – 1/200th or even only 1/400th depending on specialisation, training and

---

22 Busch, *Whaling Will Never Do for Me*, 8; Creighton, *Rites & Passages*, 46; Davis/Gallman, "American Whaling", 59; Francis, *A History of World Whaling*, 93; Hohman, *The American Whaleman*, 48, 51, 61, 242f.; Rediker, *Between the Devil and the Deep Blue Sea*, 33f.
23 Creighton, *Rites & Passages*, 42f.; Hohman, *The American Whaleman*, 228.
24 Choyce, *The Log of a Jack Tar*, 3.
25 Chatwin, "A Trade so Uncontrollably Uncertain", 98.

experience.²⁶ This system of sharing the spoils is unusual in the annals of paid labour and seems to have originated in the seventeenth-century Dutch whaling industry – or even in the time of the Vikings. It meant that not only profits were shared, but also the risk of a venture, shifting a part of it from syndicates and shipowners to the crew. Crews thus found themselves burned with the principal disadvantages both of dependent labour (lack of autonomy) and of entrepreneurship (business risk).²⁷

The sum paid out to a seaman at the journey's end was often much less than the share to which he was nominally entitled – in fact, he might well end up in debt. On the voyage, men had to purchase such everyday items as a knife, a needle or a new pair of trousers from the shipboard stores or "slop chest". This was administered by the captain, who was under orders from the shipowners to sell goods at a steep mark-up – often one hundred per cent or more – against the men's wages. This was the case aboard both British and American whalers.²⁸ Such practices prompted Walter Burns, who sailed in the brig *Alexander* of San Francisco from 1890 to 1890, to observe: "The fact is the 'lay' means nothing to sailors on a whaler. It is merely a lure for the unsophisticated. It might as well be the 1,000th lay as the 190th, for all the poor devil of a sailor gets."²⁹ The seemingly inevitable disappointment of payday is captured in a couplet that became proverbial among seamen: "Naught is naught, two is two / Young man there's nothing coming to you."³⁰

Besides the slop chest, a major drain on seamen's purses was the cost of "rigging" themselves out for a voyage. Directly before sailing, shipowners or their agents would usually commission an outfitter to provide the crew with work clothes, a sea chest or "donkey", needle and thread, cutlery, soap, razor and comb and similar items. This outfit, often consisting of inferior wares at inflated

---

26 Busch, *Whaling Will Never Do for Me*, 6; Chatwin, "A Trade so Uncontrollably Uncertain", vi; Creighton, *Rites & Passages*, 28–30, 35f.; Gilje, *Liberty on the Waterfront*, 22. For concrete examples of how profits were shared out see Eldridge, *Lewis William Eldridge's Whaling Voyage*, 4, Ferguson, *Harpooner*, 315 and Cone, *For Candlesticks & Corset Stays*, app. 4. Among the few exceptions to system of payment as a share of earnings were apprentices aboard British whalers (who received a monthly wage) and a few cases in which American whalemen were paid in oil for resale on their own account. (Chatwin, "A Trade so Uncontrollably Uncertain", vi).
27 Hohman, *The American Whaleman*, 217, 220–223; Warrin, *So Ends This Day*, 39.
28 Busch, *Whaling Will Never Do for Me*, 11; Chatwin, "A Trade so Uncontrollably Uncertain", 100; Hohman, *The American Whaleman*, 227. A detailed account of seamen's purchases from the slop chest can be found in Log PEDRO VARELA, 1881–1883.
29 Burns, *A Year With a Whaler*, 14.
30 Chippendale, *Sails and Whales*, 157.

prices, was paid for by the agent but billed to seamen at an average interest of twenty-five per cent.[31] Many seamen chafed at their inexperience and desperation being exploited. One, William Whitecar, complained the outfitter "charges double the price of good, for worthless articles, which must be taken at his prices."[32]

What was more, come payday, seamen's wages were docked by the cost of any damage to the vessel they might be blamed for as well as for any hospitalization charges they had incurred. Deserters, if caught, were made to foot the bill for their capture and lost labour. Since any earnings from a voyage were not payed out till its end, most seamen were strapped for cash for the duration and depended on advances from the captain, who kept exact records for the benefit of the vessel's owners, who levied a one-off interest of twenty-five to forty per cent on seamen's debts.[33]

In New Bedford and other whaling ports, returning seamen found themselves beset by inkeepers, merchants and other "helping hands" of the kind known to seamen as "land sharks" or "sharkers". Seamen were offered a wealth of goods and services – from room and board via grog to a visit to the brothel – for cash or on credit, often plunging them into debt before very long and leaving them with no alternative but to sign on aboard a whaler once more. This debt trap worked to the advantage of shipowners, to whom it guaranteed a steady flow of experienced labour. They would accordingly pay commission to land sharks and defer repayment of debts if a seaman was willing to go on another voyage. This system drove many seamen into a state of permanent dependency, being in debt on board to shipowners for their outfit or advances on their wages and on land to the owners' middlemen.[34]

Yet it is likely that most of the men did not end their seafaring days in debt. On the twelve voyages made between 1845 and 1879 by the barque *Marcella* of New Bedford, for example, a common seaman returned with average earnings of $11.79 and an officer with $342.07. In the case of the *James Maury* of New Bedford, which made six voyages between 1845 and 1868, the figures were $103.20 and $491.43 respectively.[35] The average American whaleman earned less than his counterpart aboard a merchant vessel, and less too than an unskilled factory

---

31 Busch, *Whaling Will Never Do for Me*, 10; Francis, *A History of World Whaling*, 100; Hohman, *The American Whaleman*, 70, 98f. For a seaman's description of such a sea chest and its contents see e.g. Beane, *From Forecastle to Cabin*, 14.
32 Whitecar, *Four Years Aboard the Whaleship*, 19.
33 Creighton, *Rites & Passages*, 35f.; Gilje, *Liberty on the Waterfront*, 23; Hohman, *The American Whaleman*, 15, 220, 250–252, 259–261.
34 Busch, *Whaling Will Never Do for Me*, 10; Hohman, *The American Whaleman*, 97, 219.
35 Hohman, *The American Whaleman*, 318. For other examples of seamen's earnings see e.g. Spears, "The Log of the Bark Emily", 251.

worker, a soldier or an agricultural labourer. An officer or captain aboard a whaler, by contrast, could expect to earn more than a similarly specialised skilled worker or tradesman on the American mainland, and distinctly more, on average, than a seaman of comparable rank in the merchant navy.[36] The largest share of the profits, however – often about seventy percent – went into the shipowners' pockets.

Fig. 13: A group of seamen from the *John R. Manta* of New Bedford in one of her boats. The photograph, taken in 1906 by Captain Henry Mandly, gives an idea of the youth of many of the seamen aboard American whalers.
Courtesy of the New Bedford Whaling Museum, item number 2000.100.86.306.1.

For most of those involved, dreams of riches foundered on the actual experience of whaling no less than did romantic notion of freedom and adventure. "Life – the sailor's life, the only one of which I now had any well shaped idea – seemed at best but a troublesome and tiresome struggle", was Charles Nordhoff's conclusion at the end of his first voyage in the mid-nineteenth century.[37] Many lower-ranking seamen did not sign on aboard a whaler for a second time if they could help it. Yet recruiting practices were such that young men were seldom in short supply. The

---

36 Busch, *Whaling Will Never Do for Me*, 9; Creighton, *Rites & Passages*, 43, 46; Hohman, *The American Whaleman*, 16, 219; Warrin, *So Ends This Day*, 36.
37 Nordhoff, *Whaling and Fishing*, 273.

demand for labour increased in line with the size of the vessels, at least until the middle of the nineteenth century.[38] The average age of the crews was accordingly low. If it was seldom quite so low as aboard the schooner *Esquimaux* of Provincetown, with the average seaman in the early 1840s aged only seventeen, it was not usually significantly higher, either.[39] A survey of New Bedford and New London whalers between 1818 and 1888 reveals the average age of white seamen to have been twenty-two to twenty-seven, that of black seamen a little higher. This pattern seems to have remained fairly consistent across the various periods of American whaling, while officers and captains – usually the oldest men on board – were aged thirty on average in 1818 and forty in 1888.[40]

The fact that captains and officers tended to be comparatively old did much to raise the average age of crews. Common seamen were hardly ever aged over thirty and often under twenty (Fig. 13).[41] Of the recruits he encountered in New Bedford around 1850, Charles Nordhoff observed that "Very few among them had beards. Most of them were very young men, or rather, overgrown boys already too large ever to become good seamen but just at that age when they would contract all the vices of the sailor."[42] Nordhoff here refers to an assumption dating back to the early modern age which held that seamen ought ideally to go to sea before the onset of puberty, since only then would they truly internalise shipboard life as well as acquiring immunity to seasickness.[43] Youth hence did not necessarily imply inexperience. George Barker, for instance, had already been a cabin boy before signing on aboard the *Alcyone* of Provincetown around 1870, aged sixteen.[44] Thomas W. Smith, who had grown up not far from London and first joined the crew of a whaler in his early twenties, had worked aboard freighters and warships from the age of six.[45] And in June 1849 Nelson Cole Haley, aged sixteen, rose to a leading position as boatsteerer aboard the barque *Charles W. Morgan* of New Bedford, having first joined a whaling crew aged eleven.[46]

---

38 With an average of .14 men per vessel ton, British whalers tended to be more closely staffed than American ones at .08 men, which is likely to have been one factor in the latter's greater productivity. Moreover, American vessels usually carried a greater proportion of trained and specialised seamen. (Davis/Gallman, "American Whaling", 58f.)
39 Currie, *Thar She Blows*, 15f.
40 Creighton, *Rites & Passages*, 213f.
41 Hohman, *The American Whaleman*, 57f.
42 Nordhoff, *Whaling and Fishing*, 27.
43 Elias, "Studies in the Genesis of the Naval Profession", 293, 298.
44 Barker, *Thrilling Adventures of the Whaler Alcyone*, 12–14.
45 Smith, *A Narrative of the Life, Travels, and Sufferings of Thomas W. Smith*.
46 Haley, *Whale Hunt*, 9.

Under orders

What positions did the men occupy aboard ship? At the top of the crew's hierarchy stood the captain, whose formal powers were scarcely limited and comparable to those of an absolute monarch. Although he was answerable to the vessel's owners afterwards – and sometimes to lawcourts and insurers, too – he was fully in control of every aspect of a voyage itself. His actions, however, were dictated not by his will alone but also by that of the vessel's owners, in whose name he transacted any business that might occur in the course of a voyage. He therefore not only had to be able to navigate the vessel, command the crew, and organise the hunting and processing of whales, he had also to possess commercial acumen. Moreover, the captain would often command one of the whaleboats during the chase itself, and his reputation hinged on his experience and success in finding and catching whales. The ideal captain therefore was not only a qualified shipmaster and an astute businessman, he was also the most skilful hunter on board. Second-in-command to the captain was the first mate – also known as the chief mate of first officer – who was responsible for translating the captain's orders into specific instructions and setting tasks accordingly. It was the first mate who would set the course, summon the men to work, supervise everyday routines and keep the ship's log. He made sure that the whaling tackle was in order and ready for use at a moment's notice, commanded one of the boats, and when a whale had been taken, it was he who organised the work needed to process it. As the captain's deputy, he had to be able to take his place in an emergency.[47]

Another rung lower in the hierarchy were a number of men who held positions of responsibility but were subject to the constant control of the captain and the first mate. These included the second mate and, depending on the size of the vessel, the third and fourth mates too. These officers, who were also known as "afterguards", each worked one watch, kept discipline aboard ship and acted as "boatheaders" in charge of one of the boats. Other of their responsibilities were less well defined but might include such tasks as keeping an eye on ongoing work or checking the rigging. Being among the most experienced men on board, they would perform some of the more skilled tasks themselves. Each officer was assigned a harpooner or a "boatsteerer", the men who threw

---

[47] Chatwin, "A Trade so Uncontrollably Uncertain", 103; Creighton, *Rites & Passages*, 28f; Davis/Gallman, "American Whaling", 56; Hohman, *The American Whaleman*, 60, 119. In the American whaling industry, many captains owned shared in their vessels. (Creighton, *Rites & Passages*, 89).

the harpoons and who naturally bore a large share of the responsibility for a voyage's success.[48]

American whalers would usually have three specialised tradesmen on board, each with responsibility for his own tasks: the ship's carpenter maintained the masts, planks and other wooden parts, the cooper did the same for the barrels that held the whale oil, and the blacksmith worked on harpoons, lances and other metal objects. These tradesmen would also keep watch aboard the vessel when the crew were out in the boats chasing whales,[49] for which they were often mocked as "idlers". But whaling was nothing without sound barrels, sharp harpoons and agile vessels, and ship's tradesmen often worked as hard as anybody on board. "Once I repaired one boat three times before breakfast", recalled John Williams, a carpenter aboard a whaler in the Indian Ocean in the 1840s.[50]

The largest group aboard were the common seamen or "foremast hands", some fifteen to twenty depending on the size of the vessel. They included trained "able seamen", experienced but untrained "ordinary seamen" and novices or "green hands" lacking both training and experience. The green hand began by performing such unskilled routine tasks as scrubbing the deck and learnt from the more experienced men along the way. It was the latter group who performed most of the tasks on board, from setting the sails to rowing the boats.[51]

One final group of men did not fit squarely into the hierarchy on board a whaler, not least because their tasks were associated with the pursuit of whales only indirectly. They were the ship's cook (sometimes known as "doctor"), the steward and – though not in all vessels – the cabin boy. The men hired as cooks, a disproportionate number of whom were black, usually had no nautical training and were not (or no longer) fit for hard physical labour. His assistant was the steward, who waited on the captain. The cabin boy had no fixed set of tasks, being employed instead for all manner of odd jobs as well as often being treated by the captain as his own personal servant.[52] In terms of their share, cook, steward and cabin boy were among the worst paid members of the crew,

---

48 Hohman, *The American Whaleman*, 119f.
49 Creighton, *Rites & Passages*, 29f.; Hohman, *The American Whaleman*, 120. An undated note in the log of the *Columbia* of Nantucket contains a list of tasks to be performed by the blacksmith by order of the captain. This included making "Ring bolts for lashing Anchors" and "Hooks for Boat Bearers" as well as staples and tongs for a variety of purposes (Log COLUMBIA, 1846–1850).
50 Williams, *The Adventures of a Seventeen-year-old Lad and the Fortunes He Might Have Won*, 110.
51 Creighton, *Rites & Passages*, 30; Hohman, *The American Whaleman*, 62, 120.
52 For a cabin boy's account of his tasks see Robinson, *A Boy's Will*, 5.

but their tasks brought them into closer contact than with the captain and his officers than common seamen. This proximity was often the source of conflict. The steward might find himself accused of being the captain's lackey, the cook held responsible for the poor food (ultimately the owners' responsibility) and the cabin boy suspected of "ratting" or informing on other crew members to the officers.[53]

***

Spatial arrangements aboard a whaleship replicated the hierarchical ordering of its crew. The largest cabin was the captain's, which was also the most comfortably appointed (comparatively speaking) and situated in the quarterdeck along the port side. The captain might enjoy such amenities as a sofa, a bed or berth designed to remain level even as the vessel pitched and rolled, and a washroom of his own (Fig. 14). The first mate too enjoyed the privilege of an aftercabin, albeit one less lavishly furnished than the captain's. Next door was a cabin shared by the second and third mates. The aft portion of the vessel adjoining the officers' cabins was traditionally known as the "steerage" in whalers, though it was not in fact the deck below the main deck traditionally associated with that term. Here, harpooners and tradesmen as well as cook, steward and cabin boy shared cabins of two or four wooden bunks. The common seamen had their bunks in the forecastle. This forward compartment, often no larger than fourteen square metres, was poorly lit and served as communal sleeping, dining and living quarters, predestining it for infestation with rats, cockroaches and other vermin. On board most whalers, because the forecastle was too small to sleep them all, the men would have to take turns using a bunk. It also tended to be both poorly ventilated and damp, being insufficiently insulated to keep out rain or the spray from waves breaking on the bow.[54] The diaries, travelogues and memoirs of common seamen have much to say about conditions in the forecastle and are unsparing in their criticism.[55] Men would spend as little time there as they could, often preferring to brave the weather on deck.

---

[53] Bolster, "To Feel Like a Man", 1194; Creighton, *Rites & Passages*, 30, 186; Ely, *There She Blows*, 65; Hohman, *The American Whaleman*, 120.

[54] Ashley, *The Yankee Whaler*, 51f.; Busch, *Whaling Will Never Do for Me*, 13; Creighton, *Rites & Passages*, 28–30; Currie, *Thar She Blows*, 35f.; Hohman, *The American Whaleman*, 71, 119f., 125–127. On some vessels, the forecastle was so infested with vermin as to make sleep impossible. See e.g. Jarman, *Journal of a Voyage to the South Seas*, 69.

[55] See e.g. Browne, *Etchings of a Whaling Cruise*, 24; Nordhoff, *Whaling and Fishing*, 43; Whitecar, *Four Years Aboard the Whaleship*, 24.

A ubiquitous experience of life on board ship was that it took place almost completely in public – in other words, its lack of privacy.[56] The layout of the vessel was such that only the captain and the first mate were exempt from this rule. To have spaces and retreats of their own not only underscored the privileges of rank, it also marked them out as the sole representatives of the middle classes: only the captain and his deputy were able to preserve something of the bourgeois division between work and leisure on board ship.[57]

Not only the arrangement of the cabins ensured a rigid spatial separation between the captain and his officers on the one side and the common seamen on the other. A manuscript containing orders from Captain Edward Davoll, who commanded six whaling voyages from New Bedford and Mattapoisett between 1847 and 1862, suggests that the officers, the steward and the cook aboard his vessels were usually restricted to the aft part of the deck, common seamen to the fore. The boundary was marked by the mainmast, and officers would shout their orders from one part of the vessel to the other. Common seamen were permitted to leave the forward part of the vessel only when ordered aft. The link between the two sections was formed by the second mate, who might keep an eye of work in the fore, but was forbidden to make any conversation beyond what was absolutely necessary.[58] This segregation by class reflected, for one thing, a process of differentiation and separation observable throughout much of North America in the nineteenth century and taking such seemingly different forms as the emergence of *Chinatowns* or a growing distinction between masculine and feminine spaces.[59] On board the vessel itself, segregation marked a symbolic border and thus had an important role to play in organising power relations.

***

Looking back at his whaling years, Charles Nordhoff concluded that "There is nothing [. . .] so difficult to grow accustomed to as the difference in rank, and consequent difference in physical comforts, which prevail on ship board."[60] Many seamen were angry at the unequal distribution of power, privilege and food embodied in the space of the whaleship. In order, however, to keep labour cheap and easy to hire, United States law gave seamen few rights or possibilities

---

56 Dening, *The Bounty*, 28.
57 Creighton, *Rites & Passages*, 31; Dillard, "A Whale of a Man", 60.
58 Davoll, *The Captain's Specific Orders on the Commencement of a Whale Voyage to his Officers and Crew*, 10f., 15.
59 Creighton, *Rites & Passages*, 31.
60 Nordhoff, *Whaling and Fishing*, 52.

for appeal, whereas captains were equipped with far-reaching powers, including the right to exact obedience from refractory seamen by force.[61] Such were the captain's powers that the political order on board ship may be defined as autocratic.

Fig. 14: Captain Benjamin D. Cleveland in his cabin aboard the *Charles W. Morgan*. Photograph by William H. Tripp, August 1916. Cleveland's first voyage in command of a whaler – the barque *Bertha* of New Bedford – had taken him, among other places, to Annobón.
Courtesy of the New Bedford Whaling Museum, item number T-183.

As in any autocracy, power aboard a whaler was subject to rules which even the captain could not escape and which went some way towards constraining his power. In his capacity as representative of the owners or the syndicate, he had to ensure as high a return as possible on the voyage and hence to keep

---

61 Lemisch, "Jack Tar in the Streets", 379.

productivity in mind when using his power. Moreover, the pursuit of whales as well as navigating stormy seas could not but forge the crew into a community united by a common purpose and destiny. The survival of each man, including the captain, depended on the skills and cooperation of all.[62] In addition, the *Second Great Awakening*, the religious revival that swept America in the 1820s, brought captains under pressure from dozens of evangelical reform groups – most notably the *American Seaman's Friend Society* – which sought to influence public opinion and legislation with the aim of improving living and working conditions on board vessels.[63]

Powerful though the captain was, enforcing rules and hierarchies on board was far from being a straightforward task, calling instead for strategic acumen.[64] The degree of and psychological and social stress to which seamen were exposed added to the challenge of keeping order. Aboard a vessel, men might be confined together for years on end with no privacy, they had to undergo extreme dangers and perform heavy physical work on an often insufficient diet. A particular strain was imposed by periods in which no whales were to be found, for every day that passed without taking a whale meant another day at sea and a smaller share at the end of it. Weeks and months of poor hunting meant long spells of painful monotony in which even experienced men's nerves might be on edge, and latent discontent and anger erupt at any time.[65] "Whalers with nothing to do are restless and dangerous", observed Greg Dening.[66] Violent altercations between seamen were particularly frequent at such times, and the ubiquity of knives, whaling tackle and tools meant that they were liable to end in serious or even fatal injury.[67] Captains had to use their authority judiciously if they were to prevent such tense situations from spiralling out of control.

What is striking about Davoll's orders quoted above is the stress placed by the captain on status distinctions. Davoll expressly forbade mingling between the steward and the boatsteerers on the one hand and the common seamen of the forecastle on the other. The orders he issued to his offers display a similar concern with preventing the emergence of confidential relations between the two sections of the vessel. He was no less emphatic in appealing to his officers' loyalty in this

---

62 Rediker, *Between the Devil and the Deep Blue Sea*, 155.
63 Creighton, *Rites & Passages*, 87, 96f.; Gilje, *Liberty on the Waterfront*, 214f.
64 Creighton, *Rites & Passages*, 115.
65 Gilje, *Liberty on the Waterfront*, 78; Hohman, *The American Whaleman*, 64, 176f.; Heffernan, *Meuterei auf der Globe*, 80.
66 Dening, *Beach Crossings*, 116.
67 See e.g. McCormick, *Two New Bedford Whalemen*, 176 (15.01.1870) & 174 (03.12.1868).

matter: "When I pull, I shall expect you all pull with me, not against me."[68] This emphasis reveals the captain's relationship with his officers to be a fragile link in a whaler's command chain. Rivalry between officers or any pointed show of disloyalty might pose serious threats to a captain's authority. Cohesion among the officers and keeping them distinct as a body from the rest of the crew was thus one of the key elements in captains' strategies for rule: anyone seeking to exert power through a hierarchical structure had to ensure that the system was not counterbalanced by friendships or other personal relations.[69]

As in other branches of seafaring, whaling captains and their officers used the threat and exercise of physical violence to ensure that work was done with the efficiency needed to make a voyage successful. Violence was a defining part of seaman's quotidian experience from the early days of American-style pelagic whaling. By no means all captains and officers ruled as tyrants, and seamen are on record as speaking in praise of their superiors.[70] Yet on the whole, the pressure exerted by shipowners to turn a profit combined with contemporary ideas about duty and discipline, and backed up with far-reaching rights to enact punishment, to produce a culture of authority in which most captains and offers assumed the role of strict and sometimes cruel taskmasters.[71]

Any number of incidents might rouse a commanding officer to fury. Captain Alden of the *Bruce*, for instance, kept pummelling the head of a young seaman with his fists and whipping him with a rope when the unfortunate boy, who had been put at the tiller, failed to keep the vessel steady in a rough sea.[72] Besides poor work, occasions for instantaneous abuse might include falling asleep on watch, cursing, slacking off and any number of lesser infractions. That captains and officers were within their rights to beat seamen with ends of rope, belying pins or with any other tool that came to hand – or, for that matter, their bare hands – was taken for granted aboard many a whaleship and merited no mention in the ship's log. This would seem also to apply to the practice of restraining seamen by putting them in irons, which was used by captains to punish minor offences – sometimes pre-emptively.[73]

---

68 Davoll, *The Captain's Specific Orders on the Commencement of a Whale Voyage to his Officers and Crew*, 12.
69 Bolster, "To Feel Like a Man", 1180; Gilje, *Liberty on the Waterfront*, 84f.
70 See e.g. Ferguson, *Harpooner*, 26.
71 Creighton, *Rites & Passages*, 87; Hohman, *The American Whaleman*, 14, 71, 120f., 125.
72 Browne, *Etchings of a Whaling Cruise*, 265–267.
73 Busch, *Whaling Will Never Do for Me*, 21f.; Creighton, *Rites & Passages*, 108f., Hohman, *The American Whaleman*, 121–124.

Alongside such frequently casual violence, a systematic practice of formal punishments emerged for graver offences, which included insubordination, attacks on officers, brawling or theft. These punishments can be divided into three broad categories. The first was known as "seizing up", in which the offender was suspended by his hands or thumbs from the vessel's ratlines in such a manner as to leave his feet barely or not all touching the deck. To remain in this position for hours on end and in public view was not only humiliating, but could also be extremely painful, particularly in a rough sea.[74] The second, which would often follow upon seizing up, was the lash (Fig. 15). Using a whip or a heavy rope, the captain would deliver a fixed number of lashes, depending on the gravity of the offence, to the seaman's bare back.[75] The pain inflicted, along with the lasting scars, made the lash the form of corporal punishment that seamen feared most. Moreover, having their vulnerability put on public display and being helpless in the face of the blows were felt by seamen as insults to their dignity and manhood. Last but by no means least, the lash bore, as Briton C. Busch puts it, "the stigma of slavery".[76]

The third punishment was imprisonment, in which the offender would be locked in a cell below the quarterdeck for a stretch of days or weeks with only bread and water for sustenance. This cell, known as the "run", was so small that even a short man could not stand upright or lie outstretched inside it. The run was neither illuminated nor ventilated, the stench being all the worse for the bilge water collected beneath it. Depending on his offence, the prisoner might also be bound be the hands, less often by the feet.[77] John Ross Browne accordingly describes the run of the *Bruce*, in which one of his shipmates was imprisoned for seven months, as a place of nearly indescribable horror.[78] The combination of corporal punishment and subsequent imprisonment was considered the severest punishment aboard a whaler, imposed by captains for such offences as desertion.[79] Instead of the run, captains might on rare occasions also have a seaman confined in a barrel.[80]

Besides these three degrees of formalised punishment, some captains and officers were in the habit of contriving penalties that underscored their power to inflict pain and testified to sadistic leanings. Cases are recorded of seamen

---

74 Barker, *Thrilling Adventures of the Whaler Alcyone*, 17–19; Busch, *Whaling Will Never Do for Me*, 23.
75 Hohman, *The American Whaleman*, 121–124.
76 Busch, *Whaling Will Never Do for Me*, 29, 31, 39.
77 Hohman, *The American Whaleman*, 121–123.
78 Browne, *Etchings of a Whaling Cruise*, 488f.
79 See e.g. Log GLOBE, 1855–1857, 05.07.1856.
80 Busch, *Whaling Will Never Do for Me*, 22f.

Fig. 15: Punishment by the lash as depicted in Browne's memoir. The artist emphasis the response of the other seamen, who are made to watch and yet turn away, whether in horror, outrage or embarrassment.
Source: Browne, *Etchings of a Whaling Cruise*, 222.

being punished for brawling by being forced into hand-to-hand combat with another man, the loser being sentenced to a severe lashing. Others were made to perch in a dangerous position on a yard or job-boom[81] or to eat refuse.[82] In 1839 Joseph Dexter, master of the barque *Emerald* of Salem, punished a seaman for brawling by having him stripped from the waist down and tied to the mizzen tack, where his bare buttocks were flogged with the cat-o'-nine-tails.[83]

The subjective experience of fear and horror aboard a whaler was not necessarily proportionate to the frequency of such punishments. As Rediker has pointed out, the decisive factor was not the degree to which corporal punishment was the rule, but that to which corporal punishment asserted the rules that applied on

---

[81] Hohman, *The American Whaleman*, 121–123.
[82] See e.g. Ships Daily Journal, entry 1/1881. National Archives and Records Administration, Records of Foreign Service Posts, Record Group 84, Loanda 1881–1891.
[83] Log EMERALD, 1838–1840, 17.01.1840. For other instances of punishments that seem sadistic see Busch, *Whaling Will Never Do for Me*, 22f.

board ship. What mattered was not so much the frequency of such punishments as their symbolic effectiveness as deterrents.[84] From his research into the famous munity on the *Bounty*, Greg Denning has concluded that Captain Bligh incurred his men's hostility not so much by the punishments he meted out as by the contempt evident in his language. This suggests that many seamen were prepared to accept ill-treatment by their superiors as unexceptional as long as the use of force was constrained by the rules of the sea and was to some extent predictable.[85]

A captain or officer seeking to bend the will of a recalcitrant seaman might therefore dispense with formalised penalties and instead resort to deliberate violations of common sense. He might try to demean his victim with insults and obscenities, or to make him live in fear by constant threats or by consistently assigning him the most difficult and dangerous tasks. Persecution of this kind might stem less from a specific intention to overcome obstinate behaviour than from personal animosity. Commanding offers might also purposely harass seamen in order to provoke them into desertion or another act of resistance that could then be punished with due severity.[86]

The systematic use of force to extract a maximum of labour left both physical and psychological marks on seamen. Physical damage might range from all manner of injuries to lifelong incapacitation or even death. Mistreatment would often go the very limits of what human beings are able to withstand and left deep mental scars too. Observers found that their first lashing brought about a lasting change in seamen's personalities.[87] Ben Ely, a seaman in the *Emigrant*, wrote that such men were henceforth "broken spirited".[88] Seamen unable or unwilling to tolerate abuse would sometimes seek escape by taking their own lives.[89]

If the goal was to secure harmonious coexistence on board ship, this reliance on force was counterproductive, contributing as it did to the emergence of multiple lines of conflict that were liable to get out of hand. Excessively harsh captains and officers incurred the enmity of individual seamen and provoked aggression and a thirst for vengeance in their turn.[90]

---

84 Rediker, "The Common Seaman in the Histories of Capitalism and the Working Class", 342f.
85 Dening, *The Bounty*; Dening, *Mr Bligh's Bad Language*.
86 Gilje, *Liberty on the Waterfront*, 218; Hohman, *The American Whaleman*, 120f., 123f.
87 Dening, *The Bounty*, 23; Hohman, *The American Whaleman*, 121–123. For another account of psychological trauma as a result of abuse see Nordhoff, *Whaling and Fishing*, 337. Herman Melville's novella *Billy Budd* offers a harrowing depiction of the destructive impact a violent regime might have on individual seamen.
88 Ely, *There She Blows*, 40f.
89 See e.g. Gilje, *Liberty on the Waterfront*, 82.
90 Rediker, *Between the Devil and the Deep Blue Sea*, 226. For exemplary accounts of such reactions see Ely, There She Blows, 14f.; Look, Journal CHARLES W. MORGAN, 1871–1874, 4.

The captain's far-reaching right to punish seamen as he saw fit and to use force in doing so have a long history and may be traceable, in the European context, to principles of military organization.[91] Memoirs by seamen – the most effective was undoubtedly Richard Henry Dana's *Two Years Before the Mast* (1840) – and campaigns by evangelical groups raised public awareness and created political pressure on the American government, and the repertoire of corporal punishments was gradually limited in the course of the nineteenth century. Since, however, there was no effective mechanism of enforcement and seamen were often unaware of their rights and opportunities for redress, legally banned penalties remained commonplace aboard many a whaler – particularly the lash, which into the mid-1860s was barely any less ubiquitous than it had been before it was outlawed in 1850.[92]

The fact that seamen had few means of redress did not, however, mean that whalemen accepted the iniquities of everyday shipboard life uncomplainingly. Vessels brought together men from different walks of life and with a wide range of experiences, exposing them to far-flung parts of the world. This made vessels the perfect place to gather knowledge and cultivate techniques of resistance. The era of American-style pelagic whaling partly coincided with the age of revolution, the era spanning the first rumblings of discontent in the American colonies in the 1760s and bourgeois uprisings in Europe of 1848/49. Both the ports of the New England and the vessels that sailed from them witnessed the increasing social tensions and conflicts of the era. In the 1760s and 70s many seamen (in both the navy and the merchant marine) and dock workers in such ports as Boston or Newport joined in the rioting crowds. Seamen were aware of uprisings in all corners of the Atlantic world, and vessels with all their tools and arms made militant resistance a plausible option for all involved.[93]

When seamen decided to rise up as a body, they usually did so in the form of stopping work. A strike would often be called in response to a particular grievance.[94] Captains tended to respond with harsh measures designed to break

---

[91] Vickers, "Maritime Labor in Colonial Massachusetts", 311.
[92] Busch, *Whaling Will Never Do for Me*, 25f., 30f.; Creighton, *Rites & Passages*, 94, 108; Gilje, *Liberty on the Waterfront*, 217f.; Hohman, *The American Whaleman*, 74–77. An example of the lash being used after 1850 is provided by the *Lapwing* of New Bedford, whose captain, William Weeks, had a recalcitrant seaman flogged in January 1854. (McCormick, *Two New Bedford Whalemen*, 102, 03.01.1854).
[93] Gilje, *Liberty on the Waterfront*, 127; Rediker, *Between the Devil and the Deep Blue Sea*, 237. On the circulation of knowledge about resistance among seamen in the Atlantic world see especially Linebaugh/Rediker, *The Many-Headed Hydra* and Scott, *The Common Wind*.
[94] For a powerful account of the events in the course of a strike during a stay at Saint Augustin, Madagascar see Log ISRAEL, 1841–1842, 29.08.–06.09.1842.

resistance by force, and their tactics were often successful.[95] Yet even a strike that had been put down might be effective. In November 1857 eight seamen in the *Brewster* of Mattapoisett laid down their tools after Captain Crary Waite had refused them shore leave in St Helena. Although Waite soon put an end to this protest by having the strikers bound in chains, for the remainder of the voyage, the men were granted comparatively generous shore leave at every landfall, often even being allowed to spend the night ashore.[96] What this incident reveals is that for its effect, a strike – not unlike a lashing – relied on its ability to render an abstract possibility tangible as a concrete threat and thereby to show up the power structures on board in their fragility. Bertolt Brecht aptly described this mechanism in his poem "In Praise of the Revolutionary": "Wherever they chase him, there / Will come disorder, and where they've expelled him / There will unrest remain."[97] By going on strike, seamen gave voice to a disaffection that might also express itself in the form of mass desertion or even mutiny – acts of resistance that seriously jeopardised a voyage's success. Captain Waite was therefore well advised to temper the demonstration of his power with subsequent concessions if he was to complete the voyage in the interests of the syndicate.

Mutiny in particular exerted its influence on the actors aboard ship as an imagined possibility rather than a real event. In whaling, mutinies were rare occurrence – but not so rare as not to be present at the back of everyone's mind. Captains and officers were aware of the threat mutiny posed to their lives, while crewmen were aware of the danger accusations of mutiny posed to theirs.[98] The very consciousness of the awful consequences of munity – that on the *Globe* of Nantucket in 1824 was a notorious example – influenced social dynamics on board whalers.[99] It was also common knowledge that the American took charges of mutiny very seriously indeed.[100] Against this backdrop, captains tended to label any resistance on the part of seamen as "mutinous" and entering it as such in the ship's log with a view to strengthening their position with to regard any subsequent legal action. It was this attitude that underlay the advice given by one seaman to another: "There is no justice or injustice on board ship, my lad", he explained. "There are only two things: duty and mutiny – mind that. All that you

---

95 See e.g. McCormick, *Two New Bedford Whalemen*, 102, 03.01.1854.
96 Log BREWSTER, 1857–1860, 19.11.1857.
97 Brecht, *Collected Plays: Three*, 122.
98 Gilje, *Liberty on the Waterfront*, 86, 253; Hohman, *The American Whaleman*, 64f., 198.
99 On the mutiny on the *Globe* see Heffernan, *Meuterei auf der Globe*.
100 When, for instance, the American consul in Valparaiso leant of the mutiny on the *Globe* in June 1824, he immediately informed the US Department of State, the commander-in-chief of the pacific squadron and the authorities in Nantucket (Heffernan, *Meuterei auf der Globe*, 179).

are ordered to do is duty. All that you refuse to do is mutiny."[101] Seamen minded to protest were accordingly keen to prevent being charged with mutiny, for instance by backing up stoppages with written demands.[102]

Crews sometimes found effective means of resisting abuses and arbitrary violence. Some seamen put up posters in their home ports detailing their grievances against their superiors. Aboard the schooner *Pedro Varela* of New Bedford, several men threw such essential tools as harpoons and lances, as well as part of the anchor winch, overboard by night in order to force their vessel to turn around.[103] Calling at St Helena in October 1879, seamen in the barque *Marcella* of New Bedford complained to the American consul, who had come on board, that the vessel was unseaworthy. Her captain, Frederick Tripp, had previously denied his men shore leave. The consul ordered an investigation, as a result of which the *Marcella* was indeed found unfit to sail and ordered to be unrigged. In his diary, Horace Palmer, a seaman observing these events from aboard the *Wanderer*, remarked that many whalers fell short of codified criteria of seaworthiness and that the *Marcella*'s crew seems to have taken advantage of this knowledge in order to settle its score with the captain.[104]

The considerable risks involved and the heterogeneity of the crews often stood in the way or organised resistance, making agreement on demands and action difficult to reach. What was more, the men all knew that their time on a particular vessel was limited. Although living and working conditions were hard aboard any whaler, there a relatively few recorded instances of strikes or other forms of collective resistance. In a survey of 3,336 voyages undertaken by American whaleships between 1820 and 1920, Briton C. Busch found 230 cases of collective strike action, a rate of just under seven per cent. Nearly nine out ten strikes sought to obtain shore leave, and about one in four was successful.[105]

Far more common than open revolt by many was subtle recalcitrance on the part of individuals. Seamen had many and often ingenious ways of expressing their refusal to cooperate. They might make tools disappear, mishear orders, obstruct work by making blunders, feign ignorance of one thing or another, or use any number of gestures and grimaces to register their contempt for the captain

---

[101] Quoted in Weibust, *Deep Sea Sailors*, 372.
[102] Creighton, *Rites & Passages*, 129f.; Hohman, *The American Whaleman*, 120f.
[103] A similar incident occurred on board the brig *Pavilion* of Holmes Hole near the mouth of the Congo in 1859. (Log PAVILION, 1858–1860, 10. & 12.08.1859) On resistance on the *Pedro Varela* and its aftermath see Hammond, *Mutiny on the Pedro Varela*. For another case of sabotage see Log PALMETTO, 1872–1875, 27.04.1873.
[104] McCormick, *Two New Bedford Whalemen*, 238f.
[105] Busch, *Whaling Will Never Do for Me*, 52f., 61.

and his officers. Some might be planning their escape, others the legal action they were going to bring on their return home to Massachusetts. Simply by not singing the usual shanties, seamen could do much to slow down hauling in the anchor and other communal tasks.[106] The risks seamen were willing to take in making their discontent known came down not least to individual needs and expectations. A shared experience was by no means experienced equally by all: a seaman who had previously been a plantation slave might find something liberating in life aboard ship, an aspect unlikely to be appreciated by men from more privileged backgrounds.[107]

"I would sleep while standing on my feet"

The difficulties encountered in organising collective resistance point to another important aspect on everyday life aboard a whaleship: the fragmentation of the crews. Two organisational principles profoundly divided common seamen as a category. The first was the system of watches. At the beginning of each voyage, the men aboard a whaler – as in other branches of seafaring – were split into two groups which were the principal units organising the rhythm of shipboard life and work: the starboard watch and the port watch. The first and the second mate usually assigned the men to one watch or the other on the first day at sea, directly after the captain's traditional address, by alternately selecting men to join their respective groups. For four hours at a time, each group would take over the tasks necessary to keeping the vessel going – handing, reefing and steering the sails, manning the crow's nest or taking the tiller. In order to prevent each watch from having to work the same times day after day, the 4 p.m. to 8 p.m. watch was divided into two shifts of two hours each, known as the "dog watches". The dog watches meant each watch found its shift reversed at the end of each day, the working day aboard a whaler beginning and ending with the changing of the watch at noon. This meant, for example, that if the starboard watch was assigned the work-intensive shift from 8 a.m. to noon on a Monday, that shift would be taken over by the port watch on Tuesday, again by the starboard watch on Wednesday and so on. This meant that – on paper, at any rate – seamen would alternately work ten – and fourteen-hour days. Since

---

106 Creighton, "Fraternity in the American Forecastle", 546f.; Creighton, *Rites & Passages*, 129f.; Gilje, *Liberty on the Waterfront*, 86; Hohman, *The American Whaleman*, 64f.; Vickers, "Maritime Labor in Colonial Massachusetts", 313. On the chances of successfully suing a captain see Creighton, *Rites & Passages*, 107.
107 Creighton, *Rites & Passages*, 59.

it usually fell to the first dog watch to gather in the sails and prepare the vessel for the night, there tended to remain little work to do during the second dog watch, the seamen using the time for carving, music-making, reading and other recreations.[108]

As soon as a vessel reached a whaling ground, the system of watches was supplanted by another and, as Charles Nordhoff put it, "the whole economy of the ship is changed".[109] Depending on the vessel's size, three to five groups were now formed, each headed by an officer or the captain along with a boatsteerer and with four men assigned to a boat.[110] While looking for whales, the captain would keep the vessel drifting slowly under small sails, thereby reducing the work needed for their upkeep and freeing the boat crews to divide up the shifts of the starboard and port watches as they saw fit. This also meant a shorter working day, at least in theory. Like the watches, boat crews were generally put together by officers soon upon leaving port. Unlike in the case of the watches, however, an important principle in the selection of boat crews was seniority, that is, a seaman's experience as a whaler and the skills and knowledge he had acquired during that time. Each boat crew was led by a boatsteerer or harpooner and ought to maintain a balance between more and less experienced men. The harpooner's responsibility for his boar meant that he had to ensure at all times that its weapons were sharp, its tools complete and its ropes at the ready, and that it was equipped with food, water, a compass and signalling flags in case it drifted off.[111]

---

108 Creighton, *Rites & Passages*, 60; Hohman, *The American Whaleman*, 115, 128f.; Rediker, *Between the Devil and the Deep Blue Sea*, 88. For a seaman's description of the make-up of watches and boat crews see Haley, *Whale Hunt*, 22f., for an account of activities during the second dog watch see Pinkham, *The Log Book of the Good Ship Alliance of Nantucket Captain Bartlett Coffin*, 13.12.1791.
109 Nordhoff, *Whaling and Fishing*, 93.
110 Around 1800 the average American whaler carried three boats. Larger vessels (mostly barques) carrying four boats were introduced in the 1830s and accounted for a majority of American whaleships by around 1850. See Kugler, "The Penetration of the Pacific by American Whalemen in the 19th Century", 21. On the boats see esp. Ashley, *The Yankee Whaler*, 57–64.
111 Creighton, *Rites & Passages*, 60f.; Ferguson, *Harpooner*, 25; Hohman, *The American Whaleman*, 115, 153; Thompson, "A Whaling Cruise in the 'Sea Fox'", 143. By 1800, whaleboats were being built in a manner that changed little between then and the end of American-style pelagic whaling. A whaleboat was built of wood, approximately eight metres long and equipped with a folding mast. Boats were usually clinker-built into the 1860s, when carvel-built boats were introduced. For a detailed account of these boats, which are considered milestones in the construction of rowing boats for their exceptional agility, speed and seaworthiness, see Hohman, *The American Whaleman*, 12, 156–158 and Kugler, "The Penetration of the Pacific by American Whalemen in the 19th Century", 21.

Once a whaling ground had been reached, all activities aboard ship were geared to finding quarry. Besides the two or three men on lookout, the captain or the first mate would also scan the horizon for a blow, flukes or any other sign of a whale.[112] Once a seaman had announced the discovery of a whale – for which "There she blows!" was the traditional call – everything shifted gear once more. Watches and shifts were ignored and all men sprang into action.[113] Depending on the number of whales sighted, some or all crews lowered their boats. Each of the six men in a boat had a precisely defined set of tasks. At its prow stood the harpooner. The harpoon itself was attached to the boat by a rope, and the harpooner would throw it as soon as the boat had come within about five metres of a whale. Its purpose was not to kill the whale – which in any case it could scarcely have accomplished – but rather to lodge itself in its blubber, weakening the whale and attaching it to the boat. As soon as the whale had been "fastened", the boat would try to put distance between itself and the whale to prevent being struck by its thrashing flukes. The harpooner now changed places with the boat's commander – an officer or the captain – and took over at the tiller. It was the commander's privilege to deliver the *coup de grâce* to the animal, by now much weakened by its struggle. The final blow came by lance or, from the mid-nineteenth century, a shot from a specially-designed front-loading rifle and was aimed below the neck, where vital arteries supplying the whale's lungs were situated.[114] While the boat went in pursuit of the whale, the commanding officer would spur his men into action by entreaties or curses, stoking them, to a frenzy in pursuit of their common goal.[115] The third-most important role in the boat after the harpooner and the commanding officer was that of the bowman, usually the most experienced among the common seamen. He worked one of the oars as well as handling the ropes that tied the whale to the boat by means of the harpoon. If the boat was fitted with a sail, this too was operated by the boatsteerer, at least when the quarry was to the lee side of the boat. Of the three other oarsmen, one was tasked with keeping the rope wet, which might otherwise catch fire as a result of the friction to which it was subject.[116]

---

112 Nordhoff, *Whaling and Fishing*, 94.
113 See e.g. Ferguson, *Harpooner*, 108.
114 In the 1850s, some whalers began to carry the "Greener Whaling Harpoon Gun". Its powerful recoil, however, meant that it was usually used only in sheltered bays and not on the open sea. (Kugler, "The Penetration of the Pacific by American Whalemen in the 19th Century", 21).
115 See e.g. Ely, *There She Blows*, 51.
116 Many seamen have given detailed accounts of the hunt in whaleboats, see e.g. Nordhoff, *Whaling and Fishing*, 63–65; Thompson, "A Whaling Cruise in the 'Sea Fox'", 143f.; Whitecar, *Four Years Aboard the Whaleship*, 57f.

Dividing seamen into watches and boat crews created boundaries and social distinctions even among common seamen. Watches might compete with one another "to see which was the better crew, being more careful in charge of the vessel and handing her tools over to the succeeding watch in better condition".[117] Boat crews too could serve as foci for men's identification, sometimes competing to outdo one another.[118] Even in the absence of any outright rivalry between boat crews, it comes as no great surprise to find that friendship and confidence were most likely to emerge within a given section of the crew.[119] Although common seamen occupied the same position in the shipboard hierarchy of status and shared many of the same experiences, the structural division of labour fostered the development of social sub-units, adding another dimension to the image of a whaler's hierarchy as divided into two great classes or castes. Such distinctions emerge more clearly from cultural histories, such as Margaret Creighton's, than from the works produced under the banner of "New Labor History". The latter, notably the works of Markus Rediker and Peter Linebaugh, place the class opposition between common seamen on the one hand and captains and officers at the centre of conflicts aboard ship, treating it as a microcosm of the conflict between capital and labour.[120]

Other factors contributed to tensions, conflicts and sometimes violent altercations that did not develop vertically, along the chain of command, but horizontally, among the seamen.[121] In most cases, the relative importance of personal animosities, rivalries over privileges, national or racial prejudice, conflicting or overlapping tasks, or general psychic and social stress is impossible to establish in retrospect. Crews were divided along multiple lines, and these lines would

---

117 Heimerdinger, *Der Seemann*, 51.
118 Creighton, *Rites & Passages*, 125; Rediker, *Between the Devil and the Deep Blue Sea*, 89. Such competitive relations are vividly described in e.g. Ferguson, *Harpooner*, 270 and Nordhoff, *Whaling and Fishing*, 143.
119 Busch, *Whaling Will Never Do for Me*, 16.
120 See e.g. Rediker, *Between the Devil and the Deep Blue Sea*, 242: "The struggles [. . .] can probably be described most accurately as class war: 'class' because the setting of conflict was the workplace and because the conflict grew directly out of the social relations of production, manifested between those buying and directing labor power and those selling and providing it; 'war' because the hostility and struggle between opposing forces for different ends was armed, violent, and nearly chronic." By contrast see Creighton, *Rites & Passages*, 121: "Men before the mast were separated from one another and allied to men aft by the lay system, the watch system, and the organization of boats' crews. They were also pulled apart by class, race, and ethnic divisions."
121 For descriptions of such conflicts see e.g. Ely, *There She Blows*, 30, 108.

often intersect.[122] Margaret Creighton has accordingly described a whaler's forecastle as a social kaleidoscope in which conflicting interests made it hard for common seamen to present a united front to the captain and his officers.[123] The high level of turnover among crews due to desertion, discharges and hiring men en route only compounded this difficulty.[124]

Both in the whaling grounds and on the way there and back, seamen's experience of everyday life aboard a whaler was mostly one of intense physical exertion. An idea of the effort involved emerges from Ben E. Ely's summary of three weeks' work in a whaling ground:

> I have left the ship at ten o'clock in the morning, and rowed hard in the boat until four o'clock in the afternoon; and then have worked at the windlass in cutting in the whale until three o'clock next morning.
>
> Then I have gone to work at trying out the oil, and for eighteen days in succession have worked constantly, with the allowance of five hours only out of the twenty-four for rest. I would frequently be so weary that I would sleep while standing on my feet.[125]

Such working days were very much the norm when whales had been found. After the chase, which might last four hours or more and was extremely tough work, the boats had to tow the carcass, weighting many tons, to the vessel, where it was attached to a chain by the root or "small" of the tail.[126] The vessel was not always to the windward of the quarry and hence able to sail towards its boats; often, the boats had to do the work of hauling up to fifty tons of dead whale back to the vessel by the power of their oars alone, which meant hours of back-breaking work.[127]

Then began the process of what was known to American whalemen as "cutting-in" and to their British counterparts as "flensing". This began by "scarfing", using long-handled "cutting-spades" to carve up the whale's blubber

---

[122] Dening, *The Bounty*, 28. Bolster comes to a nearly identical conclusion: "Boundary maintenance – between officers and men, between larboard and starboard watches, between idlers and watch standers, between skilled and greenhands – was the essence of life aboard ship, for boundaries delineated privileges, perquisites, and punishments. Though formal boundaries could flex to accommodate human relationships, they never entirely broke down, and they essentially defined the social combinations and conflicts at the heart of seafaring life." (Bolster, "To Feel Like a Man", 1180).
[123] Creighton, *Rites & Passages*, 136.
[124] Hohman, *The American Whaleman*, 64f. On desertion, discharge and other reasons why seamen might be left behind see the chapter "Passages III".
[125] Ely, *There She Blows*, 59f.
[126] Thompson, "A Whaling Cruise in the 'Sea Fox'", 145.
[127] Hohman, *The American Whaleman*, 166f.

(subcutaneous fatty tissue) into strips. This work was performed from a platform suspended from the starboard of the vessel; the blubber then being hoisted aboard by means of a windlass. If a sperm whale had been caught, the captain and the first mate would cut off its head in a process taking anywhere between two and four hours. The head was then hoisted aboard as a whole and the spermaceti removed in buckets by the men (Fig. 16). A sperm whale's head might contain up to thirty tons of whale oil and spermaceti of the purest kind and hence was considered the most precious part of the catch. The strips of blubber or "blanket-pieces" hoisted on board were then passed through the main hatch to the blubber room in the upper hold, where they were cut into "horse-pieces" measuring roughly forty-five by fifteen centimetres.[128] Cutting-in demanded all hands on deck, with only the briefest of breaks for food or sleep and shifts lasting twenty-four hours or more. Depending on how many whales had been taken and of what size, flensing might take several days or even a week or more. Everything and everybody on deck was soon drenched in blood and oil.[129]

After cutting-in came the process of boiling up the oil and storing it in casks, which American whalers called "trying out" and the British "making off". For this task, officers would usually divide the crews into two shifts, working day and night for six hours at a time until the job was done. The men began by making a fire under the two (sometimes three) try-pots installed to the aft of the foremast, stoking it first with wood and then with whale-hide. On a kind of anvil known as the "mincing-block", notches were then cut into the horse-pieces in order to increase their surface area and make them cook faster. Thus prepared, the "Bible-leaves" were left to cook until the oil had been released from the tissue and was ready to be placed into copper tanks or "coolers". Once it had cooled down, the oil was poured into casks and stowed in the hold.[130]

Turning a whale into whale oil took an average of seven days' long and dirty work. In addition to the ubiquitous blood and oil, the try-pots produced

---

[128] Hohman, *The American Whaleman*, 167–169; Whitecar, *Four Years Aboard the Whaleship*, 75.
[129] Ely, *There She Blows*, 61–63; Gilje, *Liberty on the Waterfront*, 76; Hohman, *The American Whaleman*, 170–172; Nordhoff, *Whaling and Fishing*, 129.
[130] Ashley, *The Yankee Whaler*, 52; Hohman, *The American Whaleman*, 172f. Whalers used "casks" much larger than the "barrels" which had been standardised since 1706 to hold 31.5 gallons. A cask of the kind used aboard whalers held up to four times the volume of a barrel, over one hundred gallons. In order to use the space of the hold to its full advantage, however, vessels also carried smaller casks, known as hogsheads or ryers, holding two barrels, as well as larger ones, tuns, which held eight. Since the measure used is not always clear in the sources, the amounts of oil involved cannot always be precisely stated. (Ashley, *The Yankee Whaler*, 97; Chatwin, "A Trade so Uncontrollably Uncertain", iv–v; Jarman, *Journal of a Voyage to the South Seas*, 254 n. 23).

immense heat as well as black smoke that coated all surfaces and an acrid stench combining the odours of boiling oil and burning hide.[131] As Ben E. Ely wrote of this work, "Few can imagine how our crew appeared, when every one's person was covered with oil from head to foot, and every face was blackened by the smoke of the furnaces employed in trying blubber, and with iron rust, from the hoops of our casks."[132]

Work aboard a whaleship reached its highest degree of intensity when there were whales to be killed and processed. But there was no shortage of work during the remaining time, either. Since whalers tended to be exposed to the elements for longer periods at a time than merchant vessels and hence had to do more "work" themselves – meaning that their planking was under constant strain from the sea and its movements – seamen accordingly had to spend more time making repairs and adjustments. An unpopular task not required aboard merchantmen was keeping lookout from the top of the main mast or "standing mastheads", which demanded absolute concentration from a man while he was alone and unprotected against the weather.[133] Since many vessels lacked a proper crow's nest or even a platform or similar structure, the lookout often had no choice but to suspend themselves as best they could from the royal yard.[134]

The size of a whaler's crew depended on the number of seamen needed to fill all its boats – more, in any case, than were needed merely to keep the vessel afloat. At times when the crew was not engaged in the pursuit or processing of whales, them there was a relative surplus of labour on board. A 350-ton brig, for example, which as a merchantman could have been run with a crew of twelve, was crewed with thirty-five men when used as a whaleship. This overcrewing was a benefit as far as the seamen were concerned, meaning as it did that some tasks could be performed under less pressure and hence also less dangerously, for instance in a rough sea.[135]

Captains and syndicates naturally took a less positive view of this excess of labour. Following the adage whereby "the devil makes work for idle hands", crews with little to do for weeks or months on end were thought particularly

---

[131] Hohman, *The American Whaleman*, 172f. Since the smoke given off by the tryworks blackened sails, masts and yardarms, seasoned seamen aboard other vessels were able to tell whether a whaler had already been successful by how sooty it was. (Hohman, *The American Whaleman*, 175).
[132] Ely, *There She Blows*, 63.
[133] Ferguson, *Harpooner*, 27; Gilje, *Liberty on the Waterfront*, 69; Hohman, *The American Whaleman*, 155; McCormick, *Two New Bedford Whalemen*, 107, 21.07.1855.
[134] Ashley, *The Yankee Whaler*, 6.
[135] Busch, *Whaling Will Never Do for Me*, 8; Gilje, *Liberty on the Waterfront*, 75; Hohman, *The American Whaleman*, 11f.; Whitecar, *Four Years Aboard the Whaleship*, 49f.

prone to recalcitrance, and it certainly was true that boredom and monotony exacerbated discontent among seamen.[136] Officers and masters thus contrived to have a seemingly infinite store of more or less necessary chores to keep the crew busy at all times. There were tools to be oiled, ropes to be spliced and tarred, harpoons to be sharpened, bilges to be pumped out, sails to be mended, boats to be tarred and painted, casks to be checked for leaks and – every day – decks to be swabbed.[137] Shipowners would, moreover, often allow whalers to sail before they had been fully refitted and let the crew do the work along the way in an effort to save costs. Men might, for instance, have to cover the deck in a layer of pine planks in order to protect them from the wear and tear of cutting up whales and to outfit the boats for the hunt.[138] Captains would often order further repairs and refits on the homeward leg in order to present as pristine a vessel as possible to the syndicate. Work was thus more than usually hard during the first and last weeks of a voyage.[139]

It is due in large part to the pronounced routine character of many of these shipboard tasks that historians have wondered whether a seaman's experience of work might be thought of as prefiguring that of a factory worker or an industrial wage-earner. The claim that the factory in its industrial and capitalist sense revealed itself aboard vessels as early as the sixteenth century has been most forcefully argued by Marcus Rediker. According to Rediker, seamen experienced exploitation of their labour in a form that bore essential features of industrial capitalism – notably shift-work, the ubiquity of supervision and control, the concentration of labour in a confined and relatively isolated location, strict discipline, and a division of labour that is both complex and hierarchical, broken down into precisely coordinated and synchronised tasks.[140] Other historians, including Daniel Vickers and Roland Schultz, have

---

136 Creighton, *Rites & Passages*, 72; Rediker, "The Common Seaman in the Histories of Capitalism and the Working Class", 344; Leek, Journal DELTA, 1836–1838, 25.12.1836.
137 Rediker, *Between the Devil and the Deep Blue Sea*, 95. For a seaman's account of such shipboard experiences see Eldridge, *Lewis William Eldridge's Whaling Voyage*, 1.
138 Ashley, *The Yankee Whaler*, 5; McCormick, *Two New Bedford Whalemen*, 84; Nordhoff, *Whaling and Fishing*, 43f., 54; Palmer, "The Diary of a Foremast Hand on the First Voyage of the Bark Wanderer", 4.
139 Gilje, *Liberty on the Waterfront*, 69; McCormick, *Two New Bedford Whalemen*, 228.
140 Linebaugh/Rediker, *The Many-Headed Hydra*, 149f.; Rediker, *Between the Devil and the Deep Blue Sea*, 83, 206, 290, 293; Rediker, "The Common Seaman in the Histories of Capitalism and the Working Class", 339. With regard to the organization of work aboard early modern vessels, Treinen too speaks of a "structure familiar to us from industrial enterprises." (Treinen, "Parasitäre Anarchie", 83) Alan Rice has extended the analogy of work aboard ship and industrial wage labour to include slave vessels. (Rice, *Radical Narratives of the Black Atlantic*, 59).

Fig. 16: Seamen bailing the spermaceti from the "case" or head of a sperm whale. The American artist and author Clifford Warren Ashely accompanied the barque *Sunbeam* in 1904 and took this photograph in the north Atlantic in September of that year. It gives an idea both of the physical demands imposed by work aboard a whaleship and of the importance of black labour in the late stage of American whaling.
Courtesy of the New Bedford Whaling Museum.

questioned this analogy, arguing that seafaring work bore a closer resemblance to work on a plantation or as a soldier.[141] The debate continues, and while this is not the place to conclude it, it does seem reasonable to state that a whaleship was much more like a factory than was, for instance, a merchantman, encompassing as it did an integrated process of production from the extraction of an organic resource to its processing into large quantities of fuel and lubricants.

Life and limb, holding on and spewing up

Greg Dening has observed that "A sailing vessel is a machine energized by natural forces and human vigor. Power so harnessed gives every part of a ship a trembling, beating life that transmits itself to the bodies of the sailors and all their senses. Sailors feel the rhythm, hear it, smell it, see it, have the language to describe it."[142] If we take seamen's descriptions as our benchmark, we must soon notice the prominence of a sense missing from Dening's list, namely that of taste. Food and drink were among the aspects of shipboard life that were foremost in seamen's minds. Most of their comments will be found to resemble those of Horace Palmer, who recorded this in his diary while sailing in the barque *Wanderer* of New Bedford in December 1879:

> As it is now, the food that is furnished foremast hands, would be refused by the meanest vagrant to be found crying for bread at the back door of the poor house and even such as it is, it is dealt out so sparingly that we are always hungry and, like Oliver Twist, always yearning for more.[143]

Nearly all seamen found the food on board to be inadequate: it was unwholesome, lacking variety and there was too little of it. As to the causes, there can be little doubt: Mid-nineteenth-century shipowners were more than parsimonious when it came to feeding crews, spending no more than fifteen to thirty cents per man and day on food. The "doctor" was not usually a trained cook, and captains tried to keep victualling stops to a minimum in an effort to save time and money. A law passed in 1790 obliged American whalers to carry sufficient provisions for the duration of a voyage.[144] The barrels in which food was

---

141 On the controversy surrounding this question see esp. the first issue of the *International Journal of Maritime History* (1989), which collects a number of viewpoints.
142 Dening, *Deep Times, Deep Spaces*, 25.
143 Qtd. in McCormick, *Two New Bedford Whalemen*, 248.
144 Busch, *Whaling Will Never Do for Me*, 13f.; Creighton, *Rites & Passages*, 95; Hohman, *The American Whaleman*, 71, 130. The average voyage of an American whaler lasted six weeks in the 1750s, four and a half months around 1770, twenty-nine months around 1820 and forty-two

stored, however, and in which it was taken on board before sailing were able to keep food from spoiling only for a few weeks. In the later stages of a voyage, meals accordingly were increasingly likely to consist of ingredients that were stale, in a state of partial decomposition or riddled with vermin.[145] The men nonetheless had no choice but to eat what the captain set in front of them.[146] If, moreover, the whale hunt proved unsuccessful, matters were only made worse by the pressure from syndicates to cut losses by saving on food. This gave rise to a dynamic described in the following terms by the journalist Christopher Slocum, who sailed aboard the *Obed Mitchell* of Nantucket in the 1840s:

> If the ship hapens [sic] to be out eight or ten months without being successful the captain becomes restless and is fearful of having to procure provisions at the expense of the owners or be obliged to return home before the ship is full.
>
> He then begins curtailing their provisions by a fixed allowance in this situation the crew half famished and exposed to the abuse and curses of the captain and officers they are in a sad state indeed.[147]

The staple food on board whaleships was "hardtack", a hard bread made of flour, water and salt. Old hands would crumble it into rum or hot water, or carefully tap it in order to remove the vermin that commonly infested the bread barrels. Then there was pork or beef, preserved by drying and stored in barrels of salt. Even when soaked in water for days, it was so tough, dry and salty that it was known to seamen as "salt jack" or "salt junk". Like the bread, the meat too attracted vermin and before very long was partly or wholly spoilt.[148] Ben Ely recalls that whenever the cook opened a "fresh" barrel of meat, a nauseating, putrid stench would spread throughout the vessel.[149]

For breakfast (7 a.m.), lunch (noon) and supper (5. p.m.), common seamen could expect to be served hardtack, salt horse and a bucket of tea and coffee, along with molasses as a sweetener. In addition, boatsteerers might sometimes receive potatoes, and officers butter, sugar, softer bread and sometimes minced meat. Once a week, for the sake of a change, the cook might prepare a "duff", a

---

months in the mid-nineteenth century. (Hohman, *The American Whaleman*, 86; Vickers, "Maritime Labor in Colonial Massachusetts", 270).
145 Hohman, *The American Whaleman*, 132f.
146 See e.g. Davoll, *The Captain's Specific Orders on the Commencement of a Whale Voyage to his Officers and Crew*, 8–10, 14.
147 Qtd. in Sherman, *The Voice of the Whaleman*, 41.
148 Currie, *Thar She Blows*, 37–39; Eldridge, *Lewis William Eldridge's Whaling Voyage*, 5; Gilje, *Liberty on the Waterfront*, 78; Hohman, *The American Whaleman*, 132f.
149 Ely, *There She Blows*, 9.

pudding made with flour, lard and yeast. Boiled or steamed in salt water, the duff was served with lard or molasses.[150] The captain and his officers dined in the captain's cabin, where they were served by the steward. When they had finished, the table was given over to the boatsteerers. Common seamen, by contrast, took their meals in the forecastle from a large communal vat or "kid". The famished men would often jostle for the food (Fig. 17), leading some crews to arrange for an equitable division of the contents to prevent brawling.[151]

Understandably, seamen seized any opportunity to add some variety to this tedious diet. Wherever they called, vessels would usually take on board large quantities of fruit and vegetables, to be either shared out or divided among the crew.[152] Whalers would also take on live animals to have fresh meat as required. Some captains would have an animal slaughtered for Christmas, Independence Day or Thanksgiving – usually the only holidays kept aboard American whalers. Pigs and chickens were most frequently found in vessels, though goats and cattle were no rarity, either.[153] Since a whaler's complement also included a ship's cat – to keep the inevitable mice and rats in check – and sometimes a dog, crews might find themselves competing for space with quite a few animals.[154]

Particularly in the Indian Ocean but also in the Atlantic and Pacific, seamen would catch turtles and tortoises. Unlike the other animals taken on board, these reptiles could survive for months and sometimes years, and the soup which seamen made from them was considered a delicacy.[155] A popular spot for catching turtles were the uninhabited islands in the Mozambique Channel, such as Bassas da India and Europa Island, where the men could also gather large quantities of birds' eggs.[156] While cruising, seamen might often harpoon dolphins, porpoises and pilot whales, which would sometimes accompany vessels for miles at a time.

---

[150] Hohman, *The American Whaleman*, 131.
[151] Gilje, *Liberty on the Waterfront*, 77; Hohman, *The American Whaleman*, 133–135.
[152] Gilje, *Liberty on the Waterfront*, 78; for an illustrative account in a logbook see e.g. Log BERTHA, 1883–1887, 02.03.1885.
[153] Barker, *Thrilling Adventures of the Whaler Alcyone*, 21f; McCormick, *Two New Bedford Whalemen*, 146, 25.07.1868. On the observance (or not) of holidays aboard American whaleship see Busch, *Whaling Will Never Do for Me*, 161–164, 167.
[154] Since rats were able to cause leaks by gnawing at a ship's timbers, the ship's cat had an important part to play in preventing costly refits. To lose a cat to accident or disease thus presented a major problem and was recorded as such in the logbook (see e.g. Log EMERALD, 1838–1840, 12.09.1838).
[155] See e.g. Barker, *Thrilling Adventures of the Whaler Alcyone*, 22f.; Log EMERALD, 1838–1840, 26. & 27.06.1838; Whitecar, *Four Years Aboard the Whaleship*, 96f.
[156] See e.g. Ferguson, *Harpooner*, 71; Log KATHLEEN, 1880–1884, 10.–12.06.1881; Log OHIO, 1862–1854, 02. & 07.–08.10.1863.

Captains would sometimes even lower the boats for the sake of pilot whales, whose jaws contained an oil considered precious and used, for example, by watchmakers. Captains and officers generally took a favourable view of such diversions, which kept the men in practice for the actual hunt. Dolphin meat was minced and formed into little balls, which were deep fried and served, when possible, with onions. The tastiest cuts of the pilot whale were thought to be the loin, liver and (again, deep fried) brain.[157]

Sailors also took advantage of periods of lying becalmed or cruising in placid waters for fishing. Catching a longhorn cowfish or an ocean sunfish not only brought variety to the seamen's diet, but was also a curiosity in its own right and as such worth logging.[158] In the tropical and subtropical parts of the south Atlantic, flying fish might land on deck, which were much appreciated deep fried. Crews would sometimes seek to lure them aboard by placing a lantern in the rigging at night.[159] By contrast, most seamen shunned the meat of the whales they caught. Naturally enough, it occurred to some captains to cut costs by feeding their crews on whale meat, which was available by the ton but economically useless.[160] Yet even when minced and deep fried, whale meat was considered exceptionally tough, ill-tasting and indigestible – so much so that many men preferred even salt meat to fresh whale meat.[161]

Since water too had to be stored in casks over long periods and would gradually spoil, developing a repellent odour, seamen would sweeten it with molasses and cut it with tea and coffee. The resulting beverage, known as "longlick", while not exactly pleasant-tasting in itself, had the benefit of counteracting the foulness of the food. From the dawning of the age of American-style pelagic whaling, vessels would also carry stores of rum, whisky and other alcoholic beverages, of which every seaman received a ration from the captain.[162] The health and social

---

[157] Ashley, The Yankee Whaler, 8f.; Barker, Thrilling Adventures of the Whaler Alcyone, 45–48; Eldridge, Lewis William Eldridge's Whaling Voyage, 6f.; Ferguson, Harpooner, 43; Log EMERALD, 1838–1840, 05.07.1838; Pinkham, The Log Book of the Good Ship Alliance of Nantucket Captain Bartlett Coffin, 06.12.1791 & 18.01.1792; Spears, "The Log of the Bark Emily", 247.
[158] See e.g. Log BERTHA, 1883–1887, 28.02.1885; Ely, There She Blows, 73; Ferguson, Harpooner, 49.
[159] See e.g. Barker, Thrilling Adventures of the Whaler Alcyone, 17; Stewart, "Journal Aboard the Brig JOHN H. JONES of Cold Spring Harbor", 5; Whitecar, Four Years Aboard the Whaleship, 50.
[160] Williams, The Adventures of a Seventeen-year-old Lad and the Fortunes He Might Have Won, 45.
[161] See e.g. Nordhoff, Whaling and Fishing, 130.
[162] Hohman, The American Whaleman, 132f., 136.

risks of regular drinking had to be balanced against its benefits: alcohol provided comfort amid the strains of unrelenting work, some drinks (notably beer) had nutritional value in themselves, and drinking together might ideally help the men to bond with one another. In surroundings in which distinctions between work and leisure, public and private were impossible to maintain, drinking could provide at least emotional relief from the strains of shipboard life.[163]

Fig. 17: Food is served on the foredeck in an illustration from Browne's memoir.
Source: Browne, *Etchings of a Whaling Cruise*, 143.

In the 1820s, such evangelical reform movements as the Boston Society for the Religious and Moral Improvement of Seamen or the American Seaman's Friend Society began to campaign for a ban on alcohol aboard ships, holding it responsible for vice in all its forms. More and more American whalers in the 1830s – and probably most by the 1840s – sailed as "temperance ships" carrying no liquor on board. This is said already to have applied to some three quarters of New Bedford Whalers in the early 1830s. Being declared a temperance ship did not, however, reliably indicate the absence of alcohol on board. Shipowners welcomed the temperance movement for providing them with a handy cost-cutting measure, saving them the purchase of rum and whisky by the

---

163 Gilje, *Liberty on the Waterfront*, 78; Pope, "Rev. of Marcus Rediker", 333; Rediker, *Between the Devil and the Deep Blue Sea*, 192f.

barrel, while turning a blind eye to seamen bringing their own supplies on board – at their own expense.[164]

***

In February 1841, the log of the *Charles Carroll* of Nantucket recorded that "One of our harpooniers a negro named Peter Sands was fishing off the martingales and fell overboard". In spite of the crew's best efforts, the story had a sad ending: "we cleared away and lowered the larboard boat but unfortunately for him he could not swim and before the boat got to him he sank and we saw him no more."[165] Such accidents reminded seamen of the ubiquity of mortal danger and were among the elementary experiences of whaling.[166] Storms and other forces of nature meant that the threat of a watery grave hung over every vessel that took to the high seas, and it took only an unexpectedly high wave crashing onto the deck to carry a man overboard.[167] Since whalers would sometimes follow their quarry into uncharted waters, they were more likely to come across unfamiliar reefs, crags and shallows than merchant vessels.[168] The whaling grounds in the western Indian Ocean, for example, near the Seychelles, were notorious for their perilous coral reefs. It was here that the *Foster* (1846) and the *Osceola II* (1872) of New Bedford were shipwrecked, as were the *Nautilus* (1858) and the *Hecla* (1870) of Nantucket.[169] In the Atlantic, a known danger zone was the Skeleton Coast in the north of modern Namibia, where breakers might strike a vessel unawares in the midst of dense fog and smash it against the rocky shore.[170]

The fact that even in the choppiest seas seamen were constantly handling sharp weapons, heavy tools and boiling oil meant that injuries were commonplace.[171] Falls from the rigging toppling casks in the dark hold or mishaps with

---

164 Creighton, *Rites & Passages*, 96f.; Gilje, *Liberty on the Waterfront*, 215; Hohman, *The American Whaleman*, 136. Aboard the *Emigrant*, supposedly a temperance ship, Ben Ely noticed that Captain Sherman got through no less than a barrel of gin in the course of a three-year journey. (Ely, *There She Blows*, 67f.) For an overview of the American temperance movement see Gassert/Häberlein/Wala, *Kleine Geschichte der USA*, 258–266.
165 Log CHARLES CARROLL, 1840–1843, 09.02.1841.
166 Rediker, *Between the Devil and the Deep Blue Sea*, 94, 154.
167 See e.g. Jarman, *Journal of a Voyage to the South Seas*, 129, Stewart, "Journal Aboard the Brig JOHN H. JONES of Cold Spring Harbor", 5.
168 Hohman, *The American Whaleman*, 183f., 193f.
169 "Merchants' Transcript." *Whalemen's Shipping List and Merchants' Transcript*, 26.10.1847: 136; Lund et al., *American Offshore Whaling Voyages*, 218f., 269, 428, 457.
170 See ch. 1, "Walvis Bay".
171 See e.g. Atkins, Log POLLEY, 10. & 17.08.1774.

cutting-spades might end a life in an instant. These risks were compounded by the inexperience of many of the men. Uriah Bunker, who lost his grip on the mizzenmast of the *Alliance* of Nantucket and came crashing down, receiving severe injuries to his head and arm, was aged only sixteen at the time of the accident.[172] Many, perhaps most seamen – and certain most of the American "green hands" – had grown up far inland, were unable to swim and knew little of the sea. They in particular were in danger from its unpredictability – all the more so if they fell in.[173]

The greatest danger, however, was posed by chasing whales in boats, not least because boats would be lowered even into stormy seas.[174] Unsecured harpoons might fall about in the process, injuring seamen.[175] As soon as the harpooner had struck home, the boat was exposed to a force of many tons, under which conditions even minor slip-ups, distractions and miscalculations might be fatal.[176] The clumsiness of an inexperienced green hand or the bravado of an ambitious officer might prove equally dangerous, putting entire boat crews at risk. To get caught in a fast uncoiling rope or to be struck by a broken rope could be fatal.[177]

No less fatal were the risks of direct contact with whales. Boats would try to approach their quarry from outside its field of vision, either "head to head" or from behind, "over the flukes". But as soon as a whale was struck by a harpoon, it would often begin to flail about wildly and might well cause the boat to capsize.[178] The risk of accident, however, did not remain constant. As early as 1858, William B. Whitecar observed that diminishing returns in the whaling industry led officers and boatsteerers into taking ever greater risks to match their predecessors bags. Meanwhile, the pressure to economise was also making itself felt in the quality of the equipment.[179]

In a desperate bid to escape, a harpooned whale would often tow the boat along at a considerable speed, sometimes for several hours at a time and over distance of several miles. In June 1882 Robert Ferguson, a harpooner aboard the *Kathleen* of New Bedford and cruising at the time off the coast of Angola,

---

[172] Dickson, "The Cruise of the Nantucket Ships 'Asia' and 'Alliance'", 9.
[173] Helen C. Allen "When I Went a-Whaling." New Bedford Whaling Museum, Manuscript Collections: KWM 402B. 8; Gilje, *Liberty on the Waterfront*, 79.
[174] Nordhoff, *Whaling and Fishing*, 166.
[175] See e.g. Thompson, "A Whaling Cruise in the 'Sea Fox'", 145.
[176] Hohman, *The American Whaleman*, 183f.
[177] See e.g. McCormick, *Two New Bedford Whalemen*, 182, 09.07.1879.
[178] See e.g. Jarman, *Journal of a Voyage to the South Seas*, 57f.
[179] Whitecar, *Four Years Aboard the Whaleship*, 340–344; see also Busch, *Whaling Will Never Do for Me*, 88.

observed that a stricken humpback whale "goes away as fast as it can go, dragging the boat after it with the speed of an express train."[180] This was known to seamen as a "Nantucket sleigh ride", but the term's merry ring conceals the deadly seriousness of a situation in which a whale might suddenly make a dive and drag the pursuing boat down with it.[181]

Less frequent but no less dangerous were direct attacks by whales on boats. Whales might occasionally hit a boat or a man inside it with their flukes, and humpback whales could also lash out with their long pectoral fins.[182] The greatest danger, however, was a "stove boat", when a boat was damaged or smashed by a blow from a whale's fins or flukes.[183] Sperm whales tended to put up a particularly ferocious fight and might also attack a boat by ramming or biting down on it.[184] As Charles Smith, first mate of the barque *Sunbeam* of New Bedford, remarked in 1904, the sperm whale "fights at both ends".[185] It was no rarity for members of a boat crew – or indeed all of them – to be killed in such attacks.[186] For the mothership to be sunk after being rammed by a whale was a less frequent occurrence, but such stories loomed large in seamen's imaginations. Confirmed cases are those of the *Harmony* of Rochester (1796), the *Ann Alexander* of Dartmouth (1805), the *Essex* of Nantucket (1820), the *Acushnet* of Mattapoisett (1840) and the *Kathleen* of New Bedford (1902).[187]

Besides a "stove boat", what whalemen feared most was being towed out of sight of their vessel by a whale. When that happened, a boat crew might have to spend the night on the open sea – and sometimes hold out days or even weeks.[188] Although boats were prepared for such eventualities – which were far from infrequent, especially in heavy seas – and carried provisions, navigational instruments and lanterns, lost boats were not always recovered. Cases are

---

180 Ferguson, *Harpooner*, 130.
181 Hohman, *The American Whaleman*, 160f.; Jarman, *Journal of a Voyage to the South Seas*, 9.
182 See e.g. Ferguson, *Harpooner*, 130; Jarman, *Journal of a Voyage to the South Seas*, 200f.; Leek, Journal DELTA, 1836–1838, 16.12.1836; Look 2.
183 See e.g. Jarman, *Journal of a Voyage to the South Seas*, 172.
184 See e.g. Chippendale, *Sails and Whales*, 85.
185 Ashley, *The Yankee Whaler*, 9. In one such instance, a breaching sperm whale smashed a boat belonging to the barque *Bertha* of New Bedford of the coast of Angola in 1886. (Log BERTHA, 1883–1887, 09.08.1886.)
186 Hohman, *The American Whaleman*, 13. For an impressive account of a deadly attack by a sperm whale in the seas near Mauritius see Beane, *From Forecastle to Cabin*, 148.
187 Lund et al., *American Offshore Whaling Voyages*, 21f., 52, 199f., 265, 337f.
188 Such a fate befell, for instance, a boat belonging to the schooner *Alfred* of New Bedford. (Log KATHLEEN, 1852–1855, 23.08.1854.) For a further account of such an incident see Ely, *There She Blows*, 55f.

known in which men whose boats had got lost were so desperate with hunger and thirst that they saw no choice but to eat the flesh of those who had died before them – or even to kill for that purpose, as in the case of boats gone adrift from the *Essex* of Nantucket (1820) and the *Janet* of Westport (1849).[189]

Whalemen faced life-threatening risks not only when chasing whales, but also when processing the whales they had captured and killed. The blood and flesh that spread around the vessel in the process of cutting-up attracted countless sharks,[190] which not only consumed a considerable portion of the whale,[191] but also posed a serious threat to the man perched on the slippery, half-submerged carcass, to which he had to attach a winch hook even in the heaviest of seas. Sharks would sometimes inflict severe bites on men in that position, an example being recorded aboard the *Clarkson* of Nantucket in December 1841.[192] In order to minimise the danger to themselves, whalemen would often kill as many sharks as they could before flensing began.[193]

Besides being attacked by whales, working on the carcass came with the risk of being caught between it and the vessel, of being struck by a stray winch hook or of losing one's footing and falling into the blade of a cutting-spade.[194] A further danger when cutting in was slipping on a deck slick with blood and oil or, worse still, being struck by a loose cask in a rolling sea.[195] The tryworks, when in use, were also a dangerous place to be. The oil was prone to explode on contact with seawater, and sparks from the furnace also presented an obvious fire hazard. Since sailing vessels were built largely of highly flammable materials and the deck of a whaleship tended to be steeped in oil, fires were hard to put out and could destroy a vessel in no time.[196]

---

189 Hohman, *The American Whaleman*, 13, 165f., 183f., 189f. The sinking of the *Essex* has been much researched; for an overview aimed at a general readership see Philbrick, *In the Heart of the Sea*.
190 See e.g. Whitecar, *Four Years Aboard the Whaleship*, 94.
191 See e.g. Log GLOBE, 1869–1872, 26.08.1870 and Log LOUISA SEARS, 1856–1858, 19.08.1857. When, in June 1882, the men of the *Kathleen* had taken a sperm whale off the coast of Angola, but were unable to process it till the next day as night was rapidly falling, they woke to find that sharks had left them only bones. (Ferguson, *Harpooner*, 132).
192 Log CLARKSON, 1838–1842, 08.12.1841; on the dangers posed by sharks when cutting in see Ferguson, *Harpooner*, 18, 24.
193 See e.g. Ferguson, *Harpooner*, 134; Jarman, *Journal of a Voyage to the South Seas*, 63f.
194 Hohman, *The American Whaleman*, 170–172; Jarman, *Journal of a Voyage to the South Seas*, 207.
195 See e.g. Smith, *A Narrative of the Life, Travels, and Sufferings of Thomas W. Smith*, 166f.
196 Hohman, *The American Whaleman*, 183f.; Pinkham, *The Log Book of the Good Ship Alliance of Nantucket Captain Bartlett Coffin*, 23.12.1792. For examples of whaleships lost to fire see Hohman, *The American Whaleman*, 193f.

Sailors aboard whaling vessels experienced potentially lethal dangers as a permanent threat – a threat, moreover, that was constantly being brought home to them by frequent accidents. This could barely leave them cold. A consciousness of the perils they had jointly undergone became an important part of whalemen's self-perception as a group and was expressed in the motto – still to be found inscribed on a statue in the centre of New Bedford – "A dead whale or a stove boat!"[197]

Particularly aboard American whalers, illness was as deadly a risk as accidents. Whereas British whalers were obliged by law to have a surgeon or a medically-trained officer on crew, the corresponding American law of 1790 stipulated only that a medicine chest be carried on board. The treatment of sick seamen fell to responsibility of the captain who, however, generally lacked both expert knowledge and surgical tools.[198] Little wonder, then, that seamen had many a story tell of botched treatments and their dire consequences – precipitate amputations, for instance, or the case of the captain whose kept his medicines in numbered phials: when he ran out of remedy number twelve, he prepared a mixture of numbers five and seven in the hope of producing the same effect.[199]

Caution is due when making claims about sickness and health aboard whaleships. One problem is the fact that experiences of the body are themselves historically contingent, the notorious difficulty of retrospective diagnosis is another.[200] It is striking how often ships' logs give diseases much feared at the time – "consumption", for instance (most probably tuberculosis) – as the cause of illness or death. Lesser-known or noticed diseases – such as mental and psychological conditions – are, by contrast, almost wholly absent.[201] One condition, however, whose diagnosis has been relatively immune to the changing currents of medical history and which was described then much as it is now is seasickness. On their first voyage, in particular, many men suffered from seasickness in consequence of the vessel's rolling and pitching. Weathering this first bout of seasickness accordingly marked a rite of passage, of a novice's

---

197 Whitecar, *Four Years Aboard the Whaleship*, 130f.
198 Busch, *Whaling Will Never Do for Me*, 16; Creighton, *Rites & Passages*, 95; Hohman, *The American Whaleman*, 71, 136f. For an annotated inventory of a medicine chest see Schmitt, *Mark Well the Whale!*, 144.
199 Ellis, "Whaling, Traditional", 1249; Warrin, *So Ends This Day*, 50f.
200 On the challenges of historicising disease see Leven, "Krankheiten".
201 A qualification is due with regard to mental illness, for the distinction between mental and physical illness became established only gradually in the course of the eighteenth century and many seamen would have been likely to seek somatic causes for all their complaints. On the history of the dichotomy between mental and physical illness see Stolberg, "Der gesunde Leib".

transformation into a seaman.[202] For centuries, scurvy was as constant a companion of navigation on the high seas as seasickness. Since the effectiveness of citrus fruit in preventing the disease had been known since the mid-eighteenth century, scurvy was a less frequent occurrence by the dawning of the age of American-style pelagic whaling. But this awareness alone did not mean that it had been beaten, and whaling crews in particular – who often spent months on end away from dry land, subsisting largely on hardtack and salt horse – remained prone to the disease.[203]

No less feared by whalemen than scurvy were infectious diseases, for the spread of which the cramped conditions of the forecastle, the dirty and bloody work of cutting-in, the stagnant drinking water and the poor ventilation below deck offered nearly ideal conditions. Diarrhoea and dysentery, influenza and tuberculosis seem to have been constant companions on many a voyage.[204] The most dangerous infections, however, were smallpox and yellow fever, with the latter in particular causing frequent epidemics in port cities, notably in the 1790s on the east coast of the United States. Smallpox or yellow fever were not only threatening to life of the seamen who caught them, but were also capable of spreading so quickly that there might not be enough healthy seamen on board to steer the vessel into the nearest harbour. Captains were accordingly wary of any rumours or reports of outbreaks and avoided calling at ports where smallpox or yellow fever were known to be rife.[205] Besides yellow fever, the coastal areas of Africa harboured other dangerous tropical diseases, particularly malaria.[206]

Like so much else aboard a whaler, the treatment of diseases and diseases was a question of class. Considerable detours might be made in order to allow the captain or the first mate to receive the pest possible medical attention. In June 1843, for instance, Robert Borden, master of the *Sally Ann* of New Bedford, ordered his vessel to sail more than two thousand nautical miles from Anjouan

---

[202] Creighton, *Rites & Passages*, 59; Gilje, *Liberty on the Waterfront*, 81.
[203] Hohman, *The American Whaleman*, 138f. Not all seamen were convinced of the benefits of citrus fruit in the prevention and treatment of scurvy. Seamen of the Royal Navy, who were made to take a daily ration of lime juice, were mocked by their American counterparts as "limejuicers" – hence the term "limey".
[204] Currie, *Thar She Blows*, 43.
[205] This was why, in August 1881, Captain Howland of the *Kathleen* cancelled shore leave for his crew in Zanzibar. (Ferguson, *Harpooner*, 94.)
[206] When, for instance, the barque *A.R. Tucker* of Dartmouth left Zanzibar after two weeks in port in December 1858, nearly the entire crew was down with fever within two days. (Log A. R. TUCKER, 1857–1861, 23.–26.12.1858.) On probable cases of malaria on the coast of Madagascar see e.g. Log GEORGE WASHINGTON, 1848–1849, 26.04.1849.

to find a hospital in Cape Town after he had broken his leg harpooning a whale.[207] By contrast, common seamen who fell ill or sustained severe injuries could not as a rule expect their vessel to change course. As far as captains were concerned, men who were unable to work were little more than costly ballast to be discharged at the next possible stop. Though they might be lucky enough to find a hospital there, they would have to meet the expenses themselves.[208]

Accidents and illnesses, punishments and disciplinary measures, hard physical work and a poor diet, and – by no means least – constant exposure to the elements left both physical and psychological marks on seamen.[209] The way in which whaling inscribed itself permanently on their often young bodies and subjecting them to the constant threat injury and disease was an experience that brought together, and did so not infrequently even in the early days at sea. Ben Ely, for instance, describes his first weeks aboard the *Emigrant* as "painful beyond description": "My hands were very tender, and for weeks after I sailed they were blistered and raw, so that when I hauled on a rope I would leave the marks of my hands in blood." Ely also remembered that he would sometimes cough up blood after days on end of hard work.[210]

Captains and officers exercised their power as a regime of the body. Ideas of order and discipline were translated into physical experience by means of spatial control and segregation – as well as by inflicting injuries that were both palpable and visible. Power relations on board a whaleship were represented in seamen's bodies, of which captains and officers took symbolic charge by both verbal and non-verbal communication. But seamen's bodies were not merely subjects of control, drill, discipline and subjugation. In joint rhythmical movements of the kind used in setting the sails or weighing anchor, often accompanied by the singing of shanties, common seamen gave physical expression to their sense of community as distinct from that of the captain and his officers.[211]

Whether it was on account of accident, disease or corporal punishment, many a seaman never returned from his voyage in a whaleship. Death aboard ship was never an impersonal event. It was visible to all, and to all it vividly

---

207 "Merchants' Transcript." *Whalemen's Shipping List and Merchants' Transcript*, 28.11.1843, 346.
208 Hohman, *The American Whaleman*, 138.
209 Rediker, *Between the Devil and the Deep Blue Sea*, 11; Hohman, *The American Whaleman*, 200; and more broadly on the relationship between the body, its environment and its past Foucault, *Von der Subversion des Wissens*, 91.
210 Ely, *There She Blows*, 39.
211 Edwards/Walser, "Sea Music", 400–403; Gilje, *Liberty on the Waterfront*, 81; Heimerdinger, *Der Seemann*, 18.

brought home the fragility of life at sea.[212] Having been socialised as Christians, most seamen considered proper burial to be necessary for eternal peace. Yet as seamen, they also thought it bad luck to carry corpses. A burial on land was thus only to be considered when the vessel was near the coast at the time – all the more so because a funeral and a burial plot meant expenses for which the captain would be accountable to the vessel's owners. (The burial in St Paul's churchyard in St Helena of Captain Edward Mayhew, who died in April 1857 in command of the barque *Louisa Sears* of Edgartown, cost no less than 158 dollars.[213]) Most of the men who died at sea were accordingly buried at sea, usually with a friend of the deceased saying a prayer or delivering a short eulogy. As a rule, the vessel's officers would not stand for work stopping for much longer than it took to perform these basic obsequies.[214]

After the death of seaman, the crew would usually gather at the mainmast to auction off the deceased's (typically meagre) possessions for the benefit of his dependants. Notwithstanding their own notorious poverty, seamen would often pay well over the odds for everyday objects. In so doing, they expressed both their respect for the dead man as well as their awareness that they too were in the same perilous situation. The captain or the first mate would then send profits along with a letter to the next of kin.[215]

Getting over, getting on

The conditions of life and work aboard whalers were quite distinctive in many respects and moulded the crew into no less distinctive a community, one that developed its own rules of sociability as well as its own forms of cultural expression. Perhaps the best known of these forms is "scrimshaw", in which teeth and bones – particular the jawbones of whales – are engraved with patterns, images and script. Practiced seamen might develop great skill at working with simple knives and needles, producing not only complex images, bur also carving whalebone

---

212 Whitecar, *Four Years Aboard the Whaleship*, 382.
213 Log LOUISA SEARS, 1856–1858, 26.–28.04.1857.
214 Busch, *Whaling Will Never Do for Me*, 168–170; Rediker, *Between the Devil and the Deep Blue Sea*, 195f. For a description of a burial at sea see e.g. Eldridge, *Lewis William Eldridge's Whaling Voyage*, 12f.
215 Creighton, "Fraternity in the American Forecastle", 552; Hohman, *The American Whaleman*, 139, 260; McCormick, *Two New Bedford Whalemen*, 91, 01.03.1847; Rediker, *Between the Devil and the Deep Blue Sea*, 197f.

into objects of everyday use (such as rolling pins) or sculptures, including model ships.[216]

Whalers also used the network of communication routes and transport links they created for their own system of carrying mail. Letters were highly valued as a means of keeping in touch with family, friends and loved ones. Literate seamen would often spend a good deal of time writing letters and on reading and re-reading those they had received, thereby maintain symbolic links beyond the isolated space of the vessel.[217] Those men who could not read and write themselves had other dos so for them.[218]

When to whaleships met, they would usually arrange a "gam",[219] a reciprocal visit by the two crews. In the process, the vessel that was likely to return to America the soonest would take on board a sack of mail from the other. If this vessel in its turn encountered a whaler that would get home even sooner, the mailbag would be passed on. The reverse procedure was used to convey letters to seamen. Whalers would also use much-frequented entrepôts, such as St Helena or Honolulu, to exchange incoming and outgoing mail.[220] In a bay on the coast of Floreana, one of the Galápagos Islands, seamen put up a barrel around 1800 that for decades served whalers as a letterbox. This system meant that even a letter that gave only "Atlantic Ocean" as its address would reach its destination – though it would take several months to get there.[221]

The usual times for reading and writing, for scrimshawing and mending clothes, for smoking or for tending to pets, were the second dog watch (6 to 8 p.m.) and the quitter parts of the voyage, when the vessel lay becalmed or was having little luck in finding whales. During such periods, one of the men would often play a musical instrument, sing a song or tell a story. If the captain allowed it, the crew might also play cards or stage wrestling matches.[222]

The question of whether work was to cease on Sundays and Christian holidays was controversial throughout the era of American-style pelagic whaling.

---

[216] Thousands of scrimshaws are preserved and have been closely studied – not least because some historians consider scrimshaw to be the only art form to have originated in the United States. See esp. Flayderman, *Scrimshaw and Scrimshanders*; Frank, *Dictionary of Scrimshaw Artists*.
[217] Gilje, *Liberty on the Waterfront*, 54f.
[218] See e.g. Ferguson, *Harpooner*, 9; Nordhoff, *Whaling and Fishing*, 75f.
[219] In seafaring parlance, "gam" meant "gossip" and may have derived from "game" or the verb "to gammon", meaning to chatter or boast. (Spears, "The Log of the Bark Emily", 246).
[220] See e.g. Log MERMAID, 1887–1890, 30.03.1888.
[221] Creighton, *Rites & Passages*, 171; Currie, *Thar She Blows*, 57; Hohman, *The American Whaleman*, 16, 87.
[222] Hohman, *The American Whaleman*, 16, 140f.

From the 1820s on, evangelical reform movements campaigned for Sunday – which they identified with the Sabbath – to be kept holy and free from work in order to give seamen time for their devotions. Many seamen – and captains, too – adopted this principle as their own.[223] "Fair weather but this being the sabbath I have no work done", Captain Green wrote in the log of the *Hudson* of Sag Harbor on a Sunday in April 1834.[224] Seamen might even disobey orders to lower the boats on a Sunday and were accordingly willing to accept severe penalties for the sake of the principle. On the barque *Pacific* of New Bedford, it was the officers who upheld the holiness of the Sabbath against the will of Captain Howland. "Sir, we aint going [to] lower the boats here in Sundays", one seaman recalled the first mate telling the dismayed captain. "There is six days in a week for to work [. . .]; we have and will seen whales enough in all the weekdays."[225]

Contrary, however, to this particular officer's blithe assumption, whales might well not be in evidence for weeks on end – only to show themselves on a Sunday. In such cases, nobody had an interest in letting the whales go, thereby adding to the length of the voyage and depleting its profits – including one's own lay. As William Whitecar remarked, "Three-fifths of our whaling up to this time, has been on Sunday, and, subsequently, this day of days proved equally fortunate for us." He also adduced a moral argument in favour a relaxed view of Sunday whaling: "It takes a strong religious bias to induce a man who depends upon the capture of whales for an early return to home and friends, after being separated from all that he holds dear, perhaps for years, to forego attempting their capture on a Sunday."[226] Nor were clergymen in whaling ports united in their condemnation of the practice. To Christians, fishing after all is not just a job like any other, but weighted with profound religious symbolism. Only few whaleships thus sailed as pious "Sunday whalers", meaning that they would not work on a Sunday even if a whale happened to breach alongside them. On most vessels, the captain took the moderate view that some work might be suspended, but not those tasks directly involved in finding and catching whales. This meant some respite for seamen, who would use their free time to catch up on their sleep, shave and wash their clothes.[227]

---

223 Gilje, *Liberty on the Waterfront*, 214; for a remark to that effect in a seaman's diary see Wallace, Journal CLARA BELL, 1855–1858, 15.06.1856.
224 Log HUDSON, 1833–1835, 20.04.1834.
225 Qtd. in Warrin, *So Ends This Day*, 180.
226 Whitecar, *Four Years Aboard the Whaleship*, 96.
227 Ashley, *The Yankee Whaler*, 8; Busch, *Whaling Will Never Do for Me*, 121f.; Hohman, *The American Whaleman*, 130, 178f.; Log EMERALD, 1838–1840, 08.07.1838; Nordhoff, *Whaling and Fishing*, 73.

The specific culture of whaling was also evident in a variety of rituals. Not only the skills they acquired as seamen set whalemen apart – their ability to climb the rigging, splice a rope and tie a bewildering variety of knots – but they also jointly performed symbolic acts to express their shared identity. The most widespread of these rituals was the "sailor's baptism", which was found on all oceangoing vessels. On a vessel's first crossing of the equator on a given voyage, the experienced seamen would dress up as Neptune, Roman god of the sea, and make the "green hands" perform a number of unpleasant tasks to gain admission into the ranks of seafarers. This ceremony was restricted to the common seamen, who accompanied it with fanciful tales and other celebratory rites. As for the tasks to be performed, they varied widely, from initiates being daubed in tar and lard before being shaved or dipped into the sea at the end of a rope to being made simply to stand a round of rum for the crew.[228]

Early scholarship on the social history of whaling – the work of Elmo P. Hohman, for instance – viewed the seaman's baptism merely as a rite of passage. More recent studies, however, such as those of Creighton and Rediker, have pointed to another aspect: by calling the mock ritual a "baptism" while invoking a pagan deity, the seamen put symbolic distance between themselves and bourgeois society. And by excluding the captain and his officers, the common seamen affirmed their bond, for a moment at least pitting their own set of rules against the hierarchy of the vessel.[229] "It was always a grotesque satire on institutions and roles of power. The satire could be about the sacraments of the state – the accolade of a knight – or the sacraments of the church – baptism by a priest. It could be a statement on kingship and the power over life and death."[230]

Other customs and rituals performed by some crews included the smashing of the tryworks at the start of the homeward leg as a way of symbolically inscribing the end of the hunting season into the vessel's fabric. On some vessels, the crew celebrated the one thousandth barrel of oil by frying doughnuts in the trypots.[231] Such shared tasks as weighing anchor or hoisting the mainsail were accompanied by the singing of particular shanties, which not only gave a

---

228 Gilje, *Liberty on the Waterfront*, 73; Hohman, *The American Whaleman*, 140; Rediker, *Between the Devil and the Deep Blue Sea*, 186. For a detailed account of a seaman's baptism see Haley, *Whale Hunt*, 38–42; a briefer account from the perspective of an initiate can be found in Jarman, *Journal of a Voyage to the South Seas*, 10f.
229 Creighton, "American Mariners and the Rites of Manhood", 146; Creighton, *Rites & Passages*, 120f.; Rediker, *Between the Devil and the Deep Blue Sea*, 187–189.
230 Dening, *Deep Times, Deep Spaces*, 25.
231 Helen C. Allen "When I Went a-Whaling." New Bedford Whaling Museum, Manuscript Collections: KWM 402B. 5; Busch, *Whaling Will Never Do for Me*, 160; Currie, *Thar She Blows*, 48; Eldridge, *Lewis William Eldridge's Whaling Voyage*, 5.

rhythm to the tasks at hand, but which also contributed to in-group bonding as well as relieving the stress of shipboard life. Some of these shanties openly aired grievances about the quality of the food or the treatment of the men by the officers.[232] Though not immune to change over the course of the eighteenth and nineteenth centuries, these rituals at heart remained direct and easily decoded communicative acts: "Maritime rituals were broadly accessible to and understood by an extremely diverse group of working men who came from many nations [. . .]. Such rituals served to integrate, to create cohesion, to incorporate individuals of differing backgrounds into a new and meaningful collectivity."[233]

EIn matters of religion, whaling crews were as heterogeneous as their social and cultural origins would suggest. Since whaleships offered neither the time nor the space for religious assemblies – aside from such brief moments of collective prayer as when a seaman died – religion aboard ship was largely an individual concern. Even such high Christian holidays as Christmas were observed only with a few casual gestures, if at all.[234] Faith may certainly have helped some seamen to come to terms with the privations of shipboard life, but such religiosity would have been an individual rather than a collective coping mechanism.[235]

Sailors were rather more united in their belief in "Jonahs", that is, in signs and omens. Shooting stars, the tint of the moon or particular behaviours of dolphins – these and other natural phenomena were taken as harbingers of gathering storms, changing winds or looming disaster.[236] Many seamen believed it bad luck to kill an albatross or to leave port on a Friday, the hateful *Dies infaustus*. Among the most feared omens was St Elmo's fire, an electrostatic discharge observable at the tip of the mast in stormy weather. It was believed to be sign from departed seamen announcing the death of another.[237] Some men also claimed to have seen that legendary ghost ship, the Flying Dutchman.[238] Nordhoff tells of a landfall on the coast of Madagascar around 1850, during which the crew fled the

---

232 Edwards/Walser, "Sea Music", 401; Heimerdinger, *Der Seemann*, 18, 50f. For an example of a protest shanty see Hugill, *Shanties from the Seven Seas*, 170.
233 Rediker, *Between the Devil and the Deep Blue Sea*, 198.
234 See e.g. Chippendale, *Sails and Whales*, 50f.; Thompson, "A Whaling Cruise in the 'Sea Fox'", 156f.
235 Busch, *Whaling Will Never Do for Me*, 105, 134.
236 See e.g. Browne, "Sketches of the Arabs", 4; McCormick, *Two New Bedford Whalemen*, 250.
237 Hohman, *The American Whaleman*, 139. For an example of fear triggered by an omen see Chippendale, *Sails and Whales*, 145f.
238 See e.g. Ferguson, *Harpooner*, 44, 65f.

vessel in a panic, claiming to have observed a ghost in the forecastle.[239] According to Rediker, belief in such phenomena helped seamen to rationalise their state of being at the mercy of powerful and potentially Lathan natural forces: "The seaman, whose life might be threatened on any given day, made omens central to his outlook, seeking mastery over his surroundings not only through natural observation but also through magic, ritual, and supernatural interpretation."[240]

Another distinctive feature of whaling culture was its peculiar and sometime coarse language. As seaborne traffic in the Atlantic world increased and seamen of a variety of nationalities and languages came into contact, the early modern era witnessed the emergence of a kind of maritime pidgin English, which contained a number of specifically nautical terms as well as displaying distinctive and sophisticated forms of syntax and pronunciation.[241] Oaths, imprecations and often blasphemy were a key element of this lingua franca, and some captains would ban profanity because Christian seamen would create panic by threatening God's wrath on an impious crew.

"Singing out" the whales was another peculiarity: a seaman who spotted a whale was supposed to announce his discovery by means of a loud yell, musical and eruptive, the purpose of which was to get the crew fired up for the hunt.[242] And not least by their highly specialised vocabulary were whalemen set apart from seamen in merchant or naval vessels. After all, they not only had to be capable of making a verbal distinction between a mizzen topmast and a mizzen topgallant mast, but also between the flukes of a sperm whale and the pectoral fin of a humpback.

***

Although only men worked aboard whaleships, beginning in the 1830s it was not unheard of for captains, at least of American whalers, to bring their wives and sometimes also their children on board. What had begun as an exception became, by the 1850s and 60s, an established practice, with an estimated one in five captains now sharing his quarters with his wife. More than a few seamen were resentful of sailing in what they called "lady ships" or "hen frigates". As well as generally being considered unlucky, women contributed nothing to the

---

239 Nordhoff, *Whaling and Fishing*, 202–204.
240 Rediker, *Between the Devil and the Deep Blue Sea*, 180–184.
241 Mühleisen, "I've Crossed an Ocean / I've Lost my Tongue"; Rediker, *Between the Devil and the Deep Blue Sea*, 11, 162f., 166f.
242 Davoll, *The Captain's Specific Orders on the Commencement of a Whale Voyage to his Officers and Crew*, 8; Hohman, *The American Whaleman*, 156. The term "singing out" (German *aussingen*) more broadly denotes the giving and confirmation of orders in set terms and at fixed volumes. (Heimerdinger, *Der Seemann*, 55).

success of the whale hunt while enjoying the privileges of the captain's cabin. For their part, the wives took little pleasure in the role as passive outsiders and usually accompanied their husbands only because that was what he wanted.[243]

The sphere of intimacy, sexuality and love, along with the masculine self-image of seamen, will be discussed at greater length in the chapter "Passages III". It is merely worth noting at this point that some seamen found it to be a problem or a conflict of roles to be forced to perform such "feminine" tasks as washing or mending clothes. White men in particular were reluctant to deviate from their masculine self-image any further than absolutely necessary. It therefore fell disproportionately to black men, who were often denied access to jobs with strong masculine connotations on shore too to take on service roles as cooks, stewards or cabin boys.[244]

"Slaves at sea, outcasts on shore"

It is striking how often white men, in their attempts to give expression to their experience of life and work aboard a whaleship, used the term slavery. "Both British and American seamen are subject to as horrible slavery while at sea, as any of the children of Africa in any part of the world", Ben Ely remarked with regard to corporal punishment, concluding that "No slave on shore ever suffered half so much injustice as in nine cases out of ten is practiced on board our whale-ships."[245] These may have been deliberate exaggerations aimed at satisfying the appetite of American readers for gruesome tales of the sea and focusing attention on his own memoir. Yet Ely was far from being the only seaman to draw an analogy between his own situation and slavery. Nordhoff too spoke of "slavery on board the whaleship", and the journalist Christopher Slocum had this to say about his experiences aboard the *Obed Mitchell* of Nantucket in the 1840s: "I ask what slave at the south suffers more hardships or feels more keenly

---

[243] Ashley, *The Yankee Whaler*, 50; Busch, *Whaling Will Never Do for Me*, 148f.; Creighton, "American Mariners and the Rites of Manhood", 143–145; Creighton, *Rites & Passages*, 163; Currie, *Thar She Blows*, 68. For captains' wives complaining of loneliness and boredom see Busch, *Whaling Will Never Do for Me*, 150f. and McCormick, *Two New Bedford Whalemen*, 187. For a rare example of a seaman appreciating the presence on women on board see Chippendale, *Sails and Whales*, 137f.
[244] Creighton, "American Mariners and the Rites of Manhood", 154; Creighton, *Rites & Passages*, 185f.; Ely, *There She Blows*, 40f., 86; Gilje, *Liberty on the Waterfront*, 34.
[245] Ely, *There She Blows*, 40f., 86.

the bitterness of oppression than the poor care worne sailor."[246] Of Silas Alden, master of the *Bruce* of Fairhaven, John Ross Browne observed that "He gave orders [. . .] in such a manner as plainly betokened that he considered us all slaves of the lowest cast, unworthy of the least respect, and himself our august master."[247] From his time living among seamen, Browne drew this conclusion:

> There is no class of men in the world who are so unfairly dealt with, so oppressed, so degraded, as the seamen who man the vessels engaged in the American whale fishery. [. . .]

> From the time he leaves port he is beyond the sphere of human rights: he is a slave till he returns. [. . .] Worse than all, he is the slave of others, perhaps his inferiors in every manly attribute. He is flogged for the most trifling offense, cursed when he strives to please, trampled and spit upon, without the power to resent the indignities.[248]

In a letter to his brother, Justin Martin, a seaman aboard the *Ann Alexander*, remarked it 1844 that "It would be better [. . .] to be painted black and sold to a southern planter than be doomed to the forecastle of a whale ship."[249] Their supposed resemblance to slaves did not exist in the eyes of the seamen alone: captains too might be found describing their men as slaves. American newspapers that published advertisements looking for seamen who had deserted could sometimes be found using the same images and illustrations employed in notices promising rewards for the return of escaped slaves.[250]

In fact, the life of a seaman did resemble that of an American plantation slave – the point of comparison here – in certain respects, if by no means in all. There was a peculiar tension to shipboard life, as Paul A. Gilje has remarked: "The sea simultaneously represented a passport to freedom and a life akin to slavery."[251] Captains and officers would often treat common seamen as their property, which might include cruel and arbitrary corporal punishments as well as the denial of rights. Unlike in the institution of Atlantic slavery, however, this state of subservience was by its nature temporary. As Greg Dening has observed, "it is the mark of such institutions as a ship to be temporary. A voyage begun is a voyage to be ended."[252] It was possible for seamen to be sold, hired out or bequeathed. Nor did working aboard a whaleship spell social death, which historians have found to be a key element of slavery as an institution. Some black men

---

246 Quoted in Bolster, *Black Jacks*, 219.
247 Browne, *Etchings of a Whaling Cruise*, 23; Nordhoff, *Whaling and Fishing*, 272.
248 Browne, *Etchings of a Whaling Cruise*, 504–506.
249 Quoted in Busch, *Whaling Will Never Do for Me*, 87.
250 See e.g. Medley, 23.06.1796; see also Gilje, *Liberty on the Waterfront*, 138.
251 Gilje, *Liberty on the Waterfront*, 69.
252 Dening, *The Bounty*, 40.

signed on aboard a whaler in full awareness of the hardships awaiting them, yet finding them preferable to the conditions of life and work on a plantation. The unrelenting disciplinary regime under which whalemen lived was founded on violence and as such operated in a context in which, as Marcus Rediker has pointed out, "*all* important forms of transatlantic labour were founded on violence: the army, the navy, the merchant navy, the institution of indentured labour, plantation slavery and ultimately the entire project of transatlantic settlement, production and trade."[253] Seamen, slaves, apprentices, cotton pickers and other groups of workers made similar experiences wherever the exploitation of labour relied on direct and barely regulated force, manifesting itself in the form termed "predatory capitalism" by Max Weber.[254]

***

A broad perspective on the social and cultural history of American-style pelagic whaling shows that the seamen whom it brought to the shores of Africa constituted a distinctive group of actors. They did so not only with regard to their intentions. Everyday thought and action were articulated under the formative and normative conditions and constraints of whaling and hence as the result of seamen's specific experience of their own environment.

Whalemen would have shared a good deal of this experience with seamen in merchant, naval or indeed pirate vessels. Each of these groups would have recognised being at the mercy of the forces of nature, a tough disciplinary regime and the more or less complete absence of women. To evaluate the reality of life and work aboard a whaleship, it may therefore be useful to draw on observations made in other branches of seafaring. In his sociological study of seventeenth-century Caribbean privateers, Heiner Treinen found that a vessel's crew that remains in communicative isolation from the outside world for a longer period of time and whose mode of interaction is characterised by a comparatively direct enforcement of obedience "is immensely prone to develop into a world unto itself".[255] This idea of a vessel as a world unto itself also emerges from Greg Dening's findings regarding eighteenth-century British warships. Dening stresses that hierarchies of status and relations of functional dependency permeated seamen's everyday experience of shipboard life and narrowly circumscribed their scope for action.[256] Rediker's analysis of eighteenth-century

---

253 Rediker, "Der rote Atlantik", 159.
254 Vickers, "Maritime Labor in Colonial Massachusetts", 311f.; Weber, *Wirtschaft und Gesellschaft*, 671, 838f.
255 Treinen, "Parasitäre Anarchie", 80.
256 Dening, *The Death of William Gooch*, 31.

Anglo-American merchant shipping as "a world apart" points in the same direction – a world characterised above all by the absence of family, church, state and other institutions giving structure to society.[257]

Both Dening and Rediker consider vessels to be total institutions in which everyday experience, perception and action are minutely structured by ranks and rules. This reliance on order and hierarchy also served partially to level social and cultural distinctions among the crews, thereby making the space of the vessel a de-individualised place comparable to the barracks-style socialisation of a prison or labour camp.[258] The concept of the total institution goes back to Erving Goffman, a Canadian sociologist who in 1957 used it to draw attention to the typological resemblance between such socially sequestered institutions as prisons and mental asylums.[259] But contemporary observers had already drawn analogies between vessels and prisons. Ralph Waldo Emerson, for instance, travelling as a passenger on the merchantman *Jasper* of Boston in January 1833, observed in his diary that a vessel as such was "A prison with the chance of being drowned."[260]

As this chapter has shown, whaleships too displayed these features of a total institution. In contrast to Gilje and Rediker, however, who consider seamen in whaleships to be part of an overarching social group (the "maritime proletariat") including those of the navy and merchant navy,[261] I think it worth emphasising certain distinctive features of whaling. The system of payment in lays, the high proportion of untrained green hands on board, the voyages that could last for years, often with no landfall made for months on end, the temporary labour surpluses, the competing orders of the boat crew and the watch system, and not least the mortal peril of the whale hunt itself – all these were peculiar to whaling and produced specific situations, experiences, expectations and (psycho-)social dynamics that set the experience of going to sea in a whaler apart from that of a seaman in, say, the merchant navy.

Observing the formative power of specific experiences aboard vessels in general and whaleships in particular casts doubt on a school of research in which everybody who came from across the Atlantic to the shores of Africa can only have been the agent of an imperial project. A similar point has been made the historian Nicole Ulrich, who has charged certain studies taking a postcolonial approach

---

257 Rediker, *Between the Devil and the Deep Blue Sea*, 161.
258 Dening, *Islands and Beaches*, 159; Rediker, *Between the Devil and the Deep Blue Sea*, 211f. See also the quotation from Heinrich Popitz in the chapter "Passages I".
259 Goffman, *Asylums*.
260 Emerson, "From Journals", 120.
261 Rediker, *Between the Devil and the Deep Blue Sea*, 105.

with injudiciously lumping together different groups of actors with different backgrounds and intentions. As Ulrich stresses, explorers, seamen, adventurers, tradesmen, missionaries or soldiers were "not united by a single intellectual project, but wracked by deep social and ideological cleavages."[262] In more general terms, Frederick Cooper and Ann Laura Stoler have accused some of the scholarship in the field of taking too undifferentiated an approach to "Western" actors.[263] The historian Monika Juneja has identified a process of "postcolonial closure", in which the view of the past is structured in advance by the presupposition of a ubiquitous asymmetry of power, causing ambiguous and unexpected phenomena to be ignored.[264]

Sailors who arrived on the beaches of Africa on board whalers did so as mobile workers – as semi-nomadic hunters, as it were. The logics, rules, dynamics and constraints of whaling were decisive in forming their experiences and their actions. These common seamen approached the people they encountered on the beach not as representatives of a superior power, but as poor working men in a position of subaltern dependency which many of them likened to slavery. They were, as the seaman Ben Ely summed up their predicament, "exposed to be treated like dogs or slaves at sea, and as outcasts on shore."[265]

---

[262] Ulrich, "Dr Anders Sparrman", 733.
[263] Cooper/Stoler, "Between Metropole and Colony", 16.
[264] Juneja, "Debatte zum Postkolonialismus aus Anlass des Sammelbandes 'Jenseits des Eurozentrismus' von Sebastian Conrad und Shalini Randeria", 90–93.
[265] Ely, *There She Blows*, 86.

3 A stabilising flow of goods: Saint Augustin, Madagascar, 1830–1860

"The *Clara Bell* had been leaking", recalled her captain, Charles Robbins. "It was a trifle, said I at first; but it got worse. The pumps were at it all the while, not working hard, but working. Clearly, it was time to worry."[1] At the time – the mid-1850s – the Mattapoisett whaler was cruising between the Cape of Good Hope and Madagascar. A close inspection of the hold revealed a leak at the sternpost. To Robbins, the case was clear: "Our cruise was up. Port was the place for us, so we put away."[2] The problem was that the closest shoreline, the south-western coast of Madagascar, had precious few anchorages to offer, being nearly everywhere guarded by sandbanks or coral reefs. Unlike the east coast of Africa – which the *Clara Bell* could probably not have reached quickly enough because of the northward current in the west of the Mozambique Channel – that part of the island had scarcely any sheltered bays. Accordingly, Robbins was all the more relieved when his vessel finally did reach safe moorings: "Out of the sea rose the green, luxuriantly wooded Madagascan coast, – within the coast a lovely harbor, the harbor of Augustine Bay."[3]

Saint Augustin, a crescent-shaped sandy bay surrounded by tall cliffs in the south-west of Madagascar, is where the Onilahy Congo river flows into the Mozambique Channel. Over the centuries the river's current created a gap in the coral reef that encircles much of the coast of Madagascar, a gap which made the bay the ideal refuge for vessels. Like the *Clara Bell* under Charles Robbins, such vessels not infrequently arrived in a state of disrepair, the seas to the south of Madagascar, which they had to cross after passing the Cape of Good Hope, being much battered by storms from the Antarctic. "Once every twenty-four hours, violent rain-storms of from one to four hours duration thoroughly drench the crew and vessel", recalled William Whitecar, who sailed these waters in October 1858 aboard the *Pacific* of New Bedford.[4] Charles Nordhoff gives a similar account: "Every morning, without a single exception, it rained in torrents; and every morning, without a single exception – ('no Sundays in ten fathom of water', say whalemen) – precisely at five o'clock we started out and chased whales until the sea breeze became too strong."[5]

---

1 Robbins, *The Gam*, 195.
2 Ibid., 195.
3 Ibid., 195f.
4 Whitecar, *Four Years Aboard the Whaleship*, 340.
5 Nordhoff, *Whaling and Fishing*, 182. Nordhoff had similar things to sa about the area off the eastern coast of Madagascar, which he called an "unpleasant whaling ground". (Nordhoff, *Whaling and Fishing*, 165f.)

https://doi.org/10.1515/9783110759914-006

James Prior, who sailed through the Mozambique Channel around 1812 as the surgeon of the frigate HMS *Nisus*, observed no fewer than four waterspouts simultaneously "within two miles of the ship".[6] It may come as no surprise that several whalers were shipwrecked under such conditions, including the *Rambler* of London (1825), the *Lucas* of New Bedford (1845), the *Junius* of New Bedford (1851), the *Nautilus* of Nantucket (1858) and the *Charles Carroll* of New London (1862).[7] One captain, Edward Lakeman, lost no fewer than two whalers in the seas off Madagascar: the *Malay* in 1842 and the *Emerald* in 1845, both of Salem.[8]

Saint Augustin has two names in Malagasy, the language of Madagascar: *Anantsoño* and *Ianantsony*, both after the *sono*, a plant of the family Didiereaceae endemic to the area. As with most places they visited, however, seamen coined their own names for the bay and nearby landmarks. A promontory of white rock jutting into the bay from the south was known as "Tent Rock" in tribute the Saint Augustin's reputation as a shelter.[9] It was here that whalers would usually cast anchor, safe from the storms that would sometimes churn up the seas even within the bay itself.[10] (The Malagasy word for "sea" is *ranomasina*, which means both "salty water" and "powerful water".[11]) In addition to natural shelter, Tent Rock offered an excellent sandy anchorage.[12] Though whalers would also call at other harbours on the coast of Madagascar – Nosy Be and Majunga in the north-west, Tôlanaro (Port Dauphin) in the south-east or Île Sainte-Marie in the north-east – nowhere did they drop anchor as often as at Tent Rock in the Bay of Saint-Augustin.[13] Another point in its favour was the existence of comparatively accurate charts for the area, in contrast to the rest of

---

6 Prior, *Voyage Along the Eastern Coast of Africa*, 30.
7 Jones, *Ships Employed in the South Seas Trade*, 80; Starbuck, History of the American Whale Fishery, 398f., 468f., 554f., 572f. In August 1792 the *Winterton*, a British East Indiaman carrying a rich cargo, struck a reef and sank off Saint Augustin. (Buchan, *A Narrative of the Loss of the Winterton*).
8 Starbuck, *History of the American Whale Fishery*, 392f., 404f. On shipwrecks in this area see Newitt, A History of Mozambique, 147f. In March 1856 several seamen aboard the *Montgomery* of New Bedford went on strike in the Mozambique Channel in order to prevent Captain Chapman from sailing for the southern coast of Madagascar during cyclone season. (Log MONTGOMERY, 1855–1858, 28.03.1856).
9 Boteler, *Narrative of a Voyage of Discovery to Africa and Arabia*, vol. 2, 95; Hooper, "An Empire in the Indian Ocean", 54; Manjakahery/Radimilahy, "Archaeology of St Augustine's Bay", 64; Robbins, *The Gam*, 196.
10 See e.g. Beane, *From Forecastle to Cabin*, 157f.
11 Hooper, "An Empire in the Indian Ocean", 42.
12 Beane, *From Forecastle to Cabin*, 157f.; Bialuschewski, "Pirates, Slavers, and the Indigenous Population in Madagascar", 410.
13 Haywood, "American Whalers and Africa", 97; Huddart, *The Oriental Navigator*, 92.

the western coast of Madagascar, for which only rudimentary charts existed until well into the nineteenth century.[14]

Before reaching Tent Rock, whalers would pass a low-lying islet just under ten nautical miles from the shore, known to the local population as *Nosy Ve* and to English-speaking seamen simply as "Sandy Island" (Fig. 18). Whalers found it helpful in locating the entrance to the bay.[15] If a vessel bore north-east at Sandy Island, its navigator, looking through his telescope, would soon discover an elevation on the horizon that marked the southern end of the Bay of Saint-Augustin. Soon the outline of a mountain would come into view, and if the captain made straight for that point he could be sure of passing safely through the reef without getting caught in the breakers which, owing to the nearby shallows, here set in at some distance from the coast.[16]

Seasonal boom periods

Saint Augustin was never a whaling ground – only too rarely would a humpback or any other whale find its way into the bay.[17] When whalers called here, they did so to take on provisions or, as in the case of the *Clara Bell*, to make urgent repairs. The first whalers reached these waters around 1790, when a London whaling company, Samuel Enderby & Sons, began to send vessels through the Indian Ocean to Australia. The first American vessels to sail for the Australian whaling grounds did so soon afterwards, in 1792. On their way, the *Asia* and the *Alliance*, both of Nantucket, explored potential whaling grounds in the western Indian Ocean, particularly off Madagascar. The first whaleships to sail for these waters as their primary destination rather than as a stopover were two British vessels, the *Kingston* and the *Elligood*, in 1801.[18] Both victualled at Saint Augustin, thereby becoming the first whalers known to have anchored in the bay.[19]

Yet the *Kingston* and the *Elligood* seem also to have been the last whalers to call at Saint Augustin for some time. A succession of wars, first between France

---

14 Boteler, *Narrative of a Voyage of Discovery to Africa and Arabia*, vol. 2, 96; Owen, *Narrative of Voyages to Explore the Shores of Africa*, vol. 2, 57f.
15 See e.g. Lewis, Journal ATLANTIC, 1835–1837, 30.07.1836.
16 Huddart, *The Oriental Navigator*, 92.
17 See e.g. Log HERCULES II, 1834–1836, 03.–11.09.1835.
18 Spence, *Harpooned*, 57f., 63–66; Wray/Martin, "Historical Whaling Records from the Western Indian Ocean", 213f.; see also the chapter "Passages I".
19 Log KINGSTON, 1800–1801, 09.02.–02.03.1801.

214 — 3 A stabilising flow of goods: Saint Augustin, Madagascar, 1830–1860

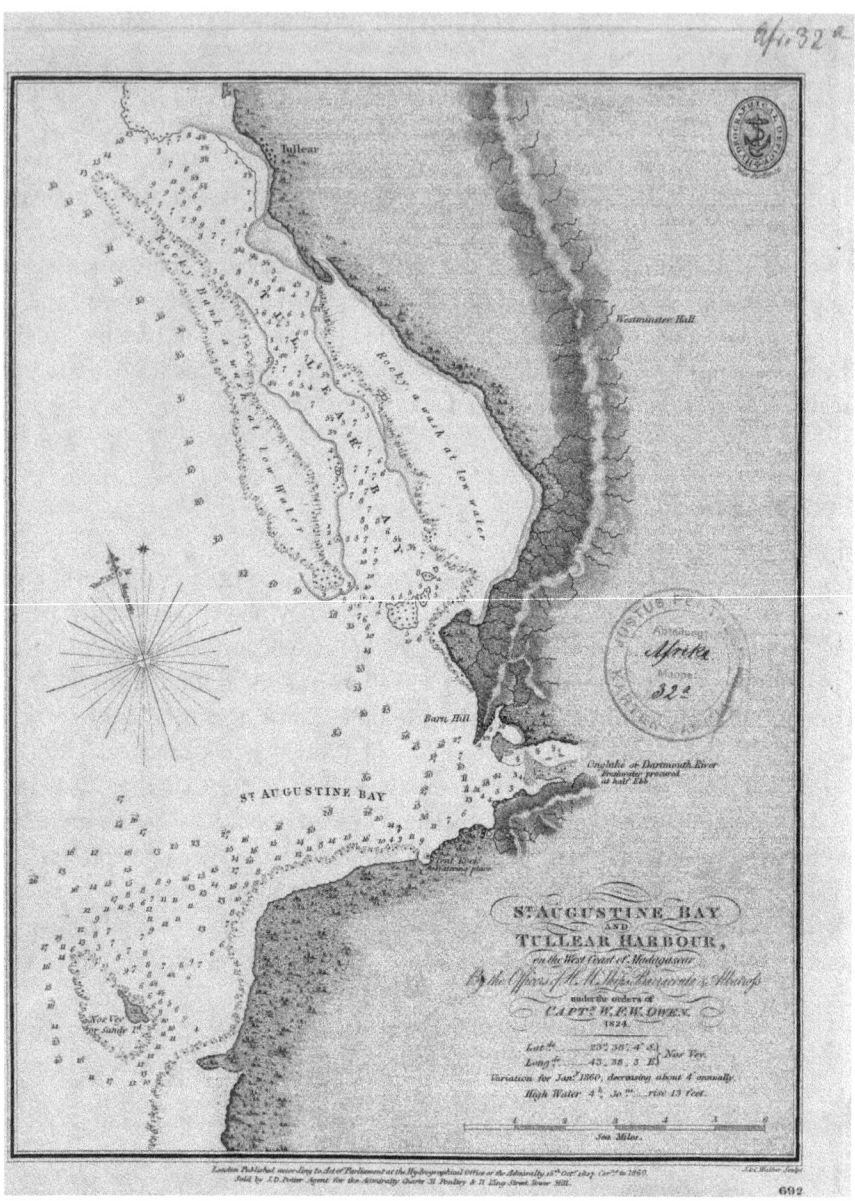

Fig. 18: The Bay of Saint-Augustine on a British Admiralty Chart of 1824 (William Fitzwilliam Owen et al. *St. Augustine Bay and Tullear Harbour on the West Coast of Madagascar*. London: Hydrographic Office of the Admirality, 1824, corrections to 1860).
Courtesy of the Gotha Research Library at University of Erfurt, SPK 40 32.a A [01,11].

and its rivals (1792–1814) and then between Britain and the United States (1812–14), stood in the way of the systematic exploitation of whale stocks in the Indian Ocean. The situation was particularly dangerous for British whalers, who under threat not only from French, Dutch and Portuguese privateers, but also from the Royal Navy, which was wont to impress British seamen into its service. To avoid these dangers, after 1798 the British whaling fleet moved the centre of its operations to the eastern Indian Ocean, exploring new whaling grounds off Timor, Australia and New Zealand.[20]

Once the wars had ended it was the resurgent American whaling industry that opened up the western Indian Ocean to sperm whaling, with new hunting grounds being established by and by. The presence of American whalers first peaked in the 1830s, by which time British whalers had all but stopped operating in the area. This was also the boom period for stopovers at Saint Augustin. "Out of thirty American whale-men who have visited this port [Cape Town] this season, twenty-five have proceeded to the eastward, and will, probably, be at St Augustine Bay", noted Isaac Chase, the US consul in Cape Town, in 1836.[21] This estimate turns out to have been pretty exact: often more than a dozen (and sometimes more than two dozen) whalers might be found at anchor in the bay at any one time[22] – twenty-eight in August 1834.[23] Such clusters were due to the seasonal pattern which whalers in the western Indian Ocean were beginning to adopt at the time. They would use the dry south-westerly winds of the winter months to sail into the northern part of these waters, cruising off Zanzibar or the Seychelles, for instance, where plenty of sperm whales were to be found from May to July. During the southern summer, from November to April, when the north-east monsoon drives rain and storms across the Indian Ocean, whalers moved south, hunting in more tranquil waters such as those off the coast of Madagascar.[24]

Whalers would usually call at Saint Augustin before moving on to the more southerly whaling grounds, i.e. in March or April. A second cluster of stopovers occurred in July and August, as the southern winter drew to a close. Many whalers sought to reach the Mozambique Channel in time to intercept humpback whales before they headed back to the Antarctic Ocean (and thus out of reach) for the summer. Whaleship might occasionally visit Saint Augustin at other times, including vessels that were calling on their way to or from the

---

20 Richards/Du Pasquier, "Bay Whaling off Southern Africa", 246.
21 "From Cape Town." *New-Bedford Mercury*, 13.05.1836, 1.
22 Lewis, Journal ATLANTIC, 1835–1837, 04.04.1836.
23 Log HUDSON, 1833–1835, 08.08.1834.
24 Haywood, "American Whalers and Africa", 101f.; Wray/Martin, "Historical Whaling Records from the Western Indian Ocean", 218–224.

Pacific whaling grounds without hunting in the Indian Ocean. By far the most stopovers, however, were made during these two periods, and it was accordingly rare for a whaler to be alone in the bay.

Saint Augustin remained well-frequented as whalers branched out from sperm whales to humpback whales in the 1840s, though slightly fewer calls overall are on record for the 1840s and 50s compared to the 1830s. After all, humpback whales were to be found nearby in the winter months, in the Mozambique Channel and off the southern coast of Madagascar. Only the outbreak of the American Civil War in 1861 brought about a sudden drop in operations, one from which the American whaling industry would never quite recover as petroleum came gradually to replace whale oil in a variety of uses. While some whalers were able to operate profitably in the Atlantic and Pacific whaling grounds, comparatively close to home, into the late nineteenth century, the costs of sailing to the remote Indian Ocean were such that American shipowners largely stopped sending their vessels there after the Civil War.[25] Only four identifiable American whalers are recorded as having called at Saint Augustin after 1865: the *Falcon* (1866), the *Desdemona* (1867), the *A.R. Tucker* (1873) and the *Platina* (1885), all of New Bedford.[26]

Trading port and tributary state

Exchange with vessels and their crews had long been a familiar phenomenon in Saint Augustin when the first whalers dropped anchor there in 1800. The first merchants had sailed into the bay in the sixteenth century, their visits becoming more frequent in the seventeenth. In order to establish what practices of interaction these contacts produced and how they might have prefigured later encounters with whalers, I shall begin by outlining the history of Saint Augustin up the end of the eighteenth century.

The question of when and from where the first inhabitants arrived on the island of Madagascar has long been the subject of scholarly debate. What we know for certain is that its population originally consisted of people of Indonesian and African origin; what is uncertain is whether the Indonesian migrants came directly across the Indian Ocean or rather indirectly, via east Africa, along existing trade routes. Connected to this is another controversial question,

---

25 Clark, "The American Whale-Fishery", 321f.
26 Log DESDEMONA, 1865–1869, 12.–20.02.1867; Log FALCON, 1865–1867, 07.–18.03.1866; Log PLATINA, 1882–1886, 05.–12.08.1885; Ricketson, *Mrs. Ricketson's Whaling Journal*, 24.–31.10.1873.

namely whether immigration from Africa was connected with that from Indonesia or occurred separately. Leaving aside the question of who arrived first, however, there can be no doubt that in the first millennium AD people from all parts of the Indian Ocean seaboard – and not only from Australia – settled in Madagascar.[27]

The local ecology imprinted itself on the course of the island's settlement. A high central plateau offering little fertile land dominates the interior of Madagascar, running from north to south and separating the east and west coasts. The coastal plains were accordingly settled earlier than the central highlands, probably in the course of the first four centuries AD. The western lowlands in which Saint Augustin is situated are divided into three climate zones: in the north, heavy seasonal rainfall supports tropical rainforest; the drier central coast is dominated by shrub-steppes; while the south is largely desert.[28]

Saint Augustin is situated at the geographical and climatic boundary between the central and the southern parts of the coastal plain. It is in this area that archaeologists have found the earliest traces of human activity in Madagascar, though it is unclear whether they were left by a settled or rather an iterant population.[29] Livestock herders settled in the area no later than the twelfth century, keeping zebus in particular. Settlement remained sparse compared to the north, with the population spread out over a multitude of villages. Archaeological research has found the population to have maintained trading links with other parts of the island as well as with the east coast of Africa. Finds including remnants of Chinese ceramics furthermore testify to indirect connections with long-distance trade routes along the Indian Ocean seaboard. Saint Augustin itself, however, most probably was not involved in coastal trade, being too far south for the monsoon winds that decisively structured the trading system in the western Indian Ocean. In contrast to the north of Madagascar, Arab merchants did not settle in Saint Augustin, which appears to have remained untouched by Islamic religion and culture.[30]

---

27 Alpers, "The Islands of Indian Ocean Africa", 8f.; Campbell, "Austronesian Mariners and Early Trans-Indian Ocean Crossings", 19f.; Campbell, "Madagascar: Prehistory and Developments to c.1500", 872f; Dewar/Wright, "The Culture History of Madagascar", 418; Hooper, "An Empire in the Indian Ocean", 41; Manjakahery/Radimilahy, "Archaeology of St Augustine's Bay", 63f.
28 Campbell, "Madagascar: Prehistory and Developments to c.1500", 873; Dewar/Wright, "The Culture History of Madagascar", 440f.
29 Dewar/Wright, "The Culture History of Madagascar", 426–428; Manjakahery/Radimilahy, "Archaeology of St Augustine's Bay", 61f.
30 Campbell, "Madagascar: Evolution of Malagasy Kingdoms", 873f.; Duffey, "China's Contact with Southern Africa", 30f.; Hooper, "An Empire in the Indian Ocean", 46f.

The population of Saint Augustin first encountered European vessels and their crews in the sixteenth century, when the burgeoning East India trade brought Western seafarers to the Indian Ocean. In August 1528, for instance, no fewer than eleven Portuguese vessels bound for India were moored in the bay. The approximately four thousand seamen, soldiers and passengers on board bartered for such provisions as sheep, chickens and beans. It was Portuguese seamen too who named the bay for St Augustine of Hippo.[31] Shipwrecked seamen are known to have come ashore at Saint Augustin on several occasions, sometimes spending years in the area before being picked up by a vessel. On one occasion in mid-1527 eight hundred men made it to the shore after two vessel from a Portuguese flotilla ran aground on a sandbank in the bay. After a year during which more and more of their number fell prey to fever, the survivors decided to make their way overland to the east coast – thereby missing the arrival of the aforementioned trading fleet in August 1528.[32]

As well as Portuguese vessels, some Dutch vessels found their way into the Bay of Saint-Augustin, as did, beginning in 1591, British ones. As the sixteenth century gave way to the seventeenth, stopovers seem to have come at the more or less predictable rate of one per year, although it should be remembered that East Indiamen often arrived in convoys of three or four vessels at a time. Since a culture of writing did not take hold in south-western Madagascar until the twentieth century, the observations recorded by seamen form a particularly important source for the history of Saint Augustin. What these records suggest is that the population at the time subsisted by a combination of means – fishing, animal husbandry and arable farming – as well as continuing to barter both with neighbouring societies as well as with societies in the island's interior. Seamen estimated the local population to number approximately five hundred, classified as Fihereña in historical and ethnographic research. Their local communities were headed by political and military leaders known as *andriana*. European seamen were known to the Fihereña as *vazaha* ("white strangers"). The coastal trade between Fihereña and *vazaha* consisted largely in the exchange of livestock – and to a lesser degree of rice and lemons – against red carnelian beads and pieces of silver.[33]

---

[31] Hooper, "An Empire in the Indian Ocean", 38f.; van den Boogaerde, *Shipwrecks of Madagascar*, 36–38; Sibree, *Madagascar Before the Conquest*, 110f.

[32] Van den Boogaerde, *Shipwrecks of Madagascar*, 30–33, 42.

[33] Campbell, An Economic History of Imperial Madagascar, 51; Campbell, "The Structure of Trade in Madagascar", 140; Hooper, "An Empire in the Indian Ocean", 54–59; Pearson, "Close Encounters of the Worst Kind", 395f. The best known memoir of Saint Augustin from the pen of a seaman is Robert Drury: *Madagascar: Or, Robert Drury's Journal, During Fifteen Years*

The number of cattle the Fihereña were able to spare and use in barter was subject to the impact of drought, floods and armed conflict with neighbouring groups. Conflicts might also arise, however, because *vazaha* were wont to interpret the non-availability of cattle as a lack of cooperation on the part of the Fihereña. To gain access to herds of cattle in the area, it was known for *vazaha* to make common cause with local *andriana* against rival neighbours. Such complications notwithstanding, seamen to and from the East Indies began to call at Saint Augustin more frequently in the early seventeenth century, taking advantage of its location on the Mozambique Channel, which was the preferred route at the time. Moreover, Saint Augustin was comparatively easy to find, making it the ideal place for convoys to regroup after having been separated in the storms of the south-eastern Indian Ocean. With this mind, Saint Augustin attracted the attention of European East India companies looking to put their provisioning infrastructure on a solid basis by establishing permanent settlements of their own in the seventeenth century.[34]

140 British settlers arrived in 1645 in order to set up a fortified compound for the East India Company on the southern shore of the Bay of Saint-Augustin. However, the poor soils of the area meant that the station soon had trouble feeding itself, all the more so because they lacked the goods that might have allowed them to barter for food. Several British soldiers were killed in conflicts with the Fihereña over cattle theft and pasturage. Famine was compounded by fever and dysentery. In this situation, the station commander made a fateful error by allying himself with of the *andriana*, incurring his enemies' hostility in

---

Captivity on that Island. London: W. Meadows, 1729. Its value as a historical source, however, is debatable. See e.g. Hooper, "An Empire in the Indian Ocean", 69 n. 6; Pearson, "Close Encounters of the Worst Kind", 402f.; Pearson/Godden, *In Search of the Red Slave*; Van den Boogaerde, *Shipwrecks of Madagascar*, 99–105, 144f. In the Malagasy language, the term *Fihereña* denotes the area between the Onilahy and Mangoky rivers. By adding the prefix *anti* (meaning people or population), it can be applied to the area's inhabitants. *Antifihereña* thus means "people from Fihereña". Scholars writing about Madagascar, however, tend simply to apply the name of the area to its inhabitants and thus to refer to "the Fihereña" as a population group – though it should noted that neither *Fihereña* nor *Antifihereña* carries an ethnic connotation. According to historical and ethnographic research, the population of Fihereña since the seventeenth century has consisted of at least nine different ethnic groups. (Kent, *Early Kingdoms in Madagascar*, 169f.; Manjakahery/Radimilahy, "Archaeology of St Augustine's Bay", 63f., 76) In the case of the Vezo, who live by fishing on the coast of Fihereña, their definition as an ethnic group and the date of their formation as such remain controversial. (Marikandia, "The Vezo of the Fihereña Coast, Southwest Madagascar").

34 Graham, *Great Britain in the Indian Ocean*, 53; Hooper, "An Empire in the Indian Ocean", 35, 39f., 55–61; Pearson, "Close Encounters of the Worst Kind", 396; Pearson/Godden, *In Search of the Red Slave*, 169f.

the process. After several more violent confrontations the remaining settlers – by now reduced to twelve – beat a hasty retreat. The Company abandoned the station in 1646.[35]

This failure notwithstanding, merchantmen continued to head for Saint Augustin. The demand they generated for cattle and drinking water caused Fihereña communities to engage in raids on one another. For their part, the *vazaha*, in their quest for timber with which to repair their vessels, did much to deplete the forests around the bay. Since the rival Fihereña factions remained more or less equally matched, none of them succeeded in permanently establishing its domination over others and building up something resembling an overarching state. In the mid-seventeenth century the Saklava state in the east began to take advantage of this situation by repeatedly attacking Fihereña communities.[36]

A new group of European actors to turn up in Madagascar in the late seventeenth century were pirates. Having been driven out the Caribbean by European navies, several pirate captains and their crews sought refuge in Saint Augustin from about 1690 onwards, among them such famous figures as Nathaniel North, John Halsey, La Buse, John Taylor and Thomas Howard.[37] These pirates – a total of up to 1500 individuals – set up encampments where they spent weeks and sometimes months while gathering provisions. While conflicts with Fihereña were no rarity, some crews also cooperated with particular *andriana* and supported them in raids on neighbouring groups for a share of the booty. As the presence of pirates became common knowledge, however, merchant vessels began to avoid the bay. From about 1700 onwards, the pirates found hardly any vessels to attack in the seas off Saint Augustin and instead focussed their activities in the mainland. By entering into alliances, setting themselves up as middlemen in commercial dealings, marrying into Malagasy families and teaching English to the local elites, they were absorbed into littoral society over the following years.[38]

---

35 Bialuschewski, "Firearms and Warfare in Late Seventeenth and Early Eighteenth-Century Madagascar", 60; Bialuschewski, "Pirates, Slavers, and the Indigenous Population in Madagascar", 401, 410; Coupland, East Africa and its Invaders, 54; Hooper, "An Empire in the Indian Ocean", 61f.; Larson, "The Origins of Malagasy Arriving at Mauritius and Réunion", 196; Pearson, "Close Encounters of the Worst Kind", 398; Van den Boogaerde, *Shipwrecks of Madagascar*, 58–60, 82f., 114.
36 Bialuschewski, "Pirates, Slavers, and the Indigenous Population in Madagascar", 411f.; Hooper, "An Empire in the Indian Ocean", 35, 39f., 62f., 66f.
37 Pearson/Godden, *In Search of the Red Slave*, 4, 10, 12; Van den Boogaerde, *Shipwrecks of Madagascar*, 176f., 179f.
38 Bialuschewski, "Firearms and Warfare in Late Seventeenth and Early Eighteenth-Century Madagascar", 60f.; Bialuschewski, "Pirates, Slavers, and the Indigenous Population in

The barter goods introduced to Saint Augustin by pirates and merchants in the seventeenth century seem to have found their way into domestic trade only to a limited degree. Archaeological research has shown that the Fihereña used such items as beads, rings, silks and bracelets – and also muskets – as grave goods in particular, as well as burying them in holy forests.[39] Although its economic importance would therefore seem to have been small, this coastal trade attracted the interest of the Sakalava kingdom, which in the seventeenth century began gradually to expand from the interior into the west of the island. The Sakalava had already incorporated the territory bordering on Saint Augustin to the north into their realm from the 1680s before attacking Saint Augustin itself in 1712 or thereabouts, probably in an effort to bring all contacts with *vazaha* under their control. The prisoners taken in these raids were sold to the *vazaha* as slaves, mostly in exchange for firearms and gunpowder. Slaves from south-western Madagascar thus ended up in the Cape Colony, in Mauritius, in the Île Bourbon, in Jakarta and in the Caribbean.[40]

Other local groups – most probably Mahafaly – attacked Saint Augustin around the turn of the century with a view to gaining control over the bay and trade there. The Sakalava state of Maroseraña, which had established itself on the banks of the Morondava Congo river, repelled these raids in a series of large-scale counter-attacks. Subsequently the Sakalava united their various states that previously had existed side by side in the west of Madagascar (known to them as *Menabe*) to a single kingdom under Andriamanetriarivo, the ruler of Maroseraña. Saint Augustin was merged with the neighbouring bay of Tulear in the north to form a tributary state in which the coastal trade was

---

Madagascar", 407–410, 412f., 419f.; Hooper, "An Empire in the Indian Ocean", 118–120; Larson, "The Origins of Malagasy Arriving at Mauritius and Réunion", 205; Newitt, *The Comoro Islands*, 19. On the role of strategic marriage between *vazaha* and Fihereña see Pearson, "Close Encounters of the Worst Kind", 409.

39 Bialuschewski, "Firearms and Warfare in Late Seventeenth and Early Eighteenth-Century Madagascar", 60; Bialuschewski, "Pirates, Slavers, and the Indigenous Population in Madagascar", 411; Pearson, "Close Encounters of the Worst Kind", 406.

40 Bialuschewski, "Pirates, Slavers, and the Indigenous Population in Madagascar", 403f., 413, 415; Bialuschewski, "Thomas Bowrey's Madagascar Manuscript of 1708", 32. Slave labour was not used in growing produce for export in Madagascar itself, where slaves worked, for instance, in the household or alongside subsistence farmers. Their position thus resembled that of agricultural or domestic servants in Europe rather than that of plantation slaves in the Caribbean or Mauritius. (Clarence-Smith, "The Economics of the Indian Ocean Slave Trade in the 19th Century", 3–5.)

monopolised by Sakalava agents. Captains were henceforth to do business with "King Baba" in Tulear and "Prince Will" in Saint Augustin.[41]

Both names were in fact official titles that were carried over successive generations. *Baba* denoted "merchant" among the Sakalava, with the prefix "King" probably meant to indicate to visiting skippers that were dealing with the merchant-in-chief. The meaning of *Will* is unclear, but the fact that he was a "Prince" underscored that his position was subordinate to that of King Baba. Implicit in this hierarchy is the superiority of Tulear of Saint Augustin, which reflects an attempt on the part of the Sakalava to divert shipping in that section of the coast to the more northerly bay. Vessels arriving at Saint Augustin would usually be asked by Prince Will to sail on to Tulear. If a captain refused, Prince Will had to obtain permission from King Baba through a messenger before concluding business in Saint Augustin.[42]

The preference for Tulear on the part of the Sakalava was probably due in large part to the latent threat posed to Saint Augustin by the Mahafaly state to the south and east. The Mahafaly controlled the area to the south of the Onilahy Congo river and sought to take advantage of that position by building trading links of their own with *vazaha*. King Baba maintained an army in Tulear to prevent the Mahafaly from extending their territory to Saint Augustin and acquiring guns through the coastal trade there. This army was also useful in raiding neighbouring societies and taking prisoners that King Baba could sell as slaves to visiting vessels in exchange for guns. The booty from such raids, their income from trade and the gifts they received in their official capacity brought wealth and influence not only to King Baba and Prince will but also to a number of military commanders. In their dealings with *vazaha*, these men and their wives displayed their eminence through guns and fine clothing.[43]

The sale of slaves, which previously had been only incidental to Saint Augustin's main trade in provisions, grew considerably in importance under Sakalava rule. Especially in the Ibara territories in the central southern part of Madagascar, the Sakalava's campaigns generated a steady flow of captives who were taken to Saint Augustin by long-distance trade routes. Yet the volume of the slave trade in Saint Augustin remained far smaller than in other coastal trading places in Madagascar, which by then were turning into slave ports. The long supply route through the sparsely-populated hinterland

---

41 Hooper, "An Empire in the Indian Ocean", 78, 89–92, 98f.
42 Ibid., 92f. For accounts of King Baba in Tulear in 1824 see Boteler, *Narrative of a Voyage of Discovery to Africa and Arabia*, vol. 2, 98f. and Owen, *Narrative of Voyages to Explore the Shores of Africa*, vol. 2, 59.
43 Hooper, "An Empire in the Indian Ocean", 93–95, 99.

meant comparatively long delivery times and high prices, meaning that Saint Augustin was not one of the preferred ports of call for slave vessels, which preferred to conduct their business along Madagascar's more densely populated northern and eastern coasts.[44]

Traffic in Saint Augustin increased in the mid-eighteenth century. The colonial wars fought in India from 1744 to 1763 between France and Great Britain brought a large number of warships to the western Indian Ocean. Besides Anjouan, Saint Augustin was the Royal Navy's principal port of call during this period and saw a large trade in provisions. British vessels may also have recruited seamen and soldiers from among the Fihereña.[45]

The introduction of rice terraces on the high plateau in the island's interior did much to stabilise the food supply around this time, in turn allowing larger and more stable political units to emerge. In the 1780s these units merged to form a large multi-ethnic state by the name of Imerina (land of the Merina). From 1810 onwards Imerina, under the rule of Radama I, sought to extend its rule from the central highlands to the island as a whole. Under the terms of a treaty concluded with Great Britain in 1817, Ramada promised to put an end to the slave trade, in return for which the British recognised his claim as "King of Madagascar" and provided the arms to underpin it. The Merina consequently launched a series of attacks on the Sakalava, taking their port of Mahajanga in the north of the island in 1824. But repeated attempts to conquer the Sakalava in the south-west of Madagascar and thereby to gain control of Saint Augustin failed.[46] The Sakalava tributary state in Saint Augustin, which had imparted a stable structure to coastal trade in the area for over a century, would continue to exist until French colonisation at the end of the nineteenth century.

Whaleships, slave ships, warships

The slave trade continued throughout the period in which whalers called regularly at Saint-Augustin. Beginning in the 1810s, the Royal Navy's operations against the slave trade caused the transit routes in the western Indian Ocean to shift. Instead of direct connections, served by large vessels, between the well-known and easily policed centres of the trade, slavers now used less conspicuous

---

44 Campbell, "The Structure of Trade in Madagascar", 137f.; Hooper, "An Empire in the Indian Ocean", 103; Pearson, "Close Encounters of the Worst Kind", 411.
45 Hooper, "An Empire in the Indian Ocean", 154, 175, 182–184, 190 n. 68.
46 Haywood, "American Whalers and Africa", 90; Hooper, "An Empire in the Indian Ocean", 223–225; Oliver, *Madagascar*, vol. 1, 63; Pearson, "Close Encounters of the Worst Kind", 395.

dhows and followed indirect routes, increasingly resorting to such lesser-known ports as Nosy Be or Mahajanga in the north of Madagascar.[47]

Slave exports increased on the western coast of Madagascar after Imerina had succeeded in banning the trade on the east coast from about 1820 onwards. A further shift occurred after 1835, when slavery was abolished in Mauritius, which previously had accounted for most the demand for slaves in the western Indian Ocean. The slave trade subsequently diminished. What remained of it took the form of smuggling, again from a different centre. It was around this time that the export of slaves from Saint Augustin reached what is likely to have been its all-time peak. At one point in 1835 no fewer than twenty-one vessels were moored in the bay, most which were probably slave ships.[48]

Since slave raids were usually made in the southern winter, slave vessels from Mauritius and La Réunion tended to come to Madagascar between March and December, when the supply was at its peak.[49] Slaves continued to reach Saint Augustin from Ibara territories,[50] albeit unreliably, it would seem. When, in March 1844, Frederick Barnard, a lieutenant of the Royal Navy, posed as a slave buyer, the local middlemen offered only a few young women for sale.[51] Twenty years earlier, another British naval officer, Thomas Boteler, had already found that "Slaves can be purchased only in limited number at St. Augustine's."[52]

The vessels of the Royal Navy that were fighting the slave trade in the western Indian Ocean knew what was going on in Saint Augustin. In 1825 HMS *Leven* succeeded in stopping the French vessel *Soleil* from leaving the bay with 172 slaves on board.[53] If the British were nonetheless unable to stop the slave trade in Saint Augustin for good, it may have been because – like Barnard – they found it to be too insignificant to bother about, instead concentrating their attention on the busier ports.[54] The volume of the slave trade

---

47 Alpers, "Becoming Mozambique", 135f.
48 Campbell, "Madagascar and the Slave Trade", 213; Newitt, *The Comoro Islands*, 21f.
49 Campbell, "Madagascar and Mozambique in the Slave Trade of the Western Indian Ocean", 167f., 179f.
50 Campbell, *An Economic History of Imperial Madagascar*, 57; Campbell, "Madagascar and Mozambique in the Slave Trade of the Western Indian Ocean", 168, 170, 173, 176; Campbell, "Madagascar and the Slave Trade", 212f.
51 Barnard, *A Three Years' Cruise in the Mozambique Channel*, 132f.
52 Boteler, *Narrative of a Voyage of Discovery to Africa and Arabia*, vol. 2, 97.
53 Ibid., 267f.; Owen, *Narrative of Voyages to Explore the Shores of Africa*, vol. 2, 115f.
54 Barnard, *A Three Years' Cruise in the Mozambique Channel*, 132f. In prohibiting the establishment of a mission station in Saint Augustin, King Baba may also have been motivated by a desire to conceal the true extent of the slave trade from the British. The ostensible reason he gave for rejecting such a request by Jesuit missionaries was that their written culture was

in the bay certainly was lower than, for instance, in north-western Madagascar. Even and its peak in the 1820s and 30s, the slave trade in Saint Augustin played a relatively minor role in the wider area.[55] The bay saw a final surge in the slave trade in the 1880s, when the power of Imerina in the interior dwindled. Many prisoners were taken in the ensuing warfare. Armed bands of Sakalava, Bara and Tsienimbala conveyed their prisoners as slaves to Saint Augustin, where they were sold to vessels from La Réunion – mostly in exchange for guns – as late as the 1890s.[56]

Most whalemen are unlikely to have seen much direct evidence of slavery in Saint Augustin. Slaves were kept in camps in the hinterland, out of sight of British patrols and of rival groups. Theodore Lewis, who visited Saint Augustin in 1836 as a surgeon aboard the *Atlantic* of Bridgeport, supposed that "Few of the slaves are seen by the whites as they are kept back in the country to work".[57] The only permanent indication of the slave trade in Saint Austin was the presence of a few middlemen, who usually stayed close to the mouths of the Onilahy and Fiherenana rivers. When a slave vessel dropped anchor the middlemen would seek to establish contact with the captain, involving a number of other intermediaries, advisors and translators in making a deal. These negotiations, however, were often as poorly structured as the delivery chains themselves, with a variety of actors at different levels competing for a share of the profits. Several weeks might pass between the arrival of a slave vessel and the delivery of its cargo, during which time there was often trouble over prices or delays.[58]

To bystanders, the slave trade came into view only in the brief moment during which the slaves were finally taken on board the vessel. Since the captains of slave vessels, however, were aware of the risk of being betrayed to the Royal Navy by seamen from other vessels, they tried to hide that part of their activities as best they could. Their fears were not misplaced. In June 1844, for instance, the *Minerva* of New Bedford reported the sighting of a suspicious-looking brig to a British frigate.[59] Experienced seamen often recognised slave vessels as such,

---

tantamount to witchcraft. (Campbell, "Crisis of Faith and Colonial Conquest", 430; Oliver, *Madagascar*, vol. 1, 77f.)
55 Campbell, "Madagascar and Mozambique in the Slave Trade of the Western Indian Ocean", 168, 170, 173, 176; Campbell, "Madagascar and the Slave Trade", 212f.
56 Alpers, "Becoming Mozambique", 135f.; Campbell, "The East African Slave Trade", 12, 16, 19f.; Campbell, *An Economic History of Imperial Madagascar*, 233, 235; Campbell, "Madagascar and Mozambique in the Slave Trade of the Western Indian Ocean", 168, 170, 173, 176; Campbell, "Madagascar and the Slave Trade", 212f.
57 Lewis, Journal ATLANTIC, 1835–1837, 30.07.1836.
58 Campbell, "Madagascar and the Slave Trade", 220–222.
59 Barnard, *A Three Years' Cruise in the Mozambique Channel*, 148–150, 156.

their attempts at concealment notwithstanding. "Came in a Spanish Slaver", recorded the log of the *Octavia* of New Bedford during a stopover in February 1838.[60] In September 1857 the log of the *Mars* of New Bedford noted the presence of "6 vessals [sic] laying at anchor here four whalers and two slavers."[61] And in February 1858 a seaman aboard the *Clara Bell* of Mattapoisett wrote in his diary: "Found ourselves in company with three French brigs – two of which are slavers."[62] Spotting slave vessels was all the easier because ordinary merchant vessels had all but ceased to frequent the bay. Since the end of the Napoleonic Wars, the European imperial powers had all acquired bases of their own in the western Indian Ocean and no longer had any need to call at Saint Augustin for supplies.[63] Whalemen and seamen aboard slavers must sometimes have spoken to one another. There is scarcely any other way for the officer who kept the *Octavia*'s log to have known that the slave vessel he mentioned had at the time been at sea for eight months and left Saint Augustin with two hundred slaves on board.[64]

Only once, however, do we find a whaleman recording his observations of slaves being taken on board. In the mid-1850s Charles Robbins of the *Clara Bell* encountered a slave vessel from La Réunion in Saint-Augustin, a scene which he later described in his memoirs. This singular account is worth quoting at length:

> A fine clipper swept up the harbor and anchored near us, the French tri-color at her peak. According to the best accounts, she had come into port to procure a cargo of laborers. Innocent word enough, – laborers! Ah, but she would take them to the island of Bourbon. There they would be paid twelve dollars a month for seven years' service.
>
> And what of that? Just this: they would never be able to buy their way out of bondage. The seven years up, they would all be in debt and would have to remain as slaves, powerless even to return home. It was slavery in disguise.
>
> Out of the remote interior of the island came that somber procession. A slave trader had them in leash. He herded them all the way to the shore, and he himself brought them, load after load, aboard the French ship. Once on deck the poor creatures were examined by a sort of veterinary, who punched their breasts, pinched their limbs and eyed their teeth as if he were appraising so much horse-flesh. Oh, it was a horrid sight! And I saw it done.
>
> In the midst of the operation a man-of-war, cruising for slavers, entered the harbor. A boat sped swiftly across the water, and the officers boarded the Frenchman. But nothing

---

60 Log OCTAVIA, 1837–1839, 02.02.1838.
61 Log MARS, 1856–1859, 07.09.1857.
62 Wallace, Journal CLARA BELL, 1855–1858, 02.02.1858.
63 Boteler, *Narrative of a Voyage of Discovery to Africa and Arabia*, vol. 2, 97.
64 Log OCTAVIA, 1837–1839, 04.02.1838.

could be contrived to save the poor wretches. The Frenchman's papers were flawless. Dastardly though the fact, it was cloaked in legal fiction. No one had a right to interfere.[65]

In his opposition to slavery and the slave trade, Robbins is likely to have represented the views of many American seamen – and certainly of those who expressed their views in print. Charles Nordhoff too recalls the horrified accounts of the cruelties perpetrated by slave traders on the coast of Madagascar which circulated aboard his vessel around 1850.[66]

Princes and captains

Since Saint Augustin became absorbed into a tributary state at the cusp of the eighteenth century, the Sakalava had done much to formalise the coastal trade and its procedures. Any vessel sailing into the bay would be met by Prince Will's pilots, interpreters and ambassadors. The function of the pilots most probably was to ensure that vessels did not go on to drop anchor off a section of the coastline under Mahafaly control but safely in Sakalava territory. The other intermediaries questioned the captain as to his commercial interests and communicated his answers via Prince Will to King Baba. King Baba would then issue instructions regarding the goods required before proceeding to the bay on person. There, the captain was obliged to visit him, offering the requisite gifts before trade could commence. Over the following days, King Baba, Prince Will and other members of the local elite made repeated visits to the vessel in order to exchange gifts and to dine with the captain and his officers.[67]

This highly formalised procedure, however, applied only to the trade in cattle, rice and slaves. The buying and selling of lemons, bananas and other fruit King Baba left to small traders. Since whaleships' demand for rice and cattle was lower than that from slavers and merchantmen, King Baba and Prince Will went to much less trouble in dealing with them. Whalers would not have encountered the delegations of up to fifty elaborately costumed dignitaries that would sometimes appear aboard East Indiamen in the eighteenth century. The somewhat muted welcome accorded to whalers may also have been due to the fact that their vessels were unarmed and hence unable to fire their guns in salute of King Baba, a show of respect usually required vessels arriving at Saint Augustin.[68]

---

65 Robbins, *The Gam*, 203f.
66 Nordhoff, *Whaling and Fishing*, 170–173.
67 Hooper, "An Empire in the Indian Ocean", 111–115.
68 Ibid., 115, 122, 126.

Yet King Baba, Prince Will and other Sakalava dignitaries would often go to meet whaleships in person. Sometimes they would all appear together, sometimes in succession – particularly when King Babar was in Tulear and unable to travel the approximately twenty kilometres to Saint Augustin on the day of a vessel's arrival.[69] King Baba and Prince Will were usually accompanied by other influential personages and family members. The purpose of these visits was, as noted in the log of the *Adeline* in June 1842, "to speak the business".[70] This included the payment of docking fees. In return for permission to moor in the bay and to gather water and timber on the banks the Onilahy, King Baba and Prince Will usually asked for a few bottles of gunpowder and some textile clothes, sometimes also for guns.[71]

Since the merchantmen who had begun visiting Saint Augustin in the seventeenth century had already significantly depleted the already sparse forests in the vicinity of Saint Augustin in their search for timbers to repair their vessels,[72] whalers are unlikely to have found much contiguous woodland nearby. Any significant reserves of timber would have been found on the banks of the Onilahy. Seamen usually cut it themselves and stocked up on drinking water at the same time.[73] Since only a flat rate was charged for the permit, some captains had their crews cut very large quantities of wood indeed. Captain Taber of the *Janus* of New Bedford, for instance, ordered no fewer than twenty boatloads of timber to be brought on board.[74] The amount of water taken by a whaler depended not least on the level of the Onilahy, which was subject to considerable fluctuations.[75]

During a whaleship's stay at Saint Augustin, King Baba and Prince Will would often pay several visits to the vessel. Sometimes one or the other would come aboard daily with their retinue. Each time they would bring "presents" – a zebu, for example – and each time they expected presents of equivalent value in return: gunpowder, clothes and brandy, or perhaps an invitation to dine

---

69 Log GRANDTURK, 1834–1836, 26. & 29.04.1835; Log HUDSON, 1833–1835, 16.04.1834; Log LEONIDAS, 1837–1839, 13.08.1838; O'Keeffe, Journal GRAND TURK, 1836–1841, 14.–16.04.1837; Tobey, Journal ROSCOE, 1846–1849, 31.08. & 01.09.1847.
70 Log ADELINE, 1840–1842, 25.07.1842.
71 Ibid., 25.07.1842; Log HUDSON, 1833–1835, 11.04.1834; Log JANUS, 1835–1837, 07.07.1836; Log JOHN AND EDWARD, 1855–1858, 09.07.1855.
72 Hooper, "An Empire in the Indian Ocean", 63.
73 Lewis, Journal ATLANTIC, 1835–1837, 30.07.1836; Log LEONIDAS, 1837–1839, 15.08.1838; Log SMYRNA, 1853–1857, 14.03.1857; Tobey, Journal ROSCOE, 1846–1849, 03.09.1847.
74 Log JANUS, 1833–1835, 09.08.1834.
75 Barnard, *A Three Years' Cruise in the Mozambique Channel*, 132f.

with the captain.[76] When visiting merchantmen, King Baba would sometimes offer slaves as gifts,[77] though no instances are recorded of slaves being given to whalers. Talk of gifts or "presents" – the term used by both sides – should not blind us to the fact that these exchanges were commercial in nature. In his capacity as the gatekeeper of trade in Saint Augustin, King Baba was a figure of key importance, and maintaining good relations with him was worth a captain's while. Captains could thus scarcely refuse the frequent visits by the potentate and his followers, even though they might disturb shipboard routines and be considered an imposition. During a stopover in April 1834, the log of the *Hudson* of Sag Harbor noted that "We are visited every day by the King Duke and some of the Princes they all go almost mad".[78] King Baba clearly came in pursuit of his own commercial interests, and captains had little choice but to receive him and his deputies. However, this did not always entail receiving them with much respect. On one occasion, Captain Robbins of the *Clara Bell* set a bucket of sweet water and several pounds of hardtack before his guests and left them to alone with these meagre offerings.[79]

It was probably also part of these efforts to maintain good relations that whaling captains could also be found participating in funeral obsequies on tent rock, the burial place of the local elites. In April 1834 the skippers of five whalers attended the funeral of a high-ranking lady, and in June 1836 several whalers sent a delegation bearing the American flag to the funeral of Prince Will.[80] Only few instances are recorded of *vazaha* visiting Prince Will at his residence, which lay on south bank of the Onilahy about a mile from its mouth.[81]

The practice of rowing out in canoes to meet visiting vessels with a view to selling the *vazaha* seashells and animals as well as produce – oranges, lemons

---

76 Log GRAND TURK, 1834–1836, 26.04.1835; Log KINGSTON, 11.02.1801; Robbins, The Gam, 200.
77 Hooper, "An Empire in the Indian Ocean", 124.
78 Log HUDSON, 1833–1835, 17.04.1834. For another remark to the same effect see Winslow, Journal WAVE, 1851–1854, 05.04.1852.
79 Robbins, *The Gam*, 200.
80 Log HUDSON, 1833–1835, 16.04.1834; Log SOUTH CAROLINA, 1835–1837, 03.07.1836; Tobey, Journal HOUQUA, 1835–1837, 04.07.1836. A detailed account of the funeral can be found in Lewis, Journal ATLANTIC, 1835–1837, 30.07.1836. A few years later a British captain, Pascoe Grenfell Hill, described Prince Will as "extreme old", which may suggest that his post was filled with a man of considerable experience. (Hill, *Fifty Days on Board a Slave-vessel in the Mozambique Channel*, 8f.)
81 Barnard, *A Three Years' Cruise in the Mozambique Channel*, 2–8; Boteler, *Narrative of a Voyage of Discovery to Africa and Arabia*, vol. 2, 269f.; Hill, *Fifty Days on Board a Slave-vessel in the Mozambique Channel*, 8f.; Log KINGSTON, 1800–1801, 10.02.1801.

and honey – had already emerged in the eighteenth century. Winds and tides permitting, up to thirty narrow canoes, each with five or six persons on board, might encircle a vessel as soon it dropped anchor. The number of small traders seeking to clamber over the bulwarks often far exceeded that of the men on board.[82] "The ship is loaded with natives", records the log of the *Izette* of Salem, which moored at Saint Augustin in March 1842.[83]

These visitors spoke a rudimentary form of English and introduced themselves by English rather than by Malagasy names. It was the convention for those who wished to do business to prefix a simple and easily understood name with a royal or noble title – "Prince Green", for example. Somebody looking to recommend himself as a pilot would call himself "captain", the records containing references to personages named "Captain Stoart", "Captain Long" or "Captain Peorgey".[84] Though seamen were likely to be amused rather than impressed, these names at least served the purpose of being memorable with a view to securing preferential treatment on future visits. In February 1844, Lieutenant Frederick Barnard of the Royal Navy noted that "We anchored at St. Augustine's Bay on February 14, and were soon surrounded by our old friends. Prince Green came on board".[85] The Malagasy "princes" and "captains" had clearly made an impression.

Some small traders asked seamen to provide them with letters of reference vouching for their trustworthiness to other whalemen.[86] They often remained on board until sunset. In payment for their wares, they accepted both US dollars and barter goods, such as beads, fabrics, bottles, tobacco or tools.[87] Writing in 1824, Thomas Boteler, an officer of the Royal Navy, found that "They understood well how to drive a bargain".[88] It seems that business was mutually satisfactory. Unlike slavers, whalers were untroubled by delays in supplying the desired goods, and logbooks repeatedly mention the plentiful availability of

---

82 Barnard, *A Three Years' Cruise in the Mozambique Channel*, 2–8, 65f.; Boteler, *Narrative of a Voyage of Discovery to Africa and Arabia*, vol. 2, 92f.; Hill, *Fifty Days on Board a Slave-vessel in the Mozambique Channel*, 8f.; Lewis, Journal ATLANTIC, 1835–1837, 05.04.1836; Log FRANCES II, 1831–1832, 29.01.1832; Log HUDSON, 1833–1835, 12.04.1834; Log KINGSTON, 1800–1801, 10.02.1801; Wallace, Journal CLARA BELL, 1855–1858, 02.02.1858; Winslow, Journal WAVE, 1851–1854, 06.04.1852.
83 Log IZETTE, 1841–1842, 11.03.1842.
84 Barnard, *A Three Years' Cruise in the Mozambique Channel*, 2–8; Hill, *Fifty Days on Board a Slave-vessel in the Mozambique Channel*, 8f.; Log FRANCES II, 1831–1832, 29.01.1832.
85 Barnard, *A Three Years' Cruise in the Mozambique Channel*, 116f.
86 Ibid., 2–8.
87 Ibid., 22–25; Wallace, Journal CLARA BELL, 1855–1858, 08.03.1857.
88 Boteler, *Narrative of a Voyage of Discovery to Africa and Arabia*, vol. 2, 92f.

livestock and fruit.[89] Only the several days it might take for King Baba to arrive, without whose permission no water, timber or other provisions could be taken on board, were apt to slow matters down.[90] Crews generally enjoyed the meat of the zebus and sheep found in the area and took advantage of their stopovers to lay in large quantities of stores. In the approximately three weeks she was moored at Saint Augustin in August 1834, the *Hudson* of Sag Harbor took on a total of four hundred barrels of water, five adult and four young zebus, seventeen sheep and goats, as well as potatoes, pumpkins, beans, grass for fodder, poultry, honey, tamarinds, lemons, sugarcane and other produce.[91]

Zebus could be obtained only from King Baba and Prince Will and, as a rule, only in exchange for firearms, with one gun buying one adult or two calves.[92] Gunpowder might also be accepted in payment, with Frederick Barnard observing the going rate to be about twenty to twenty-five pounds of gunpowder for "a beast weighing about 350 pounds".[93] A zebu weighing roughly twice a was acquired in exchange for a musket by Captain Tobey of the *Roscoe* of New Bedford in 1847.[94] Zebus were widely viewed as markers of wealth and status in southern Madagascar. They were luxury items acceptable both as bridal gifts and as sacrificial offerings; to their owners, they promised a degree of security against bad harvests.[95] Combined with their considerable economic value, this special significance was probably the reason for the monopoly over the trade in zebus claimed by the representatives of the Sakalava state.

Sheep, goats and poultry, on the other hand, were also sold by small traders, usually in exchange for clothing and gunpowder.[96] In May 1835, for instance, Captain Bartlett of the *Grand Turk* of New Bedford paid three cups of gunpowder for six sheep.[97] Traders would sometimes also demand guns in exchange for larger numbers of sheep and goats. For rice too King Baba demanded guns, whereas *vazaha* might obtain fruit and honey in exchange for

---

89 Log FRANCES II, 1831–1832, 29.01.1832; Log KINGSTON, 1800–1801, 14.02.1801; Wallace, Journal CLARA BELL, 1855–1858, 08.03.1857.
90 Haywood, "American Whalers and Africa", 91.
91 Log HUDSON, 1833–1835, 01.09.1834.
92 Log AVERICK, 1834–1836, 08.04.1835; Log HUDSON, 1833–1835, 09. & 12.08.1834; Log KINGSTON, 1800–1801, 25.02.1801.
93 Barnard, *A Three Years' Cruise in the Mozambique Channel*, 65f.
94 Tobey, Journal ROSCOE, 1846–1849, 02.09.1847.
95 Boteler, *Narrative of a Voyage of Discovery to Africa and Arabia*, vol. 2, 272; Hooper, "An Empire in the Indian Ocean", 47; Thompson, *The Life of John Thompson*, 122–124.
96 Log REAPER, 1835–1837, 14.04.1836.
97 Log GRAND TURK, 1834–1836, 05.05.1835; Log KINGSTON, 1800–1801, 24.02.1801.

beads or tools.[98] Prices remained fairly stable throughout the era of whaling in the western Indian Ocean. Only the arrival of unusually large vessels with correspondingly large crews, such as warships of the Royal Navy, might cause King Baba and Prince Will as well as the small traders to raise their demands considerably. One such case was a visit by the frigate HMS *Cleopatra*, which sailed with a crew of approximately two hundred, in the early 1840s.[99] But whalemen generally found prices in Saint Augustin to be reasonable. Of a stopover in 1847, the log of the *Ann Parry* of Portsmouth records that it was a place "wher a poor fellow gets his money worth and a litll change back."[100]

Over the years, King Baba and Prince Will, along with certain independent traders, appear to have amassed a considerable number of guns. In 1836 Theodore Lewis, the ship's surgeon mention above, observed "a great number of Muskets" being carried in Sain Augustin.[101] In the same year Asa Tobey, a seaman aboard the *Houqua* of New Bedford, was told by the armed men that they carried guns as protection against "pirats as thay call them a tribe that lives Back that want to take prosession of there teretories so as to have the trade of the ships".[102] In light of such observations, the historians Phoebe Wray and Kenneth Martin concluded that the supply of guns from whalers to local Sakalava over the years was what kept warfare in the hinterland going[103] – and hence, it might be added, the slave trade. Yet it is impossible in retrospect to verify the underlying assumption that the arms provided by the whalers – usually old, cheap muskets – would indeed have conferred military superiority on the Sakalava.[104] It must therefore remain an open question whether the coastal trade with whalers was a significant (albeit indirect) factor in encouraging conflict and slave raids in the interior.

✳✳✳

How did seamen make use of their leisure time in Saint Augustin? Some went for walks through coastal settlements and their environs.[105] Madagascar's many endemic species of flora and fauna seem to have exerted a strong fascination on

---

98 Hooper, "An Empire in the Indian Ocean", 128.
99 Barnard, *A Three Years' Cruise in the Mozambique Channel*, 65f.; Boteler, *Narrative of a Voyage of Discovery to Africa and Arabia*, vol. 2, 275; Hill, *Fifty Days on Board a Slave-vessel in the Mozambique Channel*, 11.
100 Log ANN PARRY, 1845–1847, 16.02.1847.
101 Lewis, Journal ATLANTIC, 1835–1837, 30.07.1836.
102 Tobey, Journal HOUQUA, 1835–1837, 18.03.1836.
103 Wray/Martin, "Historical Whaling Records from the Western Indian Ocean", 218.
104 On the history of guns in Africa see also the recent publications by Felix Brahm, in particular "Guns in Africa" and "Merchandise of Power".
105 Beane, *From Forecastle to Cabin*, 151; Log MARS, 1856–1859, 23.09.1857.

many of the men.¹⁰⁶ Some observed the Fihereña (Fig. 19) and visited them in their bamboo huts, but by and large seamen kept themselves to themselves, playing ball games on the beach or simply relaxing on board.¹⁰⁷

Unlike in other coastal areas of Arica, however, seamen making landfall in Saint Augustin often encountered women. As early as the eighteenth century, women were members of King Baba's official delegations which came on board visiting vessels. Some were wives and daughters of the male visitors, and given that high-status Sakalava men might marry up to twelve women, they could make up a considerable proportion of the visiting parties. The men demanded specifically feminine gifts for their women, such as mirrors, scissors or frocks. For his part, King Baba might also offer gifts in the form of slave girls, even when the vessel in question was not a slave vessel.¹⁰⁸ Women and children were also to be found in the canoes that came to do small-scale trade with incoming vessels.¹⁰⁹ "The women taking a most prominent part in this traffic", observed Frederick Barnard in August 1843.¹¹⁰ And in April 1852 John Winslow, a seaman aboard the *Wave* of New Bedford, noted that "The Deck is full of Natives all the time Men Women and children."¹¹¹

The sources we have for Saint Augustin do not answer the question to what extent encounters between seamen and local women included sexual contacts, which Ben Ely's account suggests were commonplace in the north of Madagascar.¹¹² A rare hint at such a contact is to be found in the log of the *Mars* of New Bedford, which arrived in September 1857: "As soon as the celley was down the queanes rushed on Board the deck was strewed with tight heads and when the men all chose their wife the rest all went on shore this is the devils one place."¹¹³ More explicit still is John Winslow, whose diary records twenty-five to thirty "ladies of pleasure" who remained on board well into the night.¹¹⁴

Sailors usually spent their shore leave within sight of their vessels, only seldom venturing further inland. Far from being considered a place of exotic promise, Madagascar had a reputation for being rife with dangers. In Saint

---

106 Beane, *From Forecastle to Cabin*, 157.
107 Busch, *Whaling Will Never Do for Me*, 164f.; Haywood, "American Whalers and Africa", 96; Log SOUTH CAROLINA, 1835–1837, 15.07.1836.
108 Hooper, "An Empire in the Indian Ocean", 123–125.
109 Ibid., 110f.; Tobey, Journal HOUQUA, 1835–1837, 14.03.1836.
110 Barnard, *A Three Years' Cruise in the Mozambique Channel*, 65f.
111 Winslow, Journal WAVE, 1851–1854, 05.04.1852.
112 Ely, *There She Blows*, 98; for another suggestion to that effect from Nosy Pasandava see Log REAPER, 1837–1839, 06.06.1838.
113 Log MARS, 1856–1859, 07.09.1857.
114 Winslow, Journal WAVE, 1851–1854, 15.04.1852.

234 —— 3 A stabilising flow of goods: Saint Augustin, Madagascar, 1830–1860

Fig. 19: Grinding plants in Saint Augustin. Drawing from the diary of R. Weir, a seaman who visited the bay aboard the *Clara Bell* of Mattapoisett in February 1857.
Weir, Journal CLARA BELL, 1855–1858, 08.03.1857. Courtesy Mystic Seaport.

Augustin, as elsewhere in the island, seamen often caught tropical fevers.[115] Above all, however, the men feared attacks by the indigenous population. Stories of such attacks circulated from vessel to vessel, giving Madagascar a lasting reputation as a dangerous place. Such tales did not lack foundation in fact. In 1825, for instance, several survivors of the British whaler *Rambler*, which had been shipwrecked on a reef off the north-eastern coast of Madagascar, were murdered ashore, among them her captain, Greaves.[116] A similar incident occurred in 1844 some sixty nautical miles north of Saint Augustin when several canoes attacked a boat carrying seamen from HMS *Cleopatra*, which had run aground. Eight seamen were killed.[117] In 1851 the entire crew of an American merchant vessel, the *Queen of the West*, was killed by attackers of the north-

---

115 Browne, *Etchings of a Whaling Cruise*, 267; Log MARS, 1856–1859, 11.09.1857.
116 "Marine Journal." *New-Bedford Mercury*, 30.12.1825.
117 "From Madagascar." *New-Bedford Mercury*, 21.06.1844, 2.

west coast of Madagascar.[118] And in 1858 local men attacked a French vessel which had been looking to hire workers on an unspecified part of the coastline, again killing the entire crew.[119]

Nor were *vazaha* quite safe in Saint Augustin itself. In July 1836 a seaman from the *South Carolina* of Dartmouth was attacked while cutting wood and his axe stolen.[120] Only four weeks later a crewman of the *General Pike* was shot in an altercation. Around a dozen whalers were moored in the bay at the time, and several of their captains went on land in an effort to resolve the dispute.[121] In April 1837 Thomas O'Keeffe, a seaman aboard the *Grand Turk* of New Bedford, was attacked by three men. On this occasion, however, the assailants were caught by Prince Will's men, and O'Keeffe was paid compensation.[122] Finally, in 1882 an American merchant named Emerson was robbed and murdered inland from Saint Augustin.[123]

Although such attacks were few in number, they generated a multitude of legends, yarns and concrete fears, all of which contributed to Saint Augustin's poor reputation among seafarers.[124] In 1843, for instance, Captain Alden of the *Bruce* of Fairhaven ordered the process of dropping anchor in the bay to be abandoned when he noticed that no other vessel was moored there and was afraid of being left at the mercy of potential attackers.[125] Seamen from warships would sometimes insist on arming themselves before going ashore.[126]

A more frequent cause of conflict was theft. Seamen often accused their Malagasy visitors aboard ship of having sticky fingers. The log of the brig *Penobscot* of Nantucket, which called at Saint Augustin April 1844, noted that the crew had been "Plagged badly by the Natives stealing every thing";[127] similar

---

118 "Zanzibar." *The Republican Standard*, 17.06.1852, 1.
119 "The Massacre of a French Crew at Madagascar." *The Republican Standard*, 12.08.1858, 2. For accounts of other attacks see "Marine Journal." *New-Bedford Mercury*, 30.12.1825 and "Marine Journal." *New-Bedford Mercury*, 19.09.1834, 2.
120 Log SOUTH CAROLINA, 1835–1837, 18.07.1836.
121 Log CERES II, 1835–1837, 17. & 18.08.1836.
122 O'Keeffe, Journal GRAND TURK, 1836–1841, 23.04.1837.
123 Oliver, *Madagascar*, vol. 2, 299–302.
124 Haywood, "American Whalers and Africa", 96f. The reputation of Saint Augustin among seamen is aptly summarised in this entry from the log of the barque *Reaper* of Salem: "It is one of the most miserable holes on the face of the earth, the inhabitants are but a shade above the brutes." (Log REAPER, 1835–1837, 14.04.1836).
125 Browne, "Sketches of the Arabs", 4.
126 Barnard, *A Three Years' Cruise in the Mozambique Channel*, 132f.
127 Log PENOBSCOT, 1843–1845, 10.04.1844.

remarks are recorded elsewhere.[128] Returning from shore leave, the crew of *Leonidas* of Fairhaven even found one of her boats' sails missing.[129] In order to prevent theft, some crews would stow all ropes, belaying pins, buckets and tools not in current use in the hold before mooring off Saint Augustin.[130]

Material losses aside, theft was a potential threat to the captain's authority. At sea, the captain would keep order by punishing even minor infractions severely. If visitors then came on board and were suffered to remove items with impunity, seamen might well take it as a sign of weakness on the captain's part. It was probably in order to avoid creating such an impression that Captain Gray of the *Adeline* of New Bedford resorted to a drastic measure during a stopover in 1842. When a Malagasy small trader was accused of stealing a piece of cotton fabric, Grey ordered him to be punished as he would have punished his own men, having him hung from the rigging by his arms. The alleged thief remained in that uncomfortable position until the next day, when Prince Will bought his freedom in exchange for four sheep.[131]

Saint Augustin's reputation also seems likely to have prevented many seamen from abandoning ship there, although records of *vazaha* being left behind go back a long way. As early as 1595 a Dutch expedition had left behind two seamen in the bay,[132] and such cases continued to occur. It would appear that in the seventeenth and eighteenth centuries seamen man would sometimes desert from merchantmen with a view to joining the pirates who were reputed to be based in the area and who were still the subject of many a colourful legend among seamen. The topography of the bay and its hinterland made it hard for captains to find fugitive seamen, and it became to custom instead to pay King Baba and Prince Will bounties for their capture.[133]

By the time whalers became regular visitors to Saint Augustin, King Baba and Prince Will had already established a business model along those lines, taking the initiative in offering captains to retrieve deserters and return them to their vessels against payment of a fee. "Gave the Indians one Bottle powder for detecting the Blacksmith", noted the log of the *Averick* of New Bedford in April 1835.[134] Around a year later, the escape of six seamen from the *Golconda II* of Fairhaven came to a

---

128 Lewis, *Journal* ATLANTIC, 1835–1837, 30.07.1836; Log ADELINE, 1840–1842, 25.07.1842; Thompson, *The Life of John Thompson*, 122–125.
129 Log LEONIDAS, 1837–1839, 22.08.1838.
130 Robbins, *The Gam*, 196f.
131 Log ADELINE, 1840–1842, 28. & 29.07.1842.
132 Pearson, "Close Encounters of the Worst Kind", 396.
133 Hooper, "An Empire in the Indian Ocean", 119, 133f.
134 Log AVERICK, 1834–1836, 16.04.1835.

similar end. The men had taken a boat, provisions and some one hundred dollars but were returned to the vessel almost naked, having apparently been robbed beforehand. Captain Chase nonetheless found their return to be worth a musket and a considerable quantity of gunpowder.[135] In 1855 Captain Smith of the *John and Edward* of New Bedford paid some forty yards of cloth for the capture of four deserters.[136] Other captains to enlist local potentates in retrieving fugitive seamen included Chapman of the *Montgomery* (1856) and Dougherty of the *Falcon* (1866).[137] As in other places frequented by whalers, deserters in Saint Augustin were sometimes betrayed. In March 1843 four men on the run from the *Milwood* of New Bedford encountered Fihereña who offered to help by hiding them in a hut, only to claim a bounty from the captain for revealing their whereabouts. The escapees were given the lash and put in irons.[138]

Such was the risk of being caught that fugitive seamen had better prospects for success if they hid not on land, but on another vessel. This was the course taken by a young seaman from New York who escaped from the barque *Mars* of New Bedford in September 1857 to join the crew of a French slaver moored in the Bay of Saint-Augustin.[139] It also occurred that a seaman managed to persuade men from another whaler he met on shore to hide him as a stowaway aboard their vessel.[140] Overall, and particularly in comparison to other ports in the wider area frequented by whalers, such as Port Louis or Cape Town, Saint Augustin witnessed few desertions. It reputation was such that seamen feared never to get out alive if left to their own devices, and some would-be deserters soon returned to their vessels of their own accord.[141] Only seldom did whalers come upon deserters left behind by other vessels in Saint Augustin.[142]

The end of whaling in the waters surrounding Madagascar brought a sharp decline in shipping and, with it, of the coastal trade in Saint Augustin. This decline was further accelerated by the opening of the Suez Canal in 1869, after which much of the commercial traffic in the Indian Ocean moved to its northern part. France, which conquered Madagascar in the 1880s and 1890s, found Saint Augustin to be of no economic importance and did nothing to develop its

---

135 Lewis, Journal ATLANTIC, 1835–1837, 14.07.1836; Tobey, Journal HOUQUA, 1835–1837, 21.07.1836.
136 Log JOHN AND EDWARD, 1855–1858, 16.–17.07.1855.
137 Log FALCON, 1865–1867, 17.–18.03.1866; Log MONTGOMERY, 1855–1858, 04.02.1856. For another case see Winslow, Journal WAVE, 1851–1854, 17.04.1852.
138 Thompson, *The Life of John Thompson*, 124.
139 Log MARS, 1856–1859, 24.09.1857.
140 Thompson, *The Life of John Thompson*, 125.
141 Lewis, Journal ATLANTIC, 1835–1837, 08.04.1836.
142 Log HUDSON, 1833–1835, 31.08.1834.

infrastructure.[143] Saint Augustin, which from the mid-seventeenth to the mid-nineteenth century had been an important and contested centre both of global navigation and of commerce within the island of Madagascar, became the backwater it remains today. Unlike in the case of Walvis Bay, where the connections established by whalers survived the disappearance of whaling itself, Saint Augustin found itself isolated. A more similar case, at first sight, would appear to be that of Delagoa Bay, where coastal states sought to use trade with whalers for their own advantage in times of crisis. Saint Augustin, however, relied on the victualling trade to a far greater extent than Delagoa Bay, where ivory came to predominate.

In light of Saint Augustin's subsequent development, it would seem that the most important effect of whalers and their visits to the bay lay in having stabilised the coastal trade until about 1860. The shift in imperial boundaries and spheres of influence that overtook the Indian Ocean as a result of the Napoleonic wars had already cost Saint Augustin its role as a port of call for merchant vessels. In their absence, it fell to whalers to keep goods circulating in the area and to ensure that King Baba was supplied with guns and powder. In so doing, whalers contributed to supporting the Sakalava tributary state in south-western Madagascar as it came under increasing pressure from the expanding state of Imerina.

---

143 Hooper, "An Empire in the Indian Ocean", 266f.

4 Provisioning as a power resource: Mutsamudu, Anjouan, 1835–1890

Anjouan, its outline resembling a gnawed triangle, lies at the centre of the archipelago of the Comoros. Its western tip seems to be pointing towards section of the African coastline where Mozambique borders on Tanzania; its southeastern tip reaches out towards Madagascar, some two hundred miles to the west – roughly the same distance as the African mainland in the east. As if to create a symbolic link between Africa and the island of Madagascar from which it broke off millions of years ago, a mountain range spans the island, dominating all three sides of the triangle. At their highest point, Mount Ntringui, these volcanic highlands rise to nearly 1,600 metres. Along with the three other principal islands in the group, which also rise high above the sea, Anjouan appears like a fragment of a bridge across the north of the Mozambique Channel.

English-speaking seamen usually called this island by a woman's name, "Johanna". In the local language of Shindzwani, which is closely related to Swahili, it is known as *Nzwani* and in Arabic as جوانان. The French called the island Anjouan, and since this is the most firmly established of its various names, it shall be used here throughout. For the same reason, I will refer to the island's capital as Mutsamudu, though it too has been known by various names in a variety of spellings.

Mutsamudu was not altogether easy to reach by sea. To the south of the island, reefs form an underwater wall blocking access to much of the coast. An island approximately one kilometre wide off the western coast of Anjouan, known to seamen as "Saddle Island" on account of its distinctive hills, helped vessels find their bearings. From Saddle Islands, navigators had only to sail due east until, after about ten nautical miles, the minaret of Mutsamudu's chief mosque came into view in their telescopes (Fig. 20). Since the town lacked port facilities, vessels would usually anchor several hundred metres from the shore, a little to the west of Mutsamudu. Not only did they find better anchorage there, they were also less exposed to tidal currents.[1]

Not all seamen found the idea of mooring so far from the coast in the western Indian Ocean, which after all was notorious for its stormy seas, appealing. More than one captain also preferred to take his chances closer to the beach.[2] Yet at

---

[1] Barnard, *A Three Years' Cruise in the Mozambique Channel*, 278f.; Huddart, *The Oriental Navigator*, 103; Isaacs, *Travels and Adventures in Eastern Africa*, vol. 2, 371; Prior, *Voyage Along the Eastern Coast of Africa*, 46; Smyth, *The Life and Services of Captain Philip Beaver*, 263.
[2] Log MONTEZUMA, 1846–1849, 07.03.1846; Log PALESTINE, 1839–1842, 14.05.1840.

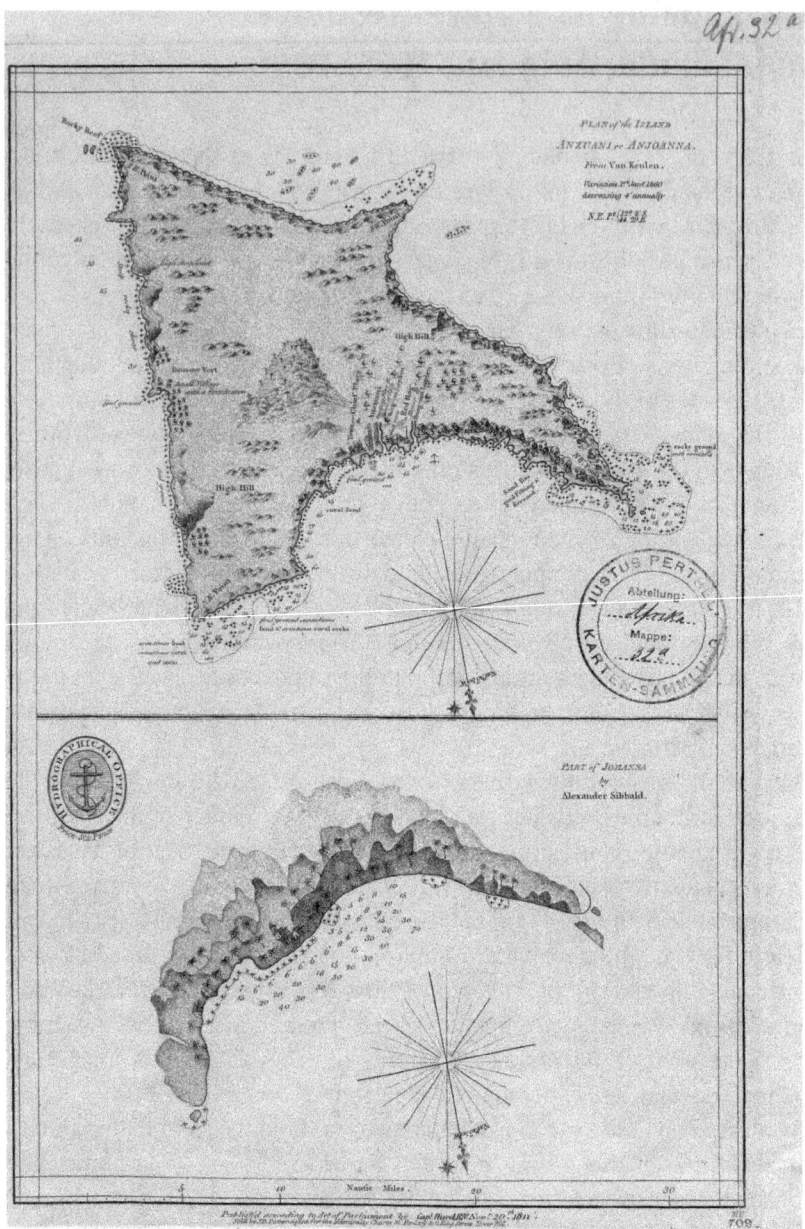

Fig. 20: Anjouan on a British Admiralty Chart of 1811, adapted from a much older map by the Dutch mapmaker Johannes van Keulen. (*Plan of the Island Anzuani or Anjoanna.* London: Hydrographical Office of the Admirality, 1811).
Courtesy of the Gotha Research Library at University of Erfurt, SPK 40 32.a A [01, 22].

least in the winter months, when the mountains shielded Anjouan from the dry south-west monsoon winds, the sea off Mutsamudu is as smooth as a windowpane – and as clear, too: seamen could sometimes see as far as the seabed and observe corals, molluscs and fish of all sizes and colours imaginable.³

From October to April, however, the north-west monsoon brings heavy rainfall and churns up the sea, leading to tall breakers off Mutsamudu. Especially in January, the winds carry heavy storms, sometimes lasting for days at a time, to the Comoros. Lacking as it does rocky offshore islands to shield it, Mutsamudu during this time is at the mercy of the raging sea, known as *bahári* in Shindzuani, the language of Anjouan. A breakwater made of rubble and built in the mid-nineteenth century was designed to offer some protection to vessels, but was useless in all but the gentlest seas.⁴ Whalers therefore did their best to avoid Mutsamudu except between May and September. Some particularly intrepid vessels still came from October to December, but only the foolhardiest in January or after.⁵ Among the latter was the *Bruce* of Fairhaven, which dropped anchor in March 1843. To avoid the vessel being smashed on the rocky shore by storm winds, Captain Alden anchored so far offshore that the men had to row a boat for three hours to land in Mutsamudu.⁶

Provided they avoided the dangerous months of the southern summer, seamen tended to find Anjouan appealing and welcoming. Even from afar, the foliage of date and coconut palms as well as banana plants could be seen to cover the island in a dense layer of green reaching from the beach to the hills (Fig. 21). At certain times of day the wind would carry the fragrance of spices from Mutsamudu far out onto the sea, bringing an alluring whiff of the exotic to seamen's noses.⁷ "How I would like to go on shore there!", the harpooner Robert Ferguson remembers thinking as his vessel, the barque *Kathleen* of New Bedford, approached the island in June 1881.⁸

---

3 Browne, *Etchings of a Whaling Cruise*, 269; Huddart, *The Oriental Navigator*, 103; Log JOSEPHINE, 1903–1905, 21.07.1904.
4 Boteler, *Narrative of a Voyage of Discovery to Africa and Arabia*, vol. 1, 160f.; Browne, *Etchings of a Whaling Cruise*, 269; Hildebrandt, "Fragmente der Johanna-Sprache", 90.
5 Alpers, "Littoral Society in the Mozambique Channel", 126f.; Wray/Martin, "Historical Whaling Records from the Western Indian Ocean", 219.
6 Browne, *Etchings of a Whaling Cruise*, 276.
7 Barnard, *A Three Years' Cruise in the Mozambique Channel*, 278f.; Boteler, *Narrative of a Voyage of Discovery to Africa and Arabia*, vol. 1, 169f.; Ferguson, *Harpooner*, 85; Haywood, "American Whalers and Africa", 196f.; Prior, *Voyage Along the Eastern Coast of Africa*, 46.
8 Ferguson, *Harpooner*, 72.

Fig. 21: View of Anjouan (probably from the north) in the memoirs of John Ross Browne, who visited the island aboard the *Bruce* of Newhaven in March 1843.
Source: Browne, *Etchings of a Whaling Cruise*, 268.

Once they had cast anchor and rowed to the shore, many seamen found their high hopes confirmed. Seen from the beach, Mutsamudu may have looked unprepossessing, concealed as it was by a stone wall nearly five metres high. Once inside the gate, however, the town presented a delightful prospect. "The scenery was grand", observed Ferguson.[9] Lanes scarcely more than two metres wide wound their way between ancient stone buildings, interspersed with little stairways, narrow creeks and orange trees. In this manner and without an obvious centre the town stretched from the beach to the slopes of Mount Ntringui, from where a citadel and it cannons kept watch over it. The narrow lanes among the closely set created a constant draft that mitigated the tropical heat and allowed brisk business to be carried on throughout much of the day.[10]

---

[9] Ferguson, *Harpooner*, 86.
[10] Browne, *Etchings of a Whaling Cruise*, 270f.; Ferguson, *Harpooner*, 86, 97; Haywood, "American Whalers and Africa", 196f.; Prior, *Voyage Along the Eastern Coast of Africa*, 22f.; Smyth, *The Life and Services of Captain Philip Beaver*, 264; Thompson, "A Whaling Cruise in the 'Sea Fox'", 151.

Following the monsoons

"Saw Spirm whales lowed 2 boats", recorded the log of the barque *Dimon* of New Bedford as she lay just off Mutsamudu on 2 July 1846.[11] Both sperm and humpback whales sometimes came very close to the port[12] – but not, on the whole, often enough to make the waters around Anjouan a worthwhile whaling ground. Whalers came to Mutsamudu for provisions, not to hunt.

This was a comparatively sudden development which began in the mid-1830s. Once the Napoleonic wars and the War of 1812 had ended, American whalers in particular – but their British counterparts, too – had begun to explore new hunting grounds in all the world's oceans. In the Indian Ocean, their attentions turned first to Zanzibar and the Seychelles in the 1820s before extending their range to Anjouan in the 1830s.[13] The dangers of seasonal storms cannot yet have been widely known when several vessels from New London – the *Ann Maria*, the *Boston*, the *Georgia* and the *John and Edward* – called at Anjouan (some of them repeatedly) in February and March 1836. Later that year, the first whalers from New Bedford and Portsmouth arrived at Mutsamudu, followed by vessels from other New England ports.[14]

This marked the beginning of a period in which whalers regularly called at Anjouan. The number of visits by individually identifiable vessels rose to about twenty-five per year in the mid-1840s and remained at that level throughout the 1850s. Leaving aside the traffic represented by dhows and canoes, for which no figures are available, whalers in some years accounted for the largest share of shipping in Mutsamudu. For the year of 1857 William Sunley, the British consul, reported to London that "American Vessels engaged in the Sperm Whale Fishery exceed in number all the vessels which come to Johanna".[15] During this period many whaleships called twice in one season: first in April or May, when the onset of the south-west monsoon gave them the opportunity to search the whaling grounds of the western Indian Ocean from south to north, and again in August, before the north-east monsoon brought stormy weather to these waters. During the southern summer these vessels usually moved south, operating, for

---

11 Log DIMON, 1845–1848, 02.07.1846.
12 Log MARIA, 1846–1849, 18.08.1847.
13 On whaling and its dynamic of exploration in the western Indian Ocean see the chapter "Passages I".
14 Log ANN MARIA, 1835–1837, 27.02.–01.03. & 08.–15.03.1836; Log GEORGIA, 1835–1837, 09.–16.03. & 12.–17.02.1836.
15 William Sunley. Report upon the Trade of the Comoro Islands for the Year Ending December 31st 1857. 31.03.1858. The National Archives, FO 19/5.

instance, off the south coast of Madagascar, before once more shifting their operations northwards, via Anjouan, in April.[16]

The whaleships that moored off Mutsamudu were almost exclusively American. Such British vessels as continued to sail for the Indian Ocean in spite of the crisis in British whaling by and large operated off Timor and the Moluccas. Only vary rarely do we find British whalers making a stopover at Mutsamudu – among them the *Foxhound* (1847), the *Sir James Ross* (1850) and the *Henrietta* and the *Surprise* (both 1854).[17] Sunley knew of only five British whalers that had called at Mutsamudu between 1851 and 1857 – set against seventy-two American ones in the same period.[18]

This boom period drew to a close with the end of the south-west monsoon in 1860 with the almost simultaneous arrival of the *Marcella*, the *Thomas Pope* and the *Swallow*, all of New Bedford.[19] The outbreak of the American civil war in the following year put a sudden stop to visits by whalers, with no more than two on record in any one year from 1861 to 1865. Only from 1868 to 1871 did traffic once more reach pre-war levels, before the decline of American whaling was felt here too. In no year after 1871 are more than six whalers known to have called at Mutsamudu.

"For ten days we have been cruising around the Comoro Islands looking for whales", noted Robert Ferguson of the *Kathleen* in September 1881. "Although there is a bounty of five dollars for the man who sights a whale, we have no luck."[20] Many whalers in the western Indian Ocean began to record such lengthy periods of inaction from the mid-1800s on. Whether the sperm whales had adapted to the pressure of hunting and grown more cautious or whether populations had already precipitously declined cannot be established with any certainty in retrospect.[21] In any case, the forces that contributed to the industry's decline were the same here as elsewhere: the impact of the American Civil War, the replacement of whale oil by petroleum in a growing number of fields, declining yields, lack of investment and high losses from dangerous operations in Arctic

---

16 Haywood, "American Whalers and Africa", 101f.; William Sunley. Report upon the Trade of the Comoro Islands for the Year Ending December 31st 1857. 31.03.1858. The National Archives, FO 19/5. 180f.
17 Log MARIA, 1846–1849, 10.–20.05.1847; Log WILLIAM LEE, 1850–1851, 12.– 25.09.1850; *The Republican Standard*, 11.01.1855.
18 William Sunley. Report upon the Trade of the Comoro Islands for the Year Ending December 31st 1857. 31.03.1858. The National Archives, FO 19/5.
19 Log MARCELLA, 1858–1861, 10.–22.07.1860; Log THOMAS POPE, 1859–1862, 28.07.–09.08.1860.
20 Ferguson, *Harpooner*, 89f.
21 Wray/Martin, "Historical Whaling Records from the Western Indian Ocean", 226f.

waters combined to make whaling unprofitable. Only a few whalers called at Anjouan in the 1880s, the last for some time being Ferguson's *Kathleen*. Not until July 1904 did another whaleship drop anchor in the port of Mutsamudu, the *Josephine* of New Bedford – apparently the very last to do so.[22]

A hub of trade and a seat of power

Their location has always predestined the Comoros to act as a bridge of sorts between the African mainland and the island of Madagascar. It may well be that the islands' earliest inhabitants, in the first century BC, were African, Indonesian and Polynesian migrants on their way to Madagascar, though another theory puts the first settlement at an earlier date. Whichever account one may find more convincing, there can be no doubt that vessels called at the Comoros to take on provisions long before whaling began the Indian Ocean. Muslim traders who, beginning in the twelfth century, expanded their operations from the Arabian sea to the eastern seaboard of Africa and the north coast of Madagascar made regular visits for victualling. Fragments of Song dynasty (960–1279) Chinese porcelain found in the islands suggest that they were connected to the Indian Ocean's long-distance trading networks even earlier. A fleet from Shiraz in Persia is known to have arrived in the tenth century. Only in the late fifteenth century, however, are the Comoros first mentioned in writing, when we find an Arab navigator, Ahmad ibn Mājid, referring to the islands as a centre of trade as well as mentioning a town in the east of Anjouan by the name of Domoni. The name "Comoros" is itself of Arabian origin, deriving from the word for "moon".[23]

Settlements such as Domoni would seem to have initially been inhabited above all by Muslim merchants – known in Anjouan as *Fani* – and their families and slaves. No later than the sixteenth century, but probably beginning already in the thirteenth or fourteenth centuries, several influential families from the Hadhramaut region in south Arabia emigrated to the Comoros. By means of a strategic marriage policy, these *Shirazi* forged strong links with the rulers on the east coast of Africa and created new markets for their goods there. The Shirazi traded with the Portuguese who settled on the Ilha de Moçambique in the

---

22 Log JOSEPHINE, 1903–1905, 20.–26.07.1904; Log MERMAID, 1887–1890, 25.07.–10.08.1888.
23 Dubins, "A Political History of the Comoro Islands", 20–29; Duffey, "China's Contact with Southern Africa", 30f.; McPherson, *The Indian Ocean*, 97; Newitt, *The Comoro Islands*, 15; Newitt, "The Comoro Islands in Indian Ocean Trade before the 19th Century", 142f.; Toussaint, *History of the Indian Ocean*, 52.

early 1500s. In the Comoros, the Shirazi founded new coastal settlements – including Sima, to the west of Anjouan – which they ruled as city-states. They ordered mosques to be built and maintained links with the religious centres of the Islamic world, so that the Comoros themselves soon became a centre of Muslim religiosity in eastern Africa. Among themselves, however, these city-states existed in perpetual rivalry. None of their rulers ever succeeded in bringing the entire archipelago under his control. Tensions existed not only between islands but also within them. In Anjouan, where a Shirazi nobleman named Hassan founded a long-lasting Afro-Arab dynasty in the fifteenth century, Domoni and Sima were locked in political rivalry. Shirazi rule, moreover, was confined to these city-states. Especially in the interior, where no urban culture developed, structures persisted which were less strongly influenced by Islam and sometimes still dominated by the descendants of the earlier arrivals, the Fani.[24]

In the early 1600s, the Comoros came to the attention of the European East India companies, which were looking to establish bases for their vessels in the western Indian Ocean. While the Portuguese, French and Dutch tried to gain footholds in Madagascar, the Mascarenes or on the coast of the east African mainland, the British East India Company relied chiefly on Anjouan for provisioning its vessels – without, however, taking possession of the island. Anjouan nonetheless fell into Britain's sphere of imperial interest, all the more so because Britain had no possessions of its own in the western Indian Ocean until it conquered the Seychelles (1810) and the Mascarenes (1811).[25]

French and Dutch as well as British vessels were frequent visitors to the Comoros and particularly to Anjouan. Although the islands soon became the site of imperial rivalries and more than one naval battle, the trading companies sought to maintain the Comoros as a free-trade area and held off from attempts at outright colonisation. The high demand for food from the East Indiamen gave a fillip both to local agriculture and to trade between the islands. To be able to deliver a sufficient quantity of cattle or goats to a particular port, for instance, required the existence of transport links across several islands. Provisions were paid for not only in barter but also in silver coin. Unlike in many

---

24 Alpers, "The Islands of Indian Ocean Africa", 8; Dubins, "A Political History of the Comoro Islands", 30, 35–37, 51; Newitt, *The Comoro Islands*, 16f.; Newitt, "The Comoro Islands in Indian Ocean Trade before the 19th Century", 143f., 159; Shepherd, "The Comorians and the East African Slave Trade", 87.
25 Alpers, "The Islands of Indian Ocean Africa", 6; Coupland, *East Africa and its Invaders*, 79, 160, 163; Newitt, *The Comoro Islands*, 17; Newitt, "The Comoro Islands in Indian Ocean Trade before the 19th Century", 141, 152f.; Newitt, *A History of Mozambique*, 174.

other coastal regions of Africa, cash payments thus already became the norm in the coastal trade in the Comoros as early as the seventeenth century.[26]

The trade in provisions led to the increased use of slave labour in farming and to conflicts, both over the control of ports and agricultural land and over access to European vessels. The Shirazi found themselves facing new rivals to their power and were forced to accept the control of the Afro-Arab Al'Masela clan, which was probably of Fani descent, over the port of Mutsamudu. It was Mutsamudu which, on account of its location and its largely reliable supply of food and drinking water, soon became the hub of shipping in the Comoros. By obtaining recognition as the supreme ruler or sultan of Anjouan from the British as well as their military support, the head of the Al'Masela succeeded in expanding his clan's rule from Mutsamudu to much of Anjouan and, in the seventeenth century, probably as far as the neighbouring island of Mohéli. Yet although they soon became the most powerful ruling dynasty in the Comoros, the influence of the Al'Masela remained limited even in Anjouan itself. Domoni, for instance, long held on to its independence, though the Al'Masela would later make it their seat – if only for a time.[27]

Besides trading with the East India companies, Comorian merchants in the seventeenth century and afterwards continued to maintain close links with Muslim traders in the western Indian Ocean and the Red Sea area. From there, they acquired goods such clothing and opium; in exchange they delivered rice and ambergris, but above all slaves. The fact that conflicts between rival groups in the Comoros frequently escalated into small-scale warfare is likely also to have been due to the prospect of taking captives, which could either be sold as slaves or be put to work in the fields. Since there were no metal reserves in the islands themselves, Comorian rulers depended on foreign trade for the iron needed to produce swords and other weapons they needed to fight these wars.[28]

The increased efforts made in the latter half of the eighteenth century to suppress piracy in the Caribbean caused many pirates to turn instead to the western Indian Ocean. Besides the coast of Madagascar, the Comoros became their preferred haunt. Among the islands, Mayotte in particular was a place where pirates would exchange news of merchant fleets in the area, sell their booty and victual their vessels. Since their East Indiamen depended on Mutsamudu for

---

26 Dubins, "A Political History of the Comoro Islands", 53f.; Hooper, "An Empire in the Indian Ocean", 166; Newitt, *The Comoro Islands*, 17f.
27 Dubins, "A Political History of the Comoro Islands", 40f., 47; Newitt, *The Comoro Islands*, 18f.; Shepherd, "The Comorians and the East African Slave Trade", 74.
28 Newitt, *The Comoro Islands*, 17–19, 21; Newitt, "The Comoro Islands in Indian Ocean Trade before the 19th Century", 157.

their own provisions, the presence of pirates in Comorian waters was a particular problem for the British, who now brought pressure to bear on the Al'Masela to get rid of the menace. So intense was British interference in Anjouan that some historians have found it to have constituted an indirect form of colonization.[29]

Especially in the eighteenth century British actors intervened repeatedly in the wars between the Al'Masela on the one hand and Mohéli and Mayotte on the other. By providing the Al'Masela with swords and firearms or by deploying British warships in the support they hoped to drive the pirates away. To the extent that these efforts were successful, they also had the unintended consequence of leading the pirates to prey on the Comorian ports on which they could longer rely for refuge. In 1701 Mayotte and Grande Comore were sacked by the notorious Nathaniel North; in 1720 the British East Indiaman *Cassandra* was lost to the pirates Edward England and Olivier Levasseur. Meanwhile, the rulers who enjoyed British support pursued their own ends and used the arms they received not least in order to capture slaves and make them work in their fields. The British would sometimes also support the Al'Masela in their internal conflicts, for instance in putting down a revolt among the rural population in the interior of Anjouan in the 1770s. It was around this time that Sultan Abdulla moved his residence from Domoni to Mutsamudu – not least, it would seem, to be closer to British vessels.[30]

From the mid-1700s on the emergence of large-scale plantations in the Mascarenes and Seychelles – both controlled by France – led to surge in the demand for slaves in the western Indian Ocean. Two societies in the north of Madagascar were among the principal suppliers of slaves: first the Sakalava, who had come from the south in the late seventeenth century to bring the north-western coast under their rule, and second the Zana Malaka, who established the kingdom of Betsimisaraka on the north-eastern coast in the late eighteenth century. Both sent expeditions of up to five hundred outrigger canoes into the Mozambique Channel in order to take prisoners. These canoes, known as *lakana* or *laka*, could be up to ten metres long and carry sixty people, and a single expedition might consist of eighteen thousand attackers. It was under the impression of such massed forces that the head of the Almadua clan, which had ruled over Domoni

---

29 Newitt, *The Comoro Islands*, 19–21; Newitt, "The Comoro Islands in Indian Ocean Trade before the 19th Century", 158f.
30 Dubins, "A Political History of the Comoro Islands", 30f.; 55–57; Newitt, *The Comoro Islands*, 19f.; Newitt, "The Comoro Islands in Indian Ocean Trade before the 19th Century", 155.

since Abdulla's departure, turned to the rulers of northern Madagascar for help in his campaign against the Al'Masela in Mutsamudu.³¹

In acceding to this request, the Sakalava and Zana Malata were motivated less by a concern for the Almadua than by their own interests: beginning in 1795, they successively raided Anjouan, Mohéli, Mayotte and Grand Comore, taking livestock, burning villages and enslaving many islanders. These captives were taken to the north coast of Madagascar, where most of them were sold to French vessels, often ending up on the plantations of Île de France (Mauritius) or Île Bonaparte (Réunion). These raids peaked between 1800 and 1816, during which period Anjouan suffered on average one major attack per year, the worst in 1808. Never, however, did the attackers succeed in taking Mutsamudu.³²

Being unable to mount a strong military opposition to these attacks, Comorian rulers turned to more powerful actors to ensure their safety. The envoys of various Comorian rulers stated their case in a number of places including Cape Town, Île de France, Bombay, Ilha de Moçambique and Madagascar. Their usual request was for a military alliance, in return for which they offered far-reaching concessions, including placing their respective islands under the protectorate of a foreign power. For their part, the representatives of foreign powers rejected such overtures, being wary both of the complex power structures within the Comoros and of the costs of any such intervention. The most they were willing to do was to send muskets, gunpowder and cannonballs or to promise diplomatic support. Only when the Portuguese fought off a band of raiders in the Quirimbas archipelago in 1816, inflicting heavy losses, and when the Sakalava kingdom was conquered by the Merina encroaching from the south in 1820 did the attacks finally cease.³³

The repeated raids by the Sakalava and Zana Malata considerably destabilised the Comoros both economically and politically. In Anjouan, the assassination of Sultan Selim in 1790 triggered a long succession struggle between the

---

31 Alpers, "Littoral Society in the Mozambique Channel", 132; Campbell, "Slavery and the Trans-Indian Ocean World Slave Trade", 168; Hooper, "An Empire in the Indian Ocean", 204, 210; Newitt, *The Comoro Islands*, 21f. Such raids were not altogether unheard of in the Comoros, which had suffered attacks by Madagascan raiders since the sixteenth century, albeit at considerably longer intervals. (Dubins, "A Political History of the Comoro Islands", 59f.)
32 Campbell, "Slavery and the Trans-Indian Ocean World Slave Trade", 168, 184; Dubins, "A Political History of the Comoro Islands", 53, 62, 65–68; Hooper, "An Empire in the Indian Ocean", 210; Newitt, *The Comoro Islands*, 22; Shepherd, "The Comorians and the East African Slave Trade", 75. For a description of Mutsamudu on the eve of the slave raids see Rooke, *Travels to the Coast of Arabia Felix and from thence by the Red Sea and Egypt to Europe*, 20–29.
33 lpers, "A Complex Relationship", 74f.; Dubins, "A Political History of the Comoro Islands", 53, 59, 65–69, 70–82, 85f.; Newitt, *The Comoro Islands*, 22f.

Al'Masela of Mutsamudu and the Al'Madwa of Domonia, who were probably descendants of Shirazi migrants. In seeking British support around 1800, Abdulla, the head of the Al'Masela, was looking not just to fend off attacks from Madagascar, but also to keep the Al'Madwa at bay.[34]

The elite of Anjouan kept up its diplomatic efforts to forge alliances with foreign powers even when the era of the slave raids had ended. To this end, Sultan Alawi – who had settled the succession struggle in his favour in 1803 – made contact with the French in Saint-Denis in Île Bonaparte in 1816, his son with the British in Port Louis in 1820. Another member of the ruling family, Said Hamza, was in Cape Town at the time, where he struck up a friendship with John Philip of the London Missionary Society. Said Hamza gave Philip permission to dispatch a missionary, William Elliot, to Anjouan – with the purpose, it would seem, of bolstering ties with the British and teaching English to the *sheriffs* of the island. This idea had not, however, been discussed with the sultan, who forbade any contact with the missionary. In the interest of preserving good relations with the British, the sultan was keen to ensure that they should never learn that the *sheriffs* of Anjouan were using the weapons and equipment provided for their defence to carry on a slave trade of their own. Nor did he want the British to get wind of the fact that the rulers of Anjouan would sometimes ally themselves with the Sakalava and launch joint attacks on neighbouring islands. Eliot left the island after about a year spent largely in isolation.[35]

A broad view of the history of Anjouan and Mutsamudu up to the early 1800s reveals four distinct eras: in the tenth century, under Fani rule, the island came under the lasting influence of Muslim Afro-Arab actors. When, beginning in the fifteenth century, the Fani were supplanted by the Shirazi, whose links with the Arab world and Islam were stronger still, city-states emerged whose relations between one another and with their neighbours – meaning other islands as well as the rural populations in their own respective hinterlands – were marked by tensions which repeatedly flared up in small-scale warfare. In the seventeenth century Mutsamudu came under the control of the Al'Masela clan, which was able to establish a long-lived sultanate not least on the income from provisioning British vessels. In spite of British support, however, it was never able to establish uncontested rule over the whole island. From the 1790s onwards the slave raids by the Sakalava and Zana Matata plunged Anjouan into a crisis, one aspect of which was the emergence of internecine struggles

---

34 Dubins, "A Political History of the Comoro Islands", 71–79.
35 Alpers, "Madagascar and Mozambique in the Nineteenth Century", 43; Coupland, *East Africa and its Invaders*, 79; Dubins, "A Political History of the Comoro Islands", 90–95, 98; Shepherd, "The Comorians and the East African Slave Trade", 78f.

among the Al'Masela themselves, who responded by trying to forge alliances with foreign powers. In each of these periods, Anjouan's position between the east African mainland and the island of Madagascar – and, later, its links to the centres of Islamic world and to European colonial powers – meant that external factors had a strong influence on events in the island. As the key point at which Anjouan intersected with the wider world, the importance of Mutsamudu as a centre of commerce and a seat of power grew as the island became woven into the fabric of the East India trade. But did whalers also constitute a comparably significant external factor in the nineteenth century?

Contested conditions

In the period of regular attacks from Madagascar, the political history of Anjouan appears as a sequence of diplomatic manoeuvres following a consistent pattern. Although their position was stronger than that of their rivals, successive Al'Masela sultans were never strong enough to keep them at bay without external support. Yet such aid as they received – from the British in particular – was never enough to assert supremacy over the island as a whole. In pursuit of this elusive goal, both the sultans and their defeated (and sometimes exiled) rivals sent delegations far and wide in search of support without ever fully winning over any colonial power. Since European actors found it hard to tell who was trying to involve them in any given situation and to what end, they preferred to keep their distance. Whilst rival forces tried to take advantage of European actors in other parts of Africa too, one aspect in which the situation in the Comoros was different was the lack of resident Europeans who might have provided information on local conditions. This basic pattern was to continue throughout the decades in which Mutsamudu was regularly visited by whalers.

Anjouan's continuing political tensions were in large part the result of a structural problem. Since the Al'Masela sultans imposed heavy taxes on the rural population while reserving the most fertile land for themselves, their rivals had an easy job finding support in the interior and encouraging opposition. Many visitors to the island got no further than Mutsamudu and were thus prone to the mistaken impression that the sultan's rule over the island was absolute. Yet at no time was there a lack of competing forces ready to fight the sultan's troops. His power, moreover, was circumscribed by all manner of advisers and powerful dignitaries, some of whom will have had more or less open designs on the sultan's position. Formally speaking, then, Anjouan was not so much an absolutist sultanate as a political oligarchy in which key political officeholders acted in a framework of often sharp mutual rivalry.[36]

This was particularly true of the years in which whalers began to call at Mutsamudu in larger numbers. Abdullah bin Alawi, who had taken over from Alawi bin Husain to rule as sultan from 1824 to 1823, pursued the goal of bringing the entire island under Al'Masela rule. To this end, he forged an alliance with Ramanataka, a Merina warlord who had had to flee Madagascar in the course of a succession struggle, settling in Anjouan with two hundred of his supporters in 1828. With their support, Abdullah succeeded in conquering Mohéli. Ramanataka was rewarded with the country estate of Pomoni in the south-west of Anjouan, where he set up plantations – the first in the history of the Comoros – and soon grew in wealth and influence. Many of the dissidents from Abdullah's rule now looked to Ramanataka and around 1830 launched a rebellion, forcing the sultan to flee to Mohéli. Yet Ramanataka too had to seek refuge there in 1832, when some of his previous allies came to consider him too powerful and began to plot against his life. The power vacuum left by Ramanataka's flight allowed Abdullah to return to Mutsamudu and reclaim the sultanate in 1833.[37]

Abdullah now sought to revenge himself on Ramanataka. To this end, he joined forces with Andriansouli, the ruler of Boina, a Sakalava kingdom in northwestern Madagascar, who had fled to Mayotte after his defeat in a power struggle. Abdullah and Andriansouli attacked Ramanataka in Mohéli in 1836 – and failed, not least because their flotilla was dispersed by a sudden storm. Abdullah was taken prisoner by Ramanataka and died the same year. A struggle over his succession now erupted in Mutsamudu: the sultanate was claimed by Abdullah's son Alawi, who faced fierce resistance from Abdullah Zebiri, the governor of Domoni. Though it threatened to escalate into a civil war, the struggle was contained by diplomatic pressure from the British, who were keen to maintain political stability. Abdullah Zebri ultimately succeeded in keeping Alawi out of office. The sultanate instead went to Abdullah Zebri's favoured candidate, his son-in-law Said Hassan, who was also a brother of Abdullah's and hence Alawi's uncle. Alawi fled, first to Mozambique and then to Mauritius, where he died in 1842. Said Hassan assumed the regnal name of Salim bin Alawi and put an end to the fighting between the islands, which had never quite ceased since Abdullah's attack on Mohéli, with a shattering assault on Mayotte. Salim died in 1855 and the sultanate to his eldest son, Abdullah, who was also the candidate

---

36 Dubins, "A Political History of the Comoro Islands", 103f., 126, 128.
37 Alpers, "Madagascar and Mozambique in the Nineteenth Century", 52; Dubins, "A Political History of the Comoro Islands", 97, 99–103; Hooper, "An Empire in the Indian Ocean", 242f.; Newitt, The Comoro Islands, 23f., 26.

favoured by the British. Abdullah remained in office until 1887 – that is, for nearly the entire period during which Mutsamudu was visited by whalers – against sometimes considerable resistance.[38]

Anjouan's trade and economy became diversified during the decades in which Mutsamudu was frequented by whalers. Besides the commercial traffic of dhows and canoes within "Indian Ocean Africa" – the name given to this mesoregion by the historian Gwyn Campbell[39] – American merchantmen in particular began to ply Comorian waters in the early 1800s. Once the War of 1812 had ended, vessels from Salem, Boston and other New England trading ports became ever more frequent visitors to the western Indian Ocean, at times dominating foreign trade in Zanzibar, in the Madagascan port of Mahajanga and in what is now Mozambique. Until the mid-nineteenth century, when they chose to concentrate on the more profitable trade with Zanzibar, American traders were also regular visitors to the Comoros, where they found cottons to be in particular demand.[40]

For their part, Comorian traders used their own vessels to export sugar, coconuts and coconut oil, rice, millet, oats, beans, ghee, honey, goats, cattle *sambi* (sago) and cowrie shells, especially to the Ilha de Moçambique. The quantities involved were quite small, however, and provisioning vessels remained an economic factor of considerable importance.[41] A few planters from Britain and the United States settles in Anjouan from the 1840s, looking to take advantage of the fertile soils for sugar cane and coconut plantations of their own. In so doing, they indirectly contributed to bolstering the position of the sultan, who levied a tax on such businesses and thus was able to increase his income considerably. Arab traders from the Persian Gulf area sailed to the Comoros in order to buy tortoiseshells and sell cloths and rugs.[42] Less is known of

---

38 Alpers, "The Islands of Indian Ocean Africa", 11; Alpers, "Madagascar and Mozambique in the Nineteenth Century", 52; Dubins, "A Political History of the Comoro Islands", 32, 106–110, 127–129; Newitt, *The Comoro Islands*, 23f.; William Sunley to the Earl of Clarendon, 19.10.1855. The National Archives, FO 19/5. 21.
39 Campbell, "Slavery and the Trans-Indian Ocean World Slave Trade", 287.
40 Bennett/Brooks, "Introduction", xxvi–xxvii; William Sunley. Report upon the Trade of the Comoro Islands for the Year Ending December 31st 1857. 31.03.1858. The National Archives, FO 19/5; William Sunley. Report upon the Trade of the Comoro Islands for the Year Ending December 31st 1858. 1859. The National Archives, FO 19/6.
41 Alpers, "A Complex Relationship", 75; William Sunley. Report upon the Trade of the Comoro Islands for the Year Ending December 31st 1857. 31.03.1858. The National Archives, FO 19/5.
42 Dubins, "A Political History of the Comoro Islands", 235; Prior, *Voyage Along the Eastern Coast of Africa*, 55. In the nineteenth century too whalers caught tortoises near the

the Indian merchants who operated from the Comoros in mid-nineteenth century as middlemen for the export of ivory from the east African mainland. Broadly speaking, however, migration from India to Anjouan can be traced as far back as the sixteenth century, when Indian merchants arrived there to do business with the Shirazi.[43]

Besides whalers and merchantmen, Mutsamudu in the 1840s was used as a victualling stop particularly by the Royal Navy. These stops were made not least with a political end in mind, namely to solidify Anjouan's ties with Britain and to keep French influence at bay.[44] Figures compiled in 1859 by the British consul, William Sunley, however, show that the number of British vessels decreased while that of French vessels increased in the course of the 1850s. Yet the single largest share in any given year was accounted for by American vessels, most of them whalers (Tab. 3). This balance seems to have remained largely consistent until the outbreak of the American Civil War. In 1864 a British naval officer, Algernon de Horsey, estimated the number of vessels calling at Anjouan to run to fifty or sixty per year, "principally whalers touching for refreshments".[45]

Since the traumatic slave raids from Madagascar, successive sultans in Mutsamudu had made it their policy to place Anjouan under the protection of an outside power. Diplomatic advances towards the British in the early 1820s did not, however, produce the desired effect. Although Britain underpinned its special relationship with the island with repeated deliveries of guns and ammunition, it sought to avoid the potentially costly burden of outright colonial annexation. By taking targeted measures to strengthen ties from the 1840s onwards, Britain was actuated above all by a desire to ward off French influence in Anjouan.[46]

Towards the end of his reign and finding British support to be wanting, Abdullah began to look around for a new protector. In 1879 he negotiated a trade agreement with an American admiral – which, however, the US Senate declined to ratify. The following year Abdullah offered both Egypt and the Ottoman Empire a kind of inter-Arab protectorate over Anjouan, but again found himself

---

Comoros, notably in atolls such as Aldabra or Assomption; see e.g. Log A. R. TUCKER, 1857–1861, 16.–17.02.1858.

[43] Jackson Haight, *European Powers and South-East Africa*, 262f.; Newitt, "The Comoro Islands in Indian Ocean Trade before the 19th Century", 149.

[44] Jackson Haight, *European Powers and South-East Africa*, 294.

[45] Horsey, "On the Comoro Islands", 262.

[46] Coupland, *East Africa and its Invaders*, 170f.; 201, 228; Jackson Haight, *European Powers and South-East Africa*, 294. For an account of a British shipment of arms to Sultan Alawi bin Husain see Smyth, *The Life and Services of Captain Philip Beaver*, 261f., for an example of the travelling diplomacy still carried on from Anjouan see Prestholdt, *Domesticating the World*, 15–18.

rebuffed.⁴⁷ Once more, only the British seemed to offer any prospect of an alliance. They, however, demanded the abolition of slavery, to which Abdullah agreed in 1883, promising the British government by treaty to set all slaves free by 1890. This announcement caused considerable disquiet among the landowning *sherifs*. They had already observed how the abolition of slavery in neighbouring islands had meant that local landowners found themselves competing with Europeans whose deeper reserves of capital allowed them soon to buy up the best land. The *sherifs* of Anjouan were afraid that their island too would be turned into a plantation economy oriented towards Europe. In 1884 opponents of abolition launched a revolt against Abdullah under the leadership of his brothers Mohammed and Osman. It was in this difficult situation that France – which had grown fearful of colonial designs on east Africa by its new rival Germany and was stepping its own activities in the western Indian Ocean accordingly – offered Abdullah a protectorate. Abdullah, who had incurred considerable debts with French banks in Mauritius in the preceding years, accepted this offer in April 1886. The French protectorate over Anjouan came into force in 1889.⁴⁸

***

Whalemen were unlikely to gather much about political conflicts and conditions in the island's interior. When on shore leave, their attention tended to be directed towards Mutsamudu's old stone buildings and their Afro-Arab inhabitants (Fig. 22). Even seasoned seamen had never seen such turbans, white gowns and oriental cutlasses as worn by the locals, for few whalers ever operated in the Arabian Sea.⁴⁹ Seamen were all the more curious to observe the local population going about its everyday business in the alleys of Mutsamudu, chewing betel nut or playing board games.⁵⁰ A particularly impressive sight was the sultan's palace in the heart of the city: its irregular layout made it resemble a vessel, with parts of it arching over the alleys in a singularly picturesque fashion. Only scant information exists as to the population of the city and the island at large. James Prior, a British ship's surgeon, in 1812 reckoned the population of Mutsamudu to number three thousand, while his captain

---

47 Booth, *The United States Experience in South Africa*, 222; Dubins, "A Political History of the Comoro Islands", 129.
48 Dubins, "A Political History of the Comoro Islands", 129–131, 234; Haywood, "American Whalers and Africa", 99f.; Newitt, *The Comoro Islands*, 34f. On slavery in the Comoros in the nineteenth century see especially Shepherd, "The Comorians and the East African Slave Trade".
49 See e.g. the quotation in Haywood, "American Whalers and Africa", 196f.
50 Thompson, *The Life of John Thompson*, 127; Thompson, "A Whaling Cruise in the 'Sea Fox'", 151.

aboard HMS *Nisus*, Philip Beaver, put it at no more than two thousand. A later naval officer, Algernon de Horsey, estimated the total population of the island at ten thousand individuals in 1862.⁵¹

The town's infrastructure, by contrast, struck seamen as less impressive. In the absence of any harbour wall, crews had no choice but to row goods to and from their vessel.⁵² Nor could skippers count on finding spare parts, skilled craftsmen or indeed any facilities for repairing their vessels. When, for instance, the barque *Rhine* of Edgartown sustained damage to the hull and the hinges of her rudder in an accident near Anjouan, her captain was left with no choice but to sail for Zanzibar, a distance of 450 nautical miles, for repairs. Seamen were similarly unimpressed with the medical facilities. In 1843 William Perry, master of the *Sally Anne* of New Bedford, preferred to be travel another two thousand nautical miles to Cape Town after a whale had broken his leg off Anjouan.⁵³ Captain Winslow of the barque *Marcella* of New Bedford died in Mutsamudu in 1852, apparently for want of adequate medical treatment.⁵⁴ Not until the 1880s do we hear of a doctor named Wilson treating seamen in Mutsamudu.⁵⁵

Another amenity sorely missed by seamen was an American consulate. Aside from a Portuguese representative, the only consulate in Mutsamudu during the period when it was frequented by whalers was the British one. It had been built between the beach and the town wall in 1847, at a time of colonial rivalry with France. After the French had established colonial rule over Mayotte in 1843, the British were keen to curb the expansion of French influence. Their fear was that by gaining control of the entire archipelago, France would control the Mozambique Channel much as Britain controlled the Strait of Gibraltar. To prevent this, Britain sought to strengthen its informal protectorate over Anjouan. In a move designed to make Anjouan seem unappealing to France, the British signed a treaty with Salim banning the slave trade in his sphere of influence in 1844. In order to consolidate diplomatic relations with Salim and keep a closer eye on French activities, Joseph Napier was named consul in 1847, one of two British sugar planters and merchants living in Anjouan at the time.⁵⁶

---

51 Horsey, "On the Comoro Islands", 261; Prior, *Voyage Along the Eastern Coast of Africa*, 48f., 52f.; Smyth, *The Life and Services of Captain Philip Beaver*, 264.
52 Ferguson, *Harpooner*, 87.
53 *Whalemen's Shipping List*, 28.11.1843.
54 Busch, *Whaling Will Never Do for Me*, 170.
55 Log MERMAID, 1883–1890, 21.02.–04.03.1888.
56 Alpers, "Madagascar and Mozambique in the Nineteenth Century", 46; Coupland, *East Africa and its Invaders*, 445f., 449; Dubins, "A Political History of the Comoro Islands", 110, 112f., 118; Horsey, "On the *Comoro* Islands", 262; Newitt, *The Comoro Islands*, 24f., 34.

Napier, however, resigned from his office and left Anjouan in 1851. The only resident Briton remaining was thus the other planter, William Sunley, who was duly installed as Napier's successor.[57] It was around this time that, probably at the urging of whaling captains, the American consul in Zanzibar asked the State Department to open a consulate in Mutsamudu. Yet his appeal fell on deaf ears,[58] and the British consulate remained the only one in Anjouan for the time being. Sunley, however, spent much of his time in Pomoni, in a former country seat of Ramanataka's, from whom he had acquired coconut and sugar plantations. He had also taken advantage of his position as consul in order to have Salim provide him with fertile land and slaves. That the British consul was operating a slave plantation was shocking news to the British officials who heard it from rivals of Abdullah's successor, Salim, who saw to it that Sunley was relieved of his duties in 1865. In view of the scant benefits Britain had so far derived from its consulate, the Foreign Office declined to appoint a successor.[59]

Tab. 3: Shipping in Mutsamudu according to figures compiled by the British consul.

Ships from . . .	1852	1853	1854	1855	1856	1857	1858
Britain and its colonies	22	13	17	17	3	6	8
France and its colonies	5	2	0	3	8	11	11
the United States	35	28	24	27	20	30	23
other countries	0	4	1	1	0	3	3
Total	62	47	42	48	31	50	55

Source: William Sunley. Report upon the Trade of the Comoro Islands for the Year Ending December 31st 1857. 31.03.1858. The National Archives, FO 19/5; William Sunley. Report upon the Trade of the Comoro Islands for the Year Ending December 31st 1858. 1859. The National Archives, FO 19/6.

In 1869 the petitions of whaling captains once more compelled the State Department to consider opening an American consulate in Mutsamudu. Yet in spite of the support of the American consul in the Seychelles, Washington once again decided against the idea. Unlike Port Louis or Zanzibar, for instance, Mutsamudu remained without a consulate that could have assisted whalers in their business dealings and other matters. The lack of a consulate also means that scarcely any information is preserved as to how often whaling captains took

---
57 Dubins, "A Political History of the Comoro Islands", 119; Newitt, *A History of Mozambique*, 324.
58 Haywood, "American Whalers and Africa", 107f.
59 Dubins, "A Political History of the Comoro Islands", 120; Newitt, *The Comoro Islands*, 34.

advantage of a stopover at Mutsamudu to discharge seamen. They may in fact have been encouraged to do so by the absence of any consular oversight or assistance.[60]

Action and suffering

"Tara and sweet potatoes are the principal articles of trade and for these nearly all the whale ships in this ocean put in here", observed J.T. Langdon, a seaman who visited Mutsamudu in June 1851.[61] The taro corms here referred to as "tara" were a popular alternative to potatoes among seamen.[62] Aside from taro corms and sweet potatoes, the provisions captains were able to lay in at Mutsamudu included rice, maize and yams as well as tropical fruit, such as coconuts, plantains and oranges. The supply of meat depended on cattle, goats and poultry; the island had neither pigs nor sheep.[63] Provisions were generally available in ample quantities. Only for the last decades of American whaling, when very few vessels still called at Mutsamudu for provisions, do we hear of difficulties in obtaining the desired amount of food.[64]

At least under Salim's rule, Anjouan's trade in provisions was considered to be the sultan's privilege. The greater part of the food taken on board by whalers appears to have been supplied from his stocks. If the British merchants who ran plantations in the interior of Anjouan in in the mid-nineteenth century wanted to sell provisions with whalers, they had to reckon with punitive taxes imposed by the sultan.[65] Only the incidental small-scale trade carried on with individual seamen was sultan happy to leave to others. This usually took the shape of several vendors taking to their outrigger canoes, a type much used in the islands, to meet incoming whaleships and clambering over the gunwales. In exchange for tobacco, they proffered seashells, dates, pineapples, banana and sugar cane, and perhaps straw hats, rose oil and ornamental blankets.

---

60 Haywood, "American Whalers and Africa", 107f.
61 Quoted in Haywood, "American Whalers and Africa", 196f.
62 Thompson, "A Whaling Cruise in the 'Sea Fox'", 154.
63 Huddart, *The Oriental Navigator*, 103; Prior, *Voyage Along the Eastern Coast of Africa*, 56; Rooke, *Travels to the Coast of Arabia Felix and from thence by the Red Sea and Egypt to Europe*, 23; Smyth, *The Life and Services of Captain Philip Beaver*, 262.
64 Log JOSEPHINE, 1903–1905, 23.07.1904; Log MERLIN, 1881–1882, 19.05.1882.
65 Haywood, "American Whalers and Africa", 102f.; 196f.

Fig. 22: An Anjouani as drawn by R. Weir, a seaman who visited Mutsamudu in September 1856 aboard the *Clara Bell* of Mattapoisett.
Source: Weir, Journal CLARA BELL, 1855–1858, 26.09.1856. Courtesy Mystic Seaport.

Many of these *Johannamen*, as some of the seamen called them, spoke English well enough for the purposes of this trade.[66]

Some seamen particularly appreciated their acquaintance with the *Johannamen* and the trading opportunities they offered at modest prices. In 1843, for instance, a seaman received one hundred coconuts in exchange for half a pound of tobacco.[67] Little wonder, then, that one seaman, George Harris, in 1832 referred to the small-scale traders as "very good people".[68] Yet other seamen found the

---

66 Allen, Diary, 14.05.1869; Allen, "When I Was Seven", 21; Allen, "When I Went a-Whaling", 2f.; Barnard, *A Three Years' Cruise in the Mozambique Channel*, 80–82; Eldridge, *Lewis William Eldridge's Whaling Voyage*, 13; Harris, Journal 1832–1833, 09.08.1832; Prior, *Voyage Along the Eastern Coast of Africa*, 57; Wallace, Journal CLARA BELL, 1855–1858, 26.09.1856, 24.08.1857.
67 Browne, *Etchings of a Whaling Cruise*, 276. On the high value accorded to tobacco in Mutsamudu see also ibid., 271.
68 Harris, Journal 1832–1833, 09.08.1832.

constant presence of the *Johannamen* to be a nuisance. The log of the *Palestine* of Salem, for instance, which put in at Mutsamudu in May 1840, complained about "Every body thinking you ought to trade with him, and for that reason they will bother and annoy you exceedingly".[69]

Probably with a view to making themselves memorable to seamen and thus receiving preferential treatment on future occasions or to encourage recommendations, the *Johannamen* would often introduce themselves by such striking names as Duke of Buccleugh, Marquis Cornwallis, Prince of Wales, Admiral Blankett or Lord Augustus Fitzroy, to give only a few examples.[70] Another element of this strategy was to ask seamen to provide them with letters of reference, the main purpose of which was to vouch for a trader's probity in future transactions.[71] In 1843 John Rosse Browne observed that "All the natives who transact business with the shipping have papers of this kind".[72] He records the content of such a letter as follows:

> This is to certify that Hozain, a native of Johanna, is an intelligent and accommodating lad. I have, on various occasions, hired him to transact business for me, and have always found him industrious and honest. I recommend any of my countrymen who visit Johanna to call at his house, if they wish a good dinner on reasonable terms.[73]

Other seamen, however, took advantage of the *Johannamen*'s ignorance of written English to compose such unflattering letters as this, replete with racist language:

> We the undersined do hereby sertify that jack America is a good washewoman and a fus rate help aboard ship we got him to wash for us while at ancor hear which was 2 weaks more or less and can say to all Americans that he is an honest feller having stole but 2 shirts from us the hole time which is sayen a grate dele as the nagers will all steal whin they git a chanse jack does all kinds of jobs on reasonable terms for tobacco or old close which is sometimes very convenient for saillers.[74]

All in all, provisioning vessels was a business of considerable importance – writing in 1858, Sunley found it to be the cornerstone of Anjouan's foreign trade. By Sunley's reckoning, each vessel bought food to the value of twenty pounds sterling. Since by this time whalers accounted for the largest share of

---

69 Log PALESTINE, 1839–1842, 15.05.1840.
70 Coupland, *East Africa and its Invaders*, 163f.; Dubins, "A Political History of the Comoro Islands", 54f.; Prior, *Voyage Along the Eastern Coast of Africa*, 47.
71 Prior, *Voyage Along the Eastern Coast of Africa*, 47.
72 Browne, *Etchings of a Whaling Cruise*, 272.
73 Ibid., 272f.
74 Ibid., 273.

visiting vessels, they were the island's key trading partners and source of currency.[75] Haywood concurs with this assessment. According to his calculations, based on the records of seamen, whalers in the 1850s spent up to ten thousand dollars a year in Mutsamudu.[76]

The sultan did not charge for drinking water, which was known as *mádži barídi* in Shindzuani. A clear mountain stream enters the sea close to the town, allowing seamen to take large quantities of water. In order to do so, they would usually tie their empty casks together with ropes and tow the resulting chain to the mouth of the stream by boat. Unlike in many another port of call, seamen found the drinking water of Anjouan to be of excellent quality. Only when the breakers created by the north-east monsoon made the mouth of the stream hard to reach by boat were there any difficulties with the water supply.[77]

Sailors' views on the cost of putting in at Mutsamudu varied considerably. Broadly speaking, food could be acquired here at comparatively low cost. In 1801 *The Oriental Navigator*, a standard mariner's handbook, described prices there as "cheap". This assessment seems to have held true into the mid-1800s. In 1840 the log of the *Palestine* of Salem records "very cheap" prices, in 1843 Browne found them to be reasonable and Sunley, writing in 1858, to be "very reasonable".[78] A cow cost eight to twelve dollars or might be had in exchange for a gun.[79] Nor were gifts to the sultan too onerous an expense. In April 1847 Captain Smith of the barque *United States* of Westport records giving Salim three lengths of cloth and a small barrel of gunpowder.[80] The mooring fees levied by the sultan were six dollars in the early 1830s and fifteen in the early 1860s, in each case charged per stay.[81] The sultan might also waive the fee, perhaps as a favour to a captain on a repeat visit. Since, however, the sultan and his agents controlled the victualling trade and exploited cheap slave labour to do so, his profits are likely to have been substantial. Browne estimated that

---

75 William Sunley. Report upon the Trade of the Comoro Islands for the Year Ending December 31st 1857. 31.03.1858. The National Archives, FO 19/5. 180f.
76 Haywood, "American Whalers and Africa", 111.
77 Barnard, *A Three Years' Cruise in the Mozambique Channel*, 278f.; Ferguson, *Harpooner*, 87, 100; Harris, Journal 1832–1833, 09.08.1832; Hildebrandt, "Fragmente der Johanna-Sprache", 91; Log GEORGIA, 1835–1837, 10.03.1836; Log PALESTINE, 19.05.1839–13.06.1842, 15.05.1840.
78 Browne, *Etchings of a Whaling Cruise*, 277; Huddart, *The Oriental Navigator*, 103; Log PALESTINE, 1839–1842, 15.05.1840; William Sunley. Report upon the Trade of the Comoro Islands for the Year Ending December 31st 1857. 31.03.1858. The National Archives, FO 19/5.
79 Haywood, "American Whalers and Africa", 104; Log JANUS, 1833–1835, 30.07.1834.
80 Log UNITED STATES, 1846–1849, 29.04.1847.
81 Harris, Journal 1832–1833; Haywood, "American Whalers and Africa", 99f.; Horsey, "On the Comoro Islands", 262.

each visit from a whaler swelled the sultan's coffers by some eighty to one hundred dollars.[82] A breakdown of costs incurred by the barque *Alto* during the four times she was moored off Mutsamudu in the mid-1850s, drawn up by her captain, Angeles Snell, shows them to have been well in excess of one hundred dollars on three of these occasions (Tab. 4).

In the 1850s, we find both the British consul in Anjouan and his American counterpart in Zanzibar reporting that shipmasters had repeatedly complained to them about the expenses associated with calling at Anjouan, and sometimes also about supply problems. Since, however, we have barely any records of whalers themselves making such complaints, Haywood assumes them to be rumours spread by Sunley himself, whose own plantations were put at a disadvantage by the sultan's monopoly.[83]

One reason why whalers could get away with paying such comparatively low prices for provisions at Mutsamudu was that agriculture in Anjouan depended on slave labour. From the 1820s to the 1840s in particular, the Comoros were an important hub in the slave trade between the east African mainland and the islands of Mauritius and Bourbon (Réunion). Since British patrols kept guard over the direct routes – that between the coast of modern Mozambique and the Mascarenes, for instance – dhows, canoes and small sailing boats now took their human cargo the short distance to the Comoros. The slaves were then sold to French vessels, which took them to the Seychelles. There, they picked up a smattering of French before being taken onwards to Mauritius or Bourbon. By taking this indirect route, slavers hoped to avoid their vessels being impounded by the Royal Navy on their last leg: if his vessel was stopped, a captain could point to the slaves' knowledge of French as evidence that he was not trading in slaves, but merely returning workers who had long been enslaved or indeed were contract workers (*engagés*) to Mauritius or Bourbon, from where their masters had recalled them to the Seychelles. Since doing so did not entail a change of ownership, the procedure did not fall under the British ban on the slave trade.[84]

This system collapsed when abolition was declared in Mauritius. Yet a few vessels continued to traffic slaves along this route into the middle of the nineteenth century. The fact that their route via the Comoros allowed the *sherifs*,

---

82 Browne, *Etchings of a Whaling Cruise*, 268.
83 Haywood, "American Whalers and Africa", 105. For a remark by Sunley to that effect see William Sunley. Report upon the Trade of the Comoro Islands for the Year Ending December 31st 1858. 1859. The National Archives, FO 19/6.
84 Alpers, *Ivory and Slaves in East Central Africa*, 214; Shepherd, "The Comorians and the East African Slave Trade", 76f.

Tab. 4: Expenses incurred by the barque *Alto* of New Bedford during her stopovers at Mutsamudu, 1854–1856.

September 1854: $116.25	August 1855: $112.87	June 1856: $73.00	August 1856: $105.87
60 bbl taro corms 60.00	48 bbl taro corms 48.00	38 bbl taro corms 38.00	40 bbl taro corms 3.00
1 bbl sweet potatoes 1.00	10 bbl sweet potatoes 10.00	8 bbl sweet potatoes 8.00	5 bbl sweet potatoes 5.00
300 coconuts 9.00	200 coconuts 1.50	120 coconuts 2.00	100 coconuts 1.00
20 doz. eggs 2.00	650 eggs 5.00	Eggs 2.00	1 bbl beans 2.00
Milk 1.25	Milk 5.00	Milk 2.75	Eggs and Milk 9.00
1 head cattle 5.00	3 heads cattle 18.50	9 heads cattle 5.00	3 heads cattle 16.00
300 pumpkins 15.00	1½ doz. chickens 1.75	Onions 1.00	1 bbl beef 16.50
1 coil copra rope 3.00	150 yam roots 1.50	Pumpkins 1.00	3 units pepper 1.00
Bristles for brooms 1.00	2 bbl beans 5.00	1 bbl beans 3.00	2 units sugar 5.00
Mooring fees 19.00	1 doz. groundnuts 2.00	1 bbl. groundnuts 2.00	1 coil hemp rope 22.00
	6 bunches bananas 1.00	Copra rope 6.00	1 piece chain 3.00
	7 gal lime juice 2.00	Bristles for brooms 0.75	2 jackknives 0.50
	150 oranges 2.00		50 portions tobacco 12.50
	1 bbl limes 1.00		Pay advanced to crew 9.37
	5 portions pepper 1.50		
	6 bottles pepper sauce 1.25		
	6 tools 1.37		
	Pay advanced to crew 4.50		

Source: Log ALTO, 1854–1857.

the land-owning upper class of Anjouan, to skim off a few slaves for themselves was not lost on the British. Nor could it be denied that Anjouan's population of African descent kept growing. The various measures taken by Great Britain from 1824 onwards to win over successive sultans to the cause of fighting the slave trade, however, were aimed not so much at suppressing slavery in Anjouan itself as at containing French influence in the Comoros. The purpose was geopolitical at least as much as it was humanitarian.[85]

The extent to which whalemen were aware of slavery in Anjouan and made a connection between it and the low prices they paid for provisions cannot be conclusively established. Only a few hints emerge in the documents left by seamen. One, J. T. Langdon, who visited Mutsamudu aboard the *St. Peter* of New Bedford, wrote in his diary that "Slavery is caried on to a considerable extent".[86] Robert Ferguson of the *Kathleen* wrote at length of the slavery he observed while on shore leave in Anjouan in August 1881. On a ramble in the island's interior he came upon a sugar plantation whose owners – an American and a Scotsman – he described as "devils" for treating their slaves so cruelly and feeding them so poorly. "When I saw four of these slaves naked and shackled, it made me so angry I could have killed the Scotchman", Ferguson recalled. "The feeling came over me, what right had these two white devils over these poor blacks to treat them like this when they had committed no crime." This rejection of slavery was not, however, universal among the crew. An officer named William Young, for instance, called Ferguson "chicken-hearted" on hearing of his horrified response.[87]

Dinner and discord

How did seamen spend their shore leave in Mutsamudu? Some of them took walks in the town and its environs, gathering coconuts, organs and bananas. They might also look for pieces of timber, notably sandalwood and rosewood, either as gifts or to be sold upon their return. Others climbed the hill to the citadel, where the notorious buccaneer William Kidd was supposed once to have dwelt. To the men, who for months on end had seen little but the sea and the

---

[85] Alpers, *Becoming Mozambique*, 135f.; Alpers, "The Islands of Indian Ocean Africa", 11; Alpers, *Ivory & Slaves in East Central Africa*, 214; Coupland, *East Africa and its Invaders*, 247, 447; Shepherd, "The Comorians and the East African Slave Trade", 91.
[86] Quoted in Haywood, "American Whalers and Africa", 196f.
[87] Ferguson, *Harpooner*, 89f.

sky, the stone buildings ad tropical vegetation were a welcome change. Sometimes seamen caught sharks off the island, which they sold in Mutsamudu.[88]

In the evenings, some crews would give ceremonial dinners on board ship, to which they invited the *sherifs* of Mutsamudu – whom they expected to return the favour in the form of an invitation to dine with them in town.[89] "We feasted royally on curried chicken, fruits, and cakes made of finely ground cocoanut meat", recalled one seaman, Louis Eldridge, whose voyage in the *Herald II* of New Bedford brought him to Anjouan from 1867 to 1869.[90] Yet such dinners might also be given against payment rather than being arranged on a reciprocal basis. Some *sherifs* used the cheap labour of their slaves to provide fancy meals at low prices. This allowed them to gain a reputation as generous hosts and to make a living by hosting numerous guests.[91]

On none of these occasions, however, was wine served. It was not least on account of the lack of taverns, brothels or other such "places of amusement", as Ferguson observed of Mutsamudu in 1881,[92] that the crews of whalers moored in the harbour would often arrange parties on board one of their vessels. The lack of more obvious amusements, however, also meant that seamen with little else to do in Mutsamudu also used their spare time for letter-writing.[93]

Sailors' testimonies often contain the observation that they scarcely encountered women in Mutsamudu. Of his time there in March 1843, for instance, John Ross Browne of the *Bruce* writes that he and another seaman had spent all day walking around the town "to see what the Johanna ladies were made of". Their best efforts notwithstanding, they caught nary a glimpse of the "dusky beauties of the town", leading Brown to conclude that the men of Mutsamudu systematically hid the women from seamen, "whose proverbial gallantry to the sex they look upon as dangerous."[94]

Other seamen recalled similar experiences. "It was next to impossible to see any of their wives or Daughters", observed the log of the barque *Palestine* of Salem, which called at Mutsamudu in May 1840. The Anjouanis clearly found "a

---

88 Browne, *Etchings of a Whaling Cruise*, 271; Eldridge, *Lewis William Eldridge's Whaling Voyage*, 13; Ferguson, *Harpooner*, 97, 100; Harris, Journal 1832–1833, 09.08.1832; Thompson, "A Whaling Cruise in the 'Sea Fox'", 151–155.
89 Log HARRISON, 1854–1857, 04.07.1855; Thompson, "A Whaling Cruise in the 'Sea Fox'", 153; Wallace, Journal CLARA BELL, 1855–1858, 24.08.1857.
90 Eldridge, *Lewis William Eldridge's Whaling Voyage*, 13.
91 Browne, *Etchings of a Whaling Cruise*, 272; Shepherd, "The Comorians and the East African Slave Trade", 86.
92 Ferguson, *Harpooner*, 87f.
93 Allen, "When I Went a-Whaling", 4.
94 Browne, *Etchings of a Whaling Cruise*, 274.

sailor after a cruise at sea" to be a menace to women.[95] Yet this notion that the men of Anjouan were shielding their women from the attention of seamen *in particular* – as a result, perhaps, of earlier encounters – is questionable. In Anjouan's Islamic culture, it was generally unheard of for married women to show themselves to strange men. An earlier British officer, Henry Rooke, writing in 1781, was probably nearer the mark on observing that the men of Mutsamudu "never allow any man to see the women".[96] It also seems that Mutsamudu was unlike many other port cities in lacking prostitutes. Only in a single source, the memoirs of Lewis Eldridge, do we hear of unspecified "slave girls" with whom the seamen had passed a "hilarious time" on the beach. Whatever hilarity is meant, however, ended with the women's departure at dusk.[97]

This lack of encounters with women gave rise to myths and rumours. Tales circulated among crews of polygamous debauchery supposedly carried on behind the walls of Mutsamudu or of the local women's suppressed desire for white men.[98] Such tales may indeed have emboldened some men in forcing their attentions on women. Having failed in his attempts to meet women in the streets, Browne and another seaman forced their way into house after catching a glance of women through a crack in the door. "Shrieking and laughing, they attempted to make their escape, through a back passage, but we were too fast for them", he frankly recalled. Yet although the seamen tried to shut the doors on the "wild damsels", they were soon beaten off by Anjouanis roused by the noise.[99]

R. Wallace, a seaman in the barque *Clara Bell* of Mattapoisett, recorded a similar episode in his diary. On observing some women at their needlework, "I entered the house by force" – only likewise to be sent packing by the men who soon arrived on the scene.[100] Other seamen found less antisocial ways of coping with the absence of women. On 4 July 1846 the American whalers moored off Mutsamudu gathered aboard the *William Badger* of Lynn to celebrate the occasion with dance, music and shots fired in salute. "Probably there was 125 Sailors onboard", records the log, "but the Ladies !0! All at home."[101]

---

95 Log PALESTINE, 1839–1842, 15.05.1840. For similar observations see Thompson, *The Life of John Thompson*, 127.
96 Rooke, *Travels to the Coast of Arabia Felix and from thence by the Red Sea and Egypt to Europe*, 24.
97 Eldridge, *Lewis William Eldridge's Whaling Voyage*, 13.
98 Barnard, *A Three Years' Cruise in the Mozambique Channel*, 88; Haywood, "American Whalers and Africa", 196f.
99 Browne, Etchings of a Whaling Cruise, 275f.
100 Wallace, Journal CLARA BELL, 1855–1858, 01.10.1856.
101 Log WILLIAM BADGER, 1845–1849, 04.07.1846.

This in some respects so baffling town of Mutsamudu was in fact a centre of Islamic religiosity. Many seamen would have heard a muezzin, seen a mosque or encountered Muslims at prayer in the streets for the first time in their lives. Some Anjouanis tried to win Christian seamen over to Islamic doctrines or invited them to their mosques,[102] and some seamen were glad to accept such invitations, though most probably out of sheer curiosity rather than any interest in conversion. On visiting mosques, seamen were impressed by what they saw. "They have large and splendidly decorated temples", an African-American seaman, John Thompson, noted in June 1843, adding: "I was astonished at the reverence and humility with which they approached the throne of grace, for they fell flat upon their faces."[103] John Ross Browne, who visited the smaller "sheik's [i.e. sultan's] mosque", also in 1843, was particularly struck by "the splendid Persian rugs of the richest texture and color" as well as by the "curiously-designed maps or charts" adorning the walls.[104] It occurred, however, that seamen caused offence, for instance by failing to remove their shoes before entering a mosque, whether from ignorance or negligence.[105] Differing opinions might also be exchanged with regard to the consumption of pork and alcohol.[106] On the whole, however, we hear very little of grave disagreements between seamen and Anjouanis over religious or cultural matters. Only aboard the *Kathleen* does there appear to have been a dangerous situation when, in 1881, a seaman threw a piece of pork at an Anjouani, thereby provoking a fight which claimed no lives even though knives were drawn.[107] Such serious conflicts as did occur generally had other causes.

Sailors took exception to the fact that visits to their vessels by Mutsamudu traders were often accompanied by theft. Once the vendors had left, crews would often notice that such tools as knives and hatchets had gone missing, or even oarlocks and other moving parts of the vessel and its boats. "Our deck is crowded with Arabs and the men forward are beginning to miss things", observed Robert Ferguson of the *Kathleen* in 1881, adding that "These people seem to steal for the love of stealing."[108] Complaints of this kind can be found

---

102 Thompson, *The Life of John Thompson*, 127; Thompson, "A Whaling Cruise in the 'Sea Fox'", 152.
103 Thompson, *The Life of John Thompson*, 128.
104 Browne, *Etchings of a Whaling Cruise*, 278f.
105 Ferguson, *Harpooner*, 86f.
106 Thompson, "A Whaling Cruise in the 'Sea Fox'", 153.
107 Ferguson, *Harpooner*, 101.
108 Ibid., 86.

in a number of logs, their exasperated keepers sometimes referring to Anjouanis as "rascals" or "liars".[109] Nor was it only the vessel's fittings that were taken. Seamen's personal possessions sometimes also disappeared – the aforementioned Lewis Eldridge's shoes, for instance, or a pipe belonging to Thomas Morrison of the barque *Avola* of New Bedford.[110] Mutsamudu's reputation among seamen – broadly positive though it was, not least on account of the low incidence of tropical diseases[111] – suffered from such cases. "Terrible time among the Arabs!!", noted the log of the barque *John Dawson* in August 1868.[112] To prevent theft, Captain Sturgis of the *Marcella* of New Bedford went so far as to ban all locals from entering the barque when she called at Mutsamudu in 1874. In 1881 Captain Howland of the *Kathleen* ordered his men to remove all small objects from deck and from the boats before entering port.[113]

While seamen complained above all of theft, the sultan found cause for annoyance in whalers ignoring his instructions. They might, for instance, defy orders not to land, which the sultan would usually issue when outbreaks of disease were reported from nearby coastal areas.[114] In 1869, for instance, the *John Dawson* dropped off two passengers from Zanzibar even though Abdullah had expressly banned landings from that island on account of an outbreak of cholera there.[115] Only a few years earlier, a cholera epidemic, which had probably been introduced from Mauritius, had claimed an estimated one in ten of the island's population.[116] Another affront was whaleships leaving without having paid the appropriate mooring fees. Finally, more than one shipmaster found the lack of an American consulate to offer a chance to get rid of undesirable seamen without fear of repercussions.[117]

As far as seamen themselves were concerned, Mutsamudu was considered anything but the best place to jump ship. In the western Indian Ocean, they far preferred Port Louis in Mauritius, were busy commercial traffic and the American

---

109 See e.g. Log JOHN DAWSON, 1867–1870, 04.08.1868; Log PALESTINE, 1839–1842, 15.05.1840.
110 Eldridge, *Lewis William Eldridge's Whaling Voyage*, 14; Log AVOLA, 1874–1877, 23.09.1877.
111 Browne, *Etchings of a Whaling Cruise*, 277.
112 Log JOHN DAWSON, 1867–1870, 03.08.1868; for similarly negative views of Mutsamudu see Log MILES, 1839–1841, 20.07.1840 and Wallace, Journal CLARA BELL, 1855–1858, 26.09.1856.
113 Log MARCELLA, 1873–1876, 13.08.1874; Ferguson, *Harpooner*, 85.
114 Log WILLIAM BADGER, 1845–1849, 01.07.1846.
115 Haywood, "American Whalers and Africa", 113.
116 Horsey, "On the Comoro Islands", 261.
117 *Commercial Gazette*, 31.01.1872; *Commercial Gazette*, 02.02.1872; Haywood, "American Whalers and Africa", 108.

consulate made for good chances of finding a new vessel before very long. But desertions were as much a part of whaling as sharks were of flensing, and Mutsamudu was no exception.[118] Some seamen may have felt themselves emboldened to desert by the town's appealing aspect. Most, however, are likely to have thought of Mutsamudu less as a place to stay than a point of transit. It might occur, for instance, that men with a mind to desert made common cause and stole a boat along with provisions, charts and navigational instruments in order to make their way onwards from Mutsamudu to Zanzibar.[119]

Captains where particularly keen to capture the fugitives in cases where they made off with part of the vessel's equipment. The sultan in Mutsamudu did his best to help skippers in this endeavour and expected to be amply repaid for his troubles. If his men succeeded in apprehending a deserter, the sultan had word sent to the captain that the man could be redeemed for a fee – five dollars per head in 1882.[120] In cases where a group of men deserted, this might soon make a tidy sum for the sultan. Captains usually tried to recoup these expenses by deducting them from their pay – which, however, they could do only if the men actually stayed on board until the lays were shared out at the end of the voyage.

The payments made by captains to the sultan may have encouraged some Anjouanis to goad seamen on shore leave into deserting, only to subsequently betray them for a reward. That at least would explain what Samuel Charles Thompson records of a man close to sultan whom he met while on shore leave in Mutsamudu in the mid-1860s: "He said to me: 'You leave ship – hide here when it sails. Plenty trouble on ship. Whale break you. You stay here, have house, plenty slave, plenty wife,' and I forget how much silver money from the Sultan, to be increased by other gifts."[121]

It has already been described how whalers in the western orientation followed seasonal patterns, guided both by the monsoon winds and by the migrations of

---

118 Log ATLANTIC, 1868–1872, 13.07.–03.08.1870; Log BREWSTER, 1857–1860, 26.08.– 08.09.1858; Log BRUNSWICK, 1856–1859, 22.–29.04.1857; Log CALLAO, 1875–1875, 12.08.–04.09.1877; Log CERES II, 1835–1837, 13.–23.05.1836; Log DIMON, 1845–1848, 26.06.–04.07.1846; Log GOVERNOR CARVER, 1854–1857, 22.05.– 01.06.1855; Log MARIA, 1846–1849, 10.–20.05.1847; Log MERLIN, 1881–1882, 14.– 21.05.1882; Log MERMAID, 1883–1890, 25.07.–10.08.1888; Log PALESTINE, 1839–1842, 14.–29.05.1840, 06.–14.05.1842; Log PETREL, 1874–1877, 23.–26.01.1877; Log THOMAS POPE, 1859–1862, 28.07.–09.08.1860.
119 For an account of such a case see Thompson, *The Life of John Thompson*, 125–128.
120 Log MERLIN, 1881–1882, 17.05.1882. For other accounts of deserters caught by the sultan's men see Log DIMON, 1845–1848, 26.03.1846; Log MARIA, 1846–1849, 20.05.1847; Tobey, Journal ROSCOE, 1846–1849, 15. & 18.06.1847.
121 Thompson, "A Whaling Cruise in the 'Sea Fox'", 152f.

humpback and sperm whales. They often called at Mutsamudu several times in the course of a single voyage, and they did so at predictable intervals. This allowed captains to hire casual labourers who signed on for an agreed period and left the vessel on its return to Mutsamudu. Unlike regular crewmen, these "seasoners" received not a share of the profits but a monthly salary, usually between five and seven dollars. Some seasoners seem to have combined a stint working aboard a whaler with their travels and agreed, for instance, to be dropped off at Zanzibar rather than returning to Anjouan.[122] Others dispensed with such arrangements and simply deserted on reaching their destination.[123]

Comorian seamen hardly ever remained aboard whalers for the duration of the voyage. The records of the New Bedford customs authorities list only two men as having arrived there from Anjouan as members of a whaling crew: Slocum James, who left again in 1866 aboard the barque *Petrel*, and Abdello Combo, who sailed for the Atlantic in 1879 in the schooner *Aurelia*.[124] It was not unheard of for Comorians to travel aboard American whalers as paying passengers, though others tried to save the fare by stowing away.[125] Anjouanis might also find short-term work as pilots. The merchantmen *Peru* of New York, for instance, paid a total of five dollars for the services of pilots in August 1832 and April 1833.[126] Whaleships, however, seldom used pilots, and those that did afterwards often found their services to have been unnecessary.[127]

Sailors often referred to Anjouanis aboard their ships by such names as "Jack" or "Sambo", and often "Jim Crow", a derogatory tag applied to blacks in the United States.[128] As in other cases of African seamen having such names applies to them by their shipmates, the motive is unclear. The difficulty English-speaking seamen had pronouncing Arab names may have been one factor, intent to disparage another.

---

122 Haywood, "American Whalers and Africa", 101; Log A. R. TUCKER, 1857–1861, 06.07.1858, 11.12.1859, 26.06.1860, 30.06.1860; Log MARCELLA, 1873–1876, 01.09.1874.
123 Log A. R. TUCKER, 1857–1861, 14.12.1858.
124 Lund et al., Whaling Crew List Database. Records were kept of the crews of outbound whalers only.
125 Log JOHN DAWSON, 1870–1872, 26.07.1871; Log PALESTINE, 1839–1842, 29.05.1840.
126 Harris, Journal 1832–1833.
127 Ibid.; Haywood, "American Whalers and Africa", 102, 196.
128 Log A. R. TUCKER, 1857–1861, 06.07.1858, 17.12.1858; Log JOHNDAWSON, 1870–1872, 26.07.1871; Log MARIA, 1846–1849, 20.05.1847.

Visits, return visits and a bombardment

A whaler putting it at Mutsamudu would usually be visited by the sultan in person. Beforehand, however, an envoy came on board to announce the impending visit to the master of the vessel and to let him know what was expected of the encounter. This included informing the captain of the gifts the sultan expected – often gunpowder and cotton stuffs – and of the general terms of the stay.[129] When the sultan himself finally came on board, he was always accompanied by an entourage.[130] Seamen generally had only the vaguest notion of who these people were and what their function was, though some are likely to have been the sultan's advisers. Among them, around 1830, was one Dr Lambert, a British ship's surgeon who had previously left the whaler *Coquette* after a dispute with the captain.[131] We find another foreigner in the sultan's retinue around 1870, this time an American by the name of Duncan, a seaman who had deserted from his vessel and subsequently converted to Islam.[132] Some of these attendants were involved in discussions concerning the purchase of provisions and may have been merchants. Since, however, the trade in provisions was the monopoly of the ruling court, there was no obvious distinction between political and commercial functionaries.[133]

The visitors displayed the signs of their high office – in the sultan's case, a jacket of purple velvet, a robe, a crown with gold ornaments and an impressive scimitar. His attendants likewise underscored their eminence by means of their dress – colourful shirts with frogging, for instance – and by wearing scimitars.[134] Captains did their best to receive their guests with due ceremony, for instance by flying their signal flags or firing their guns in salute.[135] The sultan himself cut an exceptionally gracious and courteous figure, paying compliments all round, expressing his delight at the return of earlier visitors and asking well-informed

---

129 Browne, *Etchings of a Whaling Cruise*, 268; Log ATLANTIC, 1868–1872, 29.07.1869; Log MARCELLA, 1873–1876, 11.08.1875.
130 Barnard, *A Three Years' Cruise in the Mozambique Channel*, 278f.
131 Isaacs, *Travels and Adventures in Eastern Africa*, vol. 2, 372.
132 Allen, Diary, 14.05.1869; Allen, "When I Was Seven", 21f.
133 Browne, *Etchings of a Whaling Cruise*, 268; Log MARCELLA, 1873–1876, 29.08.1874.
134 Barnard, *A Three Years' Cruise in the Mozambique Channel*, 80–82; Wray/Martin, "Historical Whaling Records from the Western Indian Ocean", 219.
135 Brott, Journal YOUNG PHENIX, 1867–1871, 25.06.1869; Haywood, "American Whalers and Africa", 105f.; Wray/Martin, "Historical Whaling Records from the Western Indian Ocean", 219.

questions.[136] Whereas Salim sometimes relied on an interpreter,[137] Abdullah seems to have spoken English proficiently enough. If a captain was sailing with his children on board, Abdullah would sometimes introduce them to his own son, born around 1860.[138]

The sultan usually paid these visits in the morning and took the opportunity to issue an invitation for a return visit. This was addressed above all at the shipmaster, who was, however, at liberty to choose such men as he saw fit to accompany him. While this usually meant officers, some captains did also allow men of lower rank to escort them. The visitors were first taken on foot to a square near the mosque. Here, they found donkeys on which they could ascend the remaining way to the sultan's residence. On their arrival, they received the salute of the palace guard. While this was given with spears in the early nineteenth century, the guard later adopted scimitars, which may be a sign of the increased dominance of Arab over African elements in Comorian culture. The seamen were then led to the main gate and thence to a great hall, where the sultan awaited them on a raised seat of state with a dozen or so attendants at his feet. All were dressed in elaborate costumes. Cushions for the visitors were placed to both sides of the sultan.[139]

The meeting began with a conversation between the sultan and the captain, which gradually broadened to include the others present. In the course of these exchanges, the sultan introduced his visitors to his wives and children, showed off his sumptuously decorated rooms and distributed compliments as well as little gifts. All this left seamen duly impressed, not least because they were also able to observe numerous retainers who would only address the sultan on their knees, kissing his hand and performing other obeisances.[140]

A ceremonial banquet marked the culmination of the visit. It was served in a dining hall whose walls were adorned with weapons and engraved elephant tusks. The company was joined by more of the sultan's retainers, bringing the number of diners to about fifty. All sat at a long heavy table, with the sultan and his senior attendants seated on a dais. Sometimes the visitors would be

---

136 Allen, "When I Was Seven", 20; Barnard, *A Three Years' Cruise in the Mozambique Channel*, 278f.
137 Barnard, *A Three Years' Cruise in the Mozambique Channel*, 80–82.
138 Allen, Diary, 19.05.1871.
139 Ferguson, *Harpooner*, 91; Prior, *Voyage Along the Eastern Coast of Africa*, 48f.; Shepherd, "The Comorians and the East African Slave Trade", 88f.
140 Allen, "When I Went a-Whaling", 2f.; Barnard, *A Three Years' Cruise in the Mozambique Channel*, 88; Boteler, *Narrative of a Voyage of Discovery to Africa and Arabia*, vol. 1, 166; Ferguson, *Harpooner*, 91; Harris, Journal 1832–1833, 09.08.1832; Haywood, "American Whalers and Africa", 196f.; Prior, *Voyage Along the Eastern Coast of Africa*, 50.

invited to spend the night at the palace and stay for breakfast the next morning.[141] Some captains took the opportunity once more to invite the sultan aboard their vessels, where he would issue another invitation in his turn, turning a stopover into a chain of reciprocal visits.[142] Sometimes the sultan would also invite visitors to one of his country seats in the interior, a privilege most frequently extended to captains already known to the sultan from earlier stays in Anjouan.[143]

As time went on, the sultans seem to have grown ever more adept at arranging these reciprocal visits in such a way as to maximise their capacity for building confidence. Of Whereas some early nineteenth-century visitors had complained of Alawi's coarse manner and poor English,[144] Abdullah, who ruled for much of the latter half of the century, seems to have left a consistently favourable impression on seamen, who emphasise his affability and multilingual fluency.[145] In a manuscript memoir, Helen Allen, who made several visits to Mutsamudu around 1870 in the barque *Merlin* of New Bedford – of which her father David was the captain – recalls that Abdullah had repeatedly suggested a marriage between herself and his son. Although Helen Allen believed the proposal to have been made in jest,[146] it actually seems quite plausible in light of Abdullah's alliance-building strategy. Salim, by contrast, who occupied the throne between the reigns of Alawi and Abdullah, struck a number of seamen as selfish and conceited.[147] He also made a fatal error, which will be discussed in the following section.

***

In April 1850 an argument broke out between several Mutsamudu victuallers and Thomas Bloomfield, captain of the *Phoenix* of New London, in the course of which Bloomfield accused the merchants of having broken previous agreements. The *Phoenix* subsequently left Anjouan under cover of darkness and without payment for provisions to the value of over one hundred dollars which

---

141 Boteler, *Narrative of a Voyage of Discovery to Africa and Arabia*, vol. 1, 163f.; Ferguson, *Harpooner*, 92.
142 Allen, "When I Went a-Whaling", 2f.; Browne, "Sketches of the Arabs", 4.
143 Brott, Journal YOUNG PHENIX, 1867–1871, 18.09.1869.
144 Boteler, *Narrative of a Voyage of Discovery to Africa and Arabia*, vol. 1, 164f.; Prior, *Voyage Along the Eastern Coast of Africa*, 50.
145 Ferguson, *Harpooner*, 91; Haywood, "American Whalers and Africa", 196f. Abdullah seems to have spent some of his youth in Scotland and attended the University of Edinburgh. (Ferguson, *Harpooner*, 92)
146 Allen, "When I Was Seven", 22; Allen, "When I Went a-Whaling", 2f.
147 Log PALESTINE, 1839–1842, 30.05.1841.

had already been taken on board.¹⁴⁸ Salim considered this a grievous affront, not least because his already fragile authority was further weakened by his apparent inability to punish such offences on the part of visiting mariners. Bloomfield's conduct would also have caused economic damage to the sultan, who controlled the trade in provisions. Nor was this the first incident of its kind: Bloomfield was only the latest in a succession of whaling captains to have sailed onwards without settling their bills or paying their mooring fees.¹⁴⁹

Whether it was chiefly on account any particular factor or rather their cumulative effect, the incident of the *Phoenix* was a slight to which Salim reacted sharply. When the next whaler put in at Mutsamudu the following month – the *Maria* of New Bedford – Salim summoned her captain, Charles Mooers, to appear before him. In the course of this interview, Salim demanded that Mooers settle the debts incurred by all whalers in Mutsamudu, a sum of eight hundred dollars. It was, Salim told him, up to Mooers to recoup the money from his defaulting countrymen.¹⁵⁰

This is not the only such case in the history of American whaling. In the Pacific islands in particular, we repeatedly hear of rulers trying to penalise a whaling captain for another vessel's misdeeds.¹⁵¹ As for Mooers, this was his first voyage in command of a whaler, and he would not get as far as the Pacific for some years yet. In any case, he rejected Salim's demand, with which he could probably not have complied even had he been minded to so: the sum demanded was in excess of the cash usually carried by whalers. Salim responded by having Mooers arrested, thereby increasing the pressure upon him.¹⁵²

The British were alarmed by the severity of Salim's reaction. To punish a captain for the infractions of others was a blatant contradiction of American law and might call forth an American intervention – an intervention not just in a dispute between one vessel's captain and the sultan of Anjouan, but in Britain's sphere of influence. It was with a view to preventing such an intervention that Josiah Napier, the outgoing British consul, tried to persuade Salim to set Mooers free. At the same time, Mooers received several visits from William

---

148 Ward, "Charles Ward to John M. Clayton", 455f.
149 *Commercial Gazette*, 31.01.1872; *Commercial Gazette*, 02.02.1872.
150 Rodman, "Samuel W. Rodman to Joseph Grinnell", 469. The account of events from the pen of the vessel's owner, Samuel W. Rodman, whom Mooers had told of the incident by letter, is one of the principal sources for this episode.
151 Chappell, "Beyond the Beach", 23.
152 "From the Indian Ocean." *New-Bedford Mercury*, 03.01.1851, 1.

Sunley, who would succeed Napier a few months later, probably with a view to obtaining better treatment for the prisoner.[153]

Although Napier tried to make the sultan aware of the potentially far-reaching consequences of his actions, Salim was at first unyielding. Indeed, the sultan threatened to go further by confiscating the *Maria* in lieu of the outstanding debt. To prevent this from happening, Mooers gave word to have her leave under the first mate's command. After two weeks, however, Salim finally bowed to British pressure and released Mooers.[154]

Salim's about-turn did not, however, resolve the dispute – at least not as far as the American military was concerned. In 1851 Francis Gregory, commander of the US Navy's Africa Squadron, which was engaged in operations against slave ships at the time, ordered USS *Dale* to sail for Mutsamudu (Fig. 23). On her arrival in August, the Dale's commander, Captain William Pearson, demanded that the sultan pay an indemnity of $20,000 for the imprisonment of Mooers and the impounding of the *Maria*. Salim let Pearson know that he had only $1,000 at his disposal, which, however, he was willing to pay. Pearson was not satisfied with this offer and ordered the *Dale* to open fire on the fort of Mutsamudu. Once the fort had been hit by a total of thirty-nine shots, Salim indicated his willingness to surrender, while maintaining that he could not possibly pay more than $1,000. This time Pearson accepted the offer, accompanied as it was by a treaty in which the sultan promised henceforth to give preferential treatment to American vessels.[155]

The bombardment of Anjouan in response to Mooers's arrest was significant not least in that was the first ever military operation of the United States in the Western Indian Ocean. That aside, however, the incident seems to have changed little: it brought about neither a permanent presence of the US Navy as in intervention force in the area nor a lasting strain in relations between whalers and the sultan. Even Mooers seems not to have harboured a grudge: in November 1851, more than a year after his address, the *New-Bedford Mercury* reported that the captain spoke of Anjouan "in high terms" and that the treaty obtained by Pearson meant that American whalers could be sure of advantageous terms there.[156] However,

---

153 Dubins, "A Political History of the Comoro Islands", 119; Rodman, "Samuel W. Rodman to Joseph Grinnell", 469.
154 Rodman, "Samuel W. Rodman to Joseph Grinnell", 469; Ward, "Charles Ward to John M. Clayton", 455f.
155 "Arrival of the Sloop of War Dale." *Whalemen's Shipping List and Merchants' Transcript*, 19.04.1853, 50; "Bombardement of Johanna by U. Sloop-of-War Dale." *The Republican Standard*, 05.02.1852, 3; Dubins, "A Political History of the Comoro Islands", 119f.; Haywood, "American Whalers and Africa", 108f.
156 "By Tuesday's Mails." *New-Bedford Mercury*, 14.11.1851, 3.

Mooers's story was subsequently embroidered as it became absorbed into mariners' lore, gaining a number of entirely fictitious accretions in the process. In the mid-1860s the tale went aboard the brig *Sea Fox* of Westport that the US Navy had bombarded Mutsamudu in order to free an American deserter who had been locked in a cell naked for his refusal to convert to Islam.[157]

Fig. 23: USS *Dale* as drawn in ink by the American artist Robert G. Skerrett. Courtesy Navy Art Collection, Washington, DC. U.S. Naval History and Heritage Command Photograph.

That the sultan too appears to have taken the matter no further may be due to the fact the American bombardment of Mutsamudu did little damage compared to earlier attacks, notably those from Madagascar. Nor was the *Dale* the first Western warship to attack Mutsamudu: in 1828 a French warship, *La Zélée*, had opened fire on the town in reprisal for the sultan's seizure of the human cargo of a shipwrecked French slaver without due compensation to the owner.[158]

---

157 Thompson, "A Whaling Cruise in the 'Sea Fox'", 151f.
158 Dubins, "A Political History of the Comoro Islands", 98f.

Indirect diplomacy

It may at first sight seem baffling to find that so momentous an event as a military attack on Mutsamudu should not have affected relations between whalers and local rulers in the long term. The extent, however, to which both sides profited from existing arrangements explains why their maintenance was considered desirable. For captains, Mutsamudu offered a comparatively cheap and reliable place to take on provisions without running an increased risk of desertion, strikes, requests for release or drunkenness on the part of the crew. Further pull factors may have helped to maintain the ports attractiveness even in the face of occasional disputes over prices and fees, notably the sultan's mostly generous hospitality and the town's picturesque appearance. The usefulness of Anjouan to whalers was circumscribed only by the difficulty of obtaining timber and the fact that it only offered a safe anchorage during the months of the south-west monsoon.

Testimony to the fact that sultans Alawi, Salim and Abdullah also expected to reap considerable benefits from whalers is given by their regular visits to vessels and their invitations to captains and officers. Their efforts to meet as many captains as possible followed the strategy of cultivating potentially useful relationships of friendship and trust – which, it was hoped, would encourage more vessels to put in at Anjouan. Not only did the income from trade and mooring fees, as well as the bounties paid for capturing deserters, do much to bolster the sultan's position domestically, they also offered the prospect of a reduced dependency on Britain and hence a wider range of political options. It is this incidental effect of whaling at the political level that strikes me as the most consequential: by trying to turn relations with whalers to its advantage in the context of its alliance-building strategies, the ruling house engaged in a form of indirect diplomacy in which whaling vessels figures as informal representatives of the United States. This representative function ascribed to them is also evident in the arrest of Mooers and the impounding of the *Maria*, both of which were intended as collective punishments. Yet since the United States showed little interest in Anjouan and was not even prepared to set up a consulate there, the whalers were unable to live up to the role in which they had been cast. Among the outside actors who influenced political conditions in the island over the course of the nineteenth century, ending in its colonisation, whalers did not play a decisive part, though they did help to stabilise the sultan's perpetually contested position. The fact that Abdullah managed to remain in office for as long as he did may also be due to the fact that his reign saw the most stopovers by whalers, which at times accounted for the largest share of shipping in Mutsamudu.

The dark side of this arrangement in which everybody might at first seem to have been a winner was that whaling is likely to have contributed, albeit indirectly, to the continuance of slavery in Anjouan. But for his earnings from whalers Abdullah would probably have had to seek an alliance with Britain earlier on in a bid to preserve his power, which would have meant agreeing to the abolition slavery earlier. The flourishing trade in provisions carried on in Mutsamudu also raises the question to what extent the demand for cheap food from whalers encouraged the use of slave labour in the island's agricultural sector.

5 Promise and endeavour: Port Louis, Mauritius, 1789–1878

Had somebody told him before setting sail as first mate in the *Thomas Pope* of New Bedford that he would one day put down the phrase "we decided" in the logbook, Nathaniel Morgan may well have shaken his head in disbelief. The simple combination of words would have struck him as fanciful, or at any rate unlikely to be encountered aboard a whaleship, where captains held sway no less autocratically than the queen of Spain – the byword, in Morgan's day, for the outright rejection of any ideas smacking of liberalism or even republicanism. To find the phrase "we decided" entered in a vessel's log must accordingly testify to the occurrence of something quite extraordinary.

The *Thomas Pope* was sailing in the northern Mozambique Channel when, in the night of 9 December 1859, a strong easterly winded picked up. Although the crew immediately struck in the foretop and reefed the mainsail, it was not enough to secure the barque against the hurricane that was sweeping the sea with ever greater force. Before very long the wind and the waves had torn away two sails and three boats, as well as stripping the deck of everything that was not nailed down. At 1 p.m. on the next day, after a fearful night, Charles Robbins saw himself forced to take the ultimate measure left to a captain in such a situation: to relieve the pressure on the vessel, he ordered parts of the masts to be cut down, in this case the topmasts and topgallant masts. To make matters worse, a topgallant yard broke while this work being carried out. The vessel narrowly survived the afternoon, and around 6 p.m. the sky finally seemed to clear. Exhausted and soaked to the bone though they were, the men began to gather the remains of her storm-ravaged rigging. Soon, however, they came to realise that the sky over the south-west Indian Ocean had deceived once more. Within an hour, the hurricane was back – indeed, "with more fury than ever", as Morgan noted in the vessel's log. The gale soon tore up the remaining sails and drove the now virtually disabled vessel north and south as it blew. Whenever her men thought the worst was behind them, they found their hopes dashed: "The hurricane continued to increase all the time", noted Morgan. In the course of 11 December the *Thomas Pope* lost her mizzenmast and her sea ladder as well as her jib-boom and flying jib-boom along with all their rigging. By the evening, when the sea finally calmed down, the barque had lost all her masts, her boats and much else besides. Only the stump of the foremast still jutted upwards defiantly. Robbins called his officers together in order to settle on what to do next. Morgan recorded the upshot of the discussion as follows: "We decided that Mauritius was the most probable port for repairs."[1]

Following the currents of the sperm whale hunt

What happened to the *Thomas Pope* is not merely a dramatic tale of fortitude in adversity. Her case stands for the many other whalers that found their way to Mauritius by accident rather than by design. This was a particularly frequent occurrence in the early days of whaling in the Indian Ocean, in the eighteenth and nineteenth centuries, when many a vessel had to make an unscheduled stop for repairs after being caught in one of the heavy storms for which these waters were and remain notorious. The *Eliza* of Boston too had sustained severe damage when she put in at Port Louis in the spring of 1795. Her commander, Charles Swain, gave a detailed account of the vessel's tribulations to the local authorities. The first disaster had been the death of Caleb Gardner, the original captain; later, she lost her anchor and rudder in a strong gale in Delagoa Bay before suffering renewed damage in stormy weather. It was only then that Swain decided to sail for Mauritius, which at the time was an island of little importance to whalers.[2]

Swain was among the earliest captains to sail a whaler into Port Louis, the island's capital and chief port. Yet earlier still, French merchants had made an attempt to exploit whale stocks in the surrounding waters. In June 1775 the *Salomon* sailed from Port Louis to hunt whales around La Réunion (then known as Île Bourbon) and the island of Sainte-Marie off eastern Madagascar. Alas, although the vessel returned safely, the crew had failed to take a single whale, and the French pursued the project of colonial whaling in the Mascarene Basin no further.[3]

The first individually identifiable whaler to sail into Port Louis was the *United States* of Nantucket in 1789,[4] although American historians Peter Duignan and Lewis Gann believe there to have been sporadic visits from New England whalers before that date.[5] Whilst there is no hard evidence for this supposition, we do know that American merchantmen began making regular calls at Port Louis in 1786 and hence would have been aware of the Mascarene Basin and perhaps its whale stocks by that date. Trade soon flourished and several American merchants

---

1 Log THOMAS POPE, 1859–1862, 10.–11.12.1859.
2 Richards/Du Pasquier, "Bay Whaling off Southern Africa", 245.
3 Du Pasquier, *Les Baleiniers Français*, 184.
4 Jones, *Ships Employed in the South Seas Trade*, 9.
5 Duignan/Gann, *The United States and Africa*, 69.

settled in the town, which was already important enough for the State Department in Washington to open a consulate in 1794.[6]

New England whalers continued to visit Port Louis during the Napoleonic wars, though the naval war forced them move across the South Seas in patterns different from those to which they had become habituated. From 1793 onwards privateers commissioned by belligerent states repeatedly seized American vessels in the bays of southern Africa, where they had been accustomed to hunt southern right whales. Those whalers who braved the South Seas in spite of the war now avoided spending months waiting to intercept southern rights in Walvis Bay or Delagoa Bay, instead moving between whaling grounds at shorter intervals. While avoiding privateers was one reason for this change, an already noticeable decline in southern right stocks may also have played a part. As their patterns of movement altered, a few American vessels began to take their pursuit of whales to the Mascarene Basin and put in at Port Louis.[7] No more than four such calls are recorded for any given year of the war, however. To most whalers, Port Louis was a last resort – a place to go for repairs that brooked no delay, as in the case of the *Eliza*. After an unsuccessful cruise, the busy port might also be the place to hear news of whales in the surrounding waters.

The ongoing war posed considerable risks to British whalers in the South Seas too. They had not to fear only the depredations of French, Spanish and Dutch privateers but also the Royal Navy, which might impress their seamen at will. Another danger came in the form of corsairs, who were made Port Louis the base for their raids throughout the western Indian Ocean. Against this backdrop, from about 1798 onwards the British whaling fleet shifted its operations in the South Seas away from the Atlantic and the bays of southern Africa towards the eastern Indian Ocean.[8]

Even after the peace treaties of Ghent and Paris (both 1814) only few whalers ventured into Mascarene waters. Britain replaced France as the colonial power and barred foreign vessels from Port Louis until 1820. Thereafter and into the mid-1830s, only one or two whaleships a year put in at Port Louis. It was during this period that both American and British vessels established the western Indian Ocean as a sperm whaling ground, working their way from north to south. They discovered the first sperm whaling grounds around the Seychelles in 1823 and

---

6 Duignan/Gann, *The United States and Africa*, 67.
7 Richards/Du Pasquier, "Bay Whaling off Southern Africa", 245.
8 Ibid., 246.

began operations off Zanzibar in 1828 before hunting in the waters off Madagascar and, finally, in the Mascarene Basin.[9]

The heyday of whaling in the Mascarene Basin dawned in the late 1830s. At least nine whalers put in at Port Louis in 1838, more than ever before. Vessels continued to frequent Port Louis throughout the 1840s, and the number of their visits again increased considerably in the latter part of the 1850s. "During the whaling season many whaling ships come in for recruiting", the American consul reported back to Washington in 1856.[10] Ten whalers called at Port Louis in the third quarter of that year alone.[11] From 1857 to 1860 the annual number of whalers ranged from seventeen to thirty-three. Since the US consulate kept records of all American-flagged vessels that sailed into Port Louis, we may treat these figures as fairly reliable. However, these records only began to be kept in 1857, and it is quite probable that the number of vessels in previous years exceeds that recorded in the incompletely preserved logbooks.[12] Although the records of the American consul do not account for British whaleships, they had in any case ceased to operate in these waters by that time. Mauritius was never of any significance to British whalers – quite unlike their American counterparts.

In order to make the port more attractive to American whalers, George Fairfield, the US consul at the time, in January 1859 asked the State Department to enter into negotiations with the British government with a view to securing tax- and duty-free status for the transhipment of whale products in Mauritius.[13] The ability to load whale oil, blubber and baleen onto freighters or other whaleships in the course of their voyage would have allowed whalers to extend their operational periods in their hunting grounds, to increase their efficiency and profitability, and to use Port Louis as their central transhipment port in the Indian Ocean. This scheme, however, seems not to have been realised. Not until 1860s do we hear of whalers using Port Louis for the transhipment of their catch, and then only in a few instances.[14]

---

[9] On whaling's dynamic of exploration in the western Indian Ocean see the chapter "Passages I".
[10] George H. Fairfield. Letter to Secretary of State, 30.06.1856. National Archives and Records Administration, Records of Foreign Service Posts, Record Group 84, Port Louis, vol. 052.
[11] George H. Fairfield. Letter to Secretary of State, 30.09.1856. National Archives and Records Administration, Records of Foreign Service Posts, Record Group 84, Port Louis, vol. 006.
[12] Ships Daily Journal, 1857–1862. National Archives and Records Administration, Records of Foreign Service Posts, Record Group 84, Port Louis, vol. 051.
[13] George H. Fairfield. Letter to Secretary of State, 10.01.1859. National Archives and Records Administration, Records of Foreign Service Posts, Record Group 84, Port Louis, vol. 006.
[14] See e.g. Log ATLANTIC, 1868–1872, 16.11.–23.12.1869; Log ATLANTIC, 1876–1879, 03.–15.05.1877, 07.–29.11.1877; Log JOSEPHINE, 1903–1905, 09.05.– 01.06.1904.

The Civil War not only halved the American whaling fleet but affected whaling operations in the Mascarene Basin in other ways too. Simply knowing of the presence of two Confederate privateers – the *Alabama* and the *Florida* – was enough to keep Union vessels out of the western Indian Ocean.[15] In 1861, the year in which the war broke out, the US consulate recorded forty-one whalers calling at Port Louis. In 1865, when the war ended, the number had fallen to one.[16]

Even once petroleum began to be extracted industrially and on a large scale, some shipowners and syndicates continued to outfit vessels for whaling. These vessels largely sailed from San Francisco for the sub-Arctic northern Pacific or from New Bedford. After the Civil War, fewer and fewer vessels made the longer journey to the Indian Ocean. The number of stopovers at Port Louis remained at well below ten for nearly each of the post-war years. Only in 1869 was there a sudden peak of eighteen – in consequence, no doubt, of an unusually profitable hunting season in these waters – but numbers declined all the more sharply thereafter.[17] The last whaler identifiable by name to sail into Port Louis in the nineteenth century was the barque *Atlantic* of New Bedford in June 1878,[18] afterwards to continue whaling in the Arctic.[19] Not until a quarter of a century later did another whaler put in at Port Louis: the *Josephine* of New Bedford called twice, in 1904 and 1906, and is likely to have been the last of her kind to do so.[20]

As far as this study and its themes are concerned, the changing fortunes of whaling around Mauritius raise the question of whether the experiences of the whalemen themselves in Port Louis affected the rise and fall in the number of stops there or whether this was due entirely to the external factors cited above. What did whalemen make of Port Louis, what were their experiences? And

---

15 Thomas Shankland. Letter to Secretary of State, 03.08.1863. National Archives and Records Administration, Records of Foreign Service Posts, Record Group 84, Port Louis, vol. 006; W. R. G. Mellen. Letter to Secretary of State, 10.10.1864. National Archives and Records Administration, Records of Foreign Service Posts, Record Group 84, Port Louis, vol. 006.
16 Ships Daily Journal, 1857–1862. National Archives and Records Administration, Records of Foreign Service Posts, Record Group 84, Port Louis, vol. 051; Ships Daily Journal, 1865–1871. National Archives and Records Administration, Records of Foreign Service Posts, Record Group 84, St. Helena, vol. 050. The Mauritius newspaper *The Commercial Gazette* likewise records hardly any calls by whalers during these years. See *The Commercial Gazette*. British Library Newspapers, MC 1358. Isuues 05.01.1864 to 29.04.1865.
17 Nicholas Pike. Letter to Secretary of State, 10.01.1870. National Archives and Records Administration, Records of Foreign Service Posts, Record Group 84, Port Louis, vol. 006.
18 *The Mercantile Record*, 18.06.1878.
19 Lund et al., *American Offshore Whaling Voyages*.
20 Log JOSEPHINE, 1903–1905, 09.05.–01.06.1904; Log JOSEPHINE, 1905–1907, 04.–26.05.1906.

what effects did their increased presence have on the port and on the town more generally? In order to answer this question, I shall begin by describing the port and the development of shipping there prior to the coming of whalers to the western Indian Ocean. I shall then discuss conditions in Port Louis during the whaling era itself with a view to establishing what consequences the visits of the whalemen may have had.

Fig. 24: The *Charles W. Morgan* of New Bedford. Previously a full-rigged ship, she appears in this photograph from 1920 rigged as a barque, as she had been since 1867. She was one of several whalers moored at Port Louis in May 1872. Today she is the only American whaler to have been preserved and as such is perhaps the best-known vessel of her day.
Courtesy Mystic Seaport.

A dream destination and a danger zone

Mauritius is surrounded by a belt of coral reefs with few gaps. Only three of the many bays carved into the shoreline by the Indian Ocean offer safe anchorage: the *Baie de Grande Rivière Noire* in the south-west, *Grand Port* in the south-east and the *Baie de Grande Rivière* in the north-west. Port Louis is situated on the latter. Seamen found reaching it to be a challenge, for they had to steer their vessels along a narrow and winding channel through the reef – so narrow that two vessels were barely able to pass one another at certain points.[21]

Nor were captains well advised to trust their charts and handbooks unconditionally. As late as 1826 we find such works mentioning offshore islands that never actually existed.[22] Experienced navigators used a rule of thumb in order safely to steer a vessel past the shallows and through the channel marked by buoys. Once they were within about fifteen miles of the island and its outline was discernible through the clouds and the mist in which it was often shrouded, the vessel had to be positioned with its prow facing squarely towards Port Louis. The rocky massif rising above the city now revealed a rectangular gap which opened onto the landscape behind. Now the object was to steer the vessel in such a manner as to keep the distinctively shaped peak of Pieter Both always in view. A navigator who managed to do so could count in crossing the reef in safety. This manoeuvre was often impeded, however, by a wind blowing from the direction of the port, forcing seamen to tack close to the wind.[23]

Rising to 820 metres, Peter Both is one of the highest peaks of the three volcanic mountain ranges which dominate the island's topography. The peculiar shape into which the south-east trade winds carved the lava at this point allowed seamen to pick out Mauritius from afar and to distinguish it from La Réunion and Rodrigues, its neighbours in the Mascarene Bay. Pieter Both is part of the Moka range, which forms a semicircle cradling Port Louis in the north and south. Seamen called the two arms of the range Citadel Hill and Signal Mountain – the fortress being situated on one and the signal station on the other. After the mountains themselves, the signal point was the first feature that seamen would notice. It controlled the traffic in the port below and hence was usually a busy place. Incoming vessels were asked to signal their name, port of origin, cargo and destination, while signals were also used to assign anchorages or give warning of storms.[24]

In between exchanging signals or sounding the depth, seamen might notice how what appeared at first sight to be a bare and forbidding rocky landscape gradually became greener and more inviting the closer they came to it. As sun-

---

21 Bernardin de Saint-Pierre, "Letters to a Friend", 23; Le Comte, *Mauritius from its Origin*, 11; Nordhoff, *Whaling and Fishing*, 257; van der Velde, "Jacob Haafner in Mauritius", 79; White, "Cape Town and Mauritius", 7; Wright, *Mauritius*, 12.
22 Wright, *Mauritius*, 28.
23 Huddart, *The Oriental Navigator*, 68; Nordhoff, *Whaling and Fishing*, 257; Wright, *Mauritius*, 12, 65.
24 Whitecar, *Four Years Aboard the Whaleship*, 294–296.

drenched casuarina groves, plantation fields and the first buildings came into view, many observers who had spent months at sea went into transports of delight.[25] "The eyes of God" were the words supposedly whispered by one officer aboard a New Bedford whaler as he caught sight of Mauritius around 1850. His shipmate Charles Nordhoff was more effusive: "My pen is not adequate to a delineation of the beauteous boldness with which the outlines of the volcanic peaks are thrown in deep, deep blue against the distant horizon, or the glorious golden effulgence in which they are enveloped as the sun sets behind them."[26]

On the whole, however, seamen had little time to indulge in such fancies. Their vessels would often be welcomed by tugboats promising to tow them safely through the channel, and pilots would usually offer their services too. As the nineteenth century progressed, the authorities increasingly formalised the process of entering port, for instance by putting down moorings, deploying steam tugs and mandating the use of a pilot.[27] The reason for these measures was that the inner harbour was too small for the traffic it had to handle. In order to prevent collisions or tangled anchors, arriving vessels had first to take moorings, marked by a bell buoy, in the so called "canal" at the upper end of the port. Only when traffic permitted would the signal point then assign them to an anchorage by the quayside, where vessels lay side by side (Figs. 25, 26 and 27). Small vessels in particular, however, might have to remain in the canal for the duration of their stay. This usually applied to whalers too, which had no cargo to discharge and hence had to give way to merchantmen. There was a separate holding area where departing vessels had to wait before the signal point gave permission to proceed.[28]

Before a vessel moored in the canal was permitted to send a boat to the shore, it had to await a visit from the port physician or "colonial surgeon", an office which had already been created under French rule to prevent the introduction of

---

25 Backhouse, *A Narrative of a Visit to the Mauritius and South Africa*, 2f.; Darwin, *Journal of Researches into the Natural History and Geology of the Countries Visited during the Voyage of H.M.S. Beagle round the World*, 483f.; Pike, *Sub-tropical Rambles in the Land of Aphanapteryx*, 55; van der Velde, "Jacob Haafner in Mauritius", 78; Whitecar, *Four Years Aboard the Whaleship*, 300.
26 Nordhoff, *Whaling and Fishing*, 256f.
27 Nordhoff, *Whaling and Fishing*, 257; Log JOSEPHINE, 1903–1905, 09.05.1904; Pinkham, *The Log Book of the Good Ship Alliance of Nantucket Captain Bartlett Coffin*, 04.10.1792; Whitecar, *Four Years Aboard the Whaleship*, 297–299.
28 George H. Fairfield. Letter to Secretary of State, 28.05.1859. National Archives and Records Administration, Records of Foreign Service Posts, Record Group 84, Port Louis, vol. 006; Nordhoff, Whaling and Fishing, 257; Log JOSEPHINE, 1903–1905, 09. & 31.05.1904; White, "Cape Town and Mauritius", 7; Whitecar, *Four Years Aboard the Whaleship*, 297–299.

epidemic diseases from the many visiting vessels. The colonial surgeon might take hours to arrive. If he found the situation on board to his satisfaction, he handed the captain a red flag, indicating permission to make contact with the shore.[29] But if the colonial surgeon found signs of infectious diseases, the vessel had to wait for several weeks in a quarantine dock. This was the fate of, for instance, the *Mechanic* of Newport in 1858 or the *Mercury* of New Bedford in 1875.[30]

To be admitted to the quarantine dock meant a considerable delay and hence was a considerable annoyance to shipmasters – all the more so because the verdict could be pronounced without there being any signs of disease on board. It was enough merely to have visited a supposed disease hotspot along the way. Even when, however, the colonial surgeon issued a clean bill of health, just waiting for his call meant an unwelcome delay. Of his arrival at Port Louis in 1863 aboard the *Java* of New Bedford, Joshua Beane recalled: "As no person is allowed to go up town or leave the vessel until she is visited by the health officer, we were obliged to wait until the next morning before having communication with the shore."[31]

Besides the colonial surgeon, the vessel would also be visited by a port official who issued the captain with a book of laws and regulations relating to the stay. In important part of this book was the key to the signal point's weather warnings.[32] For although some vessels came to Mauritius in a desperate search for shelter, Port Louis itself was poorly protected from storms ravaging the open sea. The island is situated in the middle of the south-west Indian Ocean tropical cyclone basin; the season generally last from December to May, with Mauritius particularly prone to cyclones from January to March. "You cannot compare it to anything else", recalled Jacob Haafner, a Dutch-German East Indiamen, of a storm he witnessed in Port Louis in January 1787. "Heaven and earth vanished from sight."[33] Every few years cyclones struck with particular intensity, for instance 818, 1819, 1824, 1840, 1844, 1848, 1865 and 1868. An exceptionally devastating cyclone hit the island in 1892, destroying a third of Port Louis and killing more than 1,200 people. These storms would usually smash many of the vessels lying in port against the shore. The floods they caused

---

29 Backhouse, *A Narrative of a Visit to the Mauritius and South Africa*, 3; Log GAZELLE, 1863–1866, n.d.; Pinkham, *The Log Book of the Good Ship Alliance of Nantucket Captain Bartlett Coffin*, 02.04.1793.
30 Log MERCURY, 1873–1876, 13.08.1875; Whitecar, *Four Years Aboard the Whaleship*, 331.
31 Beane, *From Forecastle to Cabin*, 137.
32 Whitecar, *Four Years Aboard the Whaleship*, 294f.
33 Quoted in van der Velde, "Jacob Haafner in Mauritius", 79f.

Fig. 25: View of Port Louis town centre and harbour (c. 1870) from a foothill of the Moka range reaching towards the town north of the Champ de Mars. The various parts of the port are clearly discernible: the inner harbour (left), the canal (centre) and the Trou Fanfaron (right). In the mid-nineteenth century three dry docks were built in the Trou Fanfaron, a harbour basin developed from a river estuary. (Pike, *Sub-tropical Rambles in the Land of Aphanapteryx*, p. 247). Source: Pike, *Sub-tropical Rambles in the Land of Aphanapteryx*, p. 96.

offered excellent breeding conditions for mosquitoes and hence promoted the spread of malaria. Floods might even occur far from the shore, with the incoming sea pushing rivers far back inland.[34]

Whalers generally avoided Port Louis in this perilous season. Sometimes, however, they had little choice but to put in to port. In May 1904, for instance, Captain Horace Smith of the *Josephine* witnessed "the greatest electric storm that I have ever been in", writing in the ship's log that he had "Never thought it could rain so fast or lighten so sharp."[35] In order to prevent cyclones from throwing anchored vessels against the shore, driving them out into the open sea or simply smashing them to pieces by the dozen – as it happened in 1773[36] – the port

---

[34] Burrun, *Port Louis*, 90; Larson, "A Census of Slaves Exported from Central Madagascar to the Mascarenes between 1769 and 1820", 197; Toussaint, *Port Louis*, 68, 96f.; Varma, *The Making of Mauritius*, 135.
[35] Log JOSEPHINE, 1903–1905, 08.05.1904.
[36] Wright, *Mauritius*, 15, 113.

authorities followed a multi-stage safety protocol. In the first stage, the signal point ordered all captains to re-join their vessels, where they were to await further instructions: to lengthen the anchor winch, to change berth or, in the worst case, to leave port immediately.[37] Beane, who arrived at Port Louis in late 1863 aboard the *Java*, reports that he heard of the British colonial administration had engaged the services of a soothsayer to foretell cyclones from the behaviour of worms.[38] Though this tale may have been much embroidered, the very existence of such rumours testifies to a ubiquitous fear that cast a shadow cast over the port's everyday bustle. This tropical dream of a place, to which many seamen would look forward for weeks in advance, could quickly turn into a zone of mortal danger.

Fig. 26: The quayside of the main harbour basin in the late nineteenth century, showing the customs office (left), Church Street (right) and ship chandleries (centre).
Source: *Illustrated Australian News*, 01.07.1892, p. 17.

From naval base to trading port

At the time when whaling in Mascarene waters began the island now known as Mauritius was already a hub for shipping in the Indian Ocean. Remains of Song dynasty (960–1279) porcelain found in the island suggest that it had long been known to the Arab merchants who called there for drinking water. Whether it corresponds to the island of *Dina-Arobi* mentioned in early Arab maps and writings remains, however, subject to debate among historians. Even earlier visitors to the island may have included Phoenician, Dravidian and Malay vessels. The

---

37 Whitecar, *Four Years Aboard the Whaleship*, 295f.
38 Beane, *From Forecastle to Cabin*, 142.

Portuguese seafarers who explored it between 1500 and 1539 gave the island at least four different names. They also introduced pigs, goats and cattle from Madagascar to ensure provisions for their vessels in the future. The first settlement, however, was established by the Dutch East India Company, which in 1638 erected a fort for the provisioning of its spice fleet in the south-east of the island. In 1839 the Dutch brought more than three hundred slaves to the island from Madagascar, modern-day Mozambique and their own trading stations in South Asia. These slaves were to clear the forests, cut ebony, tend cattle herds, and plant tobacco, vegetables and sugar cane. Many, however, were sold on to Brazil or to the Dutch colony of Batavia in south-east Asia – not least because the Company, fearful of revolts, wanted to prevent too large a slave population from forming. French, British and Dutch vessels were also occasional visitors to the island, calling mostly in order to purchase ebony. Its importance as a victualling station largely ceased when the Company opened its Station at the Cape of Good Hope in 1652. The island's population of about two hundred was gradually removed to the Cape, and in 1710 the Company abandoned the by now unprofitable island altogether. The Dutch, however, left the island not only with severe ecological damage – having caused the extinction of both dodo and the red rail, among other species – but also with a lasting name, bestowed in honour of Maurice of Nassau, Prince of Orange.[39]

The development of a port in Mauritius goes back to an expedition by the French East India company, the *Compagnie des Indes orientales*. After France's first colonial projects in Madagascar had come to naught, the Company turned its attention to the Mascarene islands as possible trading and provisioning stations. In 1715 Captain Guillaume Dufresne d'Arsel took possession of the island on behalf of the French crown, naming it "Île de France". The first French settlers arrived in 1721, followed a year later by the first French governor, Denis Denyon, and several dozen slaves. It was Denyon who named a bay in the north-west of the island for King Louis XV. A settlement at this site, Port Louis,

---

39 Allen, "The Mascarene Slave-trade and Labour Migration in the Indian Ocean during the Eighteenth and Nineteenth Centuries", 33; Allen, "A Traffic of Several Nations", 157; Barnwell/Toussaint, *A Short History of Mauritius*, 1–8; Bowman, *Mauritius*, 8–10; Duffey, "China's Contact with Southern Africa", 30f.; Le Comte, *Mauritius from its Origin*, 14–17, 58; Teelock, *Mauritian History*, 22–24, 30–46; Toorawa, "The Medieval Waqwaq Islands and the Mascarenes", 49f.; Varma, *The Making of Mauritius*, 12–18; Vink, "The World's Oldest Trade", 173. On Dutch rule in Mauritius see esp. Moree, *A Concise History of Dutch Mauritius*. Since the severe ecological damage done to island posed a threat to its strategically important reserves of wood, the French instituted a systematic forestry administration in the mid-1700s, one of the earliest state-mandated environmental protection measures in history. (Grove, "Conserving Eden"; idem, *Green Imperialism*)

was initiated by Denyon's successor, Nicolas de Maupin. Maupin found that the bay, sheltered as it was by the surrounding mountains, offered better protection from cyclones than the south-east of the island which had hitherto been favoured by settlers. The next governor, Mahé de La Bourdonnais, believed Port Louis to have the potential to grow into a strategic centre of French policy and trade in the Indian Ocean. Under his governorship, port facilities – docks, warehouses, wharves, a beacon, fortifications and barracks for up to six thousand soldiers – were built, largely by Indian labourers as well as by slaves. Port Louis henceforth assumed a key role in the Company's operations, all the more after it was driven out of India by the British in 1754 in the Second Carnatic War. With a view to promoting commerce, from about 1740 the Company allowed private merchants to acquire land in the island and to outfit vessels of their own in port Louis. To provide further encouragement to shipping, the cultivation of sugar cane was intensified and new crops – coffee, tea, cotton, indigo and spices – were planted. To make this possible, tens of thousands of slaves were now brought to the island – an average of about three thousand a year from 1769. They came first from Pondicherry (now Puducherry) and other French possessions in South Asia, and from the 1760s onwards from the what are now Madagascar, Tanzania, India, Mozambique and Malaysia, from the Comoros and Zanzibar, as well as from west Africa. For the Île de France, however, this meant falling into structural dependence: since the island's own produce was largely destined for export, feeding the rapidly growing slave population meant ensuring a steady supply of wheat, rice and fish from Madagascar and the east African mainland.[40]

The expansion of agriculture, the development of infrastructure and the concentration of mercantile capital soon caused Port Louis to grown into a flourishing town replete with shops, workshops, stables, government offices, coffeehouses, markets and streets. Merchantmen put in at the port in increasing numbers, taking advantage of its location on what was now the main route between the Cape of Good Hope and India, which had shifted from the west to the east of Madagascar.

---

40 Allen, "The Mascarene Slave-trade and Labour Migration in the Indian Ocean during the Eighteenth and Nineteenth Centuries", 33; Allen, *Slaves, Freedmen, and Indentured Laborers in Colonial Mauritius*, 14; Alpers, "The French Slave Trade in East Africa", 89f.; Bowman, *Mauritius*, 12f.; Burrun, *Port Louis*, 5–13, 20f., 24–27; Coupland, *East Africa and its Invaders*, 53, 73f.; Jackson Haight, *European Powers and South-East Africa*, 104–108; Larson, "A Census of Slaves Exported from Central Madagascar to the Mascarenes between 1769 and 1820", 196; Le Comte, *Mauritius from its Origin*, 33–37, 43, 58; Reddi, "Aspects of Indian Culture in Ile de France during the Period 1803–1810", 33f.; Teelock, *Mauritian History*, 18f., 49–67; Toussaint, *History of the Indian Ocean*, 155; Toussaint, "The Role of Trade in the Settlement of Mauritius", 117; Varma, *The Making of Mauritius*, 20–22; Worden, "Cape Town and Port Louis in the Eighteenth Century", 45f.

Shipping saw its sharpest increase after 1767, when the governor, Pierre Poivre, revoked the Company's trading monopoly. The Company had already been in bad financial shape, and Poivre gave the island's commerce a boost by declaring Port Louis a free port for French citizen and ordering its development as a naval base. Whereas seventy-eight vessels had put in at Port Louis in 1769, the number never fell below one hundred throughout the 1770s and 1780s, in some years exceeding three hundred. On some days the port gave the appearance of a forest of masts. This substantial increase in shipping was due in large part to the liberalisation of trade, in consequence of which French merchants came to use the island as an entrepôt for goods imported from Asia. European and American merchants, for instance, had no longer to sail as far as China for tea, but were able to obtain the desired commodity at Port Louis. This trade brought considerable wealth to many a merchant and landowner in Port Louis, some of which went towards the building of impressive mansions in the island's interior. This wealth, however, was generated in large part on the backs of slaves, whose share of the overall population increased as trade was liberalised. On the eve of the monopoly's revocation, some 33,000 slaves lived in Mauritius; by the late 1790s their number had grown to more than 93,000. In the mid-1770s, they accounted for three quarters of the population of Port Louis.[41]

Many of the vessels that sailed into Port Louis in the late 1700s had come from or via the north-east coast of Madagascar and carried slaves on board – or food for the slaves already in the island. At the same time, more and more merchants from South Asia settled in the port, mostly Indian Hindus and Muslims. This diversification of the town's population was reflected in the increased segregation of urban space. This development was formalised in 1800, when the authorities divided the town into six districts, divided along class and ethnic lines. Three of these districts were reserved for inhabitants of European origin. Together, they formed the *Ville Blanche*, whose boundaries were marked by the port, the *Champ de Mars* and the *Champ de Lort*. This "white city" contained government buildings, the preeminent merchant houses and the town's largest market. The remaining districts were each subdivided by class, religion and region of origin, for instance into one for free labourers of Madagascan origin and another for Arab Muslim merchants. A number of laws and by-laws was intended to restrict each group to its designated streets. Workers of African origin, for instance, were

---

41 Allen, "The Mascarene Slave-trade and Labour Migration in the Indian Ocean during the Eighteenth and Nineteenth Centuries", 34f.; Bowman, *Mauritius*, 13; Burrun, *Port Louis*, 27, 64; Jackson Haight, *European Powers and South-East Africa*, 31; Larson, "A Census of Slaves Exported from Central Madagascar to the Mascarenes between 1769 and 1820", 200f., 205; Teelock, *Mauritian History*, 19f., 133; Toussaint, *Early American Trade with Mauritius*, 1; Worden, "Cape Town and Port Louis in the Eighteenth Century", 45f., 48.

forbidden from entering the *Ville Blanche* as hawkers, where they might sell liquor to seamen in the harbour.[42]

Such strategies of segregation were always going to prove hard to enforce. Many slave women from the *Camp des Noirs de l'État*, for instance, sought out contacts with men from other districts who were of higher social rank and might be able to secure their freedom. Free black women pursued similar strategies for social advancement. What was more, every year hundreds or even thousands of slaves who had escaped from plantations in the interior arrived in the city, where they mingled with the free workers who populated the fourth and fifth districts. These districts' inhabitants also included many an impoverished worker, soldier and seaman of European descent who was not welcome in the *Ville Blanche*. For their part, the residents of the *Ville Blanche* employed many servants of African and Asian origin. In practice, the segregation of urban space was far less rigid than it may have seemed on paper.[43]

As early as 1740s, the French had already used the Île de France as a base for privateers who attacked British and Portuguese merchantmen in the Indian Ocean. The harbour at Port Louis was subsequently expanded and dredged in order to allow larger warships to berth there. In 1778 France entered the war against Great Britain on the side of the rebel colonists in America, and Port Louis was its main naval base in the Indian Ocean. When Franco-British conflict was further exacerbated by the outbreak of the Napoleonic wars, France stepped up its naval operations in the area. Between 1793 and 1810 French warships and privateers seized more than five hundred enemy vessels. Such famous corsairs as François Thomas Le Même, Jean-Marie Dutertre or Robert Surcouf sold their copious booty at knock-down prices in the market at Port Louis, which acted as a draw on merchant shipping. Once trade had been liberalised and the port opened for vessels of all nations, merchants began to arrive from Oman and east Africa – and, from 1786 onwards, the United States.[44]

---

[42] Alpers, "Becoming Mozambique", 139; Barker, *Slavery and Anti-Slavery in Mauritius*, 137; Larson, "A Census of Slaves Exported from Central Madagascar to the Mascarenes between 1769 and 1820", 200f.; Ly-Tio-Fane Pineo/Lim Fat, *From Alien to Citizen*, 121f.; Teelock, "From Mozambique to Le Morne Brabant Mountain", 281; Teelock, *Mauritian History*, 133–136; Toussaint, *Port Louis*, 30; Worden, "Cape Town and Port Louis in the Eighteenth Century", 48.
[43] Allen, Slaves, *Freedmen, and Indentured Laborers in Colonial Mauritius*, 45f.; Barker, *Slavery and Anti-Slavery in Mauritius*, 136f.; Peerthum/Peerthum, "Shattering the Shackles of Slavery", 77–84; Rosunee, "Manumission and Maroonage", 62–65; Vaughan, *Creating the Creole Island*, 125.
[44] Allen, *Slaves, Freedmen, and Indentured Laborers in Colonial Mauritius*, 11f.; Bowman, *Mauritius*, 14; Coupland, *East Africa and its Invaders*, 106f.; Duignan/Gann, *The United States and Africa*, 67; Jackson Haight, *European Powers and South-East Africa*, 112f., 145f.; Le Comte, *Mauritius from its Origin*, 37–39, 47, 49; Teelock, *Mauritian History*, 20; Toussaint, *Early*

294 — 5 Promise and endeavour: Port Louis, Mauritius, 1789–1878

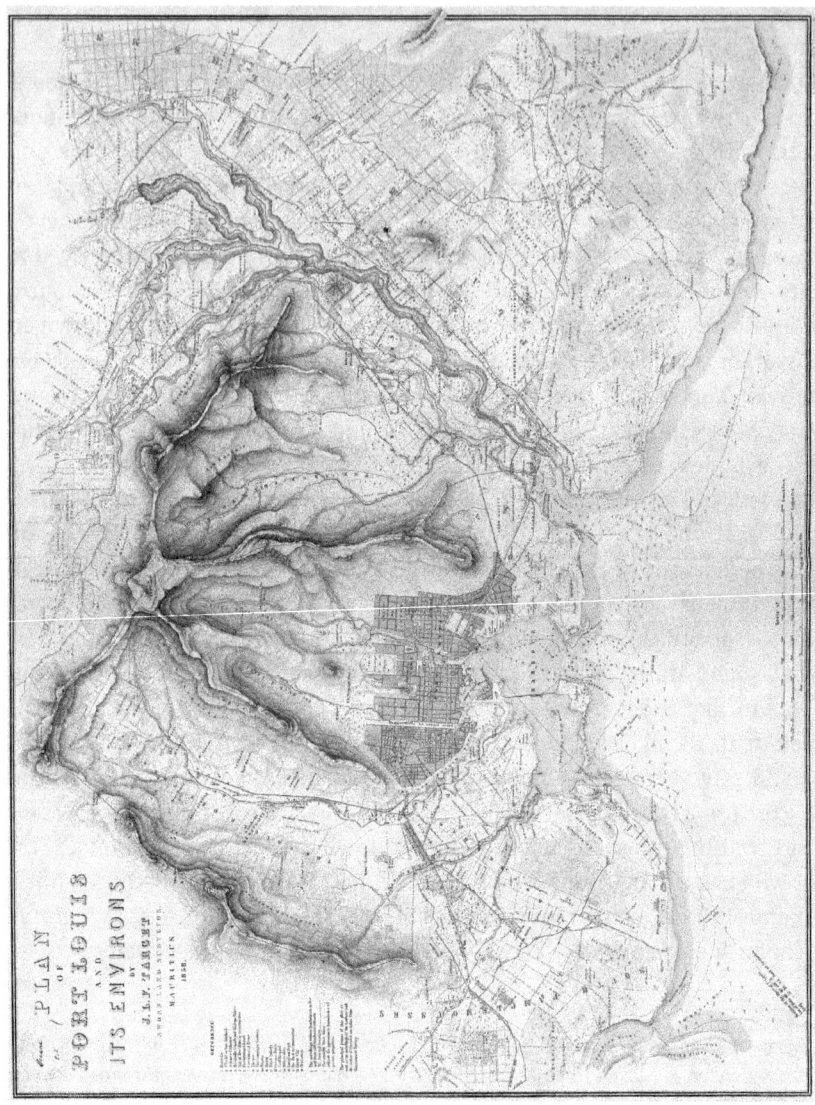

Fig. 27: Port Louis on a map of 1858 (J. L. F. Target. *Plan of Port Louis and its Environs*. Mauritius 1858).
Courtesy of the Gotha Research Library at University of Erfurt, SPK 547$112117643.

The French Revolution reached the Île de France in 1790. However, the changes it brought in its wake – including the founding of Jacobin clubs of some importance – did not amount to a social revolution. The "plantocracy" – the powerful and well-organised merchants and planters of French origin – supported some of the changes mandated for the colonies by the revolutionary authorities in Paris. But while it was willing to accept the creation of a parliament, the abolition of hereditary titles or the expropriation of the Church, it refused to implement the abolition of slavery which had been set by French parliament for 1794. In fact, the Mauritian plantocracy imported twice as many slaves after 1794 than it had before. Dependent as they were on Île de France as a naval base in their war with Britain, the French authorities were loath to pick a fight with the local magnates and made no efforts to enforce abolition.[45] This may have been the price of social peace amid revolutionary turmoil. As the Mauritian historian Auguste Toussaint concluded, "It was slavery that held the colonists together and prevented class conflict."[46]

Knowing it to be the operating base for French corsairs, the British government had already identified the Île de France as the principal threat to British shipping in the Indian Ocean. The outbreak of the Napoleonic wars roused the Admiralty into revisiting its earlier plans for eliminating this threat. In the latter part of the seventeenth century the French had heavily fortified Port Louis and concentrated their troops there in anticipation of a British naval blockade. However, in view of lack of familiarity with Mascarene waters, the danger posed by cyclones and the difficulty of putting up sufficient vessels for a blockade lasting several months, the Admiralty instead decided to invade. In November 1810 approximately twelve thousand British troops, most of whom had been recruited in India, landed in the north of the island from some seventy vessels. They made their way to Port Louis through the interior largely unopposed. Captain-General Decaen surrendered the town after a few days and without a major battle. The island formally became a part of the British Empire under the Paris Peace Treaty of 1814.[47]

American Trade with Mauritius, 7; Toussaint, *History of the Indian Ocean*, 162; Varma, *The Making of Mauritius*, 23, 31–33, 126f.; Wright, *Mauritius*, 19–26. On the history of piracy in the seas around Mauritius see Piat, *Pirates and Corsairs in Mauritius*.
45 Barnwell/Toussaint, *A Short History of Mauritius*, 92–107, 112; Coupland, *East Africa and its Invaders*, 194; Jackson Haight, *European Powers and South-East Africa*, 48; Toussaint, *Port Louis*, 46–55; Varma, *The Making of Mauritius*, 42–45.
46 Toussaint, *Port Louis*, 53.
47 Barnwell/Toussaint, *A Short History of Mauritius*, 117f.; Burrun, *Port Louis*, 16, 64; Coupland, *East Africa and its Invaders*, 139f.; Graham, *Tides of Empire*, 61f.; Ly-Tio-Fane Pineo, *In the Grips of the Eagle*, 217–226; Jackson Haight, *European Powers and South-East Africa*, 110f.; Teelock, *Mauritian History*, 157f., 167–169; Varma, *The Making of Mauritius*, 49f.

Britain's interest in Mauritius was above all strategic. Having eliminated the French threat and asserted its own security claims, Britain at first pursued no projects of its own with regard to the island, nor did it station warships at Port Louis. In the wider context of colonial policy, the newly acquired island seemed like a minor prize, a necessary evil to be maintained at as small a cost as possible. Keeping expenses low was one reason why the British administration pursued a hands-off policy with regard to the local population and barely interfered in its social, religious and cultural customs. The legal and education systems were left unchanged, and although the slave trade had been outlawed in the British Empire since 1807, in the first years of British rule the Mauritian planters were able to import more slaves than ever before. Some names were changed, most notably that of the Île de France, which reverted to the earlier Dutch designation it retains to this day. The British takeover did, however, noticeably affect the local economy. Since Britain's protectionist policy prohibited trade between its colonies and foreign merchants, Port Louis lost its status as a free port and a good deal of its commercial traffic. If it was to preserve its wealth and influence, the Franco-Mauritian plantocracy would henceforth have to concentrate on agricultural produce for which there was high demand in the British imperial marketplace. Sugar fitted the bill perfectly.[48]

The growth of whaling in the Mascarene Basin after the Napoleonic wars thus coincided with a period of structural change in Mauritius. As far as Port Louis was concerned, the most palpable effect of the sugarcane monoculture emerging in the island's interior was that virtually the only vessels still to frequent the harbour were merchantmen. From serving military, colonial and a variety of economic purposes in equal measure, Port Louis went to being a commercial port geared overwhelmingly towards exporting sugar and importing food and plantation workers.

A sugar port and its shifting forms

Sugar was no small matter in Port Louis. The decades during which whalers regularly called there coincided with the wholesale transformation of Mauritius into a sugar cane island. Before the advent of the British, a sizeable proportion of the land had been given over to the cultivation of cotton, wheat, maize and manioc. Such was the pressure of altered structural circumstances, however, that sugar

---

48 Jackson Haight, *European Powers and South-East Africa*, 141, 209; Larson, "A Census of Slaves Exported from Central Madagascar to the Mascarenes between 1769 and 1820", 201; Le Comte, *Mauritius from its Origin*, 53; Storey, *Science and Power in Colonial Mauritius*, 26; Teelock, *Mauritian History*, 21; Toussaint, "The Role of Trade in the Settlement of Mauritius", 119.

production increased fivefold between 1816 and 1826. The extent of sugar cane plantations grew tenfold by the mid-1800s. This development was encouraged by Britain's lowering of import duties on Mauritius sugar, placing the island on an equal footing with the British possessions in the Caribbean. Whereas Port Louis had exported £24.5 million worth of sugar in 1823, on the eve of this measure, by 1840 the figure had increased to £60 million and continued to do so until the early 1900s. For the first time in the island's history agriculture was the principal sector of its economy, but the proportion of agricultural production that was not intended for export was continually shrinking. The narrowing of the Mauritian economy and its increasing reliance on a cash crop monoculture left its mark on politics and society in the island, with nearly every branch of commerce, every job depending directly or indirectly on sugar.[49]

Two other developments profoundly changed life in Mauritius during the whaling era. First, between 1830 and 1835 the British governor, Sir William Nicolay, succeeded in implementing, by a combination of threats and considerable financial concessions, the abolition of slavery against the protests of the plantocracy. The measure had been in preparation since 1817, but not until 1 February 1835 were the island's slaves – an estimated 60,000 to 70,000 in a population of 100,000 – legally freed. As in other parts of the British Empire, they were to continue working for their previous masters as apprentices for a transitional period of five years. Many former slaves, however, had little enthusiasm for this scheme and fled the plantations for the coast and for towns and villages, where they settled as fishermen, small-scale farmers or tradesmen. Only seldom did planters succeed in recruiting former slaves as workers.[50]

The loss of slave labour led (second) to a considerable change in the size and composition of Mauritian population. Threated with the collapse of the plantation economy, the plantocracy and the British administration began efforts for the large-scale recruitment of indentured workers from India, Madagascar, China, the Comoros and east Africa. Around half a million of these so-called "coolies" came to Mauritius between 1834 and 1920. Although they were formally understood to

---

[49] Barnwell/Toussaint, *A Short History of Mauritius*, 131, 139f.; Bowman, *Mauritius*, 19f.; Storey, *Science and Power in Colonial Mauritius*, 26f.; Toussaint, *Port Louis*, 72; Varma, *The Making of Mauritius*, 91–108.

[50] On the history of slavery and abolition in Mauritius see Allen, *Slaves, Freedmen, and Indentured Laborers in Colonial Mauritius*; Barker, *Slavery and Anti-Slavery in Mauritius*; Filliot, *La Traite des Esclaves vers les Mascareignes au XVIIIe Siècle*; Larson, "A Census of Slaves Exported from Central Madagascar to the Mascarenes between 1769 and 1820"; Nöel, *L'Esclavage à l'Isle de France (Ile Maurice) de 1715 à 1810*; Nwulia, *The History of Slavery in Mauritius and the Seychelles*; Teelock, *Bitter Sugar*; Vaughan, *Creating the Creole Island*; Vaughan, "Slavery and Colonial Identity in Eighteenth Century Mauritius".

have done so of their own free will, they had in fact often been forcibly recruited or deceived by false promises. They were contractually bound to their employers for five-year periods, and although the conditions under which they lived and worked strongly resembled those of slaves (including physical violence and other forms of abuse), the majority of them – an estimated 283,000 – remained in Mauritius after their contracts had expired, albeit not least because many planters refused to honour their contractual obligation to give them their passage home, expecting them instead to sign on for another five-year period. This meant a rapid increase in the island's population, which had numbered only about 60,000 on the eve of its annexation by Britain. Although this increase was greater in the countryside than in the towns, it certainly did not pass Port Louis by (Tab. 5). It also brought about rapid and far-reaching changes in culture and society. Within a few decades, for instance, Hinduism became the most widespread religion in Mauritius, Morisyen creole the dominant language and rice imported from India the staple food.[51]

Visiting whalers would have experienced these structural changes only indirectly – they may, for instance, have affected the availability of provisions. For this reason, I will draw only occasionally on the extensive research literature on the history of the sugar economy, abolition and indentured labour in Mauritius, concentrating instead on the space in which seamen interacted with the population of Port Louis in the whaling era – on the harbour and its environs. My account owes a great deal to Auguste Toussaint, the doyen of modern Mauritian history and author of a monograph on the history of Port Louis.[52]

The appearance of Port Louis underwent considerable changes in the course of the whaling era, though this had little to do with one colonial power taking over from another. A fire in September 1816 half destroyed the down, and towards the end of 1818 a severe cholera epidemic broke out which claimed many lives over the succeeding months. Under the governorship of Robert Farquhar, the authorities took advantage of this loss of both buildings and population to restructure the urban space. The town was now divided into eighteen sections, and roads were paved to make them passable for vehicle traffic. The effects of the latter measure became noticeable after around 1830, when carts and carriages became a more familiar sight than the sedan chairs which had long been in use and

---

51 On the history of labour migration to Mauritius see Anderson, *Convicts in the Indian Ocean*; Carter, *Lakshmi's Legacy*; Emrith, *History of the Muslims in Mauritius*; Deerpalsingh/Carter, *Select Documents on Indian Immigration*; Hazareesingh, *History of Indians in Mauritius*; Ly-Tio-Fane Pineo/Lim Fat, *From Alien to Citizen*; Rivière, "No Man Is an Island"; Teelock, *Mauritian History*, 209, 226–260.
52 Toussaint, *Port Louis*.

Tab. 5: Population of Port Louis according to various estimates.

1826	26,615
1836	27,645
1846	45,212
1851	49,909
1861	74,128
1871	63,015
1881	66,466
1891	62,046
1901	52,652

Sources: Backhouse 4; Barker, *Slavery and Antislavery in Mauritius* 136; Varma 132.

had functioned not least as status symbols. In the 1850s the authorities had the harbour walls extended and the first dry docks built for repairing vessels.[53]

Once Britain had placed Mauritius under the administration of the Admiralty in Cape Town in 1819, more British warships began to be seen in the harbour, many of which were on patrol for slave ships in Mascarene waters.[54] The end of both the Napoleonic wars and the War of 1812 also meant that American merchant vessels began to venture forth into the Indian Ocean again.[55] All in all, the fortunes of shipping fluctuated throughout the decades in which whalers called at Port Louis. Measured in tonnage alone, traffic rose consistently until 1874 before entering a period of stagnation which lasted into the twentieth century. Counting the number of vessels reveals a steady though by no means linear decline from 1858 onwards. Two factors were at play here. First, the transition from sail to steam in the second half of the nineteenth century worked to the disadvantage of Port Louis, for its infrastructure was laid out for sailing vessels and the authorities were slow to acknowledge the need to keep up with technological change. Second, the opening of the Suez Canal in 1869 meant that more and more merchant shipping passed through the Red Sea, calling at Djibouti, Massawa or Aden rather than Port Louis.[56]

---

[53] Barker, *Slavery and Anti-Slavery in Mauritius*, 135; Barnwell/Toussaint, *A Short History of Mauritius*, 132; Toussaint, *Port Louis*, 67f., 77, 91.
[54] Coupland, *East Africa and its Invaders*, 191; Jackson Haight, *European Powers and South-East Africa*, 112.
[55] Bennett/Brooks, *New England Merchants in Africa*, xxvi–xxvii.
[56] Toussaint, *Port Louis*, 99, 110–112.

The decline of shipping would no doubt have been more drastic had there not been countervailing tendencies. One attraction was the availability of dry docks and other repair facilities which continued to attract a certain number of vessels, especially in the cyclone season. Moreover, both British and French shipping lines began to include Port Louis in the scheduled passenger itineraries, providing direct connection with London, Marseilles and Suez. Although many of these connections were short-lived, passenger traffic never wholly ceased.[57] And after 1860 in particular, whalers made their own modest contribution to keeping the number of vessels in the harbour from dropping too precipitously (Tab. 6).

Tab. 6: Shipping in Port Louis according to US consular records.

Country of origin	1859/1860	1862/1863	1863/1864	1864/1865
Great Britain & colonies	389	393	476	331
France & colonies	154	176	164	168
United States	59	46	min. 22	8
(of which whalers)	(31)	(approx. 13)	(9)	(6)
other countries	20	122	24	19
Total	622	737	min. 686	526

The consulate's reports covered twelve-month periods from 1 October to 30 September.
Sources: George H. Fairfield. Letter to Secretary of State, 10.10.1860; W. R. G. Mellen. Letter to Secretary of State, 15.10.1863; W. R. G. Mellen. Letter to Secretary of State, 10.10.1864; W. R. G. Mellen. Letter to Secretary of State, 26.10.1865. National Archives and Records Administration, Records of Foreign Service Posts, Record Group 84, Port Louis, vol. 006.

In spite of this decline, Port Louis was more heavily frequented than most ports visited by whalers in the western Indian Ocean. To whalemen more familiar with little bays than major commercial harbours, it presented quite an extraordinary sight. "The immense quantity of shipping usually found here is truly surprising", was Ben Ely's impression on arriving aboard the barque *Emigrant* in 1845.[58] And Joshua Beane, who came to Port Louis aboard the *Java* of New Bedford in 1863, described the following scene: "Immense warehouses lined the wharves, into which were packed hundreds of thousands of bags of rice and sugar, awaiting shipment to all parts of the world. The inner harbor, with depth of water sufficient to float the largest ships, was packed with craft of every nationality."[59]

---

57 Toussaint, *Port Louis*, 95f., 99.
58 Ely, *There She Blows*, 81f.
59 Beane, *From Forecastle to Cabin*, 137.

Under such circumstances, even news from remote parts of the world might reach Port Louis comparatively soon. In April 1793, for instance, the men of the *Alliance* of Nantucket heard that war had broken out between Britain and France some ten weeks after the fact.[60] Whalers were able to exchange not only world news but also information on hunting conditions in the surrounding waters. In September 1858, for instance, the crew of the *Pacific* of New Bedford heard from that of the *Martha II* of Fairhaven that there were no more humpback whales to be found in the whaling grounds north of the islands – the whales were clearly further along their southward migration to the Antarctic Ocean than usual for the time of year.[61] The likelihood of such encounters between whalers in Port Louis was generally high. The migrations of the whales, the monsoon winds and the cyclones imposed a rough seasonal rhythm on shipping in the western Indian Ocean, which meant that it was not usual for old acquaintances from different whalers to meet in port. "When we arrived at Mauritius there were a great many vessels in the harbor [. . .]. Many of the captains and officers were old friends", remembers Helen Allen, who came to Port Louis around 1870 as the daughter of Captain David Allen of the barque *Merlin* of New Bedford.[62] Seamen took advantage of such encounters to exchange news of family and friends, messages from shipowners, letters and newspapers.[63] Its considerable distance from the continental mainland notwithstanding, the port was an important hub for the circulation of information.

When seamen went shore, their first impressions tended to pick up one thing in particular: as racial segregation between urban districts gradually faded away, people of the most diverse origins could increasingly be seen to mingle in the streets. To see people side by side whose ancestors had come from various parts of Asia, Africa and Europe – and some of them indeed from the America – came as surprise to many visitors to Port Louis. This surprise was reflected in many of their letters[64] as well in the recollections of whalemen. "If a traveler is desirous of seeing the manners and customs of all the tribes of men at once, let him land at the Isle of France", declared Ben Ely, before entering on a detailed account of the people a visitor might expect to meet:

---

[60] Pinkham, *The Log Book of the Good Ship Alliance of Nantucket Captain Bartlett Coffin*, 12.04.1793.
[61] Whitecar, *Four Years Aboard the Whaleship*, 330.
[62] Allen, *Slaves, Freedmen, and Indentured Laborers in Colonial Mauritius*, 6.
[63] George H. Fairfield. Letter to Secretary of State, 10.01.1859. National Archives and Records Administration, Records of Foreign Service Posts, Record Group 84, Port Louis, vol. 006.
[64] Barker, *Slavery and Anti-Slavery in Mauritius*, 136; Toussaint, *Port Louis*, 72f.

> There he will find the turbaned Turk in his mosque; the Arab with his bald pate; the Chinaman eating with his rice sticks; the Hollander and German with their pipes; the sandy haired Scotchman with his bagpipes; the Englishman and his brown-stout; the Irishman and his whiskey; the Frenchman with his love of frogs, dancing and military glory; the American with his readiness to trade in all sorts of notions; the Jews with their golden trinkets, and money to loan on pawns; Lascars, Malabars, Hindoos, Ceylonese, Burmese, Portuguese, Spaniards, and woolly headed negroes, all mixing together, and all living after his own fashion and religion.[65]

Similar descriptions, no less reflective of contemporary stereotypes, can be found in records left by other seamen.[66] Many of them professed themselves bewildered by the scene they came upon. "From the different languages that fell on our ears we were at a loss to tell what country-men we were among", noted William Whitecar, who called at Port Louis in September 1858 aboard the *Pacific* of New Bedford. It was to be supposed, he added, "that the commingling of all their different languages must produce a most Babel-like confusion." What surprised Whitecar most of all, however, was that he encountered few white people in the streets of what was, after all, a British colonial capital and that barely anybody was able to give him directions in English when he lost his way.[67]

In his descriptions of the various population groups, Whitecar refers to their supposedly typical physical and character traits as well as to the costumes and trades associated with them, but he withholds judgment.[68] Charles Nordhoff, by contrast, shows no hesitation in describing the "Blacks" or Port Louis as thieving and the "Malabars" as lazy.[69] Whatever they may have claimed to make of what they saw, however, such attempts at ethnic categorisation of the part the seamen testify to a need to find order within a city perceived as a baffling muddle.

∗∗∗

Besides the human scene, Whitecar gave a detailed account of Port Louis's hospital, which he describes as "a large, commodious, well-ventilated building, surrounded by verandas, healthily situated, and close by the water's side."[70]

---

[65] Ely, *There She Blows*, 81f. *Lascars*, derived from the Persian *Al-ashkar* (army), was the name given by European East India companies to the seamen they recruited from the Indo-Portuguese communities of Calcutta and Madras from the eighteenth century onwards. (Pereira, "Black Liberators", 2)
[66] See e.g. Beane, *From Forecastle to Cabin*, 138.
[67] Whitecar, *Four Years Aboard the Whaleship*, 300f. A similar account can be found in Pike, *Sub-tropical Rambles in the Land of Aphanapteryx*, 56.
[68] Whitecar, *Four Years Aboard the Whaleship*, 313–318.
[69] Nordhoff, *Whaling and Fishing*, 267–269.
[70] Whitecar, *Four Years Aboard the Whaleship*, 306.

The building was situated on the edge of the harbour basin known as Trou Fanfaron and was opened in 1740 after its predecessor, completed in 1733, had been destroyed by a cyclone. An extension was added in 1851 and given over to the treatment of civilian patients, while the original building was reserved for members of British garrison.[71] The new building had two floors, each of which formed a department of its own: one for the care of Asian patients (the largest demographic in Port Louis), the other for everybody else. This meant that whites and blacks shared a ward, a far from commonplace occurrence in a colonial town and remarked upon accordingly by Whitecar.[72]

Whitecar's interest in this building should come as little surprise. After Cape Town, the hospital and its British staff offered what was probably the best medical care in the south-west Indian Ocean. Seamen were held liable for the cost of treatment themselves, at a daily rate of two shillings in 1858. Since most of them, however, lacked ready money of their own, they would often have to draw an advance from their captain. If a vessel was forced to leave an American seaman behind for a longer stay in the Port Louis hospital, it was among the duties of the American consul to put up the money for his treatment.

Sailors were well aware of this, and some of them may have welcomed a longer spell in hospital as an opportunity to leave their vessel in a legal fashion and have their passage home paid courtesy of the American consul. The hospital was open to all seamen, and indeed looking after them was one of its principal tasks, for vessels had repeatedly brought deadly diseases to Mauritius. There had been devasting smallpox epidemics in 1770, 1782 and 1792, with the latter claiming the lives of an estimated eight per cent of the population, mostly slaves.[73] The impact of the 1792 epidemic can also be traced in the logs of the *Alliance* and the *Asia*, both of Nantucket, which put in at Port Louis that year. When their commanders heard that 129 people had died of smallpox in a single day, they decided to have their crews vaccinated immediately. Not all of the seamen were vaccinated in time, however, and several them developed the illness over the next few days, including Captain Coffin of the Alliance.[74]

Although the authorities had begun to launch vaccination campaigns to counter infectious disease in the late eighteenth century, not all epidemics could be prevented. In 1813 the government saw no choice but to kill all dogs in the island in a bid to contain rabies. Cholera outbreaks in 1819, 1844 and 1854 led to

---

71 Burrun, *Port Louis*, 20f.; Toussaint, *Port Louis*, 23.
72 Whitecar, *Four Years Aboard the Whaleship*, 305–307.
73 Burrun, *Port Louis*, 86.
74 Dickson, "The Cruise of the Nantucket Ships 'Asia' and 'Alliance'"; Pinkham, *The Log Book of the Good Ship Alliance of Nantucket Captain Bartlett Coffin*, 04.10.1792.

panic in Port Louis, with thousands killed and thousands more escaping into the island's interior. Comparatively minor outbreaks followed in 1856, 1859 and 1861 before Port Louis suffered the worst epidemic of its history from 1866 to 1868, when up to 33,000 people succumbed to malaria in the town alone, with tens of thousands more dying in the countryside. Those worst affected by these epidemics were the many impoverished former slaves who lived in cramped and insanitary hovels in such places as Moka Street.[75]

The mortality rate in Port Louis – on only from epidemic disease, but across the board – exceeded that of such other colonial ports as, for instance, Calcutta. The marshes on the town's fringes and the mosquitoes they harboured were partly to blame. Another long-standing problem was rats. As early as 1786, a shocked Jacob Haafner observed that "he depredations of the rats and the hordes of these animals with which the island swarms transcend the realms of the imagination".[76]

Sanitation, however, was the major problem, and it continued to fall short of the engineering standards of the day well into the twentieth century. Although Port Louis had one of the most modern harbours in the western Indian Ocean, many parts of the town lacked both piped drinking water and adequate sewers. Most dwellings were built of wood or straw, were low-ceilinged and offered poor ventilation. Since kitchens and lavatories usually faced a courtyard, waste of all kinds had to be carried through living quarters before being dumped in the street, where it was usually left to fester in the humid climate rather than being removed. Sanitary conditions were particularly dire in the town's prisons. Deaths from fever increased even in the late nineteenth century, causing a worried colonial administration to move the troops garrisoned at Port Louis to barracks inland for their own safety. Not until the global Spanish flu pandemic of 1919 ravaged Port Louis with particular ferocity were significant investments in healthcare and sanitation made.[77]

Deceptive promises

Although it turned out to be a dangerous and indeed deadly place for a good many of them, seamen did not on the whole rank Port Louis among the notorious

---

[75] Allen, "The Mascarene Slave-trade and Labour Migration in the Indian Ocean during the Eighteenth and Nineteenth Centuries", 37; Burrun, *Port Louis*, 86f.; Teelock, *Mauritian History*, 266f.; Toussaint, *Port Louis*, 69, 96–99; Varma, *The Making of Mauritius*, 131f.
[76] Quoted in van der Velde, "Jacob Haafner in Mauritius", 79.
[77] Storey, *Science and Power in Colonial Mauritius*, 39; Teelock, *Mauritian History*, 273–277; Toussaint, *Port Louis*, 74, 92.

"fever ports" which were to be avoided at all costs. To most of them, the names of Port Louis and Mauritius would probably rather have evoked images of paradisiacal bliss, a reputation owed above all to the work of Jacques-Henri Bernardin de Saint-Pierre. This French writer and engineer had spent two years in Mauritius and made it the setting of his novel *Paul et Virginie*, published in 1788. Soon translated into several languages, the story also inspired scores of paintings and engravings as well as musical and dramatical adaptations, giving it an international popularity that was to last throughout the nineteenth century. Many readers in Europe and North America are likely to have become aware of the existence of Mauritius only through *Paul et Virginie*.[78]

Bernardin's novel outlines a romantic critique of civilisation combined with an idealisation of nature. The story is this: Paul and Virginie, both of whom have lost their fathers, grow up in Mauritius with their French mothers and two slaves. They lead a carefree life in an unspoilt natural environment and amid harmonious social condition, free of European constraints of class or estate. Aged fifteen, Virginie – who is by now in love with Paul – is taken to France by a well-meaning great aunt, only to be sent back a few years later after failing to submit to social convention and to agree to a "good" marriage. Her return is eagerly anticipated by Paul. However, the vessel aboard which Virginie returns to Mauritius is shipwrecked just off the coast. Social convention in France forbidding a woman to jump into the water and swim to safety, Virginie drowns under the eyes of Paul, who dies of grief for his lost love soon afterwards.[79]

Whether they had read it themselves or had absorbed it through one if its many retellings, many of the seamen who came to the Indian Ocean in the nineteenth century were familiar with this tragic tale. Those who not yet seen Mauritius with their own eyes were wont to imagine it as Bernardin had described it, as a kind of tropical idyll, and many of those who actually did come ashore on the island had their expectations conditioned by the novel, even in matters of detail. Pascoe Grenfell Hill, for instance, who arrived in Mauritius in the early 1840s as chaplain aboard HMS *Cleopatra*, marked all the places mentioned by name in his copy of *Paul et Virginie* and made a point of visiting them one by one as soon as he had come ashore at Port Louis.[80]

---

[78] Wright, *Mauritius*, 83. *Adventures of a Younger Son* by the British novelist Edward John Trelawny further contributed to the romance associated with Mauritius in the nineteenth century.
[79] Bernardin de Saint-Pierre, *Paul et Virginie*.
[80] Hill, *Fifty Days on Board a Slave-vessel in the Mozambique Channel*, 7f. David Allen, master of the barque *Merlin* of New Bedford, sailed in the company of his family, and his wife read *Paul et Virginie* to their children as they approached Port Louis in September 1871. (Allen, Journal 1871–1872, 03.09.1871)

Many whalemen had the same idea. Of his stay in the island in 1850, Nordhoff recalls that "I spent the balance of the day in the re-perusal of Bernardin St. Pierre's delightful story of Paul and Virginia".[81] Nordhoff was particularly interested in the sites that could still be found much as Bernardin had portrayed them. "I took out my now never failing Paul and Virginia, and with the lofty peak called Peter Botta heaving its giant head into the air before me, read over again the story of that fatal shipwreck", he continues. "Every shoal in the bay, as we sailed past it, every palm tree on the shore, every peak, towering in the blue distance, all were part and parcel of the story, the most charming of all tales of true love." Mauritius was the very embodiment of romance to this seafarer, who also visited the site where the thwarted lovers supposedly lay buried: "I trod a ground sacred to all true lovers, and with book in hand, wandered about the beach endeavoring to fix upon the spot whence Paul leaped into the flood to the rescue of his Virginia."[82]

The purported grave of Paul and Virginie was marked by a sandstone monument with iron railings, which had been erected in a picturesque copse some ten kilometres to the north-east of the harbour in the district of Pamplemousses. Many seamen took this memorial as proof of the story's authenticity and ignored its fictional character.[83] Whitecar, for instance, who visited the site in 1858, wondered why two such eminent personages had not been laid to rest in a mausoleum.[84]

Such was the desire of many seamen to visit the places described in the novel and perhaps even to discover relicts of Paul and Virginie that a tourist trade of sorts sprang up in Port Louis. Coachmen, owners of small boats and young locals offered their services as guides, promising to show visitors the fabled locations in exchange for a few coins. Some visitors chipped off pieces of the monument as souvenirs.[85] The grave and other locations mentioned in the novel thus became tourist destinations, sights to be seen, and are marketed as such to this day.

Months at sea, however, left most seamen too exhausted to explore the novel's locations further inland, let alone the mountains.[86] Aside from the monument, seamen on shore leave would usually stick to the town, which was considered an attraction in its own right. Often, it was the first time in months that they had landed at a purpose-built harbour rather than coming ashore in boats in a remote bay. " I stepped upon the stone landing place with a feeling

---

[81] Nordhoff, *Whaling and Fishing*, 260.
[82] Ibid., 261f.
[83] Ely, *There She Blows*, 81f.; Pike, *Sub-tropical Rambles in the Land of Aphanapteryx*, 81f.
[84] Whitecar, *Four Years Aboard the Whaleship*, 301f.
[85] Beane, *From Forecastle to Cabin*, 141; Nordhoff, *Whaling and Fishing*, 261f.; Whitecar, *Four Years Aboard the Whaleship*, 301f.
[86] Whitecar, *Four Years Aboard the Whaleship*, 302.

that I was once more in a civilized country", was how Joshua Beane recalled his arrival at Port Louis in 1863, delighted by the brick buildings several storeys high, by the paved roads and the ornamental fountains.[87] William Whitten, who had visited Mauritius three years earlier, aged twenty-two, remarked that Port Louis was "a fine looking place, more like civilization than anny we have been in this voige."[88] Some seamen spent most of their shore leave strolling along its streets and taking in the lively ambiance, or visiting more tranquil spots such as the park with its fountains or the cemetery close to the shore. Their curiosity might sometimes lead them to observe a funeral or, on the *Champ de Mars*, a duel.[89] Some would enjoy a French meal at a restaurant or visit the theatre on Government Street, opened in 1822, where a French-trained ensemble performed variety shows, melodramas and operas by such writers and composers as Halévy, Rossini and Meyerbeer. It was at this theatre that the crew of the *Ceres* of New Bedford attended a masked ball in 1839.[90]

Prostitutes were ubiquitous in the streets of Port Louis and would have drawn most of their custom from soldiers stationed in the island.[91] Moreover, the town had a distinctive culture of promiscuous sexuality that had emerged under French rule and in which sexual relations could and frequently did cross boundaries of class and ethnicity. "There is no girl or woman, whatever her position in society, who could claim to have an unblemished name", observed Jacob Haafner, his meaning clear enough through the euphemism of the time.[92] Although the ruling elites of the eighteenth and nineteenth centuries made a point of repeatedly bemoaning such loose morals, they too participated in an everyday culture which struck many a European visitor as dissipated. Frederick Barnard, a British naval officer, recalled the "constant succession of gaiety and amusements" to be enjoyed in Port Louis, remarking that "I never yet saw a place in

---

[87] Beane, *From Forecastle to Cabin*, 137f., 141; for similar descriptions see Pike, *Sub-tropical Rambles in the Land of Aphanapteryx*, 58 and Whitecar, *Four Years Aboard the Whaleship*, 303–305.
[88] Whitten, *A Journal of a Whaleing Voyage on Board the Barque Eureka*, 11.07.1860.
[89] Backhouse, *A Narrative of a Visit to the Mauritius and South Africa*, 3f.; Pickman, "Réunion and Mauritius", 13; Whitecar, *Four Years Aboard the Whaleship*, 308–310; Whitten, *A Journal of a Whaleing Voyage on Board the Barque Eureka*, 15.07.1860.
[90] Beane, *From Forecastle to Cabin*, 141; Burrun, *Port Louis*, 56f.; Log CERES, 1838–1839, 01.04.1839; Pike, *Sub-tropical Rambles in the Land of Aphanapteryx*, 63.
[91] Barker, *Slavery and Anti-Slavery in Mauritius*, 135.
[92] Quoted in van der Velde, "Jacob Haafner in Mauritius", 79.

which so constant a round of feasting, dancing, and late hours, is kept up".[93] Under these conditions it was not unheard of for seamen to form intimate relationships with women based neither on payment nor on compulsion. We hear of such a relationship from Charles Nordhoff, who obtained a discharge from his New Bedford whaler around 1850 and spent about seven months in Port Louis, during which time he enjoyed the "friendship" of a "brown" woman named Angelique.[94] In 1872 the cooper of the barque *John Dawson* stayed behind in Port Louis in order to marry – quite a rarity in the annals of whaling.[95]

In addition, Port Louis was one of the few places they frequented in the western Indian Ocean where whalemen might attend Christian worship. The Roman Catholic church (now cathedral) of St Louis, only a few hundred metres from the harbour, had been consecrated in 1756. The first Anglican church was opened by the British government in what had once been the arsenal in 1812 and became St James Cathedral in 1850. Since few seamen found their way there, however, Anglican clergymen opened a chapel in the harbour itself, in a disused warship, in the 1850s.[96]

For some seamen, their ramblings in Port Louis brought their first encounters with Islamic culture and religion. Muslims had been publicly performing their religious observances and celebrating their festivals since the eighteenth century. The first of several mosques opened in 1805 in the town's working-class Indian quarter. But these encounters between western seamen and Islamic culture did not always end well. The crew of the *Java* of New Bedford, for instance, which was moored at Port Louis in 1863, outraged the Muslim dock workers who had been invited for a meal on board by serving port. Some men of the *Java* gave added offence by bursting in on prayers in a mosque.[97]

Muslim sensibilities were not the only ones to be offended – sometimes deliberately, but more often inadvertently – by seamen roaming the streets of Port

---

93 Barnard, *A Three Years' Cruise in the Mozambique Channel*, 280–282; see also Barnwell/Toussaint, *A Short History of Mauritius*, 87; Toussaint, *Port Louis*, 44 and, for another contemporary view of dissipated Port Louis elites, Freycinet, *Briefe von der Uranie*, 55f.
94 Nordhoff, *Whaling and Fishing*, 258f.
95 Log JOHN DAWSON, 1870–1872, 18.06.1872.
96 Anderson, *Descriptive Account of Mauritius*, 34; Burrun, *Port Louis*, 40f., 58; Nicholas Pike. Letter to Secretary of State, 15.03.1868. National Archives and Records Administration, Records of Foreign Service Posts, Record Group 84, Port Louis, vol. 006; Pike, *Sub-tropical Rambles in the Land of Aphanapteryx*, 248; Toussaint, *Port Louis*, 25; Whitecar, *Four Years Aboard the Whaleship*, 308.
97 Beane, *From Forecastle to Cabin*, 137, 142; Storey, *Science and Power in Colonial Mauritius*, 34; Teelock, *Mauritian History*, 147f.; Worden, "Cape Town and Port Louis in the Eighteenth Century", 49.

Louis. Under French rule, the port and the adjacent central district had been the reserve of wealthy citizens of European descent, the *Ville Blanche*. Workers of African or Asian descent were allowed into this area only to perform specific tasks under supervision. Attempts to take advantage of employment in the harbour to escape by sea were punishable by death in certain cases.[98] Although the British abolished the legal basis for the segregation of urban space, it remained in place informally for decades to come. Only the devastating malaria epidemic of 1866 to 1868, which saw large-scale flight from Port Louis, cleared the path for a genuine reordering of the town.[99] Against this backdrop, it may be assumed that seamen sometimes frequented streets of the former *Ville Blanche* whose wealthy inhabitants would certainly not have welcomed their presence. These were the people of whom Ben Ely wrote in 1845 that "They all look down upon mariners as a low and degraded set of beings."[100]

Although most seamen limited their exploration of Mauritius to Port Louis, there were exception, albeit few. One was Joshua Beane, who in 1863 visited the island's interior and observed the work on a sugar plantation.[101] Even men who did not go out of their to investigate local conditions could not fail to notice the dominance of sugar within the Mauritian economy in its ubiquitous manifestations. On the harbourside, they would have noticed not only the huge warehouses where sugar was stored awaiting export but also, from 1843, the central immigration depot where contract labourers spent the first two nights after the arrival before being sent on to the plantations (Fig. 28). The town was also where workers who had escaped from a plantation sought to shake off their pursuers amid the urban bustle – much like deserters from whaleships.[102]

Whitecar's memoir is one contemporary account to discuss indentured labour, which he condemned as a particularly heinous form of slavery and which, he recalls, the entire crew of the *Pacific* found repellent.[103] Nordhoff too found indentured workers to be "treated much worse than slaves." In Port Louis, Nordhoff had heard that plantations were ruled by the lash and that desertion and suicide were commonplace; he also observed at first hand police measures to recapture escapees.[104] Thomas O'Keeffe, a seaman who arrived at Port Louis aboard the *Grand Turk* of New Bedford in 1837, found that "The cruelty with

---

98 See the description of an execution in White, "Cape Town and Mauritius", 7f.
99 Ly-Tio-Fane Pineo/Lim Fat, *From Alien to Citizen*, 122; Teelock, *Mauritian History*, 137, 143.
100 Ely, *There She Blows*, 84.
101 Beane, *From Forecastle to Cabin*, 142.
102 Ibid., 137f.; Burrun, *Port Louis*, 62f.; Nordhoff, *Whaling and Fishing*, 265f.
103 Whitecar, *Four Years Aboard the Whaleship*, 315–325.
104 Nordhoff, *Whaling and Fishing*, 265f.

Fig. 28: Bengali migrant labourers at the Port Louis docks, mid-1800s.
Source: Mouat, *Rough Notes of a Trip to Reunion, the Mauritius and Ceylon*, 35.

which they treat their slaves is beyond comprehension."[105] Even without a visit to the interior, a few days in Port Louis were enough to bring home the truth that Mauritius was not the innocent idyll portrayed in *Paul et Virginie*.

Staying behind, signing on – and arguing about it

"This day all our people went on shore to buy what things they stood in need of and they all returned at night excepting James Robinson", reads the entry for 28 October 1792 in the log of the *Alliance* of New Bedford, which was calling at Port Louis. "When we came to examine his chest", it continues, "we found no cloths and how he got them on shore there is no one can give any account."[106] After four days without a trace of Robinson, Captain Coffin hired a Boston seaman, Isaac Coleman to fill the vacancy.[107] James Robinson, it seems, was the first whaleman to desert in Mauritius.

Many more seamen were to follow in Robinson's footsteps. The promise associated with Mauritius may have been one factor in encouraging desertion, but

---

[105] O'Keeffe, Journal GRAND TURK, 1836–1841, 10.08.1837.
[106] Pinkham, *The Log Book of the Good Ship Alliance of Nantucket Captain Bartlett Coffin*, 28.10.1792.
[107] Ibid., 02.11.1792.

the bustle of Port Louis offered more tangible advantages. "Charly has gone for sure and I wish him good luck", wrote Lucien Britt, ship's carpenter aboard the *Young Phenix* of New Bedford, in his diary of a fellow seaman who had deserted in 1868, adding that "There are plenty ships mostly english so that he may get a chance to ship before long".[108] The prospect of signing on aboard a new vessel before very long – and ideally one bound for home – encouraged numerous disgruntled seamen to act on long-held plans for desertion when they reached Port Louis. Some whaleships lost a considerable proportion of their crews in this way. Eight men abandoned the *Ann Parry* of Portsmouth in 1846 and the same number the *Avola* of New Bedford in 1870.[109] The *Abigail* and the *Thomas Pope*, both of New Bedford, each lost seven men to desertion in 1859 and 1860, respectively.[110] Eleven men deserted from the *Mercury* of New Bedford while she lay at Port Louis in 1875; a further two were discharged.[111] This phenomenon was not lost on the American consul, George Fairfield, who reported back to the State Department that "Desertion from American vessels in this port especially from whalers is enormous".[112] Yet the consulate, which was bound by law to support penniless American seamen, was itself a pull factor for would-be deserters.

Although shipmasters would sometimes report deserters to the police,[113] the force itself was notoriously inefficient, even after a major attempt at reforming it was made in 1840. The Mauritian police was so understaffed that it visibly struggled even to fulfil its principal task of ensuring public safety. Muggings, robberies and other such crimes were daily and especially nightly occurrences, abetted by the complete lack of street lighting until the first gas lamps were put up in 1865.[114] Nonetheless, the police did sometimes succeed in catching fugitive seamen – in 1858 alone, these included deserters from the *North West* of New London and the *Eugenia*, the *Eliza* and the *Margaret* Scott, all of New Bedford.[115] It was around this time that Fairfield was able to tell his superiors in Washington that the police gave him "every assistance I can ask".[116]

---

108 Brott, Journal YOUNG PHENIX, 1867–1871, 12.05.1868.
109 Log AVOLA, 1867–1870, 17.–20.07.1870; Log ANN PARRY, 1845–1848, 18.10.–02.11.1846.
110 Log ABIGAIL, 1856–1860, 13.–22.10.1859; Log THOMAS POPE, 1859–1862, 18.01.–02.03.1860.
111 Log MERCURY, 1873–1876, 18.04.1875.
112 George H. Fairfield. Letter to Secretary of State, 30.09.1856. National Archives and Records Administration, Records of Foreign Service Posts, Record Group 84, Port Louis, vol. 006.
113 Log MALAY, 1837–1839, 26.06.1838.
114 Toussaint, *Port Louis*, 74, 79, 95.
115 Log EUGENIA, 1855–1858, 11.03.–30.04.1858; Ships Daily Journal, 1857–1862, National Archives and Records Administration, Records of Foreign Service Posts, Record Group 84, Port Louis, vol. 051.
116 George H. Fairfield. Letter to Secretary of State, 30.09.1856. National Archives and Records Administration, Records of Foreign Service Posts, Record Group 84, Port Louis, vol. 006.

However, in 1861 the authorities in Mauritius decided that desertion was no longer a police matter. The reasons for this decision are unclear. When, in February that year, no fewer than eleven seamen went missing from the *J.H. Duvall* of Provincetown, the police refused to give any assistance in finding the men. On complaining to the government, Fairfield was told that it was now an offence for policemen to arrest deserters.[117] After 1861 the ships' logs record very few instances of deserters being apprehended by the police.[118] This refusal to cooperate was a particular problem when the *Atlantic* of New Bedford sailed into Port Louis in May 1866. The barque's cook, James Brown, was accused of killing a fellow seaman, and Captain Wing wanted to hand him over to the authorities in the nearest port. The Mauritian police, however, denied any responsibility in the matter and prohibited the captain from bringing Brown ashore. Since Wing on no account wanted to keep the cook on board, however, it was left for the American consul to find a solution. For a payment of $250, he persuaded Captain Bourne of the *Osceola II* of New Bedford to take Brown back to face trial in the United States.[119]

But how did the seamen fare who stayed behind in Port Louis? In his memoirs, the seaman George Barker tells of two cabin boys who deserted from the *Alcyone* of Provincetown around 1870. He recounts how the boys had been beaten with ends of rope and generally maltreated throughout the voyage by Captain Baldwin. In the harbour, they confided in a man who promised to hide them until the *Alcyone* sailed, but who in fact betrayed to Baldwin for five dollars. The boys escaped from their vessel a second time soon afterwards, this time joining the crew of a merchantman bound for Melbourne.[120]

Like these two boys, most seamen who stayed behind for one reason or another seem to have tried to sign on aboard another vessel as soon as possible.[121] Those who failed to do so usually had to make their way in Port Louis under difficult conditions, even though American citizens were entitled to support from their consulate. Especially between December and May, when vessels avoided Port Louis as best they could for fear of cyclones, seamen might find themselves stuck there with no prospect of getting away and in conditions of

---

117 George H. Fairfield. Letter to Secretary of State, 25.03.1861. National Archives and Records Administration, Records of Foreign Service Posts, Record Group 84, Port Louis, vol. 006.
118 Log ATLANTIC, 1876–1879, 07.–29.11.1877; Log BREWSTER, 1860–1863, 05.06.1861; Log LANCER, 1869–1873, 05.–11.10.1870.
119 G. Robinson. Letter to Secretary of State, 30.06.1866. National Archives and Records Administration, Records of Foreign Service Posts, Record Group 84, Port Louis, vol. 006.
120 Barker, *Thrilling Adventures of the Whaler Alcyone*, 14, 19, 49–51.
121 See e.g. Whitecar, *Four Years Aboard the Whaleship*, 350; Whitten, *A Journal of a Whaling Voyage on Board the Barque Eureka*, 17.07.1860.

considerable hardship.¹²² "For want of money and other means they slept under the market-house, and ate raw stock fish for sustenance", Ben Ely recalls of two men who joined the crew of the *Emigrant* in mid-1845. "Occasionally some foreign sailors would give them a few crumbs of bread."¹²³ Such men would sometimes find employment in Port Louis – not infrequently, it seems, with the police.¹²⁴ Prospects were worse for men who had had to leave a whaleship on account of severe disease or injury and were physically unable to work in town or aboard a vessel.¹²⁵ Only if the consul was willing and able to find a place for them on board a merchant or other vessel (and to pay for it) could they hope to leave the island again.

A useful insight into what became of seamen left behind in Mauritius during the boom years of whaling in the surrounding seas is afforded by an overview produced by the US consulate for the year 1857. It reveals that of the eighty-six American seamen who stayed behind in Port Louis that year, fifty-two were discharged, thirty deserted and four died while their vessel was in port. Of these men – and of those who were already in town at the beginning of the period covered by the report – seventy-six were dependent on financial support from the consulate, and for only-twenty-one of them was the consulate able to recoup its expenses from pay owed by the respective captains. The remaining fifty-five had to supported from the consulate's own budget. Seven of these penniless seamen the consul was able to place as passengers on board vessels bound for the United States, and a total of 187 seamen left Port Louis having found work aboard a new vessel.¹²⁶ Since this last figure would seem, however, to include all the seamen who moved from one vessel to another without spending much time in Port Louis in between, it cannot be wholly assigned to the category of left-behind seamen. Nonetheless, this group was so consistently large throughout the 1850s that Anglican clergy found it necessary to open a seamen's home near the docks in order to keep destitute mariners from having to sleep on the streets.¹²⁷

***

---

122 Nordhoff, *Whaling and Fishing*, 318f.
123 Ely, *There She Blows*, 86f. For another description of a destitute seaman in Port Louis see Whitecar, *Four Years Aboard the Whaleship*, 330.
124 Pike, *Sub-tropical Rambles in the Land of Aphanapteryx*, 432; Whitecar, *Four Years Aboard the Whaleship*, 350.
125 See e.g. Whitecar, *Four Years Aboard the Whaleship*, 305–307.
126 George H. Fairfield. Letter to Secretary of State, 01.01.1858. National Archives and Records Administration, Records of Foreign Service Posts, Record Group 84, Port Louis, vol. 006.
127 Anderson, *Descriptive Account of Mauritius*, 34.

The high number of desertions, discharges and legal disputes that occurred while vessels were calling at Port Louis meant that the American consulate frequently became the site of altercations between captains and their crews. Nicholas Pike, the consul at the time, complained in 1872 that scarcely a whaleship anchored at Port Louis without such disagreements being brought before him.[128] Already in 1858 his predecessor George Fairfield had told of regular and sometimes heated arguments in his office, in the course of which he had more than once been physically assaulted by angry seamen.[129] It also happened that captains flagrantly broke the law under the very eyes of the consul, for instance by refusing to pay off discharged seamen or by leaving seamen behind against their will. This was not only illegal but placed an additional burden on the consulate, which was charged with supporting the seamen concerned.[130] Moreover, in the mid-1860s the consulate informed the State Department of its suspicion that certain shipmasters were abusing its services to register desertions that had never occurred.[131] This, it seems, was an attempt to indemnify themselves against legal claims by seamen whom they had illegally left marooned on remote islands such as Île Amsterdam.[132]

Little wonder, then, that successive consuls often took a critical attitude towards captains. Nicholas Pike, for instance, observed in 1871 "that the brutality with which seamen are treated on board our whale ships is really disgraceful".[133] Consuls would sometimes come down on the side of common seamen, thereby courting the fury of skippers, officers and shipowners. In 1846 the first mate of the barque *Ann Parry* of Portsmouth committed to her log his opinion that the American consul of the day was a "superfine villain".[134] In 1863 the

---

128 Nicholas Pike. Letter to Secretary of State, 02.01.1872. National Archives and Records Administration, Records of Foreign Service Posts, Record Group 84, Port Louis, vol. 006.
129 George H. Fairfield. Letter to Secretary of State, 08.07.1858. National Archives and Records Administration, Records of Foreign Service Posts, Record Group 84, Port Louis, vol. 006.
130 Thomas Shankland. Letter to Secretary of State, 04.02.1863. National Archives and Records Administration, Records of Foreign Service Posts, Record Group 84, Port Louis, vol. 006; Nicholas Pike. Letter to Secretary of State, 02.06.1871. National Archives and Records Administration, Records of Foreign Service Posts, Record Group 84, Port Louis, vol. 006; George H. Fairfield. Letter to Secretary of State, 25.02.1857. National Archives and Records Administration, Records of Foreign Service Posts, Record Group 84, Port Louis, vol. 006.
131 W. Hunter. Letter to W. R. G. Mellen, 24.01.1866. National Archives and Records Administration, Records of Foreign Service Posts, Record Group 84, Port Louis, vol. 011.
132 George H. Fairfield. Letter to Secretary of State, 30.06.1856. National Archives and Records Administration, Records of Foreign Service Posts, Record Group 84, Port Louis, vol. 052.
133 Nicholas Pike. Letter to Secretary of State, 14.12.1871. National Archives and Records Administration, Records of Foreign Service Posts, Record Group 84, Port Louis, vol. 006.
134 Log ANN PARRY, 1845–1848, 27.10.1846.

consul ordered the discharge of eighteen men of the *North West* of New Hampshire to protect them from the abusive regime of Captain Dunbar, who, it was claimed, had used arms against his own men, causing grievous injury to several of them.[135] A similar case occurred in 1871, when Pike ordered the discharge of several men of the *Pioneer* of New Bedford who had taken to the hills for fear of Captain Hayard.[136] An earlier consul, George Fairfield, even changed sides while arbitrating a dispute aboard the *James Edward* of New Bedford in 1857. Fairfield had initially found Captain Murray's charge of mutiny to be plausible and had twenty-five men arrested with the help of the police. On further examination of the events, however, Fairfield concluded that they had constituted a justifiable strike and agreed to the men's demands by ordering their release.[137]

Although what happened aboard American vessels lay beyond the jurisdiction of Mauritian courts, some disputes eventually came before a judge in Port Louis. In 1872, for instance, a charge of libel brought by John Pierce, master of the barque *Annie Ann* of New Bedford, against the daily *Commercial Gazette* came before the highest court in the territory. The paper had printed a letter by the barque's cook accusing Pierce of cruel mistreatment, a claim the captain vehemently denied.[138]

Port Louis differed from other ports in that whalers did not usually put in with the intention of recruiting new men. However, desertion and discharge were such frequent occurrences that many a captain found himself with little choice but to replenish his crew. The numbers involved were generally small. Of the 120 whalers known to have recruited men while in Port Louis, sixty-six hired fewer than five men, thirty-five hired five to nine, nineteen hired ten to fifteen. Interestingly, signings in Port Louis often exceeded losses, which suggest that Port Louis was a preferred place for captains to make up for earlier defections. Official records, however, are unlikely to provide the full picture, since some captains seem to have recruited men on the sly. For instance, in 1847 the first mate of the *Ann Parry* of Portsmouth accused her captain, Abiel Perry, of having logged seamen who had joined the crew at Port Louis as stowaways in an attempt to escape both the fees and the legal obligations attendant upon their formal enlistment.[139]

---

135 Thomas Shankland. Letter to Secretary of State, 04.02.1863. National Archives and Records Administration, Records of Foreign Service Posts, Record Group 84, Port Louis, vol. 006.
136 Nicholas Pike. Letter to Secretary of State, 06.02.1872. National Archives and Records Administration, Records of Foreign Service Posts, Record Group 84, Port Louis, vol. 006.
137 George H. Fairfield. Letter to Secretary of State, 25.02.1857. National Archives and Records Administration, Records of Foreign Service Posts, Record Group 84, Port Louis, vol. 006.
138 *Commercial Gazette*, 05.02.1872.
139 Log ANN PARRY, 1845–1848, 26. & 27.11.1847.

Port Louis was a particularly convenient recruiting ground above all because there was usually no shortage of destitute seamen in the town. This group included not only those seamen who had been discharged from or deserted their vessels here, but also a number of men who had fallen on hard times elsewhere in the western Indian Ocean and knew that Port Louis offered good employment opportunities. Anyone shipwrecked in these parts, for instance, would usually try to obtain a passage to Mauritius, and penniless seamen accordingly arrived aboard all manner of vessels.[140] Those seeking to leave the island, whether by working their passage or by stowing away, also included soldiers who had deserted from the local garrison.[141] Joshua Beane, who called at Port Louis aboard the *Java* of New Bedford in 1863, recalls soldiers urging whalemen to "gi' me a bloody tuck, mon", i.e. to hide them aboard their vessels.[142] Doing so could lead to serious trouble, however. In 1854 Captain Bliss of the barque *Smyrna* of New Bedford found himself charged in Port Louis with having concealed three fugitive soldiers on board and enabling their escape. Bliss denied the charge vigorously and was acquitted.[143] The indigent population of Port Louis was further swelled in the 1860s, when a period of depression caused thousands of unemployed men from the plantations to look for work in the capital.[144]

"You can get any thing you may want as you have plenty of money"

How easily (or otherwise) were provisions, water and firewood obtained by whalers in Port Louis, geared as it was towards the export of sugar? Water was the easiest to come by. In spite of an annual dry period from June to August, Port Louis generally enjoyed an ample supply of drinking water. The Moka range that rises directly above the town causes humid sea air to rise and cool off, with the resulting condensation gathering in the plateau's numerous rivers and lakes. In order to bring this water to the town, the French government in 1782 began to build an aqueduct, known after its architect as the *Canal Dayot*. Further canals

---

140 *The Mercantile Record*, 19.11.1877, 4; George H. Fairfield. Letter to Secretary of State, 27.01.1863. National Archives and Records Administration, Records of Foreign Service Posts, Record Group 84, Port Louis, vol. 006; Lutwyche, *A Narrative of the Wreck of the Meridian*; Schmitt, *Mark Well the Whale*, 78–82.
141 Nordhoff, *Whaling and Fishing*, 325.
142 Beane, *From Forecastle to Cabin*, 138.
143 Log SMYRNA, 1853–1857, 09.–14.09.1854.
144 Teelock, *Mauritian History*, 246.

were built in 1827, 1860 and 1883, and a network of iron pipes began to be laid in 1860. All these conduits, however, were prone to silting, and their coverage was unequal. The town's poorer eastern districts in particular suffered water shortages in certain years. Damage to the canals also repeatedly forced the population of Port Louis to obtain water by the bucket from distant rivers. To put an end to this problem, the authorities built a reservoir above the Champ de Mars in 1872.[145]

These recurring supply problems were of little concern to crews in the harbour, where the authorities ensured a steady supply of waters at all times – enough for a hundred vessels at once. The harbour was supplied by its own aqueduct, and seamen did not even have to bring their barrels ashore to draw water from a pipe. The downside of this system lay in the long waits it sometimes entailed. "We found [the nozzle] surrounded by seamen of every nation, hose in hand, patiently waiting their turns, while being scorched by the burning rays of a tropical sun", William Whitecar of the *Pacific* remembered an uncomfortable wait in 1858. Under these conditions, Captain Shearman's plan to fill all the vessel's casks in a single day was all too ambitious.[146]

A more complicated task was obtaining food. To do so, captains usually headed for the area around La Chausée, which became the main commercial district of Port Louis after the 1816 fire, when many merchants and small traders took advantage of the destruction by moving their business to the town centre. Moreover, from 1835 many former slaves supported themselves by small-scale farming or as fishermen, bringing their produce to market in Port Louis every morning. As the supply of food increased, a covered market was built a few hundred metres north of La Chausée – that is to say, near the harbour – in 1844. The new "Central Market" was surrounded by an iron fence and divided into four sections: one for meat and fish, another for fruit and vegetables, a third for coffee and the last – the so-called "bazaar" – for household goods, clothing, perfume and jewellery. This latter section increasingly attracted Muslim traders the Indian regions of Kutch and Kathiawar. They had come to Mauritius in the wake of the migrations of indentured Indian labourers and by 1870 dominated the bazaar.[147]

---

145 Burrun, *Port Louis*, 32–34; George H. Fairfield. Letter to Secretary of State, 10.10.1860. National Archives and Records Administration, Records of Foreign Service Posts, Record Group 84, Port Louis, vol. 006; Nwulia, *The History of Slavery in Mauritius and the Seychelles*, 23; Pike, *Sub-tropical Rambles in the Land of Aphanapteryx*, 61; Teelock, *Mauritian History*, 133; Toussaint, *Port Louis*, 79f.; Varma, *The Making of Mauritius*, 134; Wright, *Mauritius*, 15.
146 Pickman, "Réunion and Mauritius", 13; Whitecar, *Four Years Aboard the Whaleship*, 298.
147 Backhouse, *A Narrative of a Visit to the Mauritius and South Africa*, 38; Barker, *Slavery and Anti-Slavery in Mauritius*, 135; Burrun, *Port Louis*, 70f.; Pike, *Sub-tropical Rambles in the Land of Aphanapteryx*, 65f.; Toussaint, *Port Louis*, 36, 73, 88; Toussaint, "The Role of Trade in

Sailors were impressed by the variety of goods and produce on sale in the market as well as by the medley of languages and currencies they found in use there. Joshua Beane observed in 1863 that "You could buy everything that the imagination can conceive". "At nine o'clock everything is running at full blast," Beane added, "the anxious salesman often grasping your arm and shouting in your ear: 'Com' yo' een, Joe 'Merican, by 'e' yo' sumting; sam' clo's berry sheep, lak' helee, all 'e' mos', watee yo' say, Joe 'Merican?'"[148] As a rule, however, the language barrier was no barrier to commerce, since buyers and vendors alike shared a rudimentary knowledge of the main lingua francas and were able to fill the gaps with hand signals and gesticulations.[149] Greengrocers sold mainly tropical fruit of all kinds, which shipmasters were able to obtain in large quantities.[150] Howeverm vegetables – such as sweet potatoes and yams, which were kept better and hence were more suitable as provisions – were less readily available. In order to supply this need, and to avoid the lengthy bargaining that was customary in the Central Market, some captains employed the services of local commercial agents.[151] Yet even they were usually unable to provide whaleships with one of their essential commodities: there was scarcely any firewood to be had in Port Louis. Only very few vessels' logs record such a purchase.

One obstacle to commerce was the observance of Sunday as a holiday, a religious prescription which was rigorously enforced by the authorities. The ban on Sunday trading covered business in the market as well as work in the docks and even on board the vessels moored there. Although the principle was shared by many seamen, whaling captains included, its strict interpretation sometimes came as a surprise. One Sunday in January 1848 Captain Perry of the *Ann Parry* of Portsmouth was unable to obtain so much as a sack of beans.[152] Some captains thus saw little choice but to grant their crews generous shore leave, sometimes lasting all day, on Sundays.[153]

Nor were weekdays free of strictures on trade. A gun fired at five o'clock in the morning and eight o'clock in the evening signalled the opening and closing

---

the Settlement of Mauritius", 120; Varma, *The Making of Mauritius*, 98f.; Whitecar, *Four Years Aboard the Whaleship*, 303–305.
148 Beane, *From Forecastle to Cabin*, 140. On the goods available in the bazaar see also Allen, *Slaves, Freedmen, and Indentured Laborers in Colonial Mauritius*, 128f.
149 Beane, *From Forecastle to Cabin*, 141.
150 Whitecar, *Four Years Aboard the Whaleship*, 328.
151 Log GAZELLE, 1863–1866, n.d. (May 1864); Whitecar, *Four Years Aboard the Whaleship*, 303–305.
152 Log ANN PARRY, 1845–1848, 17.01.1848.
153 Log MALAY, 1837–1839, 08. & 09.07.1838; Pinkham, *The Log Book of the Good Ship Alliance of Nantucket Captain Bartlett Coffin*, 28.04.1793.

of shops and markets, and trading outside these hours was strictly prohibited.[154] In practice, most business was conducted in the mornings and evenings, since it was simply too hot when the sun stood high in the sky.[155] Shipmasters unaware of this custom and looking to buy provisions in the middle of the day might well find their efforts thwarted.

It was a peculiar feature of Mauritian agriculture to grow half the world's sugar but not enough food to feed its own population. Unsurprisingly, this imbalance provided many a whaler calling at Port Louis with opportunities for doing business on the side. The *Brewster* of Mattapoisett, for instance, sold part of her beef supply at a considerable profit in 1859.[156] In 1793 the *Alliance* of Nantucket picked up a few sacks of sugar in Mauritius, which could be sold at a good price back at home.[157] The *Alliance* had already struck a less commonplace deal in the previous year. In October 1792 Captain Coffin bought the fifty-ton schooner *Hunter* in Port Louis for "2,000 paper dollars" and used it to ship part of his catch of whale oil to the Île Bourbon. The next time the *Alliance* called at Port Louis, the captain sold the *Hunter* on at a profit of $100.[158] Common seamen, two, sought to take advantage of price differentials and business opportunities by taking whalebones, teeth and baleen to the bazaar.[159] However, there was no demand for whale oil in Mauritius, which produced enough coconut oil to provide for its needs in that respect.[160]

As far as whalers were concerned, the main problem involved in calling at Port Louis was the cost involved. "Found Mauritius a very expensive place and no Ship should go than unless obliged so to do", remarked the log of the *Splendid* of Edgartown, which had a leak repaired there in 1861, adding: "You can get any thing you may want as you have plenty of money."[161] This problem had already been communicated to the State Department three years earlier by Georg Fairfield, the American consul, who had written of the exceptionally high prices charged for food in Port Louis. A barrel of flour cost twenty-five dollars, a bushel of potatoes between seven and twelve dollars, and a pound of

---

154 Whitecar, *Four Years Aboard the Whaleship*, 296.
155 Pickman, "Réunion and Mauritius", 13.
156 Log BREWSTER, 1857–1860, 22.09.1859.
157 Pinkham, *The Log Book of the Good Ship Alliance of Nantucket Captain Bartlett Coffin*, 20.05.1793.
158 Pinkham, *The Log Book of the Good Ship Alliance of Nantucket Captain Bartlett Coffin*, 30.10.1792 & 13.05.1793. The editor of this source adds an exhaustive footnote on the use of paper currency in the early United States and its distribution abroad.
159 Whitecar, *Four Years Aboard the Whaleship*, 305, 326f.
160 Ibid., 326f.
161 Log SPLENDID, 1858–1862, 23.10.1861.

butter one dollar.[162] It was with such prices in mind that Fairfield elsewhere referred to Port Louis as the most expensive place in the world.[163]

As with so much in Mauritius, high food prices could be traced at least indirectly to sugar. Food had to be imported because sugar took up most of the island's agricultural land. The beef, for instance, bought at Port Louis in 1858 by Captain Sherman of the *Pacific*, came from animals brought from Madagascar and the Cape Colony.[164] Merchant vessels were able to make up for the comparatively high costs of provisioning through advantageous rates of tax and duty, but this was not a possibility open to whalers, who had nothing to sell in Mauritius. Captains and officers hence often had little good to say about Port Louis. To the keeper of the *Alliance*'s log, it was "the dirtyest hole that I ever saw or heard of" and populated, moreover, by a "pack of villains".[165]

The prices of parts and repairs were on a level with those charged for provisions. Tradesmen and shopkeepers were clearly aware the advantage conferred upon them by the harbour's monopoly and its status, as Captain Baldwin of the *Alcyone* of Provincetown put it, as the only "civilized port for repairs" far and wide.[166] After all, the next port where a chronometer might be readily obtained was Cape Town, more than two thousand nautical miles away. A good many of the whalers who put in at Port Louis did so only for the repair facilities, notably the dry dock, and for the maintenance of their equipment. This category included not only the *Alcyone* but also, for instance, the brig *Para* of Salem in July 1868.[167]

Workshops were lined up along the quayside like chicken coops in the market. This clustering was the result not least of the abolition slavery in 1835, after which many former slaves headed for Port Louis to find work as tradesmen, dockers or stevedores.[168] There was scarcely a repair job for which captains

---

162 George H. Fairfield. Letter to Secretary of State, 08.07.1858. National Archives and Records Administration, Records of Foreign Service Posts, Record Group 84, Port Louis, vol. 006. Before the the Mauritius rupee, which remains in use to this day, was introduced in 1876, a variety of currencies were in circulation in Port Louis and seamen were able to use American dollars. (Toussaint, *Port Louis*, 32; Whitecar, *Four Years Aboard the Whaleship*, 326)

163 George H. Fairfield. Letter to Secretary of State, 30.09.1856. National Archives and Records Administration, Records of Foreign Service Posts, Record Group 84, Port Louis, vol. 052.

164 Whitecar, *Four Years Aboard the Whaleship*, 297.

165 Pinkham, *The Log Book of the Good Ship Alliance of Nantucket Captain Bartlett Coffin*, 15.11.1792.

166 Barker, *Thrilling Adventures of the Whaler Alcyone*, 48f.

167 Allen, *Slaves, Freedmen, and Indentured Laborers in Colonial Mauritius*, 129; Barker, *Slavery and Anti-Slavery in Mauritius*, 13.

168 Allen, *Slaves, Freedmen, and Indentured Laborers in Colonial Mauritius*, 129; Barker, *Slavery and Anti-Slavery in Mauritius*, 13.

could not find specialized workers – or at least men who claimed to have the relevant skills.[169] In 1870, in a blacksmith's shop known as Smith's and Blacks, Captain Craw of the *Atlantic* of New Bedford found several carpenters to overhaul his rudder; a year later he found a sailmaker there.[170] Captain Smith of the barque *Josephine* of New Bedford hired a bricklayer for several days in May 1904 to rebuild the foundations of her tryworks. However, her log also records Smith's irritation at the slow progress of the work: "I am thoroughly disgusted with this place and with the people in it. Its [sic] the slowest place in the world. I think a ship might rot out to the water line before she could get out of here if she had any work for the people on shore to do for her."[171]

So dear were the services provided by Port Louis's exclusive repair facilities that the American consulate was inundated with complaints from shipmasters.[172] In April 1848 the *Roscoe* of New Bedford had to wait for ten days in the Canal for crucial repairs such as the installation of a new foremast. Captain Tobey had no choice but to sell several tons of whale oil to pay for the work.[173] There was, however, little that American consuls could do about this. As Nicholas Pike, who held the office from 1867 to 1872, complained, "No appeals are of any effect to get fair and liberal arrangements". Pike held these costs to have been responsible for the dwindling number of whalers calling at Port Louis in the 1860s.[174] The charges had not, however, been any lower in previous decades. Only two things in demand by seamen were to be had cheaply in Port Louis: cigars and spirits. Cigar smoking was widespread among the local population and land was set aside for the cultivation of tobacco. "Plug" tobacco for pipes and chewing, on the other hand, was an expensive import.[175]

Like cigars, spirits were produced domestically. In order to reduce their perceived impact on public morals, however, the French authorities began to pass strict licensing laws. From 1772, the sale of alcoholic beverages was restricted to so-called "Canteens" and other outlets were closed. The number of licensed premises was thus drastically reduced from 125 to four. Moreover, in an effort to

---

169 See e.g. Log MALAY, 1837–1839, 27.06.–03.07.1838.
170 Log ATLANTIC, 1868–1872, 14.11.1870 & 01.11.1871.
171 Log JOSEPHINE, 1903–1905, 24.05.1904.
172 George H. Fairfield. Letter to Secretary of State, 09.06.1858. National Archives and Records Administration, Records of Foreign Service Posts, Record Group 84, Port Louis, vol. 006.
173 Tobey, Journal ROSCOE, 1846–1849, 22.04.1848.
174 Pike, *Sub-tropical Rambles in the Land of Aphanapteryx*, 55, 432.
175 Whitecar, *Four Years Aboard the Whaleship*, 326.

reduce alcohol consumption among the other population groups, only persons considered white were eligible to trade as licensed *cantiniers*.[176]

This policy of restricting the sale of alcohol to a handful of white-owned hostelries was largely retained by the British. One unintended consequence was the proliferation of illegal distilleries whose market appears to have been above all the local garrison; alcohol-related deaths were a frequent occurrence among soldiers in the nineteenth century.[177] Coming ashore in 1858, Whitecar observed that the local population by far preferred wine to spirits.[178] But seamen usually had no difficulty in obtaining spirits in the port, and the police repeatedly arrested drunk and disorderly whalemen.[179] "All hands except 4 on liberty And many of them Beastly Drunk", records the log of the *Ceres* of New Bedford, which was moored in Port Louis in April 1839.[180] Although getting drunk in harbourside bars, most of which are likely to have been unlicensed, may have got seamen into trouble with the police, it did have the benefit of keeping the men in the vicinity of the waterfront and reducing the likelihood of their straying into the residential districts of the former *Ville Blanche*.[181] This may have been one reason why the authorities did not act more forcefully against the unlicensed sale of spirits in the harbour.

An unavoidable expense

Looking back at the *Pacific*'s stay in Port Louis in 1858, Whitecar found himself wondering why the place was so well frequented. "I cannot imagine why whalers visit this port in preference to others where they could be much better supplied", he mused,[182] and his bemusement is easy to understand in retrospect. A high risk of desertion, long waits for the colonial surgeon, the risk of being quarantined, the need to pay for the services of a pilot and perhaps a commercial agent, the uncooperativeness (from 1861) of the police, restrictions on Sunday trading and working, the expense of parts and labour, and steep hospital fees –these factors would have combined to make putting in at Port Louis seem like a considerable

---

[176] Barker, *Slavery and Anti-Slavery in Mauritius*, 131; Toussaint, *Port Louis*, 34.
[177] Backhouse, *A Narrative of a Visit to the Mauritius and South Africa*, 11f., 45; Barker, *Slavery and Anti-Slavery in Mauritius*, 135f.; Teelock, *Mauritian History*, 143.
[178] Whitecar, *Four Years Aboard the Whaleship*, 326.
[179] Whitten, *A Journal of a Whaling Voyage on Board the Barque Eureka*, 29.07.1860.
[180] Log CERES, 1838–1839, 12.04.1839.
[181] Ely, *There She Blows*, 84.
[182] Whitecar, *Four Years Aboard the Whaleship*, 325.

financial risk for captains and shipowners alike. Water and provisions were available at far lower cost elsewhere in the western Indian Ocean, and firewood was barely to be had at all. Both shipmasters and consuls repeatedly cited these as reasons why whalers did not call at Port Louis more often than they did.

But why, then, did they still do so several hundred times? The infrastructure of its harbour, which permitted even highly complicated repairs, was certainly a strong point in favour of Port Louis. It was also a reliable recruiting ground when captains found their vessels undercrewed as a result of desertion or discharge. The presence of an American consulate was the deciding factor in several cases. Moreover, we occasionally hear of whalers being able to offset the expense of calling at Port Louis by trading on the side or taking advantage of an opportunity to tranship their cargo of whale oil.

Above all, however, in the heyday of sperm whaling, Port Louis was hard to ignore. There were not really that many viable alternatives in the area, and whalers were often constrained in their choice of stopovers by monsoon winds, the cyclone season and – by no means least – whales and their seasonal and cyclical migrations. These factors constrained vessels' movements and meant that other potentially suitable harbours could not be reached without detours which were liable to be no less costly and time-consuming. The fact that Port Louis was frequented as consistently as it was from the late 1830s to the early 1860s can thus be far more convincingly explained in terms of structural push factors than the harbour's distinctive pull factors.

The demand generated by whalers for food may have made itself felt in the sales of Port Louis merchants, particularly those in the Central Market. Since, however, whalers only ever accounted for a small proportion of traffic in the harbour, they would not have constituted an economic force in their own right. By the same token, the presence of whalers in the harbour did not spell any other changes for Port Louis and its citizens, who had been accustomed to seamen, their activities and their incidental effects as familiar elements of the urban space since the eighteenth century. Only their notoriously large number of desertions set whalers apart from other vessels, but this would have been a matter of concern to the consulate rather than the population at large.

Passages III: Going ashore

"On land, behind the beach, life is lived with some fullness and with some establishment. On the sea, beyond the beach, life is partial and dependent", writes Greg Dening. "Ships are distorted segments of living – all male, disciplined, parasitic on the land, not productive. Those who come on them – sailors, missionaries, traders, soldiers – proffer very singular gestures about themselves. They display their cultures but not whole."[1] Following Marshall Sahlins, it might be added that in encounters with the unfamiliar, cultural practice "has its own dynamics [. . .] which meaningfully defines the persons and objects that are parties to it". "Nothing", Sahlins argues, "guarantees that the situations encountered in practice will stereotypically follow from the cultural categories by which the circumstances are interpreted and acted upon."[2] An item of clothing changing owners on the beach, for instance, does not imply that the participants in the exchange invested the piece of cloth with the same significance in terms of economic value, social prestige or possible ascriptions of cultural meaning.[3] On beaches, as in other contact zones, meaning was situationally highly specific, and this in turn conditioned the actors' behaviour. What kind of situations might arise from the visit of a whaleship?

As far as seamen were concerned, the first thing to note is that their perception of their vessel changed once they went ashore. Once a vessel dropped anchor, the routines that structured life at sea – hoisting and dropping the sails, or the wearying task of keeping watch in the crow's nest – ceased to apply, as did the overarching temporal regime specific to whaleships, the shifts worked by watches and boat crews. Above all, however, what came to an end was the crew's seclusion, its isolation, both social and communicative, from the outside world. While it lay in port, the vessel ceased to be a total institution.

In this section, I shall begin by outlining the reasons why vessels might decide to call into harbour and the criteria which led captains to favour one port over another. I shall then discuss typical patterns in the actions and experiences of seamen on shore before finally asking why many a seaman chose not to return to his vessel from shore leave. As in the chapter "Passages II", the discussion here owes much to the studies of nineteenth-century American whaling by Hohman, Busch and Creighton. I also draw on more general studies in the social and cultural history of seafaring, notably those of Gilje, Rediker, Dening and Heimerdinger. Given the paucity of research and sources

---

1 Dening, *Islands and Beaches*, 32.
2 Sahlins, *How "Natives" Think*, 247.
3 Dening, *Islands and Beaches*, 34.

highlighted in the introduction, I can only make occasional reference to British whaling in this period.

Dropping anchor

Ships are designed to move across the water, and to lie at anchor would seem to be inimical to their very essence. Yet several times in the course of its voyage, a whaleship would spend days or even weeks unmoved, moored in a harbour or off a coast. But why? Among the most important reasons was to take on board provisions. The average voyage of an American whaler lasted twenty-nine months around 1820 and forty-two months by the middle of the century.[4] "On such long voyages, where [. . .] the vessel is for many months at a time cruising about at sea, men are very liable to attacks of scurvy", observed Charles Nordhoff, who sailed in a New Bedford whaler around 1850.[5] Although hard tack and salt horse, the staple provisions of the nineteenth-century whaleship, could be stored over long periods, fresh food had to be taken on en route if both scurvy and discontent among the seamen were to be kept at bay. Water too could not be kept fresh and uncontaminated for the duration of a voyage. In order to keep the number of stops as low as possible, shipmasters preferred to lay in foodstuffs that would keep, such as potatoes, yams, rice and coconuts. Live animals could continue to provide fresh meat even months after being taken on board. Some species were more suitable to being kept on board than others, especially chickens, pigs and goats, as well as tortoises and turtles.[6]

Second only to food in importance to the working of a whaleship was firewood, which was needed to fuel the vessel's tryworks. Trying out a whale's blubber took several days, during which time the trypots, which sat in a brick foundation at the base of the foremast, were kept constantly bubbling. Once the fire had got going, it was able also to burn the whale's skin, but not as its sole fuel. Not was it possible to carry sufficient firewood to last the entire voyage. Taking on firewood was thus an important reason – or at least a supplementary reason – for stopping along the way.

Whaleships often had to call at port for repairs. Its constant rolling and heaving meant that a vessel was always "working". The movements of the sea caused planks to move, loosening caulk and creating cracks in the wood through which

---

4 Hohman, *The American Whaleman*, 86.
5 Nordhoff, *Whaling and Fishing*, 71.
6 See chapter "Passages II".

water might enter. An additional problem was that, as the voyage progressed and their hold filled with whale oil, whaleships' draught increased. This meant that planking which had become dry and brittle in the sun gradually went below the waterline. Wear and tear, necessitating regular repairs, affected not only the vessel's hull but also its rigging. "Everything being kept taut, the strain on the rigging, in heavy weather, is tremendous, so that some little thing or other always needs repair", recalled William Whitecar, who sailed in the *Pacific* of New Bedford from 1855 to 1859.[7] Since a whaleship would usually crisscross the oceans for several years before returning to its home port, it was usually left to the men to keep the vessel (and its boats) seaworthy by performing such tasks as caulking and painting it along the way. Not all these jobs, however, could be done at sea. In order to reach planking below the waterline, the crew had to reduce the vessel's draught by fully unloading it. Torn sails too were more easily replaced in port. And when a vessel was hunting whales in coastal waters, it might well work more efficiently if it lay at anchor while the catch was being processed.[8]

While stops of this kind might be planned or at least to some degree anticipated, whalers might also have to make altogether unscheduled stops, for instance in cases of illness or injury demanding expert attention. Although common seamen could not expect the captain to divert the vessel even in cases of severe injury, it was a different case when the captain himself was in need of medical treatment or when the incidence of disease on board ship jeopardized the voyage itself. Both these criteria applied when the barque *Monmouth* of Cold Spring Harbour called at Cape Town in 1846, with Captain Halsey suffering from dysentery and several of the men from scurvy.[9]

Unscheduled stops might also be made to take advantage of lucrative business opportunities. The space covered by whalers meant that sooner or later, they invariably found themselves in parts of the world where certain things were accorded a far greater value than elsewhere. Such value differentials could be profitably exploited, and seamen, when they got together for "gams", would exchange information on market rates in various ports and coastal regions. In February 1872, for instance, Captain Hamblin of the barque *Islander* of New Bedford bought a large quantity of sugar in Anjouan, which he sold at a

---

7 Whitecar, *Four Years Aboard the Whaleship*, 355.
8 See e.g. Nordhoff, *Whaling and Fishing*, 186.
9 Schmitt, *Mark Well the Whale!*, 55f. Events are reported to have taken an usual turn when in December 1844, the whaler *Henry Thompson* of New London left behind Captain Andrews, who had purportedly become "deranged", in Cape Town. She continued her voyage under the command of the first mate. (*Whalemen's Shipping List and Merchants' Transcript*, 18.03.1845).

profit in Mauritius several months later.[10] The *Herald II* sailed for Zanzibar in the late 1860s to take advantage of the best prices for the ambergris recently extracted from sperm whales by the crew.[11] Some skippers would also use the mobility their calling conferred upon them to pursue their own personal sidelines, sometimes on a considerable scale. Samuel Swain, for instance, commander of the British whaleship *Vigilant*, made a profit of several thousand pounds in a transaction in Timor in 1832 – whereupon he set sail for Sydney, where he bought two thousand pounds worth of shares in the Commercial Banking Company of Sidney.[12] But such cases as Swain's also help explain why shipowners were generally wary of opportunistic business deals, or at any rate such as they did not stand to profit from themselves. Every day a captain spent engaged in trade on shore meant additional expense – sometimes in mooring fees, but in any case because it was time spent away from the whale hunt.[13]

As a rule, however, captains pursued these opportunities in the name and for the benefit of shipowners, which meant keeping time spent in port as short as possible. Only at sea was the crew able to catch whales and thereby generate revenue. How seriously the injunction to avoid lying in port unnecessarily was taken can be seen from a remark in the log of the schooner *Admiral Blake* of Marion, which had put in to Jamestown, St Helena, for ten day in 1870 because the captain's wife had fallen ill: "So much time lost as we have done no business to do takin us more than on or two days at most."[14] Captains usually stopped no more often than absolutely necessary, and several months might pass between one landfall and the next. That the men might feel a yearning for shore leave was not considered sufficient reason for interrupting a journey, yet such interruptions might sometimes be forced by discontented crews. It also occurred that a captain would make a stop for the very reason of giving refractory seamen the opportunity to desert. These are aspects to which I shall return in the course of this chapter.

✳✳✳

But where did whalers choose to call? In his capacity as representative of the shipowners, the shipmaster had to consider above all the costs likely to be incurred in a given place. Away from the main hubs of maritime trading networks, provisions and firewood tended to be cheaper than in such ports of global rank

---

10 Log ISLANDER, 1871–1873, 16.–26.02. & 07.–24.07.1872.
11 Eldridge, *Lewis William Eldridge's Whaling Voyage*, 14.
12 Chatwin, "A Trade so Uncontrollably Uncertain", 100.
13 Hohman, *The American Whaleman*, 287f.
14 Log ADMIRAL BLAKE, 1869–1870, 12.04.1870.

as Cape Town or Zanzibar. These comparatively remote coastal and island locations, where economy and society were not (yet) geared towards trading with crews, often lacked specialised middlemen, allowing seamen to obtain the required goods directly from the producers. Other costs were to be considered besides provisioning. In some places, barter could only begin once more or less elaborate gifts had been made to local dignitaries, other ports might charge mooring fees or mandate hiring a local pilot.[15]

Besides lower prices, a further advantage of places away from the main trade routes was that seamen were less likely to desert. William Whitecar was just one seaman who knew that "The reason for touching at obscure places, is the great danger of losing men by desertion, which always occurs in commercial ports".[16] For one thing, these were often small settlements with few places to hide; moreover, the dearth of traffic gave seamen little opportunity to make good their escape – awareness of which seems to have changed the mind of more than one potential deserter.[17] If putting in at a major port could not be avoided – in case of urgent repairs, for instance – captains would keep the stay as short as possible and often moor some distance out to sea in order to deter deserters from swimming ashore.

Yet many captains feared desertion and factored it into their decisions only for as long as a voyage had not yet met its target and the entire crew was needed for the hunt. As a voyage neared its conclusion, by contrast, it was no rarity for captains to put their men in the way of temptation, tacitly encouraging them to desert in order to save the lay payable on arrival in the vessel's home port. One way of doing so was to tighten the disciplinary regime, meting out cruel punishments or picking on particular men as means of heightening discontent and driving seamen to despair. A longer stay in a port offering a comparatively easy escape would then be timed to coincide with the peak of these persecutions – a stratagem to which I shall return at the end of this chapter.[18]

Distance from a whaling ground was a factor to which different captains accorded different weight. On the one hand, proximity to the whaling ground meant fewer days spent getting there (and not taking whales) and hence a higher potential return overall. Yet some captains were keen to conceal their preferred whaling ground from other vessels by making their stops at some

---

15 Booth, "American Whalers in South African Waters", 281; Creighton, *Rites & Passages*, 144; Haywood, "American Whalers and Africa", 3, 82, 133.
16 Whitecar, *Four Years Aboard the Whaleship*, 25.
17 Busch, *Whaling Will Never Do for Me*, 174; Haywood, "American Whalers and Africa", 133.
18 Busch, *Whaling Will Never Do for Me*, 174; Haywood, "American Whalers and Africa", 133.

distance from their destination.[19] On the whole, however, the location of whaling grounds was not treated as a secret among whalers, nor would it have been feasible to do so given he high fluctuation among crews. Most whaling ports, moreover, were small places inimical to the keeping of secrets.[20]

Of the manner in which stops were decided upon in American whaling, Margaret Creighton has written that "Shipowners and masters conspired to choose ports and to time visits not to suit sailors' inclinations but to suit their own concern for savings and expenditures".[21] Seamen who might have had other concerns – time to recuperate, for instance – once again came up against harsh realities. Yet these visits nonetheless meant a lot to them, as the following section shows.

Coming ashore, breaking free

"The captain proposed to go into port for *refreshments*", recalls Nordhoff. His vessel, a New Bedford whaler, was cruising the western Indian Ocean around 1850 when the captain announced that she would soon be calling at a port. Which port, however, was the subject of much speculation among the crew. Nordhoff suspected that it would be "Either the blue mountains of Madagascar, or the flat, desert-like beach of the opposite African coast".[22] Just knowing that the vessel was soon to put into port was enough to electrify the crew. A whaleman's life aboard ship in many respects resembled that of a convict, and the prospect of leaving the vessel during a visit was accordingly welcomed as something of an escape.[23] For a few hours or even days, the ranks and rules of shipboard life ceased to be all-powerful. Shore leave – which, tellingly, is known as "liberty" to American seamen – was the high point of a voyage. Its emotional impact is impressively described in the memoir of Henry Dana, who sailed in a Boston merchantman in the mid-1830s: "I shall never forget the delightful sensation of being in the open air, with the birds singing around me, and escaped from the confinement, labor, and strict rule of a vessel – of being

---

19 See e.g. Nordhoff, *Whaling and Fishing*, 92.
20 Hilt, Contracts, "Risk Taking and Diversification in the American Whaling Industry", 57f.
21 Creighton, *Rites & Passages*, 141.
22 Nordhoff, *Whaling and Fishing*, 156f.
23 Busch, *Whaling Will Never Do for Me*, 173; Gilje, *Liberty on the Waterfront*, 94.

once more in my life, though only for a day, my own master. A sailor's liberty is but for a day; yet while it lasts it is perfect."[24]

Knowing that their liberty on shore was destined to be brief, many seamen sought to experience it as intensively as possible, which sometimes made their behaviour seem like an eruption of long dormant forces. "For the sailor ashore there was no future, only the here and now", observes Gilje. "He could drink, curse, carouse, fight, spend money, and generally misbehave."[25] Of a visit to Anjouan in March 1843, John Ross Browne, who sailed in the *Bruce* of Fairhaven, recalled: "A sailor let loose from a ship is no better than a wild man. [. . .] It is like an escape from bondage. D – and I felt what it was to be at liberty, and our exuberance of spirits was beyond all bounds."[26] This impression would probably have been shared by the locals who encountered seamen on leave, for the fact that seamen viewed coastal towns above all as "compensation spaces" (in Timo Heimerdinger's phrase) for the privations of shipboard life meant that conflicts with the local population were virtually inevitable.[27]

One of the pitfalls of the archive is its tendency to privilege the views of the powerful. The popular image of seamen on leave has been shaped above all by the perceptions of actors on shore, particularly the authorities in the ports concerned. The resulting story thus reads like the account of a plague: men freed from the constraints of discipline and routine descend upon taverns and brothels, get drunk, attack women, spread venereal disease, get into fights and steal what they can – all as if there were no tomorrow.[28] No wonder, then, that the historians Peter Duignan and Lewis Gann can state that "The whaler was known wherever he sailed for his violence, abusiveness, and drunkenness"[29] and that Elmo Hohman describes shore leave as an "emotional explosion" in which seamen cast off all restraint.[30] This image has its foundation in the available sources and may well offer an accurate enough depiction of what happened on many such occasions. What it reflects, however, is a specific perception conditioned by middle-class values and mores, one in which particular aspects of shore leave are foregrounded and others ignored. The following account will thus focus

---

24 Dana, *Two Years before the Mast*, 111.
25 Gilje, *Liberty on the Waterfront*, 6–12.
26 Browne, *Etchings of a Whaling Cruise*, 275.
27 Heimerdinger, *Der Seemann*, 78. For a case study of these problems in Cape Town see Hamilton, "Seamen and Crime at the Cape".
28 See e.g. Francis, *A History of World Whaling*, 104.
29 Duignan/Gann, *The United States and Africa*, 59.
30 Hohman, *The American Whaleman*, 88f.

above all on seamen's self-perception and asks what going ashore meant to the men themselves.

∗∗∗

"Mahe is many a Port for girls and rum all a Sailor wants", the seaman Ezra Goodnough noted in his diary in May 1847. Goodnough was first mate of the barque *Ann Parry* of Portsmouth, which at the time was lying in Victoria, the main port of Mahé, the largest island of the Seychelles. He added: "Go it whilst you are young for when you get old you can't."[31] It is perhaps in relation to sex that the significance of shore leave as a "compensatory counterpart to the situation of life at sea"[32] is most clearly displayed. Like Goodnough, many a seaman on shore leave sought contact with women, and the desired contact was often – if by no means always – sexual in nature. In order to understand this aspect of encounters between seamen and local females, it is essential first of all to appreciate the significance of gender in whaling.

The virtual absence of women made the whaleship a homosocial space – one in which the company was, by and large, exclusively male. Seamen were not, however, united by a common idea of what it meant to be a man. A vessel's crew brought together men who differed in age, origin, religious convictions and much else, not least in their self-image as men and their ideas of gender roles.[33] A homosocial space need not be a space in which gender homogeneity obtains.

At the same time, it was in the nature of whaling to open up specific possibilities of masculine identification. Aboard a whaleship, seamen were both workers *and* hunters. By killing whales, they exercised domination over the largest and most powerful bodies to be found on earth.[34] This experience was apt to enhance those aspects of a seaman's self-image which were generally considered eminently masculine in the cultures of Europe and North America, namely courage, strength, bravery, manual dexterity and equanimity in the face of danger. Intelligence, though it was likewise considered a masculine trait, did not have a defining role to play here. In this form of working class masculinity – which, given the low average age of crews, could not but share certain aspects of male youth cultures – it was not necessarily a problem that seamen should live for years on end with virtually no female company. In the

---

31 Quoted in Haywood, "American Whalers and Africa", 123f.
32 Heimerdinger, *Der Seemann*, 77.
33 Busch, *Whaling Will Never Do for Me*, 142; Creighton, "American Mariners and the Rites of Manhood", 151.
34 Dillard, "A Whale of a Man", 39f.

eighteenth and nineteenth centuries such places in which men barely ever met women existed on land, too – the settler outposts in the American West are only one example. And one effect of industrialisation was to shift wage labour further from the home. Given the conditions of the gendered division of labour as they obtained in Europe and North America, a variety of spaces emerged which were all but exclusively male. Ships were not unusual in this respect.[35]

Women were largely absent from whaleships – but not completely. In the chapter "Passages II", I mentioned the captains' wives and daughters who would sometimes accompany their husbands and fathers. In addition, there were cases – albeit extremely rare – of women disguised as men signing on aboard whalers.[36] But it was above all in their symbolic invocation that absent women maintained a presence on board ship: seamen would toast their mothers and loved ones, sketch their sweethearts from memory and compare the results, and write letters home. Not least did they go whaling in the hope of earning enough money to marry and start a family. Even in their absence, then, women were a factor to be reckoned with, one that helped guide seamen's actions. In the early days of American whaling, moreover, when Nantucket was the dominant port, sailing in a whaleship was a decisive factor in determining a man's eligibility for marriage: "No young woman, it was said, paid a moment's notice to the attentions of a suitor who was not a whaler", according to the historian Daniel Francis.[37] Men usually first signed on aboard a whaler aged between fifteen and seventeen – in order to prove their manhood and be in a position to marry when they returned.[38]

Although, then, women were present in whaling as an idea, their physical absence presented a challenge to the masculine self-image of many a seaman. On board ship, men had to perform tasks that were traditionally assigned to the feminine sphere – washing shirts, sewing on buttons, mending trousers. It was no rarity for white seamen to try to get their black shipmates to do these jobs for them, either for money or in exchange for favours. The three service positions – those of cook, steward and cabin boy – likewise tended to be filled by black seamen, most probably because whites were reluctant to take on these jobs. Black men, on the other hand, often found themselves barred from masculine-connoted jobs even on dry land, since many white men regarded them as less manly than themselves.[39] As the historian David Chappell has observed with regard to British

---

35 Norling, "The Sentimentalization of American Seafaring", 164f., 170.
36 Busch, *Whaling Will Never Do for Me*, 148.
37 Francis, *A History of World Whaling*, 93.
38 Norling, "The Sentimentalization of American Seafaring", 167.
39 Creighton, "American Mariners and the Rites of Manhood", 151f., 154.

whaling crews, "The work of stewards and cooks was considered effeminate and hence suited for 'smaller' races than manly Englishmen".[40]

The physical absence of women on board ship has repeatedly given rise to the supposition that seamen must have sought to satisfy their craving for love, sex and intimacy with one another. Some records left by whalemen would indeed seem to allude to such contacts or fantasies beyond what is being described. Of one of his officers, Robert Ferguson wrote in his diary in June 1880 that "Mr. Young picked me up, carried me down below and undressed me. This big, strong man is as gentle as a woman." What had happened was in fact that Ferguson, a harpooner aboard the barque *Kathleen* of New Bedford, sustained an injury to his back in an encounter with a sperm whale, whereupon the officer had made it his task to nurse Ferguson back to health. "He rubs my back and talks to cheer me up. He is very kind to me, more so than any other of my shipmates. The last thing before going to sleep, he came down and wrapped me up in blankets and fixed me up like a mother would."[41] Such descriptions of physical closeness and affection between men turn up in a number of texts by seamen. Writing of his voyage aboard the *Emigrant* from 1844 to 1847, Ben Ely recalled that he had felt compelled "to get one of my ship-mates to sleep with me" to keep warm at night.[42] There may a hidden meaning to such accounts, allowing men to give implicit expression to feelings and sexual practices of which they would not dare to speak, let alone write. On a related note, a literary scholar, Caleb Crain, has argued that the striking frequency of references to cannibalism in the writings of seamen testifies to a subtext of suppressed sexuality.[43]

Explicit references to romantic or sexual relations between seamen are few and far between, however. Margaret Creighton was able to identify only four cases in the more than one thousand relevant texts she examined; Briton C. Busch found only five among in over three thousand logbooks, diaries and consular files. These cases relate to instances of "sodomy" which, while not described in detail, appear to have become known on board and were punished with great severity by the captain. Most of these cases seem to have involved an officer or boatsteerer and a common seaman, which suggests that coercion according to rank may have been in play.[44] One such incident in January 1895 is

---

[40] Chappell, *Ahab's Boat*, 80.
[41] Ferguson, *Harpooner*, 15.
[42] Ely, *There She Blows*, 18.
[43] Crain, "Lovers of Human Flesh". An example of the American tradition of treating cannibalism as a metaphor for taboo forms of sexuality is Tennessee Williams' famous play *Suddenly, Last Summer* (1958).
[44] Busch, *Whaling Will Never Do for Me*, 147f.; Creighton, *Rites & Passages*, 190f.

recorded in the log of the *Frances A. Barstow* of San Francisco: "One of the Boatsteerers, Philip Forte, – was caught in the act of sodomy with one of the crew. – The case was reported – by one of the Fore mast hands. – Jim Keifer. – who witnessed the act".[45] Captain Edwards discharged Forte and abandoned him on the coast of Brazil, off which the brig was sailing at the time. Generally speaking, it seems reasonable to suppose that intimate or sexual relations between men, consensual or otherwise, were more frequent than the sources would suggest, since the parties involved would have tried to conceal them for fear of punishment. Yet the case of the *Frances A. Barstow* equally shows that it is no less plausible to suppose that there was no scope for consensual relations to form in the first place. The lack of private spaces aboard a whaleship made secrecy virtually impossible, the only exceptions being the quarters of the captain and the first mate. How often whalemen had intimate contact with one another there or elsewhere aboard ship must, for lack of reliable sources, remain an unanswered question.[46]

The sources have more to say about sexual contact between men on shore leave and local women. In Lāhainā, for instance, a Hawaiian port much visited by whalers, a doctor in the 1840s assumed that during the whaling season, whalemen had sex with local women in four hundred cases per day.[47] Such encounters served men not least to prove their own virility, both to themselves and to each other. Prostitutes offered their services in many ports. "The old man came on board (after playing billards all day) and brought five whoares with him and spent the evening [. . .] pulling them around half of the night there was a plenty of brandy drank by the bloody whoares", noted Ezra Goodnough of the *Ann Parry* – the "old man" being none other than her captain, James Dennett.[48] For his part, Goodnough bought clothes for a prostitute in Mahé, in return expecting her exclusive attentions for as long as the vessel lay in port. This woman, to whom Goodnough referred as "my wife", was also to maintain a monogamous relationship with him during the *Ann Parry*'s future visits to Mahé. "We can hire the girls in Mahe to remember us, that is more the girls at home will do", he drily observed in his diary.[49] The woman Goodnough describes, who accepted his gifts in return for a promise to "remember" him, exemplifies how prostitutes turned the desires of seamen on shore leave to

---

45 Quoted in Warrin, *So Ends This Day*, 208.
46 Busch, *Whaling Will Never Do for Me*, 147f; Creighton, *Rites & Passages*, 190f., 193f.; Gilje, *Liberty on the Waterfront*, 37–39.
47 Hilt, "Risk Taking and Diversification in the American Whaling Industry", 34.
48 Quoted in Haywood, "American Whalers and Africa", 123f.
49 Quoted ibid., 123f.

their own advantage. Relations between seamen and prostitutes were not, on the whole, characterized by one-sides exploitation. "In actuality, sailors and prostitutes used each other", according to Busch.[50]

Yet seamen also sought sexual contacts with women in places where no prostitutes plied their trade. Although it seems easy to assume that these were all acts in which imbalances of power were exploited, whether by taking advantage of economic inequality or in the form of outright rape, this would be using too broad a brush. Research on Oceania has shown, for instance, that contacts between seamen and local women took place under divergent cultural norms and that attempts at explaining them are bound to fall short if they operate with the conceptual equipment of only one of the cultures involved.[51]

***

"I have had some dificulty with the things that aleas [alas?] sailors getting drunk, getting in prison, deserting and so on", Captain Samuel Braley wrote in his diary in his diary while his vessel, the *Harrison* of New Bedford, lay in the port of Victoria in Mahé. "One by the name of Walker is now in prison", he continued, "sentenced to one years hard labour for stabbing a Police-man."[52] To the captain, the time spent at Victoria was nothing but trouble, a perception shared by several shore-based actors. In a letter written in 1854, William Mullen, the US consul in Zanzibar, complained that "During my residence in Zanzibar (seven years) I have never known an American Whale Ship to be at this port without causing much trouble".[53] And trouble was indeed what seamen on shore leave regularly caused, often in the form of violence.

Since captains imposed strict disciplines on board and often imposed heavy penalties for brawling, hostile seamen would often wait until they next made landfall to settle their scores, which they sometimes did in vicious fights. One man of the barque *George and Susan* of New Bedford stabbed another in the back with a knife while on shore leave in Moçâmedes in southern Angola, to cite just one particularly savage incident.[54] Violence might also erupt among seamen when some men refused to return to their vessels from shore leave.[55] But violence on shore was by was by no means strictly an affair between seamen. A typical

---

50 Busch, *Whaling Will Never Do for Me*, 142.
51 Igler, "Diseased Goods"; see also Busch, *Whaling Will Never Do for Me*, 155.
52 Log HARRISON, 1854–1857, 16.05.1855.
53 Quoted in Haywood, "American Whalers and Africa", 21.
54 Log GEORGE AND SUSAN, 1865–1868, 15.04.1866.
55 See e.g. Eldridge, *Lewis William Eldridge's Whaling Voyage*, 12.

incident is recorded in the log of the barque *Globe* of New Bedford, which called at Moçâmedes in February 1859

> When he [the captain] went on shore he told the Boats crew to stay by the Boat, but John Main & dBartholomew Newton left the Boat & went up to a house & got Drunk. John Main Drew a knife on a Portugue & also threw stones at him. when he came on Board the Captain Put him & Newton in Irons. Main wilst in Irons thretned to see the Captains hearts Blood & said he should like to put a knife up to the handle in his guts.[56]

Such eruptions of violence on the part of seamen might have further-reaching consequences, as the following example shows. While on shore leave in Zanzibar in August 1846, six to eight men of the *Ann Parry* of Portsmouth got violently drunk and picked a fight with several local men on the beach, one of whom, a senior customs official by the name of Thabet, was killed in the ensuing struggle. When the ruler, Saʿīd ibn Sulṭān, heard of this, he complained to the American consulate and demanded that the perpetrator be punished – a perpetrator, however, whom he could not name, since the men had flown the scene to take refuge in their vessel. Since her captain, Dennett, had been taken ill on shore, the consul passed the sultan's demand on to Perry, the first mate. Perry had three of the men involved put in irons and soon after was able to report to the consul that one of them had confessed to the killing. That, at least, was how the consul chose to interpret the message. In fact, the accused had confessed only to his involvement in the brawl, not to having killed Thabet. Nor was a judicial enquiry by the qadi, which had the support of the consul, able to identify the guilty party – much to the dismay of the Zanzibaris. Saʿīd ibn Sulṭān and the qadi were not alone in suspecting the Americans of having altered the confession with a view to protecting the killer. The failure to bring him to justice led to angry protests in the streets and threats against Americans from among the local population.[57]

The victim of seamen's violence in this case was a customs officer. This may have been a coincidence, but generally speaking, seafarers – perhaps on account of their experience of the way captains ruled their vessels – confronted local officials with what Rediker calls a "militant attitude toward arbitrary and excessive authority".[58] Such conflicts were particularly likely to end in seamen being arrested. This was an annoyance to captains, for a man in gaol meant a longer time lying in port and all the expense that entailed. If a captain found

---

56 Log GLOBE, 1858–1861, 26.09.1859.
57 Gray, *History of Zanzibar*, 214–216; Haywood, "American Whalers and Africa", 114f., 118; see also the source documents excerpted in Bennett/Brooks, *New England Merchants in Africa*, 366–372.
58 Rediker, *Between the Devil and the Deep Blue Sea*, 250.

the prisoner to be dispensable or unlikely to be released soon enough, the man might well be left behind without further ado.[59]

It has already been mentioned that outbreaks of violence among seamen on shore leave were often the consequence of drunkenness. "All hands except 4 on liberty And many of them Beastly Drunk", records the log of the *Ceres* of New Bedford of a visit to Port Louis in April 1839.[60] Indeed, drink was often the first thing sought by disembarking seamen, and there were canny vendors on hand in nearly every port to ensure that they found it.[61] Nor was this urge restricted to common seamen. During a stopover on the east coast of Madagascar in 1875, the log of the barque *Mercury* recorded: "Capt is very sick I think it is on count of drink too much rum".[62]

With sex, violence and drinking dominating popular images of seamen on shore leave, it is all too easy to forget that the men often enjoyed more sedate recreations. In 1856, the log of the barque *Globe* of New Bedford can be found recording that "Part of the crew went on shore to hav a run in the sand and returned on Board at sunset".[63] Some men struck out on their own to visit a market, attend religious worship or go an ramble in the interior. Some were content simply to enjoy the sight of landscapes, animals, plants, buildings or indeed people that struck them as unusual and on which other, less mobile men of their class were unlikely ever to set eyes.[64] "The shade of the trees in the interior of the island; the tall, luxuriant grass; the extreme richness of the vegetation, and the grateful perfume of the wild flowers, were all indescribably refreshing", was John Ross Browne's impression of an island off the coast of Madagascar in 1843. "Eager to see every thing on the island [. . .] I ascended the peak, or highest part, from which a splendid view may be had of the whole island, and the adjacent parts of the coast of Madagascar."[65] Working aboard a whaler enabled such men as Browne to visit coastal areas all around the world

---

59 One such case was that of the *Harrison* of New Bedford, which had to leave behind a man in Mahé in May 1855 after he had received a prison sentence for assaulting a policeman. (Log HARRISON, 1854–1857, 17.05.1855) Prison terms posed a deadly risk to seamen. Browne, for instance, writes of his fear of being gaoled in Zanzibar: "I have it from the best authority that two thirds of the white men imprisoned in this fort fall victims to the fever." (Browne, *Etchings of a Whaling Cruise*, 374).
60 Log ISRAEL, 1841–1842, 12.04.1839.
61 Creighton, *Rites & Passages*, 149.
62 Log MERCURY, 1873–1876, 26.07.1875.
63 Log GLOBE, 1855–1857, 05.10.1856.
64 Creighton, *Rites & Passages*, 147f.
65 Browne, *Etchings of a Whaling Cruise*, 225f.

and to observe the cultural, social, linguistic and religious customs and peculiarities of their inhabitants. Not for nothing has the historian Stephen Currie called whalemen "the first American tourists".[66]

***

Not only captains but common seamen too took advantage of opportunities to trade in foreign ports. The oldest European sea law, the twelfth-century Rolls of Oléron, had already permitted seamen to carry their own merchandise aboard ship and to sell it on their own account. In the early modern era, this tradition was observed both in the Atlantic economy and the East India trade, and many seamen welcomed the opportunity to supplement their income.[67]

Once again, whalers were a special case. On the one hand, the long distances covered by whalemen allowed them to profit from global value differentials – nor least because they were often exempt from the scrutiny of customs authorities and hence in a comparatively advantageous position for smuggling.[68] On the other hand, however, most common seamen aboard whaleships owned nothing that they might have profitably traded. The one important exception to this rule was tobacco. "When we left home, we all took along ten to twenty pounds each; not only for our own use, but to trade with the natives at the different islands we might stop at", recalls John Williams, who sailed aboard a whaler in the Indian Ocean in the early 1840s. Williams took ten pounds of tobacco with him on the voyage – although he was not himself a smoker.[69]

The tobacco carried by seamen was usually plug tobacco, which for purposes of barter and exchange was cut into sticks of about thirty grams.[70] Unlike Williams, most seafarers were themselves tobacco users, often chewing it while at work and smoking it in a pipe in their leisure hours. Robert Jarman, a British seaman, relished pipe-smoking as a "bond of sociability" uniting the members of the crew:

> After the work of the day is over, in fine weather, all hands assemble on the forecastle; and the pipe is the prelude to the yarn, of his home, or his friends. In bad weather it shortens the time, warms and comforts him. Alone, in the night-watches it is his company, and

---

[66] Currie, *Thar She Blows*, 51. Creighton too refers to whalemen as "some of America's first global tourists". (Creighton, *Rites & Passages*, 147).
[67] Rediker, *Between the Devil and the Deep Blue Sea*, 130–132.
[68] See e.g. Whitecar, *Four Years Aboard the Whaleship*, 31f.
[69] Williams, *The Adventures of a Seventeen-year-old Lad and the Fortunes He Might Have Won*, 50; see also Nordhoff, *Whaling and Fishing*, 42.
[70] Galton, *The Narrative of an Explorer in Tropical South Africa*, 18.

tends to raise agreeable reflections in his mind, of the friends he hopes to enjoy a whiff with again. In short, it is his tie of contentment, without he has no pleasure.[71]

Elmo Hohman estimates that a seaman might consume anywhere between fifty and one hundred kilograms of tobacco over the course of a three-year voyage. This was generally more than could be carried in a sea-chest, and seamen thus took advantage of stops to resupply themselves with tobacco wherever prices allowed. Whaleships usually also carried an additional supply of tobacco in the stores administered by the captain, the so-called "slop-chest", but the mark-up was often more than five times the retail price. Seamen avoided this source as best they could,[72] preferring instead to barter tobacco among themselves. "Money is not a medium aboard a whale-ship", recalled William Whitecar of his voyage aboard the *Pacific* in the 1850s:

> Tobacco takes its place and is the currency; [. . .] as most men coming to sea, whether they use the weed or not, provide themselves with a considerable quantity of it, some of the old hands accumulated quite a stock; several of them numbering their acquisitions by the hundred pounds.[73]

Tobacco functioned as a cash substitute not only on board ship but also on land – and indeed on a global scale, being welcomed in barter even on the remotest beaches and farthest-flung islands. "I had nothing with me but a few plugs of tobacco, with which to purchase curiosities", recalls John Ross Browne of his visit to Anjouan in March 1843.[74] Depending on the locality, seamen might also be able to sell items to which they accorded little value themselves. When, for instance, the *Mermaid* of New Bedford arrived on the coast of what is now Ghana in the late nineteenth century, "each man ransacked his chest or sea-bag and unearthed trinkets of various kinds", as the seaman Harry Chippendale records in his memoirs. "There were needles, thread, hooks, lines, dominoes, bone rings made from whales' teeth, and a varied assortment of cheap jewelry to catch the eyes of the African maidens."[75] Caleb Hunt, who kept the log of the schooner *S.R. Soper* of Provincetown, recalled this of a stop at the Îles de Los on the coast of the modern Republic of Guinea in 1866: "A

---

71 Jarman, *Journal of a Voyage to the South Seas*, 66.
72 Busch, *Whaling Will Never Do for Me*, 11; Goodridge, *Narrative of a Voyage to the South Seas*, 30; Hohman, *The American Whaleman*, 135.
73 Whitecar, *Four Years Aboard the Whaleship*, 31f.
74 Browne, *Etchings of a Whaling Cruise*, 269.
75 Chippendale, *Sails and Whales*, 78.

crew of negroes came aboard [. . .]. They are ready for trading anything, for almost nothing, giving 20 fathoms of line for a sewing needle."[76]

Experienced shipowners made sure their vessels were amply supplied with cheap goods for the sole purpose of barter (Fig. 29). Whitecar speaks of the "tawdry articles" carried by the *Pacific* "to trade with the semi-civilized natives of the East India and Madagascar Isles."[77] The items in question were usually clothing, cotton studs, jewellery, metal objects, knives, beads, spirits or gunpowder.[78] Captains would sometimes exchange these goods on a large scale; at other times they passed on small quantities to seamen to trade as they saw fit. "No one of the crew but myself was the possessor of a cent of money", recalls Nordhoff of a group of seamen on shore leave in Mahé around 1850. "But all had what is called 'trade', such as calico, tobacco, beads, etc., which they could here readily barter for such purchases as they desired to make."[79] And Lewis Eldridge, who visited Port Dauphin in Madagascar aboard the *Herald II* in the late 1860s, recalls: "The captain had given each of the crew a bar of soap to trade for fruit with the natives. In this manner we purchased our peanuts also, for the soap was a rarity in these parts and looked upon slightly in awe."[80]

Since seamen were paid only at the end of the voyage and had scarcely any money of their own in the meantime, they often asked the Captain for an advance on their lay before going on shore leave.[81] It was no rarity for a seaman to spend all the money he could draw in matter of days. Contemporary observers were quick to put this down to the general irresponsibility of seafarers and hence as further confirmation of what drunkenness and violence had led them to suspect.[82] But there was a dimension to these "deliberate acts of transgression after weeks of discipline and privation" that pointed beyond their immediate context.[83] Displays of hedonism on shore leave may also be interpreted as expressions of resistance to the norms and values of an emergent middle-class society.[84] It was known, for instance, for some seamen to spend a lot of money on hiring horse-drawn carriages

---

[76] Log S.R. SOPER, 1865–1866, 07.01.1866.
[77] Whitecar, *Four Years Aboard the Whaleship*, 25.
[78] Hohman, *The American Whaleman*, 247.
[79] Nordhoff, *Whaling and Fishing*, 246.
[80] Eldridge, *Lewis William Eldridge's Whaling Voyage*, 10.
[81] Hohman, *The American Whaleman*, 255.
[82] Rediker, *Between the Devil and the Deep Blue Sea*, 146f.
[83] Heimerdinger, *Der Seemann*, 77f.
[84] Gilje, *Liberty on the Waterfront*, 12.

to have themselves driven roaring drunk through a port's streets.[85] Gilje interprets this aping of bourgeois manners as a targeted subversion of meaning-bearing insignia, one directed against both the vessel's hierarchy and the values of landlubber society. By so pointedly violating class boundaries, Gilje argues, seamen were expressing a culture of anti-authoritarian opposition.[86]

This culture was surely one reason why seafarers were not always welcomed by shore-dwelling communities. Of going ashore at Port Louis in the mid-1840s, Ben Ely recalls that "There was little pleasure in being among the inhabitants, for they all look down upon mariners as a low and degraded set of beings". A seaman, Ely continues, "could find no companionship except in some tavern or grog-shop."[87] This sense of being unwelcome might be not only a cause but also an effect of their behaviour: "A tar is avoided and gazed upon as an ass or a lion, and because people expect no good of him, and show him no civility, he is often reckless in his conduct."[88]

A career as a seaman was generally considered disreputable in broad sections of nineteenth-century bourgeois society. Life and work at sea scarcely conformed to middle-class ideas of respectability. Seamen did not live in houses and maintained no spatial segregation between black and white. Whalemen, moreover, made their living by hunting, an activity viewed as primitive. All in all, seafarers "seemed to represent the very worst qualities of an old order", as Margaret Creighton put it with regard to their social standing in the United States. "Their work was too erratic, their hands too soiled, their company too mixed, and their ships too far from home to be acceptable to the middle-class arbiters of status."[89] Even where class prejudice was not an issue, previous experience of seafarers was often enough to make littoral societies wary of their behaviour.

Whalers would sometimes encounter European or American missionaries in the ports they visited. This posed a problem for the missionaries, whose claims for the superiority and the ideals of European civilisation were apt to be contradicted by the seamen's conduct. Seamen, as far as missionaries were concerned, represented exactly the immoral elements of western civilisations whose spread to Africa and elsewhere they sought to prevent.[90] A former seaman who had tried to establish himself as a merchant in the south of what is now Namibia was described in 1879 by Tobias Fenchel, in a dispatch to his missionary society, as a

---

85 Creighton, *Rites & Passages*, 147; Gilje, *Liberty on the Waterfront*, 105.
86 Gilje, *Liberty on the Waterfront*, 12–14.
87 Ely, *There She Blows*, 84.
88 Ibid., 85.
89 Creighton, *Rites & Passages*, 77.
90 Busch, *Whaling Will Never Do for Me*, 107; Creighton, *Rites & Passages*, 153.

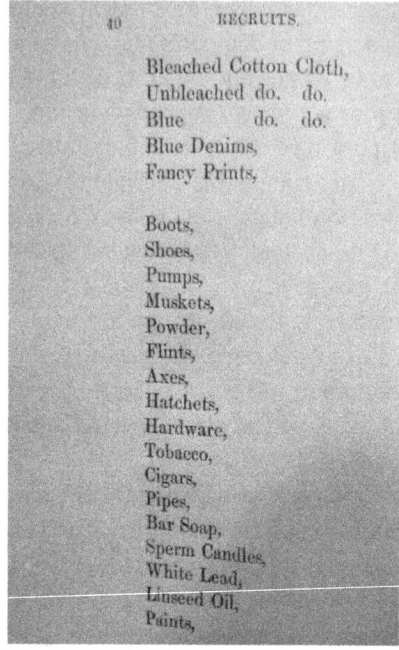

Fig. 29: These pre-printed kit lists for whalemen, of a type provided for captains by New Bedford stationers, mention numerous items intended for barter on shore. The list on the left is from the barque *King of Tyre*, that on the left from the full-rigged ship *Christopher Mitchell*, both probably from the 1850s or 1860s.
Source: Brown University Library, John Hay Library, Manuscript Collections, Carleton D. Morse whaling collection: Box 4, Folders 2 & 3.

"dissolute sea-captain" and "truly a blight" upon religious endeavours.[91] The low esteem in which missionaries held seafarers was widely reciprocated. Where missionaries preached the virtues of piety, self-restraint and long-suffering, seamen were apt to see weakness and effeminacy. And where missionaries – themselves signally lacking forbearance – not only preached abstinence, but campaigned for taverns and brothels to be closed, the fierce hostility of seafarers could come as no surprise.[92] Like missionaries, the authorities in colonial ports saw seamen as a problem for the ideal of order they were aiming for – above all those white seamen who had deserted or been discharged and now haunted the waterfront. From the perspective of colonial policy, the presence of destitute whites constituted a threat

---

91 *Berichte der Rheinischen Missions-Gesellschaft*, Jahrgang 1879, 317.
92 Creighton, *Rites & Passages*, 155.

to the racially structured social order, as the historian Harald Fischer-Tiné has shown with regard to Calcutta in the 1850s and 1860s.[93]

Whether from authorities, missionaries or other actors: seamen on shore leave often encountered rejection. Many of their writings testify to sadness and disappointment at the way they were treated. "I expected a hearty reception", recalls John Ross Browne of a meeting with two American merchants on the north-west coast of Madagascar in the mid-1840s. Both, however, spoke only to the captain and refused to dignify the common seaman with so much as a glance. "I had forgotten", Browne continues, "that I was dressed in a greasy whaling suit".[94]

***

So powerful is this popular image of shore leave as a moment of eruptive debauchery that it is easy to forget that even this part of a voyage often meant hard work for seamen. It might be necessary, for instance, to unload barrels of oil and baleen, either to check them for damage or to sell them in order to pay for major repairs to the vessel.[95] Such repairs too called for physical labour on the part of the men.[96] But it was above all cutting timber that meant that many stops were about work as much as play. Whaleships usually had to stock up on firewood several times in the course of a voyage, and often enough at each stop. For the men, this might mean days or even weeks of cutting wood.[97] Since there were often no suitable forests close to the beach, logs often had to be carried to the vessel from the interior. Less time-consuming, though scarcely less arduous, was the process of laying in drinking water. Common procedure was for the crew to tie a number of casks to one of the boats and tow them to the shore to be filled. Again, however, the nearest suitable watering place might be some distance from the beach, meaning that casks had to be rolled over sometimes considerable distances into the interior – and, when full and accordingly many times heavier, back.[98] This was hard and sometimes dangerous work. "While rolling casks in the water to raft them Andrew Anderson was drowned and could not recover his body", reads an entry in the log of the barque *Sunbeam* of New Bedford, which had made landfall on the coast of what is now Gabon in 1879.[99]

---

93 Fischer-Tiné, *Low and Licentious Europeans*, 90–130.
94 Browne, *Etchings of a Whaling Cruise*, 237.
95 Starbuck, *History of the American Whale Fishery*, 166.
96 See e.g. Log ELIZA ADAMS, 1883–1887, 12.02.1885.
97 Browne, *Etchings of a Whaling Cruise*, 225; Nordhoff, *Whaling and Fishing*, 147.
98 See e.g. Log GLOBE, 1869–1872, 11.02.1871.
99 Log SUNBEAM, 1878–1879, 19.08.1879.

It also meant work for the crew if the captain succeeded in obtaining livestock. For instance, while calling at the Cape Verdean island of Fogo, the *Alexander Barclay* of New Bedford acquired forty pigs, which had to be brought on board and suitably accommodated.[100] An even greater challenge was getting live cattle into boats and from there onto the vessel.[101] Nor was that the end of it. "The Bullock began to snort and shortly he got loose, clearing the decks and running about them furiously, either knocking down, jumping over, or through everything that came in his way", was how Henry Nichols, cooper of the barque *Emerald* of Salem, recorded an incident in the logbook in 1839. "All this time the ship's company were in the rigging."[102]

In spite of the hard work and the experience of social marginalisation, seamen generally looked forward to shore leave as a much-needed change from the privations of shipboard life. Merely approaching the shore was enough to spark both fanciful anticipation and concrete expectations. Of his years as whaleman, Nordhoff recalls: "I never sailed into a port in my life, that the crew, or a portion of them, at any rate, had not prepared their minds for a day's liberty".[103] If for any reason shore leave was cancelled, the men's disappointment was commensurate with their expectations. "Bitter lamentations at their hard fate succeeded the announcement to the green hands, of the impossibility of their getting on shore; they could scarcely believe that the captain could refuse them such a favor", remembers Nordhoff of one such occasion. "That night sundry schemes were laid for running off from the vessel, and thus gratifying their wishes without the consent of the captain, whom they regarded as a cruel monster."[104]

With such reactions in mind, it will come as no surprise to find that shore leave being cancelled often gave rise to serious tensions aboard whalers. Indeed, such disagreements were the most frequent cause of strikes in American whaling.[105] "The trouble came to a head when Captain Costa announced that there would be no shore liberty at Cape Town", reports Chippendale of such a case in the early 1900s:

> With fire in their eyes they went aft and demanded shore liberty, but the captain was obdurate. After more swearing and cursing the men armed themselves with belaying pins, knives, and chain hooks, and, going to the davits, dropped the boat's falls to the deck in the attempt to lower the boats.

---

100 Log ALEXANDER BARCLAY, 1837–1839, 12.–16.01.1838.
101 See e.g. Eldridge, *Lewis William Eldridge's Whaling Voyage*, 11.
102 Log EMERALD, 1838–1840, 08.05.1839.
103 Nordhoff, *Whaling and Fishing*, 57f.
104 Ibid., 57f. For similar remarks see Phillips, Journal ADMIRAL BLAKE, 1868–1870, 31.05.1869.
105 Busch, *Whaling Will Never Do for Me*, 54; Gilje, *Liberty on the Waterfront*, 14.

Only by the threat of force were the captain and his officers able to divert the men from their purpose:

> Captain Costa, the three officers, and the harpooners [. . .] armed themselves with revolvers, with which they soon cowed the mutinous seamen. The Stars and Stripes was then hauled to the masthead upside down, denoting mutiny, which soon brought help in the shape of the Cape constabulary.[106]

Captain Costa's may have been ill-advised to cancel the shore leave demanded by the crew, but from his perspective, it was certainly prudent not to countenance his men's attempt to resolve the matter by force. For if a crew succeeded in using industrial action or other means to obtain "liberty" against the captain's will, his authority sustained lasting damage. This was the case with the barque *Reaper* of Salem, which sailed into Port Dauphin in February 1839 for a stop which the crew had forced by threatening a strike. Over the following days, Captain Neal found himself under pressure to make further concessions "or the purpose of keeping the crew quiet", as he noted in the log. The men repeatedly got roaringly drunk in the harbour and ultimately persuaded Neal to allow them to bring prostitutes on board overnight. "Last night there was a complete hell on board", remarked the exasperated captain.[107]

***

Consulates were one of the principal arenas in which struggles over "liberty on shore" and other aspects of shore leave played out. Most of the seamen who turned to a consulate – whether in person or by means of a petition – did so because they felt they had been unfairly treated. The consul, they hoped, would intervene and ensure that justice was done. Although a law passed in 1840 and strengthened in 1856 expressly gave American seamen the right to put their concerns before a consul, captains would usually try to prevent them from doing so. They feared not only damage to their authority, but also a longer stay in harbour and other unforeseeable difficulties. It was not unheard of for a captain to go so far as to have a man put in irons to keep him from talking to the American consul.[108]

The network of consulates which the United States began to build in the 1790s was intended above all to support the country's overseas trade, and the consuls appointed by the State Department accordingly were mostly American merchants familiar with local conditions. These consuls were less familiar with

---

106 Chippendale, *Sails and Whales*, 120f.
107 Log REAPER, 1837–1839, 27.02.–12.03.1839.
108 Busch, *Whaling Will Never Do for Me*, 64, 77f.

Fig. 30: A canoe at the prow of an American whaler in one of the few preserved photographs of such a scene. The date and location of this photograph – originally a hand-coloured lantern slide – are unknown, but since other lantern slides acquired at the same time are known to depict Dakar (in modern Senegal) and Banjul (in what is now The Gambia), this image too may have been taken near one of these towns.
Courtesy New Bedford Whaling Museum, item number 2003.103.10.

conditions aboard whalers, and they had little experience to guide them in the jurisdictional duties imposed on them by law in 1792.[109] Many consuls were out of their depth when it came to their legal obligation of safeguarding the rights of seamen against abuse, and those who had the relevant expertise or acquired it in the course of their duties often found themselves swamped by sheer volume of complaints.[110]

Adjudicating on a dispute aboard a whaler was no easy matter for a consul. A consul taking the time to interview the parties to a conflict or even to investigate its background with a view to appreciating the divergent positions was likely to be

---

109 Busch, *Whaling Will Never Do for Me*, 65; De Santis/Waldo Heinrichs, "United States of America".
110 Hohman, *The American Whaleman*, 78f.

considered partisan by the captain. And since every day a vessel spent lying in harbour cost money, such a consul would at least have been thought a nuisance by shipmasters with an eye on the balance sheet. In order to deflect such hostility, consuls would often choose the path of least resistance, which generally meant foregoing any deeper examination and adopting the captain's view of the matter. The path of least resistance might also mean visiting the vessel and having the parties state their case on board before dispensing justice in such a way that would not delay the vessel's onward journey. Such attempts at arbitration often demanded concessions from both sides – for instance, by asking seamen on strike to return to work and captains to grant shore leave. It also occurred that a consul would advise a captain to discharge a seaman perceived as being at the heart of the dispute.[111]

Many seamen knew from experience that American consuls tended to side with the captain. Looking back at discussions in the fo'c'sle of the *Bruce* of Fairhaven in the mid-1840s, Browne recalls how those of his shipmates "who had been to sea before knew too well that consuls are, in many instances, but the aiders and abettors of the cruelties of captains".[112] One element of the problem was that American consuls were not salaried, but instead had to support themselves on the income generated by their official duties. A consul, in other words, earned his money not least by notarising vessels' papers and officially certifying hires, discharges and desertions. If a consul acquired a reputation as a champion of the common seaman, American vessels might well prefer to call at other ports and in so doing cut into his earnings. The fact that many consuls continued to trade as merchants while in office further meant that they stood to gain by maintaining good relations with captains.[113] Yet although consuls more often than not found in their favour, captains' fears were not entirely groundless. Consuls were able to impose hefty fines on captains, officers and shipowners, and they had had their disposal the extreme sanction of declaring a vessel unseaworthy, thereby terminating its voyage and inflicting maximum damage on its owners.[114]

Whether before consuls or during their onshore recreations, seafarers tended not to appear as a crew but rather individually or in small groups.[115] Their practices during, intentions for and experiences of their periods of "liberty" were, as this section has shown, more diverse than popular imaginings of such situations would suggest.

---

111 Busch, *Whaling Will Never Do for Me*, 64, 78, 80.
112 Browne, *Etchings of a Whaling Cruise*, 303.
113 Hohman, *The American Whaleman*, 80f.
114 Busch, *Whaling Will Never Do for Me*, 79f.
115 Creighton, *Rites & Passages*, 140.

Staying behind

"Sunday the 25 the starboard of the watch went ashore and on runing five of the men runway with boat we never found him again", records the log of the *Mercury* of New Bedford for July 1875, when the barque lay off the east coast of Madagascar.[116] Thousands of similar entries are to be found throughout the material history of whaling. It would be only a slight exaggeration to state that wherever whalers dropped anchor, seamen stayed behind. "There were now, of the thirty who sailed from home in the vessel, but twenty-one remaining", writes Whitecar of the homeward journey of the *Pacific* in late 1858, adding that "even this is a much larger proportion of the original crew than is usually carried home from a voyage of such length as ours".[117] Whitecar's observation is confirmed by research into crew fluctuation in American whaling, with many vessels displaying far higher rates of turnover than the *Pacific*.[118] An exceptional case, as recounted by Elmo P. Hohman, was surely that of the *Montreal* of New Bedford, which sailed in November 1857 with a crew of thirty-nine. In the course of her voyage, the *Montreal* hired 158 men and lost a total of 139: seventy-nine were discharged, thirty deserted, seven died, five were left behind, two were held back on consul's orders and one moved to another vessel; the remaining fifteen left for reasons unknown.[119] In Hohman's study of fifteen voyages made by American whalers between 1843 and 1862, of an initial total of 489 seamen, 143 deserted (29.2%), 166 were discharged (33.9%) and sixteen (3.3%) died.[120] A study drawing on a wider set of data has yet to be produced, and hence the role of desertion in crew fluctuation cannot be reliably established. The estimates of Busch and Hohmann suggest that as many as two thirds of the crew may have deserted on some journeys.[121] What is certain is that there was scarcely a voyage during which there was not at least one desertion.

But why did so many men desert?[122] According to Chippendale – who himself sailed in a number of American whalers in the Atlantic around 1900, ultimately rising to the rank of captain – most did so "because of brutal treatment

---

116 Log MERCURY, 1873–1876, 25.07.1875.
117 Whitecar, *Four Years Aboard the Whaleship*, 339.
118 Hohman, *The American Whaleman*, 62.
119 Ibid., 63.
120 Ibid., 316.
121 Busch, *Whaling Will Never Do for Me*, 24, 92; Francis, *A History of World Whaling*, 108.
122 Desertion – the act of leaving an enforced community without permission and with no intention of returning – was and is a concept in criminal law that captains sometimes used freely for their own ends. Since, however, seamen made it their own – unlike the concept of mutiny, which presents a comparable case – I feel justified in using it here.

from the captain or some officer".[123] If ill usage was not enough to drive men away, the other hardships and privations of whaling described in the chapter "Passages II" certainly were. Moreover, since the absolute domination exercised by the captain over his vessel left men with little hope of changing the conditions under which they lived and worked, "they could at least", in Rediker's phrase, "escape it by using their fast feet".[124]

As the main push factor in causing desertions, Hohman describes a general sense of restlessness brought about by conditions on board.[125] This feeling was certainly familiar to Nordhoff, who jumped ship during a stop at Mahé around 1850. "I was", he writes, "heartily tired of the monotony and dirt of a whaleship, as well as of the ignorance and brutality of those whom I was compelled to own as shipmates in the forecastle. These fellows [. . .] were to me day by day growing more unendurable." The possibility of deserting was, in Nordhoff's telling, never far from the men's minds and their conversation: "Nothing is more common in a whaleship's forecastle than to hear the crew, even at an advanced stage of the voyage, speak of their hopes to escape at the next port."[126] Plans had already been made during the approach to the Seychelles:

> Of our entire crew, leaving out of consideration the boatsteerers and officers whose interests were of course identified with the vessel, none but one Portuguese and the black cook really cared to stay. Each of the others had a plan for making good his own escape. Some thought to take one of the ship's boats [. . .]. Some thought to procure a passage to a neighboring island in a small coasting pinnace. Others yet were convinced that they would be able to subsist in the mountain region of Mahé.[127]

Browne had similar recollections. Of the *Bruce*'s stop at Zanzibar in May 1843, he writes: "We had assembled in the forecastle every evening since we made land, to concert measures for ridding ourselves of the many grievances under which we labored. [. . .] The cruelties and oppressions to which we were subjected; the necessity for some change, were discussed with fierce imprecations upon the head of the tyrant."[128] Since the law prohibited seamen from unilaterally terminating their employment and the captain's consent was hard to obtain, desertion was usually – short of dying – the only way to escape a whaleship.[129]

---

123 Chippendale, *Sails and Whales*, 139.
124 Rediker, *Between the Devil and the Deep Blue Sea*, 100.
125 Hohman, *The American Whaleman*, 62, 68f.
126 Nordhoff, *Whaling and Fishing*, 235.
127 Ibid., 234.
128 Browne, *Etchings of a Whaling Cruise*, 302f.
129 Hohman, *The American Whaleman*, 68f.

But the decision to jump ship need not always be a direct reaction to the hardships of whaling. As the historian Thomas F. Heffernan notes, "Desertions took place on well-run ships, and seamen stayed with badly run ones."[130] Seamen on shore might sometimes hear of opportunities for easier money – whether aboard a merchant vessel or prospecting for gold in California, Australia or Alaska. If temptation was strong enough, even seamen (and indeed officers) who were generally content with their lot or enjoyed a privileged position on board might desert.[131] Particularly in Oceania, the prospect of starting a new and better life elsewhere was a strong pull factor. The tropical coral islands of Polynesia and Micronesia exerted a strong attraction that was heightened by seamen's yarns and made them look like good places for a new start. Several thousand seamen deserted in such islands over the course of the nineteenth century; three thousand deserters from whaleships are estimated to have lived in Oceania in the mid-1800s alone.[132] Many of these men were African Americans, to whom the memory of North America was associated with oppression and discrimination and to whom returning there seemed a less enticing prospect than it was to many of their white shipmates.[133]

When vessels had no luck in the whale hunt, desertion might strike seamen as a sound economic choice. If a man could expect to run a deficit – that is, to have incurred debts with the vessel's owners in excess of his likely share of the profits – desertion could seem a good way of escaping this looming debt. Ports that were much visited by whalers offered good prospects to deserters of finding work aboard a vessel that was doing better and hence was likely to pay more.[134] Aside from the reasons discussed here, seamen may have had all manner of other and often altogether personal reasons for deserting. Sometimes an argument, an insult or a frustrating experience was enough to make a man jump ship. Some men simply preferred a roving lifestyle and were reluctant to spend more than a few months at a time in one place – even if that place was itself in motion, like a ship.

---

130 Heffernan, *Mutiny on the Globe*, 58.
131 Busch, *Whaling Will Never Do for Me*, 89, 95; Hohman, *The American Whaleman*, 68f.; Log BERTHA, 1883–1887, 18. & 19.12.1884; Starbuck, *History of the American Whale Fishery*, 112. Even captains were known to desert, albeit very rarely. One such case was that of William Swain, who commanded the *Matilda* of London from 1836 to 1840, when he made good his escape in the Bay of Islands, New Zealand. (Chatwin, "A Trade so Uncontrollably Uncertain", 109–111, 143).
132 Currie, *Thar She Blows*, 41; Ellis, "Whaling, Traditional", 1253.
133 Busch, *Whaling Will Never Do for Me*, 90.
134 Gilje, *Liberty on the Waterfront*, 21; Hohman, *The American Whaleman*, 65.

Others had only ever signed on aboard a whaler to reach places where gold had been found and deserted as soon as they got there.[135]

***

Of two men who had been left behind by his vessel months before in Port Louis, William Whitecar learnt in 1858 that they were now working for the harbour police; a third had signed in aboard another whaler.[136] These men had done comparatively well for themselves, for other deserters in Port Louis were reduced to begging in the streets for a living.[137] In most cases, however, it is impossible to establish what became of deserted seamen. It would nonetheless be a worthwhile for research, promising as it does an insight into phenomena of subaltern mobility which so far have received scant attention. The number of entries relating to desertion in the logbooks that have been preserved hint at the extraordinary spatial connections enabled by whaling. The case of a seaman who signed on aboard the *A.R. Tucker* of Dartmouth in Oceania and deserted in Zanzibar on 1 July 1860 is only one of many suggestive examples.[138] In the absence of any research on this topic the question of what lay ahead for a deserter can be answered only in general terms. One thing that is certain is that the escape itself was often fraught with difficulties. The simplest and hence most common way of deserting was simply not to return to the vessel from shore leave. Whenever they could, seamen would wait until the day before the vessel was due to sail, by which time the captain would have made his preparations for departure had had little time to spare for chasing after deserters.[139] "Many times the sailing of a vessel was held up by desertions on the last liberty day, while extensive search was made for the deserters", recalls Harry Chippendale of his voyage aboard the *Greyhound* in the early 1900. "This man-hunt seldom produced any results, as the deserters were always hidden."[140]

Since, however, captains often denied shore leave to seamen whom they suspected of being minded to desert, many found themselves left with no choice but to swim ashore under cover of darkness. Captains were aware of this and would often moor their vessels at some distance from the coast, thereby adding to the difficulty and danger of this mode of escape – all the more so because many

---

135 Gilje, *Liberty on the Waterfront*, 86; Starbuck, *History of the American Whale Fishery*, 112; Vickers, "Rev. of Marcus Rediker", 313.
136 Whitecar, *Four Years Aboard the Whaleship*, 350.
137 Ely, *There She Blows*, 86f.
138 Log A. R. TUCKER, 1857–1861, 01.07.1860.
139 For two examples of many see e.g. Log ADELINE GIBBS, 1875–1878, 15. & 16.05.1876 and Log DESDEMONA, 1873–1876, 04.03.1874.
140 Chippendale, *Sails and Whales*, 139.

seamen were unable to swim and often managed to keep afloat only by clinging on to a piece of wood. Of a night in the late 1860s when the *Herald II* lay off Victoria, Lewis Eldridge recalls how "during the anchor watch we heard a cry out over the water, a cry like that of a drowning person". He continues:

> We discovered that Mike was missing and we took a boat to shore in an effort to find him. The third day we located him; he had escaped and swum to an old derelict about half a mile from our ship. By the time he reached the anchor chain of this old ship he was too exhausted to climb on board. His cries brought the ship-keeper to his rescue and he stayed on board until the officers found him three days later.[141]

Other potentially deadly perils facing a seaman trying to swim ashore included sharks, currents, hypothermia and breakers. Some deserters accordingly headed first for a vessel anchored closer to the shore in the hope of finding refuge there among the common seamen in the forecastle before covering the remaining distance by night.[142] When seamen deserted as a group, they often avoided the dangers of swimming by stealing one of the vessel's boats. This also made desertion possible in cases when a vessel was not at anchor but close enough to the coast for the deserts to reach it by boat.[143]

The first priority of any deserter who had made it safely to the shore was to conceal himself until his vessel's departure. Some men managed to disappear in the streets of the harbour district, others took to the woods in the interior.[144] "On my last night of shore liberty, I gave a loafer at the Connaught Arms (a place frequented by sailors) a half-crown to hide me, which he did in a small room over the tavern", is how Chippendale made good his escape from his vessel, then lying in Cape Town, in the early 1900s. "I then paid him a shilling a day to bring me food and watch for the sailing of the *Clara L. Sparks*. At the end of the fourth day the old whaler sailed out of the harbor and I breathed a lot easier."[145] Willing accessories like this "loafer" could be found in many ports, but to use their services was not without risk: if a skipper announced a reward for the seizure of a fugitive seaman, many such "helpers" found the temptation hard to resist.[146] In some places, taking both the seaman's money for hiding him and then the bounty for betraying him became a regular business model. One such place was the Azores, where – as Chippendale recalls –

---

141 Eldridge, *Lewis William Eldridge's Whaling Voyage*, 12.
142 Busch, *Whaling Will Never Do for Me*, 98; Creighton, *Rites & Passages*, 145.
143 Browne, *Etchings of a Whaling Cruise*, 449f.; Busch, *Whaling Will Never Do for Me*, 92.
144 Creighton, *Rites & Passages*, 145.
145 Chippendale, *Sails and Whales*, 122.
146 See e.g. the account of two cabin boys and their attempts to desert in Barker, *Thrilling Adventures of the Whaler Alcyone*, 14, 19, 49–51.

"Some of the people there would encourage desertions, hide the deserter, wait until a reward was posted for his capture (either by the captain or the consul) then turn him in and claim the reward".[147]

A deserter who managed to remain undiscovered until his vessel had sailed could expect to face a new set of challenges. Fugitive seamen were usually completely penniless and had to obtain food, shelter and clothing in a strange environment. Many of them struggled to do so, not least on account of language difficulties.[148] We hear, for instance, of an escaped whaleman who died in the streets of Zanzibar in the 1840s after several years spent sleeping rough and begging for his livelihood.[149] It seems that few deserters managed to establish themselves permanently in the places where they had left their vessel.[150]

In this situation, a vital resource for deserters was their country's consulate – if there was one. The United States had charged its consuls with the task of providing food, shelter and medical care to its destitute citizens and to arrange, wherever possible, for their passage home. Although many consuls were unable or unwilling to meet this obligation, some were so swamped with the claims of deserted seafarers that they could scarcely manage to deal with them all even if they were willing to do so. For instance, by the time the US consulate in Mahé opened in 1868, there were already sixty deserters waiting for consular assistance.[151]

Given these difficulties, many deserters sooner or later signed on aboard another whaler. Some may have hoped for better living or working conditions than offered by their last vessel, others would simply have been desperate to get away.[152] Since most whalemen were not trained mariners, they stood little chance of finding work aboard a merchant vessel. Many deserters held out for a vessel that was homeward bound and would reach North America before too long. But even if they manged to get aboard such a vessel, this did not necessarily mean an end to their odyssey. A case in point is that of George Barron and Merrit Wilson, who had deserted from the *Janus* of New Bedford in Moçâmedes (in modern Angola) in February 1863. Soon afterwards, they signed on aboard the barque *Thomas Pope*, which was bound for the United States. She made a last call at St Helena, where she happened to meet the *Janus*. Captain Robbins of the *Thomas Hope* wasted no time returning the deserters to their previous vessel.

---

147 Chippendale, *Sails and Whales*, 139.
148 Hohman, *The American Whaleman*, 67f.
149 Putnam, "A Visit to Zanzibar", 404f.
150 Creighton, *Rites & Passages*, 146; Currie, *Thar She Blows*, 42.
151 Hohman, *The American Whaleman*, 78f., 110f., 127.
152 See e.g. Nordhoff, *Whaling and Fishing*, 325.

The two men, however, had no intention of staying here. Wilson jumped overboard the same night, no doubt hoping to reach another vessel or the shore. Barron did the same the night after; the captain sent a boat in pursuit, but it was too dark to find him. It is unknown whether either of them ever reached the shore.[153]

***

The way captains dealt with desertions followed a peculiar logic. Depending on the circumstances, they sought sometimes to prevent and sometimes to encourage desertions – and sometimes even to force them. "Masters might set men free or kick them out of the ship. Or they might watch them like hawks and hunt them like slaves", as Creighton puts it.[154] The former approach – preventing seamen from deserting – naturally prevailed throughout most of the journey. A strong fluctuation within the crew posed a threat to the success of the voyage, and all the more so if experienced men had to be replaced by comparatively inexperienced ones. In 1861 George Fairfield, the American consul in Port Louis, reported to the State Department that "The loss of each man from a whale ship at the commencement of a cruise is, at a low estimation, equivalent to a loss of one hundred dollars to the ship".[155] British whalers in particular suffered high rates of desertion; the consequent loss of skills hastened the decline of British whaling.[156] Moreover, most whalemen were in debt to shipowners for their clothing and advances on their pay – expenses with which shipowners were saddled if a seaman deserted.[157]

Shipowners and captains accordingly took both tactical and strategic measures to reduce the risk of desertion. Shipowners or their agents tried to assess a candidate's propensity to desert even when putting together a crew and choosing their hires accordingly.[158] A strategic instrument which has already been mentioned was the choice of stops. Potential deserters were likely to be deterred by remote ports away from the main shipping routes, which offered little prospect of getting away even if a seaman made good his escape from the vessel itself. Nordhoff, for instance, writes of his hesitation to jump ship during a visit to the Seychelles around 1850: "I judged, from what the boatsteerers told me of the

---

153 Log JANUS, 1862–1865, 11. & 14.03.1863.
154 Creighton, *Rites & Passages*, 141.
155 George H. Fairfield. Letter to Secretary of State, 25.03.1861. National Archives and Records Administration, Records of Foreign Service Posts, Record Group 84, Port Louis, vol. 006.
156 Chatwin, "A Trade so Uncontrollably Uncertain", 112f.; Starbuck, *History of the American Whale Fishery*, 112.
157 Creighton, *Rites & Passages*, 92.
158 See e.g. Nordhoff, *Whaling and Fishing*, 40.

islands, that it would be almost impossible to get safely away from a whaleship there, unless some merchant vessel was just then in port, in which to take passage".[159] "Whaling captains", he realised, "always chose a 'liberty' port with an eye to the facilities it affords for retaking fugitives."[160] Many seamen would think twice before deserting in places where communication was difficult and the "natives" might prove unpredictable. Contemplating desertion in the Indian Ocean in the 1840s, John Williams decided to wait until his vessel called somewhere "where white people lived".[161]

One advantage of small islands was that fugitive seamen were easier to find. In some locations shipmasters could also draw on the support of the local police or other actors who would find deserters and return them to their vessels for a reward – the cost of which was to be borne by the deserter himself.[162] In order to prevent the greater part of crew from deserting together or going on strike while on shore leave, seamen were allowed to go ashore only in the company of their respective watch or boat crew. As long as one group, the free watch, was ashore, the other had to keep the anchor watch on board. This system ensures that half the crew were aboard at any time. The make-up of the free and anchor watched did not necessarily correspond to that of starboard and port watches. When, for instance, the *Clara Bell* of Mattapoisett put in at the Seychelles in June 1856, the "Yankies" formed one watch and the "Portuguese" the other.[163] Calling at Zanzibar in 1843, Captain Alden of the *Bruce* of Fairhaven tried to keep his men from deserting by stoking their fears. John Ross Browne remembers Alden warning the crew that "The natives will murder you if you go outside the town. You'd better keep in sight of the ship, and not trust 'em. [. . .] I'll send a boat for you at sundown, and if you ain't on the beach, look out!"[164] According to Busch, the planning of a voyage and its stops, the rules aboard ship and the way captains organised shore leave all followed the logic of the prison: "The system on board was designed to discourage easy escape."[165]

Desertion was a threat not only to a voyage's profitability, but also to the captain's authority. To abscond successfully was to reveal to the crew the limits

---

159 Nordhoff, *Whaling and Fishing*, 218.
160 Ibid., 235.
161 Williams, *The Adventures of a Seventeen-year-old Lad and the Fortunes He Might Have Won*, 47.
162 Busch, *Whaling Will Never Do for Me*, 97; Creighton, *Rites & Passages*, 144.
163 Wallace, Journal CLARA BELL, 1855–1858, 15.06.1856.
164 Browne, *Etchings of a Whaling Cruise*, 303f.
165 Busch, *Whaling Will Never Do for Me*, 102.

of his rule. A seaman who deserted removed his body from the captain's influence, thereby asserting his freedom and autonomy. It was, as Margaret Creighton puts it, "the ultimate tool of protest" of a sailor – and the only one that, if successful, went unpunished.[166] If deserters were caught, however, the punishment was likely to be all the more severe, not least to minimise the damage to the captain's authority. After two men had deserted from the *Bruce* of Fairhaven while on shore leave in Zanzibar in 1843, Captain Alden berated the remaining crew: "Yes, they're gone; an' I suppose you'll all be tryin' it next. You'd better not! *I'll* catch 'em, and, d – n their souls, I'll warm their backs. I'll see whether my crew will leave me or not!"[167] The thwarted fugitives would usually be put in irons or imprisoned in the run – at least until the vessel had sailed, but for often days or even weeks afterwards. Additional punishments – notably the lash – were also imposed.[168] Little wonder, then, that deserters who had been seized often desperately tried to escape again. For instance, the cooper aboard the *A.R. Tucker* of Tucker of Dartmouth, David Ashton, who had deserted in April 1858 in Silhouette (one of the Seychelles) and been apprehended after a few days, jumped overboard as the barque put out to sea.[169]

However, captains pursued their goal of preventing desertion only for as long as it was worth their while. Once the vessel was homeward bound with its hold was full of whale oil, a desertion promised a saving rather than an expense, for the fewer seamen returned home, the larger the payout for those who did – including the captain himself.[170] Towards the end of voyage, then, some captains more or less systematically encouraged their men to jump ship. The best places to do so were ones where there was no American consulate or other authority likely to interfere, for if a seaman presented himself to the consul to demand a regular discharge rather than simply deserting, further expenses were to be feared.[171] It was not unheard of for a captain to leave a man behind deliberately while he was on shore leave and then to log him as a deserter.[172] Walter Hammond found himself in such a situation when the *Pedro Varela* of New Bedford called at the Azores: "The captain offered me shore-

---

166 Creighton, *Rites & Passages*, 104; Creighton, "Fraternity in the American Forecastle", 545.
167 Browne, *Etchings of a Whaling Cruise*, 304.
168 Busch, *Whaling Will Never Do for Me*, 97; Hohman, *The American Whaleman*, 67f. The punishment of attempted desertion by imprisonment was outlawed in the United States by the 1915 Seamen's Act. (Warrin, *So Ends This Day*, 84).
169 Log A. R. TUCKER, 1857–1861, 21.–27.04.1858.
170 Creighton, *Rites & Passages*, 144.
171 Busch, *Whaling Will Never Do for Me*, 91, 149.
172 Ibid., 92–95.

leave on two conditions – that I would stay away from the consulate and that I would agree not to return – namely, desert." What had happened was that Captain Corvelho had had an insurrection by several men in protest at the poor conditions on board brutally put down. Hammond supposed that the captain had hoped to rid himself of several seamen who might later testify against him for using excessive force by encouraging them to desert in the Azores. Hammond knew that "If he would once classify me as a deserter, anything I might say thereafter would carry little weight" and accordingly declined the offer: "I told him I didn't want to stay on board any more than he wanted me to, and suggested that he give me a discharge. I definitely would not agree to refrain from lodging a complaint."[173]

Since seamen like Hammond knew what skippers were up to and resisted their inducements to desert – especially at the end of what promised to be a profitable voyage – some captains decided not to leave the mater to chance.[174] Of the strategy pursued towards inexperienced recruits by the master of the *Sea Fox*, Chippendale recalls:

> It was custom for the Captain Gilbane type of whaling skipper not to treat such men too badly at the beginning [. . .], but to wait until the last season, then go the limit and give them hell, so that would desert ship [. . .]. They would then be logged as deserters, and I was told their voyage money would be confiscated and divided among the owners, agents, and the skipper.[175]

***

Besides desertion, the most common way for a seaman to be left behind was being discharged. American seamen in the nineteenth century were subject to a legal framework which strictly governed the discharge of seamen and consequently caused much legal wrangling. A law passed in 1803 required that if a seaman was discharged en route, he was to receive three months' wages in addition to his pay up do that date along. This payment and the legality of the discharge were to be witnessed by the American consul (assuming there to be one in the place of discharge), who was entitled to a fifty cent processing fee for each of these points as well 2.5 per cent of the pay due to the seaman. The consul was initially to hold the pay due to the man in its entirety in trust and to use it to pay for his passage back to the United States. This procedure faced captains with considerable difficulties. As far as the average captain was concerned, discharging a

---

173 Hammond, *Mutiny on the Pedro Varela*, 69.
174 Creighton, *Rites & Passages*, 92; Hohman, *The American Whaleman*, 201.
175 Chippendale, *Sails and Whales*, 160f.

seaman in a place where there was an American consulate meant a lot of red tape – costly formalities that might well delay the voyage. Moreover, whalemen did not receive fixed wages, but were paid a share of the profits, which were calculated at the journey's end. In order to estimate what a seaman was owed, the captain had to make a complicated tally of all takings and expenses to date and submit it to the consul's scrutiny.[176]

Seamen were aware of the consuls' duty towards them, as they were of their right to request reimbursement of their hospital fees from the consul. Since many seamen were in poor health, those seeking a discharge did so, where possible, in a place provided with both a hospital and an American consulate.[177] By the same token, captains sought to prevent this from happening – unless the man concerned was likely to be unfit for work for a longer period of time on account of illness or injury, or if he was a "seasoner", one who signed on aboard a whaling vessel for a specified part of its voyage.[178]

Whether a captain acceded to a man's request for a discharge depended on a variety of factors. A common seaman usually seemed more dispensable than, for instance, an experienced harpooner or a specialised tradesman. Another question was whether a replacement might be found locally. In the case of injury, discharging a man would usually strike a captain as more expedient than dragging him along, which caused some seamen to wound themselves in a desperate attempt to obtain a discharge. Nordhoff recalls a particularly drastic case: "A man who had vainly tried to desert from his vessel, having been several times retaken when making the attempt, deliberately laid his left wrist on a chopping block and cut off the hand, exclaiming as he did so, 'Now you'll have to let me go.'"[179] Since captains were also keen to rid themselves of troublemakers, seamen might also hope to hasten their discharge by making a show of their discontent – though in doing so they risked severe punishment.[180]

John Ross Browne, who shipped on the *Bruce* of Fairhaven as a common seaman in 1842, secured his discharge in Zanzibar in May 1843 by presenting Captain Alden with a capable and willing replacement he had found locally.

---

176 Busch, *Whaling Will Never Do for Me*, 24, 63, 69f., 91.
177 Hohman, *The American Whaleman*, 78f. In such ports as Lāhainā (Hawai'i) or Callao (Peru), which were much frequented by whalers, the hospital bills charged to the American and British consulates for the care of discharged seamen ran to tens of thousands of dollars per year. In order to escape the burden of maintaining sick and indigent seamen, American consuls were able to compel whalers bound for the United States to take them on board. (Busch, *Whaling Will Never Do for Me*, 73, 82).
178 Busch, *Whaling Will Never Do for Me*, 67; Hohman, *The American Whaleman*, 68.
179 Nordhoff, *Whaling and Fishing*, 245.
180 Busch, *Whaling Will Never Do for Me*, 91; Hohman, *The American Whaleman*, 68.

Still, Browne was apprehensive about the possibility of Alden refusing the exchange: "I was, indeed, somewhat bereft of my senses, and had difficulty in controlling my feelings". All the greater was Browne's relief when the deal was finally done: "We went up to the consuls to sign the papers and settle accounts. I did not feel sure of my release till I held the written discharge in my own hand; then, for the first time in my life, I felt what it really was to be FREE!"[181]

Browne's was, however, an exceptional case. Captains were usually unwilling to grant discharges except in cases of severe injury or illness.[182] And yet it also occurred that a skipper would try to force a man's resignation against his will – if only out of personal animosity. Some captains bought seamen's consent to being discharged in ports without a consulate by issuing them with an IOU allowing the man to claim his lay from the shipowners at a later date. Since this order could be redeemed only in the vessel's home port, which it was uncertain that the seaman would ever reach, this procedure favoured the captain and the syndicate.[183]

Since captains minded to avoid their legal obligations preferred to call at ports without a consulate if they wanted to discharge seamen, it is in many cases – perhaps in most – impossible to tell whether a discharge was consensual or not. Entries in logbooks referring to consensual discharge on the one hand and desertion on the other ought in any case to be taken with caution. Cases in which "masters simply dumped such men ashore out of sight of the consul [. . .] and then logged them as deserters" were, as Hohman observes, no rarity.[184]

There was another way besides desertion and discharge that seamen might get left behind. Sometimes a captain would simply abandon a seaman he had grown to detest. The advantage, as far as the captain was concerned, was that this saved the time and expense involved in the formal discharge of a seaman – including, of course, the need to pay him off. Abandoning a man was, however, illegal under US law, and since such cases were hence not usually recorded in ships' logs, their frequency is difficult to gauge. Logs often fail to spell out whether a man left behind had been discharged or abandoned – perhaps in an attempt to make a case of abandonment look like a regular discharge.[185] The abandonment of a seaman tended to go in record only if the case went to court in some form or another – or when the captain was so certain of the lawfulness of

---

181 Browne, *Etchings of a Whaling Cruise*, 324f.
182 Hohman, *The American Whaleman*, 68.
183 Busch, *Whaling Will Never Do for Me*, 72.
184 Ibid., 70.
185 Ibid., 25; Macdonald, *Cinderellas of Empire*, 20.

his action that he had it logged. Such was the case with the brig *Pavilion* of Holmes Hole, whose captain had two seamen left behind in Cabinda in August 1859 after accusing them of damaging the ship's equipment.[186]

Sailors might also not return to their vessel because they had been arrested by the police while on shore leave and the captain was not prepared to wait for their release. In cases of grave offences on board – such as attempted mutiny – captains would deliver the accused seamen to the authorities in the nearest port, where they would often receive severe punishments. If there was an American consul in the vicinity, he would usually press for the accused to be taken to for trial in the United States by the next vessel. This was not, however, an option likely to find favour with the captain, since he stood to lose additional men who would be summoned as witnesses. It was no rarity for men to be exchanged between whalers which lay in harbour, and this was a useful way of resolving tensions among the crew that could be put down, for instance, to a personal dispute between a seaman and an officer. Ideally, this would be in everybody's best interest, since an exchange of men by mutual consent neither delayed a vessel's onward sailing nor caused additional expense.[187]

∗∗∗

"For shore-dwellers", Heimerdinger observes, "shore leave represents the only situation in which they become aware of sailors, who are hidden from view in the course of their work on board ship. A sailor visible to a shore-dweller is invariably a sailor operating in a state of exception."[188] This insight is important for understanding the situations in which littoral societies in Africa encountered seamen. As a rule, captains called into to port in order to enable the voyage to continue (by making repairs, by taking on food, water, and firewood, or by hiring new hands) or to increase its productivity (by pursuing commercial sidelines, by obtaining news and information, or by transhipping oil and baleen). For most seamen, however, a stopover meant above all an opportunity to escape from the cramped conditions and hardships of shipboard life. In the few days' grace this afforded them – days to which seamen felt entitled and for the sake of which they were prepared to take industrial action – they did all they could to compensate for their everyday privations. For many and perhaps most seamen this meant indulging in as much drink and sex as they could find and generally to do all the things they were prevented from doing on board ship. Littoral societies

---

186 Log PAVILION, 1858–1860, 10. & 13.08.1859.
187 Busch, *Whaling Will Never Do for Me*, 24, 91.
188 Heimerdinger, *Der Seemann*, 77.

hence often experienced seafarers as troublemakers and were accordingly wary of them. Yet solitary rambles, attending church and buying souvenirs were equally part of being ashore – as was the hard work of fetching water, cutting wood and transhipping casks. Many men did not return to their vessels: deserted, discharged and abandoned seamen lined the whaling routes in their thousands. They too were – to use Heimerdinger's phrase – "seamen in a state of exception".

6 Under the sign of abolition: Cabinda, 1850–1855

"The water that flows from the river is a different color, and does not seem to mingle with the water of the ocean", Lucy Smith observed in her diary for 24 June 1870. On that day, she had reached the mouth of the Congo river aboard the *Nautilus* of New Bedford, of which her husband George was captain. Of the zone where the waters met, she wrote: "You could see a long distance the difference in the color in a strait [sic] line, and it seemed to be but a few feet deep and the ships rudder would stir up the green water underneath."[1] The water of the Congo not only looked different from that of the Atlantic and flowed in a different direction, it also tasted different.[2] Whales too seem to have appreciated this difference: humpback whales came to the mouth of the Congo during their annual migration from the Antarctic ocean, perhaps deliberately swimming into the sweet water pouring from the river in order to kill the barnacles and amphipods which infested their skin. More importantly still, the Congo estuary – one of the most productive ecosystems on the African coast – was a rich feeding ground for the whales.[3]

After heavy rains in the interior, the Congo river flows into the sea at a speed of up to seven knots, producing a current that could be felt even one hundred or more kilometres out from the coast. It occurred that whaling crews had to take to their boats in order to tow their vessel past the river's mouth, as the sails did not offer enough propulsion to cross the current.[4] This presented mariners with another challenge. If a vessel wished to approach the coast near the mouth of the river from the west, it had to sail against the onrush of the Congo's waters. If, however, a vessel was coming from the north, it had another current to struggle against: the Benguela, which, coming from the Antarctic, here – close to the equator – merges into the South Equatorial Current. The wind, which blows almost invariably from the south-west, made life hard for vessels coming from the north and west alike.[5] The mouth of the Congo was best reached *with* the Benguela and hence from the south, which was the route taken by most whalers, if not by most merchant vessels.

---

1 Smith, Journal NAUTILUS, 1869–1874, 24.06.1870.
2 Travassos Valdez, *Six Years of a Traveller's Life in Western Africa*, vol. 2, 77.
3 Burton/Burton, "Humpback Whale", vol. 9, 1260; Walker, "African Fisheries", 656.
4 Log GLOBE, 1855–1857, 30.06.1856.
5 Martin, "Cabinda and Cabindans", 82.

https://doi.org/10.1515/9783110759914-010

At the currents' end

Tracking, chasing, catching, flensing and trying out: by the time they reached the mouth of the Congo, whalers had usually been working for weeks on end. "Last week we chased whales every day in the hot sun", reads the diary of Robert Ferguson, who arrived in the area as harpooner aboard the *Kathleen* of New Bedford in mid-1882.[6] Humpback whales could reliably be found on the coast of what is now Angola, from where the barque was coming, between May and September. Since, however, the longest section of this coast offers few sheltered bays, vessels that went humpbacking there lacked opportunities for taking on food, drinking water and firewood. It was at the end of a hunt in the area that Andrew Heyer, captain of the barque *Wanderer* of New Bedford, wrote to his brother Tobias: "Try to get something to eat for we have nothing for the past month but Bread Hash, and I never eat that stuff. We are all out of preserved meats". It was high time to put into port, for which Heyer chose a bay some thirty nautical miles north of the mouth of the Congo and known to seamen as the best – that is, the safest and most spacious – anchorage far and wide: "We are now steering in for the land, bound for Cabenda".[7] As early as 1700, the French navigator and slaver Louis de Grandpré had called this place the "paradise of the coast".[8]

Today the name Cabinda usually denotes the Angolan exclave and province which comprises a major part of the Zaire lowlands. Historically, however, the name refers only to the coastal portion of this territory.[9] Its origins is uncertain. Portuguese navigators had initially called the bay *Baia das Almadias* or "Bay of Canoes".[10] According to a common account, around 1500 a Portuguese captain there encountered an official (*mafouk* or *mafuka*) of the coastal state of Ngoyo by the name of Binda. The Portuguese may have heard this man addressed as "Mafuka Binda" and named the place accordingly. On the other hand, it is also quite possible that Cabinda is a Kikongo or Kimbundu term composed of the prefix *ka* and the noun *binda*, denoting a water vessel and by extension a bay.[11] Whichever version one might take to be the more plausible, the name is certainly old. Even in one of the earliest written accounts of the bay – by Andrew Battell, who reached it around 1590 after having been taken prisoner by the Portuguese from

---

6 Ferguson, *Harpooner*, 133.
7 McCormick, *Two New Bedford Whalemen*, 183.
8 Martin, "Cabinda and Cabindans", 84f.
9 Martin, "Family Strategies in Nineteenth-Century Cabinda", 66.
10 Martin, "Cabinda and Cabindans", 80; Pinto, *Cabinda e as construções da sua história*, 97.
11 Pinto, Cabinda e as construções da sua história, 97–99.

an English privateer – it is referred to as "Cabenda".[12] This name remained in use with nineteenth-century American whalemen, often in such variants as "Kabenda" or "Kabendy".

Adolf Bastian, a German explorer who visited in 1873, reported that "the Bay of Cabinda offers a picturesque vista, with a ridge broken up by peaks enclosing the cluster of villages known as Cabinda from the south". He also observed how "in Cabinda, being a half-enclosed bay, the Calema [breakers] are never as strong as they would be along a coast fully exposed to the Atlantic billows, and hence landing there is seldom perilous."[13] The bay has a coastline of approximately ten kilometres, offering several good anchorages for whalers (Fig. 31) – anchorages which they would often gradually move north, following the usual northward course taken in humpbacking.[14] The coast slopes very gently down towards the sea, and since whales had little opportunity to escape their pursuers by diving deep (and did not sink far when killed), whalers were able to hunt their quarry over a large area. Whalers would sometimes anchor as far as ten nautical miles out to sea, where the water was still comparatively shallow at approximately twenty metres.[15] However, whaleships were largely alone in finding this situation to their advantage. Large merchant vessels with deep draughts had to steer clear of the shoreline. And although the breakers caused by this shallow coast are weaker in the bay than elsewhere in the area, even lighter vessels had a hard time getting much closer to the shore than one nautical mile. As commercial shipping has come to rely on ever larger ships, Cabinda has declined as a commercial port and is now overshadowed by the deep water ports of Luanda in the south and Port-Gentil in the north.[16]

The bay of humpback whales

"Succeeded in striking the cow", the log of the barque *Globe* of New Bedford records for 24 August 1870. This occurred around noon off the coast of Angola. One of the boats had fastened onto a female humpback, but just as the third mate was poised to deliver the *coup de grâce*, the wounded animal suddenly lashed out and, as the log records, "struck the boat, & stove her". The boat's

---

12 Battell, *The Strange Adventures of Andrew Battel of Leigh*, 42.
13 Bastian, *Die deutsche Expedition an der Loango-Küste*, vol. 1, 17.
14 See e.g. Log FALCON, 1879–1882, 27.09.1881.
15 Log LEONIDAS, 1860–1863, 01.08.1862.
16 Martin, "The Cabinda Connection", 55; Martin, *The External Trade of the Loango Coast*, 1; Soyaux, *Aus West-Afrika*, 258.

The bay of humpback whales — 365

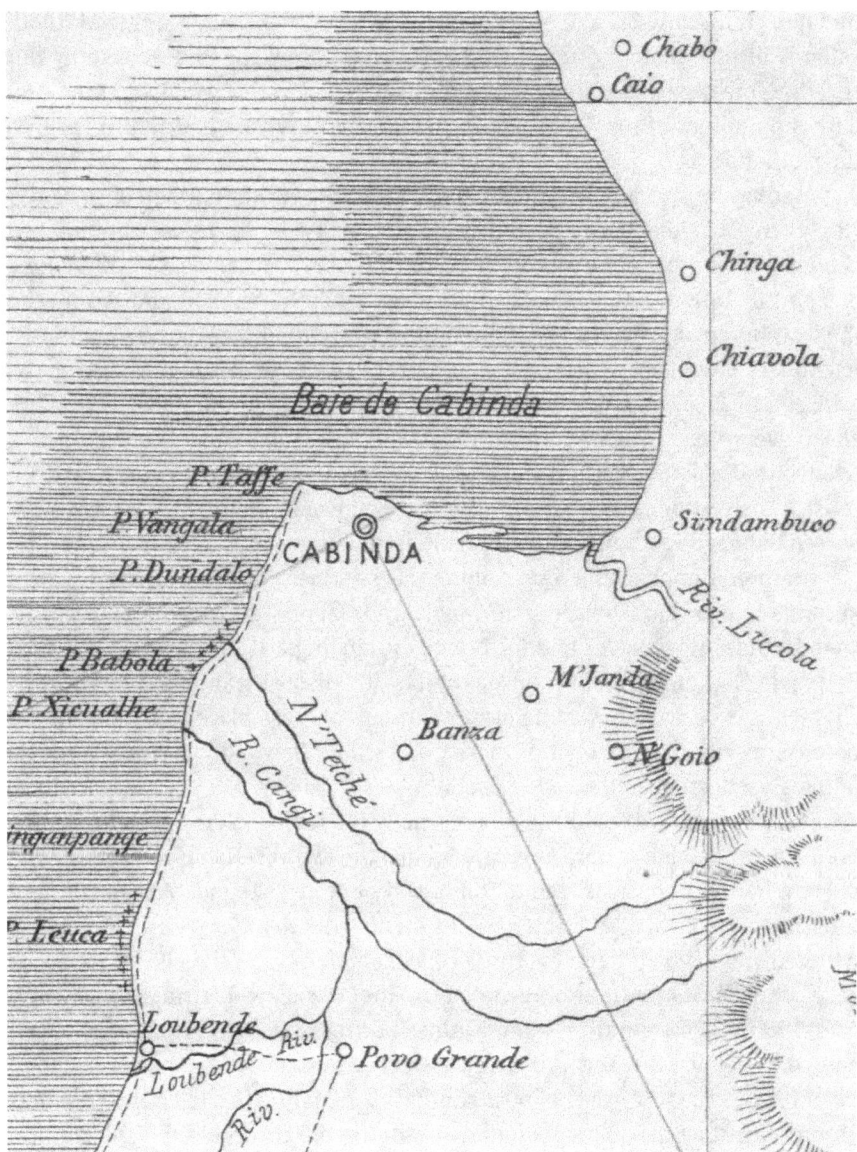

Fig. 31: Extract from the map "Carte de la commission de délimitation" showing Cabinda (no date, probably late nineteenth century).
Courtesy of the Gotha Research Library at University of Erfurt, SPK 40 26.II B [05, 01].

inmates clung to wreckage and cut the rope to prevent being dragged under water. But the whale did not dive. Instead it went on the attack, lashing out several more times, killing one man and severely injuring another. Only after dark did another of the *Globe*'s boats rescue the survivors and return them to the mother ship.[17]

Among the species they pursued in the eighteenth and nineteenth centuries, many whalemen considered the humpback whale to pose the greatest challenge – and not only because it could lash out for whaleboats with its long pectoral fins. By trying to flee at high speed when harpooned and fighting to the last, humpback whales drove their pursuers to the limits of their abilities.[18] As Robert Ferguson, who was whaling off the coast of Angola aboard the *Kathleen* in 1882, noted in his diary: "It's hard work and they give us a merry chase every time".[19] It was this arduous and dangerous pursuit of humpback whales that was the main reason why whalers sailed for the central African coast. "There are lots of whales", observed Ferguson. "Hardly a day passes but we see them. To catch up to them is a different matter."[20]

On their humpbacking routes along the west coast of Africa, whalers called at numerous locations in modern Angola and Gabon – besides Cabinda, these were Luanda, Moçâmedes and the Congo estuary in particular, but also Ambriz, Benguela, Equimina, Lobito or Mayumba. If I discuss Cabinda alone in this chapter, it is because it was the most important of these places for whaling and because trying to include all of these ports would inevitably exceed the scope of the present study.

It is impossible to establish when exactly the first whalers began to operate off the coast of what is now Angola. Perhaps the two vessels dispatched to Walvis Bay by the Dutch East India Company between 1726 and 1729 also visited the Angolan coast. At any rate, one of them – the *Acredam* – returned home with redwood, which her crew cannot have obtained in Walvis Bay.[21] As in the case of the *Acredam*, the routes taken by the vessels which sailed from Nantucket in the 1760s and 1770s for "Guinea" or the "Coast of Africa" are not recorded in details. It seems probable, however, that American whalers began to head for the coast of what is now southern Angola by the later 1780s. It was around this time that the populations of southern right whales off the coast of southern Africa began to be exploited, and the island of Baía dos Tigres, which

---

17 Log GLOBE, 1869–1872, 24.08.1870.
18 Hohman, *The American Whaleman*, 148; Leek, Journal DELTA, 1836–1838, 16.12.1836.
19 Ferguson, *Harpooner*, 134.
20 Ibid., 192.
21 Dekker/De Jong, "Whaling Expeditions of the West India Company to Walvis Bay", 54f.

is situated north of the mouth of the Kunene Congo river, is one of these whales' preferred mating and calving grounds.[22]

Southern rights did not, however, make it as far as the mouth of the Congo, nor did whalers find their way there in the hunt for sperm whales, for which the waters are too shallow. Only as their interest shifted to humpback whales did whalers begin to pay attention to Cabinda.[23] As with many whaling grounds, the boom period set in quite abruptly, in the case of Cabinda in the mid-1850s. At least eleven whaleships are known to have visited the bay in August 1854, and their numbers remained high throughout the following years. These were all American vessels, British whaling in the South Seas having largely collapsed in the 1840s and that of France earlier still. The end of whaling in Cabinda came no less abruptly in the mid-1880s. Whereas at least six whaleships called at Cabinda in 1886, American whalers ceased to visit the bay afterwards.

Whalers usually arrived in Cabinda towards the end of the southern winter, in the months of August, September and October, having worked their northwards along the coast over the course of the season.[24] Some vessels traced the triangular humpbacking route between St Helena, Baía dos Tigres and Cabinda twice in a season and hence called twice at Cabinda, once in the middle and once near the end of the southern winter.[25] By contrast, it virtually unheard of for a whaleship to sail into the bay in the months of the southern summer.

The time a whaleship spent in Cabinda depended above all on whether it arrived near the close of the season or was planning to continue humpbacking in the Gulf of Guinea. In the former case, a vessel might spend up to five weeks in the bay – as did the barque *Bertha* of New Bedford, which lay there from late September to early November 1880.[26] The latter, however, was the more common scenario, with whalers usually staying for less than a week. Others passed Cabinda without stopping, reluctant to waste even a day that might be spent in pursuit of their quarry.[27]

As in the cases of Walvis Bay and Annobón, however, a stop at Cabinda could be used for hunting as well as for victualling, with humpback whales appearing within sight of the coast – and often in large groups. A vessel might

---

22 On the migration routes of southern right whales off the south-western coast of Africa see the chapter "Passages I".
23 This shift and the resultant practice of "humpbacking" is discussed in the chapter "Passages I".
24 Haywood, "American Whalers and Africa", 71.
25 See e.g. Log SUNBEAM, 1878–1882, 29.–30.07. & 04.–18.10.1881.
26 Log BERTHA, 1878–1881, 25.09.–01.11.1880.
27 See e.g. Log TRITON, 1868–1871, 22.06.– 04.07.1869.

often lower its boats while moored in the bay.[28] "All 3 boats cruising for humpbacks", reads an entry in the log of the brig *Pavilion* of Holmes Hole, which had put in at Cabinda in August 1859.[29] If one of the boats succeeded in taking a whale, the vessel would usually follow it to the site of the carcass to begin flensing it. Speed was of the issue when operating in these coastal waters, where whalemen almost invariably found themselves fighting countless sharks for their catch. If a crew had to wait till the next day to continue flensing – whether on account of dusk or a lull in the wind – they might wake up to find there was nothing left for them to do. As the log of *Sunbeam* of New Bedford remarks with the genre's typical bluntness: "It was calm and could not get the ship to the whale and shark eat him".[30]

Since many whalers shifted their moorings over the course of their stay without the exact positions being logged, it is often impossible to ascertain where exactly a vessel lay in the bay or when it arrived at and departed from this location. This makes it difficult to quantify whalers' calls at Cabinda: the logs do not always reveal whether a mooring constituted a scheduled visit or merely one of many stops along the humpbacking route. Since no consular files, newspapers or other sources from Cabinda itself exist for the period in question, there is no documentation against which the entries in the logs might be verified.

Palms and slavery

While there can be no doubt of Cabinda's significance to whalers, it remains to be established whether whalers were of significance to Cabinda. It was not one of the remote places so often favoured by whalers. At the time of the first whalers' arrival, Cabinda had already been a hub of Atlantic commerce – and the slave trade in particular – for more than two hundred years. In order to assess the importance of contacts with whalers to the local littoral society, it is accordingly necessary first to understand Cabinda's relations with the Atlantic sphere in their historical growth and the point they had reached during the whaling era. Perhaps the best historian of these developments is Phyllis Martin, and it is on her research that much of the following account relies.[31]

---

28 Log GLOBE, 1869–1872, Juni & Juli 1870; Log KATHLEEN, 1852–1855, 11.–13.08.1854; Log PAVILION, 1858–1860, 04.–10.08.1859; Log WAVE, 1869–1870, 16. & 17.07.1870.
29 Log PAVILION, 1858–1860, 21.08.1859.
30 Log SUNBEAM, 1878–1882, 13.08.1879; see also Log TRITON, 1868–1871, 11.09.1870.
31 Even before the emergence of a separatist movement in the mid-twentieth century, much of the historical writing on Cabinda addressed (implicitly or explicitly) the question of what

Portuguese navigators arrived at the Congo estuary in the 1480s and 1490s, establishing contacts that laid the foundations for the longstanding connection between Portugal and this coastal area. The elites of the Congo Empire, which had emerged south of the river in the fourteenth century, entered into close economic and political relations with the Portuguese. From the 1570s onwards, these relations increasingly took the shape of indirect colonial rule: Portugal erected forts along the coast and made viceregents of some local rulers while going to war against other who rejected Portuguese suzerainty. Cabinda was part of the Ngoyo Empire, which appears to have emerged to the north of the river around the year 1600, and was not directly affected by events in the south. The lower reaches of the Congo, several kilometres wide and populated with crocodiles and hippopotamuses, presented a virtually insuperable boundary.[32] The Ngoyo ruler was known as the *mangoyo* and, like several other west African potentates, was forbidden from laying eyes upon the sea, a taboo that limited his influence on the coast. He resided at Mbanza Ngoyo, situated some thirty kilometres or two days' march away from the coast on the fringes of the densely wooded Mayombe highlands, which in turn form part of the great central African rainforest. The Ngoyo state was represented in the bay by an overseer. This official, known as *mafouk* – or, depending on the source, as *mafuka, mafuk, mafouca* or *mambouk* – charged taxes and duties on commercial transactions, goods which he delivered annually to the *mangoyo*. Taking advantage of his powerful position, the *mafouk* was usually also a businessman in his own right, and the holders of this office soon became wealthy and influential personages.[33]

It was in the seventeenth century that Cabinda grew into a hub of Atlantic shipping. Portuguese slave ships began to visit the bay around 1670 and found middlemen willing to provide them with slaves in the form of prisoners, convicts and abductees from the savannas bordering the Congo Basin to the south. These middlemen acted as agents, wholesalers and interpreters, organising slave transports along two routes: the captives were either ferried across the river and then

---

state ought to rule Cabinda – if any. Narratives seeking to justify the Portuguese claim over the bay against other colonial powers emerged already in the eighteenth and nineteenth centuries and continue to shape the Lusophone debate. Alberto Oliveira Pinto published a critical examination of this discourse in 2006 under the title *Cabinda e as construções da sua história (1783–1887)*.

32 Martin, "The Cabinda Connection", 48–50; Newitt, "Angola in Historical Context", 20, 22f.; Volavka, *Crown and Ritual*, 104.

33 Martin, "Cabinda and Cabindans", 83; Martin, *The External Trade of the Loango Coast*, 97f.; Martin, "Family Strategies in Nineteenth-Century Cabinda", 69. The interdiction on rulers catching sight of the sea also applied in Dahomey, among other places. (Hargreaves, "The Atlantic Ocean in West African History", 8)

taken to Cabinda overland, or they were taken first to the coast and thence to Cabinda by sea. Both routes required boats, and slavery was instrumental in establishing a practice of coastal navigation that was to exert a lasting influence on life in the bay. The slave boats were built mainly of kapok timber and could carry up to two hundred passengers; some were fitted with sails made of raffia and the vines of climbing plants for rigging.[34] In order to protect their dominant position, the middlemen soon banned Europeans from taking up residence in the bay, the exception being a Dutch trading post which seems to have exited for a few years around 1670. The crews of the slave ships were even prohibited from spending the night ashore. Yet the middlemen were also aware of the importance of good personal relations with their trading partners. They learnt Portuguese, which soon became the lingua franca of commerce in the region, and sometimes saw to it that their sons received a European education. The first such case of which we know occurred in 1687, when a *mafouk* sent his son to school in England.[35]

In the late seventeenth century, Dutch, English, Spanish and French vessels began to sail for Cabinda, which by now was one of the principal harbours for the export of slaves south of the Gulf of Guinea, alongside Loango and Malemba. Although they broke Portugal's domination of the slave trade, no trading company succeeded in establishing a long-term monopoly in the area – not least owing to resistance on the part of the *mafouk*. In 1723 the British Royal African Company erected a fort in the bay only for it to be destroyed by Ngoyo and Portuguese soldiers that same year. In the following years Cabinda was increasingly visited by French slave ships from Nantes, which were looking to meet the growing demand for labour in France's Caribbean possessions. French gradually replaced Portuguese as the lingua franca in the bay, where up to twenty-three vessels lay at anchor at once in the 1770s – most of them, it is likely, French.[36] In 1783, however, Portugal dispatched four warships to Cabinda carrying some 400 soldiers and 150 tradesmen, who were tasked with monopolising the slave trade and building the fort of Santa Maria de Cabinda. This

---

34 Birmingham, *Trade and Conflict in Angola*, 156f.; Martin, "Cabinda and Cabindans", 82–85; Martin, "The Cabinda Connection", 51; Miller, *Way of Death*, 208–212; Newitt, "Angola in Historical Context", 28; Silva, *Dutch and Portuguese in Western Africa*, 172; Young, "Angola", 209.
35 Martin, "Cabinda and Cabindans", 85f.; Martin, *The External Trade of the Loango Coast*, 68.
36 Birmingham, *Trade and Conflict in Angola*, 157; Martin, *The External Trade of the Loango Coast*, 76–85; Martin, "Family Strategies in Nineteenth-Century Cabinda", 73; Vansina, *Paths in the Rainforests*, 204; Vaz, "The Trans-Atlantic Slave Trade and the African Origins of the Peoples of Grenada", 115–123.

plan, however, was thwarted by the resistance of Ngoyo, which made common cause with the French to destroy the fort in 1784.[37]

This situation benefited no one as much as it did the middlemen, who came to wealth and power while the slave trade – specifically, the loss of young people it caused – drained the interior economically and destabilised it both socially and politically. The middlemen controlled activities in the bay through kinship networks, the most important of which were the Nkata Kolombo, the Nsambo and the Npuna. The Nkata Kolombo ruled over the village of Taffe, which lay directly behind the entrance to the bay and hence was the first port of call for many vessels. On a slope rising above Taffe lay Chioua – the name translates as "great fish market" – a village controlled by the Nsambo. Chioua was the hub of trade with the interior and the best place from which the observe the movements of vessels in the bay. Some two kilometres to the south of Chioua, where Npuna ruled over the village of Simulambuco, the narrow Lukola Congo river flows into the Atlantic – a place much favoured by crews in search of drinking water.[38]

In exchange for their services and the use of the bay's material resources, the middlemen demanded barter goods, the lesser portion of which they passed on the *mangoyo* via the *mafouk*. Their economic power allowed them to forge relations of loyalty and dependence with followings of several hundred people each and thereby to form a political power base.[39] The fact that Ngoyo derived only a small profit from trade in the bay and was unable to control its middlemen effectively set in motion a gradual decline in the kingdom's fortunes in the late 1700s. As was the case elsewhere in Africa, the slave trade in Cabinda had allowed its middlemen to develop a state-like organisational structure. When, in the early nineteenth century, the office of *mangoyo* in Mbanza Ngoyo fell vacant without a successor, the middlemen and their families attained the peak of their power and exerted full and autonomous control over the bay.[40]

The policy of abolition which took hold in parts of the Atlantic World during the early 1800s brought about profound structural change in the slave trade.

---

37 Birmingham, *Trade and Conflict in Angola*, 157f.; Klein, *The Middle Passage*, 26; Klein, "The Portuguese Slave Trade From Angola in the Eighteenth Century", 896 n. 4; Martin, *The External Trade of the Loango Coast*, 87–91; Martin, "Family Strategies in Nineteenth-Century Cabinda", 73; Miller, Way of Death, 608–610; Newitt, "Angola in Historical Context", 39; Pinto, *Cabinda e as construções da sua história*, 219f.; Volavka, *Crown and Ritual*, 63.
38 Martin, "Family Strategies in Nineteenth-Century Cabinda", 67–69.
39 Martin, "The Cabinda Connection", 48; Martin, "Family Strategies in Nineteenth-Century Cabinda", 70f.
40 Martin, "Family Strategies in Nineteenth-Century Cabinda", 69f.

British pressure in particular meant that British, French and Dutch vessels all but ceased to sail into the bay. Their absence, however, was more than compensated by Brazilian and Cuban-Spanish slave ships, for the plantation economies of South America and the Caribbean continued to rely heavily on slavery and were experiencing a period of growth after the Haitian revolution, which had caused a decline in French sugar production. Ibero-Atlantic slavers now shifted their routes from the central to the south Atlantic, and Portuguese resumed its primacy as lingua franca in Cabinda, pushing out French.[41]

The growing importance of Brazil for trade in Cabinda brought a new generation of middlemen to influence.[42] A prime exponent was Francisco "Chico" Franque, whose father, a *mafouk*, had sent him to Brazil for his education. Taking advantage of his contacts there – in the following years, he would several times meet important slave traders and, on occasion in Rio de Janeiro, even the exiled prince regent of Portugal – Franque became the richest and most powerful man in Cabinda. Using his private army, he drove the Nsambo from Chioua, renaming it Porto Rico and establishing his own residence there on an elevation. Around its base there grew a considerable settlement of former slaves who had returned from Brazil and were now apparently in Franque's employ. This residence, grouped around an impressive central house, not only symbolised Franque's power but also served as a widely visible landmark for navigation. Unlike the early middleman elite, Franque allowed the establishment of trading posts in the bay – at least by Brazilian merchants – and maintained good relations with the Portuguese colonial authorities in the south. The governor in Luanda reciprocated by recognising him as "king" as well as appointing him a Portuguese honorary colonel, which allowed him to fly the Portuguese flag from his vessels and provide them with Portuguese papers, thereby reducing the likelihood of their being intercepted by British patrols.[43]

In spite of the increasing measures taken towards Abolition in the Atlantic World, the slave trade in Cabinda increased in volume after 1822. In that year, the government of Brazil, which had just won its independence from Portugal,

---

[41] Martin, "Family Strategies in Nineteenth-Century Cabinda", 71–80; Miller, *Way of Death*, 514f.; Strickrodt, "Die brasilianische Diaspora in Westafrika im 19. Jahrhundert", 199f.

[42] Of the estimated two million people who were enslaved in the area of modern Angola and transported across the Atlantic between the late sixteenth and the early nineteenth century, approximately one million ended up in Brazil. (Young, "Angola", 209)

[43] Bastian, *Die deutsche Expedition an der Loango-Küste*, vol. 1, 213; Martin, "Cabinda and Cabindans", 87; Kerdijk, *Reisjournaal van Lodewijk Kerdijk*, 115f.; Martin, "Family Strategies in Nineteenth-Century Cabinda", 71–80; Pinto, *Cabinda e as construções da sua história*, 219, 239; Volavka, *Crown and Ritual*, 63.

introduced an import duty on slaves. In order to cut costs, Brazilian vessels switched from the Portuguese-controlled ports of Luanda and Benguela, where they had to pay export duties, to Cabinda, which was not under Portuguese rule.[44] The fact that Cuba, Brazil, Spain and Portugal, under British pressure, prohibited the slave trade in increments between 1810 and 1842, did not at first put a stop to the trade but merely pushed it into illegality. An estimated 1,153,000 slaves crossed the Atlantic between 1821 and 1843, most of them to Brazil. During this period, Cabinda became the hub of the slave trade on the Loango coast. The majority of slaves brought to Rio de Janeiro in the 1820s and 1830s were taken there via Cabinda.[45] When, in January 1826, the British survey vessels *Leven* and *Barracouta* visited the bay, they found five slave ships lying at anchor there, four of them Brazilian.[46] "It is impossible for a vessel touching for a few hours, as we did, at Kabende, to obtain stock", complained Thomas Boteler, an officer aboard HMS *Barracouta*, "for it is an article of trade of such inferior consequence to slaves, ivory, or red wood, that few engage in it, and indeed those only who have not means to engage in any other traffic."[47]

An Anglo-Portuguese accord reached in 1817 gave the Royal Navy the right to search vessels sailing under the Portuguese flag that were suspected of carrying slaves – but not in the Bay of Cabinda itself.[48] The Palmerston Act of 1839, however, granted additional powers to Britain's naval squadrons in the fight against the slave trade and stepped up the pressure in Cabinda too. Henceforth slave ships would enter the bay only for the minimum time necessary to take on board their human cargo, and many sought moorings elsewhere, notably in the Congo estuary, whose dense mangrove forests made it hard to police. Since slaves could no longer be held in the bay itself, they were hidden away in fortified camps or "barracoons" two or three hours' march from the coast. In 1842 British forces found and destroyed five such barracoons holding a total of approximately 1,100 slaves; their suspected proprietor was Franque.[49]

---

44 Martin, "The Cabinda Connection", 52; Martin, "Family Strategies in Nineteenth-Century Cabinda", 73; Pinto, Cabinda e as construções da sua história, 224f.; Vansina, *Paths in the Rainforests*, 204.
45 Klein, *The Middle Passage*, 75; Martin, *The External Trade of the Loango Coast*, 144; Martin, "Family Strategies in Nineteenth-Century Cabinda", 73; Pinto, *Cabinda e as construções da sua história*, 215–218; Salau, "Illegal Slave Trade, Brazil"; Strickrodt, "Die brasilianische Diaspora in Westafrika im 19. Jahrhundert", 200; Stubbs, "Abolition of the Slave Trade, Brazil", 4.
46 Owen, *Narrative of Voyages to Explore the Shores of Africa, Arabia, and Madagascar*, vol. 2, 171.
47 Boteler, *Narrative of a Voyage of Discovery to Africa and Arabia*, vol. 2, 355.
48 Graham, *Great Britain in the Indian Ocean*, 113.
49 Martin, *The External Trade of the Loango Coast*, 144f.; Martin, "Family Strategies in Nineteenth-Century Cabinda", 73f.; Pinto, *Cabinda e as construções da sua história*, 236f., 246.

In spite of the increased pressure brought to bear by the Royal Navy, such middlemen as Franque or the heads of the Nkata Kolombo family continued to use their own fleets to traffic slaves for several years more. Other local potentates recognised that the slave trade was bound to decline and sought alternative sources of income. Manuel José Puna, for instance, the chief of the Npuna, hired out canoes to Portuguese small traders and generally made friendly overtures to the Portuguese: he sent both his sons to school in Coimbra, petitioned for Portuguese colonisation of Cabinda in 1853 and in 1871 travelled to Lisbon to meet the royal couple in person. Portugal rewarded him with the title "Baron of Cabinda" and other honorifics. Puna later broadened his power base in Cabinda by placing himself at the head of the ancient Ngoyo kingdom.[50]

Cabinda's slave trade finally collapsed in the mid-1860s. The Brazilian and Cuban traders had grown wary of the risk involved or had run up such debts that they were no longer able to pay the local middlemen.[51] The role of slaves as Cabinda's most lucrative export was soon taken over by palm products and palm oil in particular; other exports now included rubber, groundnuts, ivory, copal, coconuts, orcein and coffee. To take advantage of this trade, the first European companies set up branches in Cabinda (Fig. 32) and made their own arrangements for the transport of goods from the interior. Middlemen like Franque, who had invested in the slave trade to the last, were able only to draw limited profit from this trade. More successful were the Nkata Kolombo, who continued to levy fees from merchant vessels and leased land to European trading companies. A new generation of middlemen – including two of Franque's nephews – carved out a niche as suppliers and warehousemen to the Dutch *Afrikaansche Handelsvereeniging* or to the Liverpool-based company of Hatton & Cookson. Unlike the old slave trading elites, however, these new middlemen operated from a position of dependency and sometimes even as servants. In terms of wealth and influence, the end of the slave trade saw the elites of Cabinda relegated to the second division.[52]

---

50 Dennett, *Seven Years Among the Fjort*, 30f.; Martin, "Family Strategies in Nineteenth-Century Cabinda", 75f., 80, 83; Pinto, *Cabinda e as construções da sua história*, 228f., 237f., 240, 251–255; Volavka, *Crown and Ritual*, 65. Controversy surrounds the continued existence of Ngoyo as a state in the latter part of the nineteenth century; see Volavka, *Crown and Ritual*, 104f.

51 Martin, "Family Strategies in Nineteenth-Century Cabinda", 80. However, local potentates in Madeira continued to keep slaves. See e.g. Monteiro, *Angola and the River Congo*, vol. 1, 205 and Despatch 49/1883, National Archives and Records Administration, Records of Foreign Service Posts, Record Group 84, Loanda, vol. 004, Despatch Book, 1880–1892.

52 Dennett, *Seven Years Among the Fjort*, 28f.; Martin, "Cabinda and Cabindans", 87f.; Martin, *The External Trade of the Loango Coast*, 150–153; Martin, "Family Strategies in Nineteenth-Century Cabinda", 81f.; Pinto, *Cabinda e as construções da sua história*, 247–251. For a description of the premises of the *Afrikaansche Handelsvereeniging* in Cabinda see Bastian, *Die deutsche*

Fig. 32: A trading post in Cabinda drawn after a photograph from the 1880s.
Source: Dennett, *Seven Years Among the Fjort*, 2.

As a preliminary conclusion, it may be noted that when whaling took off in Cabinda in the 1850s, the bay underwent processes of profound economic diversification and political change. Phyllis Martin supposes that the local rulers welcomed whalers as potentially compensating for the decline of the slave trade. However, their strategy of charging high fees for drinking water, firewood and provisions only served to deter whalers, who ceased to visit the bay after about 1870 as a result.[53] Martin's conclusions are based on Portuguese sources and the observations of Europeans in the area, but not on documents left by the whalers themselves. In my account of the interaction between whalemen and the littoral society of Cabinda, I shall examine the question of whether Martin's interpretation can stand up when tested against the seafarers' own records.

Expedition an der Loango-Küste, vol. 1, 16. Consequential though it was, the establishment of a Portuguese protectorate over Cabinda falls outside the scope of the present discussion. It coincided – but was not connected – with the end of whaling in nearby waters. On the establishment of the Portuguese protectorate and the crucial Treaty of Simulambuco see esp. Martin, "The Cabinda Connection", 53 and Pinto, *Cabinda e as construções da sua história*, 255–269.
53 Martin, "Family Strategies in Nineteenth-Century Cabinda", 81.

Before attempting to answer this question, I should point out that the economy of Cabinda's littoral society, while geared towards the slave trade, was by no means limited to it. Not only were manioc, maize, peas, beans, bananas and other crops grown in the area, but seventeenth-century accounts already tell of a successful fishing industry. Every morning, hundreds of men took to the sea in dugout canoes to catch sardines, breams, rays and even sharks, using – either singly or in combination – nets, spears, basket traps and fishing lines. The resulting catch was not for subsistence alone but was also sold to the neighbouring Mayombe highlands. Besides fish, the people of Cabinda also sold salt to communities in the interior, which they produced by evaporating sea water in large pans. The local rulers maintained a strict monopoly over the salt trade in the bay and punished any unlicensed dealings.[54]

Cabinda also maintained maritime trading connections with neighbouring societies, though they were long overshadowed by the slave trade. Exports included redwood, copper and raffia clothing. The local men were considered skilled boatbuilders and coastal navigators. Perhaps taking their inspiration from the slave ships they saw in the bay, in the nineteenth century they built not only rowing boats but also ocean-going two-mast schooners or *palhabotes* weighing up to thirty tons.[55]

In the mid nineteenth-century Taffe, the most densely populated section of the bay, had an estimated population of five to six thousand – about half the area's total. Villages emerged from the forest that reached up to the beach at many points without ever joining up to form a town.[56] For the local population, the sea was not merely a reservoir of material resources. Water in general and the sea in particular had in important part to play in the way littoral societies in west central Africa made sense of life and the world, in how they perceived and explained nature and the cosmos, and in the meaning they gave to elemental experiences. Rivers, lagoons and the ocean were home to a variety of sacred or divine beings, such as Tchiama, the holy snake, or Yemaja, the mother of god in Yorùbá mythology.[57] Much research has been done on the meaning of the sea to the BaKongo and the BaWoyo – to which the littoral society of Cabinda

---

54 Barbot/Casseneuve, "A Voyage to Congo River", 511; Bastian, *Die deutsche Expedition an der Loango-Küste*, vol. 1, 76; Martin, "Cabinda and Cabindans", 80–82, 58; Martin, "Family Strategies in Nineteenth-Century Cabinda", 69; Pinto, *Cabinda e as construções da sua história*, 226.
55 Martin, "Cabinda and Cabindans", 82, 88f.
56 Martin, "Family Strategies in Nineteenth-Century Cabinda", 65. For a list of individual places found in Cabinda in 1873 see Bastian, *Die deutsche Expedition an der Loango-Küste*, vol. 1, 213–215.
57 Nehusi, "Water", 708; Volavka, *Crown and Ritual*, 68.

belonged – most notably by the missionary and ethnographer Karl Edvard Laman, the social anthropologist Wyatt MacGaffey and Kimbwandènde Kia Bunseki Fu-Kiau, a specialist in cultural studies.[58] Although their findings do not apply specifically to Cabinda but, insofar as they can be localised, to neighbouring parts of Zaire lowlands, according to Phyllis Martin they largely apply to Cabinda too.

To put it in somewhat simplified terms, the people of Cabinda viewed the universe as comprising two parts: this world was inhabited by human beings, the other world by their spirits and ancestors. The barrier between the two worlds was the sea, while rivers, lakes and other bodies of water acted as intermediaries of various kinds.[59] For instance, one sacred place, the shrine of Lusunsi, was situated on a stream in the northern part of Cabinda. Lusunsi was an ancestral deity who ruled over the sea, wind and rain, over fishing and also over navigation. Any designated Ngoyo ruler had to commune with Lusunsi before taking office. This communion took the form of two ceremonies performed with the aspirant at the shrine by the rain priest. The votary offerings and royal insignia kept there by the rain priest included two large iron anchors which had evidently been salvaged from shipwrecks.[60]

The question of how cosmological ideas – regarding, for instance, the workings of Lusunsi – might have influenced littoral societies in their interactions with seafarers has been much discussed by scholars. One of MacGaffey's principal claims, for instance, is that the BaKongo considered the European who arrived aboard ships to be *simbi*, that is, spirits of the dead which had crossed over from the realm of their ancestors.[61] As late as 1826, a local potentate asked British seamen to act out their own death, as his own people were unwilling to believe that white men could die.[62] The idea that European actors were messengers from the hereafter was to prove consequential not only in the early stages of missionary activity and Christianisation but also for the slave

---

[58] The key works of these authors on this topic are Fu-Kiau, *African Cosmology of the Bântu-Kângo*; Laman, *The Kongo*; MacGaffey, *Religion and Society in Central Africa*; MacGaffey, "The West in Congolese Experience". For ethnographic accounts from the era of whaling in the bay see Bastian, *Die deutsche Expedition an der Loango-Küste*, vol. 1, 76–78, 164f., 182, 214f., 242f.; Bastian, *Die deutsche Expedition an der Loango-Küste*, vol. 2, 166f., 170, 231; Dennett, *Seven Years Among the Fjort*, 10f. and Monteiro, *Angola and the River Congo*, vol. 1, 254.
[59] Martin, "Cabinda and Cabindans", 83.
[60] Volavka, *Crown and Ritual*, 11f., 57., 86, 120–123; see also Bastian, *Die deutsche Expedition an der Loango-Küste*, vol. 1, 219, 224; Bastian, *Die deutsche Expedition an der Loango-Küste*, vol. 2, 171.
[61] MacGaffey, "Dialogues of the Deaf", 257, 267.
[62] Boteler, *Narrative of a Voyage of Discovery to Africa and Arabia*, vol. 2, 357.

trade in the area. Since, however, commerce with whalers in Cabinda was controlled by an elite whose conduct was shaped by long experience of dealing with European actors (and sometimes by travelling to Europe) and thus may be said to have conformed to Max Weber's idea of instrumental rationality, I will pursue this aspect no further. Whether or not whaleships and whalemen were taken for *simbi* appears to have had no bearing on the contact situations as they played out on the beach – at least none that left its mark in the sources.[63]

Mention has already been made of how slave traders were pushed into illegality by abolitionist measures. Visiting seamen were well aware of what was going on in Cabinda, sometimes being eyewitnesses to clandestine operations: "They took on about 450 and [. . .] weighed anchor and stood to sea", Joseph Underwood recorded in the log of the *Sea Eagle* of Boston in 1845. "She was just one hour and 35 minutes from the time she anchored taking on board a load of slaves and getting under weigh again. Quick work. It's a pity such smart people are not engaged in better business."[64] In 1858 the men of the *John and Edward* of New Bedford observed a coaster of the type used for slave-running by Franque.[65] Such incidental remarks as Underwood's aside, the records reveal no value judgements with regard to slavery. Most follow the pattern of the following entry in the log of the barque *Louisa Sears* of Edgartwon, which encountered a suspected slave ship near Cabinda in April 1857: "At 2 P.M. saw a Topsail Schooner soposed her to be a Slaver bound towards the coast of Africa."[66]

However, whalers in Cabinda were witnesses not only to the slave trade but also to its suppression. When the *Louisa Sears* once more put in at Cabinda, in September 1857, her crew heard of three slave ships that had recently been seized there. This may have been the cause of a dispute aboard the *Petrel*, a merchant vessel anchored alongside the *Louisa Perry*, with the whaler's log recording how "the second mate off the bark Pettrel was put a shore becaus he wouldent agree to take Slaves".[67] On a stopover at Cabinda in 1854, the barque *Kathleen* of New Bedford received a visit from the captain of a slaver that had

---

[63] This may be the place to remark that for their part, whalemen did not consistently obey the dictates of instrumental rationality while calling at Cabinda. Writing in the log of the *Nye* of Dartmouth, which lay at Cabinda in October 1855, John Howland remarked: "Got some trade the sabath is not respected here". (Log NYE, 1853–1856, 07.10.1855)

[64] Quoted in Brooks, *Yankee Traders, Old Coasters, and African Middlemen*, 114. Since she arrived at Cabinda in January and is not mentioned in any of the reference works on American whaling, the *Sea Eagle* is likely to have been a merchantman rather than a whaler.

[65] Log JOHN & EDWARD, 1855–1858, 30.07.1858.

[66] Log LOUISA SEARS, 1856–1858, 04.04.1857.

[67] Log LOUISA SEARS, 1856–1858, 18. & 20.09.1857.

been impounded by the Royal Navy. Having apparently escaped arrest, the skipper was now stranded in Cabinda.[68] Whalers in Cabinda would often observe British warships on anti-slave-trade patrols[69] and sometimes the seizure of a slave ship. In 1859 one captain of the Royal Navy even allowed the crews of the *Globe* of New Bedford and the *Keoka* of Westport to loot a slave ship before having it scuttled.[70]

The records contain only one reference to American whalers dabbling in the slave trade themselves. In 1865 an American seaman, Edward Baxter, appeared before the Portuguese authorities in Moçâmedes, a colonial outpost on the southern coast of what is now Angola. Baxter had escaped from the *Governor Carver*, a Westport whaling bark, and now accused Thomas Percy, her captain, of having taken on board slaves in the bay. The Portuguese, however, charged Baxter with making false accusations and threw him into gaol, where he contracted a severe fever. After five months, he was handed over to the American consul in Luanda, who considered Baxter to be a deserter and sentenced him to another spell in prison.[71] In the absence of other sources relating to this case, Baxter's accusation is impossible to verify or refute.

"Paying them their price and waiting their time"

"Have to give presents to King Jack, Kinge Fine, & the Governer", notes the log of the barque *Cicero* of New Bedford, which arrived at Cabinda in 1875.[72] The log of the barque *Nye* of Dartmouth, which called in 1855, her log records that she had "had a visel from the kings of Kabenda."[73] This was not the *Nye*'s first visit to Cabinda. She had already put in there during the previous humpbacking season and on that occasion received several eminent personages, first "King Jack, king of Kabenda", and later "comodore port", who demanded a mooring fee.[74]

---

68 Log KATHLEEN, 1852–1855, 04. & 05.08.1854. The Dutch merchant Lodewijk Kerdijk also records meeting two slave captains who had lost their vessels in Cabinda in 1857. (Kerdijk, *Reisjournaal van Lodewijk Kerdijk*, 114)
69 See e.g. Log MORNING STAR, 1883–1888, 02.10.1885.
70 Log GLOBE, 1858–1861, 18.08.1859; Log KEOKA, 1858–1860, 18.08.1858.
71 Despatches 20 & 22/1866. National Archives and Records Administration, Records of Foreign Service Posts, Record Group 84, Loanda, vol. 002, Despatch Book, 1864–1879.
72 Log CICERO, 1874–1875, 22.06.1875.
73 Log NYE, 1853–1856, 07.10.1855.
74 Ibid., 08.08.1854.

Sailors who came to Cabinda found it to be the done thing for several dignitaries to call upon them at once,[75] though we also hear of captains going ashore to visit them. "I went on shore and called on the King, where I received very greate attention. I think he (King Porter) is as good a man as Kabenda can produce", reads an entry in the log of the *John and Edward* of New Bedford, which lay at Cabinda in September 1858.[76] Mariners had little idea just who exactly these men were and what their function was. Four names that keep cropping up in the records are "King Jack" (or "Prince Jack"), "King Fine", "King Porter" (or "Commodore Port") and the "governor". It seems that all these names in fact denoted titles of authority and that, for instance, the "King Jack" of 1880 was not the same person who had held that title in 1860. These men usually met a captain with several of their men in attendance. They dressed in such western garments as frock coats and hats and might further underscore their wealth by adding highly polished shoes, brass buttons, coloured scarves or wigs to their attire.[77] In 1859 seamen found themselves faced with a man whose suit was made of a Union Jack.[78] In his diary, Robert Ferguson, who came to Cabinda aboard the *Kathleen* in 1882, describes the appearance of one such potentate as follows:

> One [canoe] came alongside with a great chief in it, all decorated up with a battered high hat on his head. The band on the hat was a red ribbon and on the side was the wing of some brilliant bird. His coat was a British soldier's red coat with a pipe-clayed belt. For pants he wore a pair of woman's drawers with ruffles on them. He had on a pair of large gum boots with brass spurs on his heels. He wore a collar that once was white but now was far from being clean. There were medals of brass and silver on the breast of his coat. On the shoulders, hanging down in front, were old-fashioned epaulets. He was the big chief and would allow no one to board the ship until he led them. Captain Howland invited him on board. Evidently they had met before because the chief said, "How do you do, Captain Howler."[79]

According to Phyllis Martin, both "King Jack" and "King Fine" were representatives of the Nkata Kolombo family, which controlled the coastal village of Taffe and hence that section of the bay in which most crews first made landfall. The power of the Nkata Kolombo rested on two main pillars. First, they acted as

---

75 See e.g. Boteler, *Narrative of a Voyage of Discovery to Africa and Arabia*, vol. 2, 349f.
76 Log JOHN & EDWARD, 1855–1858, 27.09.1858.
77 Boteler, *Narrative of a Voyage of Discovery to Africa and Arabia*, vol. 2, 349; Kerdijk, *Reisjournaal van Lodewijk Kerdijk*, 117; Smith, Journal NAUTILUS, 1869–1874, 03.08.1871.
78 Log U.S.S. MARION, 43f.
79 Ferguson, *Harpooner*, 136f. For another description of a Cabindan ruler, this one dating from 1826, see Boteler, *Narrative of a Voyage of Discovery to Africa and Arabia*, vol. 2, 351f.

middlemen for trade in Cabinda and for the slave trade in particular. It was in their canoes, for instance, that slaves were carried onto vessels. Second, Nkata Kolombo men periodically held the office of *mafouk*, the local representative of the Ngoyo state. Although Ngyoyo was in decline during the period of whaling in the bay, the *mafouk* still commanded a certain authority, levying fees from moored vessels and engaging in commerce. Representatives of European powers who came to Cabinda with a cause to plead – measures towards ending the slave trade, for instance – usually negotiated with the *mafouk*, thereby bolstering the position of the Nkata Kolombo.[80]

Cabinda offered ample drinking water, particularly during the periods when it was frequented by whalers – that is, the rainy season, the months of the southern winter known locally as *vou vulu* or *tepamvulu*, the "wet half of the year".[81] A crew looking to obtain water, however, had another family to deal with. The mouth of the Lukola Congo river, known as the best watering place in Cabinda, was ruled by Npuna in the village Simulambuco. The family belonged to the Ngoyo elite but was involved in the slave trade to a lesser degree than the Franques or the Nkata Kolombo. Its most influential member in the mid-nineteenth century was probably Manuel José Puna, who – like Francisco Franque – had spent his youth in Brazil.[82] Franque himself had driven the Nsambo from Chioua in mid-nineteenth century and to the end of his life remained one of the most powerful figures in Cabinda. No sooner had a vessel entered Taffe Point, the entrance to the bay, than its crew could see Franque's great house on the hillside. He or one of his proxies may indeed have been the unspecified "governor" mentioned in several logbooks – Franque had after all had himself declared the Portuguese representative in Cabinda by the colonial authorities in Luanda.[83]

We owe one of the rare accounts of a meeting with Franque to the merchant Lodewijk Kerdijk of Rotterdam, who visited Porto Rico in 1857. In his diary Kerdijk recounts how Franque received him at home, himself seated on a chair and surrounded by slaves and other subordinates lying on mats at his feet. Franque wore none of the insignia typically sported by west African potentates, appearing instead in boots, white trousers, a plain grey jacket and a black tie – the style, in other words, usually worn by his American and European trading partners. He struck Kerdijk as resembling "een meester timmerman in zondags kleederen" ("a master carpenter in his Sunday best") – all the more so for having

---

[80] Martin, "Family Strategies in Nineteenth-Century Cabinda", 67–69, 77, 79; Pinto, *Cabinda e as construções da sua história*, 230–236, 240.
[81] Bastian, *Die deutsche Expedition an der Loango-Küste*, vol. 2, 231f.
[82] Martin, "Family Strategies in Nineteenth-Century Cabinda", 67–69, 79f.
[83] Ibid., 71–80.

put up pictures of Catholic saints in his house. No women were to be seen in this house, and it seemed to Kerdijk that they were banned from entering it, being confined instead to a number of huts at the rear of Franque's estate.[84]

As a rule, however, Cabinda's various rulers visited newly arrived vessels in person rather than receiving their captains ashore. Sometimes they went aboard a vessel individually, sometimes as a group. When "Prince Jack" called upon the British survey vessels *Leven* and *Barracouta* in 1826, he came with six of his daughters.[85] On each occasion, the shipmaster was asked to pay a mooring fee, the size of which and the manner of its payment were up for negotiation. One constant was that payment was always in kind, never in cash. And nearly always (there were exceptions) did captains find the rulers' demands to be excessive: "The head men of Kabendy cum on Board for poart Charges in the way of Cloth Musketts and Bread & & wich cum to a great sum in all", noted the log of the brig *Leonidas* of Westport in 1856.[86] For a stopover in Cabinda in March 1879, Captain Ricketson of the schooner *Pedro Varela* of New Bedford paid a total of 82 yards of cotton fabric, 16 pounds of tobacco, 30 pounds of soap, three pen-knives and sixteen pipes.[87] Another visit in the following year was paid for with 82 yards of cotton fabric, 10 pounds of tobacco, 25 pounds of soap, three pen-knives and thirty-six pipes.[88] By contrast, Robert Ferguson found Captain Howland of the *Kathleen* to have struck an advantageous deal with a local ruler in 1882: "All he got did not amount to five dollars' worth, but he went away well pleased."[89]

In return for their payments, shipmasters were entitled, for the duration of their stay, to engage in commerce and to gather drinking water and firewood. "Two days after the King's visit, the vessel paid his representative thirty fathoms of blue cloth for the privilege of cutting wood, procuring water, and trading for recruits", writes Carl Haywood with regard to the visit of the *Nye* in 1854.[90] What many captains did not at first realise was that additional charges might be incurred when actually taking advantage of these rights, particularly when it came to water and firewood. The local rulers clearly tried to draw the utmost material advantage from the whalers' visits, in which they evidently saw an opportunity to make up – at least in part – for the loss of the lucrative

---

84 Kerdijk, *Reisjournaal van Lodewijk Kerdijk*, 115–119.
85 Owen, *Narrative of Voyages to Explore the Shores of Africa, Arabia, and Madagascar*, vol. 2, 171.
86 Log LEONIDAS, 1855–1857, 01.12.1856.
87 Log PEDRO VARELA, 1881–1883.
88 Ibid.
89 Ferguson, *Harpooner*, 136f.
90 Haywood, "American Whalers and Africa", 72; see also Ferguson, *Harpooner*, 136f.

slave trade.[91] A group of German scientists who planned to open a research station near the Congo estuary in mid-1870s ultimately decided against Cabinda, finding it to be "swarming [. . .] with an infestation of princes", against whose unreasonable demands the Germans had no recourse.[92]

What kind of trade did whalemen engage in once they had obtained the license to do so from the rulers of Cabinda? In the case of the schooner *Pedro Varela* of New Bedford, which put in to the bay in 1879 and 1880, in each case at the beginning of the humpbacking season, the log provides an detailed account:

Tab. 7: Provisioning of the *Pedro Varela* in Cabinda.

March 1879	April 1880
Cargo loaded:	*Cargo loaded:*
4,050 sticks wood	4,050 sticks wood
400 ears corn	600 ears corn
192 eggs	600 oranges
150 oranges	204 eggs
96 chickens	84 chickens
72 bunches bananas	70 pumpkins
60 pumpkins	60 bananas
25 bushels sweet potatoes	60 ducks
18 ducks	8 bushels sweet potatoes
2 goats	1 goat
Cargo unloaded:	*Cargo unloaded:*
300 yards unbleached cotton cloth	317 yards bleached cotton cloth
252 yards printed cotton cloth	218 yards unbleached cotton cloth
139 yards bleached cotton cloth	22 yards blue twill
18 yards blue cotton cloth	50 yards printed cotton cloth

Source: Log PEDRO VARELA, 1881–1883.

Provisions and firewood for cloth – that, in simplified terms, was the pattern of the barter in which Captain Ricketson engaged in Cabinda. The local demand for textiles is also evident from other vessels' records. In August 1854 Frederick Howland, captain of the *Nye*, traded in calico (as well as soap) for oranges, bananas, pigs and chickens.[93] Cloth had already stood in for currency at the height of the slave trade, accounting for up to eighty per cent of the barter goods imported by

---

91 Martin, "Family Strategies in Nineteenth-Century Cabinda", 81.
92 Bastian, *Die deutsche Expedition an der Loango-Küste*, vol. 1, 26.
93 Log NYE, 1853–1856, 10. & 11.08.1854.

slave ships. The importance of cotton clothing, known locally as *peças de facenda*,[94] derived from their function as status markers. By wearing *peças de facenda*, the Cabindan population set itself apart from slaves and inhabitants of the hinterland alike, the latter dressing mainly in the fibres of the raffia palm. To wear *peças de facenda* meant signalling one's own success, specifically one's access to commodities imported from faraway places, and by extension one's power or nearness to power. Even dowries were usually paid in *peças de facenda* at this time.[95] Local merchants evidently took advantage of whalers to maintain the supply of cottons even after the end of the slave trade. Whaleships also brought everyday commodities such as soap, knives and hatches, all for barter – there are no records of cash payments.[96]

As far as provisions were concerned, the single most important commodity – at least by volume – were oranges. "Plenty of oranges but not much of any other fruit", records the log of the barque *Adeline Gibbs* of New Bedford, which lay in Cabinda in 1877.[97] During one visit in 1870, the *Globe* of New Bedford took on a cargo of some 1,100 oranges.[98] Other items that were frequently acquired included sweet potatoes, maize, pumpkins, groundnuts and yams as well as fruit and livestock, as the records of the *Pedro Varela* show.[99] For captains to buy fish to add to their crews' diet was, by contrast, something of a rarity.[100]

The victualling trade in Cabinda appears to have been organised by small traders, though it is unclear in what relation they stood to particular rulers and whether they paid them taxes or similar fees. When the *Kathleen* dropped anchor in the bay in 1854, she was welcomed by thirty *malungu*. Vendors from these craft came aboard to sell oranges, groundnuts, pineapples, plantains and lemons as well as pigs, goats, parrots and monkeys.[101] The log of the *Nye*, which also visited in 1854, records: "Had lots of canoes of to trad fruit &c."[102]

---

94 Travassos Valdez, *Six Years of a Traveller's Life in Western Africa*, vol. 2, 73.
95 Boteler, *Narrative of a Voyage of Discovery to Africa and Arabia*, vol. 2, 356f.; Martin, "Cabinda and Cabindans", 92; Martin, *The External Trade of the Loango Coast*, 107–109, 112; Martin, "Power, Cloth and Currency on the Loango Coast", 5–8; Owen, *Narrative of Voyages to Explore the Shores of Africa, Arabia, and Madagascar*, vol. 2, 173; Travassos Valdez, *Six Years of a Traveller's Life in Western Africa*, vol. 2, 73f.
96 Haywood, "American Whalers and Africa", 73f.
97 Log ADELINE GIBBS, 1875–1878, 01.08.1877.
98 Allen, Journal GLOBE, 1869–1872, 09.08.1870.
99 See e.g. Log GLOBE, 1855–1857, 02.07.1856; McCormick, *Two New Bedford Whalemen*, 175, 10.08.1869.
100 See e.g. Log JOHN & EDWARD, 1855–1858, 26.09.1858.
101 Log KATHLEEN, 1852–1855, 04. & 05.08.1854.
102 Log NYE, 1853–1856, 06.08.1854.

Lucy Smith in 1871 noted how vendors boarded the *Nautilus* to sell fruit,[103] as did the log of the *John and Edward* in 1858, which records: "Traded a little with a few Natives who came on board for that purpose."[104]

The *malungus* used by these traders were up to nine metres long; sometimes two would be lashed together to form a single vessel. Some of the traders knew English, but all spoke Portuguese. Since, by the mid-1800s, there was scarcely an American whaler whose crew did not number at least one Portuguese speaker, communication presented few difficulties.[105] It seems that the trade may have become more centralised in later years: when the barque *Bertha* of New Bedford was moored in the bay in July 1880, she was visited by only one vendor per day.[106] Not all Cabindan *malungu* approached whalers to sell provisions: if a vessel was flensing a humpback carcass at the time, locals might seek to buy whale meat.[107] We also hear of rare instances of Cabindan men offering their services as pilots to guide whaleships through the bay's shallows and rocks.[108]

Captains differed in their assessments of the business done in the bay. "Several Natives visited the vessel – brought off some Fowls, Yams, Egges, &c but they asked such an exharegent price for that I did not buy much", records the log of the *John and Edward* of one transaction near Cabinda in September 1858.[109] Nor did her master find commerce in the bay itself to be any more satisfactory, describing the local merchants as dishonest.[110] The log of the *Desdemona*, by contrast, had at least one positive thing to say about the local population in October 1875: "Our Kabenda stay having got the best recruit taken on the voyage."[111]

While captains were busy acquiring food, water and firewood, many seamen took advantage of a visit to Cabinda, with its many species of birds and monkeys, to acquire exotic pets.[112] "One of the Boatsteerers bought a monkey,

---

103 Smith, Journal NAUTILUS, 1869–1874, 02.08.1871.
104 Log JOHN & EDWARD, 1855–1858, 26.09.1858; see also Ferguson, *Harpooner*, 136f.; Log GLOBE, 1869–1872, 07.08.1870; Log WAVE, 1869–1870, 15. & 16.07.1870.
105 Ferguson, *Harpooner*, 136f.; Monteiro, *Angola and the River Congo*, vol. 1, 143.
106 Log BERTHA, 1878–1881, 13.07.1880.
107 Ferguson, *Harpooner*, 192f.
108 Log LEONIDAS, 1855–1857, 30.11. & 08.12.1856.
109 Log JOHN & EDWARD, 1855–1858, 25.09.1858.
110 Ibid., 26.09.1858.
111 Log DESDEMONA, 1873–1876, 25.10.1875.
112 Monteiro, *Angola and the River Congo*, vol. 1, 53f. The souvenirs from this part of the coast brought home to New England by seamen also included hippopotamus, elephant and sperm whale tusks decorated with engravings. Specimens are preserved in such collections as that of

Capt would have got a Parrot", noted Lucy Smith in 1871 aboard the *Nautilus*.[113] "There is nothing doing but trading with the natives for fancy grass mats, parrots, monkeys, chickens, and small pigs", observed Robert Ferguson of the *Kathleen* in 1882, adding that "Sailors will make pets of almost any living thing."[114] For his own part, Ferguson acquired a parrot, but his colleagues went further: "The ship looks like a menagerie; large and small monkeys, some black and some grey; fifteen or twenty parrots; a lot of parakeets, chickens, ducks, and at least six small black pigs. The cooper has a dozen small singing birds. One of the Portuguese has the ugliest-looking owl that I ever saw."[115] This acquisitiveness with regard to animals seems to have been something of a tradition aboard the *Kathleen*, on whose maiden voyage in 1854 the crew had bought a total of thirty-five chickens, fourteen pigs, twelve parrots and five goats in Cabinda.[116] Other vessels' crews took similar advantage of visits to the bay.[117] The local population did not, however, keep cattle, and sheep were hard to come by.[118]

Crews obtained drinking water obtained above all from the Lukola Congo river, which flows into the Atlantic in the south of the bay. Although the Lukola was easily accessible and carried ample water, seamen did not always have an easy time filling their casks with it since the Npuna, who controlled the mouth of the river, levied fees for doing so. This was not itself an unfamiliar practice in many places visited by whalemen. In Cabinda, however, many captains took exception to it, having already paid a substantial fee to a representative of the Nkata Kolombo which was supposed to cover water. The fact that different sections of the bay were under the control of different rulers was at odds with the experience and expectations of most captains – at least of those captains who were not already familiar with Cabinda and its ways and who had not been told what to expect there.

"Sent a raft of cask on shore, but was not allowed to take it off until the Capt of the Port had been onboard & received the Port charges", records the log of the *John and Edward* in September 1858. Before the men were allowed to fill the casks, Captain Smith had to receive three Npuna delegates, whom he paid one

---

the New Bedford Whaling Museum, but the origin of individual items is usually impossible to establish. (Stuart Sherman, personal communication to the author, 04.05.2010)

113 Smith, Journal NAUTILUS, 1869–1874, 03.08.1871.
114 Ferguson, *Harpooner*, 136f.
115 Ibid., 145.
116 Log KATHLEEN, 1852–1855, 10.08.1854.
117 See e.g. Log GLOBE, 1869–1872, 08.08.1870.
118 Boteler, *Narrative of a Voyage of Discovery to Africa and Arabia*, vol. 2, 356.

musket, six pieces of strip iron and twenty shawls and other items of clothing. "They wanted [. . .] more but I would not give it to them", noted Smith.[119] Negotiating a price and loading the water kept the *John and Edward* in port for two days.[120] At another time and in another place such a delay need not have been a problem, but in September, as the humpback whaling season was drawing to a close, every day lost was an immense annoyance.

The Npuna rulers knew that whalemen were in a hurry – and sought to capitalise on this knowledge. An instance of their strategy of exacting high fees for drawing water is recorded in the log of the *President II* of New Bedford, which came to Cabinda in June 1876. "Capt. went ashore to see the Goverer and Kings about getting water. Had considerable trouble." The log continues: "They went to the value of $20. for the privilege of getting water one barrel or 500. They want Bread, Flour, Butter, Sugar, Soap, Tobacco, Cloth, &c. The four Kings, for the privilege of trading, and take their time to get it."[121] Whalers like the *President II*, which urgently needed fresh water after weeks of humpbacking and were loath to waste a day while the season continued, often had no choice but to accede to Npuna demands. After all, they had just sailed along the coast of what is now Angola, an area with very few accessible watering places, and many captains knew of no reliable alternative to Cabinda in the area. Again, the local rulers were able to take advantage of their virtual monopoly. Although her captain, William Robinson, at first refused to pay the asking price, the crew of the *President II* was in urgent need of water. After a few days later, Robinson once more went ashore to negotiate. "Today they concluded to let us get water after detaining us until 2 P.M. Had to give them one Barrell of molasses, about 200 lbs Bread, 5 pieces of meat, 6 lbs of Tobacco, and various other things. But we must have some water as it would use up so much time to go to some other place for it", is how the log records the outcome. The stay at Cabinda left Robinson with a sour taste: "It is a very poor place for a whaler. Although you can get wood and water by paying them their price and waiting their time."[122]

Some whalers tried to avoid payment by drawing water without the consent of the Npuna – who, however, would not stand for any such attempts. "Sent a boat & crew to fill the casks with water [. . .] the Natives came down and took the Boat & every thing in her and wouldn't give them", was the experience of the *Bertha* in 1880. Her captain was the same William Robinson who had commanded the *President II* on her visit to Cabinda in 1876. Over the next few days,

---

119 Log JOHN AND EDWARD, 1855–1858, 24.09.1858.
120 Ibid., 26.09.1858.
121 Quoted in Haywood, "American Whalers and Africa", 73.
122 Quoted ibid.

Robinson had to go ashore repeatedly to negotiate a payment to the local "Kings" in exchange for the return of the boat and the permission to take water.[123] In the case of the *George and Mary* of New Bedford, which came to Cabinda in November 1878, the rulers impounded the casks rather than the boat. "One the Kings took the Casks from us and turned the Water Out", the log records.[124] The same thing happened to the crew of the barque *Desdemona* of New Bedford, which came to fill its casks in August 1874.[125]

Whalers in Cabinda were charged not only for drinking water but also for firewood. Indeed, since many whaleships had had their tryworks in operation for weeks on end, their need for wood was often even greater than that for water. Some vessels stopped for wood alone.[126] Whalemen coming to the bay for the first time may have been surprised by the steep prices charged and their unrelenting enforcement by the Npuna, but this was nothing new in Cabinda. As early as the eighteenth century we hear slave traders complaining of the sanctions with which local rulers responded to any attempts at avoiding payment.[127]

Amid its terminal decline in the final third of the nineteenth century, the American whaling industry concentrated its efforts on humpback whaling. In view of Cabinda's importance as a centre for these operations and probably also in response to the difficulties of provisioning there at reasonable prices, in 1878 New Bedford shipowners began regularly – albeit not annually – to send a tender to the bay. The vessel in question was the *Lottie Beard*, a three-mast schooner that also called at St Helena and sometimes Luanda (Fig. 33). This tender acted as a kind of floating base, supplying whalers in the bay with food, tools, parts and firewood. It may seem absurd to hear of wood being transported over thousands of miles from Massachusetts to what was, after all, one of the most densely wooded places whalers were likely to find on the African coast.[128] Yet such was the expense of putting in at Cabinda that shipowners must have thought it made economic sense. Before returning home to New Bedford, the *Lottie Beard* took on board barrels of whale oil and baleen, thereby freeing up space aboard the whaleships themselves and allowing them to spend longer working the whaling grounds. The schooner also carried passengers in both directions, for instance captains' wives who accompanied their

---

123 Log BERTHA, 1878–1881, 22.–24.10.1880.
124 Log GEORGE AND MARY, 1877–1879, 07.11.1878.
125 Log DESDEMONA, 1873–1876, 18.08.1874.
126 See e.g. Log SEA FOX, 1871–73. 08.–11.08.1873.
127 Martin, "Cabinda and Cabindans", 82.
128 Owen, *Narrative of Voyages to Explore the Shores of Africa, Arabia, and Madagascar*, vol. 2, 172.

husbands for only part of the voyage or discharged seamen on their way back to North America.

The first season in which the *Lottie Beard* is recorded as having sailed for Cabinda is that of 1878, the last that of 1886. The schooner would usually arrive in the bay in September or October, towards the end of the humpback whaling season (Tab. 8). Since whaleships out in pursuit of humpbacks often encountered one another – whether hunting off the coast of Angola or during a stopover in Jamestown – news of the tender's movements spread rapidly, and captains may indeed have been informed of her schedule before they set sail. The log of the *Sunbeam* for 7 October 1880 records "10 ships here waiting for Lottie Beard". She arrived in the bay three days later.[129]

Tab. 8: Number of American whalers in Cabinda during a visit by the *Lottie Beard*.

24 October to 11 November 1878	8
10 October to 20 October 1879	7
10 October to 25 October 1880	12
? September to ? September 1881	15
? September to 7 October 1885	5
14 September to 30 September 1886	7

Source: figures compiled from logbooks

Come September or October of the years in which she sailed for Cabinda, the *Lottie Beard* exerted a magnetic pull on the American humpback whaling fleet in the Atlantic. Fifteen whaleships lay in Cabinda in September 1881, more than ever before or since. Whalers that transhipped their catch to the tender remained in the bay for longer than in previous years. The *Sunbeam*, for instance, stopped for only one day in July 1881 to replenish its stores of firewood – in October of that year, by contrast, when the *Lottie Beard* was present, she stayed for two weeks.[130] Other whalers even spent four weeks in Cabinda, for instance the *Morning Star* of New Bedford in October and November 1886.[131] It is doubtful whether these prolonged stays added to the wealth of the local rulers, for whalers were now able to buy firewood as well as food from the tender. Only the revenue from licences to draw water would have increased with the surge in whaling traffic.

---

129 Log SUNBEAM, 1878–1882, 07. & 10.10.1880.
130 Ibid., 29.–30.07. & 04.10.–18.10.1881.
131 Log MORNING STAR, 1883–1888, 10.09.–11.10.1886.

Cabinda was both a provisioning stop and a hunting ground in its own right on the humpbacking route followed by American whalers. As a "liberty port", however – one in which skippers moored for longer periods of time and granted their men shore leave – skippers preferred Jamestown in St Helena, which they visited at the season's beginning and after its close. Yet circumstances sometimes made it necessary or expedient to allow shore leave in Cabinda too. "We will go to Kabenda in about 8 weeks (if we don't see whales) to give liberty [. . .] for he won't anchor at St. Helena this time", Myra Allen Heyer, wife of Captain Andrew Heyer, wrote from the barque *Wanderer* of New Bedford to her brother-in-law in 1880.[132]

Fig. 33: The *Lottie Beard* of New Bedford (painting; date unknown).
Source: Spinner Publications SCNL 0175.

The local rulers appear to have placed no restrictions on crews on shore leave. In that respect, they differed from their seventeenth- and eighteenth-century predecessors, who had prohibited visiting seamen from remaining ashore any longer than necessary – no doubt with a view to preventing the establishment of European middlemen and to preserve their own dominance over the slave trade. By contrast, Franque and other nineteenth-century "big men" pursued different

---

132 McCormick, *Two New Bedford Whalemen*, 209.

strategies for safeguarding their power, even allowing European companies to set up trading posts in Cabinda.¹³³ Since, however, Cabinda was never much frequented by seamen on shore leave, no infrastructure ever emerged to serve or to profit from them. It had little to offer whalemen, lacking as it did taverns, brothels and other amenities familiar from other ports. Such men as did come ashore were often left with little to do but go on rambles though villages and the interior, combined perhaps with a bit of hunting.¹³⁴ Robert Ferguson of the *Kathleen* describes such an excursion in July 1882:

> I went on shore to look around and found it a nice clean place kept in good order. The huts were made of bamboo and the fronts of them were swept clean and flattened down. [. . .] Chickens were running all around, with parrots among them, just like pigeons at home. Some of the natives have pigs, small black ones, and some have a few ducks that are fed mostly on peanuts, which seem to be plentiful.¹³⁵

Life in the bay as Ferguson witnessed it offered seamen few inducements to desert. On the contrary, the western coast of Africa was reputed among crews to be rife with lethal dangers. Their fears were far from groundless. Particularly in the summer months, many seamen contracted malaria, yellow fever and other infectious diseases along the tropical coasts. "Mate came on board sick with fever", records the log of the *Sunbeam* at the end of her visit to Cabinda in 1884.¹³⁶ The area's fever was notorious enough to enter sailing lore, for instance the popular shanty "Blow, Boys, Blow", which contains the verses: "Say, wuz ye niver down the Congo River? / Ooh! Yes, I've bin down the Congo River. / O Congo she's a mighty river, / Where fever makes the white man shiver".¹³⁷ Yet seafarers may also have mistakenly associated scurvy with west Africa and its climate, for it was at that point of the voyage – when a vessel coming directly from North America reached the western coast of Africa – that the first symptoms were apt to appear.¹³⁸ If seamen defied such perils to desert in Cabinda, the local rulers were happy to assist in capturing them – in return, we may suppose, for a reward. "King Porter and his tribe had Cout him Brought him on Board", records the log of the *Globe* of New Bedford of a man who had jumped ship in Cabinda in 1856. Captain Tripp had him severely punished: "Seased him

---

133 Martin, "Cabinda and Cabindans", 85–88; Martin, "Family Strategies in Nineteenth Century Cabinda", 81f.
134 See e.g. Log LOUISA SEARS, 1856–1858, 20.09.1857.
135 Ferguson, *Harpooner*, 136f.
136 Log SUNBEAM, 1882–1886, 23.06.1884.
137 Hugill, *Shanties from the Seven Seas*, 172; I here reproduce the verses without the chorus in the middle.
138 Rediker, *Between the Devil and the Deep Blue Sea*, 46f.

up in the Misen Rigen and let him Remain for 2 hours and then Took him down and at sunset Put him down in the after Hole in irons."[139]

Even in Cabinda, in spite of such risks, a few seamen managed to escape their vessels. Some of them managed to make their way as far as Luanda, where there was an American consulate. One such seaman was Daniel Lehr, who had deserted from the *Clarice* of Edgartown and appeared before the American consul in 1881.[140] Two other men who had jumped ship in Cabinda presented themselves in Luanda in September 1884. Frank Fisher and William Smith had deserted from the barque *Mermaid* in mid-August. They had been victimised, they said, by Captain Sherman, who had beaten them without provocation and tried to make them eat refuse.[141] For such seamen to reach Luanda, more than four hundred kilometres south of Cabinda, was by no means a foregone conclusion. Knowing this, some Captains took advantage of a stop at Cabinda to rid themselves of troublesome seamen without having to explain themselves to a consul. This was the fate of Philip Langklin and James Made of the brig *Pavilion* of Holmes Hole in 1859. They had been suspected of throwing items of equipment overboard with the aim of terminating the voyage, and Captain Adams wasted no time in abandoning them in the bay.[142]

The risk of desertion increased considerably when the *Lottie Beard* or another merchant vessel lay at anchor in Cabinda. To disgruntled seamen, such vessels represented the prospect of returning home sooner rather than later, and the prospect induced many of them to ask their captains for a discharge. While captains did always refuse these requests,[143] they were generally loath to let able-bodied seamen go before the end of a voyage – all the more so if it meant giving them the statutory three months' pay in addition to their lay. Careful skippers therefore remained on their guard to prevent desertion – even in Cabinda. In one such instance, recorded in the log of the *Clarice* of Edgartown in 1881,

---

139 Log GLOBE, 1855–1857, 05.07.1856.
140 Robert Newton to the US consul in Lisbon, 26.01.1881, National Archives and Records Administration, Records of Foreign Service Posts, Record Group 84, Loanda, vol. 004, Despatch Book, 1880–1892.
141 National Archives and Records Administration, Records of Foreign Service Posts, Record Group 84, Loanda, vol. 007, Ships Daily Journal, 1881–1891, entry 1/1881.
142 Log PAVILION, 1858–1860, 10. & 13.08.1859. American whaling captains would sometimes also leave men behind in more southerly locations in Angola beyond the consul's reach, for instance in Moçâmedes; see Despatches 125/1877 & 21/1878, National Archives and Records Administration, Records of Foreign Service Posts, Record Group 84, Loanda, vol. 002, Despatch Book, 1864–1879.
143 See e.g. Log MORNING STAR, 1883–1888, 28.09.1886; Log BERTHA, 1878–1881, 21.10.1880.

"This Morning the Falcon shifted her anchorage father outside so as to keep the men from runing away".[144]

If mobility from vessels to the beaches was small, there was more movement in the opposite direction. The slave trade had given rise to a specialised workforce in the bay, with men involved in transporting slaves in one way or another and women preparing food for the captives. By way of payment, they received a share of the barter goods carried by the vessels, thereby contributing to the steady flow of imported goods (particularly clothing) into the bay.[145] The end of the slave trade in the 1870s brought about the collapse of this sector within a few years. The effect on the local economy was dramatic, causing a wave of labour migrations which also affected visiting whalers.

The smaller part of the workforce set free (as it were) by abolition was able to find new employment in the bay itself, some as boatbuilders, others in the new local branches of European trading companies. Many more, however, left Cabinda. One reason why moving away to make a living so soon became a commonplace occurrence was that it had historical precedents. Already in the seventeenth century, many young Cabindan men went travelling in search of work, forming caravans along the coast or into the interior, founding new settlements or establishing diaspora communities in places as distant as Luanda. In the mid-1800s, this practice began to spread to new areas of employments, with Cabindans going to works as fishermen in Moçâmedes, dockers in Benguela or servants in Luanda. As early as 1841 boats from Cabinda arrived daily in Luanda, and by 1882 the Cabindan community in the capital of the Portuguese colony was said to number some one thousand persons. Labour migrants from the region of the Congo estuary became known as *Cabindas* or *Cabinda-men* even if they were not from Cabinda itself, and the sobriquet was confidently adopted by some of those to whom it was applied as a badge of professionalism and a ticket to advancement.[146]

One of the *Cabindas'* preferred sectors was shipping. The tradition of boatbuilding in Cabinda meant that many of the men possessed artisanal and navigational skills of the kind appreciated by shipmasters. Merchantmen whose recruiting ground for African workers had previously been the coast of what is

---

144 Log CLARICE, 1878–1882, 27.09.1881.
145 Martin, "Cabinda and Cabindans", 92.
146 Burton, *Two Trips to Gorilla Land and the Cataracts of the Congo*, vol. 2, 26; Martin, "Cabinda and Cabindans", 86, 89–91; Martin, "The Cabinda Connection", 48–50; Martin, "Family Strategies in Nineteenth-Century Cabinda", 76. The Portuguese generally called people from Cabinda *Fiote*, a term in decreasing use for reason of its derogatory implications. Many of the bay's inhabitants now prefer ro call themselves *Ibinda*, after the language spoken there.

now Liberia, then ruled by the Kru, in the 1850s began to hire mainly *Cabindas*. Cabindan men were also to be found in the crews of illegally operating slave ships.[147]

Some whalers also recruited *Cabindas* in the bay, some of whom worked as seasoners, for a term of weeks or months, others became full members of the crew. The records of the New Bedford customs authority name sixteen men who came to the United Stated aboard whaleships between 1877 and 1883.[148] Yet this figure surely underestimates the actual number of *Cabindas* employed in whaling, since they are always identifiable as such in the sources. Names found in ships' logs such as "Antone Kabenda" or "Manuel Cabenda" are obvious enough, but *Cabindas* might also be entered under such names as "Jim John" or "Alfred Fine".[149] And since these mobile workers were to be found not only in the bay itself, but throughout the coast of modern Angola, there is no reliable way of establishing how many of the men who signed on aboard whaleships in Luanda, Benguela or Ambriz were originally from Cabinda. The *Platina* of New Bedford, for instance, took on board ten *Cabindas* in Luanda for a one-year term as seasoners in 1881.[150]

What we do know is that the bay was not one of the American whaling industry's major sources of labour. Only few of the whalers who came to Cabinda hired additional men, mostly only one and never, in all the recorded cases, more than four (the *Sunbeam* in July 1881[151]). Seasoners would usually stay only for one or two whaling seasons at a time, that is, for six months or a year.[152] In so doing, many of them pursued a strategy much like that of the American seamen they met on board ship: they were young men who hoped that a few years at sea would earn them enough money to build a house and support a family on their return home.[153] Like so much in whaling, however, the outcome of this project was bound to be uncertain. Antonio Cabenda, for instance – whose name testifies to his origins and who worked aboard the schooner *Charles W. Morse* of New

---

147 Brooks, *Yankee Traders, Old Coasters, and African Middlemen*, 285; Zeuske, "Mongos und Negreros", 77–80. On the recruitment of Kru as seamen see Tonkin, "Creating Kroomen".
148 Lund et al., *New Bedford Crewlist Database*.
149 Ibid.
150 Robert Newton to the US consul in Lisbon, 26.01.1881, National Archives and Records Administration, Records of Foreign Service Posts, Record Group 84, Loanda, vol. 004, Despatch Book, 1880–1892.
151 Log SUNBEAM, 1878–1882, 30.07.1881.
152 Log PEDRO VARELA, 1878–1880, 29.03.1879 & 13.04.1880.
153 Martin, "Cabinda and Cabindans", 91.

Bedford in the late 1880s – was clearly unlucky in his choice of vessel. He repeatedly quarrelled with Captain Morris, who accused Cabenda of stealing food and sentenced him to several spells, each lasting days at a time, of punitive labour. In 1888, the seaman took advantage of a stop at São Miguel in the Azores to make good his escape.[154]

Besides dispatching the *Lottie Beard*, the American whaling industry in the 1880s pursued a second strategy for reducing the expenses incurred by its humpbacking fleet on the west coast of central Africa: Luanda, which since 1576 had been the administrative centre of Portugal's colonial possessions in what is now Angola, was to replace Cabinda as the key port on this stretch of coast.

American whalers had occasionally put in at Luanda since the mid-1800s, but it never became a hub in their network of routes. "Whaling Vessels on the coast seldom come here but keep more to the North and South", Robert Newton, the US consul in Luanda, reported in 1877.[155] There were four reasons why American whalers tended to avoid the principal Portuguese trading port. First, trade in Luanda was controlled by Portuguese merchants and their middlemen who sought to profit from selling previsions to ships' crews and thereby drove up the prices for food and firewood. Second, the fact that Luanda was much frequented by merchantmen made for a higher risk of desertion, offering disgruntled seamen of an easy passage home.[156] Third, the Portuguese authorities demanded formalities and charges for stopping Luanda which whalers preferred to avoid.[157] Fourth and last, whalers usually reached Luanda in the middle of the humpbacking season, when they had to follow their quarry northwards and had little time to call into port.

Another reason why whalers preferred to put in at Cabinda was that shipmasters had initially expected that by doing business directly with African actors, they would be able to provision their vessels at advantageous rates – as was the case in Annobón. However, experience soon showed that Cabinda was neither nor even an effective deterrent to desertion. It may well be that costs in Cabinda were even higher than they were in Luanda, even though, as a rule, colonial trading ports tended to be the most expensive places for whalers to call at.

---

154 Log CHARLES W. MORSE, 1887–1890, 04.–09.08.1887, 05.–07.03. & 22.–23.04.1888.
155 Despatch 131/1877, National Archives and Records Administration, Records of Foreign Service Posts, Record Group 84, Loanda, vol. 002, Despatch Book, 1864–1879.
156 Haywood, "American Whalers and Africa", 68.
157 Robert Newton to the State Department, 18.02.1881, National Archives and Records Administration, Records of Foreign Service Posts, Record Group 84, Loanda, vol. 004, Despatch Book, 1880–1892.

In July 1881 Frederick Taber, master of the barque *Sunbeam* of New Bedford, appeared at the American consulate in Luanda with a view to settling that question. Taber asked the consul, Robert Newton, to prepare a table of all the costs incurred by a whaler on a visit to Luanda. The resulting calculation Taber proposed to take to Cabinda in October, when much of the American humpbacking fleet could be expected to gather there, to discuss it with his colleagues and to compare it with the expenses associated with mooring in the bay. The whalemen, noted Newton, "are not pleased with St. Helena or Cabinda and wish to change their meeting station to Mossamedes or Loanda".[158] Informing the Portuguese governor António Eleutério Dantas of this intention, Newton requested concessions for the American whaling fleet. Dantas was happy to oblige and in August reduced the mooring fees for whalers to 400 réis (approximately 40¢) per day in addition to a one-off payment of 1,500 réis ($1.62) for the statutory visit of the harbour surgeon. An additional charge would allow whalers to store their barrels in the customs authority's warehouse. "Now the charges are so moderate that I should think it would not keep vessels from coming to a port where they will find greater facilities in arranging Provisions or anything they may require, than in any other port on the coast", reported Newton to the State Department.[159]

Whalers did indeed subsequently sail for Luanda more often, with fourteen of their vessels lying at anchor there at once in October 1883[160] – a number virtually equivalent to the entire humpbacking fleet. Yet Luanda was apparently still not attractive enough entirely to supplant Cabinda as a stopover for whalers. The fleet continued to put in at Cabinda until American-style pelagic whaling ended in these waters in 1886. For Luanda itself proved far from unproblematic as a port: the drinking water was of poor quality, whereas rum, wine and gin were cheap and readily available. Many seamen indulged freely and some, weakened by the climate and tropical diseases, paid the ultimate price. "Several of the ships have already lost some men, big strong men who were carried off in one day", observed Robert Ferguson, who came to Luanda aboard the *Kathleen* in October 1883. "I think the big strong men go first, especially the men who

---

158 Robert Newton to the Portuguese governor, 14.07.1881, National Archives and Records Administration, Records of Foreign Service Posts, Record Group 84, Loanda, vol. 004, Despatch Book, 1880–1892.
159 Robert Newton to the State Department, 16.09.1881, National Archives and Records Administration, Records of Foreign Service Posts, Record Group 84, Loanda, vol. 004, Despatch Book, 1880–1892.
160 Letter from Robert Newton, 13.12.1884, National Archives and Records Administration, Records of Foreign Service Posts, Record Group 84, Loanda, vol. 003, Despatch Book, 1879–1885.

drink the heaviest. The men think liquor keeps the fever away, but it is the worst thing they can take."[161]

Among seamen, Luanda was even more notorious than Cabinda as a fever spot. Soon after the *Kathleen* had put out from Luanda in November 1883, she met with another New Bedford whaler for a gam. "Tonight we gammed the Milton", wrote Ferguson in his diary. "She had sailed out of St. Paul de Loanda with us. Two of her men died of the fever. The *Falcon* lost three men, the *Niagara* two, the *Sea Ranger* three, the *Stafford* two, and the *Pioneer* one."[162] The opportunity for another gam arose a few days later, this time with the crew of the barque *Petrel*, who told Ferguson that "The Petrel lost three men from fever and the Mars two while they were at St. Paul".[163] Ferguson's general view of Luanda was accordingly negative: "This is a sickly port and we are lucky to be getting out of it."[164]

Whalers as a compensatory element

In the introduction to this chapter, I framed its remit as testing Phyllis Martin's assertions with regard to whaling in Cabinda. To restate them in the form of two claims: first, the rulers of Cabinda treated whalers as an opportunity to compensate at least partially for the loss of the slave trade, which is why they demanded such high prices for drinking water, firewood and provisions; second, these practices deterred whalers and caused their visits to cease after about 1870.[165]

Examining the records of American whaling in Cabinda confirms the first of these claims while refuting the second. Logbooks indeed have much to say about the exorbitant prices charged for the use of the bay's resources and the resulting conflicts, above all over drinking water drawn from the Lukola Congo river. These difficulties did not, however, mean that whalers stopped putting in at Cabinda after 1870, nor did it even lead to a decline in their numbers. By dispatching the tender *Lottie Beard* to Cabinda, the whaling industry found a way of supplying its vessels with food and firewood that did not rely on the good will of local potentates. A total of fifteen whalers came to Cabinda while the *Lottie Beard* was lying in the bay in September 1881, more than in any single year before or since. Attempts made around the same time to develop Luanda as a substitute that

---

161 Ferguson, *Harpooner*, 231.
162 Ibid. 235.
163 Ibid., 239. "St. Paul" here refers to "St Paul de Loanda", the English designation in use at the time.
164 Ferguson, *Harpooner*, 235.
165 Martin, "Family Strategies in Nineteenth-Century Cabinda", 81.

would enable whalers to avoid Cabinda failed to take hold on account of Luanda's significant drawbacks.

Unlike in Annobón or Walvis Bay, whalers at no time firmed the largest or the most important portion of shipping in Cabinda. To whalers, the bay was one of several stops along their humpbacking route, while to the littoral society of Cabinda, whalers were only one of a variety of actors who came from the sea to the bay. For Cabinda's rulers, whaling could never be more than an element in their projects of making up for the economic losses incurred by the abolition of the slave trade and of securing their power by diversifying their strategies. For Cabindans contemplating migration to find work too whaleships were only one of several options and by no means the preferred one; most young men tended to look for work in ports such as Benguela or Luanda rather than aboard vessels. In the period of transition from the slave trade to other forms of coastal trade, whaling left traces in Cabinda without making a decisive impression on the subsequent course of events. What the contacts between crews and the littoral society of Cabinda exemplify is that whalers sometimes confronted African littoral society from a position of weakness. Lacking alternatives and under pressure of time, there was little they could do but to accept the terms and above all the prices imposed by local rulers. Even attempts to obtain drinking water without payment were quickly and effectively suppressed.

7 The emergence of a west African whaling community: San Antonio, Annobón, 1825–1950

The *Vesta* was the kind of vessel seamen called "unlucky". By the time the Edgartown brig reached St Helena in 1846, nearly exactly one year after setting sail, the crew had already been riven by numerous conflicts. Her captain, Edward Mayhew, on several occasions felt compelled to enforce discipline with his fist or the end of a rope – or with the dreaded cat-o'-nine-tails. Several seamen had taken stops at the Azores and the coast of Brazil as opportunities to jump ship. And now the *Vesta* had arrived at Jamestown, seven of her men went on strike, demanding that Mayhew provide better food. As it became clear that the American consul would, contrary to their hopes, not intervene on their behalf, two of the men abandoned the strike. The other five stood firm, giving in only once the captain had had them put in irons and ordered the *Vesta* to continue her voyage did they too give up. Although Mayhew had once more asserted his authority, he appears to have concluded that the crew's diet might after all warrant improvement.[1] In order to take on fresh food and water, he sailed for São Tomé, the principal hub of marine traffic in the Gulf of Guinea. To Mayhew, who was commanding a whaleship for the first time, the island is likely to have seemed the obvious choice. Looking back, however, he may well have regretted his decision.

The first in link in the chain of unfortunate events that now began was a warning shot fired by Portuguese soldiers at the *Vesta* as she was sailing into the island's main port, Ana Chaves Bay on 11 June. The crew had apparently forgotten to raise her flag, thereby arousing the suspicions of the harbour patrol, who probably feared an imminent attack by pirates. No less a shock were the prices charged for food by the local traders, and Mayhew ordered the anchor to be raised that same night without having bought so much as an egg.

The *Vesta* made her next attempt to acquire provisions in the neighbouring island of Príncipe, where the brig weighed anchor in the port of Santo António. In the days that followed, Mayhew managed at least to obtain some yams, a boatload of coconuts and fresh waters. To his disgruntled men, however, the stop presented a welcome opportunity to desert. Several seamen who had repeatedly defied the captain and his officers went absent without leave. Some returned of their own

---

[1] Log VESTA, 1845–1846, 04.06., 25.06., 13.08., 07.09. & 08.10.1845 and 02.01., 25.01., 29.01., 10.02. & 03.04.–09.04.1846. For the following paragraphs see Log VESTA, 1845–1846, 11.–22.06.1846. A preliminary version of this chapter was published in 2014: Schürmann, "Die Wale, ihre Jäger und der Strand von Annobón".

volition after a few days. To find the others, Mayhew assembled a search party made up of reliable men, which finally succeeded in rounding up the deserts and returning them to the vessel by force.

All in all, the *Vesta*'s stopovers in São Tomé and Príncipe cost what any captain would have found to be unconscionable amounts of time and money. The events recounted here confirm the picture of these islands that emerges from the records of other whalers too. Harvey Phillips, for instance, who came to Príncipe aboard the schooner *Admiral Blake* of Marion, found that "These people set too high a prise on their produce we cannot trade with them".[2] Given the exorbitant prices charged and the risk of desertion, São Tomé and Príncipe were unsuitable as victualling stops for whaleships. When it came to taking on provisions in the Gulf of Guinea, experienced skippers preferred an island that was virtually off the map (or chart) as far as commercial shipping concerned. This island was Annobón.

"Humpbacks all round"

In many places associated with whaling, contacts between seafarers and littoral societies left traces in records and traditions of various kinds. By contrast, in the case of Annobón nearly the only sources we have are the logs and diaries seamen kept aboard ship as well as their later accounts and memoirs. No written records were produced in the island itself, whose inhabitants trusted in the spoken word. Missionaries, who began to arrive in 1885, were the first residents to produce written records over a longer period of time. Only a few newspapers published in St Helena mention Annobón as the previous stop of whalers calling at Jamestown.[3]

Since whalemen's own records are by nature incomplete, they can offer no more than clues as to how often vessels visited Annobón and whether they did so with any regularity. The first whalers to reach the island are unlikely to have done so on purpose, "discovering" it more or less in passing while hunting sperm whales in the Gulf of Guinea. Sperm whaling in these waters began in the 1760s, when Nantucket vessels searched the Atlantic for new whaling grounds. There may already have been encounters between islanders and whalemen in this period, but evidence is lacking. The first confirmed visits of whalemen to

---

[2] Phillips, Journal ADMIRAL BLAKE, 1868–1870, 08.07.1869. For a similar assessment see Log TRITON, 1868–1871, 22.07.1869.
[3] *The St. Helena Herald*, 18.08. & 29.09.1853, 20.07.1854 and 01.05., 17.07. & 11.09.1856; *The St. Helena Chronicle*, 14.08.1852.

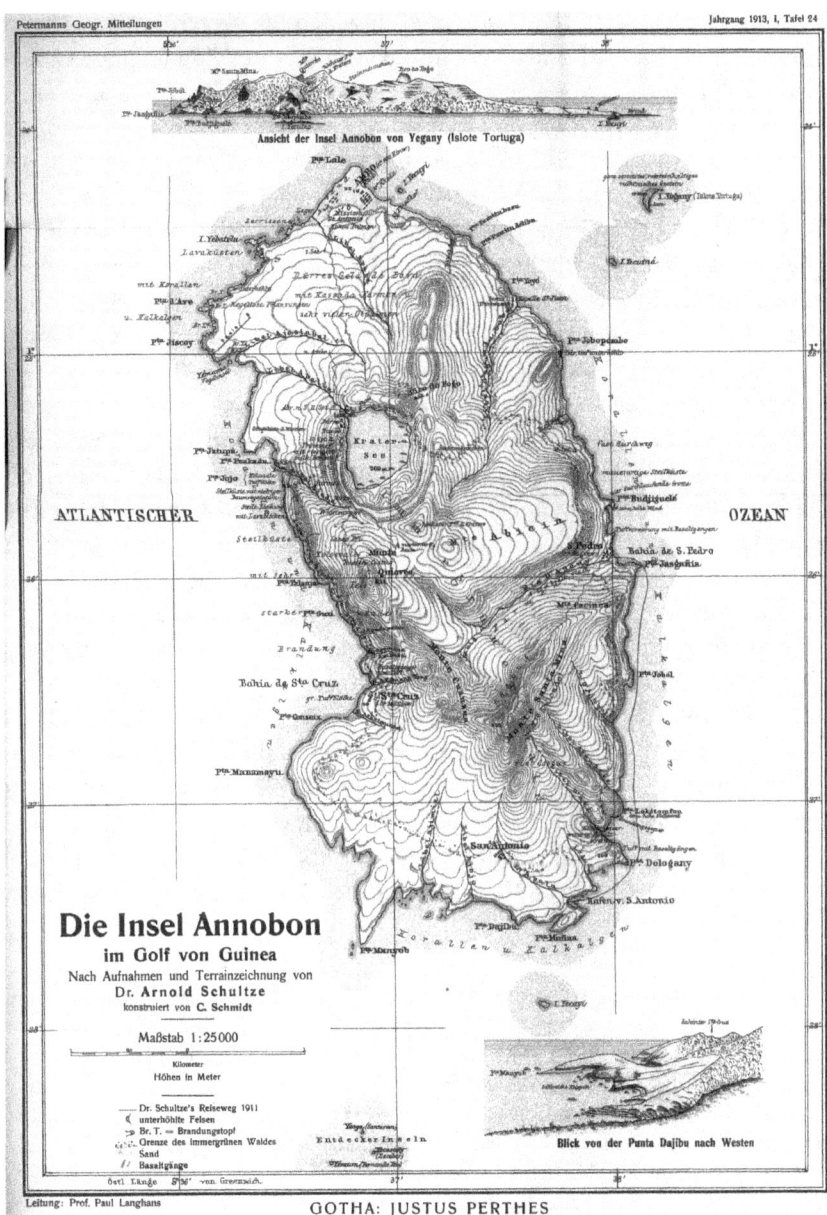

Fig. 34: Annobón on a German map of 1913. (Arnold Schultze. "Die Insel von Annobon im Golf von Guinea." 26 × 37 cm, 1:25.000. *Dr. A. Petermann's Mitteilungen aus Justus Perthes' Geographischer Anstalt* 59 [1913]: T1 24).
Courtesy of the Gotha Research Library at University of Erfurt, SPA 4° 00100 [059,01].

Annobón occurred in the 1820s, a period in which the search for new sperm whaling grounds took on a new dynamism. The first individually identifiable whaler to call at the island was the brig *Minerva* of New Bedford, which moored there twice for three days in January and February 1826.[4]

For the 1830s, 1840s and 1850s we have evidence of up to five visits by whalers per year – a figure which, given the incompleteness of sources, represents a minimum, a caveat which applies to all figures given here.[5] The 1860s and 1870s saw the most whalers in Annobón, with evidence, for instance, of eight visits in 1870. It was around this time that more and more whaleships sailed for west Africa in pursuit of humpbacks, which congregated off the coast of modern Angola and Gabon between May and October.[6] Although the American Civil War, the shrinking demand for whale oil and other difficulties meant that whaling in general was an industry in decline, the Atlantic whaling grounds were less affected by these developments than those in the Pacific and Indian Oceans, offering lower operational costs by virtue of their comparative proximity to the New England whaling ports. All the whalers known to have visited Annobón were American, for American vessels had by this time largely pushed their British competitors out of the whaling grounds of the mid- and south Atlantic.

The sea around Annobón is exceedingly deep. Humpback whales came very close to its shores, which was no small advantage as far as whalemen were concerned.[7] "Humpbacks all round", declared the log of the *Globe* of New Bedford for 8 October 1869, soon after the barque had weighed anchor off Annobón.[8] The island was able to serve whalers both as an operational base and a victualling station. It might happen that a whale breached alongside a vessel while it was taking on supplies, almost as if it had been expecting its hunters.[9] When putting in at Annobón, many captains thus kept part of the crew circling the island in

---

4 Log MINERVA, 1825–1827, 24.–26.01. & 10.–11.02.1826. The *Minerva*'s crew caught a sperm whale off the island.
5 Haywood estimates five to ten whalers per year to have visited Annobón in the mid-nineteenth century. (Haywood, "American Whalers and Africa", 76)
6 Brito/Picanço/Carvalho, "Small Cetaceans off São Tomé", 3f.; Carvalho et al., "Temporal Patterns of Population Structure of Humpback Whales in West Coast of Africa (B1–B2 Substocks) Based on Mitochondrial DNA and Microsatellite Variation"; van Waerebeek/Ofori-Danson/Debrah, "The Cetaceans of Ghana"; Weir, "Occurrence and Distribution of Cetaceans off Northern Angola", 228–231; Weir, "A Review of Cetacean Occurrence in West African Waters from the Gulf of Guinea to Angola", 10f.
7 Aguilar, "Aboriginal Whaling off Pagalu (Equatorial Guinea)", 386.
8 Log GLOBE, 1869–1872, 08.10.1869.
9 See e.g. Allen, Journal GLOBE, 1869–1872, 09.10.1869; Log BERTHA, 1878–1881, 14.08.1880; Log SUNBEAM, 1878–1882, 20.09.1880.

boats in the hope of finding whales.[10] Some whalers also took advantage of the stop to stow the whale oil produced in the last weeks' humpbacking securely away in the hold, something that was not always easily done on the high seas.[11]

In the 1880s, the decline of American whaling began to be felt in the Atlantic whaling grounds too. Although whaleships continued to sail for Annobón, the number of their confirmed visits can be seen to have dropped sharply. The last individually identifiable whalers to call at Annobón did so in the early 1900s. One was the brig *Sullivan* of Norwich, which lay at anchor off the island for eleven days in October 1906.[12]

The remotest place in the Gulf of Guinea

To whalemen, who generally approached it from the south-east, following the migration routes of their quarry, the island was an impressive sight, with the sloped of the volcanoes Pico Surcado and Pico do Fogo dropping steeply into the Gulf of Guinea. The island is a mere three kilometres wide, but its peaks seem to each the clouds. "Several larger and several smaller cliffs", remembered Georg Tams, a surgeon from Hamburg who came to Annobón aboard a merchantman in 1842, "rose above the water some distance south of the islands, in appearance like sentries defying the mighty billows".[13] Writing in his diary in 1869, Harvey Phillips, approaching the island from the south in the *Admiral Blake* and sailing along its coast, noticed that "There does not appear to be much senth [i.e. sand] to this island but quite high & ruged."[14] The sheer cliff face was occasionally broken by streams flowing into the sea, and the various nooks and ledges in the basalt rock provided nesting places for countless birds. In order to reach the only spot where Annobón opened up to the sea, vessels had to sail to the north of the island. Only here was the coast not too steep or too rocks to land a boat, and only here was there a beach (Fig. 34).[15]

---

10 Allen, Journal GLOBE, 1869–1872, 11.10.1869; Log DRACO, 1868–1871, 02.–09.09.1871; Log LEONIDAS, 1860–1863, 03.–08.09.1862; Log GLOBE, 1869–1872, 11., 13. & 16.10.1869; Log BERTHA, 1878–1881, 15.–27.08.1880; Log DESDEMONA, 1876–1879, 14.08.1877; Log GEORGE AND SUSAN, 1865–1868, 07. & 11.08.1867; Log STEPHANIA, 1847–1850, 03.–14.08.1850.
11 Log ADELINE GIBBS, 1875–1878, 07.09.1876; Log CHARLES W. MORGAN, 1878–1881, 13.–16.08.1879.
12 Log SULLIVAN, 1905–1907, 05.–15.10.1906.
13 Tams, *Die Portugiesischen Besitzungen in Süd-West-Afrika*, 186.
14 Phillips, Journal ADMIRAL BLAKE, 1868–1870, 12.06.1869.
15 Allen/Thomson, *A Narrative of the Expedition Sent by Her Majesty's Government to the Niger River in 1841*, vol. 2, 52; Schultze, *Die Insel Annobon im Golf von Guinea*, 132; Tams, *Die*

In order find an anchorage on the precipitous sea bed, vessels had to sail as close to the beach as possible. This was not a task to be taken slightly, for a vessel might be seized by a sudden gust of wind and driven onto the rocks of which the beach was by no means free.[16] Behind the beach lay the town of San Antonio de Palé, known to seamen – if they knew any name for it – simply as San Antonio.[17] From the deck of the *Albert*, a paddle troopship that was part of the British Niger expedition of 1841–42, the merchant William Simpson, described the scene in the following terms: "The town occupies a considerable extent of ground; at one end of it there stands, prominently, a church, provided with bells, which we hear ringing for matins and vespers, from this church the main street extends, west, a quarter of a mile, and constitutes the chief part of the village."[18]

No inhabited place in the Gulf of Guinea was farther from the mainland than San Antonio,[19] which lies 190 nautical miles off Cape Lopez in what is now Gabon. Even São Tomé, the closest island, is about 100 nautical miles away. Annobón is not only the remotest but also the smallest of the four volcanic islands in these waters. At roughly eighteen square kilometres, its surface area is about fifteen per cent of Nantucket's or 0.6 per cent of that of Zanzibar.

Crosses, canoes and coconuts

"I was struck by the regular pattern to which this town was built", wrote Georg Tams of San Antonio in 1842. But in what respects was it "regular"? "It was

---

Portugiesischen Besitzungen in Süd-West-Afrika, 191. There is at least one recorded case of a whaleship successfully anchoring off the south of the island. (Log GEORGE AND SUSAN, 1865–1868, 05.–14.08.1867)

16 Allen/Thomson, *A Narrative of the Expedition Sent by Her Majesty's Government to the Niger River in 1841*, vol. 2, 65.

17 The name Annobón was known to seamen in various forms, such as "Annabona" or "Annobone". San Antonio de Palé appears in the sources and in the scholarly literature variously as "Santo António", "Cidade da Praia", "Cidade da Porto", "Palea", "Ambo" and in the abbreviated form "Palé". Both "Palea" and "Palé" are likely to be derived from *playa*, the Spanish word for "beach". (Caldeira, *La Leyenda de Lodã*, 74; Cunha Matos, *Corografia historica das ilhas de Tomè, Principe, Anno Bom, e Fernando Po*, 87; Fry, "Annobon", 149)

18 Simpson, *A Private Journal Kept during the Niger Expedition*, 70.

19 There were other settlements in Annobón besides San Antonio, but they appear to have been inhabited only seasonally (perhaps at harvest time) and to have been unoccupied for much of the year. (Allen/Thomson, *A Narrative of the Expedition Sent by Her Majesty's Government to the Niger River in 1841*, vol. 2, 59)

intersected crosswise by two long, broad streets which met at the centres, and at each of the four ends there stood a charming chapel."[20] Not only had the people of Annobón arranged their town "crosswise", the entire island was covered in crosses – and in other tokens of Christianity. In San Antonio and in the surrounding countryside the paths were lined with innumerable wooden crosses as well as with shrines, chapels and effigies of saints.[21] "Many small churches and crosses [. . .] met the eye at every few steps", William Simpson observed in the island's interior in 1841.[22] The account of the British Niger expedition likewise records that "The main street is a line of crosses."[23] One of these crosses, which the Annobonese carried on such occasions as funerals, was six metres tall (Fig. 35),[24] in addition to which all the islanders wore wooden crosses around their necks. The Spanish missionaries who arrived on the island in 1885 counted no fewer than nineteen chapels there.[25]

It was singular society indeed that whalers encountered in Annobón, and the ubiquity of Christian symbols was one of its most striking features – all the more so because prior to 1885 visits by representatives of the Christian churches had been few and far between. However, the first slaves to have been brought to Annobón in the sixteenth century had already been baptized by Augustinian priests.[26] In the subsequent centuries, the population descended from these slaves had preserved forms of Catholic religiosity, to which they added spiritual ideas of their own.

The Catholic elements in the Annobonese faith were strengthened by Capuchin friars from Italy, who visited the island several times between 1726 and 1753. They took a comparatively tolerant view of non-Christian practices and

---

20 Tams, *Die Portugiesischen Besitzungen in Süd-West-Afrika*, 194f.
21 Allen/Thomson, *A Narrative of the Expedition Sent by Her Majesty's Government to the Niger River in 1841*, vol. 2, 56, 61, 63; Tams, *Die Portugiesischen Besitzungen in Süd-West-Afrika*, 191, 199. In 1916 the Portuguese historian Raimundo José da Cunha Matos identified several of Annobón's churches and chapels by name: Nossa Senhora da Conceição, Miseridordia, Santana, José and Santo Antonio. (Cunha Matos, *Corografia historica das ilhas de Tomè, Principe, Anno Bom, e Fernando Po*, 87) What is unclear, however, is whether these names were introduced by the Spanish missionaries or antedate their arrival.
22 Simpson, *A Private Journal Kept during the Niger Expedition*, 72.
23 Allen/Thomson, *A Narrative of the Expedition Sent by Her Majesty's Government to the Niger River in 1841*, vol. 2, 56. On the Niger expedition see Sundiata, *From Slaving to Neoslavery*, 45.
24 For a description of a funeral ceremony in October 1841 see Allen/Thomson, *A Narrative of the Expedition Sent by Her Majesty's Government to the Niger River in 1841*, vol. 2, 53–57.
25 Barrena, "La Isla de Annobón", 131.
26 Caldeira, "Medo e religião popular na ilha de Ano Bom", 2; Covey, "São Tomé", 335.

Fig. 35: A funeral in San Antonio, 1841, as depicted in the report of the British Niger Expedition.
Source: Allen/Thomson, *A Narrative of the Expedition Sent by Her Majesty's Government to the Niger River in 1841*, vol. II 64.

found their own teaching welcomed in return. A more hostile reception was accorded to other eighteenth-century missionaries who had taken it upon themselves to enforce orthodox forms of the Catholic liturgy in Annobón.[27]

The main church built by the people of Annobón was known as the *Gueza gany* and dedicated to the Blessed Virgin Mary. An adjacent building erected by Portuguese missionaries, by contrast, was allowed to go to ruin. The *Gueza gany* was a narrow wooden building, thirty metres long, set at one end of the longest street in the east of San Antonio. At the east of the building stood the high altar, with the vestry behind it. The nave was decorated with hundreds of images of saints placed on the mud floor, which doubled as a graveyard. "Graves all over the church", observed the log of the *Pedro Varela* of New Bedford in 1883.[28] Two or three bells hung from the exterior of the *Gueza gany* and were rung at sunrise and sunset by the *sanguistã gueza nganyi*, a verger who,

---

27 Caldeira, "Medo e religião popular na ilha de Ano Bom", 3–6, 9, 13f.; Caldeira, "Uma ilha quase desconhecida", 101.
28 Log PEDRO VARELA, 1881–1883, 01.05.1883.

besides the religious teachers of *metiscolo*, was one of Annobón's most influential figures.[29] The Spanish missionaries who arrived in 1885 were surprised to find that these local *padres* had not only preserved the knowledge of such prayers as the *Padre nuestro* or the *Ave María* in both Latin and Portuguese but also administered the sacraments of the Church and observed its feasts – albeit in a modified form and in tandem with non-Christian rituals.[30]

***

Since the mid-sixteenth century, Annobón's singular society had developed largely untouched by outside influences. Like the other islands in the Gulf of Guinea, Annobón was uninhabited when was its discovered by Portuguese navigators in the latter part of the fifteenth century. João de Santarém and Pedro Escobar first sighted the volcanic island in 1471 or 1472, and the first to set foot on its beach is likely to have been Ruy Sequeiro. He was inspired by the day of this event – one new year's day in the late 1400s, the exact year is not recorded – to name the island *Anno Bon* or "good year". The Portuguese crown formally claimed the island in 1494, but unlike in its other west African colonies did not take over its administration. In view of the island's remoteness and small size, it was left to private landowners to develop the island as they saw fit. Another reason for this relative indifference was that Annobón's hilly terrain made it unsuitable for the large-scale cultivation of sugar cane, which at the time was one of Portugal's principal economic interests.[31]

As few sources from the island are preserved and few historians have examined what little there is, the following remarks on the history and society and Annobón must needs be tentative. While the historian Arlindo Manuel Caldeira has reconstructed the island's history up to the end of eighteenth century,[32] no such work has been done for the nineteenth. Historians are apt to be no less

---

29 Allen/Thomson, *A Narrative of the Expedition Sent by Her Majesty's Government to the Niger River in 1841*, vol. 2, 55f.; Barrena, "La Isla de Annobón", 131; Caldeira, "Organizar a liberdade", 10; Caldeira, "A 'republica negra' de Ano Bom", 56f., 62; Simpson, *A Private Journal Kept during the Niger Expedition*, 70f.
30 Barrena, "La Isla de Annobón", 131. For transcripts of several religious stories from Annobón recorded in the nineteenth century see Schuchardt, "Kreolische Studien VII", 198f.
31 Caldeira, "Escravidão e liberdade", 624; Caldeira, "Organizar a liberdade", 1; Caldeira, "A 'republica negra' de Ano Bom", 48; Caldeira, "Uma ilha quase desconhecida", 100; Silva, *Dutch and Portuguese in Western Africa*, 41; Solow, "Capitalism and Slavery in the Exceedingly Long Run", 724f.
32 Caldeira, "Escravidão e liberdade"; Caldeira, "Medo e religião popular na ilha de Ano Bom"; Caldeira, "Organizar a liberdade"; Caldeira, Organizing Freedom; Caldeira, "A 'republica negra' de Ano Bom"; Caldeira, "Uma ilha quase desconhecida".

puzzled life in Annobón during this period than were the seamen who went ashore there. Nor has there been any ethnographic research to speak of, which may well be related to the fact that Equatorial Guinea, of which Annobón is now part, has been a dictatorship for more than forty years.³³

In 1494, the same year that Portugal claimed sovereignty over the island, King Dom Manuel I handed over its running to one of his liegemen. It was this aristocrat or his descendants who, between 1543 and 1565, arranged for the transfer of small groups of slaves from São Tomé or Angola to Annobón, where they were to establish a settlement and plant cotton. To feed these slaves, domestic animals were brought to the island along with manioc, sweet potatoes, orange trees and other crop plants. Once a year, a Portuguese vessel coming from São Tomé or Príncipe would call at Annobón to take on a cargo of cotton. Contacts with passing vessels were more frequent than with the neighbouring islands. Although Annobón was out of the way of the main commercial shipping routes, captains would occasionally be forced to put in there by storms or lulls, or by a shortage of food or water. The islanders took advantage of such opportunities to barter for goods that it was otherwise unable to obtain to produce itself, such as clothing, tools or weapons. This trade largely escaped the supervision of the Portuguese government, whose nominal presence was limited to the person of an administrator (*feitor* or *governador*). Besides the *feitor*, no more than seven Europeans ever lived on the island at any one time, and just how effectively they were able to control a slave population likely to have been more than one thousand strong is open to question. Aside from the cotton ships and occasional vessels that had strayed from their course, Annobón had very few contacts with outside actors throughout the sixteenth and seventeenth centuries. Dutch vessels occupied the island for a month in 1605 and again

---

33 Under the rule of President Obiang Nguema, Equatorial Guinea is widely to be considered to be one of Africa's most repressive dictatorships, a state that many observers have called "fascist". On this see esp. Liniger-Goumaz, *Äquatorialguinea*. In 2005 the American Association of Jurists reported that Nguema's regime was denying the population of Annobón even rudimentary healthcare, education and communication infrastructure. (American Association of Jurists, "The Need to Name a New Special Rapporteur for Equatorial Guinea", 4) Amnesty International in 1994 reported the arrest and execution of opposition activists in Annobón who had protested against the cancellation of supply flights. (Amnesty International, "A Missed Opportunity to Restore Respect for Human Rights", 3, 8) Scientists and journalist have reported that the government has been dumping toxic and nuclear waste from Western corporations in Annobón since the 1980s. (O'Keefe, "Toxic Terrorism", 87, Richter, "Giftmüllexporte nach Afrika", 320; Smoltczyk, "Volltanken in Malabo", 88)

from 1660 to 1664. Similarly brief were the visits of Capuchin friars from Spain and Italy, who came as missionaries in 1645, 1647 and 1654.[34]

The last *feitor* vanished without a trace in the early eighteenth century. His fate is unknown, but whether he left, was killed or did a natural death, his disappearance set in motion what may well be the earliest process of decolonisation in African history. The people of Annobón henceforth lived in a state of *de facto* independence. Several attempts by Portugal to re-establish control over the island never made it past the planning stage, while others were fended off by local resistance. In one such attempt, a missionary charged with reasserting Portuguese rule had to leave after short stay in 1744; in another, in 1755 an emissary from the governor of São Tomé suffered severe ill-treatment at the hands of the local population. Another clergyman who came to the island in 1757 fled in fear of a revolt after a brief stay. Two black missionaries from São Tomé sent to the island by the Portuguese authorities in 1770 likewise left after a hostile response from the islanders, though at sixteen months they held out longer than most. In each of these cases, the men who had been chased from Annobón afterwards explained that popular resistance was directed above all against the Portuguese claim to the island.[35]

In view of such recalcitrance and the economic insignificance of the island – which, unlike São Tomé and Príncipe, never became a hub of the Atlantic slave trade – the Portuguese crown concluded that Annobón was not worth the effort. it was useful, however, as a bargaining chip in the negotiations following the war with Spain from 1776 to 1777. In an effort to put an end to decades of strife between the two Iberian nations and in return for territory in Brazil, Queen Maria I ceded the islands of Annobón, Fernando Póo (now Bioko) and Corisco to Spain

---

34 Caldeira, "Escravidão e liberdade", 624–629, 631–633; Caldeira, "Medo e religião popular na ilha de Ano Bom", 2; Caldeira, "Organizar a liberdade", 1–3; Caldeira, "A 'republica negra' de Ano Bom", 48–51; Castro/Calle, *Origen de la colonización española en Guinea Ecuatorial*, 25f.; Liniger-Goumaz, *Historical Dictionary of Equatorial Guinea*, 30; Cunha Matos, *Corografia historica das ilhas de Tomè, Principe, Anno Bom, e Fernando Po*, 83f.; Solow, "Capitalism and Slavery in the Exceedingly Long Run", 724f.; Sundiata, Equatorial Guinea, 18. On the Dutch occupations of Annobón see esp. Caldeira, "Uma ilha quase desconhecida", 102. For the account of a British East Indiaman which had hoped to put in at Annobón for supplies in 1689 but was prevented from reaching it by the winds see Ovington, *A Voyage to Suratt in the Year 1689*, 54–58.

35 Caldeira, "Escravidão e liberdade", 635–639; Caldeira, "Organizar a liberdade", 4f.; Caldeira, "Medo e religião popular na ilha de Ano Bom", 3f.; Caldeira, "A 'republica negra' de Ano Bom", 52–54; Caldeira, "Uma ilha quase desconhecida", 103f.

in 1777. By establishing their own bases in west Africa, the Spanish hoped to secure a cheaper supply of slaves for their Caribbean possessions.[36]

In November 1778 a Spanish flotilla of three vessels, carrying 150 men between them, sailed from Montevideo to the Gulf of Guinea in order to take possession of Annobón and Fernando Póo. However, the expedition ended in disaster, with the Annobonese declaring they would sooner die than have white men on the island. When the Spanish tried to press home their claim at gunpoint, a section of their troops mutinied and Spanish slaves took the side of the Annobonese. The Spanish were left no choice but to take flight. One of the expedition's leaders, José Varela y Ulloa, afterwards gave a pessimistic assessment of the prospects for a Spanish colony in Annobón. The island's soil, he explained, were poor, as were its anchorages, and in any case it was too remote from the usual shipping routes. Spain, he argued, would do better to focus on colonising Fernando Póo and constructing slave forts in west African than wasting its efforts on Annobón. The Spanish crown followed this advice. In 1785 it transferred the task of supplying its Caribbean colonies with slaves to the newly founded Real Compañía de Filipinas, which relied heavily on slave trading structures established by other colonial powers and made no further attempts to colonise Annobón. Like Portugal before it, Spain left Annobón to look after of itself.[37]

In the days when American whalers were operating in the surrounding waters, the island once again became the object of imperial rivalry between European powers. The local population initially remained untouched by these developments. In 1807 Britain declared an interest in the Spanish possessions in the Gulf of Guinea, finding them to offer strategically convenient naval bases for the campaign against the slave trade off the coast of west Africa. In 1817 Spain agreed to fall in with British abolitionist policy, thereby securing its

---

36 Caldeira, "Medo e religião popular na ilha de Ano Bom", 5; Caldeira, "Uma ilha quase desconhecida", 105; Castro/Calle, Origen de la colonización española en Guinea Ecuatorial, 18; Creus, "Cuando las almas no pueden ser custodiadas", 518; Miller, *Way of Death*, 487. On the Spanish-Portuguese treaty of El Pardo see Ndongo Bidyogo, *Historia y tragedia de Guinea Ecuatorial*, 19–21; The passages of the treaty relating to Annobón are reprinted in Cantús, "Fernando Poo", 28 & 37.

37 Caldeira, "Escravidão e liberdade", 639; Caldeira, "Organizar a liberdade", 5; Caldeira, "Medo e religião popular na ilha de Ano Bom", 5; Caldeira, "A 'republica negra' de Ano Bom", 55; King, "Evolution of the Free Slave Trade Principle in Spanish Colonial Administration", 46–49; Liniger-Goumaz, *Historical Dictionary of Equatorial Guine*a, 30; Liniger-Goumaz, *Small Is Not Always Beautiful*, 9; Maris-Wolf, *Encyclopedia of the Middle Passage*, 39; Ndongo Bidyogo, *Historia y tragedia de Guinea Ecuatorial*, 23f.; Sundiata, *Equatorial Guinea*, 18f.; Sundiata, *From Slaving to Neoslavery*, 19; Usera y Alarcon, *Memoria de la isla de Fernando Poo*, 35f.

claim to the islands while depriving them of their importance as entrepôts for the slave trade.[38]

Like the Portuguese before them, the Spanish now used the islands as bargaining chips. In 1828 Spain offered to sell Britain both Fernando Póo and Annobón, an offer which Britain, after some hesitation, accepted in 1839. Yet in the face of disagreement about the price and resistance to the sale in Spain, then in the throes of a civil war, the Spanish government rescinded the offer. The islands' territorial status remained contested for the next few decades. By raising flags, erecting signs and making the occasional expedition, both Spain and Britain sought to underpin their claim to Fernando Póo and (to a lesser extent) to Annobón. France in 1856 and Germany in 1885 dispatched vessels to incorporate Annobón into their own respective empires, in each case being prevented from following through by diplomatic pressure from Spain. Yet Spain itself had difficulty in asserting its control over Annobón. The schooner *Santa Teresa*, which sailed for the island in 1859 in order to recruit labourers, met so much local resistance that it left without having made a single hire. Several visits by Spanish missionaries in the 1860s likewise did not lead to the establishment of a permanent mission station.[39]

Only when international recognition of its colonial claims was threatened at the Berlin Conference did Spain establish an effective presence in the Gulf of Guinea. In 1885 the government merged its west African possessions into a single colony, known as *Guinea Española*, and in August of that year six Claretians established a Catholic mission in Annobón. By this time, the islanders had run their own affairs for about two hundred years.[40]

∗∗∗

Although Annobón played a marginal part both in colonial policy and in Atlantic shipping, its seclusion was relative rather than absolute. Circumstantial evidence points to relations between Annobón and other islands in the Gulf of Guinea. For instance, the missionaries who took up work in Annobón in 1885 observed

---

38 Creus, "Cuando las almas no pueden ser custodiadas", 518.
39 Caldeira, "Uma ilha quase desconhecida", 105; Cantús, "Fernando Poo", 355, 558; Creus, "Cuando las almas no pueden ser custodiadas", 519; Liniger-Goumaz, *Äquatorialguinea*, 8f.; Liniger-Goumaz, *Historical Dictionary of Equatorial Guinea*, 30; Liniger-Goumaz, *Small Is Not Always Beautiful*, 9; Ndongo Bidyogo, *Historia y tragedia de Guinea Ecuatorial*, 26f.; Sundiata, *From Slaving to Neoslavery*, 43–45; Usera y Alarcon, *Memoria de la isla de Fernando Poo*, 39f.
40 Caldeira, "Organizar a liberdade", 5; Caldeira, "Medo e religião popular na ilha de Ano Bom", 6; Caldeira, "A 'republica negra' de Ano Bom", 55f.; Creus, "Cuando las almas no pueden ser custodiadas", 519, 532. On the history of the Christian mission in Annobón see esp. Creus, *Action missionnaire en Guinée Équatoriale*.

remarkable similarities between the creole languages that had emerged in Annobón, São Tomé and Príncipe. People's names too bore a striking resemblance to each other across the islands.[41] In addition, more recent ethnographic research has shown that the inhabitants of Annobón and Fernando Póo used similar musical instruments and were familiar with similar dances.[42] Relations between island societies in the Gulf of Guinea are also suggested by the origin myth of the Wovea population of Ndame (also known as Ambas), a rocky island off the south-western coast of modern Cameroon. This myth portrays the Wovea as as the descendants of a man from Fernando Póo who was shipwrecked on that coast (probably in the seventeenth century) and married a local woman.[43]

There are, however, other explanations for these phenomena than direct exchange between the islands. It is possible, for instance, that the slaves taken from São Tomé to Annobón might have preserved certain linguistic traits and cultural practices over centuries even without subsequent contact with São Tomé. Some customs may also have been introduced by political prisoners from Cuba, several hundred of whom the Spanish transported to Fernando Póo and possibly to the other islands in the 1860s and 70s.[44]

What also remains largely unknown is the extent to which Annobón was touched by the Atlantic slave trade. The historian Dolores García Cantús supposes that its inhabitants notorious refractoriness meant that slave ships visited the island less often than, for instance, São Tomé, Príncipe or the Cape Verde Islands.[45] It certainly seems that Annobón was not a regular stop on the Atlantic slaving routes. Yet slavers, like other vessels, were prone to drift off course, and in such cases they might indeed visit Annobón, if only to take on food and water before continuing their journey across the Atlantic.[46] According to Caldeira, shipping around the island peaked between 1770 and 1772, during which period a total of 64 vessels put in there, but it is impossible to tell how many of them were slave ships.[47] What is certain is that Annobón never became a hub of the slave trade – unlike São Tomé, which around 1800 was one of the world's

---

41 Barrena, "La Isla de Annobón", 130f.
42 Aranzadi, "A Drum's Trans-Atlantic Journey from Africa to the Americas and Back after the end of Slavery".
43 Ardener, "The Wovea Islanders of Ambas Bay".
44 Sundiata, *From Slaving to Neoslavery*, 50–54.
45 Cantús, "Fernando Poo", 46.
46 Caldeira, "Escravidão e liberdade", 630f.; Maris-Wolf, *Encyclopedia of the Middle Passage*, 39; Cunha Matos, *Corografia historica das ilhas de Tomè, Príncipe, Anno Bom, e Fernando Po*, 90.
47 Caldeira, "Uma ilha quase desconhecida", 101.

leading slave markets.⁴⁸ It also seems that, as piracy in west African waters experienced a resurgence in the first third of the nineteenth century, pirates sought refuge in Annobón. A story circulating aboard American whaleships and merchantmen in 1832 told of a large band of pirates lying in wait on shore of Annobón to raid any vessel anchoring there.⁴⁹ Whether there was substance to this particular rumour or not, it seems that piracy did not present a continuing problem around Annobón, for no attacks are recorded.

It does, however, seem to have occurred that slave ships abducted Annobonese who had come aboard to trade. One of several indications to that effect can be found in the report of the British Niger Expedition under Henry Dundas, which visited the island for a week in October 1841. According to the report, locals had told of having obtained guns by barter in order to fend off attacks from slavers.⁵⁰ When these attacks were supposed to have taken place is, however, left vague. It must be remembered that in the 1830s and 40s, Britain claimed the islands in the Gulf of Guinea for a claim, a claim supposedly justified by British efforts to suppress the slave trade. Official British references to the slave trade from that era hence deserved to be treated with caution. This applies no less to the report of John and Richard Lander, explorers who in 1830 came to the Gulf of Guinea in search of the mouth of the river Niger. The Landers claimed that the inhabitants of Annobón lived in permanent fear of slave traders, but since they had neither visited the island themselves nor gave any source for their claim, it is of no great value.⁵¹

By contrast, the resistance which the Annobonese put up to Spanish and Portuguese attempts at colonisation in the eighteenth and nineteenth centuries may indeed be understood as motivated by a fear of enslavement born from the experience of slave ships. Even in the twentieth century, it was a common imprecation in Annobón to wish enslavement by a passing vessel on somebody.⁵² At the dawn of the whaling era around Annobón, slave ships had become a rarity in these waters, and references to the slave trade in the records of whalers are few. In 1826 the *Minerva* of New Bedford encountered a French brig just off the island;

---

48 Covey, "São Tomé", 336.
49 Torrey, *Torrey's Narrative*, 45.
50 Allen/Thomson, *A Narrative of the Expedition Sent by Her Majesty's Government to the Niger River in 1841*, vol. 2, 59f. Tams, by contrast, who visited in 1842, has this to report: "They are strangers to weapons of all kinds, their only dangerous instrument being the knife they carry in order to cut open coconuts to satisfy their hunger and thirst." (Tams, *Die Portugiesischen Besitzungen in Süd-West-Afrika*, 199)
51 Lander/Lander, *Journal of an Expedition to Explore the Course and Termination of the Niger*, vol. 2, 307.
52 Caldeira, "Medo e religião popular na ilha de Ano Bom", 8.

it had come from Martinique and appeared to be a slave ship.[53] In 1841 members of the British Niger Expedition found a wreck on the coast of Annobón which they took to that of a Spanish slaver.[54] And during the visit of the brig *Leonidas* of Westport in March 1856, a schooner anchored off the island which Captain Grinnell supposed to be a slave ship.[55] On 1859 the crew of the barque *Globe* of New Bedford came upon the wreck of a slaver and retrieved its anchor.[56]

In all these cases, we have only the speculations of seamen to go by; whalemen do not provide documentary evidence of the activities of slavers in the island. Nor did they encounter many other vessels in nearby waters. Merchantmen would make occasional visits to take on provisions or ballast, and patrols of the Royal Navy in the area were rarer still.[57] Writing in 1842, Georg Tams wondered why shipping in the Gulf of Guinea largely passed Annobón by, concluding that "provisions, though plentifully available here, are far more early acquired on the islands closer to the coast". As for slave ships, he added: "Yet in order to serve as a stop on a voyage to Brazil or Havana, Annabon is too close to the coast. In addition to which the irregular nature of the winds in those parts means that the crossing to Guinea may take twenty-four, thirty or forty days and hence the ships try to avoid Annabon if they at all can."[58] Winds and currents indeed put Annobón in an awkward location for vessels crossing the Atlantic to or from America on a horizontal east-west path. For whalers, by contrast, who followed the migration of the humpback whale sail into the Gulf of Guinea from the south, Annobón was the closest island in these waters.

***

How did the population of Annobón support itself? It seems that the island's tropical flora and fauna, in addition to the crops introduced in the sixteenth century, were enough to make it self-sufficient in food. There are no records of famine. On the contrary: according to the few visitors who saw the island's interior in the nineteenth century, fruit was abundant there. "The ground was in places quite covered in fallen fruits", recalled Tams.[59] Although estimates of

---

53 Log MINERVA, 1825–1827, 21.04.1826.
54 Allen/Thomson, *A Narrative of the Expedition Sent by Her Majesty's Government to the Niger River in 1841*, vol. 2, 50.
55 Log LEONIDAS, 1855–1857, 22.03.1856.
56 Log GLOBE, 1858–1861, 26.09.1859.
57 Allen, Journal GLOBE, 1869–1872, 09. & 10.09.1870; Bastian, Afrikanische Reisen, 272; Log GLOBE, 1869–1872, 09.09.1870; Haywood, "American Whalers and Africa", 76.
58 Tams, *Die Portugiesischen Besitzungen in Süd-West-Afrika*, 198.
59 Tams, *Die Portugiesischen Besitzungen in Süd-West-Afrika*, 200; for similar observations see Log PEDRO VARELA, 1881–1883, 05.04.1882.

the population of Annobón in the nineteenth century vary wildly (Tab. 9), the variance is far more likely to be due to the rather rough nature of these estimates than to significant waves of mortality. William Simpson noticed a good many elderly people living in Annobón in 1842, which he took as an indication of the islanders' general good health.[60]

Drinking water was gathered every morning in coconut shells from *Lago a pot*, the lake formed by the crater of Pico Surcado, and taken to San Antonio – largely by the young, as members of the British Niger Expedition observed in 1841.[61] But the coconut palm not only provided water vessels, it was Annobón's principal source of raw materials. A large coconut grove stretched out on one side of San Antonio.[62] In the mid-twentieth century the scientist Aurelio Basilio observed islanders using the wood and fronds of the coconut palm to make chairs and baskets and roof their dwellings; from the fruits themselves they made wine and extracted oil.[63] The British Niger Expedition found large fenced-in manioc patches in the interior.[64] Fences were also to be found in San Antonio itself, enclosing the yards in which pigs and chickens were kept.[65] Simpson also observed the Annobonese growing crops in enclosed "provision-grounds" to keep them safe from pigs and goats.[66]

To go fishing, the islanders fashioned light dug-out canoes known as *batélu* or *bate* from the trunks of the kapok tree. As Tams observed, these canoes usually had room for only two occupants.[67] When Basilio came to Annobón in the 1950s, he found approximately 120 *batélus* in service, most which could carry two or four passengers. Some were single-seaters, while six of them war large craft able to carry up to ten men.[68] Fishing in *batélus* was a male preserve, as

---

60 Simpson, *A Private Journal Kept during the Niger Expedition*, 70, 72.
61 Allen/Thomson, *A Narrative of the Expedition Sent by Her Majesty's Government to the Niger River in 1841*, vol. 2, 61f.; Tams, *Die Portugiesischen Besitzungen in Süd-West-Afrika*, 193.
62 Tams, *Die Portugiesischen Besitzungen in Süd-West-Afrika*, 194.
63 Basilio, *Caza y pesca en Annobon*, 81.
64 Allen/Thomson, *A Narrative of the Expedition Sent by Her Majesty's Government to the Niger River in 1841*, vol. 2, 61, 63. Simpson also records enclosed vegetable gardens in the island's interior as well fenced-in patched abutting their houses. (Simpson, *A Private Journal Kept during the Niger Expedition*, 72) Yet in this instance we find the Niger Expedition reporting the opposite. (Allen/Thomson, *A Narrative of the Expedition Sent by Her Majesty's Government to the Niger River in 1841*, vol. 2, 59)
65 Tams, *Die Portugiesischen Besitzungen in Süd-West-Afrika*, 195.
66 Simpson, *A Private Journal Kept during the Niger Expedition*, 72.
67 Basilio, *Caza y pesca en Annobon*, 80; Caldeira, "Organizar a liberdade", 7; Caldeira, "A 'republica negra' de Ano Bom", 58; Tams, *Die Portugiesischen Besitzungen in Süd-West-Afrika*, 187, 190.
68 Basilio, *Caza y pesca en Annobon*, 80.

was the making of palm wine. Women, on the other hand, did the main share of work in the gardens, where they grew chiefly manioc and yams. Such gardens appear to have been private property, whereas fruit trees grew freely and were available to all.[69] In spite of references to private property, Annobonese society appears to have been geared towards subsistence rather than the production of surplus for profit.[70] No other island society in the Atlantic world is likely to have equalled Annobón's self-sufficiency – both economic and political – in the eighteenth and nineteenth centuries.

Tab. 9: Estimates of the population of Annobón in the nineteenth century.

1836	3,500[a]
1841	3,000[b]
1842	1,000[c]
1845	900–3,000[d]
1846	4,000[e]
1858	2,000[e]
1861	2,000–3,000[d,f]
1896	1,411[e]

Sources: [a]Móros y Morellon/Rios, *Memorias sobre las islas africanas de España*, 22f.; [b]Allen/Thomson, *A Narrative of the Expedition Sent by Her Majesty's Government to the Niger River in 1841*, vol. 2, 59; [c]Simpson, *A Private Journal Kept during the Niger Expedition*, 72; [d]Unzueta y Yuste, *Islas del Golfo de Guinea*, 213; [e]Caldeira, "Uma ilha quase desconhecida", 108; [f]Travassos Valdez, *Six Years of a Traveller's Life in Western Africa*, vol. 2, 63.

Chummies

At 11 o'clock on 4 September 1870 the *Globe* of New Bedford dropped anchor at Annobón. Merchants from the island had already been on board for an hour.[71]

---

69 Caldeira, "Organizar a liberdade", 6f.; Caldeira, "A 'republica negra' de Ano Bom", 57. For an Annobón fisherman's song ("Ôdjai omé sa babub" / "The sea is angry today"), recorded some years ago as part of an oral history project, see Lêdjam, *Cancionero oral Annobonés*, 72.
70 Caldeira, "Organizar a liberdade", 7; Caldeira, "A 'republica negra' de Ano Bom", 59.
71 Log GLOBE, 1869–1872, 04.09.1870.

Nearly every contact between whalemen and Annobonese began at sea. Merchants would usually take to their *batélus* as soon as the outline of a vessel appeared on the horizon, rowing out to meet it in anything from three to twenty canoes. It was no rarity for them to cover many nautical miles in the process. Many seamen were amazed at how nimbly the islanders clambered up the sides of a whaleship on the open sea:[72] "It has always been a mystery how they could do that with the ship under full sail and going along before a good breeze, it seemed as if an army had arrived", recalled Lucy Smith, who came to Annobón in 1870 aboard the barque *Nautilus* of New Bedford, of which her husband George was captain.[73]

Crews calling at Annobón for the first time tended not to be prepared for the sudden arrival of these traders. As they came aboard, the voices of the islanders mingled with those of the officers shouting their orders from the quarterdeck in frantic confusion.[74] Seamen would sometimes jostle traders for space on deck.[75] Charles Allen, third mate of the *Globe*, found the visitors' conduct to be "half crazy". Allen was, however, prepared: some of the crew knew Annobón and had already put aside surplus shirts and trousers to offer in barter.[76]

When Lucy Smith and her husband stepped out of their cabin onto the deck of the *Naultilus*, they were hailed with the greeting "be my chummie".[77] "Chummy" was a commonplace term aboard ship for a close friend,[78] and the Annobonese had learnt to use it for their own ends. They came with garlands of flowers and with bead and shell necklaces, which they offered to put around

---

[72] Allen/Thomson, *A Narrative of the Expedition Sent by Her Majesty's Government to the Niger River in 1841*, vol. 2, 47; Log BERTHA, 1883–1887, 02.03.1885; Log GLOBE, 1869–1872, 08.09.1870 & 06.09.1871; Log MINERVA, 1825–1827, 10. & 11.02.1826; Haywood, "American Whalers and Africa", 171f.; Log GEORGE AND SUSAN, 1865–1868, 05.08.1867; Log JANUS, 1837–1839, 10.04.1838; Log SUNBEAM, 1878–1882, 19.09.1880; Ricketson, Journal 1885, 17.04.1885; Smith, Journal NAUTILUS, 1869–1874, 15.09.1870; Thompson, "A Whaling Cruise in the Sea Fox", 147.
[73] Lucy P. Smith. "My Adventures Afloat." 1925. Martha's Vineyard Museum: Record Unit 207, Whaling and the Vineyard, 1793–1925, Series VI, Subseries C, Box 4, Folder 3. 4; see also Lucy P. Smith. "My Adventures Afloat, or Leaves from my Log Book." 1925. Martha's Vineyard Museum: Record Unit 207, Whaling and the Vineyard, 1793–1925, Series VI, Subseries C, Box 4, Folder 3. 9. On Lucy Smith and the writing of her diary see Teller, *Twelve Works of Naive Genius*.
[74] Log PEDRO VARELA, 1881–1883, 01.04.1882; Ricketson, Journal 1885, 17.04.1885.
[75] Phillips, Journal ADMIRAL BLAKE, 1868–1870, 13.06.1869.
[76] Allen, Journal GLOBE, 1869–1872, 07. & 08.10.1869.
[77] Lucy P. Smith. "My Adventures Afloat." 1925. Martha's Vineyard Museum: Record Unit 207, Whaling and the Vineyard, 1793–1925, Series VI, Subseries C, Box 4, Folder 3. 4.
[78] Jarman, *Journal of a Voyage to the South Seas*, 101.

seamen's necks, thereby making them "chummies".[79] This status imposed both duties and obligations: for the duration of his stay, an islander would keep his chummy supplied with fruit, eggs and other necessities, for which he expected a present in return at the end of the vessel's stay. In particular demand were trousers, shirts, hats and other items of clothing as well as (of course) tobacco. "The men instantly displayed great eagerness for tobacco", noted Tams on his arrival in March 1842: "even on the first day I had already exhausted my little supply." Cash, on the other hand, was refused, the islanders having no use for it.[80]

Annobonese traders appear not to have made their initial visits to whaleships with major transactions in mind, offering only small amounts of fruit, small animals or fish. The point was above all to establish chummy relations.[81] "Each one grabs one of the crew & presents him with coconuts & orinnges & Requests him to be his Chum during the stay of the vessel", observed Harvey Phillips in 1869. "The native Has armed himself with A string of native beads Said to be the handy work of the girls on shore This He will throw around your neck also as A token of Friendship and then with a deal of pomp & more Broken English pronounce his naim which he tells you not to forget."[82] The names by which the islanders introduced themselves to visiting seamen is a topic I shall address in due course. With regard to the practice of making chummies, it is worth noting here that the Annobonese pursued a commercial strategy quite similar to that of some contemporary island societies in Oceania. Tahitian traders too rowed out to meet whalers and offered seamen personal friendship for the duration of their stay, one aspect of which was the exchange of gifts.[83]

The islanders' visits were not limited to the day of its arrival. In fact, they usually came aboard ship every day. "The deck full of natives" is an entry to be

---

[79] According to Zamora Loboch, the Annobonese, when speaking among themselves, referred to the Americans as *Jabonñi*. This statement, however, applies to the twentieth century, and it is uncertain when the term entered use and whether it was current in the nineteenth century. (Zamora Loboch, *Notícia de Annobón*, 69)

[80] Phillips, Journal ADMIRAL BLAKE, 1868–1870, 13.06.1869; Smith, Journal NAUTILUS, 1869–1874, 15.09.1870; Lucy P. Smith. "My Adventures Afloat." 1925. Martha's Vineyard Museum: Record Unit 207, Whaling and the Vineyard, 1793–1925, Series VI, Subseries C, Box 4, Folder 3. 4f.; Lucy P. Smith. "My Adventures Afloat, or, Leaves from my Log Book." 1925. Martha's Vineyard Museum: Record Unit 207, Whaling and the Vineyard, 1793–1925, Series VI, Subseries C, Box 4, Folder 3. 9; Tams, *Die Portugiesischen Besitzungen in Süd-West-Afrika*, 201; Thompson, "A Whaling Cruise in the Sea Fox", 147–149.

[81] Log JANUS, 1837–1839, 09.04.1838; Phillips, Journal ADMIRAL BLAKE, 1868–1870, 13.06.1869; Thompson, "A Whaling Cruise in the Sea Fox", 147–149.

[82] Phillips, Journal ADMIRAL BLAKE, 1868–1870, 13.06.1869.

[83] Chappell, "Beyond the Beach", 23.

found daily in similar form in the logs of many whalers moored off Annobón.[84] The islanders that appeared under the guise of traders were always men, and their most pressing demand was often for clothing.[85] Even as they pulled up alongside a vessel in their *batélus* they would proffer fruit and call out something like "Dash me a shirt or trousers, and me give all these."[86] Other phrases quoted in the sources include "Anno Bon man – he good man – he no rogue man – dash (give) him coat, he sell you cocoa-nut" or "Annobon poor fellow, no have shirt, no have trouwsa."[87] This should not, however, be taken to mean that Annobonese traders appeared throughout in the role of supplicants, being instead both confident and price-conscious.[88] The allure which clothing made from textiles held for the islanders is evident from an observation made by Lucy Smith. When, sitting on deck, she began to knit stockings for her son, she found herself surrounded and closely watched by islanders. "It seemed as wonderful to them as wireless telegraph does to me", she recalled.[89] Caldeira assumes that textile clothing – which, it is worth noting, the Annobonese did not wear in their everyday lives – was not only a status marker but also served religious purposes, being worn for wedding and burial ceremonies.[90]

Besides clothing, the Annobonese were interested in cloth (including old sailcloth), salt meat, wire, needles, shackles, knives, brandy, tobacco, iron parts of all kinds as well as (rarely) firearms and gunpowder.[91] Samuel Chalmers Thompson, a seaman who came to Annobón in the mid-1860s aboard the brig *Sea Fox* of Westport, gives the following description of trade on board ship:

> They crowded on deck. An officer took some plug tobacco, and for a piece as big as his thumb, they would sell a bunch of bananas or plantains, a basket of oranges or eggs, a bag of cocoanuts, till the ship looked like a wholesale fruit store. No kind of money was of any use there. Tobacco seems to be the most universal medium with the outlying tribes.[92]

---

84 See e.g. Log DESDEMONA, 1869–1872, 02.07.1870; Log PEDRO VARELA, 1881–1883, 02. & 04.04.1882.
85 Simpson, *A Private Journal Kept during the Niger Expedition*, 70.
86 Ibid., 73.
87 Allen/Thomson, *A Narrative of the Expedition Sent by Her Majesty's Government to the Niger River in 1841*, vol. 2, 51, 58.
88 Allen, Journal GLOBE, 1869–1872, 04.09.1870.
89 Lucy P. Smith. "My Adventures Afloat." 1925. Martha's Vineyard Museum: Record Unit 207, Whaling and the Vineyard, 1793–1925, Series VI, Subseries C, Box 4, Folder 3. 6.
90 Caldeira, "Organizar a liberdade", 7.
91 Ibid., 7; Haywood, "American Whalers and Africa", 78f.; Log GLOBE, 1869–1872, 11.09.1871; Log SAMUEL & THOMAS, 1846–1848, 12.–14.05.1847; Phillips, Journal ADMIRAL BLAKE, 1868–1870, 16. & 19.06.1869.
92 Thompson, "A Whaling Cruise in the Sea Fox", 147–149.

Shipmasters were interested above all in buying fruit and vegetables, which the islanders were able to offer in great abundance. Oranges, bananas, coconuts, pineapples, sweet potatoes, limes, lemons, tamarinds and peppers would be taken on board by the hundred, if not by the thousand.[93] When the *Canton II* of New Bedford sailed from Annobón in the mid-1890s, "Our yardarms were strung from end to end with bunches of bananas", as the seaman Harry Chippendale recalled.[94] Groundnuts, eggs, guavas, yams and fish were traded in smaller quantities. The islanders also sold small numbers (single or double digits) of chickens, goats and pigs to visiting vessels,[95] and in at least one instance appear to have offered a captain ropes they had made of coconut fibres.[96]

While the provisioning trade took place under the captains' supervision and was recorded accordingly, it is less easy to establish what common seamen bartered. They are likely to have been interested above all in palm wine, and the islanders knew ways of getting the drink past vigilant seamen. Seamen also bought shells, baskets and other small objects, probably as souvenirs.[97] By the time whalers began to operate in the Gulf of Guinea, the Annobonese had already developed the pattern of their trading strategies with ships' crews.[98] It was, however, with the advent of whaling that this trade reached its greatest intensity, and in the nineteenth century whalers were the principal source of goods which the islanders were unable to produce themselves.[99]

---

[93] Log BERTHA, 1878–1881, 28.08.1880; Log GLOBE, 1869–1872, 09. & 14.10.1869; Log SAMUEL & THOMAS, 1846–1848, 12.05.1847. The barque *Ospray* of New Bedford took on board about 2,000 oranges during a week's stay in September 1872; see Log OSPRAY, 1871–1874, 14.09.1872. In many cases, however, it is hard to ascertain the exact quantities traded, since logs often give such vague units as "boat load" or "bushel". Although the latter was in theory a standardised measure of volume, aboard whaleships it seems to have meant simply a basketful of no particular size.

[94] Chippendale, *Sails and Whales*, 44.

[95] Allen, Journal GLOBE, 1869–1872, 07.09.1870; Allen/Thomson, *A Narrative of the Expedition Sent by Her Majesty's Government to the Niger River in 1841*, vol. 2, 51; Log DESDEMONA, 1873–1876, 31.07.1875; Log FALCON, 1887–1890, 21.07.1888; Log GLOBE, 1869–1872, 09. & 14.10.1869; Log NYE, 1853–1856, 08. & 09.06.1855; Log PALMETTO, 1872–1875, 12.–18.06.1873; Log PEDRO VARELA, 1881–1883, 11. & 12.04.1882; Log SAMUEL & THOMAS, 1846–1848, 12.05.1847; Phillips, Journal ADMIRAL BLAKE, 1868–1870, 16. & 19.06.1869.

[96] Log DESDEMONA, 1869–1872, 03.07.1870.

[97] Allen/Thomson, *A Narrative of the Expedition Sent by Her Majesty's Government to the Niger River in 1841*, vol. 2, 53; Log GLOBE, 1869–1872, 09. & 14.10.1869; Log PEDRO VARELA, 1881–1883, 01.04.1882.

[98] Caldeira, "Organizar a liberdade", 7.

[99] Haywood, "American Whalers and Africa", 80.

The whalemen brought another innovation which had not featured in earlier contacts with crews. Around 1870 – at the peak, that is, of American humpback whaling in the Gulf of Guinea – the commercial interests of the Annobonese underwent a change. They now sought to acquire not only clothing but also whale meat. As Charles Allen, for instance, recorded for 13 September 1871: "Traded away the Hump Back meat for potatoes & Bananas".[100] Since whalemen had no use for whale meat, considering it a waste product, this new interest on the part of the islanders opened up new commercial opportunities. Besides trading the meat of the humpback whales they took in these waters, some vessels' crews now began to hunt pilot whales and porpoises for the express purpose of bartering their flesh for fruit in Annobón.[101] "The natives of Anno-Bon are very fond of Blackfish [pilot whale] we would liked to get more for trade", noted Annie Holms Ricketson in 1885.[102] The development on the part of the islanders of a taste for the flesh of whales killed by American seamen coincided with a development to be discussed at the end of this chapter: the emergence of Annobonese whaling.

***

Not only at sea but also on land, encounters between seamen and Annobonese were dominated by trade. Traders usually piled up their fruit on the beach. In 1870 Lucy Smith of the *Nautilus* observed how traders asked for a small item of clothing in exchange for a small pile of fruit and a larger item for a larger pile. Captain Smith's desire to purchase a single large quantity of fruit rather than several piles of different sizes was rebuffed by the islanders. Smith saw these as evidence of their inability to perform basic addition.[103] By selling fruit only in comparatively small lots, however, the Annobonese traders may have pursued a strategy of doing business with individual seamen rather than the captain as representative of the crew as a whole. Making many small transactions instead of a single large one not only increased each trader's scope for negotiation, it also spread the risk in case one trading partner withheld payment. Some captains tried to get their way by not allowing the crew to go ashore until provisions had

---

100 Allen, Journal GLOBE, 1869–1872, 13.09.1871.
101 Allen, Journal GLOBE, 1869–1872, 12.10.1869; Log GLOBE, 1869–1872, 09., 12. & 14.10.1869; Log WASHINGTON FREEMAN, 1868–1870, 02.08.1870; Phillips, Journal ADMIRAL BLAKE, 1868–1870, 15.06.1870. In the last third of the nineteenth century, we sometimes hear of inhabitants of the mainland coast of west Africa rowing out to meet whaleships and asking for whale meat. (Ferguson, *Harpooner*, 132f.)
102 Ricketson, Journal 1885, 16.04.1885.
103 Lucy P. Smith. "My Adventures Afloat, or, Leaves from my Log Book." 1925. Martha's Vineyard Museum: Record Unit 207, Whaling and the Vineyard, 1793–1925, Series VI, Subseries C, Box 4, Folder 3. 10.

been secured. In so doing, they made their own concern – to settle the purchase of provisions quickly – that of the traders, who wanted to do business with as many seamen as possible.[104]

Sometimes Annobonese traders would ask seamen to provide them with letters of reference, which they could then display in future trading encounters as evidence of their integrity. Some traders, Lucy Smith observed, came aboard brandishing veritable fistfuls of such papers. Yet the seamen who wrote them did not always keep to their side of the bargain, sometimes warning that the bearer was in fact a swindler. This may in part have been a response to actual cases of fraud, but other cases are likely to have been jokes at the expense of the illiterate islanders.[105]

On the whole, however, barter between Annobonese and crewmen seems to have been mutually satisfactory. This is suggested not only by the decades over which the island was frequented by whalers but also by the fact that the records contain very few hints at conflict. Some men may have felt the need to vent their exasperation at the bustle caused on deck by the arrival of Annobonese traders,[106] and one captain even ordered a gun to be fired to deter theft of tools.[107] Yet even that incident seems to have had no further repercussions. A more typical remark is that recorded by Annie Holmes Ricketson on the sailing of the *Pedro Varela* in April 1885: "There was a great shaking of hands and bidding us good bye and many good wishes."[108]

However, seamen who had hoped to take advantage of the Annobonese and found instead canny trading partners capable of turning the tables on them were apt to be loo less kindly on their practices. "If you give one of them your Chest & contents he wold want your trunk & bedding and I donot think he wold be satisfied then", noted Phillips in March 1869.[109] And even Annie Holmes Ricketson complained that the value of the presents that the islanders expected from their chummies was twice that of the fruit they had supplied.[110]

***

---

[104] Log SARAH, 1873–1876, 01.–03.05. & 02.11.1874.
[105] Lucy P. Smith. "My Adventures Afloat, or, Leaves from my Log Book." 1925. Martha's Vineyard Museum: Record Unit 207, Whaling and the Vineyard, 1793–1925, Series VI, Subseries C, Box 4, Folder 3. 10.
[106] Allen/Thomson, *A Narrative of the Expedition Sent by Her Majesty's Government to the Niger River in 1841*, vol. 2, 51; Phillips, Journal ADMIRAL BLAKE, 1868–1870, 16.06.1869; Ricketson, Journal 1885, 20.04.1885.
[107] Tams, *Die Portugiesischen Besitzungen in Süd-West-Afrika*, 189.
[108] Ricketson, Journal 1885, 26.04.1885.
[109] Phillips, Journal ADMIRAL BLAKE, 1868–1870, 23.06.1869.
[110] Ricketson, Journal 1885, 26.04.1885.

Once traders had made first contact with the crew and the vessel had dropped anchor, it was the usual practice for a representative of the island to board the vessel, where he would introduce himself as its "governor". Like the "chummy" system, the manner in which the representative presented himself to the seamen resembled practices of oceanic island societies elsewhere, with European status insignia appropriated as tokens of eminence.[111] Besides the title of governor – the Portuguese title of *capitão-mor* was also sometimes used – these consisted above all of clothes and jewellery (Fig. 36). The governor who came aboard the *Nautilus* in 1870 was dressed in parts of European military uniforms and wore a felt hat and a ring on his little finger as well as other brass rings. Whether the governor donned this attire only to signify his rank in meetings with seamen or whether he wore it on the island, too – perhaps to highlight his exclusive access to outside actors and the goods they brought – remains unclear. The governor's importance was further emphasised by an attendant carrying his walking stick and his parasol. This retainer was referred to by the governor as his steward and hence by a term familiar to seafarers,[112] the steward being the captain's personal servant aboard a whaleship. Samuel Chalmers Thompson, whose voyage in the *Sea Fox* from 1865 to 1867 brought him to Annobón, noticed other titles being borrowed from whalers: "Instead of a prime minister, they have the king's first and second mates. Instead of the lord high admiral, they have the king's boat-steerer."[113] These dignitaries were often in attendance when the *capitão-mor* came aboard. In 1838 the log of the *Janus* records that she was visited by the "Govenner & about 10 or 15 of the head Men."[114]

The governor usually introduced himself as the island's head or, in one instance, as the "mouth" of its people. From the captain, he demanded a fee in the form of clothes, promising in return to supply the vessel with water, firewood

---

111 On the appropriation of European status symbols in Hawaii see Sahlins, *Historical Metaphors and Mythical Realities*, 29–31.
112 Lucy P. Smith. "My Adventures Afloat." 1925. Martha's Vineyard Museum: Record Unit 207, Whaling and the Vineyard, 1793–1925, Series VI, Subseries C, Box 4, Folder 3. 5f.; Lucy P. Smith. "My Adventures Afloat, or, Leaves from my Log Book." 1925. Martha's Vineyard Museum: Record Unit 207, Whaling and the Vineyard, 1793–1925, Series VI, Subseries C, Box 4, Folder 3. 10. The governor sometimes also wore a red robe see Allen/Thomson, *A Narrative of the Expedition Sent by Her Majesty's Government to the Niger River in 1841*, vol. 2, 48. For other descriptions of the governor's costume see Caldeira, "Organizar a liberdade", 9, Tams, *Die Portugiesischen Besitzungen in Süd-West-Afrika*, 187 and Thompson, "A Whaling Cruise in the Sea Fox", 147–149.
113 Thompson, "A Whaling Cruise in the Sea Fox", 147–149; see also Allen/Thomson, *A Narrative of the Expedition Sent by Her Majesty's Government to the Niger River in 1841*, vol. 2, 58.
114 Log JANUS, 1837–1839, 09.04.1838.

and food. In the case of the *Janus*, the governor also demanded to spend one night aboard the vessel with his retinue. A similar practice is recorded in other sources, though not in their majority. In those that do mention it, the governor is reported to have claimed that a night on board was a customary entitlement.[115]

Mention of an Annobonese governor or *capitão-mor* can already be found in eighteenth-century sources. Caldeira assumes his role to have been that of a figurehead without and power within the island itself and acting as the islanders' deputy only in contacts with ships' crews.[116] This interpretation is supported by an observation made both by nineteenth-century whalers and by earlier visitors to the island in the eighteenth century: a governor or *capitão-mor* remained in office while a certain number of vessels called at the island – irrespective of the time it took for that number to be reached. Depending on how successful trade had been under the governor, a committee – the report of the 1841 Niger Expedition mentions a "government" consisting of five men; Caldeira, drawing on Portuguese sources, calls it a council of elders – then decided whether to renew his term of office or replace him with another man. The number of vessels constituting a term appears to have changed over time. Whereas late-nineteenth-century sources cite ten or twelve ships, some eighteenth-century ones set the number at only two. This would suggest that governors' terms were increased over the course of the nineteenth century, perhaps with a view to letting them acquire more experience in negotiating with captains.[117]

The idea that the governor held no sway ashore is challenged, however, by an observation made by seamen aboard the *Pedro Varela* of New Bedford. While the schooner lay off Annobón in 1883, the governor died and the crew witnessed

---

115 Allen/Thomson, *A Narrative of the Expedition Sent by Her Majesty's Government to the Niger River in 1841*, vol. 2, 49; Log SAMUEL & THOMAS, 1846–1848, 12.05.1847; Tams, *Die Portugiesischen Besitzungen in Süd-West-Afrika*, 187f.

116 Caldeira, "Organizar a liberdade", 9; Caldeira, "A 'republica negra' de Ano Bom", 60. A hint to that effect can already be found in the report of the British Niger Expedition: "Whether they have any other privilege or jurisdiction, it was impossible to learn with certainty." (Allen/Thomson, *A Narrative of the Expedition Sent by Her Majesty's Government to the Niger River in 1841*, vol. 2, 58)

117 Allen/Thomson, *A Narrative of the Expedition Sent by Her Majesty's Government to the Niger River in 1841*, vol. 2, 57f.; Barrena, "La Isla de Annobón", 130; Caldeira, *La Leyenda de Lodã*, 77; Caldeira, "Organizar a liberdade", 9; Caldeira, "A 'republica negra' de Ano Bom", 61; Lucy P. Smith. "My Adventures Afloat." 1925. Martha's Vineyard Museum: Record Unit 207, Whaling and the Vineyard, 1793–1925, Series VI, Subseries C, Box 4, Folder 3. 6; Lucy P. Smith. "My Adventures Afloat, or, Leaves from my Log Book." 1925. Martha's Vineyard Museum: Record Unit 207, Whaling and the Vineyard, 1793–1925, Series VI, Subseries C, Box 4, Folder 3. 10; Thompson, "A Whaling Cruise in the Sea Fox", 147–149; Travassos Valdez, *Six Years of a Traveller's Life in Western Africa*, vol. 2, 65.

his elaborate funeral. Annie Holmes Ricketson, the captain's wife, has left us a detailed account of the ceremony. It began with the *sanguistã gueza ngyani* summoning the traders from the vessel to the house of the governor, who lay in state on the floor, dressed in his official garb and wrapped in white cloths. The body was then placed on a stretcher and carried to the main church or *Gueza gany*. Hundreds of people then joined the procession, many of them wearing textile clothing and some wooden masks. Some beat drums, most danced, including the pallbearers. Women cried and screamed. Two islanders dressed entirely in red opened the church door, and guns were fired as the body was carried in. A grave was dug directly in front of the altar and consecrated by the *sanguistã gueza ngyani*. Thereupon the governor's wide bade farewell to her husband. Several islanders then lowered the body on ropes, a curtain was dropped from the altar and once more guns were fired.[118] The elaborate nature of this ceremony and the fact that the deceased was buried at the foot of the altar suggests that the governor was indeed an eminence in the eyes of his own people. What does not follow from the source, however, is whether this level of respect was accorded to all holders of the office or whether this was a special case.

Fig. 36: The governor of Annobón, as drawn in the log of the brig *Samuel and Thomas* of Provincetown, May 1847.
Source: Log SAMUEL & THOMAS, 1846–1848.

---

118 Log PEDRO VARELA, 1881–1883, 26.04.–01.05.1883.

The only islander besides the governor or *capitão-mor* to feature as an individual in seamen's records was a "priest", probably the *sanguistã gueza ngyani*. He too would sometimes board a visiting vessel, albeit not as regularly as the governor. The priest's visits took place mainly at weekends, and some seamen suspected this was a ploy to obtain better prices – for the the *sanguistã gueza ngyani* too came to offer fruit and animals.[119]

Firewood was an essential resource for whalemen, who were able to obtain it in Annobón by one of three means: they could cut and chop up trees themselves, they could pay islanders to do so or they could buy firewood that had already been specifically prepared. Only few whalers ever availed themselves of the first option. The forest closest to the beach covered the slopes of Pico Surcado, and it seems that seamen were permitted to cut wood there without having to pay an extra charge to the governor. But to send the crew up the hill to cut down trees and carry the wood back to was several days' work, and few captains seem to have thought it worth the trouble.[120] Instead, they nearly always tried to buy wood from the islanders or to hire Annobonese men to cut wood for them.[121] "Paid 6 men for working on wood", records, for instance, the log of the *Samuel and Thomas* of Provincetown in 1847.[122] In 1842 Georg Tams observed in San Antonio that some islanders had already "piled up a good deal of chopped wood next to their houses in order that they might sell it to ship, and our ship too got a whole canoe full of it for a few bottles of brandy".[123] Prices, it seems, were subject to negotiation between captains and vendors. It might take several visits on shore for a captain to obtain the desired amount of wood at an acceptable price.[124] Only few logbooks record the quantity of wood bought in Annobón, with figures ranging from three to fifteen "boat loads".[125] This being an imprecise measure, however, it gives us no reliable idea of the number of trees cut down in Annobón for the benefit of whalers.

Nor can the amount of drinking water available on the island to seamen be established reliably. Some logs mention a number of rafts, others measure the water taken on board in casks or barrels. Since it tends to be unclear to what

---

119 Phillips, Journal ADMIRAL BLAKE, 1868–1870, 20.06.1869; Log PEDRO VARELA, 1881–1883, 02., 08. & 11.04.1882.
120 Allen/Thomson, *A Narrative of the Expedition Sent by Her Majesty's Government to the Niger River in 1841*, vol. 2, 49f.; Simpson, *A Private Journal Kept during the Niger Expedition*, 70.
121 See e.g. Allen, Journal GLOBE, 1869–1872, 05.09.1870; Log GLOBE, 1869–1872, 12.10.1869.
122 Log SAMUEL & THOMAS, 1846–1848, 13.05.1847.
123 Tams, *Die Portugiesischen Besitzungen in Süd-West-Afrika*, 201.
124 See e.g. Ricketson, Journal 1885, 23. & 24.04.1885.
125 Log DESDEMONA, 1869–1872, 24–28.07.1871; Log FALCON, 1887–1890, 21.–25.07.1888.

degree these measures were standardised, comparisons are difficult to make. We can perhaps say that the 260 barrels loaded by the *Desdemona* in 1875 constituted an unusually large amount, whereas the seventy barrels taken on by the *Janus* in 1838 represented a comparatively small quantity of water. Most of the figures recorded lie somewhere in between.[126]

As for firewood, crews were not charged extra for drinking water in Annobón. They did, however, have to gather it and get it on board themselves. To this end, they usually roped together empty barrels to form a chain, which was then towed to the nearest watering place by boat (Fig. 37). Accounts differ as to the location of that place and how easy it was to reach. The British Niger Expedition of 1841 had only to run a hose from the vessel to a brook close to the beach and was then able to fill the barrels using the vessel's pumps.[127] Some whalers' logs, by contrast, tell of arduous treks into the interior, with seamen spending several hours in search a suitable source, the water found close to the beach sometimes being described as too brackish to drink.[128] The likeliest explanation for this seeming inconsistency is seasonal variation: as rain and fog caused the level of *Lago a pot* to rise, the lake fed streams such as the *Libel Apalia* (or *Libel Apalé*) and increased the supply of water at near the coast. The river closest to San Antonio, which would have been the first place many seamen looked for potable water, was known to the Annobonese as *Agua Pata*.[129]

"Some of the men had terrible names, both vulgar and profane", was how Lucy Smith recalled her horror at the moment when Annobonese traders introduced themselves by name. "Men on different vessels that touched there would give them a name and tell them it was good [. . .] and they did not know enough of the English language to know it was wrong."[130] English-sounding names, it seems, were the legacy of earlier encounters with visiting seamen, and a few seamen, it seems, made a joke of giving their "chummies" wildly inappropriate ones. By and large, however, the names by which islanders introduced themselves on board ship were innocuous enough: Ben Williams, John Bull or Young America.[131] Tams observed that the Annobonese began each

---

126 Log DESDEMONA, 1873–1876, 31.07.–05.08.1875; Log JANUS, 1837–1839, 09.04.1838.
127 Allen/Thomson, *A Narrative of the Expedition Sent by Her Majesty's Government to the Niger River in 1841*, vol. 2, 64f.
128 Log JANUS, 1837–1839, 11.04.1838; Log PALMETTO, 1872–1875, 14.06.1873; Log SAMUEL & THOMAS, 1846–1848, 13.05.1847.
129 Cunha Matos, *Corografia historica das ilhas de Tomè, Principe, Anno Bom, e Fernando Po*, 87; Schultze, *Die Insel Annobon im Golf von Guinea*, 132.
130 Lucy P. Smith. "My Adventures Afloat." 1925. Martha's Vineyard Museum: Record Unit 207, Whaling and the Vineyard, 1793–1925, Series VI, Subseries C, Box 4, Folder 3. 5.
131 Thompson, "A Whaling Cruise in the Sea Fox", 147–149.

Fig. 37: View of the island of Annobón, as drawn (originally in colour) in the log of the brig *Samuel and Thomas* of Provincetown, May 1847.
Source: Log SAMUEL & THOMAS, 1846–1848.

conversation with a seaman by asking his name and used the names they had learnt in later encounters. Among themselves, Tams noticed, they used Portuguese names, such as Christovão, Miguel or Antonio.[132]

How did the Annobonese communicate with seamen? Under conditions of relative isolation, they had developed a creole language known as Fá d'Ambô.[133] Among the crews of most nineteenth-century American whalers there would have been a few seamen who spoke Portuguese or a related creole – Bravanese, for instance – and were able to understand at least the rudiments of Fá d'Ambô. Tams, who spoke Portuguese himself, writes of the governor speaking "in barely comprehensible Portuguese".[134] Meanwhile, the report of the Niger Expedition tells of the Annobonese speaking "a patois mixed up of Portuguese and the language or languages of their ancestors".[135] The islanders had also acquired a basic English vocabulary in their encounters with seamen: "Each of then knew enough English to introduce himself with the words 'me friend to you, and you friend to

---

132 Tams, *Die Portugiesischen Besitzungen in Süd-West-Afrika*, 197.
133 Lipski, "The Spanish Language of Equatorial Guinea", 171f.; Post, *Pidgins and Creoles*, 191f.; Schuchardt, "Kreolische Studien VII", 199, 225. On Fá d'Ambô see also Barrena, *Gramática annobónesa*.
134 Tams, *Die Portugiesischen Besitzungen in Süd-West-Afrika*, 187.
135 Allen/Thomson, *A Narrative of the Expedition Sent by Her Majesty's Government to the Niger River in 1841*, vol. 2, 58.

me'", reports Tams.[136] There was accordingly a foundation for communication in such situations, and gesticulations often did the rest, particularly when it came to bartering.[137]

***

"All hands came off except Robert Scott & John C Coon (Boatsteerer) it is supposed that they have deserted", Charles Allen, the third mate of the *Globe*, noted in his diary on 11 October 1869.[138] The barque had lain off Annobón for three days. When, the following day, three more men jumped ship – William Leane, Charles Guiscard and Andrew Chase[139] – Captain Tripp decided to go ashore with three of his officers to hunt down the fugitives. Over the course of the day, all were found – and found in a dreadful state. "The natives had refused them any thing to eat", noted Allen. Given that some of the men were on the brink of starvation, Tripp had no trouble having them put in irons and locked up aboard the *Globe*.[140]

Whether the reason was a general distrust of Europeans or fear of the sanctions to be expected from irate shipmasters, the Annobonese population displayed not the slightest willingness to support fugitive seamen, let alone to shelter them permanently. Nor did the small island offer much prospect of hiding out for days on end, and even less of ever leaving it on any vessel other than a whaler. Only very few seamen attempted desertion during a stay at Annobón, and we know of only three who succeeded: Henry Domings escaped from the brig *Leonidas* of Westport in 1862, Claud Payot from the *Admiral Blake* of Marion in 1869 and Sam Thomas from the barque *Janet* of New Bedford in 1879. Nothing is known of their subsequent fate.[141]

In 1877 the crew of a British warship met a Portuguese seaman in Annobón who claimed to have been left behind by an American whaler, the *Josshawk*. According to the man, the captain had ordered his vessel to put out while the man was ashore, drunk on palm wine. The British took him to the American

---

136 Tams, *Die Portugiesischen Besitzungen in Süd-West-Afrika*, 187; see also Allen/Thomson, *A Narrative of the Expedition Sent by Her Majesty's Government to the Niger River in 1841*, vol. 2, 58, Móros y Morellon/Rios, *Memorias sobre las islas africanas de España*, 27; Lucy P. Smith. "My Adventures Afloat." 1925. Martha's Vineyard Museum: Record Unit 207, Whaling and the Vineyard, 1793–1925, Series VI, Subseries C, Box 4, Folder 3. 6.
137 Tams, *Die Portugiesischen Besitzungen in Süd-West-Afrika*, 187.
138 Allen, Journal GLOBE, 1869–1872, 11.10.1869.
139 Ibid., 11.10.1869; Log GLOBE, 1869–1872, 10.–13.10.1869.
140 Allen, Journal GLOBE, 1869–1872, 14.10.1869.
141 Log ADMIRAL BLAKE, 1869–1870, 21.06.1869; Log JANET, 1877–1879, 09.03.1879; Log LEONIDAS, 1860–1863, 31.08.1862.

consulate in Luanda, but neither the consul nor the Portuguese authorities there gave his story any credence – particularly because no whaleship of that name was ever known to have existed.[142]

Another example confirms that Annobón was among the last places where any seaman would have wanted to be left behind. During a stay in Annobón in May 1847 the cook of the *Samuel and Thomas* asked Captain Swift to be discharged. Swift agreed – unusually enough – but after only a few hours ashore the cook changed his mind and asked to be taken back on board.[143] This cook may well be the only seaman ever to have asked for a discharge in Annobón. In two other cases of men remaining in Annobón it is uncertain whether it happened by consent or whether the captain left them behind against their will.[144]

Since barely a seaman ever remained in Annobón if he could help it, captains were comparatively generous in granting shore leave there. It even occurred that the entire crow was allowed to ashore at once, as distinct from the usual practice of being divided into groups or watches.[145] Some seamen took advantage of longer stays ashore to enjoy their chummies' hospitality, sometimes even spending the night at their houses.[146]

But how did seamen spend the remainder of their time in Annobón? "I went to see the lake", was the answer given by John Coguin, who came to the island aboard the *Globe* in 1869 along with Charles Allen.[147] Many men, like Coguin, took walks into the island's interior or at least around San Antonio.[148] The watch below of the schooner *Admiral Blake* of Marion caught six wild boar while ashore.[149] The local population observed the seamen in their activities with equal measures of curiosity and suspicion. Of his visit in the mid-1860s, Samuel Chalmers Thompson writes:

> When we landed for shore-leave, the beach was black with people. If one of us looked at a child it generally cried. As I sat by my "chum's" hut, a young woman passed by at

---

[142] Despatch Book, 1864–1879. National Archives at College Park, MD, Loanda, vol. 002; Records of Foreign Service Posts, Record Group 84. Letter dated 17.11.1877 to the Portuguese governor.
[143] Log SAMUEL & THOMAS, 1846–1848, 15.05.1847.
[144] Log GLOBE, 1869–1872, 13.09.1871; Log PRESIDENT II, 1862–1864, 18.02.1864.
[145] Log GLOBE, 1869–1872, 10.09.1871; Log SAMUEL & THOMAS, 1846–1848, 15.05.1847; Log CHARLES W. MORGAN, 1878–1881, 17.08.1879; Log FALCON, 1887–1890, 22.07.1888. See also Haywood, "American Whalers and Africa", 79.
[146] Haywood, "American Whalers and Africa", 77; Thompson, "A Whaling Cruise in the Sea Fox", 147–149.
[147] Log GLOBE, 1869–1872, 12.10.1869.
[148] Log PEDRO VARELA, 1881–1883, 09.04.1882.
[149] Log ADMIRAL BLAKE, 1869–1870, 19.06.1869.

intervals carrying water. She would look at me, throw back her head, and laugh convulsively; simply because I had a white skin and wore clothes, and she had a black skin and did not wear clothes.[150]

Islanders might follow seamen by the hundred,[151] as Simpson too recalls: "Immediately on our setting foot ashore, we were surrounded by immense numbers of all classes, anxious to gain a sight of us."[152]

Such unwanted attention did not deter some seamen from having parties on the beach and enjoying a good deal of palm wine.[153] Others, however, found stopovers in Annobón to be fairly trying experiences. The lack of the usual port infrastructure – taverns and prostitutes – was one reason, the commotion caused by traders on board another. "Our last day at this Island, or at least I hope so", noted the seaman who kept the log of the *Tropic Bird* in September 1882, "as I am tired to death of this canibles."[154] Charles Allen of the *Globe* had even harsher, flagrantly racist words for Annobón and its inhabitants: "The darkies are thicker than fiddlers. I never saw such a nasty hole for a ship to go to in my life. [. . .] I dont think that I ever saw or heard of such a miserable hole as this. [. . .] I have been ashore to day and of all the meanest holes this beats all. there is nothing but hills Rocks woods & Niggers &c."[155] Whether such invective was representative of seamen's opinion is, however, open to question. In the log of the barque *Mercury* of New Bedford, for instance, Annobón is described simply as a "good place for get wood and water sweet potatoes and fruit and fowl."[156]

As was the case elsewhere, captains going ashore in Annobón were keen to distinguish themselves from common seamen and to underscore their position of eminence. Daniel Ricketson, for instance, who came to Annobón several times in the 1880s as captain of the *Pedro Varela* of New Bedford, and his wife were frequent dinner guests of the governor. The couple also visited the *sanguistã gueza nganyi*, and on one occasion Mrs Ricketson brought a stereoscope and some photographs ashore to show to the islanders. Excursions were made to Pico Surcado and *Lago a pot*, and the Ricketsons also exchanged small presents with their Annobonese hosts.[157]

---

150 Thompson, "A Whaling Cruise in the Sea Fox", 147–149.
151 Log PEDRO VARELA, 1881–1883, 02. & 10.04.1882.
152 Simpson, *A Private Journal Kept during the Niger Expedition*, 71.
153 Log PEDRO VARELA, 1881–1883, 29.04.1883.
154 Quoted in Haywood, "American Whalers and Africa", 79f.
155 Allen, Journal GLOBE, 1869–1872, 08., 09. & 12.10.1869.
156 Log MERCURY, 1873–1876, 27.08.1874.
157 Log PEDRO VARELA, 1881–1883, 02., 05., 10. & 22.04.1882 and 26.–29.04.1883.

Christian seamen did not usually attend services at the *Gueza gany*. Only Annie Holmes Ricketson reports having visited the church and another chapel one Saturday in April 1885. In the service she observed, she describes islanders as singing hymns, making votive offerings of fruit and small wooden objects, and lighting oil lamps for the dead. Her account is written from the perspective of a distanced observer and suggests no active involvement on her part.[158]

***

Annobonese did not only come aboard whaleships to engage in commerce. We hear, for instance, of cases – albeit rare – of islanders spending the night on deck at the invitation of the chummies, one such case being recorded in the log of the *Nautilus* of New Bedford in 1870.[159] Local men might also take on casual work aboard a vessel, as on the barque *Bertha* of New Bedford, which had "4 Men from Shore to Work on Board" in 1880.[160] In 1885 Annie Holmes Ricketson engaged the services of a local man to do her laundry.[161] On shore too the arrival of a whaleship presented islanders with opportunities for employment, opportunities which, as far as we know, were taken only by men. Some offered their services as guides and porters to seamen who wanted to visit the island's interior,[162] others rowed whalemen ashore in their *batélus*, and some Annobonese rowed to meet vessels approaching on the horizon in the hope of being engaged as pilots to guide them to their anchorage – apparently with little success.[163] Other islanders sought to benefit from the presence of vessels in other ways, for instance by asking captains for medical help.[164]

When captains employed Annobonese, it was more often for whaling itself than for odd jobs. In 1879 Thomas Ellis of the *Charles W. Morgan* hired two islanders, who went by the names of Jim Crow and Thomas Blond. After two months of humpbacking, the vessel returned them to Annobón. For their services, they received the same pay as untrained American seamen would have

---

158 In another episode, the Ricketsons tried to escape pushy traders in San Antonio de Palé by entering chapel. Undeterred, the traders pushed chickens, pigs and potatoes at them through the chapel's windows. (Ricketson, Journal 1885, 25.04.1885)
159 Lucy P. Smith. "My Adventures Afloat, or, Leaves from my Log Book." 1925. Martha's Vineyard Museum: Record Unit 207, Whaling and the Vineyard, 1793–1925, Series VI, Subseries C, Box 4, Folder 3. 9.
160 Log BERTHA, 1878–1881, 14.08.1880.
161 Ricketson, Journal 1885, 21. & 23.04.1885.
162 Log PEDRO VARELA, 1881–1883, 05.04.1882.
163 Log BERTHA, 1883–1887, 02.03.1885; Log PEDRO VARELA, 1881–1883, 12. & 25.04.1882; Phillips, Journal ADMIRAL BLAKE, 1868–1870, 11.08.1870.
164 Ricketson, Journal 1885, 21.04.1885.

done – which is remarkable not least because there was no money economy in Annobón at the time.[165] Four Annobonese signed on aboard the *Bertha* in August 1880. Over a year later, in October 1881, they left the barque in Cabinda, where they joined the *Clarice* of Edgartwon, which was to take them home.[166] Such "seasoners" were not, however, necessarily hired for months at a time. In August 1870, Captain Blake of the *Admiral Blake* employed five Annobonese who joined in hunting humpback whales for five days.[167]

Conversely, it was also known for captains to hire Annobonese men not as seasoners, but for the duration of the voyage, at the end of which they would return to the United States with their vessels. A young islander joined the *Stephania* of New Bedford as cabin boy in 1850,[168] and Captain Gifford of the barque *Mercury* of New Bedford signed on five Annobonese in 1876.[169] In September of the same year, a stopover by the *Adeline Gibbs* of New Bedford had tragic consequences. Captain Snell took four men on board: William Wilson, William Liping, Jack Dollar and Samuel Young. After only two weeks in the barque Wilson committed suicide by hanging himself, whereupon the captain decided to bury him at sea and to return the remaining islanders to Annobón.[170]

Yet shipmasters did not always succeed in hiring men in Annobón. "Capt. [. . .] went on shore & tried to ship a man but could not", records the log of the *Admiral Blake*, the keeper of which tellingly adds: "I don't blame them."[171] Nor did all islanders who embarked on a whaleship do so with the captain's consent. In July 1888, for instance, the crew of the *Falcon* of New Bedford found two Annobonese men on board who had stowed away when she had called at Annobón the day before.[172]

Given the patchy documentary evidence, the total number of Annobonese employed aboard American whaleships in the nineteenth century cannot be reliably established. Besides the cases cited here, the clearance documents of the New Bedford customs authorities contain the names of many more Annobonese men who had come to the United States aboard whalers and continued to be employed in whaling (Tab. 10). In New Bedford, some of these men found employment that took them back to their native island. Such was the case with

---

165 Log CHARLES W. MORGAN, 1878–1881, 11.06. & 18.08.1879.
166 Log BERTHA, 1878–1881, 28.08.1880 & 01.10.1881.
167 Log ADMIRAL BLAKE, 1869–1870, 17.–21.08.1870.
168 Log STEPHANIA, 1847–1850, 28.08.1850.
169 Log MERCURY, 1873–1876, 20.04.1876.
170 Log ADELINE GIBBS, 1875–1878, 29.09.1876.
171 Log ADMIRAL BLAKE, 1869–1870, 21.06.1869.
172 Log FALCON, 1887–1890, 26.07.1888.

John Bonny and Henry Joseph, who reached Annobón aboard the *Greyhound* in August 1880. Since the papers of the customs authority record only the crews of outbound vessels and not of those returning to port, however, they do not tell us on board which vessels these men left the island in the first place.[173]

"Obé, cussá balea"

Traders came on board as usual when the *Sarah* of New Bedford approached Annobón on 20 April 1874 – fifty-one in total, clambering over the gunwales in ones and twos. Yet contrary to the expectations of all who sailed in her the *Sarah* did not succeed in reaching her anchorage. A strong current and ill winds drove the barque – which must have been very light at the time, her crew having only transhipped her barrels of whale oil in St Helena in January – away from the island. By the next day, the *Sarah* was fifty-five miles from Annobón, and the islanders were still on board. "The natives feal very bad think that we intend to carry them away", as her log records. Progress back to Annobón was slow, with the island not coming into view until 25 April. This seems to have restored the islanders' trust, who now took the boats and began to tow the *Sarah*, although it still took another four days for the barque finally to reach her anchorage.[174]

The *Sarah* was not the only whaleship that had to be towed by boats in order to reach the northern side of Annobón against a steady south-westerly wind. Islanders would sometimes row out in their *batélus* to meet struggling vessels and offer help.[175] As Georg Tams observed in 1842, "the irregular nature of the wind is the cause of much grievance to seamen in these parts and often highly dangerous".[176] Tams assumed that this unpredictability was the main reason why slave vessels avoided Annobón, and he may well have been right.[177] And yet the brief remark in the *Sarah*'s log suggests that the islanders had some knowledge and awareness of the slave trade.

As the incidents and encounters described here show, the people of Annobón were able to distinguish between different kinds of people who came across the sea. They were aware of the threat posed by a slave ship and of the danger of a colonial power-grab embodied by certain visitors to their island –

---

173 Schürmann, "Neue Hilfsmittel zur amerikanischen Walfanggeschichte", 256f.
174 Log SARAH, 1873–1876, 20.–30.04.1874.
175 See e.g. Phillips, Journal ADMIRAL BLAKE, 1868–1870, 04.06., 10.08. & 14.08.1870.
176 Tams, *Die Portugiesischen Besitzungen in Süd-West-Afrika*, 186.
177 Sundiata, *From Slaving to Neoslavery*, 13.

even if that visitor was a clergyman. The British Niger Expedition of 1841 reached Annobón aboard a steamship – perhaps the first ever to be seen there. On that occasion, the vessel was welcomed not by throngs of merchants but merely by a single *batélu* bearing the governor's messenger. Only once this messenger had ascertained that the British did constitute a threat did the islanders set in motion their usual routines. The report of the expedition describes what happened next:

> The *Governor's Mate* having satisfied himself, waved his hat towards the shore, to signify that all was right, when in a few minutes crowds of men, women, and children, were seen rushing to the beach, numerous canoes were pushed off from three points, and in a very few more we were surrounded by about sixty, containing from one to four men each, laden with goats, pigs, fowls, bananas, plantains, cassada, sweet potatoes, pines, tamarinds, but very few yams.[178]

No such precautions were taken when whalers were in the offing. The islanders recognised the vessels from afar – perhaps by their boats, perhaps by their sails black with the soot of the trypots. And in the whalemen they recognised an opportunity to obtain, by bartering considerable yet apparently dispensable quantities of fruit and livestock, goods they were unable to produce themselves. The chummy system provided the Annobonese with an effective strategy for arranging trade with seamen to their advantage. The clothes, tools and other items introduced into the island through this trade were of consequence for its political, economic and religious life. Though it is impossible to quantify their impact in detail, for a century these goods and the men that brought them constituted the principal outside influence on Annobón.

***

The encounters with American whalemen had another profound effect on Annobón, one which so far has only been alluded to, though it shaped life on the island well into the twentieth century. This was the emergence of an Annobonese whaling industry, which will be discussed in the remainder of this chapter.

American-style pelagic whaling found many imitators. Although most of them sailed from European ports, littoral and island societies in other parts of the world also adopted this way of hunting whales. The Maori in Polynesia, for instance, began outfitting whaleships of their own in the 1840s to compete with European and North American vessels. Hawaiian whaling began around the same time. In the Azores, where coastal whaling had been practised since at

---

[178] Allen/Thomson, *A Narrative of the Expedition Sent by Her Majesty's Government to the Niger River in 1841*, vol. 2, 47f.

Tab. 10: Annobonese workers and seamen aboard New Bedford whalers.

Year	Name	Vessel
1847[a]	Benjamin Fluker	Braganza
1850[b]	? (one man)	Stephania
1859[c]	Jim Hen	Roswell King
	Dick Holland	
	John Lewis	
1862[c]	John Black	Willis
	Tom Black	
1865[c]	James Luce	Ocean
1865[c]	Tom Walker	President
1865[c]	Thomas Coffin	Leonidas
1866[c]	John Foster	Adeline Gibbs
1866[c]	John Duff	George Howland
	John Eden	
	Peter Wilson	
1867[c]	John Bonney	Ansel Gibbs
1868[c]	John Bonney	Cornelia
1868[c]	Robert Jackson	Wash. Freeman
1868[c]	Jose Annabon	Rainbow
	John Bonney	
1868[c]	John Foster	Robert Morrison
1868[c]	Joseph Thompson	U. D.
1871[c]	Jose Annabon	Young Phenix
	John Bonney	
1872[c]	Joseph Stephens	Falcon
1874[c]	Thomas Adams	George and Susan
	Thomas Sambo	
1874[c]	John King	Hadley
1875[c]	John Bonney	Gazelle
	Henry Joseph	
1876[d]	? (five men)	Mercury
1876[e]	William Wilson	Adeline Gibbs
	William Liping	
	Jack Dollar	
	Samuel Young	
1876[c]	William Jackson	John and Winthrop
1876[c]	James Lyons	Varnum H. Hill
1876[c]	John Batists	Cohannet
	John Cruss	
1876[c]	John Davis	Petrel
1876[c]	Antonio Jose	Cohannet
1876[c]	John Lewis	Minnesota
1876[c]	Antonio Santos	Cohannet

Tab. 10 (continued)

Year	Name	Vessel
	Antonio Thomas	
1876[c]	Tom Tobey	Minnesota
1877[c]	Thomas Bowlin	George and Susan
1877[c]	Sandy Bill	James Allen II
1877[c]	John Bonn	John Howland
1877[c]	John Davis	Amelia
1877[c]	John King	Pioneer
1877[c]	Antone Stabon	Hadley
1877[f]	Jack Fiddle	Desdemona
1878[c]	William Jackson	Ocean
1878[c]	James Matthews	Caleb Eaton
1878[c]	Andre Potter	Isabella
1878[c]	Charles Blackburn	Ocean
	John Forman	
1878[c]	Frank Morgan	Niger
1878[c]	John Wilson	Tropic Bird
1879[c]	John Bonny	Greyhound
1879[c]	Henry Joseph	Greyhound
1879[c]	Thomas Havit	Caleb Eaton
1879[c]	James Mathews	Mattapoisett
1879[c]	Thomas Wood	Caleb Eaton
1880[c]	Chas. Blackboy	Pioneer
	John Forman	
1880[c]	Jack Lombo	Seine
1880[g]	? (four men)	Bertha
1883[c]	John Davis	Eliza Adams
1884[c]	John Boy	Aurora
	James Mathews	
1884[c]	Benicia Boy	Stafford
1885[c]	John Wilson	Pedro Varela
1885[c]	John Davie	Mermaid
1886[c]	James Mathews	Aurora
1886[c]	James Matthews	Sunbeam
1888[h]	Tom Cooper	Falcon
	Barney Cooper	

Sources: [a]"Died." *New-Bedford Mercury,* 22.03.1850, 3; [b]Log STEPHANIA, 1847–1850, 28.08.1850; [c]Lund et al., New Bedford Crewlist Database; [d]Log MERCURY, 1873–1876, 20.04.1876; [e]Log ADELINE GIBBS, 1875–1878, 29.09.1876; [f]Log DESDEMONA, 1876–1879, 18.08.1877; [g]Log BERTHA, 1878–1881, 28.08.1880; [h]Log FALCON, 1887–1890, 26.07.1888.

least the 1830s, whaling firms were established in in the 1850s that set up to ten vessels to hunt sperm whales in the Atlantic following the American model. Chilean shipowners too began to adopt these practices around 1860.[179] What is far less well known is that African societies also took up whaling – notably three island societies in the Gulf of Guinea which had witnessed American operations in the nineteenth century. These were Annobón, Fernando Póo and Ndame (Ambas), a rocky island off the south-western coast of modern Cameroon.[180]

When exactly the people Annobón began whaling is uncertain. It may well be that the seasoners who worked aboard American vessels acquired whaling skills which they were then able to use independently. That is the theory of Aurelio Basilio, a scientist who visited Annobón in the 1950s and asked the islanders to explain their whaling technique.[181] Yet it is also conceivable that the Annobonese observed American whaling from the shore, gradually developing their own skills by doing so. This is suggested by the observations of seamen in the 1870s, according to whom islanders rowed their *batélus* out to the flensed carcasses of humpback whales killed by American whalers and cut out meat for themselves.[182]

What is certain is that whaling was well established in the island by the time Spanish missionaries arrived in 1885. Alongside Basilio's account, the observations of Padre Epifanio Doce, published in the missionary journal *La Guinea Española*, form the principal source on Annobonese whaling. Between them, these texts provide a fairly comprehensive picture of whaling practices in Annobón.

Initially, it would more often than not have been fishermen or children playing on the beach who observed a whale's blow on the horizon. By the 1940s, however, the Annobonese had set up an observation post. Alerted by the cry of "Bloo!" – in imitation, most likely, of American whalemen – experienced fishermen came running to size up the whale. For the islanders largely restricted their whaling to juveniles up to about five tons. Larger whales were virtually impossible to land using *batélus*, and in the worst case, an adult might

---

179 Chappell, "Beyond the Beach", 44f.; Ellis, "Azorean Whaling", 65; Housby, *The Hand of God*, 15f.; Lebo, "Hawaii's 19th-Century Whaling Economy", 109; Pastene/Quiroz, "An Outline of the History of Whaling in Chile", 80f. On whaling in the Azores see also Clarke, *Open Boat Whaling in the Azores*.
180 On whaling in Fernando Póo and Ndame (also known as Ambas) see Ardener, "The Wovea Islanders of Ambas Bay", Barthelmeß, "Walfang in der Bucht von Biafra" and Ittmann, "Der Walfang an der Küste Kameruns".
181 Basilio, *Caza y pesca en Annobon*, 90.
182 Allen, Journal GLOBE, 1869–1872, 11.09.1870; Log GLOBE, 1869–1872, 09.09.1870.

drag its pursuers out onto the open sea, leaving them at the mercy of the wind and the current.[183]

If the whale in question was a juvenile, the islanders would push two or three *batélus* into the water, each manned by a harpooner and two or three oarsmen. In order to remain unnoticed by the whale for as long as possible, initially only one of the *batélus* approached it, if possible from behind. If the harpooner hit his target, one of the rowers raised his oar as a signal to the other boats, which then came rushing to aim their own harpoons at the calf. They often also had to distract of fend off the calf's mother, which was likely to attack the *batélus* with its pectoral fin.[184]

If and when the men did finally succeed in killing their quarry with a spear, the *batélus* lined up to tow the carcass ashore. Like American whalemen, they gave rhythm to their work by communal singing. One of these songs, which was recorded some years ago by an oral history project, complains of the hard work of towing a whale, comparing it with the long distance from San Antonio to Mábana, the remotest village in the south-west of the island:[185]

Tanzul êê . . .	**Tenzúl, eh eh**
Tenzúl-Mábana, ê . . .	Tenzúl Mábana, eh . . .
Mábana lôndji mtêê . . .	Mábana is far away . . .
Ê . . .	Eh . . .
Ê, Mábana lôndji mtêê	Eh, Mábana is far away

A good many islanders had meanwhile gathered on the beach to welcome their hunters with songs and cheering. Some would go to meet the *batélus* in the shallow water, using sticks and stones to fend off the sharks that were attracted by the carcass. Once the boats had reached the beach, the crowd joined in dragging the whale ashore, usually singing, to the accompaniment of a drum beaten

---

183 Basilio, *Caza y pesca en Annobon*, 80–83; Basilio, *La vida animal en la Guinea Española*, 123; Doce, "Pequeña Tragedia en la Pesca de la Ballena", 447; "La Isla de Annobón." *La Guinea Española*, 10.09.1910; Zamora Loboch, *Notícia de Annobón*, 68
184 Basilio, *Caza y pesca en Annobon*, 81f.; Basilio, *La vida animal en la Guinea Española*, 122f.; "La Isla de Annobón." La Guinea Española, 10.09.1910; Zamora Loboch, *Notícia de Annobón*, 68f.
185 Lêdjam, *Cancionero oral Annobonés*, 72. The song is translated here from Lêdjam's Spanish version. The words, however, were already published by Miguel Zamora Loboch in 1961 (Zamora Loboch, *Notícia de Annobón*, 70). On the oral traditions of Annobón see also Creus/Brunat, *Cuentos Annoboneses de Guinea Ecuatorial*; Laurel, "El cristianismo en la tradición oral de Annobón" and Ortega, "La voz, el ritmo y la memoria".

by an elder: "Obé, cussá balea, obé!" (Come on, we must pull in the whale, come on!).[186]

In order to underscore the size of the captured whale and thus the success of the hunt, the father of the first harpooner climbed on the carcass. Mothers thereupon placed their children onto the whale in order that its strength and dexterity might rub off on them and turn them into brave hunters. The meat was distributed in the following day, which was observed as a holiday by the Annobonese. Drums carried the news across the island; men came running to the beach with knives and women brought baskets.[187]

The Annobonese hunted whales for the sake of their meat. They had no use for their oil, nor do they appear to have traded in whale products. Since the islanders did not depend on whale meat to be self-sufficient in food, the hunt remained on a small scale. It is estimated that one to three whales were caught per year, and always – at least in the documented cases – in July or August. Keeping whaling limited to that season may be due to the fact that this swas when humpback whales – known to the Annobonese as *jonjó balea* or "horned whales" on account of the knobs (tubercles) on their skin – gave birth to their young off the island. There may, however, also be a connection with the dry period in the Gulf of Guinea, which peaks in July and August.[188]

When it came to sharing out the meat, the head went to the man whose harpoon had been the first to strike home; the man with the second greatest share in the hunt's success received the tail end. The remaining carcass was put at the disposal of the people at large, with each man and woman permitted to take their cut. This practice, however, seems to have been considered unjust by many and sometimes to have led to fighting and injury. It was accordingly reformed some time in the first half of the twentieth century. A council was now formed, which in turn nominates experts who cut the meat into strips approximately the width of a hand and graded them by quality. First, the three men who made the first attack on the whale each received a strip of the highest quality, three to four metres in length. Smaller strips were then portioned out to the other men involved in the hunt and to the owners of the harpoons, lances,

---

186 Basilio, *Caza y pesca en Annobon*, 86f.; Doce, "Pequeña Tragedia en la Pesca de la Ballena", 448; "La Isla de Annobón." La Guinea Española, 10.09.1910.
187 Basilio, *Caza y pesca en Annobon*, 87f.; Doce, "Efemérides Annobonesas", 419f. For another song sung in Annobón to celebrate the catching of whale see Lêdjam, *Cancionero oral Annobonés*, 89.
188 Aguilar, "Aboriginal Whaling off Pagalu (Equatorial Guinea)", 386; Ardener, "The Wovea Islanders of Ambas Bay"; Reeves, "The Origins and Character of 'Aboriginal Subsistence' Whaling", 86f.; Zamora Loboch, *Notícia de Annobón*, 68–72.

batélus and ropes used. Only then was the rest of population allowed to compete for the remainder.[189]

Whaling tackle seems to have private property in Annobón. Whereas the islanders were able to make their own canoes and ropes (the latter from palm fibres), harpoons (*ojacu*) were in short supply in an island lacking any metal reserves or metalworking trade of its own. Harpoons were thus obtained from American whalers – some by barter, while others were salvaged from whales that had been struck but not finished off and ultimately washed up on the island's beaches with a harpoon still embedded in them.[190]

The shortage of harpoons is likely to have been one reason why the islanders often took considerable risky to prevent a whale from getting away once the first blow had been struck. In 1934 four men were killed following a harpooned female humpback whale out onto the open sea. In 1908 an islander is said to have stabbed a humpback whale to death in a desperate struggle while swimming, the whale having previously capsized all the *batélus* pursuing it. In 1949 a group of hunters had to fight a cow for its calf all the way to the beach, with the mother seeking to defend her young (by now dead) until the water grew too shallow. Several men were badly hurt.[191] It was no doubt witnessing or hearing of such exploits that caused a Norwegian captain to remark, "These people are devils in the sea."[192]

While the islanders were developing their own culture of whaling, the modern whaling industry took hold in the Gulf of Guinea. It seems not to have had any serious consequences for the islanders until the mid-twentieth century. The first Norwegian factory ship began operating in the Gulf of Guinea in 1912, and it was so successful that by the following year five such vessels were hunting whales there. In 1914 the number again rose to seven floating factories with a total of twenty catchers. Their principal quarry was humpback whales, but they also hunted blue and fin whales, which had previously been of no commercial interest. One company acquired a concession for the waters around Fernando Póo. Around 1914 vessels belonging to the Spanish *Sociedad de la Pesqueria Hispano-Africana* were also operating in the Gulf of Guinea and are likely to have used Annobón as an anchorage. In 1922 a Franco-Norwegian company aiming to gain a monopoly over whaling in the area obtained a concession

---

189 Basilio, *Caza y pesca en Annobon*, 88; Zamora Loboch, *Notícia de Annobón*, 68–72.
190 Basilio, *Caza y pesca en Annobon*, 81; Basilio, *La vida animal en la Guinea Española*, 123; Schultze, *Die Insel Annobon im Golf von Guinea*, 133.
191 Basilio, *Caza y pesca en Annobon*, 83–86; Basilio, *La vida animal en la Guinea Española*, 124; Doce, "Pequeña Tragedia en la Pesca de la Ballena", 447.
192 Quoted in Basilio, *Caza y pesca en Annobon*, 86.

from the Spanish government for whaling off Annobón. These operations were so profitable that in 1925 three factory ships sailed from Europe for the Gulf of Guinea. However, the rivalry between them reached an intensity that reduced the profits of all companies involved, in whaling was suspended indefinitely in 1926. Some factory ships returned to the Gulf of Guinea several times between 1930 and 1937, but stocks appear by then to have been reduced to the brink of extinction, and these operations were soon discontinued.[193]

Modern whaling operations returned to the Gulf of Guinea in 1949. This time, however, they were largely shore-based. Sopecoba, a Franco-Norwegian company, opened a whaling station at Port-Gentil (Cape Lopez), from which catcher boats set out to hunt humpback whales together with a factory ship, the *Jarama*. In 1951 a Norwegian company opened a whaling station on São Tomé. Whale stocks in the Gulf of Guinea had not, however, recovered to a degree that would have made either of these enterprises viable, and both folded in 1952. A last attempt at commercial whaling in these waters, made in 1959, likewise ended in failure.[194]

Short-lived though they were, the whaling operations begun around 1950 nonetheless appear to have caused a steep decline in the humpback whale population. The Annobonese would barely have been able to catch whales themselves by this time, although the island's arms still depicted a whaling scene (since replaced by trees).[195] When Equatorial Guinea gained independence from Spain in 1968, missionaries and other Europeans were banished from Annobón. Since then, scarcely any news of whaling has left the island. Several whales are known to have been caught in the 1970s, but it is unknown whether whaling continued beyond that period or is still practised today.[196] However, whales and whaling continue to feature in the island's oral tradition and in the memory of Annobonese exiles.[197]

---

193 Doce, "Noticias de la Colonia", 103; Schultze, *Die Insel Annobon im Golf von Guinea*, 133; Tønnessen/Johnsen, *The History of Modern Whaling*, 214f., 318f.
194 Aguilar, "Aboriginal Whaling off Pagalu (Equatorial Guinea)", 385; Tønnessen/Johnsen, *The History of Modern Whaling*, 654.
195 Aguilar, "Aboriginal Whaling off Pagalu (Equatorial Guinea)", 386; Basilio, *Caza y pesca en Annobon*, 90; Liniger-Goumaz, *Historical Dictionary of Equatorial Guinea*, 31.
196 Aguilar, "Aboriginal Whaling off Pagalu (Equatorial Guinea)", 386.
197 Creus/Brunat, *Cuentos Annoboneses de Guinea Ecuatorial*, 37, 46, 56; Zamora Loboch, "Los Paraisos Imposibles", 2.

8 Whaleships into migration vehicles: Furna, Brava, 1770–1920

"The 'Gee' is found aboard of almost one whaler out of three", a recently established journal of arts and letters from New York City, *Harper's New Monthly Letters*, reported in 1856. But what was a "Gee"? "The word 'Gee' (g hard) is an abbreviation, by seamen, of Portugee, the corrupt form of Portuguese", explained the author. The term, however, did not in fact refer to men from the Portuguese mainland but rather to seamen from Portugal's island possessions in the Atlantic, from Cape Verde and the Azores. The author knew what he was talking about. He was none other than Herman Melville, who between 1841 and 1843 had worked aboard the whalers *Acushnet*, *Lucy Ann* and *Charles and Henry*. He based several stories and novels on his experiences, including *Moby Dick*, though it found few readers in Melville's lifetime. "The 'Gees' are always ready to be shipped", was one thing Melville had learnt about these men. "Any day one may go to their isle, and on the showing of a coin of biscuit over the rail, may load down to the water's edge with them." Melville also knew where they were to found in America: "'Gees' are occasionally to be encountered in our seaports, but more particularly in Nantucket and New Bedford."[1]

Melville's article not only shows that Cape Verdean seamen had an important part to play in mid-nineteenth-century American whaling, it also suggests that their presence in New England did not go unnoticed. Nor did it go unnoticed on the other side of the Atlantic, in the Cape Verde archipelago itself. There too the experience of Cape Verdean seamen was a subject for writers, among them the poet Jorge Barbosa from the island of São Vicente. One hundred years after Melville shipped aboard his first whaler, Barbosa wrote "Irmão", a poem about an imaginary brother who might have been Melville's contemporary:[2]

Cruzaste Mares	You have crossed the seas
na aventura da pesca da baleia,	in pursuit of whales
nessas viagens para a América	on those trips to America
de onde ás veses os navios não	from where the ships sometimes
voltam mais.	never return

What were "those trips to America" that Cape Verdean seamen made aboard whaleships, and what about them inspired poets on both sides of the Atlantic?

---

[1] All quotations in this paragraph are from Melville, "The 'Gees'", 357–360.
[2] Quoted in Almeida et al., *Cape Verdeans in America*, 46f.

In this chapter, I shall trace the history of encounters and interactions between American whalemen and Cape Verde islanders. My focus will be on the place that plays the principal in this story, the island of Brava.

The brave

"Almost straight skyward out of the ocean", was how the sheer cliffs of Santo Antão struck Nelson Cole Haley of the barque *Charles W. Morgan* in 1849.[3] To seamen like Hayley, the silhouette of towering volcanic islands emerging on the horizon and filling the space between sea and sky must have presented an impressive spectacle. After the Canaries, which whalemen seldom set eyes upon, the Cape Verde Islands contain the highest peaks to rise from the Atlantic. The tallest of these is Pico de Fogo, which today – as it was in the whaling era – is the archipelago's only active volcano. It was, as Lewis Eldrifge of the the *Gerald II* of New Bedford noted in the late 1860s, "An awe inspiring sight, even though nothing but a brown sun-baked rock of giant proportions rising 9,000 feet above the surface of the sea".[4]

Arranged in the shape of a broken horseshoe, the Cape Verde Islands form Africa's westernmost outpost. If we count the smaller crags on which fishermen sometimes set up camp, the archipelago consists of twenty-one islands, ten of which may be classed as "major" islands by virtue of their size. Nine islands are permanently inhabited. Even the easternmost island, Boa Vista, is more than three hundred nautical miles away from the African mainland, and Santo Antão, the westernmost of the major islands, lies approximately 450 nautical miles from the shore. The islands are usually grouped according to geology or climate. Geological criteria suggest a distinction between western islands, which tend to be rocky and mountainous (*ilhas montanhosas*), and the flat and sandy islands in the east (*ilhas rasas*). Climatic conditions, by contrast, differ most markedly between the arid northern islands exposed to the predominant north-easterly winds (windward islands or *barlaventos*) and the leeward islands (*sotaventos*) in the south, which enjoy at least seasonal rainfall.[5]

As the most south-westerly of the Cape Verde Islands, Brava is a *sotavento montanhoso*. To its steep and rocky coast, formed by a now extinct volcano, it owes both its name (*Brava* meaning "the wild" or "the brave") and its relative

---

[3] Haley, *Whale Hunt*, 35.
[4] Eldridge, *Lewis William Eldridge's Whaling Voyage*, 7.
[5] Duncan, *Atlantic Islands*, 158; Lobban, *Cape Verde*, 6; Meintel, *Race, Culture, and Portuguese Colonialism in Cabo Verde*, 15, 19.

isolation. Brava is the least accessible of the larger Cape Verde Islands and, with a surface area of approximately sixty-seven square kilometres, the smallest.[6] "It bore a wild and awful appearance: rock rose upon rock for hundreds of feet, until their heights were lost amid the dark and frowning clouds, which hung in gloomy grandeur over the barren and precipitous sides of the mountain", was the first impression recorded by Ben Ely as he approached the island aboard the barque *Emigrant* in the mid-1840s. "We could, when miles distant, hear the roar of the breakers as they dashed in mad fury against these weatherbeaten monuments of ages past, throwing their white foam for a hundred feet up their dark and rugged sides", he added.[7] Since Brava, in common with the other islands in the archipelago, lacks an insular shelf that could slow down the onrushing sea, while also having treacherous shallows that make coastal navigation tricky, approaching the island is difficult and safe anchorages are few. The best option was and remains a fragment of a crater in the island's northeast, the rim of which partly rises above sea level to form a bay resembling a broken bowl (Fig. 39). This is Furna, the island's principal harbour, a role it acquired early on as it faces the neighbouring island of Fogo. From Furna, a twisted footpath (Fig. 38) of just about three kilometres leads to the island's main settlement, Nova Sintra, traditionally known to locals simply as *Vila*, "the Town".[8]

"Off and on"

The presence of whales in the surrounding waters was well known to the inhabitants of Brava and the other Cape Verde Islands – they could, after all, sometimes be seen from the shore. By the 1680s, ambergris and oil were being extracted from beached whales. While local fishermen may occasionally have set out to catch a whale, there was no systematic whaling.[9] In 1791 a civil servant in Santiago, the largest and most populous of the islands, wrote that he failed to understand why

---

6 Duncan, *Atlantic Islands*, 182; Meintel, "Cape Verdean Transnationalism", 30.
7 Ely, *There She Blows*, 43f.
8 Duncan, *Atlantic Islands*, 182; Meintel, "Cape Verdean Transnationalism", 30; Meintel, *Race, Culture, and Portuguese Colonialism in Cabo Verde*, 19.
9 Carreira, *The People of the Cape Verde Islands*, 9, 42f.; Holloway, "Making Waves", 118; Lobban/Saucier, "Whaling", 241; Thomas, *Adventures and Observations on the West Coast of Africa*, 334.

whale stocks in Cape Verdean waters were not being exploited. By failing to do so, he argued, Portugal was foregoing a source of considerable profit.[10] The memorandum's complaint that the colonial admiration was leaving whaling to other countries may thus be read as lamenting an opportunity hitherto not seized. It may also be taken to indicate that American or European whalers were already operating around Cape Verde by this time.[11] However, there is no evidence for that suggestion.

What is certainly true is that at the dawn of American-style pelagic whaling, the route between New England and the Cape Verde island was already much frequented by shipping. North American merchantmen probably first visited the islands in 1643, and over the course of the eighteenth century at least 936 voyages to Cape Verde were made by slave ships from Rhode Island alone. For American vessels seeking to sail on the reliable westerlies of the North Atlantic in order to reach west Africa as quickly as possible, travelling via Cape Verde was almost inevitable. They often took advantage of the stop to barter tobacco for goat hides and salt and to pick up news of prices and commercial opportunities on the mainland coast. British whalers too travelled to Cape Verde by a familiar route. In the seventeenth century, British cod fishermen – up to one hundred vessels per year – had begun to call there on their way to Newfoundland in order to acquire the salt they used to preserved their catch.[12]

As with many whaling grounds, it is impossible to establish exactly when it was first reached by whalers. Records of the routes taken across the Atlantic by Nantucket vessels of the 1760s and 70s have largely not been preserved, though we may suppose them to have been – initially, at least – the same as those taken by merchant vessels.[13] Among the earliest American vessels recorded as having called at Cape Verde are the brig *Polly*, which anchored off the south-eastern

---

10 Carreira, *The People of the Cape Verde Islands*, 44. The historian Donald Warren refers to several attempts made in the eighteenth and nineteenth centuries to establish coastal whaling in Brava, São Nicolau and Maio. (Warrin, *So Ends This Day*, 307) Since neither the scholarly literature on the subject nor the records of American whalers mention such attempts, they must have been short-lived and unsuccessful. It may be that, in the early days of whalers frequenting Cape Verde, crews came on land to process their catch and hired local labour to assist them. (Brooks, "Cabo Verde", 122)
11 Carreira, *The People of the Cape Verde Islands*, 44.
12 Brooks, *Yankee Traders, Old Coasters, and African Middlemen*, 30; Duncan, *Atlantic Islands*, 188; Lobban, *Cape Verde*, 28f.; Meintel, *Race, Culture, and Portuguese Colonialism in Cabo Verde*, 38. On the salt trade in Cape Verde see esp. Brooks, "Cabo Verde", 113.
13 Busch, "Cape Verdeans in the American Whaling and Sealing Industry", 104; Meintel, *Race, Culture, and Portuguese Colonialism in Cabo Verde*, 46f.

island of Maio in 1774, and the *Sea Flower*, which put in to Boa Vista in 1776.[14] European whaleships reached Cape Verde by the mid-1780s, when vessels belonging to the Dunkirk shipowner William Rotch, among them the *Renomee*, explored whaling grounds in the area.[15] British whalers followed no later than 1787, when the *Adventure*, the *Kent* and the *Intrepid* called at Santiago.[16]

In spite of the maritime wars that plagued the following years, by the end of the eighteenth century whaleship were regular visitors to the ports and bays of Cape Verde.[17] In this early phase of whaling in the island's waters, extending into the 1820s, vessels called mainly at Santiago and the *ilhas rasas*, while scarcely any stops are recorded for Brava and the other *ilhas montanhosas*. Whalers, it seems, were following the routes established by commercial shipping, which likewise relied on Santiago (for trade) and the *ilhas rasas* (for salt). The sealing boom in the Falkland Islands, South Georgia and the South Shetland Islands from about 1790 to 1825 also meant that some whaleships, both British and American, sailed equipped for both kinds of hunting. These vessels stopped at the *ilhas rasas* to stock up on the salt they needed to preserve seal pelts.[18]

It cannot be ascertained with any certainty how many whaleships arrived in Cape Verde during this period and indeed later. According to Carreira, a total of twenty-five whalers put in to Praia (the port of Santiago) alone between 1812 and 1827.[19] However, many – indeed, probably most – whalers passed through the islands in a manner known to seafarers as "off and on". This procedure involved the captain or an officer being rowed ashore to take on provisions without the vessel dropping anchor or furling its sails completely. These flying visits, made not least in order to avoid paying mooring fees and other charges, are not included in the shipping records kept by harbour authorities and consulates.[20] The US consulate in Praia estimated the number of American whaleships passing through Cape Verde to have been around sixty per year in the 1830s.[21] Since, however, most of these stops could be confirmed only with reference to logbooks –

---

14 Log POLLEY, 1774–1775, 24.–27.06.1774; Extract of a Letter from the Governor & Council of St. Helena date the 12th June 1776 together with Extract of Proceedings of said Governor & Council of the 22d May Proceeding. British Library, India Office Records H/122, 407–410.
15 Du Pasquier, *Les Baleiniers Français de Louis XVI à Napoléon*, 141, 147, 152f., 185.
16 Jones, *Ships Employed in the South Seas Trade*, 6.
17 Carreira, *The People of the Cape Verde Islands*, 44.
18 Busch, "Cape Verdeans in the American Whaling and Sealing Industry", 104f. For an account of such a stay in Boa Vista from the perspective of a British sealer see Goodridge, *Narrative of a Voyage to the South Seas*, 29f.
19 Carreira, *The People of the Cape Verde Islands*, 45.
20 Busch, "Cape Verdeans in the American Whaling and Sealing Industry", 109.
21 "Custom-House." *Columbian Courier, or Weekly Miscellany*, 21.01.1803, 3.

which, as discussed in the introduction, are preserved only for approximately one in three voyages – any estimate must needs remain unsubstantiated.

1814 marked the end both of the War of 1812 and of the Napoleonic Wars (at least at sea), ushering in a period of relative safety and tranquillity on the world's oceans. The ability to operate unhindered by hostile navies benefited the American whaling industry, which reached its all-time peak in the 1830s and 40s. It was during this period that British, French and other European whalers fell behind their more productive American competitors and gradually disappeared from the scene. This boom in American whaling was also felt in Cape Verde. The islands were a stop not only for vessels operating in the Atlantic, but also for those sailing to or from whaling grounds in the Pacific and Indian Oceans. In Haywood's estimate, around one American hundred whalers per year came to Cape Verde between 1825 and 1875. While Santiago remained among their chief ports of call, the *ilhas rasas* came to be supplanted above all by Brava, Fogo and São Vicente.[22] During this period, a dozen or more whaleships might be found lying at Furna at any one time, as a passenger aboard the *Julius Caesar* of New London observed in 1851: "The bay itself was full of life and activity; nineteen vessels were sailing back and forth while taking on fresh supplies."[23]

Whalers usually came to Cape Verde for supplies – not to hunt whales. Such sperm whales as occurred there could not be found reliably enough for the area to become established as a whaling ground.[24] If a vessel did catch a whale in the archipelago, it was usually as a result of a chance encounter. What they did encounter more often were pilot whales, which were hunted as bycatch and for target practice.[25] Cape Verdean waters were also rich in fish, offering a welcome opportunity to add variety to the notoriously drab fare served on board whaleships.[26]

An outward-bound whaler in the nineteenth century would usually pass through Cape Verdean waters from north to south, making brief stops – usually "off and on" – at various islands. A concrete depiction of such an itinerary was given by John Ross Brown, whose account of his voyage in the *Bruce* of Fairhaven was published by the *National Intelligencer* in 1844. Browne writes this of the vessel's passage through Cape Verde:

---

22 Haywood, "American Whalers and Africa", 67.
23 Quoted in Warrin, *So Ends This Day*, 113f.
24 "Custom-House." *Columbian Courier, or Weekly Miscellany*, 21.01.1803, 3. Also to be found in Cape Verdean waters were fin whales. See e.g. Pinkham, *The Log Book of the Good Ship Alliance of Nantucket Captain Bartlett Coffin*, 07.11.1791.
25 See e.g. Log EMERALD, 1838–1840, 29.06.1838.
26 See e.g. Pinkham, *The Log Book of the Good Ship Alliance of Nantucket Captain Bartlett Coffin*, 09.11.1791.

On the 26th of October we made the Isle of Sal [. . .]. Early on the following morning we ran down for the Isle of May [Maio], where we procured late Papers from the United States, containing Congressional news of much interest. Our next stoppage was at Bonavista [Boa Vista], from which island we proceeded to St. Jago [Santiago]. At Port Praya we took in a supply of oranges, bananas, coco-nuts, and other tropical fruits.[27]

Cape Verde continued to receive such visits until the end of American-style pelagic whaling in the early twentieth century. Although the industry's decline was felt here too, the islands' relative proximity to New England meant that vessels continued to ply these waters even after they had abandoned whaling grounds in the Indian Ocean and elsewhere. It was during this late phase of whaling, in September 1904, that the *Sunbeam* of New Bedford called at Brava and São Nicolau. Among those on board was Clifford Warren Ashley, an American artist and writer. Ashley had been commissioned by *Harper's Monthly Magazine* – for which Melville had written on the "Gees" nearly half a century earlier – to write an article about whaling. His notes, sketches and photographs provide a valuable complement to the seamen's own records, and I will repeatedly draw upon them in the remainder of this chapter.[28]

Colonial rule, slavery and feudalism

By the time the first whalers reached the islands, Cape Verde had long been a hub of Atlantic navigation. That position, however, was due above all to Santiago and São Vicente, whereas Brava's role for shipping was marginal. To give a sense of the social order encountered there by whalemen, it is worth briefly outlining the archipelago's history and that of Brava's in particular.

Portuguese seamen came across the hitherto uninhabited archipelago in the 1450s. The islands may already have been visited from the western coast of Africa since the thirteenth century, and perhaps Phoenician or Arab mariners had discovered them even earlier. But their settlement began in the 1460s, when Prince Fernando of Portugal has several dozen Portuguese, Genoese, Flemings and Sephardic Jews taken to Santiago and Fogo. The Genoese merchants among them were to establish sugar cane plantations on the model of Madeira. However, peopling the islands was a slow process. In order to encourage it, in 1466 the Portuguese crown awarded settlers the privilege of undertaking

---

27 Browne, "Sketches of the Arabs", 4.
28 Ashley's article appeared under the title "The Blubber Hunters" in no. 112 (1905) of the magazine. His photographs were published in 1982 by the Old Dartmouth Historical Society in Hall, *Sperm Whaling from New Bedford*.

trading expeditions to the coast of west Africa. In the course of these voyages, commercial agents or *lançados* brought several thousand slaves from the Senegambia region to Santiago and Fogo. One result of these voyages was the emergence in Cape Verde of a creole language, *Criulo*, which remains in use today. Yet plans for the large-scale cultivation of sugar cane foundered on the geological makeup of the islands and their irregular rains. The slaves were instead set to work growing cotton and weaving it into cloths (*pano* and *barafula*) used in barter by the *lançados*. With the exploration and colonization of the Americas, beginning in 1492, the islands assumed another role. Situated as it was at the crossing of the routes taken by European vessels to west Africa on the one hand and South America on the other, Cape Verde was destined to serve as a provisioning station for Atlantic trade. Brava, however, was untouched by this development and for the time being remained uninhabited – unlike the neighbouring island of Fogo, where a few cotton fields were planted between 1480 and 1500.[29]

In view of their changing role within its colonial strategies, the Portuguese crown assumed direct control of the islands in the sixteenth century and made changes to their agricultural sector. Now focussing on the market of passing vessels and their crews, the Portuguese ordered fruit to be grown and livestock – especially pigs and goats – to be raised. Fertile holdings were placed as *donatários* in the hands of settlers, who acted as feudal lords or *capitãos* over these domains and had them worked by slaves. This model was most successful in the *sotaventos* and above all in Santiago, where Ribeira Granda emerged as the islands' chief port, which it was to remain into the eighteenth century. In the *ilhas rasas*, Portugal exploited natural reserves of salt, some of which was used to preserve goat meat and the remainder sold to passing vessels. The islands also served Portugal as an entrepôt for their west African. Unlike their trading stations on the mainland, Cape Verde was not threatened by attack from the interior, though privateers from Portugal's European rivals did on several occasions sack Cape Verdean ports. From Santiago, merchants carried *pano*, *barafula* and salt to the mainland, returning with furs and other barter goods, allowing merchantmen

---

29 Brooks, *Eurafricans in Western Africa*, 59–63; Brooks, "Cabo Verde", 104, 106; Carreira, *The People of the Cape Verde Islands*, 5–7; Davidson, *The Fortunate Isles*, 23, 25, 29; Duncan, *Atlantic Islands*, 18f., 21, 158, 181; Halter, *Between Race and Ethnicity*, 2–4; Lobban, *Cape Verde*, 11, 16f., 23; Lobban/Lopes, *Historical Dictionary of the Republic of Cape Verde*, xix; Meintel, *Race, Culture, and Portuguese Colonialism in Cabo Verde*, 31–34; Silva, *Dutch and Portuguese in Western Africa*, 40f., 83, 85, 318, 326; Vieira, "The Fortunate of the Fortunates", 206f., 226f., 233f. It was from the Senegambia, whose western tip the Portuguese encountered as the first patch of green along the arid coastline of western Africa, that the islands derived their name of *Cabo Verde* or "Green Cape".

Colonial rule, slavery and feudalism — 451

Fig. 38: Furna as seen from the island's interior in a photograph by Clifford Warren Ashley, who visited Cape Verde aboard the *Sunbeam* in September 1904.
Courtesy of the New Bedford Whaling Museum, item number 1974.3.1.6.

to pick up African goods from the warehouses of Ribeira Grande without themselves having to sail to the African mainland.[30]

These measures paved the way for economic prosperity, though its sole beneficiaries were a small group of powerful merchants and the crown itself. It was, moreover, fragile and crisis-prone, depending to a large extent on the intensity of shipping. Many of the vessels that put in to Santiago for provisions were slave ships. In the sixteenth century hundreds of slaves annually were taken from the west coast of Africa via Ribeira Grande principally to the Spanish colonies in the Caribbean but also to Brazil, Central America and Europe. Like cargo, these "commercial slaves" (*escravos de commercio*) were held at Ribeira Grande to await onward shipment; only a few of them remained in Cape Verde as working slaves (*escravos de commercio*).[31] The proportion of slaves and their descendants in the overall population nonetheless grew rapidly and soon far exceeded that of the settlers. In 1582 a missionary estimated the European population of Santiago and Fogo to number some one hundred persons; meanwhile, the slave population at the time is said to have reached 14,000.[32]

All these developments passed Brava by. It is doubtful whether the island had any human inhabitants in the sixteenth century. It has been surmised that fugitive slaves took refuge there, but no proof has been offered in support of the claim. Only one source suggests an early presence of settlers, while others record the earliest settlements in the seventeenth century. It does, however, seem that the inhabitants of Fogo sometimes used the neighbouring island to pasture their goats.[33]

Settlement of Brava began no later than 1624 with the arrival of farmers who had come to Cape Verde from Madeira. The eruption of a volcano in Fogo in 1680 brought an influx of refugees to Brava. Following the model of agriculture established in Fogo, the new arrivals raised goats and produced cotton stuffs, living and working as small-scale farmers and artisans mostly around Nova Sintra. But unlike in the other agricultural islands, hardly any slaves were employed in Brava. The island's topography is dominated by steep hillsides

---

30 Brooks, *Eurafricans in Western Africa*, 59–63; Brooks, "Cabo Verde", 106; Busch, "Cape Verdeans in the American Whaling and Sealing Industry", 105; Davidson, *The Fortunate Isles*, 27f.; Duncan, *Atlantic Islands*, 4, 22, 161, 168f., 171f., 176f., 184–191; Lobban, *Cape Verde*, 20, 22f.; Silva, *Dutch and Portuguese in Western Africa*, 318, 326; Vieira, "The Fortunate of the Fortunates", 206f., 226f., 233f.
31 Carreira, *The People of the Cape Verde Islands*, 9f.; Lobban, *Cape Verde*, 24; Meintel, *Race, Culture, and Portuguese Colonialism in Cabo Verde*, 37.
32 Davidson, *The Fortunate Isles*, 26; Meintel, *Race, Culture, and Portuguese Colonialism in Cabo Verde*, 24, 84.
33 Duncan, *Atlantic Islands*, 171, 182f.; Meintel, *Race, Culture, and Portuguese Colonialism in Cabo Verde*, 21.

inimical to large-scale farms or plantations, to the *morgadios* and *capelas* familiar from Santiago. The farms that developed in Brava were small, and most of the work was done by the settlers themselves.[34]

While Atlantic commerce continued by and large to ignore Brava in the seventeenth century, other islands – and Santiago in particular – saw increasing traffic. This was due not only to the islands' location but also to their visibility. Until the widespread introduction of the marine chronometer in the late eighteenth century, vessels had no way of establishing their exact longitude on the open sea. Volcanic islands like Cape Verde, which were visible from afar, offered a rare opportunity for doing so. This was another reason why so many captains in command of Africa-bound merchantmen made sure they passed through Cape Verde.[35] The trade in goods between the islands and the coastal region now occupied by Senegal, Gambia, Guinea-Bissau, Guinea and Sierra Leone grew in parallel to the slave trade.[36] It turned out to be so lucrative that the Portuguese crown rescinded the settlers' trading privileges in 1640 and established a company of its own with a monopoly on Cape Verde trade.[37]

Around 1700 the population of Brava saw considerable growth within just a few decades (Tab. 11). From 1720 and throughout the eighteenth and nineteenth centuries the island saw the highest population growth anywhere in Cape Verde.[38] One factor here was the decline in cotton production, particularly in Santiago, where intensive farming had done lasting damage to the soil. What was more, the colonial government began to see a connection between the high incidence of malaria in Ribeira Grande in particular and the nearby marshes, and the capital was accordingly moved to Praia in 1770.[39] Brava was now much closer than before to the colony's capital and began to attract interest for its temperate climate. The small farmers who came to settle the island were joined by members of Santiago's upper crust, who built summer residences to escape heat and disease. Many Portuguese officials also took up residence in Brava, whose landscape is reminiscent of northern Portugal.[40]

---

34 Duncan, *Atlantic Islands*, 222, 235f.; Greenfield, "In Search of Social Identity", 16; Meintel, *Race, Culture, and Portuguese Colonialism in Cabo Verde*, 21.
35 Duncan, *Atlantic Islands*, 3.
36 Davidson, *The Fortunate Isles*, 26; Duncan, *Atlantic Islands*, 198f., 206f., 210, 242; Meintel, *Race, Culture, and Portuguese Colonialism in Cabo Verde*, 41.
37 Meintel, *Race, Culture, and Portuguese Colonialism in Cabo Verde*, 41.
38 Ibid., 22; Patterson, "Epidemics, Famines, and Population in the Cape Verde Islands", 293.
39 Patterson, "Epidemics, Famines, and Population in the Cape Verde Islands", 301.
40 Brooks, "Cabo Verde", 121; Meintel, *Race, Culture, and Portuguese Colonialism in Cabo Verde*, 21; Patterson, "Epidemics, Famines, and Population in the Cape Verde Islands", 301f.; Travassos Valdez, *Six Years of a Traveller's Life in Western Africa*, vol. 1, 153.

The decline of the cotton industry meant an increased role for commerce and the slave trade. Both received a boost from the defeat of Portugal's rival France in the Seven Years' War. Between 1757 and 1777 alone, Portugal's chartered company transported more than 28,000 slaves via the archipelago and Portuguese Guinea – the territories were united to form the colony of Cabo Verde e Guiné in 1778 – to north-eastern Brazil. Meanwhile, orchella weeds – gathered principally in Fogo and the source of the dye orcein – became a major export in trade with the west African coast. American vessels also became regular visitors to Cape Verde once the United States had won their independence.[41]

What kind of society did whalemen encounter in Brava in the late eighteenth and early nineteenth centuries? In spite of the failure of the cotton and sugar plantations, the structures of feudalism and slavery that had been established for their benefit endured. The islands remained a Portuguese colony until 1975. Portugal banned the slave trade in 1858 and outlawed slavery itself in 1869 – the last European state to do so. Yet Cape Verde was not a typical slave society. In Brava, as in all the islands, an eventful history gave rise to a highly diversified social structure with many a distinctive and complex trait.[42]

Broadly speaking, Cape Verdean society in the eighteenth and nineteenth centuries may be divided into three classes. At the top were the *brancos* (whites), who in turn were divided into two groups: first the *filhos fo reino* or *reinóis*, those of European birth (including Madeira and the Azores) who were posted to Cape Verde by Church or crown; second the much larger group of *brancos da terra* and *brancos de dinheiro*, the locally-born descendants of settlers. After several generations, this latter group usually had some African ancestry too. Although the *brancos da terra* and the *brancos de dinheiro* formally ranked below the *reonóis*, in fact the *capitãos* among them held the decisive resources of land, labour and money under oligopolistic control. The holders of *morgadios* and *capelas* (church lands) in particular enjoyed the lifestyle of rich feudal lords. Like the sugar barons in plantation colonies of Latin America, the Caribbean and the Indian Ocean, they often ruled over what were effectively states within a state.

---

41 Brooks, "Cabo Verde", 120–123; Duncan, *Atlantic Islands*, 160; Meintel, "Cape Verdean Transnationalism", 29; Meintel, *Race, Culture, and Portuguese Colonialism in Cabo Verde*, 42f.
42 The three following paragraphs on Cape Verdean society in the eighteenth and nineteenth centuries are based on Bigman, *History and Hunger in West Africa*, 99; Brooks, "Cabo Verde", 106–110; Brooks, *Eurafricans in Western Africa*, 60; Brooks, *Western Africa and Cabo Verde*, 32–36; Carreira, *The People of the Cape Verde Islands*, 23–26; Davidson, *The Fortunate Isles*, 26; Duncan, *Atlantic Islands*, 236; Halter, *Between Race and Ethnicity*, 3f., 79–81, 84f., 298; Lobban, *Cape Verde*, 22–29, 32, 34, 48, 50–58; Meintel, *Race, Culture, and Portuguese Colonialism in Cabo Verde*, 23f., 86f.; Patterson, "Epidemics, Famines, and Population in the Cape Verde Islands", 306 and Silva, *Dutch and Portuguese in Western Africa*, 83, 107–109, 116–118, 123f., 136, 142f.

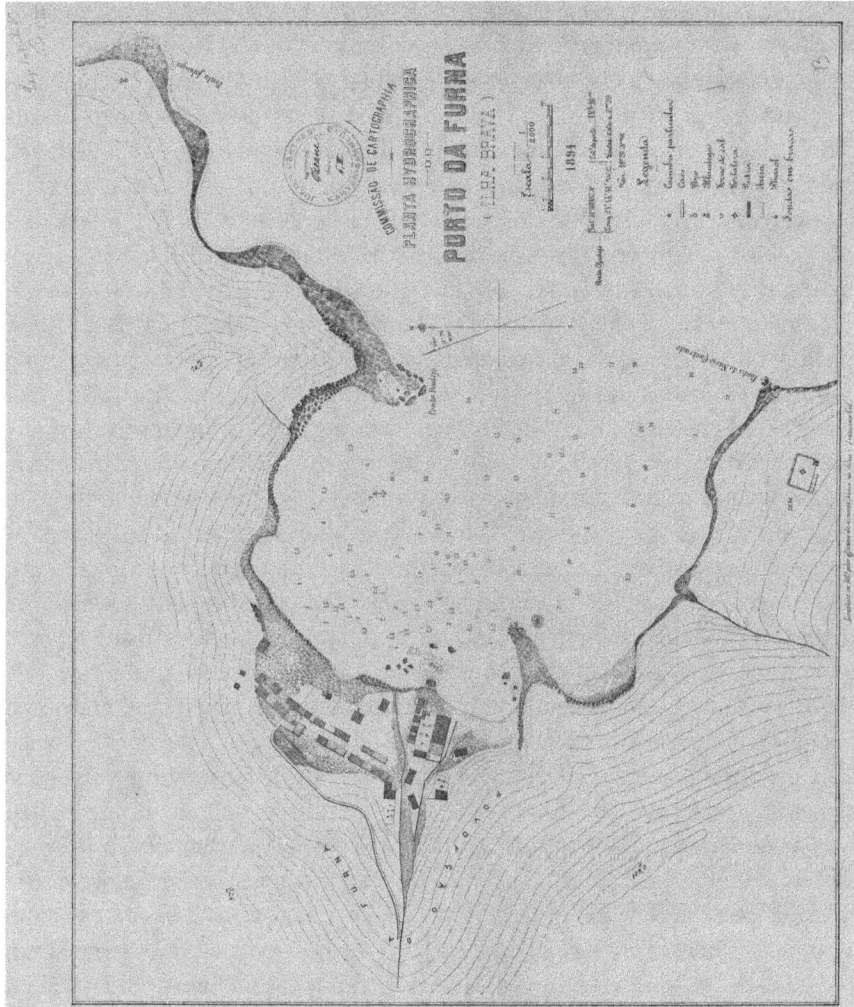

Fig. 39: Furna on a Portuguese sea chart of 1894 (*Planta Hydrographica do Porto da Furna [Ilha Brava]*. 1:2,000. Comissão de cartographia, 1894).
Courtesy of the Gotha Research Library at University of Erfurt, SPK 547$112327877.

The next lower class consisted of those who were neither *reinóis* or *brancas* nor slaves. This group was far from homogeneous but can be broadly divided into an upper (e.g. merchants, government, small farmers) and a lower middle class (e.g. tradesmen, tenant farmers, soldiers, freed slaves). Many members of this middle class were convicts, émigrés, exiles, orphans and refugees from Portugal. These *degredados* and *exterminados* had been sent to Cape Verde since the early sixteenth century, and another 2,500 joined them between 1802 and 1881 alone.

The third group were the *escravos* or slaves, who were divided into three subgroups; first the *escravos boçais* born in mainland Africa, second the *escravos naturais* born in Cape Verde and third the *escravos de confissãoi* or baptised slaves. Like the other classes, the slave population was heterogeneous in origin, being descended from at least twenty-seven different west African societies. As in other slaveholding societies in the Atlantic world, slaves in Cape Verde had no rights and received no pay. Yet since large-scale farming there declined over time, slaveholders usually owned only a few slaves – an average of three or four in the mid-1850s. Brava was one of the islands in which landholdings tended to be particularly small, and where master and slave lived in close quarters on small farms, relations tended to be less governed by violence than in other slave societies. By contrast, in Santiago and other islands divided into larger estates, many *brancos* ruled no less cruelly than their counterparts in Latin America and elsewhere. Moreover, since the seventeenth century it had become an established practice to free one's *escravos*. Since slaves required food, housing and supervision, they were a constant source of expense to their owners, whereas natural conditions meant that they were able to generate agricultural revenue only during limited periods of the year. The *brancos* thus came to realise that using cheap seasonal labour was more profitable in the long term than keeping slaves. Landowners increasing took the occasion of feast days and weddings, as well as droughts and other misfortunes, to free some of their slaves, whose population declined from 14,000 in the sixteenth century to just over 5,000 by the mid-nineteenth century. The overall population of the inlands increased about tenfold during this period.

At no point were marriages between members of different groups or classes prohibited by the authorities, and sexual relations between masters and female slaves were the norm. By the seventeenth century, most of the island's inhabitant could claim both European and African ancestry. Only the owners of the *morgadios* maintained strict and systematic endogamy in order to preserve their inherited privileges over crown lands. Since physical traits ceased to be a reliable indicator of class membership, formerly racialised terms came to function as status markers: a *branco* or white was now anybody enjoying the privileges of wealth in land (*brancos da terra*) or money (*brancos de dinheiro*). Acoording to this classification, a "white" slaveowner might well be darker-skinned than his "black" slave.[43]

Tab. 11: Population figures for Brava in the eighteenth and nineteenth centuries.

1700	100
1720	1,200
1723	200
1774	3,190
1775	2,115
1800	3,000
1807	6,950
1831	9,320
1834	3,990
1841	4,000
1844	4,600
1851	4,300
1861	6,557
1862	6,824
1867	5,874
1872	8,673
1878	8,151
1885	9,013
1900	9,200

Sources: Carreira, *The People of the Cape Verde Islands*, 50; Lobban, *Cape Verde*, 49; Patterson, "Epidemics, Famines, and Population in the Cape Verde Islands", 294f.

***

The reason I have discussed the class stratification of Cape Verdean society is above all to bring into sharper relief some of the peculiarities of Brava and its population – of the people, that is, whom whalemen most often encountered in this corner of the ocean. Since Brava was settled comparatively late and its hilly terrain prevented the establishment of large farms, the island never had either a large slave population or a feudal social order. The African element in the population was smaller than elsewhere in Cape Verde, and most of Brava's inhabitants

---

[43] Brooks, "Cabo Verde", 109; Davidson, *The Fortunate Isles*, 31f.; Duncan, *Atlantic Islands*, 234; Lobban, *Cape Verde*, 54; Meintel, *Race, Culture, and Portuguese Colonialism in Cabo Verde*, 82, 174.

were descended from immigrants from Madeira and the Azores. Those among them who did own slaves usually lived one roof with them on small farms.⁴⁴

What was grown on these farms was determined above all by their location. The island's craggy and mountainous terrain contains different regional climates. Tropical crops could be grown in its hotter low-lying parts while the uplands were suitable for the cultivation of coffee. Whatever they grew for sale, farmers usually also reserved a plot of land adjacent to their house on which to grow vegetables and a keep a few chickens, pigs and goats. Unlike in other of the Cape Verde Islands, farmers in Brava could also take advantage of several mineral springs for irrigation – at least in the lowlands.⁴⁵

Its comparatively high humidity also helped ensure that Brava was suffered from famine to a lesser degree than the other islands. From the 1850s onwards, the ill-advised policies of the colonial administration – destroying fragile vegetation through intensive cultivation, raising large herds of pigs and goats, and settling a population too large for the islands' ecological resources – led to recurring famines. Since the colonial government offered the population no chance of escape and, until the mid-nineteenth century, provided no material support to speak of, the mortality rate among humans and livestock alike was high. Famines generally occurred in the wake of droughts. The islanders distinguished between short droughts (*secas suaves*) and severe droughts (*secas extremas*), which lasted for two to three years. Approximately one drought in three was severe, and twenty-four are recorded from the mid-eighteenth to the mid-nineteenth century. In three of these cases (1775–1775, 1831–1833 and 1863–1865), the succeeding famine claimed the lives of twenty-five to forty percent of the population – some twenty to thirty thousand people on each occasion. Some islands lost half, some villages all their inhabitants. Up to ninety-five percent of livestock perished. Famines were in turn often followed by severe epidemics of smallpox or cholera, with the countless bodies and carcases encouraging the proliferation of rats and insects which acted as vectors of disease among a weakened population. A malaria epidemic in 1870 killed an estimated thirty per cent of Cape Verde islanders.⁴⁶

---

44 Bigman, *History and Hunger in West Africa*, 97; Duncan, *Atlantic Islands*, 182; Lobban, *Cape Verde*, 33; Meintel, *Race, Culture, and Portuguese Colonialism in Cabo Verde*, 15, 19, 76f.; Patterson, "Epidemics, Famines, and Population in the Cape Verde Islands", 293, 298.
45 Meintel, *Race, Culture, and Portuguese Colonialism in Cabo Verde*, 20f.; Moran, "The Evolution of Cape Verde's Agriculture", 70.
46 Bigman, *History and Hunger in West Africa*, 80; Brooks, "Cabo Verde", 106f.; Busch, "Cape Verdeans in the American Whaling and Sealing Industry", 108; Carreira, *The People of the Cape Verde Islands*, 15f.; Duncan, *Atlantic Islands*, 197; Halter, "Cape Verdeans in the U.S.", 35; Meintel, *Race, Culture, and Portuguese Colonialism in Cabo Verde*, 55–59, 63; Patterson, "Epidemics, Famines, and Population in the Cape Verde Islands", 303, 312.

For their part, the islanders subsumed famine, death and other effects of drought under the rubric of *crises*. With regard to later interactions with whalemen, one strategy in particular of surviving these *crises* is worth highlighting. It was known for legally free men and women to go to the ports and to sell themselves to vessels as slaves. During the disastrous famine of 1773–1775, slave ships were able to make off with entire families in exchange for food.[47] The Portuguese government bore much of the blame for a drought turning into a *crises*. The colonial authorities and the chartered company that long held the islands' economy in the grip of its monopoly accorded greater importance to the export of agricultural produce and the provisioning of vessels than it did to feeding the people. The government continued with the sale of food to crews even in times of drought and famine.[48] At the same time, until the early nineteenth century the Portuguese – both to protect their trading monopoly and to prevent slaves from escaping – banned all islanders, the *reinóis* excepted, from owning boats. In so doing, they prevented the emergence of a fishing industry that might have provided crucial relief in times of famine.[49] Whalers too were made painfully aware of this lack of boats. It was not unheard of for captains to post a sentry alongside a boat used to land on one of the Cape Verde Islands to prevent it from being stolen.[50]

While their disastrous effects may be ascribed to the colonial government, the incidence of drought was due to climatic conditions. Cape Verde is situated in the semi-arid Sahel region and may be considered the westernmost outpost of the Sohara. They are situated at the northern edge of the intertropical convergence zone, which is subject to seasonal shifts. As a rule, the islands could expect rainfall when the convergence zone and its humid south Atlantic winds moved northwards. Since the presence of basalt made the soil porous and unable to retain sufficient groundwater, this period between July and August was crucial to the supply of water for human, animal and plant life. Usually, however, the rain only gets as far as the *sotaventos*, and in some years even they remain to the north of the convergence zone. When the rain did come, it was far from being an unmixed blessing. Arable land accounts for only approximately 1.65 per cent of the islands' surface area, and heavy rain was liable to erode fragile topsoil left exposed by the destruction of natural vegetation and

---

47 Bigman, *History and Hunger in West Africa*, 80f.; Brooks, "Cabo Verde", 122; Meintel, *Race, Culture, and Portuguese Colonialism in Cabo Verde*, 55f.
48 Bigman, *History and Hunger in West Africa*, 81f.; Brooks, "Cabo Verde", 122–124.
49 Brooks, "Cabo Verde", 101, 107, 120, 123f., 127, 131; Brooks, *Western Africa and Cabo Verde*, 31, 33; Tuckey, *Narrative of an Expedition to Explore the River Zaire*, 32.
50 Perkins, *Na Motu*, 39.

cause landslides. Yet in the long run, the wind, which in Cape Verde usually blows from the north-east, was an even greater cause of soil erosion.[51]

Only in the mid-nineteenth century, and particularly after the *crises* of 1862 to 1865, did Portugal begin to take systematic measures to support the islanders. The famine-stricken population were offered work in building roads into the islands' inaccessible interior or in the plantations of São Tomé, Príncipe and Guinea-Bissau. Those who took up the offer received food and a small cash payment. The colonial government was thus able to exploit the famine for its own ends, channelling labour into its own projects and offering jobs that few would have taken on but for fear of starvation. Conditions in road building and on the plantations were akin to slavery, and many workers lost their lives to accidents or disease. Those who could preferred to try their on the coast and sign on aboard a whaler or another vessel. The construction crews this became the last resort of those unable to find work at sea: women and children.[52]

Although Brava tended to suffer less from drought and famine than the other islands Tab. 12), this was by no means always the case. For instance, the famine of 1773–1775 claimed more than 1,500 lives in Brava, whereas that of 1785–1789 caused no deaths there at all – the islanders were even able to send food to the starving population of Boa Vista. At such times, Brava's problem was refugees escaping famine on other islands.[53]

Trade and its cost

"Went on Shore and Vewed their Huts and traded with them", records the log of the *Polly* of Nantucket for a stop at Maio on 25 June 1774.[54] The log is one of the earliest records of a whaler off the coast of Africa and shows that by then Cape

---

[51] Bigman, *History and Hunger in West Africa*, 71; Brooks, "Cabo Verde", 102; Carreira, *The People of the Cape Verde Islands*, 14f.; Lobban, *Cape Verde*, 5f.; Meintel, "Cape Verdean Transnationalism", 27; Meintel, *Race, Culture, and Portuguese Colonialism in Cabo Verde*, 56f.; Moran, "The Evolution of Cape Verde's Agriculture", 67; Patterson, "Epidemics, Famines, and Population in the Cape Verde Islands", 291, 312.

[52] Bigman, *History and Hunger in West Africa*, 82; Brooks, "Cabo Verde", 133f.; Lobban, *Cape Verde*, 52, 63; Meintel, *Race, Culture, and Portuguese Colonialism in Cabo Verde*, 63f.; Patterson, "Epidemics, Famines, and Population in the Cape Verde Islands", 311. On the working conditions endured by plantation labourers in São Tomé and Príncipe see Clarence-Smith, "Creoles and Peasants in São Tomé, Príncipe, Fernando Póo and Mount Cameroun", 494–496.

[53] Meintel, *Race, Culture, and Portuguese Colonialism in Cabo Verde*, 21; Patterson, "Epidemics, Famines, and Population in the Cape Verde Islands", 307f.

[54] Quoted in Haywood, "American Whalers and Africa", 137.

Tab. 12: Droughts and famines in Brava in the eighteenth and nineteenth centuries.

1704–1712
1747
1754–1755
1773–1775
1790–1791
1804
1810
1830–1833
1845–1846
1853–1855
1856–1859
1863–1866
1883–1886
1889–1890
1892
1896–1897
1900

Sources: Moran, "The Evolution of Cape Verde's Agriculture", 71; Patterson, "Epidemics, Famines, and Population in the Cape Verde Islands", 304f.

Verde was already a trading place known to seafarers. But what were whalers able to obtain there? Most frequently mentioned in the logs of vessels that called at Brava were fruit and vegetables, notably oranges, bananas and plantains, squashes, pineapples, grapes, potatoes, yams, and figs. Livestock – particularly pigs, goats and chickens, and sometimes ducks – was also taken aboard, albeit in small numbers. Eggs were another frequent purchase.[55] Provisions aside, seamen would sometimes acquire souvenirs, curios or pets – the crew of the London sealer *Princess of Wales*, for instance, in 1820 bought a monkey in Santiago.[56]

The volume of commerce generated by whalers in their stay at Brava varied considerably. The *Columbia* of Nantucket, which stopped for a day in September 1846, bought four thousand oranges, two hundred eggs and eleven

---

[55] Brock, Journal LEXINGTON, 1853–1856, 06. & 07.07.1853; Ely, There She Blows, 43–45, 182; Goodridge, *Narrative of a Voyage to the South Seas*, 30; Log BERTHA, 1878–1881, 17.–28.11.1878 & 11.–21.11.1879; Log CERES, 1838–1839, 08. & 09.11.1838; Log EMERALD, 1838–1840, 28. & 29.06.1838; Log GENERALSCOTT, 1875–1878, 16.11.1875; Log PEDRO VARELA, 1878–1880, 22. & 23. 11.1878; Log SPLENDID, 1858–1862, 10.–13.01.1859; Nichols, *Eastward Around the World on the Barque Emerald*, 20.
[56] Goodridge, *Narrative of a Voyage to the South Seas*, 30.

pigs.[57] The schooner *Pedro Varela* of New Bedford, which called in 1878, loaded one thousand oranges, two hundred eggs, fifteen chickens, twelve ears of maize, three chickens and a basketful of sweet potatoes.[58] In other (perhaps most) cases, the quantities traded were distinctly smaller. Captain Stanford of the *Hibernia* was unable to find more than two pigs in Brava in August 1842, as was Captain Sturgis, who arrived aboard the *Herald II* in 1867m two years after a severe famine.[59] There was no reliable way of knowing in advance what provisions would be available. "Sent a boat on shore for trade but met with poor luck", records the log of the schooner *Admiral Blake* of Marion of a stop at Brava in 1869.[60]

Visiting seamen were not oblivious to suffering in times of *crises*. "We made a call to obtain such articles as these poor islanders have to dispose of, such as pigs, goats and poultry", recalled Gurdon Alleyn, who came to Cape Verde as master of the barque *Nathaniel S. Perkins* of New London in 1848.[61] In view of the recurring famines, it seems unlikely that the population should have had food and livestock to sell to ships' crews. Such, however, were the limits imposed on economic activity by the Portuguese authorities intent on protecting their monopoly that neither the majority population of *pardos* (the descendants of European settlers and African women) nor the freed slaves (*pretos livres*) had much chance of selling anything else.[62]

Portuguese regulations also limited the range of items whalemen were able to use in barter to obtain goods in Cape Verde. Indeed, it was under the impression of the trade brought to the islands by whalers that the colonial authorities imposed additional import restrictions between 1825 and 1844. In an attempt to protect the Portuguese monopoly, the importation of goods including tobacco, cotton, ironware, shoes, tea, wine, gunpowder, and bread and flour was either banned completely or declared the preserve of Portuguese vessels. By law, every transaction required official permission.[63] In practice, however, harbour officials tended to ignore the letter of the law and instead tried to derive personal advantage from the trade by levying "taxes" of their own.[64] Several references can be found to trade carried on in

---

57 Log COLUMBIA, 1846–1850, 27.09.1846.
58 Log PEDRO VARELA, 1878–1880.
59 Eldridge, *Lewis William Eldridge's Whaling Voyage*, 8; Log HIBERNIA, 1842–1843, 04.–06.08.1842. For similar difficulties provisioning in Santiago see Log NAVIGATOR, 1849–1854, 06.10.1849.
60 Log ADMIRAL BLAKE, 1869–1870, 15.02.1869.
61 Allyn, *The Old Sailor's Story*, 64.
62 Brooks, "Cabo Verde", 116; Busch, "Cape Verdeans in the American Whaling and Sealing Industry", 105.
63 "Commercial." *New-Bedford Mercury*, 23.09.1825, 2.
64 Carreira, *The People of the Cape Verde Islands*, 59; Haywood, "American Whalers and Africa", 58.

defiance of government restrictions. The crew of the *Nathaniel Perkins* used clothing for barter,[65] and in Brava in 1878 Captain Ricketson of the Pedro Varela sold cotton cloth, one of the pillars of the Portuguese monopoly.[66] Nor were common seamen deterred from using tobacco as the basic unit of exchange.[67]

Another effect of Portugal's restrictive policy was plain for seamen to see. Unlike almost everywhere else in west African waters, small traders in canoes hardly ever rowed out to meet their vessels. As already related, the Portuguese authorities, in an attempt to both to prevent smuggling and to keep slaves from escaping, made it illegal for the Cape Verde islanders to build or own boats, a prohibition which remained in force into the early nineteenth century. Many seamen were puzzled by the absence of canoes, so familiar from ports such as Annobón or Cabinda, finding that it "gives to the port the appearance of a deserted settlement" – as James Hingston Tickey, a British explorer, remarked in Praia in 1816.[68] The records reveal virtually nothing about the actors with whom seafarers traded on shore. Haywood supposes them to have been small farmers, *pardos* and *pretos livres*, who welcomed an additional market for their produce.[69]

***

A notorious problem confronted by whalers in Cape Verde was the expense such a visit was likely to entail. Since the decline of cotton farming in Santiago and Fogo, the colony had largely ceased to generate export revenues, and Portugal looked to visiting vessels to make up at least some of the shortfall. An export duty on goods sold to vessels had already been introduced in the sixteenth century, and in the eighteenth and nineteenth centuries were added anchorage feed and high charges for drinking water provided to vessels. The income thus generated was considerable, particularly in Mindelo in the island of São Vicente, which in the late 1830s became a coaling station much frequented by steamships.[70]

Whalers too were a welcome source of revenue for the government – much to their chagrin. "4 Dollars was Requierd as costomaryes dues which I objected to", complained the captain of the *Kingston* of London about the charges levied

---

65 Allyn, *The Old Sailor's Story*, 64.
66 Log PEDRO VARELA, 1878–1880.
67 See e.g. the diary of Albert Peck of the *Chili* of New Bedford, excepts from which are transcribed in Haywood, "American Whalers and Africa", 166–168.
68 Tuckey, *Narrative of an Expedition to Explore the River Zaire*, 20.
69 Haywood, "American Whalers and Africa", 67; see also Tuckey, *Narrative of an Expedition to Explore the River Zaire*, 35.
70 Duncan, *Atlantic Islands*, 161, 164; Silva, *Dutch and Portuguese in Western Africa*, 85–88; Vieira, "The Fortunate of the Fortunates", 209. On the history of the port of Mindelo see Gatlin, "A Socioeconomic History of São Vicente de Cabo Verde".

when the vessel put in at Maio in 1800.[71] Nor had the Portuguese yet run out of ideas for how to generate extra income. Customs regulations were further tightened in 1842, and in 1846 tonnage dues were introduced on top of the existing mooring fee, with an additional one hundred réis charged per gross ton.[72]

An additional difficulty was posed by widespread corruption – a consequence of the cash-strapped administration's policy of paying its officials only small salaries, if any. Portugal expected its colonial officials – even those in government and other leading positions – to raise such taxes and duties as they needed to support both themselves and the Portuguese garrisons. But as a Cape Verdean proverb put it: no blood can be taken where there is no vein.[73] Little revenue could be extracted from a largely impoverished population, leaving officials all the keener to make money from visiting vessels. Brandy would usually persuade colonial surgeons not to waste too much time over health inspections,[74] and customs officials could be bribed to turn a blind eye to any business captains might wish to conduct in defiance of import and export regulations. The fact that slaves were smuggled through Cape Verde into the mid-nineteenth century and that livestock and drinking water were sold to crews even amid severe drought and famine is due not least to corruptible officials.[75] This state of affairs was both a curse and a blessing to whalemen. While they were able to trade as they saw fit, unencumbered by official strictures, they could never quite predict what would be demanded in return. The bribes sometimes struck seamen as so extortionate that the officials struck them as "importunate beggars" – in the phrase of Edward Perkins, who came to São Nicolau aboard an American whaler in 1848.[76]

Whalemen responded to the cost of making regular stops at Cape Verde by resorting to a practice discussed earlier: "off and on". Vessels steered well clear of ports, sending only boats ashore – often in bays a good distance from the major towns of Praia, Ribeira Grande and Mindelo. There, seamen were able to obtain provisions without any involvement with officialdom and without having to pay duties or bribes, bartering directly with small farmers and traders.[77]

---

[71] Log KINGSTON, 1800–1801, 21.03.1800.
[72] "Cape de Verds." *New-Bedford Mercury*, 27.05.1842, 1; "From the Coast of Africa." *New-Bedford Mercury*, 29.05.1846, 1.
[73] "Câ pode t'ra sangue undi qui beia câ'sta." (Parsons, *Folk-lore from the Cape Verde Islands*, vol. 2, 205) The collection consists of tales and gathered in 1916 and 1917 among Cape Verdean immigrants in Massachusetts, Rhode Island and Connecticut.
[74] Ellis, *West African Islands*, 124f.
[75] Bigman, *History and Hunger in West Africa*, 78f.; Brooks, "Cabo Verde", 122f.; Ellis, *West African Islands*, 128; Tuckey, *Narrative of an Expedition to Explore the River Zaire*, 20.
[76] Perkins, *Na Motu*, 36.
[77] Haywood, "American Whalers and Africa", 58.

Fig. 40: Port official in Furna, probably at the desk of the custom house. Photograph by Clifford Warren Ashely taken during his visit to Brava aboard the *Sunbeam* in September 1904.
Courtesy of the New Bedford Whaling Museum, item number 1974.3.1.212.

This practice was not lost on the authorities which, in the 1840s, took two measures to suppress them. In 1848 the administration exempted whalers from the mooring fee if their stay did not exceed four calendar days.[78] And already in 1845 the Portuguese had decreed that vessels were permitted to call at the officially designated ports only, on pain of fines of at least $1,000 or, in the case of repeat offenders, confiscation. The official justification was that vessels had been known to help slaves and criminals escape. Furna, which hitherto had been an informal port, was now counted as an official one, while Fajã de Água, in the north-west of Brava, was promoted to the rank of that islan's principal harbour, if only on

---

78 "Important to Whalers." *New-Bedford Mercury*, 23.03.1849, 1.

paper. The governor added to Furna's infrastructure of a custom house (Fig. 40) and a few shops by ordering the construction of a small fort.[79]

In spite of the penalties threatened, whalers largely ignored the new rules laid down by Portugal.[80] For their part, the authorities wasted no time in making an example of several American whaleships accused of unauthorised mooring, among them the brig *Sarah Louisa* of New Bedford.[81] But the Portuguese show of force ended in failure. The United States found Portugal's conduct to be unlawful and dispatched USS *Jamestown* to Cape Verde, which freed the whaleships unopposed in early 1846.[82] It seems that Portugal afterwards ceased to take a heavy-handed approach towards whalers, though it did rescind the previous exemption from mooring fees in 1884. Whaleships were henceforth charged a flat fee of $6.96 for putting into a Cape Verdean port.[83]

"Drinking spirits & playing with the wenches"

Cape Verde provides particularly abundant examples of the practice of leaving seamen behind during a stopover. The islands were often the first stop a whaleship made after leaving its home port and were thus eminently suited, in the view of many a captain, as a place to rid themselves of seamen who had proved dispensable during the first leg of the journey, whether by reason of clumsiness, (sea) sickness or recalcitrance. "It is the practice of some Masters of American Whalers; when they are dissatisfied with any portion of the crew with which they left the U. S.; [. . .] to treat them in such manner that the men are glad to run away the first opportunity", observed Benjamin Tripp, Jr., the American consul in Brava, of this practice, further noting that "The Master affords them the opportunity by going to some such place as the Island of Brava in this Consulate, where nearly the whole male inhabitant are good sailors, and taking these discontents ashore in the boat while the vessel lays off and on under sail". In order to avoid charges of having illegally abandoned their men, it was known for captains to stoke the desire for escape in certain men before providing them with opportunities to do so when in Brava. "The result is just as the Master

---

[79] Haywood, "American Whalers and Africa", 62; "Important to Whalers." *New-Bedford Mercury*, 02.05.1845, 2; "Memoranda." *Whalemen's Shipping List and Merchants' Transcript*, 29.04.1845, 31; Travassos Valdez, *Six Years of a Traveller's Life in Western Africa*, vol. 1, 154.
[80] "Memoranda." *Whalemen's Shipping List and Merchants' Transcript*, 29.04.1845, 31.
[81] "At Isle of Sal . . ." *New-Bedford Mercury*, 09.01.1846, 3.
[82] "Naval." *New-Bedford Mercury*, 20.03.1846, 1.
[83] Haywood, "American Whalers and Africa", 59.

wishes", observed Tripp, "the men [. . .] run to the mountains. The Master obtains men of the Island without difficulty and the vessel goes to sea, having exchanged a part of the crew without depositing the Papers or having any communication with the Consular Agent or Custom House."[84]

In this manner, whalers left behind dozens of men each year in Cape Verde. Sooner or later most of these men found their way to the American consulate. Some had been removed from their vessels by a ruse, having, for instance, been plied with drink.[85] Charges of misconduct against captains were, as a rule, hard to prove. The difficulty is exemplified by a trial conducted in Boston in 1855, in which Sylvanus Gage, a seaman in the *South America* of New Bedford, accused Captain Washington Walker of having abandoned him during a stopover at Santiago. Walker denied the allegation, claiming that Gage had left the *South America* of his own free will. Since Gage could offer no evidence to the contrary, the charges were dropped.[86]

By contrast, seamen who did have a mind to desert tended not to choose Cape Verde as the place to do so. For one thing, the islands were inhospitable and offered little incentive to stay. Then there was the problem that most vessels to call at the islands did so at the beginning of their voyage and not on their way home. Cape Verde was thus not a good place for anyone hoping to get back to America soon.[87] Only men from Cape Verde who had gone to the United States aboard a whaleship might take advantage of a stop there in the course of a later voyage to desert, having used, as it were, a whaleship to secure a free passage home.

Shipowners and captains were alert to this risk and sought to prevent desertion by denying shore leave to men they suspected of the intention to desert – especially in Brava. In 1877 a shipowner by the name of Lawrence sent the following written order to Simeon Church, captain of the schooner *Charles Colgate* of New London: "Do not let Jose de Pena Boatsteerer go on shore at Cape de Verdes."[88] If an experienced and hence valuable seaman nevertheless made good his escape, a captain might offer islanders a bounty for his capture.[89] The desertion of an inexperienced seaman, by contrast, tended to be of little concern. Cape Verde held no shortage of men willing to fill the position for modest

---

84 All quotations in this paragraph are from Haywood, "American Whalers and Africa", 63.
85 Busch, "Cape Verdeans in the American Whaling and Sealing Industry", 109.
86 "Serious Charges." *The Republican Standard*, 10.05.1855, 2.
87 Among the exceptions confirming this rule is the case of a deserter from an American whaleship living as a clockmaker in Santo Antão in the 1840s. (Bridge, *Journal of an African Cruiser Comprising Sketches of the Canaries*, 28)
88 Quoted in Busch, "Cape Verdeans in the American Whaling and Sealing Industry", 109.
89 Haywood, "American Whalers and Africa", 64.

pay. Some skippers hence were comparatively generous in granting shore leave in Cape Verde, at least if the vessel was not merely passing "off and on".[90] Cape Verdean seamen who were thought unlikely to desert might also be permitted to visit friends and family.[91]

***

How did seamen pass the time whole on shore leave in Brava and the other islands? There were few obvious leisure activities to speak of. John Ross Browne, who came to Praia in 1842 aboard the *Bruce* of Fairhaven, took a dim view of the place: "I saw but little to interest me at Porto Praya. The town is filthy and dilapidated, and the inhabitants a race of poor, half-starved, mulatto Portuguese, living under an oppressive form of government".[92] It seems that the only activity in which seamen regularly indulged was excessive drinking, references to which can be found in many logs and other sources. In 1800 the captain of the *Kingston* of London noted that "Joshu Dix Boatsteerer got Intoxicated on shore" in Santiago,[93] and the log of the barque *Mattapoisett* of Westport records riotous behaviour in São Vicente in 1851: "Some drunk and crazy some sober some riding donkeys some raising the devil with the Govenor."[94] Strong drink was available to seamen, in exchange for small amounts of tobacco, from local traders who distilled spirits from fermented coconut water and sugar cane.[95] "Its being strong enough to satisfy any dram drinker", was how one mid-nineteenth-century seaman, Albert Peck, appraised its quality, adding that "The natives all seemed to be anxious that we should go into their houses and tast their 'denk' for which they expected a piece of tobacco."[96] To have to turn down such invitations for want of goods to barter presented some seamen with a serious problem. As Lewis Eldridge noted of a visit aboard the *Herald II* in the late 1860s: "At Brava none of the crew except Mike had anything to drink".[97]

More often than not, however, prices were low enough to allow seamen to get quickly and thoroughly drunk. This sometimes presented captains with serious problems. Edward Hussey of the *Richmond II* of New Bedford had to have

---

[90] Creighton, *Rites & Passages*, 141f.
[91] See e.g. Log ADELINE GIBBS, 1875–1878, 08.11.1875; Log BERTHA, 1878–1881, 11.11.1879; Log PETREL, 1874–1877, 24.10.1874.
[92] Browne, *Etchings of a Whaling Cruise*, 150f.
[93] Log KINGSTON, 1800–1801, 22.03.1800.
[94] Log MATTAPOISETT, 1851–1851, 23.03.1851.
[95] Meintel, "Cape Verdean-Americans", 352; Warrin, *So Ends This Day*, 131f.
[96] Quoted in Haywood, "American Whalers and Africa", 65.
[97] Eldridge, *Lewis William Eldridge's Whaling Voyage*, 9.

several inebriated men returned to the barque by force when they failed to return from shore leave. Nor did they go back quietly, as the log records: "When taken on board the ship was very disobedient made much nois went into the forecastle & broke up the chests & ladder also threattened to kill the first man that came to rescue them or dared to come into the forecastle".[98] Behaviour of this kind might also get seamen into trouble with the police or the military. One such incident occurred in August 1843, when a group of men, much the worse for drink, turned up in a village in Santiago to resume a brawl that one of their number had begun earlier.[99] For their part, captains were usually keen to avoid involving the local police, since arrests or even court cases were apt to delay the onward voyage. Only when a skipper accused seamen of a severe offence, notably attempted mutiny, did he call on the Cape Verdean authorities.[100] Captains did, however, regularly appear before consuls to seek assistance in dealing with refractory seamen.[101]

The surprisingly large number of consulates in Cape Verde testifies to the islands' importance to Atlantic shipping. In the mid-nineteenth century, eleven countries – among them Greece, Austria and Brazil – maintained no fewer than twenty-seven consulates and diplomatic missions. The United States alone employed two consuls (in Praia and Mindelo) and five vice-consuls (in Sal, Maio, Fogo, Boa Vista and Brava). The first American consul in Cape Verde had been appointed by the State Department in 1818. This was Samuel Hodge of Massachusetts, who had taken up residence in the islands as wholesaler and smuggler in 1816.[102] In view of the large number of American seamen who came to the islands aboard whalers and sealers as well as merchant and military vessels, the chief ports of Praia and Mindelo witnessed the establishment not only of American consulates but also of American cemeteries.[103] Britain too opened several consulates in Cape Verde around this time, the first British consul being John Rendall, a merchant resident in Boa Vista.[104]

---

98 Quoted in Haywood, "American Whalers and Africa", 65.
99 Bridge, *Journal of an African Cruiser Comprising Sketches of the Canaries*, 23f.
100 "At St. Jago, Cape de Verds . . ." *New-Bedford Mercury*, 21.08.1835, 3.
101 Haywood, "American Whalers and Africa", 66.
102 Brooks, *Western Africa and Cabo Verde*, 101; Brooks, *Yankee Traders, Old Coasters, and African Middlemen*, 130, 149f., 173; Busch, "Cape Verdeans in the American Whaling and Sealing Industry", 105; Duignan/Gann, *The United States and Africa*, 63; Duncan, *Atlantic Islands*, 240; Lobban, *Cape Verde*, 34–36; Travassos Valdez, *Six Years of a Traveller's Life in Western Africa*, vol. 1, 46.
103 Busch, "Cape Verdeans in the American Whaling and Sealing Industry", 105; Meintel, *Race, Culture, and Portuguese Colonialism in Cabo Verde*, 48.
104 Bigman, *History and Hunger in West Africa*, 79; "By the Mails." *New-Bedford Mercury*, 08.07.1825, 2.

Sailors on shore leave were particularly likely to find prostitutes – or, at any rate, women whom seamen took to be prostitutes – in larger ports such as Praia and Mindelo. "Employed in recreation on shore drinking spirits & playing with the wenches", the log of the brig *Mattapoisett* of Westport records for one stop in 1849.[105] It seems that contacts between seamen and Cape Verdean women contributed significantly to the spread of venereal disease, with syphilis and gonorrhoea particularly widespread in Brava and other islands much frequented by whalers.[106] Besides other infectious diseases – notably Malaria, Tuberculosis, measles and whooping cough – they were among the principal causes of death in Cape Verde. Medical care, whether for seamen or islanders, was virtually non-existent. Only in the mid-nineteenth century did professional physicians begin to practise in the islands and were the first small hospitals set up in Praia and Mindelo.[107]

One approach taken by the colonial authorities to containing epidemic diseases was to declare particular islands quarantine zones and to prohibit vessels from landing there. Boa Vista, which suffered a yellow fever epidemic in 1846, was one such case. Whalers who defied official orders may well have been involved in spreading diseases to other islands in spite of such precautions. Yellow fever ultimately claimed the life of Ferdinand Gardiner, the American consul in Praia.[108] In 1868 Brava too suffered a yellow fever epidemic which killed at least forty-one.[109]

Inform and assist

In December 1818 a sixteen-gun pirate vessel sailed into Sal Rei, the port of Boa Vista. The pirates sacked the custom house and robbed local residents, killing several of them. Through a British whaler, the *Nelson*, news of the attack reached *Lloyd's List*, the London shipping paper, and thus reached shipowners, captains, insurers and other actors in the trade.[110] As this case illustrates, the knowledge gleaned by whalemen in the course of their voyages would often spread far beyond their own vessel. And since whalers often followed different routes from

---

[105] Wing, Journal MATTAPOISETT, 1849–1853, 14.10.1849.
[106] Haywood, "American Whalers and Africa", 67.
[107] Patterson, "Epidemics, Famines, and Population in the Cape Verde Islands", 302.
[108] "From Cape Verde Islands." *New-Bedford Mercury*, 18.06.1847, 1; "From the Coast of Africa." *New-Bedford Mercury*, 29.05.1846, 1; "Sickness at Cape de Verds." *New-Bedford Mercury*, 25.12.1846, 1.
[109] Patterson, "Epidemics, Famines, and Population in the Cape Verde Islands", 299.
[110] "The Marine List." *Lloyd's List*, 23.02.1819, 1.

those taken by commercial or naval vessels, they were sometimes privy to information that was potentially relevant but not readily available to other maritime actors. For instance, in November 1791 seamen from HMS *Medusa* and *Scorpion* went on board the *Alliance* of Nantucket to ask Captain Bartlett Coffin which of the Cape Verde Island was the best place to obtain drinking water.[111] Such instances of whalers acting the source of knowledge that subsequently entered into circulation can be found in many waters, but Cape Verde presents a particularly striking case. Just how striking can be seen with reference to news of political unrest in the archipelago.

During the whaling era, social and political tensions in the islands repeatedly erupted in unrest. Whalemen became eyewitnesses to these events and sometimes recounted them to American on their return home. The unrest in Cape Verde was in part connected with Portugal's revolution and its aftermath. Following an officers' revolt in Porto the previous year, liberal constitutionalists in 1821 formed a constituent assembly which put an end to absolutism. The new democratic constitution, however, only survived until 1824, when it was toppled in a counter-revolution by forces working towards a restoration of the previous order. These conflicts fostered the development of liberal, conservative and left-wing parties and movements, whose struggles over the next few decades twice flared up in the form of civil war and were also felt in the Portuguese colonies. The liberal revolution of Porto led to a similarly motivated uprising in Boa Vista and Santiago as early as 1821, and a revolt of tenant farmers and slaves in 1822 was likewise a consequence of events in Portugal. That political events in the colonial metropole could spread so quickly and forcefully was due in large part to the Portuguese practice of transporting hundreds of political prisoners to Cape Verde as *degredados*. Many were put to forced labour in a penal garrison in Praia, which soon acquired a reputation as a hotbed of subversion.[112]

Yet while the *degredados* may have been the numerically dominant supporters of liberalism in Cape Verde, the cause also had its adherents among the wealthy *brancos* – although the proportion of conviction to opportunism may be assumed to have varied.[113] In 1832 they are reputed to have attempted to establish an independent republic of "Donna Maria" in the islands.[114] The most consequential revolt

---

111 Pinkham, *The Log Book of the Good Ship Alliance of Nantucket Captain Bartlett Coffin*, 13.11.1791.
112 Brooks, "Cabo Verde", 109f., 129f.; Carreira, *The People of the Cape Verde Islands*, 28; "From Cape de Verds." *New-Bedford Mercury*, 25.05.1821, 1; Meintel, *Race, Culture, and Portuguese Colonialism in Cabo Verde*, 87.
113 Brooks, "Cabo Verde", 129f.; Carreira, *The People of the Cape Verde Islands*, 28.
114 "Portugal." *New-Bedford Daily Mercury*, 23.01.1832, 1.

of this period, however, was launched by soldiers of absolutist sympathies, several hundred of whom rose up in Santiago in February 1835. These soldiers proclaimed their adherence to the Miguelite cause which had been defeated in the "Liberal Wars" of 1828 to 1834, killing a dozen of their officers and pillaging Praia for several days before fleeing the islands aboard two captured vessels.[115] The upper-class *morgados* took advantage of the unrest to order militias of their own to march on Praia, thereby demonstrating their power to the Portuguese government, which duly refrained from any further attempts to curb their influence.[116] It may have been under the impression of the soldiers' mutiny, which had revealed the fragility of the social and political order, that Santiago's slave population rose up a few months later, although that revolt was quickly suppressed. In 1841, again in Santiago, tenant farmers rose up in protest at increased taxation.[117] News of these and other events reached the American public through newspapers, which in turn relied on seamen for their information – and often on whalemen.[118]

✱✱✱

Nor were whalemen oblivious to the recurring droughts and famines that bedevilled Cape Verde. "There has been no rain for four years it is hard for the local Portuguese to eke out a living", noted Robert Ferguson on reaching São Vicente aboard the barque *Kathleen* in 1880.[119] News of drought and famine in Cape Verde had reached North America long before, transmitted first by seamen and then, from 1818 onwards, also by the US consulate. In 1810 the *New-Bedford Mercury* reported on a famine in Maio, in which the livestock had perished, the people too enfeebled to work and everything "in the utmost distress imaginable".[120] The New England public were to read of several more such disasters in the following years.[121]

A spate of such stories appeared in New England papers while Cape Verde was in the grips of a famine that began in 1830. It was to last for four years and become one of the most severe in the history of the islands. At least one third of

---

115 Brooks, "Cabo Verde", 131; "From Cape de Verds." *New-Bedford Mercury*, 15.05.1835: 2; "Look out for Pirates." *New-Bedford Mercury*, 22.05.1835, 1; "The Cape de Verd Mutineers." *New-Bedford Mercury*, 22.05.1835, 2; "The Cape de Verd Mutineers." *New-Bedford Mercury*, 05.06.1835, 1; "The Pirates at Port au Praya." *New-Bedford Mercury*, 26.06.1835, 1; "The Portuguese Pirates." *New-Bedford Mercury*, 24.07.1835, 2.
116 Brooks, "Cabo Verde", 131.
117 Carreira, *The People of the Cape Verde Islands*, 28f.
118 See also e.g. "From the Cape de Verds." *New-Bedford Daily Mercury*, 18.01.1832, 2.
119 Ferguson, *Harpooner*, 36.
120 "From Isle of May." *New-Bedford Mercury*, 23.11.1810, 2.
121 See e.g. "Marine Diary." *New-Bedford Mercury*, 30.06.1815, 3.

their population died – an estimated 30,000 islanders; some sources put the figure at forty per cent – and unlike in earlier famines, all inhabited islands were affected. The death toll in Brava was about 3,000. Although the famine had been preceded by a long *seca extrema* and could thus have been foretold, the Portuguese authorities took no measures to prevent it. The governor, Duarte de Mequitela, even declared that keeping the islanders fed was not among his duties and rejected demands for the purchase and stockpiling of food. Revenues from the last orchella harvest, which might used to provide relief, were instead sent to fund the civil war in Portugal.[122] Amid the war, the Portuguese elites had few thoughts to spare for the colonies, least of all for Cape Verde and Portuguese Guinea. When news of the latest *crises* reached Lisbon, two or three vessels were dispatched with food which ended up being sold in Cape Verdes at prices that only the rich could afford.[123]

Whalemen and other seamen witnessed the unfolding catastrophe in Furna, Praia and other ports. Their observations and eyewitness began to reach the New England public in mid-1832, when both shipmasters and the American consul submitted harrowing stories to Massachusetts newspapers such as the *New-Bedford Daily Mercury* and the *Boston Daily Advertiser and Patriot*, where they were sometimes treated as front-page news.[124] "It was no uncommon thing to see women and children gathering from the streets old bones, that had been thrown away, and eagerly devouring them", reported one such article.[125] Captain Moniz of the *Funchal*, a merchantman which lay off Maio in late October 1832, heard of hundreds of dead in Brava and Fogo.[126] The captain of the *Eliza Grant* of New York reported that the famine had claimed lives in all islands save for Maio, where supplies were also running low.[127]

Not all the bearers of such bad news left it at that. Some also solicited donations for the purchase of food which was to be sent to Cape Verde. The leading figure in these efforts was Joseph Ryder, a Salem sea-captain who had commanded

---

[122] Bigman, *History and Hunger in West Africa*, 82; Meintel, *Race, Culture, and Portuguese Colonialism in Cabo Verde*, 59f.; Patterson, "Epidemics, Famines, and Population in the Cape Verde Islands", 305, 309. Estimates of the lives lost in the drought of 1831 to 1833 range from 12,000 to 30,000. (Busch, "Cape Verdeans in the American Whaling and Sealing Industry", 105; Duncan, *Atlantic Islands*, 197)
[123] Bigman, *History and Hunger in West Africa*, 81; Brooks, "Cabo Verde", 131.
[124] "Famine at the Cape de Verds." *New-Bedford Daily Mercury*, 06.06.1832; "From Cape de Verds." *New-Bedford Mercury*, 22.02.1833, 1; "From Cape de Verds." *New-Bedford Mercury*, 25.04.1834, 2; Patterson, "Epidemics, Famines, and Population in the Cape Verde Islands", 309.
[125] "From Cape de Verds." *New-Bedford Daily Mercury*, 10.10.1832, 2.
[126] "News from the Cape de Verds." *New-Bedford Daily Mercury*, 20.11.1832, 2.
[127] "Cape de Verds." *New-Bedford Daily Mercury*, 04.12.1832, 2.

merchantmen on several visits to the islands. Ryder told the *New-Bedford Daily Mercury* that the islanders had despaired of receiving aid from Portugal or the rest of Europe and were pinning their hopes on the United States.[128] In October 1832, rallies to gather donations, organised by Ryder, were held in Boston, New Bedford, Salem and other ports.[129] Meanwhile the US consul in Cape Verde, William Merrill, sent another eyewitness account of the ongoing disaster to the New England press.[130]

Following these early rallies and the coverage they received in the press, the campaign developed a momentum of its own. Calls for donations and rallies spread beyond Massachusetts to other parts of New England and further afield to New York and Philadelphia. Several tens of thousands of dollars' worth of food and cash donations were gathered at public rallies and in churches and schools. The first consignment of food – two vessels full – left Boston on 19 October. "I well remember the thrill of compassion that pervaded the community at home, on hearing that multitudes were starving in the Cape de Verd islands", was how Horace Briggs, later an officer in the US Navy, recalled the campaign. "Without pausing to inquire who they were, or whether entitled to our assistance, by any other than the all-powerful claim of wretchedness, the Americans sent vessel after vessel, laden with food, which was gratuitously distributed to the poor."[131] The American consul and the government of Cape Verde were to be in charge of distributing the relief. Ryder was able to mobilise a total of eleven vessels, including two naval vessels stationed in New Bedford and Fairhaven.[132] Even before these vessels had sailed, several whaleships took supplies to Cape Verde. Among them were the *Two Brothers* of New Bedford, which carried flour, bread, beans and mackerel to Fogo in August 1832.[133]

Although American relief efforts took the local authorities by surprise, they appear to have been sufficient at least to prevent the situation from deteriorating further.[134] Among the islanders, American aid laid the foundations of a longstanding sense of friendship with the United States. A local council in Santo Antão, for instance, passed a motion of gratitude addressed to the city of

---

128 "From Cape de Verds." *New-Bedford Daily Mercury*, 10.10.1832, 2.
129 "New-Bedford Communication." *New-Bedford Daily Mercury*, 16.10.1832, 2.
130 William G. Merrill, "Letter to the Editor." *New-Bedford Daily Mercury*, 27.10. 1832, 2.
131 Bridge, *Journal of an African Cruiser Comprising Sketches of the Canaries*, 22.
132 Meintel, "Cape Verdean Transnationalism", 29; Meintel, *Race, Culture, and Portuguese Colonialism in Cabo Verde*, 60; Patterson, "Epidemics, Famines, and Population in the Cape Verde Islands", 309; Warrin, *So Ends This Day*, 25f.
133 Log TWO BROTHERS, 1832–1833, 09. & 11.08.1832.
134 Brooks, "Cabo Verde", 131.

Philadelphia.¹³⁵ When, in 1843, the US Navy sent warships to Praia and Mindelo as part of its efforts to stop the slave trade, memories of the American relief efforts helped win acceptance for their presence. As Horatio Bridge, by now purser aboard the sloop USS *Saratoga*, recalled of his arrival in Cape Verde in August 1843: "The memory of the aid extended by Americans has not yet faded, nor seems likely to fade, from the minds of those who were succored in their need."¹³⁶

Echoes of the 1830–1833 *crises* were heard when, in the 1850s, Cape Verde once again suffered severe famines. Again, relief came aboard American vessels, with the US Navy alone providing 40,000 rations of food. This time, however, aid came to Cape Verde not only from the United States, but also from the Canary Islands and Brazil as well as from Madeira.¹³⁷ It seems that Portugal was keen to prove that it was capable of taking swift action, not least under pressure from mounting rivalry between European colonial powers. Something of the kind is implied in a remark by Albert Peck, a seaman who came to Santo Antão aboard the *Chili* of New Bedford in the mid-1850s. Citing a Cape Verdean recruit, Peck noted in his diary that the colonial administration had ordered American aid shipments to be confiscated, only to sell the goods to the starving populace itself.¹³⁸

In later famines – notably that of 1863–1866, the worst since the 1830s – a new group of actors emerged, one which brought considerable resources to bear in its efforts to mobilise aid for the people of Cape Verde. This group was made up Cape Verdean immigrants to New England and their descendants, who had grown into a minority to be reckoned with.¹³⁹ As in the aid campaign of the 1830s, whalers took a leading part in facilitating this movement of people.

From *Pardos* and *Pretos* to *Bravas* and *Gees*

"We left New Bedford with a skeleton crew, which meant of course that Captain Gilbane was planning to complete the ship's crew at the Cape Verde Islands, where labor for whaleships was cheap", recalled Harry Chippendale, who had

---

135 Meintel, *Race, Culture, and Portuguese Colonialism in Cabo Verde*, 60; Patterson, "Epidemics, Famines, and Population in the Cape Verde Islands", 309f.
136 Bridge, *Journal of an African Cruiser Comprising Sketches of the Canaries*, 22f.
137 Patterson, "Epidemics, Famines, and Population in the Cape Verde Islands", 310f.; Thomas, *Adventures and Observations on the West Coast of Africa*, 328; on the *Crises* of the 1850s see also "From the Cape de Verds." *The Republican Standard*, 04.03.1852, 3.
138 Haywood, "American Whalers and Africa", 166–168.
139 Patterson, "Epidemics, Famines, and Population in the Cape Verde Islands", 311.

sailed in the *Sea Fox* around 1900.[140] When a captain sailed with a skeleton crew – the bare minimum of men needed to keep a vessel going, sometimes only seven or eight (though usually more) – it was in the expectation of signing on further men along the way, to be hired as seasoners in the whaling grounds. This was not least part of a business strategy. The American whaling industry took advantage of its fleet's global reach to profit from global cost disparities on the labour market – in other words, to recruit workers were they were the cheapest.[141] Chippendale's account indicates that Cape Verde had long been a key part of this system, a seemingly inexhaustible reservoir of cheap and willing workers – and who were, as Chippendale continues, treated accordingly. "The men were lured on board in complete ignorance of what they were getting into and were invariably paid off in experience, a lot of abuse, and not much else".[142]

This practice of recruiting hands en route was not altogether new. As early as the sixteenth century, European vessels on long voyages hired (or sometimes impressed) workers or pilots in the faraway waters they plied. What had previously been practised ad hoc became a systematic policy in the eighteenth and nineteenth centuries. Kru from what is now Liberia, so-called "Lascars" and "Manila-men" from south and south-east Asia, and Kanakas from Oceania were foremost among the thousands of men who took on paid work aboard vessels.[143] The *Sea Fox* was one of many American whalers to take on crew at Brava. "In due course the boats came back loaded with Bravas. I felt sorry for the poor beggars when I saw them come over the rail laden with their small bundles", Chippendale recalled. "They made me think of cattle on their way to be slaughtered."[144]

American whalers' preference for Cape Verdean labour had already been remarked upon earlier in the nineteenth century. Before a parliamentary select committee, the British shipowner Samuel Browning declared in 1847 that "The American vessels are short-handed when they sail from their own coasts, and they generally put into the Cape de Verd Islands. A ship taking four boats generally ships at the Cape de Verd Islands about two men for each boat."[145] This is confirmed by Gurdon Alleyn, who came to Cape Verde in 1845 as master of the *Charles Henry* of New London. Alleyn recalled how "It was customary for whalers to stop at these islands [. . .] to ship young men on a lay represented

---

140 Chippendale, *Sails and Whales*, 159.
141 Warrin, *So Ends This Day*, 268f.
142 Chippendale, *Sails and Whales*, 159.
143 Bolster, *Black Jacks*, 54f.; Chappell, "Ahabs Boot", 178, 188, 195.
144 Chippendale, *Sails and Whales*, 160.
145 Gibson et al., *First Report from the Select Committee on Navigation Laws*, 127.

by a fraction whose denominator was much larger than its numerator."[146] The number of hands hired on such occasions might be considerable. In 1887 the *Francis Allyn*, having left New London with a skeleton crew, shipped no fewer than seventeen men at Brava. Twelve men signed on aboard the *Charles Colgate* when she called there in 1875 – and another thirteen managed to stow away.[147]

What made Cape Verde in particular such a rich recruiting ground for the American whaling industry? The guiding consideration was expediency: the prevailing winds and currents meant that nearly every whaleship that crossed the Atlantic from New England came near the islands. Since many of the islanders were keen to emigrate, captains found no shortage of young men willing to work hard for low pay, to suffer the privations of shipboard life uncomplainingly and generally to be little trouble to their officers. Melville, in the article cited at the beginning of this chapter, observed that "His docile services being thus cheaply to be had, some captains will go the length of maintaining that 'Gee' sailors are preferable [. . .] to American sailors".[148] Indeed, hiring these men was such good business that whalers put in at Cape Verde even when famine meant that no provisions were to be had.[149] "We found in the course of the voyage that nearly every whaler sails from home three or four hands short intending to stop at these islands where famine is often the reigning monarch", noted Albert Peck in 1856.[150]

We can only estimate the total number of men from Brava and the other Cape Verde Islands who signed on aboard whalers. Since most vessels, rather than mooring in the harbour, send their boats to the coast "off an on" to escape the attention of the authorities, many (probably most) hires went undocumented by the authorities on shore. Writing to the State Department in 1868, Benjamin Tripp, the US consul, described how "The Master obtains men of the Island without difficulty and the vessel goes to sea, having exchanged a part of the Crew without depositing the Papers or having any communication with the Consular Agent or Custom House".[151] This procedure suited the Cape Verdean recruits, who were likely to be charged hefty emigration fees by harbour officials.

---

146 Allyn, *The Old Sailor's Story*, 64.
147 Busch, "Cape Verdeans in the American Whaling and Sealing Industry", 109; Warrin, *So Ends This Day*, 212.
148 Melville, "The Gees", 357.
149 Busch, "Cape Verdeans in the American Whaling and Sealing Industry", 107; Busch, *Whaling Will Never Do for Me*, 42; Haywood, "American Whalers and Africa", 62.
150 Quoted in Busch, "Cape Verdeans in the American Whaling and Sealing Industry", 107; for other remarks by seamen on recruitment practices in Cape Verde see e.g. Log CLARICE, 1878–1882, 17.12.1878 and Williams, *The Adventures of a Seventeen-year-old Lad and the Fortunes He Might Have Won*, 35.
151 Quoted in Busch, "Cape Verdeans in the American Whaling and Sealing Industry", 109.

Against this backdrop, any estimate of recruitment numbers must be treated with caution. Taken together, however, the records of American whalers do reveal a clear tendency. Beginning in the last third of the eighteenth century, we hear of individual Cape Verdean men signing on aboard whalers. By the 1820s, they had become a regular sight. In 1830, an estimated seventy-six men of Lusophone heritage worked in the New Bedford whaling fleet, at least eleven of them from Cape Verde.[152] The importance of Cape Verdean labour grew after the American Civil War, when a crisis-stricken whaling industry had trouble hiring qualified Americans. Between them, the ninety-two whaleships that sailed from New Bedford in 1865 carried a total of 2,658 seamen, an estimated 688 of whom – roughly one in four – came from the Portuguese islands in the Atlantic. By 1900, when only 169 men sailed from New Bedford in whaleships, Cape Verdeans were the largest single group among them, numbering an estimated seventy-four (or forty-four per cent). Across all whaling ports, the proportion of Cape Verdean and Azorean whalemen was approximately twenty per cent in the 1860s, rising to approximately thirty-five per cent by the 1880s. More Cape Verdean and Azorean men also rose to the rank of captain, commanding twenty voyages in the 1870s, fifty-seven in the 1880s and forty-seven in the 1890s.[153] Tripp estimated that in 1868 some four thousand men had left Brava alone aboard whaleships either temporarily or permanently – of a population of around twelve thousand.[154] In 1874 Eduardo Augusto de Sá Nogueira Pinto de Balsamão, the secretary-general of the Cape Verdean government, set the number of men who left Brava by sea at an average of one hundred per year.[155] The proportion of seamen of Cape Verdean heritage reached its peak in the early twentieth century, when they were in the majority aboard several whaleships.[156]

One of the last New Bedford whaleships, the schooner *Arthur V.S. Woodruff*, called at São Vicente in December 1917. Captain Edwards took the opportunity of hiring no fewer than eighteen men.[157] Cheap Cape Verdean labour, which had merely supplemented the crews of American whalers a century earlier, had now

---

152 Warrin, *So Ends This Day*, 84f.
153 Busch, "Cape Verdeans in the American Whaling and Sealing Industry", 110; Busch, *Whaling Will Never Do for Me*, 42; Holloway, "Making Waves", 122; Warrin, *So Ends This Day*, 178, 190f., 265.
154 Haywood, "American Whalers and Africa", 60; Meintel, "Cape Verdean Transnationalism", 30. Tripp's estimate seems somewhat exaggerated and fails to clarify whether the figure refers only to natives or Brava or includes men from other islands who found their way onto whaleships via Brava.
155 Carreira, *Descrições oitocentistas das Ilhas de Cabo Verde*, 48f.
156 Holloway, "Making Waves", 125.
157 Log ARTHUR V. WOODRUFF, 1917–1920, 26.12.1917.

become the industry's mainstay. Portugal's colonial policy produced droves of men with a desire to escape, and but for their desperation, American whaling might have come to an even earlier end.[158]

***

Harry Chippendale also remembered that "The natives of the Cape Verde Islands were always called Bravas".[159] The fact that the name was applied to men from other islands underscores Brava's importance as a reservoir of labour. But did the island really account for the largest of proportion of the Cape Verdeans who joined whaling crews? Alongside São Nicolau, Brava certainly was the island most frequently visited by American whalers hoping to make new recruits.[160] The fact that approximately half the Cape Verdean immigrants in New Bedford got there from Brava testifies to its key role.[161] What is less clear, however, is how many of the men taken on at Brava had previously come from other islands in the hope of finding work aboard a whaleship. It may well be that the notion, widespread among whalemen, that the men of Brava stood on particularly intimate terms with the sea and displayed superior boatsmanship concealed the fact that many of the hands hired there were actually from other islands.

This notion was a myth in any case. Although nowhere in Brava is more than five kilometres from the shore, most islanders had no special relationship with the sea. The majority population of *pardos* and *pretos* lived in the island's hilly interior, and well into the nineteenth century there was scarcely anybody among them who had ever fished, learnt to swim or so much as seen a ship at close quarters. When we read of some seamen observing "Bravas" swimming out to meet their vessels, this would seem to have been a skill acquired by the islanders for that very purpose. This idea did not occur to American seamen, most of whom were unable to swim and were duly impressed, to the point of believing that these men must be singularly close to the sea.[162] This impression tended not to be confirmed by the islanders' performance aboard ship, "A green 'Gee being of all green things the greenest", as Melville noted.[163]

---

[158] Busch, "Cape Verdeans in the American Whaling and Sealing Industry", 116; Warrin, *So Ends This Day*, 296.
[159] Chippendale, *Sails and Whales*, 134.
[160] Warrin, *So Ends This Day*, 53, 85.
[161] Halter, *Between Race and Ethnicity*, 131f.
[162] Busch, "Cape Verdeans in the American Whaling and Sealing Industry", 108; Duncan, *Atlantic Islands*, 236; Meintel, *Race, Culture, and Portuguese Colonialism in Cabo Verde*, 16.
[163] Melville, "The Gees", 358.

As the nineteenth century went on, however, the myth of the "Bravas" and their familiarity with the sea increasingly became an accurate expectation. Since whalers were particularly frequent callers at Brava, the island also became the scene of discharges and desertions – which, in turn, created a supply of experienced seamen for captains to draw upon. In 1875 Samuel R. Howland of the *Kathleen* hired an officer in Brava, and in 1878 Captain Robinson took two harpooners aboard the *Bertha*.[164] With such skills on offer, some whalers no longer stopped a Brava merely to flesh out their skeleton crews, but also to replace less qualified men.[165]

Unlike those recruits who had already gathered experience aboard ship, most of the islanders who joined crews as "green hands" came from poor rural backgrounds. Social shifts following the abolition of slavery had swelled the population of these *pardos* and *pretos livres* in the mid-nineteenth century.[166] By contrast, whalemen scarcely ever had dealings with *brancos*.[167] Given the clandestine nature of "off and on" recruitment, however, precise information regarding the men's background is hard to come by. The authorities were largely left in the dark. "The majority of whaleships do not anchor in our ports but remain under sail along the coast, taking on those they need", a government official in Brava complained in 1880, "and not even the police are a guarantee as agents of authority in these matters, because it has happened that they have been the first to embark, leaving their swords on the beach as a testimonial."[168]

Why did so many *pardos* and *pretos livres* from Brava and other islands seek employment aboard whaleships? One key motivating factor has already been discussed: for the impoverished majority of the islanders, vessels offered the only escape from recurring famine. A job at sea meant regular food and drink, and at least in some cases it might also mean being able to send money home to one's family.[169] "Make some money and help support our family. There was no choice but to take the chance", was how Joseph Ramos, who had come to the United States aboard a whaler, explained his reasons in an interview published in 1982.[170] Remittances from their menfolk at sea were important enough for those left behind to give them a special name: they were known in Brava as *dinheiro do mar* or "money of the sea".[171]

---

164 Log BERTHA, 1878–1881, 23.11.1878; Log KATHLEEN, 1875–1879, 16.10.1875.
165 Quoted in Halter, *Between Race and Ethnicity*, 69.
166 Meintel, *Race, Culture, and Portuguese Colonialism in Cabo Verde*, 70.
167 Busch, "Cape Verdeans in the American Whaling and Sealing Industry", 105f.
168 Quoted in Warrin, *So Ends This Day*, 105.
169 Halter, "Cape Verdeans in the U.S.", 35; Haywood, "American Whalers and Africa", 59–61.
170 Quoted in Halter, *Between Race and Ethnicity*, 68f.
171 Duncan, *Atlantic Islands*, 237.

The extent to which Cape Verdean seamen actually succeeded in sending home money is, however, uncertain. Shipowners generally took advantage of their recruits' desperate situation to pay them smaller lays than American seamen of the same rank would have received.[172] Yet given the islands' generally low standard of wealth, a seaman's earnings would certainly have had the capacity to improve the lives of his relations at home – at least in theory.[173] But in practice, the various deductions (described above in the chapter "Passages II") meant that precious little was left by way of *dinheiro do mar*. As Ramos recalled, "We didn't make any money whaling because they discounted everything – food, clothing . . .".[174]

If economic hardship and existential peril made people desperate to emigrate, young men faced the additional burden of military service. Alongside its regular troops garrisoned in the island, the *primeira linha*, Portugal maintained a far larger militia, the *segunda linha*. Its commanders were *morgados* and *branco da terra*, who used the force as a de facto private army to safeguard their own interests, though legally it was an arm of the Portuguese government. All physically fit young men were subject to being drafted into its service.[175]

A call-up to the *segunda linha* did not simply mean submitting to a fixed period of basic military training. It was widely feared as a voyage with no return, for the generally poor supply of food extended to the armed forces and meant that many a conscript did not survive military service.[176] In the whaling era, recruits faced the additional danger of being sent to serve on the African mainland, in Portuguese Guinea, where many were killed by disease or in combat.[177] So feared was service in the *segunda linha* that many young men resorted to self-mutilation or even suicide to avoid it.[178] In 1874 the secretary-general of the Cape Verdean government reported that it was a daily occurrence for desperate young men facing the draft to jump off cliffs or into the sea.[179] Whether they were seeking to escape famine or conscription, shipping aboard a whaler

---

172 Creighton, *Rites & Passages*, 9; Haywood, "American Whalers and Africa", 60f.
173 Haywood, "American Whalers and Africa", 13f.
174 Quoted in Halter, *Between Race and Ethnicity*, 103.
175 Attempts by a Portuguese prefect to dissolve the *segunda linea* foundered on *morgado* resistance in 1834. (Brooks, "Cabo Verde", 109, 131)
176 For an account of the poor physical condition of conscripts in the *seguda linha* see Ellis, *West African Islands*, 128, Tuckey, *Narrative of an Expedition to Explore the River Zaire*, 16 and – as early as 1693 – Phillips, *A Journal of a Voyage Made in the Hannibal of London*, 184.
177 Carreira, *The People of the Cape Verde Islands*, 50f.
178 Busch, "Cape Verdeans in the American Whaling and Sealing Industry", 106.
179 Carreira, *The People of the Cape Verde Islands*, 48f.

482 — 8 Whaleships into migration vehicles: Furna, Brava, 1770–1920

offered the mass of propertyless *pardos* and *pretos livres* a chance to escape and a strategy for survival.

✶✶✶

"My oldest brother had shipped out from New Bedford on a whaling boat. When I heard he was coming to the Cape Verde Islands, I was on the lookout for him", Joseph Andrade told an interviewer in 1983. "When he arrived I asked him to ask the captain to give me a chance and he did."[180] Andrade was eighteen years old and living in São Nicolau when he signed on aboard a whaleship in 1914. Recruits who had no experience of going to sea, little English and who were, moreover, often the youngest on board usually joined the lowest ranks of seamen as "green hands". Those among them who had joined the crew as seasoners, for only one leg of a voyage, received a wage agreed upon in advance, usually six to eight dollars a month – less charges for the slop chest and other expenses. The large number of men who stayed for the duration of the voyage and returned with the vessel the United States received a lay in accordance with standard whaling practice. Given their desperate situation, they often had no choice but to accept a "long lay", the smallest share offered. Whereas American green hands could sign on for a share of 1/150 or 1/200, Cape Verdean men usually received smaller shares, between 1/225 and 1/275.[181] What opportunities, then, did they have to rise to better-paid positions?

As a rule, seamen of Cape Verdean origin faced worse prospects for advancement than did white Americans. In a study of 251 voyages between 1862 and 1882, the historian Briton Busch found that while 23.7 per cent of men were from Cape Verde or the Azores this was true of only about in ten officers.[182] "Portuguese seamen, like African-Americans, might over time rise to positions of Authority, but the odds were against them", Busch concludes.[183] Like their African American counterparts, Cape Verdean seamen often found that whites would not treat them as equals – even if they were of equal rank. Chippendale recalled how Captain Gilbane of the *Sea Fox* had berated the men hired at Brava as "'Portuguese bastards' and many other names too vulgar to put into print".[184] White seamen often considered Cape Verdean men to be black on account of their skin tone – whereas the *pardos*, who accounted for the majority

---

180 Quoted in Halter, *Between Race and Ethnicity*, 69.
181 Busch, "Cape Verdeans in the American Whaling and Sealing Industry", 110; Haywood, "American Whalers and Africa", 61.
182 Busch, "Cape Verdeans in the American Whaling and Sealing Industry", 108.
183 Busch, *Whaling Will Never Do for Me*, 43.
184 Chippendale, *Sails and Whales*, 160.

of Cape Verdean recruits, did not think of themselves as black and were not thought of as such at home. To find themselves thus demoted was a new and disconcerting experience for many of these men. For instance, a seaman named Mingo, who had shipped aboard a whaler in Boa Vista in 1774, complained to his captain that some of his shipmates had called him a "negro". It is likely that Mingo not only bristled at the perceived slur, but had a concrete danger in mind: at the time, to be considered a negro meant being at risk of enslavement. It may have been with this danger in mind that Mingo tried to jump ship at the Caribbean island of Saint Thomas.[185] Whether Cape Verdean whalemen were subject to racial discrimination on board – and if so, to what kind – was down to physical traits which other seamen took to denote racial characteristics. "Just before dark the captain came on board bringing in the boat three or four strong-looking islanders, black and with wool so curled that they could hardly touch their heels to the deck", was how the harpooner Nelson Haley remembered the arrival of recruits from Santo Antão on board the *Charles W. Morgan* in 1849. "The only way they were different from the regular African Negro was in language", he observed of the men to whom he elsewhere referred as "nigger Portuguese".[186]

Given the history of Brava's settlement, recruits from the island were usually lighter-skinned than those from islands such as Santo Antão. In the racial vocabulary of the day, many of their white shipmates would have thought of them as "dagoes", a corruption of the common Spanish name *Diego* applied to people from Spain and Portugal as well as their colonies.[187] For instance, in his diary, Horace Palmer, who sailed in the *Wanderer* from 1878 to 1880, describes another seaman as a "wool headed Dago".[188] The term's pejorative nature is more evident in another remark by Palmer, in which he referred to a seaman named Phillip de Gomes as "the miserable Dago boat steerer".[189]

Racist attitudes of the kind reflected in such terms as "nigger" or "dago" were not expressed in verbal abuse alone. In 1900, soon after the schooner *Era* set sail from New Bedford, one of the officers declared that he was not prepared to work with a seaman from Cape Verde – in this instance, Captain Comer decided to replace the officer.[190] Racism imposed limits on the advancement of Cape Verdean seamen not faced by their white colleagues: they were slower to

---

185 Warrin, *So Ends This Day*, 24f.
186 Haley, *Whale Hunt*, 36.
187 Busch, *Whaling Will Never Do for Me*, 43; McCormick, *Two New Bedford Whalemen*, 225.
188 Palmer, "The Diary of a Foremast Hand on the First Voyage of the Bark Wanderer", 1.
189 Quoted in McCormick, *Two New Bedford Whalemen*, 241, 25.10.1879.
190 Busch, "Cape Verdeans in the American Whaling and Sealing Industry", 115.

rise through the ranks, so that even in the course of long careers at sea, many did not rise above of the position of boatsteerer or that of a low-ranking officer.[191]

For Cape Verdean seamen to rise to the rank of captain was even rarer. All in all, masters from Cape Verde and the Azores commanded 325 voyages of American whaleships. Approximately half these voyages took place before 1900 – twenty in the 1870s, fifty-seven in the 1880s and forty-seven in the 1890s. The fact that the other half of these voyages coincided with the last two decades of American whaling in the early twentieth century reflects how reliant on Cape Verdean labour the industry had by then become.[192]

Some of these Cape Verdean captains had reached their position as stand-ins for captains who were unable to complete the voyage. In such cases, the first mate moved up to command the vessel. This did not always happen without conflict. Joseph Roderick, of Brava, first mate of the barque *Charles W. Morgan* of New Bedford, took the place of the captain, Arthur Gibbons, during a stop at Durban after Gibbons had fallen ill during the voyage. The crew at first refused to work under his command. Only under pressure from the American consul did the men agree to weigh anchor. This did not, however, settle the matter for long. Tension flared up again, and Roderick was replaced during another stop at Durban five weeks later.[193]

Other Cape Verdean seamen had happier careers as captains. Anthony Benton, for instance, commanded five New Bedford whalers between 1878 and 1899.[194] At least ten Cape Verdean captains were natives of Brava. Between them, they commanded twenty-nine American whaleships (Tab. 13).

***

"He came to me and asked for something to eat in English", recalled Albert Peck of Antonio, a recruit who joined his vessel (probably the *Chili* of New Bedford) in Santo Antão.[195] Some islanders had picked up a rudimentary English vocabulary in their interactions with crews, and it comes as no surprise to find that food was one of the subjects covered. To work aboard a whaleship, however, required a command of other aspects of the English language, nautical terminology in particular. Captains and officers expected there orders to be understood and showed little patience when they were not. For their part, many Cape Verdean seamen were interested in learning English with a view to emigrating to the United

---

191 Warrin, *So Ends This Day*, 303.
192 Busch, *Whaling Will Never Do for Me*, 42; Warrin, *So Ends This Day*, 178, 190f., 265.
193 Warrin, *So Ends This Day*, 216.
194 Ibid., 196–198.
195 Quoted in Haywood, "American Whalers and Africa", 166–168.

Tab. 13: Brava-born captains of American whaleships.

Name (year of birth)	Ships commanded (voyages)
John Da Lomba (c. 1876)	*William A. Graber* (1920)
John T. Gonsalves (1858)	*Rising Sun* (1890–1893)
	Eunice H. Adams (1893–1894)
	Baltic (1894–1897)
	Golden City (1901–1903)
	Eleanor B. Conwell (1904–1907)
	Bertha (1907–1909)
	T. Towner (1911–1914)
	William A. Graber (1914–1916, 1922)
	A. M. Nicholson (1917–1920)
	Charles W. Morgan (1920–1921)
Frank M. Lopes (1884)	*Pedro Varela* (1917–1919)
Louis M. Lopes (1877)	*A. E. Whyland* (1902, 1912–1915)
	Bertha (1910)
	Margarett (1917–1919)
	Claudia (1919)
	Cameo (1920–1921)
Severino D. Pierce (?) (c. 1817)	*Magnolia* (1858–1862)
	Europa (1862–1867)
	Thriver (1870–1871)
Valentine Roza (c. 1873)	*Canton II* (1907–1910)
	Morning Star (1910–1914)
Antonio Jose Senna (1859)	*Pedro Varela* (1891–1894)
Ayres J. Senna (1857)	*Golden City* (1897–1899)
	Adelia Chase (1901–1905, 1906)
Joseph H. Senna	*Carleton Bell* (1906–1916)
(1881, son of Ayres J. Senna)	*Claudia* (1919–1922)
Antone Sylvia (1877)	*Fannie Byrnes* (1879–1884)

Sources: Warrin, *So Ends This Day*, 290f., 323–5; Lund et al., *American Offshore Whaling Voyages*.

States. For instance, John Brown, a native of Brava, took lessons in reading and writing from the harpooner Robert Ferguson aboard the *Kathleen* of New Bedford in the early 1880s.[196]

Among themselves, however, Cape Verdean seamen usually spoke Portuguese or *Crioulo*, which they also used with seamen from other Lusophone islands, notably Madeira and the Azores. Particularly from the mid-nineteenth century onwards – by which time most American whalers employed several

---

[196] Ferguson, *Harpooner*, 52.

seamen of Lusophone origin – this led to the emergence of Portuguese or *Crioulo*-speaking sub-communities in separation from their English-speaking shipmates.[197] The latter sometimes cavilled at "Gees" forming groups. "If there are half a dozen together in the forecastle, they jabber and chatter their unmusical jargon from morning until night", remembered William Whitecar of his voyage aboard the *Pacific* from 1855 to 1859.[198] The author of the log of the *Zone* of Fairhaven was more hostile still, writing in 1855 that "We have got plenty of music on deck now for there is [. . .] a pig squealing, or a goat bleating; and if that is not enough to satisfy, go forward and you can hear a half dozen of 'Dagos' jabbering Portuguese."[199] Cape Verdean seamen probably chose to associate with other speakers of Portuguese or *Crioulo* not least in order not to be thought of as black – seamen from the Azores in particular tended to be lighter-skinned than their counterparts from Cape Verde.[200]

English-speaking captains and officers tended to take a dim view of Portuguese or *Criuolo* being spoken aboard ship. One problem was that seamen could make derogatory remarks about their superiors with impunity in a foreign language. It was above all with this issue in mind that some captains banned the use of any language other than English.[201] On a later voyage of the aforementioned *Pacific* in 1868, an officer had one seaman put in irons for two days and another locked in the run after he had caught them speaking Portuguese on deck.[202]

The separation of "Gee" communities was less palpable at work than it was in the seamen's meagre leisure time – during the second dog watch between 6 and 8 p.m. or during quieter stretches of a voyage, while playing cards, making music or on shore leave.[203] One night in March 1838, Robert Smith Owens of the Warren observed how "The 4 Portuguese amused themselves / no one seemed to take any notice of them forward". Drawn by the sound of their guitar playing, Smith went to join the group. "They feel pleased by being taken notice of – and because they are darkies as sailors call them – they do not associate with them", he found.[204] Sometimes, open conflict erupted on board between English and Portuguese-speaking factions of the crew – above all when one felt

---

197 Warrin, *So Ends This Day*, 59.
198 Whitecar, *Four Years Aboard the Whaleship*, 42.
199 Quoted in Warrin, *So Ends This Day*, 61f.
200 Busch, "Cape Verdeans in the American Whaling and Sealing Industry", 115.
201 Busch, *Whaling Will Never Do for Me*, 20, 44f.
202 Warrin, *So Ends This Day*, 59f.
203 Busch, "Cape Verdeans in the American Whaling and Sealing Industry", 114.
204 Owen, Journal HARRENA, 1837–1840, 05.03.1838.

that it was being unfairly treated by the captain or one of the officers.[205] During one stop at Jamestown, St Helena in early 1888, the "Gees" left the vessel in a body and refused to return. Captain Heyer was forced to interrupt the voyage for six weeks as a result of their industrial action.[206]

But did the "Gees" also include Cape Verdean slaves looking to escape aboard a whaler? That, at least, was reason cited by the Portuguese authorities for imposing restrictions on the vessels. At least in Brava, however, there were barely any slaves who might have shipped with a whaler. The issue became irrelevant when, in 1858, the Portuguese government decreed that slavery would be abolished – originally in 1878, a date which was then moved forward to 1869. Slave trafficking in Cape Verde had already come to an end in the early 1840s, when the US Navy stationed vessels of its newly-formed Africa Squadron in Praia and Mindelo.[207] As in other west African waters, whalers operating near Cape Verde were eyewitnesses both to the slave trade and to its suppression. US Navy vessels sometimes asked whalers to share any observations of suspicious activity. In 1850, for instance, officers of USS *Portsmouth* made enquiries to this end of the *Condor* and the *Coral* of New Bedford and of the *Samuel and Thomas* of Mattapoisett.[208]

It is unlikely that whalers involved themselves in trafficking slaves. Both the high prices charged in the islands and the considerable risk of detection made such a sideline seem not worth the trouble – all the more so because whalers usually came to Cape Verde at the beginning of their voyage, while other money-making ventures tended to be pursued towards in its later stages. Yet the possibility that whalers might on rare occasions have dabbled in the slave trade cannot be altogether excluded. According to an item in the *New-Bedford Mercury* – the plausibility of which it is impossible to assess for lack of other sources – in February 1833 the Brazilian authorities arrested the captain of the *Enterprise* of New Bedford on the charge of attempting to sell two men who been taken aboard at São Nicolau as slaves. He was then tried and sentenced to nine years in prison. The article took the captain's side in claiming

---

205 Busch, *Whaling Will Never Do for Me*, 44.
206 Log MERMAID, 1887–1890, 21.02.–04.03.1888.
207 Brooks, *Yankee Traders, Old Coasters, and African Middlemen*, 118, 289f.; Busch, "Cape Verdeans in the American Whaling and Sealing Industry", 105; Duignan/Gann, *The United States and Africa*, 32f.; Jacobsen, "The African Squadrons", 29; Lobban, *Cape Verde*, 37–40; Morison, "The United States Africa Squadron at the Cape Verde Islands"; Warrin, *So Ends This Day*, 154. A rich vein of information on Cape Verde as a base of the Africa Squadron is Log USS MARION, 1858–1860.
208 Log USS PORTSMOUTH, 1850–1851, 30.10., 07.11. & 13.11.1850.

that the men had been ordinary Cape Verdean recruits and the accusation of slavery an act of revenge on the part of disgruntled seamen.[209] The judges seem to have agreed when the case went to appeal two weeks later and let the captain off with a fine.[210]

From *Bravas* and *"Gees"* to *Americanos*

"It was a form of passport", recalled Joseph Ramos, who was introduced above, of signing on aboard a whaleship.[211] Like many young Cape Verdean men at the time, to him it was above all a means of getting away from the islands. And get away they did, sometimes to far-flung parts of the world. In the 1840s, a Cape Verdean seaman settled in one of the Ogaswara Islands in the western pacific and turned his hand to farming, with some success. Another, Antonio Pereria, became a prominent merchant on the south Pacific atoll of Fakaofo in the 1860s. An estimated four hundred Portuguese-speaking men were living in Hawaii in 1876, the large majority of whom came there aboard whalers from Cape Verde and the Azores.[212] However, most of the men who realised their desire to emigrate by means of a whaleship were not drawn to the other end of the world. They were quite content to make it to the other side of the Atlantic, seeking a discharge when their vessel arrived in its home port. By the mid-nineteenth century, they had become a common sight in New England's principal whaling ports. As Herman Melville observed, writing for *Harper's* in 1856: "To see a 'Gee' there is no need to go all the way to Fogo, no more than to see a Chinaman to go all the way to China. 'Gees' are occasionally to be encountered in our seaports, but more particularly in Nantucket and New Bedford."[213]

The earliest recorded instances of men who shipped in Cape Verde settling in the United States date from the 1820s.[214] According to the historian Medina dos Santos, the first of these immigrants was Jose Silva, who was born in Brava and became an American citizen in Nantucket in 1824.[215] In the 1860s, emigration

---

209 "Atrocious Outrage." *New-Bedford Mercury*, 21.06.1833, 2.
210 "Ship Enterprise." *New-Bedford Mercury*, 04.07.1833, 1.
211 Quoted in Halter, *Between Race and Ethnicity*, 103.
212 Warrin, *So Ends This Day*, 183, 236f.
213 Melville, "The Gees", 360.
214 Meintel, "Cape Verdean Transnationalism", 29.
215 Carreira, *The People of the Cape Verde Islands*, 43.

by means of whaleships became a routine practice, with an estimated 350 men leaving the islands in that manner each year.[216]

By law, anyone intending to leave the islands was required to the present himself to the Portuguese colonial authorities with his passport. In practice, however, this requirement was neither respected nor enforced, rendering official statistics for emigration from Cape Verde largely meaningless. Many of those seeking to emigrate would have had difficulty obtaining a passport in the first place, possessing neither the documents necessary to the application nor the money to the pay the fees involved. Portugal finally lifted the requirement in 1914, having apparently found it impossible to enforce.[217]

The use of vessels as instruments of individual plans for emigration was a side-effect of whaling observable elsewhere too. Other island societies in the world's oceans, the Azores and Hawaii among them, underwent similar experiences. In each case, the loss of manpower to whaling brought serious consequences in its train. In the mid-1840s the Hawaiian government found it to be a severe problem that several hundred young men were leaving the islands each year aboard whalers. It estimated that by that time a fifth of all men aged between fifteen and thirty had shipped from the islands permanently or temporarily.[218]

In a report produced in 1874, the secretary-general of the Cape Verdean government observed that "On the island of Brava . . . there is a great disproportion between the male and female sexes". It had arisen, he continued, "because a large part of the male population yield to their dominant passion and embark on board the whaling vessels to obtain a more satisfying way of life."[219] Emigration aboard whaleships meant the emigration of men, and the women they left behind soon formed a sizeable majority in the islands concerned. Official statistics for Brava record a marked surplus of women, at times outnumbering men by nearly two to one (Tab. 14). If we may assume the ratio among children to have been roughly even, the imbalance among adults would have been even greater than the numbers suggest. It was not easy, the administrator of the *concelho* of Brava noted in 1880, to find any men aged between fourteen and thirty left on the island.[220]

---

216 Meintel, "Cape Verdean Transnationalism", 30.
217 Carreira, *The People of the Cape Verde Islands*, 59–61.
218 Lebo, "Hawaii's 19th-Century Whaling Economy", 105, 111.
219 Quoted in Carreira, *The People of the Cape Verde Islands*, 48f.
220 Carreira, *The People of the Cape Verde Islands*, 50.

Tab. 14: Distribution of sexes in Brava, 1867–1878.

Year	Population	Male	Female
1867	5,874	2,426 (41.30%)	3,448 (58.70%)
1872	8,617	3,669 (42.58%)	4,948 (57.42%)
1875	6,584	2,480 (37.67%)	4,104 (62.33%)
1878	8,158	3,547 (43.48%)	4,611 (56.52%)

Source: Carreira, *The People of the Cape Verde Islands*, 50.

For the women of Brava, this development made life difficult not only because it reduced the supply of marriageable men – married men too signed on aboard whaleships. Though most of them will have done so with the intention of returning home in due course, a large proportion ended up settling in the United States.[221] Their wives, once the realisation dawned on them, permanently donned widow's weeds. These black-clad women were known locally as *viúvas americanas*, "American widows".[222] For the men too saying goodbye to their families was often a painful experience. In the early 1900s the Bravan poet Eugénio de Paula Tavares expressed the sorrow of the moment of parting in a song in the local *crioulo* which became widely popular, entitled *Morna de despedida* ("The Farewell *Morna*").[223]

But not all the men who shipped aboard whalers left never to return. Many returned after a few years' whaling – some for a spell, others for good. In the 1860s, a regular pattern of circular migration can be seen to emerge: men left the islands in their youth, spent some time working aboard whaleships and on shore in the United States, before returning home with the money they had saved to marry. Having done so, they would once more ship with a whaler to make money enough to buy a house and land in Cape Verde.[224]

The harpooner John Ferguson spent the period from 1880 to 1884 living and working with such a man aboard the *Kathleen*. This was John Brown, of whom Ferguson recalled: "He said that if he had five hundred dollars coming to him, he would go home to Brava. He has a piece of land there, five acres, that he

---

221 Halter, *Between Race and Ethnicity*, 73–75.
222 Carreira, *The People of the Cape Verde Islands*, 50; Meintel, "Cape Verdean Transnationalism", 30; Warrin, *So Ends This Day*, 59. A similar term, "whaling widows", was applied in American whaling ports such as Nantucket or New Bedford to women whose husbands were away on the whale hunt.
223 Quoted in Duncan, *Atlantic Islands*, 237. On Bravan *crioulo* see Meintel, *The Creole Dialect of the Island of Brava*.
224 Meintel, "Cape Verdean Transnationalism", 31.

bought with money from his last voyage." It seems that Brown was systematic in preparing his return to his native island: "There is a little two-room house on it built of stone, which he has rented until he gets back. He said that [. . .] he could live there a long time by selling chickens at ten or fifteen cents apiece, and having a goat for milk, and raising some pigs. He said he was going to buy an old boat, fix it up so he could fish, as there are plenty of fine fish to be caught."[225] Men like Brown did not depend on whalers to get them home: in the 1870s, 1880s and 1890s they also travelled to Brava – sometimes dozens at a time – as passengers on American merchant vessels.[226]

Nor did Cape Verdean immigrants to the United States depend on whaling for their subsequent employment. In the port cities of New England, where textiles supplanted whaling as the dominant industry around 1900, they worked above all in the many cotton mills. A sizeable number worked in the port district as cooks or in ropemaking. Work was also to be found in the rural areas of southeastern Massachusetts, particularly in the strawberry and blueberry fields of Plymouth County, Buzzard Bay and Cape Cod.[227] Several thousand workers were needed there throughout the year and twice the usual number at harvest time. By the early 1900s, many women and children as well as men came directly from Cape Verde to find seasonal work picking berries, earning anywhere between one hundred and five hundred dollars at a time. These workers crossed the Atlantic, not aboard whaleships, but as passengers on merchant vessels.[228]

As aboard whaleships, Cape Verdean immigrants in the United States barely ever associated with the African-American population, of which few would have considered themselves part. For the Cape Verde islanders differed from North America's other major communities of African origin in two major respects: first, they were usually Catholic rather than Protestant; and second, they or their ancestors had not come across the Atlantic as slaves. There was little to which could relate in the stories of enslavement, deportation and oppression that played so large a part in the formation and tradition of African-American identity. Perhaps more consequential still was an awareness that being considered "black" was to find one's chances of social advancement severely curtailed. By gladly accepting the label of "Gees", Cape Verdean immigrants emphasised the Portuguese element of their heritage over the African. For their part, American immigration officials did not consistently classify Cape Verdeans as "black", but often as "white"

---

225 Ferguson, *Harpooner*, 109.
226 Carreira, *The People of the Cape Verde Islands*, 49.
227 Halter, *Between Race and Ethnicity*, 5, 131f.; Warrin, *So Ends This Day*, 304.
228 Halter, *Between Race and Ethnicity*, 73–75; Meintel, "Cape Verdean-Americans", 18f., 23f.; Meintel, "Cape Verdean Transnationalism", 31f.; Rogers, "Cape Verdeans", 198.

or sometimes as "black Portuguese". Since, however, other Portuguese-speaking immigrant groups in the United States kept the darker-skinned islanders at a distance, Cape Verdeans formed a largely self-contained community, intermarrying and forming their own religious and social organisations. In the twentieth century, they came to refer to themselves as "Cape Verdean Americans".[229]

A man who returned to Brava having made good money in the United States was no longer considered the *pardo* or *preto* as which he had left. These men came to be known by their fellow islanders as *americanos*. And though the savings accumulated through whaling and other work may not have been particularly impressive by American standards, many *americanos* were rich men in Cape Verde. By returning home, these men turned the game played by the American whaling industry and its hiring practices to their own advantage, exploiting value differentials across long distances. For *americanos*, spatial mobility was the key to social mobility. The houses and the land they acquired in Brava were often bought from *brancos* who had become impoverished in successive crises. Particularly in the 1920, when Cape Verde was in the grip of severe economic depression, many *brancos* saw no alternative but to sell their once stately houses to *americanos*, some of whom, in their pre-emigration lives as *pardos* and *pretos*, might have worked there as servants.[230]

As John Brown's earlier remarks suggest, *americanos* bought land and houses above all to be in a position to support themselves as subsistence farmers. The experience of recurring famine is likely to have been a decisive factor in shaping this aspiration. In Brava, this development meant that the share of land given over to subsistence farming grew to a far larger degree than in the other islands.[231] The *americanos* made their mark on Brava in other ways, too: their money encouraged the opening of shops and the lavish celebration of Catholic feasts. Yet they were probably also the vectors for the rapid spread of syphilis and tuberculosis from which the island suffered in the late nineteenth century.[232] English was

---

229 Duignan/Gann, *The United States and Africa*, 364; Halter, *Between Race and Ethnicity*, 1; Rogers, "Cape Verdeans", 199; Williams, "Rethinking the African Diaspora", 114f. On the processes of identification and self-understanding among Cape Verdean Americans in the twentieth century see Pilgrim, "Free Men Name Themselves'" and on the community's broader social and cultural history Coli/Lobban, *The Cape Verdeans in Rhode Island* and Nunes, *A Portuguese Colonial in America*. On the meaning of the history and practice of emigration for identity formation in present-day Cape Verde see LaPorte, "The Continuities of Modernity".
230 Carreira, *The People of the Cape Verde Islands*, 54f.
231 Busch, "Cape Verdeans in the American Whaling and Sealing Industry", 109.
232 Carreira, *The People of the Cape Verde Islands*, 51; Lobban/Lopes, *Historical Dictionary of the Republic of Cape Verde*, 47; Patterson, "Epidemics, Famines, and Population in the Cape Verde Islands", 302.

increasingly to be heard in Furna, Nova Sintra and elsewhere in Brava. "I found that nearly all the men and some of the women speak our language", Benjamin Tripp, the American consul, noted as early as 1868. "The people of Brava are constantly going to and coming from the United States."[233]

"The Lifeline that binds us"

As was the case elsewhere, the seemingly incidental consequences of whaling survived the industry's decline in Brava too. *Merca*, as the Unites States was known in Brava *Crioulo*,[234] became the destination of a mass emigration movement that by the late nineteenth century had already ceased to rely on whaleships. Observing that family, friends, neighbours or acquaintances had achieved relative prosperity in New England, more and more islanders felt emboldened to follow them. In the words of one Bravan *Morna*, "Americano tem dolar, tem dolar coma burro!" – "The *Americano* has money, he has money to burn!"[235] The passenger traffic between Cape Verde and New England that developed independently of whaling has been thoroughly studied, most notably by Marilyn Halter.[236] I shall restrict myself here to a brief sketch in order to show how phenomena of entanglements produced by whaling could take on lives of their own.

The decline of the American whaling coincided with the rise of the steamship, meaning that by the late nineteenth century, the price of old whaleships was falling. Used fishing boats, so-called *Gloucester fishermen*, were also cheaply available in New England. In 1892 a Cape Verdean immigrant, Antonio Coelho, took advantage of this situation to realise a novel business idea. He bought an aged fishing vessel, the sixty-four-ton schooner *Nellie May*, and had her sail as a freight and passenger vessel between Providence and Furna. As her captain, Coelho hired a man who knew the route well: a former whaling skipper.[237]

Since few whalers still visited Cape Verde while the desire to emigrate remained high, setting up a regular service to and from the United States promised to be good business, and Coelho's example was followed by a number of other Cape Verdean immigrants, some of whom – for instance Roy Texeira, Henrique Mendes or Antonio Cardoza – became well-known entrepreneurs. Following a

---

233 Quoted in Meintel, "Cape Verdean Transnationalism", 30.
234 Meintel, "Cape Verdean Transnationalism", 31.
235 Quoted in Halter, *Between Race and Ethnicity*, 73.
236 Halter, *Between Race and Ethnicity*; Halter, "Cape Verdeans in the U.S.".
237 Cohn/Platzer, *Black Men of the Sea*, 92; Halter, *Between Race and Ethnicity*, 5; Halter, "Cape Verdeans in the U.S.", 36.

pattern familiar from whaling, they formed investment and ship-owning syndicates, buying up superannuated sailing vessels and refitting them for passenger and commercial traffic. In New England, these vessels soon became known as "Brava packet boats" or simply "packets", and their business as the "Brava packet trade".[238]

Many of these packets had previously plied the route between New England and Cape Verde as whalers: the *Sunbeam* (purchased and refitted in 1909), the *Carleton Bell* (1916), the *Bertha* (1917), the *Valkyria* (c.1920), the *Greyhound* (1921), the *A.M. Nicholson* and the *William A. Graber* (both 1922) or the *Margarett* (1922), to name but a few. The crews of these packets also tended to be recruited from among whalemen. Quite a few of the captains and officers who moved from whalers to packets were from Cape Verde, including John Da Lomba, Isaac Azulay and Joseph Senna, all of whom were born in Brava. In the case of the barque *Greyhound*, her captain Benjamin Costa remained with his vessel when she was converted to the packet trade in 1921.[239]

Like the *Greyhound*, some ninety percent of Brava packet boats sailed from New Bedford, the remainder from Providence. The journey to Cape Verde took approximately thirty-five days if all went well, the return forty-five. A packet would usually travel this route twice a year, in spring and autumn respectively. A single passage cost somewhere between fifteen and fifty dollars, depending not least on the vessel's condition. Packets were usually clapped-out vessels forced across the Atlantic as fast as they would go, and shipwrecks were no rarity. Some shipowners, however, made a point of advertising their comparatively luxurious vessels – Roy Texeira's *Coriolanus*, for instance, which covered an orchestra (Fig. 41).[240]

Sailing to Cape Verde, packets carried letters, parcels and newspapers – Cape Verdean Americans would often send their relatives household goods and, in times of drought, maize, beans and preserved meats.[241] The letters usually contained cash. Particularly in Brava, remittances from the United States were an essential supplement to many families' income. Such was this reliance on American money that a letter lacking dollar bills came to be known as a *carta seca* or "dry letter".[242]

---

238 Halter, "Cape Verdeans in the U.S.", 36.
239 Cohn/Platzer, *Black Men of the Sea*, 94; Warrin, *So Ends This Day*, 265f., 290, 295.
240 Cohn/Platzer, *Black Men of the Sea*, 91–93, 95–98, 101; Halter, *Between Race and Ethnicity*, 40, 69f., 73; Meintel, "Cape Verdean Transnationalism", 31f.; Rogers, "Cape Verdeans", 198.
241 Halter, *Between Race and Ethnicity*, 81f.; Meintel, "Cape Verdean Transnationalism", 31f.
242 Halter, *Between Race and Ethnicity*, 69, 73.

To receive a *carta seca* was all the more unusual given that many islanders could neither read nor write. Written communications were further hampered by the fact that written Portuguese differed considerably from everyday spoken *Crioulo*, so much so that it was not enough for recipients of such letters to have them read to them by friends – they usually required translation. Instead of writing letters, most emigrants seeking to communicate with friends and family therefore preferred to ask a passenger of their acquaintance to communicate messages in person. Bravanese creole developed a work for this kind of oral letter, too – namely *mantenha*, a noun formed from the verb *manter*, meaning keep, preserve or look after. Besides the sender's news and greetings, a *mantenha* would often contain information regarding employment opportunities in south-eastern Massachusetts, thereby helping those minded to emigrate find a suitable moment for doing so.[243]

On the way back to New England, the vessels would carry as many passengers as it was possible to squeeze in. Many a schooner laid out for fifty or sixty passengers now carried hundreds, most of them friends, relatives or neighbours of men who had earlier travelled this route aboard a whaleship. Very few emigrants sailed for the United States without some form of personal connection there. Cape Verdean emigration can thus be understood as a typical case of chain migration. By the end of the nineteenth century, packets had already replaced whalers as the preferred means of emigration from Cape Verde.[244]

Like those islanders who left aboard whalers, the passengers on Cape Verde packets were mostly impoverished *pardos* and *pretos*. Families would sometimes pool their savings to enable one of their number to travel to the United States. This was usually a young man; women were a minority among emigrants. Such women and children as might be found on board a packet (Fig. 42) were usually the families of male emigrants who had decided to stay in America.[245] Those women who were not sailing to join their husbands were often – if oral traditions in Cape Verde are to be believed – "disreputable" or otherwise socially isolated women looking to start new lives or who were urged to do so.[246]

The Brava packet trade in its quantitative dimension has been exhaustively studied by Marilyn Halter, according to whom at least 23,168 persons emigrated from Cape Verde to the United States between 1860 and 1940, and most of them

---

[243] Meintel, "Cape Verdean Transnationalism", 31.
[244] Halter, *Between Race and Ethnicity*, 68; Meintel, "Cape Verdean Transnationalism", 31f.
[245] Halter, *Between Race and Ethnicity*, 46, 69, 73, 84.
[246] Meintel, "Cape Verdean Transnationalism", 31.

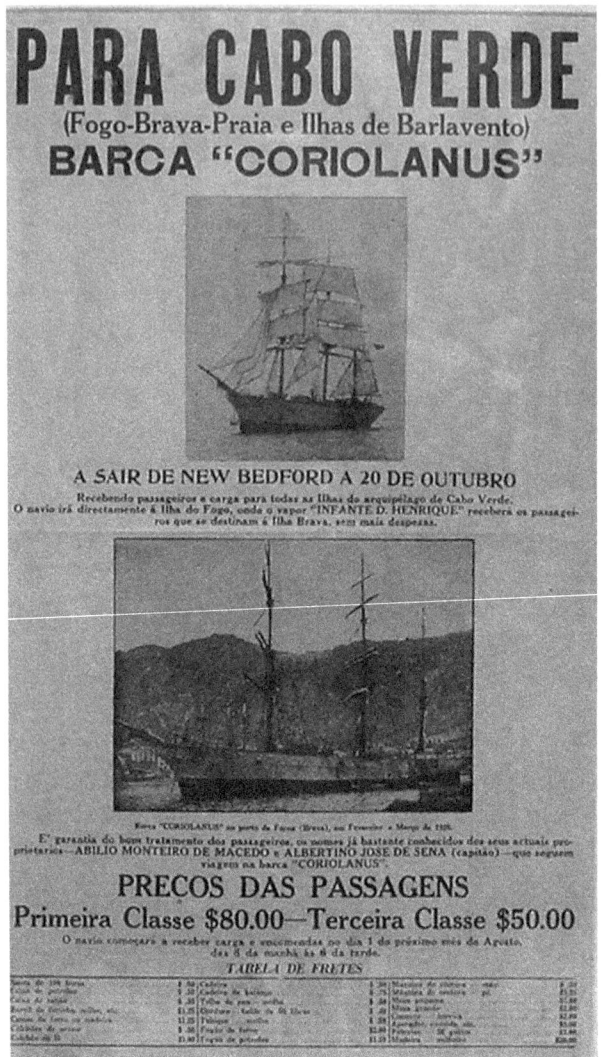

Fig. 41: The barque *Coriolanus* on a 1926 handbill advertising the packet as a luxury travel option.
Courtesy of the New Bedford Whaling Museum.

between 1890 and 1920. In some years, more than one thousand immigrants landed at New Bedford, and more than two thousand in 1914. That these figures represent a minimum is due to the fact they do not account for clandestine migration: the Cape Verdean authorities were no more aware of all who left than were their American counterparts of all arrivals. Like whaleships before them, packets often anchored away from the ports and took emigrants aboard illegally, preferably under cover of darkness. Such passengers would be put ashore on the coast of New England in a similar fashion before the vessel reached New Bedford.[247]

Fig. 42: Immigrants arriving at New Bedford aboard the *Savoia* on 5 October 1914. Although they feature prominently in this photograph, women were usually a minority among the passengers aboard packets arriving from Cape Verde.
Courtesy of the New Bedford Whaling Museum, item number 1981.61.725.

---

247 Halter, *Between Race and Ethnicity*, 37, 39, 52. In Boston in 1864 Captain James Phinney of the barque *Susan Jane* of New Bedford was tried on a charge of having landed several Bravan migrants in the United States illegally. ("Attached." *The Republican Standard*, 24.11.1864, 2; "Courts." *The Republican Standard*, 03.11.1864, 2) Since 1840 American whaling captains had been legally required to present consular certification for each man hired along the way upon return the United States, but the rule was largely ignored by skippers and immigration authorities alike. (Busch, "Cape Verdeans in the American Whaling and Sealing Industry", 106)

According to Halter, Bravas formed the single largest group among Cape Verdean immigrants to the United States, accounting for nearly a third (32.6 per cent) of the total. This figure tallies roughly with Carreira's estimate, which puts the number of immigrants from Brava at just about six thousand. The remainder came mostly from the other *Sotaventos*, above all Fogo (28.5 per cent), while the *Barlaventos* contributed only around a quarter of the total.[248] New Bedford's Cape Verdean American community generally put on a celebration to welcome new arrivals: crowds would gather on the quayside, dancing and playing music, while some climbed on board bearing gifts before the incoming packet had even completed mooring.[249]

The coming and going of the packets changed life in Brava profoundly. Each spring and autumn, Furna's harbour was bustling with packets while *pardos* and *pretos* looking to emigrate gathered on shore with their families. Weddings, christenings and other family and social occasions were timed to coincide with the arrival of the packets and their cargo of mail and relatives.[250] Looking back at the peak of the packet trade, the Cape Verdean writer Jorge Barbosa gives a vivid impression of what event the vessels' arrival must have been. To quote a passage from his poem "Ilhas", published in 1935:[251]

–Seló . . . Seló! . . .	–Seló [ahoy] . . . Seló . . .
Americanos que chegam . . .	Americanos arrive . . .
Na balbúrdia do cais	In the clamour of the dock
há lágrimas de alegria,	there are tears of joy,
fugidios cristais	elusive crystals
iluminando os olhos das mulheres . . .	illuminating the eyes of the women . . .
Foguetes	fireworks
estalam no ar por toda a Brava	exploding in the air all over Brava
contagiando a harmonia	infecting the harmony
de cores	of the colours
e de flores	and flowers
da gracílima paisagem.	of the delicate gracílima landscape.

---

248 Halter, *Between Race and Ethnicity*, 41f.
249 Meintel, "Cape Verdean Transnationalism", 32.
250 Carreira, *The People of the Cape Verde Islands*, 73; Meintel, "Cape Verdean Transnationalism", 32.
251 Barbosa, *Obra Poética*, 40. English translation: Vieira et al., "The Whale in the Cape Verde Islands", 7.

E depois . . . lá vão outra vez, tristonhos, os emigrantes . . .	And then . . . they leave again, woefully, the emigrants . . .
: América! Mar largo! Amores distantes, saudades crioulas das mornas de Eugénio! . . . –Seló [ahoy] . . . Seló . . .	: America!! Vast sea Distant loves, Creole yearnings for the mornas of Eugénio!

Scarcely anybody in Cape Verde could not have been aware of large-scale emigration to *"Merca,* which was the subject of much controversy among islanders. To some, the mass exodus meant a loss of manpower that would stymie the islands' economic development; against this view, others argued that the emigrants" remittances more than outweighed any such losses. Moreover, returnees brought experiences and ideas to Cape Verde that would ultimately contribute to economic, social and political progress. This was probably the majority position, and it had a prominent advocate in Eugénio Tavares, who argued that the government should support emigration to the United States rather than seeking to prevent it. For the men of Brava in particular, Tavares continued, emigration was an existential matter, a choice between freedom and slavery. It was for each man to decide whether he wanted to spend his life as a beast of burden in the accursed fields of Fogo or whether to accept the challenges of starting a new live as a free worker in a civilised country.[252]

For a while, the colonial government seemed to be adopting Tavares's position. In 1914 it made emigration easier by doing away with the need for a passport, and in 1917 it reformed the educational system with a view to improving literacy and hence the prospects of emigrants for permanent residence in the United States.[253] These policies were, however, short-lived. Passports were reintroduced during the First World War, and in 1919 the government began to charge emigrants the equivalent of thirty dollars. Further restrictions on prospective male emigrants of draft age were imposed in 1920.[254]

The Brava packet trade went into steep decline between 1921 and 1924. In 1915 the US Senate had urged restrictions on immigration and not least on poorly educated immigrants. It was to these measures that the educational reforms enacted by the colonial government in 1917 were responding, but in February of that year, Congress passed an Immigration Act prohibiting immigration aboard whalers. It

---

252 Carreira, *The People of the Cape Verde Islands*, 62–64.
253 Ibid., 61f.
254 Ibid., 64f.

was no longer legal for foreign seamen to be discharged in American ports. Exemptions could initially be obtained, and some Cape Verdean Americans took legal training, offering their advice in matters of immigration law to the owners and captains of packets.[255]

As the rules came to applied more restrictively and as addition laws were passed, however, legal immigration to the US from Cape Verde had become virtually impossible by 1924. The Emergency Quota Act of 1921 limited further immigration by each designated group to three per cent annually of its 1910 population. Cape Verdeans, who were officially classified as Portuguese citizens and hence as south Europeans, now found themselves competing for the few thousand remaining permits with prospective immigrants from countries such as mainland Portugal and Spain. In 1924 another Immigration Act reduced the quotas to two per cent of a group's population in 1890 and mandated that all prospective immigrants must obtain visas before travelling to the United States.[256] Furna, which had previously been thronging with prospective emigrants several times a year, became a ghost town.[257] Cape Verdean poets, who previously had composed doleful *mornas* on mass emigration, now found equal sadness in its sudden end. As Jorge Barbosa wrote in his poem "Irmao", which was quoted at the beginning of this chapter:[258]

A América . . .	America. . .
a América acabou-se para ti . . .	America is finished for you
Fechou as portas a tua expansão!	she closed her doors to your expansion!
Essas Aventuras pelos Oceanos	These adventures across the oceans
já não existem . . .	no longer exist. . .
Existem apenas	they only live
nas histórias que contas do passado,	in the tales you recount of your past,
com o canhoto atravessado na boca	with a pipe hanging in your mouth
e risos alegres	and with joyful laughter
que não chegam a esconder	that will never hide
a tua melancolia . . .	your melancholy

The Brava pocket trade was something altogether new in Atlantic history. For the first time, a large group of African migrants crossed the Atlantic westwards

---

255 Carreira, The People of the Cape Verde Islands, 61f.; Lobban, *Cape Verde*, 64; Warrin, *So Ends This Day*, 272f.
256 Meintel, "Cape Verdean Transnationalism", 33.
257 Duignan/Gann, *The United States and Africa*, 364.
258 Quoted in Almeida et al., *Cape Verdeans in America*, 46f.

of their own free will and aboard means of transport they themselves controlled.[259] Cape Verdean Americans to this day remain the largest Cape Verdean community anywhere in the world, numbering (depending on the criteria applied) between 50,000 and 200,000 individuals in the latter part of the twentieth century. Most of them continue to live in and around the former whaling ports of New England, especially in New Bedford, Boston, Providence, Rhode Island, Nantucket, Bridgeport and New Haven.[260] The names of some packets still resonate there – the *Coriolanus*, the *Savoia* and the *Arcturus*, but above all that of the schooner *Ernestina*. The last of the packets, the *Ernestine* continued to ply the route between Massachusetts and Cape Verde until 1965 and today lies as a museum ship in New Bedford harbour. Virginia Gonsalves was born in Cape Verde and became a teacher in the United States. "There have always been the boats", she observed in 1983, "that's the lifeline that binds us."[261]

**

The case of Cape Verde in general and of Brava in particular provides a vivid illustration of how the incidental social consequences of whaling could take on lives of their own. Characterised though it was by settler colonialism and slavery, the society whalemen encountered in Cape Verde was not that of a typical slave-owning plantation economy. Famines and the practice of freeing slaves (itself economically motivated) reduced the proportion of slaves from a large majority to a small minority between the sixteenth and the nineteenth century. Slavery aside, the principal structuring force in Cape Verdean society was the dichotomy between the moneyed and landed class of *brancos* and the majority population, largely propertyless, of *pardos* and *pardas*, of *pretos* and *pretas livres*. Although this dichotomy was perpetuated by a racist system of classifying the population, Cape Verdean society did allow for an element of social mobility that included mobility between "races".

In the late eighteenth century, under pressure from poverty, famine and dangerous military service, the first *pardos* and *pretos* tried to escape Cape Verde, if only for a time, by vesselping aboard a whaler. The number of Cape Verdean recruits increased markedly in 1820s, with more and more of them looking to reach North America – and to stay there. By the mid-nineteenth century, this practice had grown into mass migration, taking thousands of Cape

---

259 Halter, "Cape Verdeans in the U.S.", 36.
260 Busch, "Cape Verdeans in the American Whaling and Sealing Industry", 115f.; Duignan/Gann, *The United States and Africa*, 364f.; Lobban, *Cape Verde*, 58; Rogers, "Cape Verdeans", 198.
261 Quoted in Halter, *Between Race and Ethnicity*, 70.

Verdean men to North America. As this movement became divorced from whaling in the final third of the nineteenth century, Cape Verdean women as well as well as men followed their friends, relatives and neighbours as passengers aboard merchant vessels as well as whalers. In 1892 Cape Verdean American entrepreneurs inaugurated a regular passenger and cargo service between New England and Cape Verde. This was the Brava packet trade, which was carried on mainly with redundant whaleships. Until the tightening of American immigration laws between 1921 and 1924 put a sudden stop to the trade, far more than 20,000 individuals had sailed from Cape Verde to the United States aboard whalers, merchant vessels and packets.

The entanglements engendered by whaling between Brava and New England – the transoceanic movement of people, goods and ideas in both direction – may be adduced as evidence of what recent global historians have discussed in terms of ever denser networks of connectivity. Yet the case of Brava also reveals an aspect less frequently mentioned by scholars, and that is how the global dynamics of recent history have also produced countervailing, disconnective effects, specifically the phenomenon of connective regression. This can be observed in Brava with the collapse of the packet trade in the early 1920s. The end of American whaling and the restrictive turn in US immigration policy largely put an end to migration from Cape Verde to New England. The number of European and US consulates and diplomatic missions in the islands fell sharply. In the nineteenth century, the State Department had found it absolutely essential to maintain a consulate in Brava, the smallest and outermost of the Cape Verde Islands – a notion which today would no doubt be rejected as preposterous.[262] Furna, which just over a century ago was regularly visited by prospective and returning emigrants and their families, who brought it to life with their celebrations, is now a backwater visited almost exclusively by boats from the neighbouring islands.[263] For all the progress made in transport and communication, Brava today is more isolated than it was a hundred years ago.

---

[262] Duncan, *Atlantic Islands*, 240.
[263] Meintel, "Cape Verdean Transnationalism", 28, 34.

Conclusion: Homeward bound

When a whaler set sail for the last leg of its journey, the log would usually record it as "homeward bound". Often, these words were not put down like any others. The writer might make the letters particularly prominent, adding flourishes or an exclamation mark – or several. Returning home meant a lot to seamen. Home meant no longer having to eat "hardtack" and "salt horse" and sharing a bunk with cockroaches. Home meant no longer having to chase recalcitrant whales or to watch out for irritable officers. Home meant – and that was not the least of it – sleeping through the night.

Outward bound, many of the men (or rather boys) aboard a whaler were still inexperienced "green hands"; by the time they were homeward bound, they were considered seasoned mariners. They knew the difference between Madagascar and Málaga and could tell the blow of a southern right from that of a Bryde's whale. They knew how to brace a yard, how to tack and to beat to windward and much else besides. They had explored beaches in Africa and other far-flung places. They had a good many stories to tell.

The problem was that nobody wanted to hear it all. To friends and relatives on shore – if they were not seafarers themselves – the language in which seamen communicated during their months and years aboard ship was a mystery. If seamen wanted people to listen, they had to translate their experiences into stories that connected with wider reserves of knowledge and frames of reference – stories that were relatable and could be framed in more general terms. In that respect, homeward bound seamen faced challenges not unlike those confronting scholars presenting the past in the form of a story – of history. What are the frames of reference with which the present study and its findings connect, and in what conceptual language can these findings be expressed?

The currents in which whales move within the ocean form layers, moving at different speeds and flowing in different directions. Deep water currents sometimes circulate in the opposite direction to those on the surface. In some coastal areas, major rivers such as the Congo pour enormous quantities of water into the ocean, forming currents of their own and running athwart others. Eighteenth- and nineteenth-century seamen knew little of this. To them, the part they were familiar with, the surface current, was the whole, was the oceanic current as such.

The past too encompasses a variety of contradictory currents. Each present seeks to identify some of them as the principal ones, as the currents synonymous with history as such. With regard to Africa, European expansion, the Atlantic slave trade and colonialism continue to be the major currents that make up the grand historical narratives. Set against these currents, whalers and their multifarious relations with African littoral societies form a significant undercurrent. The connections between spaces and societies established by these currents were often different in kind from those created by the three dominant currents. Some of them were altogether novel in character. But it was nonetheless an undercurrent, not least because it circulated largely unnoticed by the chroniclers of its time – much as the deep ocean currents circulate many fathoms below a whaleship at the surface. The vessels' erratic courses and informal communication networks, seamen's peculiar language and the laws governing their life aboard ship, the convoluted paths by which *Bravas*, deserters and *Cabindas* travelled far and wide – all these were, to outsiders, aspects of a remote and alien world, one that made only isolated appearances in hegemonic discourses.

Yet even though outsiders might often have failed to notice it, in washing up against the deep beach of African history, this undercurrent changed littoral societies. In some places, it wrought profound transformations, in others, the effects were merely superficial or situational. How deeply it affected life on the coast and sometimes in the hinterland too always depended on local conditions and circumstances – the currents, as it were, with which that embodied by the whalemen collided.

As a rule, the effects of the undercurrent were strongest where whalemen were the only actors to visit a particular place from the sea over a longer period of time – or at least the only ones to do so with any regularity. Along the whaling grounds surrounding the African continent, Walvis Bay, Annobón, Saint Augustin and Furna were such places. Here, the undercurrent served an integrative purpose, tying local societies into maritime networks of communication and trade or at least helping to ensure that existing connections did not break off. In Saint Augustin, the undercurrent brought a stream of firearms and ammunition that helped the tributary state of Sakalava to maintain a degree of independence in the face of an expanding Imerina.

In Furna, the undercurrent attracted numerous young men prepared to let it carry them away, far from recurring famine and from conscription into Cape Verde's dreaded militia. In Walvis Bay, the ǂAonîn drove their cattle to the shore when the whaleships arrived. In both places, the undercurrent redirected movements in the hinterland, causing action increasingly to become strategically oriented towards the sea. And in both places, whaling was outlived by its incidental effects. Taking their cue from the recruitment of *pardos* and *pretos* by whalers in Furna, Cape Verdean American actors separated the movement of islanders across the Atlantic from whaling by setting up the Brava packet trade. In this case, the undercurrent produced a new culture of navigation and migration, taking several hundred people annually and at least 23,000 in total across the Atlantic. This phenomenon, which has its origins in whaling, is of eminent significance as the only great movement of people from Africa to the Americas that did not take place under duress, as part of the Atlantic slave trade. Walvis Bay's transformation into a trading port of international repute likewise shows how long-distance relations established by whaling could take on lives of their own. What both cases demonstrate is how the emergence and deepening of global connections in the nineteenth century was not limited to the processes usually referred to when today's historians discuss the main currents of global integration.

The undercurrent tended to be weaker in places where whalemen were only one of several groups of actors to come to the beach from the sea. In Delagoa Bay, Mutsamudu and Cabinda, whalers brought additional dynamism to activities that had begun even before their arrival. Mediator figures such as Prince Will in Saint Augustin or the governor of San Antonio – both negotiators specialising in the sale of provisions – had begun to emerge and be institutionalised before they ever had to deal with whalers. Yet visiting whaleships posed special challenges to such middlemen, for instance in the large quantities of firewood they required. In Cabinda, the dominant figures of the coastal trade – Francisco Franque, for instance, or the heads of the Nkata Kolombo family – recognised an opportunity to make up for the decline in the slave trade and to diversify their commercial strategy, thereby securing their own dominant position. In Mutsamudu, Sultan Abdullah was even more decisive in using his relations with whalers to strengthen his position against challengers from within and without. Local potentates in both places were able to turn trade with whalers to their economic and political advantage while making sure that they were its prime beneficiaries. In a manner similar to Saint Augustin, the undercurrent produced a stabilising effect in Cabinda and Mutsamudu by helping coastal rulers to assert themselves against rivals from the hinterland. Occasional conflicts – the most striking of which was the bombardment of Mutsamudu by USS *Dale* – did not alter the fundamental pattern.

A monopoly on coastal trade was what the Portuguese too hoped to gain by their activities in Delagoa Bay, where whalers bought their provisions from the Ronga states. Here, the undercurrent eroded Portugal's claims, thereby exposing the weakness of the putative colonial power, encouraging the British in their own designs on the bay and ultimately deepening the animosity between the contenders. Whereas the Portuguese in Delagoa Bay never succeeded in imposing effective rules on the trade carried on by whalers and sanctioning infractions, the African rulers in Cabinda displayed considerable efficiency in this regard, for instance when it came to exacting payment for drinking water from the Lukola river. This vividly illustrates how whalers on African beaches were always dependent in their activities on the cooperativeness of local rulers. Lacking alternatives and often under pressure of time, they tended to be at a disadvantage when negotiating prices with experienced middlemen.

Of all the places discussed here, the undercurrent was at its weakest in Port Louis, where traffic was busiest. Yet this made Mauritius all the more important to whalers. Captains and shipowners took advantage of its facilities for transhipment and repairs, while common seamen found it to be rich in promise, not least of a happy escape. Desertion – a particularly frequent occurrence in Port Louis but not unheard of in any of the other beaches visited over the course of this study – was a distinctive feature of life and work aboard a whaler, one that shows how these peculiar rules and customs could play out when a vessel called into port.

By signing on aboard whalers – for an entire voyage or as seasoners, but in any case often in pursuit of their own plans for emigration – men from littoral societies in Africa reached strange and distant parts of the world. Some stayed there, others moved on or returned home. Whether in person or by sending letters, goods and remittances, they brought knowledge, information, objects and other resources to their native coasts, where they did much to change lifeworlds. The example of Furna in particular shows how the undercurrent set off such transfer processes. Something similar can be observed with regard to Annobón and the islanders' adoption of American whaling practices. This made Annobón one of very few littoral societies in Africa to hunt whales – and to keep doing so even when American whaling had become a thing of the past.

***

This sketch of some of the undercurrent's more notable effects is far from giving a complete picture. Yet the picture it does reveal is highly diverse, showing a wide spectrum of primary and secondary effects, varying in both nature and degree. The question thus arises of whether it is possible to arrive at a more precise definition of the undercurrent. It is not, I would argue, easily conceptualised in theoretical terms. Any such conceptualisation would inevitably render the diversity of effects (both direct and incidental) invisible behind the veil of generalisation. If anything can serve to identify the undercurrent concretely, I would suggest a colour. The seas of history have taken on a polychromatic aspect since historians began to assign colours to their currents. Some call the Atlantic black in order to distinguish it as an Afro-American cultural space, others label the Pacific white in recognition of the racist policies of the United states and Australia and their ongoing effects. Some historians speak of the red seas of the age of revolution or the green Atlantic of the Irish diaspora. The undercurrent to which whaling gave rise was not limited to any one sea; its topography was transoceanic. I would like to propose calling this undercurrent grey.

Not only is grey the colour of many whales' skin. As a cold colour, it may also be taken to stand for the history of violence and suffering inflicted upon them – and for the merciless economic rationale that led to commercial whaling and its effects examined here. Everyday life for whalemen was grey, too – just how bleak and dreary is worth remembering against the romanticised image of a seafarer's life in the age of sail that is still with us. Grey can neither shine nor dazzle. And the whalemen themselves often operated in grey areas, for instance by taking on provisions "off and on" in an attempt to avoid mooring fees, or in the countless instances of seamen being left behind which were entered into logbooks as regular discharges. And grey is not least the natural appearance of the undercurrent, which flows too far below the surface to be reached by the light of the sun that gives the ocean its blue appearance.

Unlike the black, green or red Atlantic, the grey undercurrent does not invite identification or encourage tradition to accrete around it. It is barely suitable for the purposes of a politics of knowledge, guided by present interests, of the kind which is so often imposed on discourses of African history. This suggests another meaning of the colour grey: here, it points beyond the dichotomy of black and white, of villains and victims, which is still the paradigmatic structure of many historical narratives, particularly concerning Africa. The grey undercurrent offers no lessons for the present –nor, I believe, should it do so. By depicting past times and worlds which seem distant and alien to those alive today, it ought instead to convey a sense of the difference of the past and, by implication, the contingency of the presence.

Of course, the present study is far from being the only possible narrative of the events described – it is no more so than the grey undercurrent is the only metaphor in which it might be couched. In their movements around the world, whalers traversed a plurality of times, spaces and not least of cultural frames of reference which helped different societies make sense in their different ways of their encounters on the beaches. An American seaman's "ocean" was not the same thing as the *sagri* of an Annobonese woman, the *hurib* of an ǂAonîn or the *ranomasina* of a Vezo from Saint Augustin. By pointing to the terms in which littoral societies in Africa conceptualised the sea and the beach, whales and the men who hunted them, I have tried to convey something of the presence of many voices and, with them, of the possibility of alternative meanings. It is for the further pursuit of such possibilities that, I hope, the present study will have prepared the ground.

Fig. 43:
Source: Scammon, *The Marine Mammals of the North-western Coast of North America*, 80.

Archival Sources

Archives

Archiv- und Museumsstiftung Wuppertal
    Schriftarchiv, Archiv der Rheinischen Mission
British Library, London
    India Office Records
    Newspaper Collections
Brown University Library
    John Hay Library, Manuscript Collections, Carleton D. Morse whaling collection
Cold Spring Harbor Whaling Museum
Houghton Library
Martha's Vineyard Museum, Edgartown
    Gale Huntington Research Library
Mystic Seaport
    G.W. Blunt White Library, Manuscript Collection
Nantucket Atheneum
    Whaling journals
Nantucket Historical Association
    Research Library, Manuscript Collections
The National Archives, London
    Foreign Office Records
National Archives and Records Administration, Washington, D.C./College Park
    Records of Foreign Service Posts, Record Group 84
National Maritime Museum, London
    Caird Archive and Library
New Bedford Free Public Library
    Newspapers
    Whaling Collection Archives
New Bedford Whaling Museum
    Manuscript Collections
    Whaling logbooks and journals
Peabody Essex Museum, Salem
    Phillips Library, Manuscript Collections
Providence Public Library
    Nicholson Whaling Manuscript Collection
Rhode Island Historical Society, Providence
    Manuscript Collections
School of Oriental and African Studies, London
    Library, Archives & Special Collections, CWM/LMS/South Africa Journals

Logbooks

For the sake of convenience, all logbooks consulted for this study are listed here in alphabetic order, with their respective authors (if known) in second position. References to this list are marked "Log" in the footnotes to the main text.

Abigail, 1856–1860. Mystic Seaport, G.W. Blunt White Library, Manuscript Collection: Log 845.
Adeline, 1840–1842. New Bedford Whaling Museum, Whaling logbooks and journals: KWM 046.
Adeline Gibbs, 1875–1878. New Bedford Whaling Museum, Whaling logbooks and journals: KWM 0006.
Admiral Blake, 1869–1870. William Robinson. Providence Public Library, Nicholson Whaling Manuscript Collection: Wh A238 1869L.
Alexander Barclay, 1837–1839. Martha's Vineyard Museum, Gale Huntington Research Library: Book 8.
Alto, 1854–1857. Angles Snell. New Bedford Whaling Museum, Whaling logbooks and journals: KWM 0014.
Ann, 1791–1792. Coffin Whippey. Nantucket Historical Association, Research Library, Manuscript Collections: Log 9.
Ann Maria, 1835–1837. Mystic Seaport, G.W. Blunt White Library, Manuscript Collection: OLog 3.
Ann Parry, 1845–1847. Phillips Library, Peabody Essex Museum, Manuscript Collections: 656 1845A.
A. R. Tucker, 1857–1861. G. W. Beebe. New Bedford Free Public Library, Whaling Collection Archives.
Arab, 1838–1840. New Bedford Whaling Museum, Whaling logbooks and jour- nals: ODHS 0380A.
Arab, 1849–1852. Samuel T. Braley. New Bedford Whaling Museum, Whaling logbooks and journals: KWM 0255.
Argo, 1808–1811. Charles Gardner. Nantucket Atheneum, Whaling journals: Log 11.
Arthur V. Woodruff, 1917–1920. New Bedford Whaling Museum, Whaling logbooks and journals: KWM 0521.
Asia, 1791–1794. Sylvanus Crosby. Nantucket Historical Association, Research Library, Manuscript Collections: LOG 335 Negative R54.
Atlantic, 1868–1872. New Bedford Free Public Library, Whaling Collection Archives.
Atlantic, 1876–1879. New Bedford Free Public Library, Whaling Collection Archives.
Averick, 1834–1836. Humphrey Shearman. New Bedford Whaling Museum, Whaling logbooks and journals: KWM 0024.
Avola, 1867–1870. Andrew C. Briggs. New Bedford Whaling Museum, Whaling logbooks and journals: KWM 0025.
Avola, 1874–1877. Thomas Morrison. New Bedford Whaling Museum, Whaling logbooks and journals: KWM 0026.
Bertha, 1878–1881. Providence Public Library, Nicholson Whaling Manuscript Collection: Wh B538 1878L.
Bertha, 1883–1887. Benjamin D. Cleveland. New Bedford Whaling Museum, Whaling logbooks and journals: KWM 0229.

Boston Packet, 1794–1795. Hezekiah Pinkham. Nantucket Historical Association, Research Library, Manuscript Collections: Reel 27, Copy 1.
Brewster, 1857–1860. G. W. Blunt White Library, Mystic Seaport Museum, Manuscript Collection: Log 73.
Brewster,1860–1863. Mystic Seaport, G.W. Blunt White Library, Manuscript Collection: Log 91.
Brunswick, 1856–1859. New Bedford Whaling Museum, Whaling logbooks and journals: KWM 0473.
Callao, 1875–1875. New Bedford Free Public Library, Whaling Collection Archives.
Ceres, 1838–1839. Stephen Peirce. Mystic Seaport G.W. Blunt White Library, Manuscript Collection: Log 90.
Ceres II, 1835–1837. New Bedford Whaling Museum, Whaling logbooks and journals: KWM 0047.
Charles Carroll, 1840–1843. Charles Gilchrest. Nantucket Historical Association, Research Library, Manuscript Collections: LOG 359.
Charles Colgate, 1863–1865. Mystic Seaport, G.W. Blunt White Library, Manuscript Collection: Coll. 25 vol. 109.
Charles W. Morgan, 1878–1881. New Bedford Free Public Library, Whaling Collection Archives.
Charles W. Morse, 1887–1890. New Bedford Whaling Museum, Whaling logbooks and journals: KWM 0048.
Cicero, 1874–1875. New Bedford Whaling Museum, Whaling logbooks and journals: KWM 0840.
Clarice, 1878–1882. Daniel A. Anthony & B. D. Cleveland. Providence Public Library, Nicholson Whaling Manuscript Collection: Wh C5915 1878L.
Clarkson, 1838–1842. Joseph C. Chase. Nantucket Historical Association, Research Library, Manuscript Collections: LOG 41.
Columbia,1846–1850. Joseph C. Chase. Nantucket Historical Association, Research Library, Manuscript Collections: LOG 43.
Desdemona, 1865–1869. Peleg Lawrence. New Bedford Whaling Museum, Whaling logbooks and journals: KWM 0068.
Desdemona, 1869–1872. New Bedford Whaling Museum, Whaling logbooks and journals: KWM 0069.
Desdemona, 1873–1876. New Bedford Whaling Museum, Whaling logbooks and journals: KWM 0070.
Desdemona, 1876–1879. Providence Public Library, Nicholson Whaling Manuscript Collection: Wh D449 1876L.
Dimon, 1845–1848. New Bedford Free Public Library, Whaling Collection Archives.
Draco, 1868–1871. Andrew M. Braley. New Bedford Whaling Museum, Whaling logbooks and journals: ODHS 0831.
Eliza Adams, 1883–1887. New Bedford Whaling Museum, Whaling logbooks and journals: KWM 0075.
Emerald, 1838–1840. William H. Nichols. Peabody Essex Museum, Phillips Library, Manuscript Collections: 656 1838E2.
Eugenia, 1855–1858. New Bedford Free Public Library, Whaling Collection Archives.
Falcon, 1865–1867. New Bedford Whaling Museum, Whaling logbooks and journals: ODHS 0905.
Falcon, 1879–1882. Lysander Gallt. New Bedford Whaling Museum, Whaling logbooks and journals: KWM 0087.
Falcon, 1887–1890. New Bedford Whaling Museum, Whaling logbooks and journals: KWM 0088.

Forrester, 1844–1845. William Thomas. Mystic Seaport, G.W. Blunt White Library, Manuscript Collection: Log 508.
Frances II, 1831–1832. Charles Pierce & Jedidiah Whipshield. New Bedford Whaling Museum, Whaling logbooks and journals: KWM 0090.
Gazelle, 1863–1866. Frederick H. Lawrence. New Bedford Whaling Museum, Whaling logbooks and journals: KWM 0716.
General Scott, 1875–1878. New Bedford Whaling Museum, Whaling log- books and journals: ODHS 0210.
George and Mary, 1877–1879. New Bedford Whaling Museum, Whaling logbooks and journals: ODHS 0502.
George and Susan, 1865–1868. New Bedford Free Public Library, Whaling Collection Archives.
George Washinton, 1848–1849. Mystic Seaport, G.W. Blunt White Library, Manuscript Collection: Log 1032.
Georgia, 1832–1833. Gaosynor B. Gates. Mystic Seaport, G.W. Blunt White Library, Manuscript Collection: Log 1022.
Georgia, 1835–1837. G. W. Blunt White Library, Mystic Seaport Museum, Manuscript Collection: OLog 16.
Gertrude Howes, 1867–1869. Peabody Essex Museum, Phillips Library, Manuscript Collections: LOG 1867G2, B23 F1.
Globe, 1855–1857. Mystic Seaport, G.W. Blunt White Library, Manuscript Collection: Log 80.
Globe, 1858–1861. Providence Public Library, Nicholson Whaling Manuscript Collection: Wh G562 1858L.
Globe, 1869–1872. John Coguin. New Bedford Whaling Museum, Whaling logbooks and journals: ODHS 0255.
Governor Carver, 1854–1857. Nantucket Historical Association, Manuscript Collections: LOG 237.
Grand Turk, 1834–1836. David H. Bartlett. New Bedford Whaling Museum, Whaling logbooks and journals: ODHS 0327.
Harrison, 1854–1857. Samuel T. Braley. New Bedford Whaling Museum, Whaling logbooks and journals: KWM 0261.
Hercules II, 1834–1836. New Bedford Free Public Library, Whaling Collection Archives.
Hibernia, 1842–1843. Pardon Tripp. New Bedford Free Public Library, Whaling Collection Archives.
Hudson, 1833–1835. Henry Green. Mystic Seaport, G.W. Blunt White Library, Manuscript Collection: Log 209.
Islander, 1871–1873. New Bedford Whaling Museum, Whaling logbooks and journals: KWM 0113.
Israel, 1841–1842. Stephen Peirce. Mystic Seaport, G.W. Blunt White Library, Manuscript Collection: Log 90.
Izette, 1841–1842. Phillips Library, Peabody Essex Museum, Manuscript Collections: LOG 1831I2.
Janet, 1877–1879. Henry M. King. Mystic Seaport, G.W. Blunt White Library, Manuscript Collection: Log 843.
Janus, 1833–1835. John Swift. New Bedford Whaling Museum, Whaling logbooks and journals: ODHS 0391A.
Janus, 1835–1837. John Swift. New Bedford Whaling Museum, Whaling logbooks and journals: ODHS 0391B.

Janus, 1837–1839. Mystic Seaport, G.W. Blunt White Library, Manuscript Collection: Log 225.
Janus, 1862–1865. John C. Silvester. Providence Public Library, Nicholson Whaling Manuscript Collection: Wh J35 1862L.
John & Edward, 1855–1858. Martha's Vineyard Museum, Gale Huntington Research Library: Book 98.
John Dawson, 1867–1870. Abram Gifford. New Bedford Whaling Museum, Whaling logbooks and journals: KWM 0120.
John Dawson, 1870–1872. New Bedford Free Public Library, Whaling Collection Archives.
Josephine, 1903–1905. Horace P. Smith. New Bedford Whaling Museum, Whaling logbooks and journals: ODHS 0633A.
Josephine, 1905–1907. Horace P. Smith. New Bedford Whaling Museum, Whaling logbooks and journals: ODHS 0633B.
Kathleen, 1852–1855. New Bedford Whaling Museum, Whaling logbooks and journals: KWM 0125.
Kathleen, 1875–1879. New Bedford Free Public Library, Whaling Collection Archives.
Kathleen, 1880–1884. New Bedford Free Public Library, Whaling Collection Archives.
Keoka, 1858–1860. Charles D. Baker. New Bedford Whaling Museum, Whaling logbooks and journals, ODHS 0344.
Kingston, 1800–1801. Thomas Dennis. New Bedford Whaling Museum, Whaling logbooks and journals: KWM 0263.
Lancer, 20.04.1869–25.04.1873. Collins. New Bedford Whaling Museum, Whaling logbooks and journals: KWM 0265.
Leonidas, 1837–1839. Providence Public Library, Nicholson Whaling Manuscript Collection: Wh L5852 1837L.
Leonidas, 1855–1857. New Bedford Free Public Library, Whaling Collection Archives.
Leonidas, 1860–1863. J. Chase. New Bedford Free Public Library, Whaling Collection Archives.
Leviathan, 1800–1801. Charles Gardner. Nantucket Historical Association, Research Library, Manuscript Collections: LOG 241.
Louisa Sears, 1856–1858. Edward C. Luce. Mystic Seaport, G.W. Blunt White Library, Manuscript Collection: Log 832.
Malay, 1837–1839. Peabody Essex Museum, Phillips Library, Manuscript Collections: LOG 1837M.
Marcella, 1858–1861. Benjamin Ellis. Bedford Whaling Museum, Whaling logbooks and journals: ODHS 0175.
Marcella, 1873–1876. Henry W. Brigham. New Bedford Whaling Museum, Whaling logbooks and journals: KWM 0134.
Maria, 1846–1849. Charles C. Mooers. Nantucket Historical Association, Manuscript Collections: LOG 152.
Uss Marion, 1858–1860. Henry Eason. Mystic Seaport G.W. Blunt White Library, Manuscript Collection: Log 902.
Mars, 1856–1859. New Bedford Whaling Museum, Whaling logbooks and journals: KWM 0137.
Mattapoisett, 1851–1851. Isaac W. Macomber. New Bedford Whaling Museum, Whaling logbooks and journals: ODHS 1121A.
Mercury, 1873–1876. John A. Vieira. New Bedford Whaling Museum, Whaling logbooks and journals: KWM 0361.

Merlin, 1881–1882. George F. Allen. New Bedford Whaling Museum, Whaling logbooks and journals: ODHS 0755.
Mermaid, 1883–1890. James H. Sherman. New Bedford Whaling Museum, Whaling logbooks and journals: KWM 0142.
Mermaid, 1887–1890. James H. Sherman. New Bedford Whaling Museum, Whaling logbooks and journals: KWM 0142.
Miles, 1839–1841. Martha's Vineyard Museum, Gale Huntington Research Library: Book 100.
Minerva, 1825–1827. Henry B. Gifford. Nantucket Historical Association Research Library, Manuscript Collections: LOG 184.
Montezuma, 1846–1849. Prince Lawton. New Bedford Whaling Museum, Whaling logbooks and journals: KWM 0148.
Montgomery, 1855–1858. New Bedford Free Public Library, Whaling Collection Archives.
Morning Star, 1883–1888. New Bedford Free Public Library, Whaling Collection Archives.
Navigator, 1849–1854. Nantucket Historical Association, Research Library, Manuscript Collections: LOG 162.
North America, 1797–1799. Charles Gardner. Nantucket Historical Association, Research Library, Manuscript Collections: LOG 128.
Nye, 1853–1856. John W. Howland, Jr. New Bedford Whaling Museum, Whaling logbooks and journals: KWM 0160.
Ocean Rover, 1859–1862. New Bedford Whaling Museum, Whaling logbooks and journals: ODHS 0376A.
Octavia, 1837–1839, Providence Public Library, Nicholson Whaling Manuscript Collection: Wh O21 1837L.
Ohio, 1862–1854. Andrew Hillman. New Bedford Whaling Museum, Whaling logbooks and journals: ODHS 0020.
Osceola II, 1857–1859. New Bedford Free Public Library, Whaling Collection Archives.
Ospray, 1871–1874. New Bedford Free Public Library, Whaling Collection Archives.
Palestine, 1839–1842. Phillips Library, Peabody Essex Museum, Manuscript Collections: LOG 1839P.
Palmetto, 1872–1875. New Bedford Free Public Library, Whaling Collection Archives.
Para, 1867–1871. George H. Folger. Peabody Essex Museum, Phillips Library, Manuscript Collections: 656 1867P.
Pavilion, 1858–1860. Elbridge A. Adams. Martha's Vineyard Museum, Gale Huntington Research Library: Book 15.
Pedro Varela, 1878–1880. New Bedford Whaling Museum, Whaling logbooks and journals: KWM 0761.
Pedro Varela, 1881–1883. Annie H. Ricketson. New Bedford Whaling Museum, Whaling logbooks and journals: KWM 0167.
Penobscot, 1843–1845. Oliver C. Spencer. Nantucket Historical Association, Manuscript Collections: LOG 201.
Petrel, 1874–1877. Martha's Vineyard Museum, Gale Huntington Research Library: Book 12.
Platina, 1882–1886. New Bedford Free Public Library, Whaling Collection Archives.
Plato, 1833–1834. New Bedford Whaling Museum, Whaling logbooks and journals: KWM 0215.
Polley, 1774–1775. Samuel Atkins. Providence Public Library, Nicholson Whaling Manuscript Collection: Wh P773 1774j.

Uss Portsmouth, 1850–1851. New Bedford Whaling Museum, Whaling logbooks and journals: ODHS 0123.
President II, 1862–1864. New Bedford Free Public Library, Whaling Collection Archives.
Reaper, 1835–1837. Benjamin Neal. Phillips Library, Peabody Essex Museum, Manuscript Collections: 656 1835R.
Reaper, 1837–1839. Benjamin Neal. Peabody Essex Museum, Phillips Library, Manuscript Collections: 656 1837R3.
S. R. Soper, 1865–1866. Caleb F. Hunt. New Bedford Whaling Museum, Whaling logbooks and journals: KWM 0188.
Samuel & Thomas, 1846–1848. Joseph B. Hersey. New Bedford Whaling Museum, Whaling logbooks and journals: KWM 0364.
Sarah, 1873–1876. New Bedford Whaling Museum, Whaling logbooks and journals: KWM 0266.
Sea Fox, 1871–73. New Bedford Whaling Museum, Whaling logbooks and journals: KWM 0183.
Smyrna, 1853–1857. George Bliss. Providence Public Library, Nicholson Whaling Manuscript Collection: Wh S667 1853j.
South Carolina, 1835–1837. William W. Taylor. New Bedford Whaling Museum, Whaling logbooks and journals: KWM 0411.
Splendid, 1858–1862. New Bedford Free Public Library, Whaling Collection Archives.
Stephania, 1847–1850. New Bedford Whaling Museum, Whaling logbooks and journals: KWM 0130.
Sullivan, 1905–1907. William C. Hegarty. New Bedford Whaling Museum, Whaling logbooks and journals: KWM 0469.
Sunbeam, 1878–1882. Frederick P. Taber. New Bedford Free Public Library, Whaling Collection Archives.
Sunbeam, 1882–1886. New Bedford Free Public Library, Whaling Collection Archives.
Thomas pope, 1859–1862. New Bedford Whaling Museum, Whaling logbooks and journals: KWM 0091.
Triton, 1868–1871. Robert G. Brightman. New Bedford Whaling Museum, Whaling logbooks and journals: ODHS 0252.
Two Brothers, 1832–1833. New Bedford Free Public Library, Whaling Collection Archives.
Union, 1795–1796. Nantucket Historical Association, Research Library, Manuscript Collections: LOG 9.
Union, 1796. Nantucket Historical Association, Research Library, Manuscript Collections: LOG 9.
United States, 1846–1849. Joseph E. Smith. New Bedford Whaling Museum, Whaling logbooks and journals: ODHS 0517.
U.S.S. Marion, 1858–1860. Henry Eason. Mystic Seaport, G.W. Blunt White Library, Manuscript Collection: Log 902.
Vesta, 1845–1846. Horatio W. Tilton. Mystic Seaport, G.W. Blunt White Library, Manuscript Collection: Log 846.
Washington Freeman, 1868–1870. Severine D. Pierce. New Bedford Whaling Museum, Whaling logbooks and journals: ODHS 0102
Wave, 1869–1870. Henry M. Hall. New Bedford Whaling Museum, Whaling logbooks and journals: KWM 0543.
William Badger, 1845–1849. H. M. Bonney. G. W. Blunt White Library, Mystic Seaport Museum, Manuscript Collection: Log 34.
William Lee, 1850–1851. Nicholas C. Anthony. Manuscripts Collection, G. W. Blunt White Library, Mystic Seaport Museum, Log 37.

Diaries

The diaries and journals of seamen consulted for this study are listed alphabetically by author, the names usually – unlike in the case of many logbooks – being known. References to this list are marked "Journal" in the footnotes to the main text.

Allen, Charles F. Journal on the Bark GLOBE of New Bedford, 06.03.1869– 21.05.1872. Providence Public Library, Nicholson Whaling Manuscript Collection: Wh G562 1869j.
Allen, Harriet C. Diary, 23.06.1868–12.04.1872. New Bedford Whaling Museum, Whaling logbooks and journals: KWM 0401.
Allen, Harriet C. Diary, "When I Was Seven." New Bedford Whaling Museum, Whaling logbooks and journals: KWM 402A.
Allen, Harriet C. Diary, "When I Went a-Whaling." New Bedford Whaling Museum, Whaling logbooks and journals: KWM 402B.
Allen, Helen C. Diary, 01.01.1871–12.04.1872. New Bedford Whaling Museum, Whaling logbooks and journals: KWM 0402.
Brock, Eliza. Journal LEXINGTON, 1853–1856. Nantucket Historical Association, Research Library, Manuscript Collections: LOG 136.
Brott, Lucien A. Journal YOUNG PHENIX, 06.11.1867–19.04.1871. New Bedford Whaling Museum, Whaling logbooks and journals: ODHS 1156.
Gardiner, A. W. Journal to India, 1819. Houghton Library.
Harris, George O. Journal of a Voyage to the East of the Cape of Good Hope, 18.02.1832–06.06.1833. Phillips Library, Peabody Essex Museum, Manuscript Collections: Acc 2005.014.
Leek, Smith W. "Smith Leek's Book. A Small Journal of his Life and Transactions of Whale in the Ship 'Delta' from July 21st, 1836, to April 16th, 1838." Mystic Seaport, G.W. Blunt White Library, Manuscript Collection: RF 579.
Lewis, Theodore. Journal ATLANTIC, 1835–1837. Mystic Seaport, G.W. Blunt White Library, Manuscript Collection: Log 822.
Look, Hiram W. Journal CHARLES W. MORGAN, 1871–1874. Mystic Seaport, G.W. Blunt White Library, Manuscript Collection: Log 409.
O'Keeffe, Thomas. Journal GRAND TURK, 1836–1841. Providence Public Library, Nicholson Whaling Manuscript Collection: Wh G751 1836jo.
Owen, Robert "Diary 1837, 1838, 1839, 1840 of a Whaling Voyage to the Eastward in the Ship Harrena, 05.04.1837–12.02.1840." New Bedford Whaling Museum, Whaling logbooks and journals: KWM 0098.
Palmer, Horace L. The Diary of a Foremast Hand on the First Voyage of the Bark Wanderer – Whaler of New Bedford, 1878–1880. New Bedford Whaling Museum, Whaling logbooks and journals: ODHS 0409.
Phillips, Harvey R. My Journal in the ADMIRAL BLAKE, 04.12.1868–18.11.1870. New Bedford Whaling Museum, Whaling logbooks and journals: KWM 0007.
Ricketson, Annie H. Journal of Annie Holmes Ricketson, 1885. New Bedford Whaling Museum, Whaling logbooks and journals: KWM 0168.
Smith, Lucy P. Journal on the Bark NAUTILUS, 06.10.1869–21.05.1874. Providence Public Library, Nicholson Whaling Manuscript Collection: Wh N3145 1869j.

Stewart, Charles J. Journal Aboard the Brig JOHN H. JONES of Cold Spring Harbor: New York to Liberia and Return, 1861–62. Cold Spring Harbor Whaling Museum.
Tobey, Asa Journal HOUQUA, 1835–1837. Providence Public Library, Nicholson Whaling Manuscript Collection: Wh H774 1835j.
Tobey, Asa Journal ROSCOE, 1846–1849. Providence Public Library, Nicholson Whaling Manuscript Collection: Wh R793 1846j.
Wallace, R. Journal CLARA BELL, 1855–1858. Mystic Seaport, G.W. Blunt White Library, Manuscript Collection: Log 164.
Whitten, William H. "A Journal of a Whaleing Voyage on Board the Barque Eureka." 1857–1861. Martha's Vineyard Museum, Gale Huntington Research Library: Book 69.
Wing, Frederick A. Journal MATTAPOISETT, 07.06.1849–01.12.1853. Providence Public Library, Nicholson Whaling Manuscript Collection: Wh M435 1849j.
Winslow, John. Journal WAVE, 1851–1854. Providence Public Library, Nicholson Whaling Manuscript Collection: Wh W355 1851j.

Newspapers

Columbian Courier, or Weekly Miscellany (New Bedford)
The Commercial Gazette (Port Louis)
Illustrated Australian News (Melbourne)
Lloyd's List (London)
The London Gazette
The Medley, or, Newbedford Marine Journal
The Mercantile Record (Port Louis)
New-Bedford Daily Mercury
New-Bedford Mercury
The New York Times
The Republican Standard (New Bedford)
The St. Helena Chronicle (Jamestown)
The St. Helena Herald (Jamestown)
Whalemen's Shipping List and Merchants' Transcript (New Bedford)

Published Sources

Alexander, James E. *An Expedition of Discovery into the Interior of Africa, Through the Hitherto Undescribed Countries of the Great Namaquas, Boschmans, and Hill Damaras.* 2 Vols. London: Colburn, 1838.
Allen, William, and Thomas R.H. Thomson. *A Narrative of the Expedition Sent by Her Majesty's Government to the Niger River in 1841.* 2 Vols. London: Bentley, 1848.
Allyn, Gurdon L. *The Old Sailor's Story: Or, a Short Account of the Life, Adventures and Voyages of Capt. Gurdon L. Allyn, Including Three Trips Around the World.* Norwich: Gordon Wilcox, 1879.
Almada, Francisco Vaz, de. "Treatise of the Misfortune that befell the Great Ship 'São João Baptista', 1622." In *The Tragic History of the Sea, 1589–1622: Narratives of the Shipwrecks of the Portuguese East indiamen São Thomé (1589), Santo Alberto (1593), São João Baptista (1622), and the Journeys of the Survivors in South East Africa*, edited by Charles R. Boxer, 189–271. Cambridge: Cambridge UP, 1959.
Anderson, John. *Descriptive Account of Mauritius: Its Scenery, Statistics &c with Brief Historical Sketch.* Mauritius: L. A. Denny, 1858.
Andersson, Charles J. *Lake Ngami; or, Explorations and Discoveries During Four Years' Wanderings in the Wilds of Southwestern Africa.* London: Hurst & Blackett, 1856.
Andersson, Charles J. *The Okavango River: A Narrative of Travel, Exploration and Adventure.* New York: Harper & Bros., 1861.
Andersson, Charles J. *Trade and Politics in Central Namibia 1860–1864: Diaries and Correspondence of Charles John Andersson.* Edited by Brigitte Lau. Windhoek: National Archives, 1989.
Ashley, Clifford W. *The Yankee Whaler.* 1926. New York: Dover Publications, 1991.
Backhouse, James. *A Narrative of a Visit to the Mauritius and South Africa.* London: Hamilton, Adams & Co., 1844
Barbosa, Duarte. *A Description of the Coasts of East Africa and Malabar in the Beginning of the Sixteenth Century.* London: Hakluyt Soc., 1866.
Barbosa, Jorge. *Obra Poética.* Lisbon: Imprensa Nacional – Casa da Moeda, 2002.
Barbot, James, and John Casseneuve. "A Voyage to Congo River." In *A Description of the Coasts of North and South-Guinea; and of Ethopia Inferior, vulgarly: Angola: Being a New Account of the Western Maritime Countries of Africa.* Vol. 5. Edited by John Barbot, 497–522. London: Churchill, 1732.
Barker, George. *Thrilling Adventures of the Whaler Alcyone: Killing Man-eating Sharks in the Indian Ocean, Hunting Kangaroos in Australia.* Boston: Tudor Press, 1916.
Barnard, Frederick L. *A Three Years' Cruise in the Mozambique Channel, for the Suppression of the Slave Trade.* London: Richard Bentley, 1848.
Barrena, Natalio. "La Isla de Annobón: Un Paso para su Conocimiento." *La Guinea Española* 25.08.1909: 130–1.
Barros, João, de. "Extracts from 'Da Asia'". In *Records of South-Eastern Africa.* Vol. 6. Edited by George M. Theal, 1–306. Kapstadt: Government of the Cape Colony, 1900.
Bastian, Adolf. *Afrikanische Reisen: Ein Besuch in San Salvador, der Hauptstadt des Königreichs Kongo, Ein Beitrag zur Mythologie und Psychologie.* Bremen: Strack, 1859.

Beane, Joshua F. *From Forecastle to Cabin: The Story of a Cruise in Many Seas, Taken from a Journal Kept each Day, wherein Was Recorded the Happenings of a Voyage around the World in Pursuit of Whales*. New York: Editor Pub. Co., 1905.

Berichte der Rheinischen Missions-Gesellschaft. Volume 1879. Barmen.

Bernardin de Saint-Pierre, Jacques-Henri. "Letters to a Friend." In *Travellers: Classic Journals & Accounts of Travellers to Mauritius*, 13–26. Grand Baie: Christian le Comte, 2008.

Bernardin de Saint-Pierre. *Paul et Virgine*. Edited by Pierre Trahard. Paris: Garnier, 1964.

Bird, John, ed. *The Annals of Natal: 1495 to 1845*. 2 Vols. Kapstadt: Struik, 1965.

Boteler, Thomas. *Narrative of a Voyage of Discovery to Africa and Arabia, Performed by His Majesty's Ships Leven and Barracouta, from 1821 to 1826, under the Command of Capt. F. W. Owen, R. N.* 2 Vols. London: Richard Bentley, 1835.

Bovill, John H. *Natives under the Transvaal Flag*. London: Simkin/Marshall/Hamilton/Kent, 1900.

Brecht, Bertolt. *Collected Plays: Three*. Edited by John Willett. London/New York: Bloomsbury, 1997.

Bridge, Horatio. *Journal of an African Cruiser Comprising Sketches of the Canaries, the Cape de Verds, Liberia, Madeira, Sierra Leone, and other Places of Interest on the West Coast of Africa*. New York/London: Wiley and Putnam, 1845.

Brito, Bernardo Gomes, de. "The Wreck of the Galleon 'São João' on the Coast of Natal in the Year 1552." In *East Africa*, edited by Malyn D. D. Newitt, 99–113. Burlington: Ashgate, 2002.

Browne, John R. *Etchings of a Whaling Cruise: And History of the Whale Fishery, with Notes on a Sojourn on the Island of Zanzibar*. London, New York: Harper, 1846.

Browne, John R. *J. Ross Browne: His Letters, Journals and Writings*. Edited by Lina Fergusson Browne. Albuquerque: U of New Mexico P, 1969.

Browne, John R. "Sketches of the Arabs." *New-Bedford Mercury* 12.01.1844: 4.

Buchan, George. *A Narrative of the Loss of the Winterton, on Her Passage to India, the 20th of August 1792, on a Reef of Rocks off the Island of Madagascar. With the Names of the Passengers & Officers that Were Saved and Lost*. London: C. Whittingham, 1820.

Burke, Edmund. *The Writings and Speeches of Edmund Burke, Vol. III: Party, Parliament, and the American War, 1774–1780*. Edited by Warren M. Elofson and John A. Woods. Oxford: Clarendon Press, 1996.

Burns, Walter N. *A Year With a Whaler*. New York: Outing Publishing, 1913.

Carreira, António, ed. *Descrições oitocentistas das Ilhas de Cabo Verde*. Lissabon 1987.

Cécille, Jean-Baptiste. "Bericht des Kommandanten Cécille über die Fahrt der Korvette l'Héroïne." *Die ältesten Reiseberichte über Deutsch-Südwestafrika: Schluss*. Translated and edited by Eduard Moritz. Mitteilungen aus den deutschen Schutzgebieten 31 (1918): 138–43.

Chapman, James. *Travels in the Interior of South Africa, Comprising Fifteen Years' Hunting and Trading; with Journeys across the Continent from Natal to Walvis Bay, and Visits to Lake Ngami and the Victoria Falls*. 2 Vols. Kapstadt: Balkema, 1971.

Chase, Owen. *Narrative of the Most Extraordinary and Distressing Shipwreck of the Whale-Ship Essex, of Nantucket, Which Was Attacked and Finally Destroyed by a Large Spermaceti-Whale, in the Pacific Ocean; with an Account of the Unparalleled Sufferings of the Captain and Crew During a Space of Ninety-Three Days at Sea, in Open Boats, in the Years 1819 & 1820*. New York: W. B. Gilley, 1821.

Chippendale, Harry A. *Sails and Whales*. Cambridge: Riverside Press, 1951.

Choyce, James. *The Log of a Jack Tar*. 1891. Maidstone: G. Mann, 1973.

Comstock, William. *The Life of Samuel Comstock, the Terrible Whaleman: Containing an Account of the Mutiny, and Massacre of the Officers of the Ship Globe, of Nantucket, with

His Subsequent Adventures, and His Being Shot at the Mulgrave Islands, also, Lieutenant Percival's Voyage in Search of the Survivors. Boston: J. Fisher, 1840.

Couto, Diogo, do. "Narrative of the Shipwreck of the Great Ship 'São Thomé', in the Land of Fumos, in the Year 1589." In *The Tragic History of the Sea, 1589–1622: Narratives of the Shipwrecks of the Portuguese East indiamen São Thomé (1589), Santo Alberto (1593), São João Baptista (1622), and the Journeys of the Survivors in South East Africa*, edited by Charles R. Boxer, 53–104. Cambridge: Cambridge UP, 1959.

Dana, Richard H. *Two Years Before the Mast. A Personal Narrative of Life at Sea*. New York: Harper, 1840.

Darwin, Charles. *Journal of Researches into the Natural History and Geology of the Countries Visited during the Voyage of H.M.S. Beagle round the World*. New York: D. Appleton & Co., 1878.

Davoll, Edward S. *The Captain's Specific Orders on the Commencement of a Whale Voyage to his Officers and Crew*. Old Dartmouth Historical Sketch 81. New Bedford: Old Dartmouth Historical Society, 1981.

Defoe, Daniel. *Second Thoughts are Best: Or a Further Improvement of a Late Scheme to Prevent Street Robberies*. London: W. Meadows, 1729.

Dennett, Richard E. *Seven Years Among the Fjort: Being an English Trader's Experiences in the Congo District*. London: S. Low, Marston, Scarle, & Rivington, 1887.

Devereux, William C. *A Cruise in the "Gorgon", or, Eighteen Months on H. M. S. "Gorgon", Engaged in the Suppression of the Slave Trade on the East Coast of Africa*. London: Bell and Daldy, 1869.

Doce, Epifanio. "Efemérides Annobonesas." *La Guinea Española* 10.11.1947: 418–20.

Doce, Epifanio. "Noticias de la Colonia: de Annobón." *La Guinea Española* 29.03.1936: 102–3.

Doce, Epifanio. "Pequeña Tragedia en la Pesca de la Ballena." *La Guinea Española* 10.09.1949: 447–9.

Duminy, François R. *Duminy-dagboeke – Duminy Diaries*. Edited by Johan L. Franken. Kapstadt: Die Van Riebeeck-vereniging, 1938.

Een, Thure G. *Memories of Several Years in South-western Africa, 1866–1871*. Windhoek: Namibia Scientific Society, 2004.

Eldridge, Lewis W. *Lewis William Eldridge's Whaling Voyage*. New Bedford: Reynolds Printing, 1939.

Ellis, Alfred B. *West African Islands*. London: Chapman and Hall, 1885.

Ely, Ben E. S. *There She Blows: A Narrative of a Whaling Voyage in the Indian and South Atlantic Oceans*. Middletown: Wesleyan UP, 1971.

Emerson, Ralph W. "From Journals." In *American Sea Writing: A Literary Anthology*, edited by Peter Neill, 118–27. New York: Library of America, 2000.

Emmerton, Ephraim A. "A Visit to Eastern Africa, 1843–1844." In *New England Merchants in Africa: A History Through Documents, 1802 to 1865*, edited by Norman R. Bennett and George E. Brooks, 258–9. Boston: Boston UP, 1965.

Enderby, Charles. *Proposal for Re-establishing the British Southern Whale Fishery through the Medium of a Chartered Company, and in Combination with the Colonisation of the Auckland Islands, as the Site of the Company's Whaling Station*. Third Edition. London: E. Wilson, 1847.

"Extractos da Relação do Naufragio da nao 'Santiago'." In *Records of South-Eastern Africa*. Vol. 1. Edited by George M. Theal, 330–42. Kapstadt: Government of the Cape Colony, 1898.

Ferguson, Robert. *Harpooner: A Four-year Voyage on the Barque Kathleen, 1880–1884*. Philadelphia: U of Pennsylvania P, 1936.
Freycinet, Rose Marie Pinon, de. *Briefe von der Uranie: Tagebuch einer Reise um die Welt, geschrieben 1817 bis 1820*. Edited by Michael Uszinski. Berlin: Verl. der Pioniere, 2011.
Fynn, Henry F. *The Diary of Henry Francis Fynn*. Edited by James Stuart and D. McK. Malcolm. Pietermaritzburg: Shuter and Shooter, 1969.
Galton, Francis. *The Narrative of an Explorer in Tropical South Africa*. London: John Murray, 1853.
Gardner, Edmund. *Captain Edmund Gardner of Nantucket and New Bedford: His Journal and His Family*. Edited by John M. Bullard. New Bedford: Bullard, 1958.
Gibson, Thomas M. et al. *First Report from the Select Committee on Navigation Laws; together with the Minutes of Evidence Taken before them*. House of Commons Papers, Reports of Committees 232, 1847.
Goodridge, Charles M. *Narrative of a Voyage to the South Seas*. London: Hamilton & Adams, 1832.
Grant, Gordon. *Greasy Luck: A Whaling Sketchbook*. Mineola: Dover Publications, 2004.
Hahn, Carl H. *Carl Hugo Hahn Tagebücher 1837–1860/Diaries: A Missionary in Nama- and Damaraland*. Edited by Brigitte Lau. 4 Vols. Windhoek: Dep. of National Education, 1984/1985.
Hahn, Emma S. *The Letters of Emma Sarah Hahn: Pioneer Missionary among the Herero*. Edited by Dorothy Guedes and Peter Reiner. Windhoek: Namibia Scientific Society, 1993.
Haley, Nelson C. *Whale Hunt: The Narrative of a Voyage by Nelson Cole Haley, Harpooner in the Ship Charles W. Morgan, 1849–1853*. New York: Ives Washburn, 1948.
Hall, Elton W., ed. *Sperm Whaling from New Bedford: Clifford W. Ashley's Photographs of Bark Sunbeam in 1904*. New Bedford: Old Dartmouth Historical Society, 1982.
Hammond, Walter. *Mutiny on the Pedro Valera: The Adventures of a Twentieth Century Whaleman*. Mystic: The Marine Historical Association, 1956.
Hart, Joseph C. *Miriam Coffin: Or, the Whale-Fisherman; a Tale*. New York: G. & C. & H. Carvill, 1834.
Hatfield, Edwin F. *Saint Helena and the Cape of Good Hope, or, Incidents in the Missionary Life of the Rev. James M. Gregor Bertram of St. Helena*. New York: Edward H. Fletcher, 1852.
Hazen, Jacob A. *Five Years Before the Mast, or, Life in the Forecastle Aboard of a Whaler and Man-of-War*. New York: International Book Co., 1853.
Hill, Pascoe G. *Fifty Days on Board a Slave-vessel in the Mozambique* Channel, *in April and May 1843*. New York: J. Winchester, New World Press, 1843.
Hodges, Samuel. "Samuel Hodges to Henry Clay, Sao Tiago, August 22, 1825" In *New England Merchants in Africa: A History Through Documents, 1802 to 1865*, Norman R. Bennett and George E. Brooks, 102–4. Boston: Boston UP, 1965.
Holden, Horace. *A Narrative of the Shipwreck, Captivity and Sufferings of Horace Holden and Benj. H. Nute, who Were Cast Away in the American Ship* Mentor, *on the Pelew* Islands, *in the Year 1832; and for Two Years Afterwards Were Subjected to Unheard of Sufferings Among the Barbarous Inhabitants of Lord North's Island*. Boston: Russell, Shattuck & Co., 1836.
Horsey, Algernon, de. "On the Comoro Islands." *Journal of the Royal Geographical Society of London* 34 (1864): 258–63.
Huddart, Joseph. *The Oriental Navigator: Or, New Directions for Sailing to and from the East Indies, China, New Holland, &c &c. &c.* Second Edition. London: R. Laurie & J. Whittle, 1801.
Hugill, Stan, ed. *Shanties from the Seven Seas: Shipboard Work-songs and Songs Used as Work-songs from the Great Days of Sail*. Second Edition. London et al.: Routledge & Paul, 1984.

Isaacs, Nathaniel. *Travels and Adventures in Eastern* Africa, *Descriptive of the Zoolus*, Their Manners, Customs, etc. etc. with a Sketch of Natal. 2 Vols. London: E. Churton, 1836.
Jarman, Robert E. *Journal of a Voyage to the South Seas, in the "Japan", Employed in the Sperm Whale* Fishery, *Under the Command of Capt. John May*. 1838. Melbourne: Edition Renard, 2009.
Kleinschmidt, Franz H. "Kleinschmidts Aufzeichnungen über Kl. Windhuk und die Damaras, 1843." *Die ältesten Reiseberichte über Deutsch-Südwestafrika, Teil 2: Die Berichte der Rheinischen Mission bis zum Jahre 1846*, edited by Eduard Moritz, 155–70. Windhoek: Namibia Wissenschaftliche Gesellschaft, 2000.
"La Isla de Annobón." *La Guinea Española*, 10.09.1910: 131–2.
Lander, Richard, and John Lander. *Journal of an Expedition to Explore the Course and Termination of the Niger; with a Narrative of a Voyage down that River to its Termination*. 2 Vols. New York: Harper, 1833.
Lavanha, João B. "Shipwreck of the Great Ship 'Santo Alberto', and Itinerary of the People, who Were Saved from it, 1593. 1597." In *The Tragic History of the Sea, 1589–1622: Narratives of the Shipwrecks of the Portuguese East indiamen São Thomé (1589), Santo Alberto (1593), São João Baptista (1622), and the Journeys of the Survivors in South East Africa*, edited Charles R. Boxer, 107–86. Cambridge: Cambridge UP, 1959.
Lay, William, and Cyrus M. Hussey. *A Narrative of the Mutiny, on Board the Ship Globe, of Nantucket, in the Pacific Ocean, Jan. 1824, and the Journal of a Residence of Two Years on the Mulgrave Islands, with Observations on the Manners and Customs of the Inhabitants*. New London: W. Lay & C. M. Hussey, 1828.
Layrle. "Bericht des Schiffsleutnants Layrle über den Walfang im südlichen Atlantischen Ozean." *Die ältesten Reiseberichte über Deutsch-Südwestafrika: Schluss*. Translated and edited by Eduard Moritz. Mitteilungen aus den deutschen Schutzgebieten 31 (1918): 136–8.
Lêdjam, Nánāy-Menemôl. *Cancionero oral Annobonés*. Barcelona: CEIBA, 2008.
Lucas, Fielding, jr. *A General Atlas Containing Distinct Maps of All the Known Countries in the World, Constructed from the Latest Authority*. Baltimore: F. Lucas, 1823.
Lutwyche, Alfred. *A Narrative of the Wreck of the Meridian, on the Island of Amsterdam*. Sydney: Waugh and Cox, 1854.
Lys, W. H. "Letter from W. H. Lys, Esqre., to P. G. Brin, Esqre." In *Records of South-Eastern Africa*. Vol 6. Edited by George M. Theal, 41. Kapstadt: Government of the Cape Colony, 1900.
Marryat, Frank, and Robert E. Branston. *Borneo and the Indian Archipelago: With Drawings of Costume and Scenery*. London: Longman, Brown, Green and Longmans, 1848.
Melville, Herman. "The 'Gees'" In *Great Short Works of Herman Melville*, edited by Warner Berthoff, 355–61. New York: Perennial, 2004.
Milbert, Jacques G. *Voyage Pittoresque a l'Île de France, au Cap De Bonne Espérance et à l'Île de Ténériffe*. Paris: Nepveu, 1812.
Milburn, William. *Oriental Commerce; Containing a Geographical Description of the Principal Places in the East Indies, China, and Japan, with their Produce, Manufactures, and Trade*. London: Black, Parry & co, 1813.
Monteiro, Rose. *Delagoa Bay: Its Natives and Natural History, etc.* London: G. Philip & Sons, 1891.
Móros y Morellon, José, de, and Juan Miguel de los Ríos. *Memorias sobre las islas Africanas de España: Fernando Poo y Annobon*. Madrid: Comp. Tipogr., 1844.

Morrell, Benjamin. *A Narrative of Four Voyages: To the South Sea, North and South Pacific Ocean, Chinese Sea, Ethiopic and Southern Atlantic Ocean, Indian and Antarctic Ocean, from the year 1822 to 1831*. New York: J. & J. Harper, 1832.

Teixeira da Mota, A. *Cinco Séculos de Cartografia das Ilhas de Cabo Verde*. Lisbon: Junta de Investigações do Ultramar, 1961.

Mouat, Frederic J. *Rough Notes of a Trip to Reunion, the Mauritius and Ceylon; with Remarks on their Eligibility as Sanitaria for Indian Invalids*. Calcutta: Thacker, Spink & Co., 1852.

Murphy, Robert C. *A Dead Whale or a Stove Boat: Cruise of "Daisy" in the Atlantic Ocean, June 1912 – May 1913*. Boston: Houghton Mifflin, 1967.

Nichols, William H. *Eastward Around the World on the Barque Emerald*. Edited by Henry C. Nichols. Salem: Naumkeag Publications, 1973.

Nordhoff, Charles. *Whaling and Fishing*. New York: Dodd, Mead & Co., 1855.

Notes and Queries: A Medium of Intercommunication for Literary Men, General Readers etc. Twelfth Series, Vol. III. London: J. Edward Francis, 1917.

Oliver, Samuel P. *Madagascar: An Historical and Descriptive Account of the Island and its Former Dependencies*. 2 Vols. London, New York: Macmillan, 1886.

Olmsted, Francis A. *Incidents of a Whaling Voyage: To Which Are Added Observations on the Scenery, Manners and Customs, and Missionary Stations of the Sandwich and Society Islands*. New York: D. Appleton, 1841.

Ovington, John. *A Voyage to Suratt in the Year 1689: Giving a Large Account of That City and Its Inhabitants and of the English Factory There: Likewise a Description of Madiera, St. Jago, Annobon, Cabenda, and Malemba (upon the coast of Africa), St. Helena, Johanna, Bombay, the City of Muscatt, and its Inhabitants in Arabia Felix, Mocha, and other Maritime Towns upon the Red-Sea, the Cape of Good Hope, and the Island Ascention*. London: Jacob Tonson, 1696.

Owen, William F. W. "The Bay of Delagoa." In *Records of South-Eastern Africa*. Vol. 2. Edited by George M. Theal, 465–79. Kapstadt: Struik, 1964.

Owen, William F. W. *Narrative of Voyages to Explore the Shores of Africa, Arabia, and Madagascar, Performed in H. M. Ships Leven and Barracouta under the Direction of Captain W.F.W. Owen, R.N., by Command of the Lords Commissioners of the Admiralty*. 2 Vols. New York: Harper, 1833.

Palgrave, William C. *The Commissions of W. C. Palgrave: Special Emissary to South West Africa 1876–1885*. Edited by E. L. P. Stals. Kapstadt: Van Riebeeck Society, 1990.

Parsons, Elsie W. C. *Folk-lore from the Cape Verde Islands*. Vol. 2. Cambridge, New York: American Folk-lore Society, 1923.

Pereira, Duarte P. *Esmeraldo de Situ Orbis*. Lisbon: Imprensa Nacional, 1892.

Perkins, Edward T. *Na Motu; or, Reef-rovings in the South Seas: A Narrative of Adventures at the Hawaiian, Georgian and Society Islands*. New York: Garrett & Co, 1854.

Philip, John. "Letter from the Reverend Dr. Philip to P. G. Brink, Esqre." In *Records of South-Eastern Africa*. Vol. 9. Edited by George M. Theal, 41–5. Kapstadt: Government of the Cape Colony, 1903.

Phillips, Thomas. *A Journal of a Voyage Made in the Hannibal of London, Ann. 1693, 1694; from England to Cape Monseradoe in Africa; and thence along the Coast of Guiney to Whidaw, the Island of St. Thomas; and so Forward to Barbadoes; with a Cursory Account of the Country, the People, their Manners, Forts, Trade, &c*. London: Awnsham & John Churchill, 1732.

Pickman, Dudley L. "Réunion and Mauritius, 1803–1804, The Journal of Dudley Leavitt Pickman, 1799–1804" In *New England Merchants in Africa: A History Through Documents, 1802 to 1865*, edited by Norman R. Bennett and George E. Brooks, 8–14. Boston: Boston UP, 1965.

Pike, Nicolas. *Sub-tropical Rambles in the Land of Aphanapteryx: Personal Experiences, Adventures, and Wanderings in and around the Island of Mauritius*. New York: Harper & Brothers, 1873.

Pinkham, Andrew. *The Log Book of the Good Ship Alliance of Nantucket Captain Bartlett Coffin, 1791–1794*. Edited by Rod Dickson. Perth: Rod Dickson, 2006.

Prior, James. *Voyage Along the Eastern Coast of Africa, to Mosambique, Johanna, and Quiloa; to St. Helena; to Rio de Janeiro, Bahia, and Pernambuco in Brazil, in the Nisus Frigate*. London: Richard Phillips, 1819.

Putnam, Horace B. "A Visit to Zanzibar, 1847." In *New England Merchants in Africa: A History Through Documents, 1802 to 1865*, edited by Norman R. Bennett and George E. Brooks, 403–6. Boston: Boston UP, 1965.

Rath, Johannes. "Aus dem Tagebuch Raths." *Die ältesten Reiseberichte über Deutsch-Südwestafrika: Die Berichte der Rheinischen Mission bis zum Jahre 1846*. Translated and edited by Eduard Moritz. Mitteilungen aus den deutschen Schutzgebieten 29 (1916): 228–9.

Ravenstein, Ernest G. *A Journal of the First Voyage of Vasco da Gama, 1497–1499*. London: Hakluyt Soc., 1898.

Reenen, Sebastiaan V., van. "Tagebuch über die Fahrt des Schiffes 'Meermin'." *Die ältesten Reiseberichte über Deutsch-Südwestafrika: Schluss*. Translated and edited by Eduard Moritz. Mitteilungen aus den deutschen Schutzgebieten 31 (1918): 194–202.

Ricketson, Annie H. *Mrs. Ricketson's Whaling Journal: The Journal of Annie Holmes Ricketson on the Whaleship A. R. Tucker, 1871–1874*. New Bedford: Old Dartmouth Historical Society, 1958.

Ritter, Carl. "Über das historische Element in der geographischen Wissenschaft." *Abhandlungen der Königlichen Akademie der Wissenschaften zu Berlin* 1833: 41–67.

Robbins, Charles H. *The Gam: Being a Group of Whaling Stories*. Salem: Newcomb & Gauss, 1913.

Robinson, Charles H. *A Boy's Will: An Experience*. Providence: The Hillery Press, 1934.

Rodman, Samuel W. "Samuel W. Rodman to Joseph Grinnell, Dedham, August 17, 1850." In *New England Merchants in Africa: A History Through Documents, 1802 to 1865*, edited by Norman R. Bennett and George E. Brooks, 468–9. Boston: Boston UP, 1965.

Rooke, Henry. *Travels to the Coast of Arabia Felix and from thence by the Red Sea and Egypt to Europe, Containing a Short Account of an Expedition Undertaken Against the Cape of Good Hope*. London: R. Blamire, 1783.

Santos, João, dos. "Ethopia oriental." In *Records of South-Eastern Africa*. Vol. 7. Edited by George M. Theal, 1–182. Kapstadt: Government of the Cape Colony, 1901.

Scammon, Charles M. *The Marine Mammals of the North-western Coast of North America, Described and Illustrated; together with an Account of the American Whale-fishery*. San Francisco, New York: Carmany/Putnam, 1874.

Scheppmann, Heinrich. "Von der Kapstadt nach der Walfischbai, 1847." *Die ältesten Reiseberichte über Deutsch-Südwestafrika: Die Berichte der Rheinischen Mission bis zum Jahre 1846*. Translated and edited by Eduard Moritz. Mitteilungen aus den deutschen Schutzgebieten 29 (1916): 237–8.

Scheppmann, Heinrich. "Von Rehoboth nach der Walfischbai, 1845." *Die ältesten Reiseberichte über Deutsch-Südwestafrika: Die Berichte der Rheinischen Mission bis zum Jahre 1846*. Translated and edited by Eduard Moritz. Mitteilungen aus den deutschen Schutzgebieten 29 (1916): 238–41.

Schmelen, Johann H. "Kurzer Bericht Schmelens über seine Reise nach der Walfischbai." *Die ältesten Reiseberichte über Deutsch-Südwestafrika*. Translated and edited by Eduard Moritz. Mitteilungen aus den deutschen Schutzgebieten 28 (1915): 221–2.

"Secours donnés bâtiments de l'état aux navires baleiniers du commerce." *Annales Maritimes et Coloniales* 20, no. 2 (1835): 189–91.

Sibree, James. *Madagascar Before the Conquest: The Island, the Country, and the People, with Chapters on Travel and Topography, Folk-Lore, Strange Customs and Superstitions, the Animal Life of the Island, and Mission Work and Progress Among the Inhabitants*. London: T. F. Unwin, 1896.

Simpson, William. *A Private Journal Kept during the Niger Expedition, from the Commencement in May, 1841, until the Recall of the Expedition in June, 1842*. London: Shaw, 1843.

Smith, Thomas W. *A Narrative of the Life, Travels, and Sufferings of Thomas W. Smith. Comprising an Account of his Early Life, his Travels during Eighteen Voyages to various Parts of the World, during which he was Five Times Ship Wrecked, thrice on a Desolate Island and near the South Pole, once upon the Coast of England, and once on the Coast of Africa*. 1844. Edited by Damien Sanders. Dinan: Nunatak Press, 2009.

Smyth, William H. *The Life and Services of Captain Philip Beaver, late of His Majesty's Ship Nisus*. London: J. Murray, 1829.

Spears, John R. "The Log of the Bark Emily, as Kept by L. R. Hale, Third Mate – 1857–60." *Harper's Monthly Magazine* 107 (1903): 242–51.

"Tagebuch des Schiffes Boode." *Die ältesten Reiseberichte über Deutsch-Südwestafrika: Schluss*. Translated and edited by Eduard Moritz. Mitteilungen aus den deutschen Schutzgebieten 31 (1918): 42–60.

Tams, Georg. *Die Portugiesischen Besitzungen in Süd-West-Afrika: Ein Reisebericht*. Hamburg: Kittler, 1845.

Thomas, Charles W. *Adventures and Observations on the West Coast of Africa, and its Islands: Historical and Descriptive Sketches of Madeira, Canary, Biafra, and Cape Verd Islands; their Climates, Inhabitants, and Productions. Accounts of Places, Peoples, Customs, Trade, Missionary Operations, etc., etc., on that Part of the African Coast Lying between Tangier, Morocco, and Benguela*. New York: Derby & Jackson, 1860.

Thompson, John. *The Life of John Thompson, a Fugitive Slave: Containing his History of 25 Years in Bondage, and his Providential Escape*. Worcester 1856.

Thompson, Samuel C. "A Whaling Cruise in the 'Sea Fox'". *The Yale Review* 15, no. 1 (1925): 141–61.

Tindall, Joseph. *The Journal of Joseph Tindall: Missionary in South West Africa, 1839–55*. Edited by B. A. Tindall. Kapstadt: Van Riebeeck Society, 1959.

Torrey, William. *Torrey's Narrative: Or, the Life and Adventures of William Torrey*. Boston: A. J. Wright, 1848.

Travassos Valdez, Francisco. *Six Years of a Traveller's Life in Western Africa*. Vol. 2. London: Hurst & Blackett, 1861.

Tuckey, James H. *Narrative of an Expedition to Explore the River Zaire, Usually Called the Congo, in South Africa, in 1816 Under the Direction of Captain J. K. Tuckey: To Which Is Added, the Journal of Prof. Smith, Some General Observations on the Country and Its*

Inhabitants and an App.: Containing the Natural History of That Part of the Kingdom of Congo Through Which the Zaire Flows. London: John Murray, 1818.

Usera y Alarcon, Géronimo M. *Memoria de la isla de Fernando Poo*. Madrid: T. Aguado, 1848.

Van der Stell, Simon. "Extracts from a Despatch from Commander Simon van der Stell and Council to the Chamber of XVII." In *The Annals of Natal: 1495 to 1845*. Vol. 2. Edited by John Bird, 44–53. Kapstadt: Struik, 1965.

Vigne, Randolph. "James Archbell's 'Beschrijving der Walvischbaai en omliggende plaatsen aan de westkust van Africa' in 1823: An English Translation with Introduction and Notes." *Cimbebasia* 13 (1991): 29–36.

Ward, Charles. "Charles Ward to John M. Clayton, Zanzibar, July 4, 1850." In *New England Merchants in Africa: A History Through Documents, 1802 to 1865*, edited by Norman R. Bennett and George E. Brooks, 455–7. Boston: Boston UP, 1965.

White, Moses H. "Cape Town and Mauritius, 1802. Journal Kept on Board the Ship 'Herald' from Boston to Cape of Good Hope &c. Richard Derby, Esquire, Commander." In *New England Merchants in Africa: A History Through Documents, 1802 to 1865*, edited by Norman R. Bennett and George E. Brooks, 1–8. Boston: Boston UP, 1965.

White, William. *Journal of a Voyage Performed in the Lion Extra* Indiaman, *from Madras to Columbo, and Da Lagoa Bay, on the Eastern Coast of Africa, (where the Ship was Condemned) in the Year 1798*. London: John Stockdale, 1800.

Whitecar, William B. *Four Years Aboard the Whaleship: Embracing Cruises in the Pacific, Atlantic, Indian, and Antarctic Oceans, in the Years 1855, '6, '7, '8, '9*. London, Philadelphia: Lippincott/Trübner, 1860.

Williams, John G. *The Adventures of a Seventeen-year-old Lad and the Fortunes He Might Have Won*. Boston: Collins Press, 1894.

References

Monographs, Articles and Websites

Aguilar, Alex. "Aboriginal Whaling off Pagalu (Equatorial Guinea)." *Reports of the International Whaling Commission* 35 (1985): 385–6.
Ahmad, Aijaz. "The Politics of Literary Postcoloniality." *Race & Class* 36, no. 1 (1995): 1–19.
Alden, Dauril. "Yankee Sperm Whalers in Brazilian Waters, and the Decline of the Portuguese Whale Fishery (1773–1801)." *The Americas* 20, no. 3 (1964): 267–88.
Alexander, Karen. "Women at Sea." In *Encyclopedia of American Literature of the Sea and Great Lakes*, edited by Jill B. Gidmark, 480–3. Westport: Greenwood Press, 2001.
Allen, Richard B. "The Mascarene Slave-trade and Labour Migration in the Indian Ocean during the Eighteenth and Nineteenth Centuries." In *The Structure of Slavery in Indian Ocean Africa and Asia*, edited by Gwyn Campbell, 33–50. London; Portland: Frank Cass, 2004.
Allen, Richard B. *Slaves, Freedmen, and Indentured Laborers in Colonial Mauritius*. Cambridge: Cambridge UP, 1999.
Allen, Richard B. "A Traffic of Several Nations: The Mauritian Slave Trade, 1721–1835." In *History, Memory and Identity*, edited by Vijayalakshmi Teelock and Edward A. Alpers, 157–77. Port Louis: Nelson Mandela Centre for African Culture/University of Mauritius, 2001.
Almeida, Raymond A., Meintel, Deirdre, Platzer, Michael K. H., Tchuba, the American Committee for Cape Verde. *Cape Verdeans in America: Our Story*. Boston: The American Committee for Cape Verde, 1978
Alpers, Edward A. "Becoming Mozambique: Diaspora and Identity in Mauritius." In *History, Memory and Identity*, edited by Vijayalakshmi Teelocka and Edward A. Alpers, 117–25. Port Louis: Nelson Mandela Centre for African Culture/University of Mauritius, 2001.
Alpers, Edward A. "A Complex Relationship: Mozambique and the Comoro Islands in the 19th and 20th Centuries." *Cahiers d'Etudes Africaines* 161 (2001): 73–95.
Alpers, Edward A. "The French Slave Trade in East Africa (1721–1810)." *Cahiers d'Études Africaines* 10, no. 37 (1970): 80–124.
Alpers, Edward A. "The Islands of Indian Ocean Africa." In *The Western Indian Ocean: Essays on Islands and Islanders*, edited by Shawkat M. Toorawa, 1–19. Port Louis: Hassam Toorawa Trust, 2007.
Alpers, Edward A. *Ivory and Slaves in East Central Africa: Changing Pattern of International Trade in East Central Africa to the Later Nineteenth Century*, London: Heinemann, 1975.
Alpers, Edward A. "Littoral Society in the Mozambique Channel." In *Cross Currents and Community Networks: The History of the Indian Ocean World*, edited by Himanshu Prabha Ray and Edward A. Alpers, 123–41. New Delhi: Oxford UP, 2007.
Alpers, Edward A. "Madagascar and Mozambique in the Nineteenth Century: The Era of the Sakalava Raids (1800–1820)." *Omaly sy Anio* 5–6 (1977): 36–53.
Alpers, Edward A. "State, Merchant Capital, and Gender Relations in Southern Mozambique to the End of the Nineteenth Century: Some Tentative Hypotheses." *African Economic History* 13 (1984): 23–55.
American Association of Jurists. "The Need to Name a New Special Rapporteur for Equatorial Guinea." United Nations, Commission on Human Rights. (2005). Accessed November 25, 2014. http://www.ecoi.net/file_upload/iz5_G0511794.pdf.

Amnesty International. "A Missed Opportunity to Restore Respect for Human Rights." Al-Index AFR 24/01/94 (1994). Accessed November 25, 2014. http://www.amnesty.org/en/library/asset/AFR24/001/1994/fr/67f1cc4f-ec19-11dd-85b9-0939011eabc9/afr240011994en.pdf.

Anderson, Clare. *Convicts in the Indian Ocean: Transportation from South Asia to Mauritius, 1815–53*. New York: St. Martin's, 2000.

Aranzadi, Isabela, de. "A Drum's Trans-Atlantic Journey from Africa to the Americas and Back after the end of Slavery: Annobonese and Fernandino Musical Cultures." *African Sociological Review* 14, no. 1 (2010): 20–47.

Ardener, Edwin. "The Wovea Islanders of Ambas Bay." *Nigeria* 59 (1958): 308–21.

Auböck, Maria. "Afrika südlich der Sahara: Fragmente zur sukzessiven Marginalisierung." In *Globalgeschichte 1450–1620: Anfänge und Perspektiven*, edited by Friedrich Edelmayer, Peter Feldbauer, and Marija Wakounig, 75–94. Wien: Promedia 2002.

Ballard, Charles. "Trade, Tribute and Migrant Labour: Zulu and Colonial Exploitation of the Delagoa Bay Hinterland 1818–1879." In *Before and after Shaka: Papers in Nguni History*, edited by J. B. Peires, 100–24. Grahamstown: Institute of Social and Economic Research, Rhodes University, 1981.

Barker, Anthony J. *Slavery and Anti-Slavery in Mauritius, 1810–33: The Conflict between Economic Expansion and Humanitarian Reform under British Rule*. Basingstoke, Hampshire: Macmillan et al., 1996.

Barnwell, Patrick J., and Auguste Toussaint. *A Short History of Mauritius*, London; New York: Longmans, Green & Co., 1949.

Barrena, Natalio. *Gramática annobónesa*. Madrid: Instituto de Estudios Africanos, 1957.

Barthelmeß, Klaus. "Auf Walfang: Geschichte einer Ausbeutung." In *Von Walen und Menschen*, edited by Knuth Weidlich, 4–51. Hamburg: Historika Photoverlag, 1992.

Barthelmeß, Klaus. "Walfang in der Bucht von Biafra (Golf von Guinea, Westafrika)." *Fluke* 11 (2005): 8–10.

Basberg, Bjørn L. "Two Hegemonies – Two Technological Regimes: American and Norwegian Whaling in the 19th and 20th Century." Paper presented at the XIV International Economic History Congress, Helsinki, 2006. Accessed January 22, 2013. http://www.helsinki.fi/iehc2006/papers3/Basberg.pdf.

Basilio, R. P. Aurelio. *Caza y pesca en Annobon: Aves de la isla. La pesca de la ballena*. Madrid: Instituto de Estudios Africanos & Consejo Superior de Investigaciones Cientificas, 1957.

Basilio, R. P. Aurelio. *La vida animal en la Guinea Española*. Madrid: Instituto de Estudios Africanos, Consejo Superior de Investigaciones Científicas, 1952.

Bayart, Jean-François. "Postcolonial Studies: A Political Invention of Tradition?" *Public Culture* 23, no. 1 (2011): 55–84.

Beale, Thomas. *The Natural History of the Sperm Whale, to which Is Added, a Sketch of a South-Sea Whaling Voyage*. London: John van Voorst, 1839.

Beer, Esmond S., de. "The Early History of London Street-Lighting." *History* 25, no. 100 (1941): 311–24.

Benjamin, Walter. *The Arcades Project*. Transl. Howard Eiland & Kevin McLaughlin. Cambridge: Belknap, 1999.

Bennett, Norman R. and George E. Brooks. "Introduction." In *New England Merchants in Africa: A History Through Documents, 1802 to 1865*, edited by Norman R. Bennett and George E. Brooks, xxiii–xxxiii. Boston: Boston UP, 1965.

Berat, Lynn. "Genocide: The Namibian Case against Germany." *Pace International Law Review* 5, no. 1 (1993): 165–210.

Best, Peter B. "The Presence of Right Whales in Summer on the West Coast of South Africa: The Evidence from Historical Records." *African Journal of Marine Science* 28, no. 1 (2006): 159–166.

Best, Peter B. and Graham J. B. Ross. "Catches of Right Whales from Shore-Based Establishments in Southern Africa, 1792–1805." *Reports of the International Whaling Commission*, Special Issue 10 (1986): 275–289.

Best, Peter B. and Cherry Allison. "Catch History, Seasonal and Temporal Trends in the Migrations of Humpback Whales along the West Coast of Southern Africa." Paper SC/62/SH5 presented to the IWC Scientific Committee, 2010. Accessed January 22, 2013. http://iwcoffice.org/_documents/sci_com/SC62docs/SC-62-SH5.pdf.

Bialuschewski, Arne. "Firearms and Warfare in Late Seventeenth and Early Eighteenth-Century Madagascar." In *War and Peace in Africa*, edited by Toyin Falola and Raphael Chijioke Njoku, 57–71. Durham: Carolina Academic Press, 2010.

Bialuschewski, Arne. "Pirates, Slavers, and the Indigenous Population in Madagascar, c. 1690–1715." *The International Journal of African Historical Studies* 38, no. 3 (2005): 401–25.

Bialuschewski, Arne. "Thomas Bowrey's Madagascar Manuscript of 1708." *History in Africa* 34 (2007): 31–42.

Bigman, Laura. *History and Hunger in West Africa: Food Production and Entitlement in Guinea-Bissau and Cape Verde*. Westport: Greenwood Press, 1993.

Birmingham, David. *Trade and Conflict in Angola: The Mbundu and their Neighbours under the Influence of the Portuguese, 1483–1790*. Oxford: Clarendon Press, 1966.

Bixler, Raymond W. "Anglo-Portuguese Rivalry for Delagoa Bay." *The Journal of Modern History* 6, no. 4 (1934): 425–40.

Bolster, W. Jeffrey. *Black Jacks: African American Seamen in the Age of Sail*. Cambridge: Harvard UP, 1998.

Bolster, W. Jeffrey. "'To Feel Like a Man': Black Seamen in the Northern States, 1800–1860." *The Journal of American History* 76, no. 4 (1990): 1173–99.

Booth, Alan R. "American Whalers in South African Waters." *South African Journal of Economics* 32, no. 4 (1964): 278–82.

Booth, Alan R. *The United States Experience in South Africa, 1784–1870*. Kapstadt & Rotterdam: A. A. Balkema, 1976.

Botelle, Andrew and Kelly Kowalski. *Changing Resource Use in Namibia's Lower Kuiseb Valley: Perceptions from the Topnaar Community*. Roma: Institute of Southern African Studies / National University of Lesotho, 1997.

Bowman, Larry W. *Mauritius: Democracy and Development in the Indian Ocean*. Boulder/London: Westview Press, 1991.

Brahm, Felix. "Guns in Africa." In *Oxford Research Encyclopedia of African History*, edited by Thomas Spear. Oxford, 2020. http://dx.doi.org/10.1093/acrefore/9780190277734.013.700 (12.08.2022).

Brahm, Felix. *Merchandise of Power: Der Waffenhandel zwischen Europa und Ostafrika (1850–1919)*. Frankfurt a. M./New York: Campus, 2022.

Brito, Cristina, Cristina Picanço and Inês Carvalho. "Small Cetaceans off São Tomé (São Tomé and Príncipe, Gulf of Guinea, West Africa): Species, Sightings and Abundance, Local Human Activities and Conservation." Paper SC/62/SM8 presented to the IWC Scientific

Committee, 2010. Accessed May 25, 2011. http://iwcoffice.org/_documents/sci_com/SC62docs/SC-62-SM8.pdf.

Broadhead, Susan H. "Angola: History and Government." In *Encyclopedia of Africa South of the Sahara*, edited by John Middleton, 37–40. New York: C. Scribner's Sons, 1997.

Brooks, George E. "Cabo Verde: Gulag of the South Atlantic: Racism, Fishing Prohibitions, and Famines." *History in Africa* 33 (2006): 101–35.

Brooks, George E. *Eurafricans in Western Africa: Commerce, Social Status, Gender, and Religious Observance from the Sixteenth to Eighteenth Century*. Ohio et al.: Ohio UP, 2003.

Brooks, George E. *Yankee Traders, Old Coasters, and African Middlemen: A History of American Legitimate Trade with West Africa in the Nineteenth Century*. Boston: Boston UP, 1970.

Brooks, George E. *Western Africa and Cabo Verde, 1790s–1830s: Symbiosis of Slave and Legitimate Trades*. Bloomington: Authorhouse, 2010.

Bruton, M. N. *The Essential Guide to Whales*. Kapstadt: David Philip Publishers/The MTN Cape Whale Route, 1998.

Budack, Kuno F. R. "The ǂAonîn or Topnaar of the Lower !Kuiseb Valley and the Sea." *Khoisan Linguistic Studies* 3 (1977): 1–42.

Burrun, Breejan. *Port Louis, Mauritius*. Pereybere: Christian le Comte, 2009.

Burton, Maurice and Robert Burton. "Humpback Whale." In *International Wildlife Encyclopedia*. Vol. 3, edited by Maurice Burton and Robert Burton, 1258–60. Tarrytown: Marshall Cavendish Corp., 2002.

Busch, Briton C. "Cape Verdeans in the American Whaling and Sealing Industry, 1850–1900." *American Neptune* 45 (1985): 104–16.

Busch, Briton C. *Whaling Will Never Do for Me: The American Whaleman in the Nineteenth Century*. Lexington: UP of Kentucky, 1994.

Caldeira, Arlindo M. "Escravidão e liberdade: notas para uma história da ilha de Ano Bom." In *O reino, as ilhas e o mar oceano: Estudos em homenagem a Artur Teodoro de Matos*, edited by Avelino Freitas de Meneses and João Paulo de Oliveira e Costa, 623–43. Lisboa/Ponta Delgada: Universidade dos Açores, 2007.

Caldeira, Arlindo M. "La leyenda de Lodã, o de cómo Rolando, compañero del emperador Carlomagno, defendió la isla de Annobón de una invasión terrible." *Oráfrica: Revista de Oralidad Africana* 6 (2010): 71–89.

Caldeira, Arlindo M. "Medo e religião popular na ilha de Ano Bom: Uma aproximação histórica (séculos XVI-XIX)." University paper, 2007. Accessed September 14, 2012. http://cvc.instituto-camoes.pt/eaar/coloquio/comunicacoes/arlindo_caldeira.pdf.

Caldeira, Arlindo M. "Organizar a liberdade: Independência de facto na ilha de Ano Bom durante os séculos XVIII e XIX." Paper presented at Hofstra Cultural Center. *Between Three Continents: Rethinking Equatorial Guinea of the Fortieth Anniversary of its Independence from Spain*, April 2–4, 2009. Accessed September 14, 2012. http://www.hofstra.edu/pdf/Community/culctr/culctr_guinea040209_VIIBcaldeira.pdf.

Caldeira, Arlindo M. "Organizing Freedom: De Facto Independence on the Island of Ano Bom (Annobón) during the Eighteenth and Nineteenth Centuries." *Afro-Hispanic Review* 28, no. 2 (2009): 293–310.

Caldeira, Arlindo M. "A 'republica negra' de Ano Bom: Invencao de uni 'Estado' entre duas colonizacoes." In *Trabalho forçado africano: Experiências coloniais comparadas*, edited by Adriana Pereira Campos, 47–65. Porto: Campo das Letras, 2006.

Caldeira, Arlindo M. "Uma ilha quase desconhecida: Notas para a historia de Ano Bom." *Studia Africana* 17 (2006): 99–109.
Campbell, Gwyn R. "Austronesian Mariners and Early Trans-Indian Ocean Crossings." In *Navigating African Maritime History*, edited by Carina E. Ray and Jeremy Rich, 19–32. St. John's: International Maritime Economic History Association, 2009.
Campbell, Gwyn R. "Crisis of Faith and Colonial Conquest: The Impact of Famine and Disease in Late Nineteenth-Century Madagascar." *Cahiers d'Études Africaines* 32, no. 127 (1992): 409–53.
Campbell, Gwyn R. "The East African Slave Trade, 1861–1895: The 'Southern' Complex." *The International Journal of African Historical Studies* 22, no. 1 (1989):1–26.
Campbell, Gwyn R. *An Economic History of Imperial Madagascar, 1750–1895: The Rise and Fall of an Island Empire*. Cambridge: Cambridge UP, 2005.
Campbell, Gwyn R. "Madagascar and Mozambique in the Slave Trade of the Western Indian Ocean 1800–1861." In *The Economics of the Indian Ocean Slave Trade in the Nineteenth Century*, edited by William G. Clarence-Smith, 166–93. London: F. Cass, 1989.
Campbell, Gwyn R. "Madagascar and the Slave Trade, 1810–1895." *The Journal of African History* 22, no. 2 (1981): 203–27.
Campbell, Gwyn R. "Madagascar: Evolution of Malagasy Kingdoms." In *Encyclopedia of African History*, edited by Kevin Shillington, 873–5. New York: Fitzroy Dearborn, 2005.
Campbell, Gwyn R. "Madagascar: Prehistory and Developments to c.1500." In *Encyclopedia of African History*, edited by Kevin Shillington, 872–73. New York: Fitzroy Dearborn, 2005.
Campbell, Gwyn R. "Slavery and the Trans-Indian Ocean World Slave Trade: A Historical Outline." In *Cross Currents and Community Networks: The History of the Indian Ocean World*, edited by Himanshu Prabha Ray and Edward A. Alpers, 286–305. New Delhi: Oxford UP, 2007.
Campbell, Gwyn R. "The Structure of Trade in Madagascar, 1750–1810." *The International Journal of African Historical Studies* 26, no. 1 (1993): 111–48.
Carreira, António. *The People of the Cape Verde Islands: Exploitation and Emigration*. London: Hurst, 1982.
Carson, Rachel L. *Geheimnisse des Meeres*. München: Biederstein, 1952.
Carter, Marina. *Lakshmi's Legacy: The Testimonies of Indian Women in 19th Century Mauritius*. Stanley, Rose-Hill: Éditions de l'océan Indien, 1994.
Carvalho, Inês, Jacqueline Loo, Matthew Leslie, Meredith Thornton, Jaco Barendse, Cristina Pomilla, Tim Collins and Howard Rosenbaum. "Temporal Patterns of Population Structure of Humpback Whales in West Coast of Africa (B stock)." Paper SC/61/SH6 presented to the IWC Scientific Committee, Madeira, Portugal, 2009. Accessed May 15, 2012. http://iwcoffice.org/_documents/sci_com/SC62docs/SC-62-SH8.pdf.
Castro, Mariano L. de, and Luisa de la Calle. *Origen de la colonización española en Guinea Ecuatorial (1777–1860)*. Valladolid: Secretariado de Publicaciones, Universidad de Valladolid, 1992.
Chapelle, Howard I. *The History of American Sailing Ships*. New York: W.W. Norton & Co., 1935.
Chappell, David A. "Ahab's Boat: Non-European Seamen in Western Ships of Exploration and Commerce." In *Sea Changes: Historicizing the Ocean*. edited by Bernhard Klein and Gesa Mackenthun, 75–90. London: Routledge, 2004.
Chatterton, E. Keble. *Whalers and Whaling: The Story of the Whaling Ships up to the Present Day*. Philadelphia: J. B. Lippincott, 1926.

Christopher, Emma. "From the ›Ballad-Singing Monkey‹ to the ›Cunning Savages‹: The Voyage to Found a British Colony on the Orange River, 1785–1786." *South African Historical Journal* 61, no. 4 (2009): 750–65.

Christopher, Emma. *A Merciless Place: The Fate of Britain's Convicts after the American Revolution*. New York: Oxford UP, 2011.

Clancy, Dave. *Wreckhunter*. 2001–2012. Accessed September 15, 2022. http://wreckhunter.net.

Clapham, Phillip J. and Scott C. Baker. "Whaling, Modern." In *Encyclopedia of Marine Mammals*, edited by William Perrin F., Bernd Wursig and, J. G. M. Thewissen, 1239–43. San Diego: Academic Press, 2004.

Clarence-Smith, William G. "Creoles and Peasants in São Tomé, Príncipe, Fernando Póo and Mount Cameroun, in the Nineteenth Century." In *Primeira reunião internacional de história de Africa: Relação Europa-Africa no terceiro quartel do século XIX*, edited by Maria E. Madeira Santos, 489–99. Lisboa: Reunião Internacional de História de África, 1989.

Clarence-Smith, William G. "The Economics of the Indian Ocean Slave Trade in the 19th Century: An Overview." In *The Economics of the Indian Ocean Slave Trade in the Nineteenth Century*, edited by William G. Clarence-Smith, 1–20. London: Frank Cass, 1989.

Clarence-Smith, William G. *The Third Portuguese Empire, 1825–1975*. Manchester: UP, 1995.

Clark, A. Howard. "The American Whale-Fishery, 1877–1886." *Science* 9, no. 217 (1887): 321–24.

Clarke, Robert. *Open Boat Whaling in the Azores: The History and Present Methods of a Relic Industry*. Cambridge: University Press, 1954.

Clayton, Jane. "Nantucket Whalers in Milford Haven, Wales." *Historic Nantucket* 56, no. 1 (2007): 4–7.

Clifford, James. *Routes: Travel and Translation in the Late Twentieth Century*. Cambridge: Harvard UP, 1999.

Cohen, Margaret. *The Novel and the Sea*. Princeton et al.: Princeton, UP, 2010.

Cohn, Michael, and Michael K. H. Platzer. *Black Men of the Sea*. New York: Dodd, Mead, 1978.

Coli, Waltraud B., and Richard A. Lobban. *The Cape Verdeans in Rhode Island*. Providence: Rhode Island Heritage Commission/Rhode Island Publication Society, 1990.

Comores online, 1998–2014. Accessed September 15, 2022. http://www.comores-online.com.

Cone, Laurence. *For Candlesticks & Corset Stays: Long Island's Yankee Whalers*. Cold Spring Harbor: The Whaling Museum Society, 2007.

Cooper, Allan D. "American Corporate Investments in Namibia." *Africa Today* 30, no. 1/2 (1983): 23–31.

Cooper, Frederick. "Was nützt der Begriff der Globalisierung? Aus der Perspektive eines Afrika-Historikers." In *Globalgeschichte: Theorien, Ansätze, Themen*, edited by Sebastian Conrad, 131–61. Frankfurt a. M.: Campus, 2007.

Cooper, Frederick, and Ann L. Stoler. "Between Metropole and Colony: Rethinking a Research Agenda." In *Tensions of Empire: Colonial Cultures in a Bourgeois World*, edited by Frederick Cooper and Ann L. Stoler, 1–58. Berkeley: U of California P, 1997.

Coupland, Reginald. *East Africa and its Invaders: From the Earliest Times to the Death of Seyyid Said in 1856*. Oxford: Clarendon Press, 1968.

Couzens, Tim. "Robert Grendon: Irish Traders, Cricket Scores and Paul Kruger's Dreams." *English in Africa* 15, no. 2 (1988): 49–91.

Covey, Eric. "São Tomé." In *Encyclopedia of the Middle Passage*, edited by Toyin Falola and Amanda Warnock, 335–36. Westport, London: Greenwood Press, 2007.

Crain, Caleb "Lovers of Human Flesh: Homosexuality and Cannibalism in Melville's Novels." *American Literature* 66, no. 1 (1994): 25–53.
Creighton, Margaret S. "American Mariners and the Rites of Manhood, 1830–1870." In *Jack Tar in History: Essays in the History of Maritime Life and Labour*, edited by Colin D. Howell and Richard J. Twomey, 143–63. Fredericton: Acadiensis P, 1991.
Creighton, Margaret S. "Fraternity in the American Forecastle, 1830–1870." *The New England Quarterly* 63, no. 4 (1990): 531–57.
Creighton, Margaret S. *Rites & Passages: The Experience of American Whaling, 1830–1870.* Cambridge, New York, Melbourne: Cambridge UP, 1995.
Creus, Jacint. *Action missionnaire en Guinée Équatoriale, 1858–1910: perplexités et naïvétés à l'aube de la colonisation.* Lille: Presses Universitaires du Septentrion, 2002.
Creus, Jacint. "Cuando las almas no pueden ser custodiadas: El fundamento identitario en la colonización española de guinea ecuatorial." *Hispania. Revista Española de Historia* 67 (2007): 517–40.
Creus, Jacint, and Antònia Brunat. *Cuentos Annoboneses de Guinea Ecuatorial.* Malabo: Centro Cultural Hispano-Guineano Ediciones, 1992.
Cunha Matos, Raimundo José, da. *Corografia historica das ilhas de S. Tomè, Principe, Anno Bom, e Fernando Po.* São Tomé: Imprenza Nacional, 1916.
Currie, Stephen. *Thar She Blows: American Whaling in the Nineteenth Century.* Minneapolis: Lerner Publications, 2001.
Damme, Patrick van, and Veerle Van den Eynden. "Topnaar or Hottentot? The People on the Top Revisited." *Afrika Focus* 8, no. 3/4 (1992): 215–21.
Davidson, Basil. *The Fortunate Isles: Study in African Transformation.* Trenton: Africa World Press, 1989.
Davis, Lance E., and Robert E. Gallmann. "American Whaling, 1820–1990: Dominance and Decline." In *Whaling and History: Perspectives on the Evolution of the Industry*, edited by Bjørn L. Basberg, Jan Erik Ringstad, and Einar Wexelesen, 55–65. Sandefjord: Kommandør Chr. Christensens Hvalfangstmuseum, 1993.
Davis, Lance E., Robert E. Gallman and Teresa D. Hutchins. "The Decline of U.S. Whaling: Was the Stock of Whales Running Out?" *The Business History Review* 62, no. 4 (1988): 569–95.
Dedering, Tilman. *Hate the Old and Follow the New: Khoekhoe and Missionaries in Early Nineteenth-Century Namibia.* Stuttgart: Steiner, 1997.
Deerpalsingh, Saloni, and Marina Carter. *Select Documents on Indian Immigration: Mauritius, 1834–1926.* Second Edition. Moka: Mahatma Gandhi Institute, 1996.
Dekker, Pieter, and Cornelis De Jong. "Whaling Expeditions of the West India Company to Walvis Bay." *Namibia Scientific Society Journal* 46 (1998): 47–63.
Dening, Greg. *Beach Crossings: Voyaging Across Times, Cultures, and Self.* Philadelphia: U of Pennsylvania P, 2004.
Dening, Greg. *The Bounty: An Ethnographic History.* Melbourne University History Monographs 1. Parkville: History Dept., University of Melbourne, 1988.
Dening, Greg. *The Death of William Gooch: History's Anthropology.* Lanham: UP of America, 1988.
Dening, Greg. "Deep Times, Deep Spaces: Civilizing the Sea." *Sea Changes: Historicizing the Ocean.* edited by Bernhard Klein and Gesa Mackenthun, 13–36. London: Routledge, 2004.
Dening, Greg. *Islands and Beaches: Discourse on a Silent Land – Marquesas, 1774–1880.* Honolulu: UP of Hawaii, 1980.

Dening, Greg. *Mr Bligh's Bad Language: Passion, Power and Theatre on the Bounty.* Cambridge: Cambridge UP, 1994.

Dening, Greg. "Performing on the Beaches of the Mind: An Essay." *History and Theory* 41, no. 1 (2002): 1–24.

Dening, Greg. "A Poetic for Histories: Transformations That Present the Past." In *Clio in Oceania: Toward a Historical Anthropology*, edited by Aletta Biersack, 347–80. Washington: Smithsonian Institution Press, 1991.

Dentlinger, Ursula. *The !Nara Plant in the Topnaar Hottentot Culture of Namibia: Ethnobotanical Clues to an 8,000-year-old Tradition.* Munger Africana Library Notes 38. Pasadena: California Institute of Technology, 1977.

De Santis, Hugh, and Waldo Heinrichs. "United States of America: The Department of State and American Foreign Policy." In *The Times Survey of Foreign Ministries of the World*, edited by Zara Steiner, 575–81. London: Times Books, 1985.

Dewar, Robert E., and Henry T. Wright. "The Culture History of Madagascar." *Journal of World Prehistory* 7, no. 4 (1993): 417–66.

Dickson, Rod "The Cruise of the Nantucket Ships 'Asia' and 'Alliance': In Consort to the Indian Ocean and the Coast of New Holland, Australia 1791–94." *Historic Nantucket* 56, no. 1 (2007): 8–13.

Dolin, Eric J. *Leviathan: The History of Whaling in America.* New York, London: W. W. Norton & Co., 2007.

Duffey, Alexander E. "China's Contact with Southern Africa: The Ceramic Record." *Namibia Scientific Society Journal* 56 (2008): 27–42.

Duignan, Peter J., and Lewis H. Gann. *The United States and Africa: A History.* Cambridge, New York: Cambridge UP, 1984.

Duncan, T. Bentley. *Atlantic Islands: Madeira, the Azores and the Cape Verdes in Seventeenth-Century Commerce and Navigation.* Chicago, London: U of Chicago P, 1972.

Du Pasquier, Thierry. "Catch History of French Right Whaling Mainly in the South Atlantic." *Reports of the International Whaling Commission* Special Issue 10 (1986): 269–74.

Du Pasquier, Thierry. *Les Baleiniers Français de Louis XVI à Napoléon.* Paris: Henry Veyrier, 1990.

Eckert, Andreas, Ingeborg Grau and Arno Sonderegger, eds. *Afrika 1500–1900: Geschichte und Gesellschaft.* Wien: Promedia-Verl., 2010.

Eco, Umberto. *Inventing the Enemy: Essays.* Boston: Houghton Mifflin Harcourt, 2012.

Edwards, Craig, and Robert Walser. "Sea Music" In *Encyclopedia of American Literature of the Sea and Great Lakes*, edited by Jill B. Gidmark, 400–03. Westport: Greenwood Press, 2001.

Eldredge, Elizabeth A. "Sources of Conflict in Southern Africa, c. 1800–30: The 'Mfecane' Reconsidered." *The Journal of African History* 33, no. 1 (1992): 1–35.

Elias, Norbert. "Studies in the Genesis of the Naval Profession." *The British Journal of Sociology* 1, no. 4 (1950): 291–309.

Ellis, Richard. "Azorean Whaling." In *Encyclopedia of Marine Mammals*, edited by William F. Perrin, Bernd Wursig, and J. G. M. Thewissen, 64–7. San Diego: Academic Press, 2004.

Ellis, Richard. *Men and Whales.* New York: Alfred A. Knopf, 1991.

Ellis, Richard. "Whaling, Aboriginal." In *Encyclopedia of Marine Mammals*, edited by William F. Perrin, Bernd Wursig, and J. G. M. Thewissen, 1227–35. San Diego: Academic Press, 2004.

Ellis, Richard. "Whaling, Traditional." In *Encyclopedia of Marine Mammals*, edited by William F. Perrin, Bernd Wursig, and J. G. M. Thewissen, 1243–53. San Diego: Academic Press, 2004.
Emrith, Moomtaz. *History of the Muslims in Mauritius*. Vacoas: Editions Le Printemps, 1994.
Erkkilä, Antti, and Harri Siiskonen. *Forestry in Namibia, 1850–1990*. Joensuu: U of Joensuu, 1992.
Eynden, Veerle van den, Patrick Vernemmen, and Patrick van Damme. *The Ethnobotany of the Topnaar*. Gent: Universiteit Gent, 1992.
Fage, J. D., and William Tordoff. *A History of Africa*. London/New York: Routledge, 2002.
Falkus, Malcolm. "The Early Development of the British Gas Industry, 1790–1815." *The Economic History Review* 35, no. 2 (1982): 217–34.
Falkus, Malcolm. "Lighting in the Dark Ages of English Economic History: Town Streets before the Industrial Revolution." *Trade, Government and Economy in Pre-Industrial England: Essays Presented to F. J. Fisher*, edited by Donald C. Coleman and A. H. John, 248–73. London: Weidenfeld and Nicolson, 1976.
Falola, Toyin, ed. *Africa. Vol. 1: African History Before 1885*. Durham: Carolina Academic Press, 2000.
Farr, James B. "A Slow Boat to Nowhere: The Multi-Racial Crews of the American Whaling Industry." *The Journal of Negro History* 68, no. 2 (1983): 159–70.
Fegley, Randall. *Equatorial Guinea*. World Bibliographical Series 136. Oxford: Clio, 1991.
Feldbusch, Thorsten. *Zwischen Land und Meer: Schreiben auf den Grenzen*. Würzburg: Königshausen & Neumann, 2003.
Filliot, J. M. *La Traite des Esclaves vers les Mascareignes au XVIIIe Siècle*. Paris: ORSTOM, 1974.
Fischer-Tiné, Harald. *Low and Licentious Europeans: Race, Class, and "White Subalternity" in Colonial India*. New Delhi: Orient BlackSwan, 2009.
Flayderman, Norman. *Scrimshaw and Scrimshanders; Whales and Whalemen*. New Milford: N. Flayderman, 1972.
Fleisch, Axel. "Angola: Abolition of Slave Trade." In *Encyclopedia of African History*, edited by Kevin Shillington, 76–7. New York: Fitzroy Dearborn, 2005.
Florentino, Manolo. "Slave Trade between Mozambique and the Port of Rio de Janeiro, c. 1790–c. 1850: Demographic, Social and Economic Aspects." In *Slave Routes and Oral Tradition in Southeastern Africa*, edited by Benigna Zimba, Edward A. Alpers, and Allen Isaacman, 63–90. Maputo: Filsom Entertainment, 2005.
Forster, Honore. "'The Cruise of the Whaler Gipsy': Some Recent Developments in the Archives of British Whaling in the Pacific." *The Journal of Pacific History* 21, no. 2 (1986): 110–1.
Foucault, Michel. *The Archaeology of Knowledge and the Discourse on Language*. Transl. A. M. Sheridan Smith. New York: Pantheon, 1972.
Foucault, Michel. *Von der Subversion des Wissens*. München: Hanser, 1974.
Foulke, Robert C. "Voyage Narratives." In *Encyclopedia of American Literature of the Sea and Great Lakes*, edited by Jill B. Gidmark, 461–4. Westport: Greenwood Press, 2001.
Francis, Daniel. *A History of World Whaling*. Markham, Ontario, New York: Viking, 1990.
Frank, Stuart M. *Dictionary of Scrimshaw Artists*. Mystic: Mystic Seaport Museum, 1991.
Fry, C. H. "Annobon: A South Sea Island in the Gulf of Guinea." *The Nigerian Field* 27 (1962): 147–61.
Fu-Kiau, Kimbwandènde K. B. *African Cosmology of the Bântu-Kângo: Tying the Spiritual Knot – Principles of Life & Living*. Brooklyn: Athelia Henrietta Press, 2001.

Galbraith, John S. *Reluctant Empire: British Policy on the South African Frontier, 1834–1854*. Westport: Greenwood, 1978.
Gassert, Philipp, Mark Häberlein, and Michael Wala. *Kleine Geschichte der USA*. Stuttgart: Reclam, 2007.
Gewald, Jan-Bart. *Herero Heroes: A Socio-political History of the Herero of Namibia, 1890–1923*. Oxford, Kapstadt, Athens: James Currey et al., 1999.
Gewald, Jan-Bart. "Untapped Sources: Slave Exports from Southern and Central Namibia up to c. 1850." In *The Mfecane Aftermath: Reconstructive Debates in Southern African History*, edited by Carolyn Hamilton, 417–35. Johannesburg: Witwatersrand UP, 1995.
Gilje, Paul A. *Liberty on the Waterfront: American Maritime Culture in the Age of Revolution*. Philadelphia: University of Pennsylvania Press, 2004.
Gillis, John R. "Islands in the Making of an Atlantic Oceania, 1500–1800." In *Seascapes: Maritime Histories, Littoral Cultures, and Transoceanic Exchanges*, edited by Jerry H. Bentley, Renate Bidenthal, and Kären Wigen, 21–37. Honolulu: U of Hawai'i P, 2007.
Ginzburg, Carlo. *The Cheese and the Worms: The Cosmos of a Sixteenth-Century Miller*. Transl. John & Anne Tedeschi. Baltimore: Johns Hopkins UP, 1992.
Gockel, Klaus. *Mission und Apartheid: Heinrich Vedder und Hans Karl Diehl*. Köln: Köppe, 2010.
Goffman, Erving. *Asylums: Essays on the Social Situation of Mental Patients and Other Inmates*. New York: Anchor Books, 1961.
Graham, Gerald S. *Great Britain in the Indian Ocean: A Study of Maritime Enterprise, 1810–1850*. Oxford: Clarendon Press, 1967.
Graham, Gerald S. "The Migrations of the Nantucket Whale Fishery: An Episode in British Colonial Policy." *The New England Quarterly* 8, no. 2 (1935): 179–202.
Graham, Gerald S. *Tides of Empire: Discursions on the Expansion of Britain Overseas*. Montreal, London: McGill-Queen's UP, 1972.
Gray, Alastair C. "'Light Airs from the South': Whalers' Logs in Pacific History." *The Journal of Pacific History* 35, no. 1 (2000): 109–13.
Gray, Alastair C. "Trading Contacts in the Bismarck Archipelago during the Whaling Era, 1799–1884." *The Journal of Pacific History* 34, no. 1 (1999): 23–43.
Gray, John. *History of Zanzibar: From the Middle Ages to 1856*. London: Oxford UP, 1962.
Greenfield, Sidney M. "In Search of Social Identity: Strategies of Ethnic Identity Management Amongst Capeverdeans in Southeastern Massachusetts." *Luso-Brazilian Review* 13, no. 1 (1976): 3–18.
Griffiths, Charles L., L. Van Sittert, A. C. Brown, B. M. Clark, P. A. Cook, J. H.M. David, B. R. Davies et al. "Impacts of Human Activities on Marine Animal Life in the Benguela: A Historical Overview." *Oceanography and Marine Biology: An Annual Review* 42 (2004): 303–92.
Grove, Richard H. "Conserving Eden: The (European) East India Companies and Their Environmental Policies on St. Helena, Mauritius and in Western India, 1660 to 1854." *Comparative Studies in Society and History* 35, no. 2 (1993): 318–51.
Grove, Richard H. *Green Imperialism: Colonial Expansion, Tropical Island Edens and the Origins of Environmentalism, 1600–1860*. Cambridge: Cambridge UP, 1996.
Gruntkowski, Nina, and Joh Henschel. "!Nara in Topnaar History." In *!Nara: Fruit for Development of the !Khuiseb Topnaar*, edited by Joh Henschel, Rudolf Dausab, Petra Moser, and John Pallett, 39–48. Windhoek: Namibia Scientific Society, 2004.
Günzel, Stephan, ed. *Raum: Ein interdisziplinäres Handbuch*. Stuttgart, Weimar: Metzler, 2010.

Habermas, Jürgen. *On the Logic of the Social Sciences*. Cambridge: Polity, 1990.
Halter, Marilyn. *Between Race and Ethnicity: Cape Verdean American Immigrants, 1860–1965*. Urbana: U of Illinois P, 1993.
Halter, Marilyn. "Cape Verdeans in the U. S." In *Transnational Archipelago: Perspectives on Cape Verdean Migration and Diaspora*, edited by Luís Batalha and Jørgen Carling, 35–46. Amsterdam: Amsterdam UP, 2008.
Hamilton, C. I. "Seamen and Crime at the Cape, c. 1860–1880." *International Journal of Maritime History* 12 (1989): 1–35.
Harding, Leonhard. *Geschichte Afrikas im 19. und 20. Jahrhundert*. München: Oldenbourg, 1999.
Hargreaves, John D. "The Atlantic Ocean in West African History" In *Africa and the Sea*, edited by Jeffrey C. Stone, 5–13. Aberdeen: Aberdeen University African Studies Group, 1985.
Harries, Patrick. "Labour Migration from the Delagoa Bay Hinterland to South Africa 1852–1895." In *The Societies of Southern Africa in the 19th and 20th Centuries Vol. 7*, edited by Institute of Commonwealth Studies London, 61–76. London: University of London, Institute of Commonwealth Studies, 1981.
Hartmann, Wolfram. "Early Dutch-Namibian Encounters." In *Namibia and The Netherlands: 350 Years of Relations*, edited by Huub Hendrix, 9–19. Windhoek: Ambassade van het koninkrijk der Nederlanden, 2006.
Haywood, Carl N. "American Contacts with Africa: A Bibliography of the Papers of the American Whalemen." *African Studies Bulletin* 10, no. 3 (1967): 82–95.
Hazareesingh, Kissoonsingh. *History of Indians in Mauritius*. London: Macmillan, 1975.
Heffernan, Thomas F. *Mutiny on the Globe: The Fatal Voyage of Samuel Comstock*. New York/London: W. W. Norton & Co., 2002.
Heijer, Henk J. den. *Goud, Ivoor en Slaven: Scheepvaart en handel van de Tweede Westindische Compagnie op Afrika, 1674–1740*. Zutphen: Walburg, 1997.
Heimerdinger, Timo. *Der Seemann: Ein Berufsstand und seine kulturelle Inszenierung, 1844–2003*. Köln: Böhlau, 2005.
Henrichsen, Dag. *Herrschaft und Alltag im vorkolonialen Zentralnamibia: Das Herero- und Damaraland im 19. Jahrhundert*. Basel: Basler Afrika Bibliographien, 2011.
Henriksen, Thomas H. *Mozambique: A History*. London, Kapstadt: Rex Collings/David Philip, 1978.
Hildebrandt, Johann M. "Fragmente der Johanna-Sprache." *Zeitschrift für Ethnologie* 8 (1876): 89–96.
Hilton, Anne. *The Kingdom of Kongo*. Oxford: Clarendon, 1985.
Hoerder, Dirk. "Crossing the Waters: Historic Developments and Periodizations before the 1830s." In *Connecting Seas and Connected Ocean Rims: Indian, Atlantic, and Pacific Oceans and China Seas Migrations from the 1830s to the 1930s*, edited by Donna R. Gabaccia and Dirk Hoerder, 12–41. Leiden: Brill, 2011.
Hoernlé, A. Winifred. "The Social Organization of the Nama Hottentots of South-West Africa." *American Anthropologist* 27, no. 1 (1925): 1–24.
Hohman, Elmo P. *The American Whaleman: A Study of the Conditions of Labor in the Whaling Industry*. New York, London, Toronto: Longmans, Green & Co., 1928.
Holloway, Memory. "Making Waves: Cape Verdeans, Whaling and the Uses of Photography." In *Transnational Archipelago: Perspectives on Cape Verdean Migration and Diaspora*, edited by Luís Batalha and Jørgen Carling, 113–30. Amsterdam: Amsterdam UP, 2008.

Hoppe, Fritz. *Portugiesisch-Ostafrika in der Zeit des Marquês de Pombal (1750–1777)*. Berlin: Colloquium, 1965.
Housby, Trevor R. L. *The Hand of God: Whaling in the Azores*. London, New York, Toronto: Abelard-Schuman, 1971.
Igler, David. "Diseased Goods: Global Exchanges in the Eastern Pacific Basin, 1770–1850." *The American Historical Review* 109, no. 3 (2004): 693–719.
Iliffe, John. *Africans: The History of a Continent*. Cambridge: Cambridge UP, 2007.
Isaac, Rhys. *The Transformation of Virginia, 1740–1790*. Chapel Hill: University of North Carolina Press, 1982.
Isaacman, Allen F. *Mozambique: The Africanization of a European Institution, the Zambesi Prazos, 1750–1902*. Madison: U of Wisconsin P, 1972.
Isaacman, Allen F., and Barbara Isaacman. *The Tradition of Resistance in Mozambique: Anti-Colonial Activity in the Zambesi Valley 1850–1921*. London et al.: Heinemann, 1976.
Ito, Masaaki. "Changes in the Distribution of the !Nara Plant That Affect the Life of the Topnaar People in the Lower Kuiseb River, Namib Desert." *African Study Monographs* Suppl. 30 (2005): 65–75.
Ittmann, Johannes. "Der Walfang an der Küste Kameruns." *Zeitschrift für Ethnologie* 81 (1956): 203–17.
Jackson, Gordon. *The British Whaling Trade*. Bedford, Row, London: A & C Black, 1978.
Jackson Haight, Mabel V. *European Powers and South-east Africa: A Study of International Relations on the South-east Coast of Africa, 1796–1856*. London: Routledge & Kegan Paul, 1967.
Jacobsen, Steven B. "The African Squadrons." In *Encyclopedia of the Middle Passage*, edited by Toyin Falola and Amanda Warnock, 27–31. Westport/London: Greenwood Press, 2007.
Jenkins, James T. *A History of the Whale Fisheries: From the Basque Fisheries of the Tenth Century to the Hunting of the Finner Whale at the Present Date*. London: Witherby, 1921.
Jenkins, Keith, and Alun Munslow, eds. *The Nature of History Reader*. London: Routledge, 2004.
Jones, A. G. E. "The British Southern Whale and Seal Fisheries." *The Great Circle* 3, no. 1 (1981): 20–9.
Juneja, Monica. "Debatte zum Postkolonialismus aus Anlass des Sammelbandes ‚Jenseits des Eurozentrismus' von Sebastian Conrad und Shalini Randeria." *WerkstattGeschichte* 34 (2003): 88–96.
Kent, Raymond K. *Early Kingdoms in Madagascar, 1500–1700*. New York et al.: Holt, Rinehart and Winston, 1970.
Kienetz, Alvin. "The Key Role of the Orlam Migrations in the Early Europeanization of South-West Africa (Namibia)." *The International Journal of African Historical Studies* 10, no. 4 (1977): 553–72.
Kinahan, Jill. *By Command of their Lordships: The Exploration of the Namibian Coast by the Royal Navy, 1795–1895*. Windhoek: Namibia Archaeological Trust, 1992.
Kinahan, Jill. *Cattle for Beads: The Archaeology of Historical Contact and Trade on the Namib Coast*. Uppsala: Dep. of Archaeology and Ancient History, 2000.
Kinahan, Jill. "Heinrich Vedder's Sources for his Account of the Exploration of the Namib Coast." *Cimbebasia* 11 (1989): 33–9.
Kinahan, Jill. "The Historical Archaeology of Nineteenth Century Fisheries at Sandwich Harbour on the Namib Coast." *Cimbebasia* 13 (1991): 1–27.

Kinahan, Jill. "The Impenetrable Shield: HMS Nautilus and the Namib Coast in the Late Eighteenth Century." *Cimbebesia* 12 (1990): 23–61.

Kinahan, John. "Human and Domestic Animal Tracks in an Archaeological Lagoon Deposit on the Coast of Namibia." *The South African Archaeological Bulletin* 51, no. 164 (1996): 94–8.

Kinahan, John. *Pastoral Nomads of the Central Namib Desert: The People History Forgot.* Windhoek: Namibia Archaelogical Trust; New Namibia Books, 1991.

Kinahan, John, John Pallett, John Vogel, John Ward, and Malan Lindeque. "The Occurence and Dating of Elephant Tracks in the Silt Deposits of the Lower !Khuiseb River, Namibia." *Cimbebasia* 13 (1991): 37–43.

King, James F. "Evolution of the Free Slave Trade Principle in Spanish Colonial Administration." *The Hispanic American Historical Review* 22, no. 1 (1942): 34–56.

Klein, Bernhard, and Gesa Mackenthun. "Das Meer als kulturelle Kontaktzone." In *Das Meer als kulturelle Kontaktzone: Räume, Reisende, Repräsentationen*, edited by Bernhard Klein and Gesa Mackenthun, 1–16. Konstanz: UVK, 2003.

Klein, Herbert S. *The Middle Passage: Comparative Studies in the Atlantic Slave Trade.* Princeton: Princeton UP, 1978.

Klein, Herbert S. "The Portuguese Slave Trade From Angola in the Eighteenth Century." *The Journal of Economic History* 32, no. 4 (1972): 894–918.

Kock, Victor, de. *Those in Bondage: An Account of the Life of the Slave at the Cape in the Days of the Dutch East India Company.* London: George Allen & Unwin, 1950.

Köhler, Oswin. "Die Topnaar-Hottentotten am unteren Kuiseb." In *Ethnological and Linguistic Studies in Honour of N. J. van Warmelo: Essays Contributed on the Occasion of his Sixty-fifth Birthday 28 January 1969*, edited by The Ethnological Section, 99–122. Pretoria: Government Printer, 1969.

Krüger, Gesine. *Kriegsbewältigung und Geschichtsbewusstsein: Realität, Deutung und Verarbeitung des deutschen Kolonialkriegs in Namibia 1904 bis 1907.* Göttingen: Vandenhoeck & Ruprecht, 1999.

Kugler, Richard C. "The Penetration of the Pacific by American Whalemen in the 19th Century." *The Opening of the Pacific: Image and Reality.* Maritime Monographs and Reports 2, 20–7. London: National Maritime Museum, 1971.

Laman, Karl. *The Kongo.* 4 Vols. Stockholm: Victor Petterson, 1953–1968.

Larson, Pier M. "A Census of Slaves Exported from Central Madagascar to the Mascarenes between 1769 and 1820." In *L'esclavage à Madagascar: Aspects historiques et résurgences contemporaines. Actes du Colloque international sur l'esclavage, Antananarivo, 24–28 septembre 1996*, edited by Ignace Rakoto, 131–45. Antananarivo: Institut de civilisations, Musée d'art et d'archéologie, 1997.

Larson, Pier M. "The Origins of Malagasy Arriving at Mauritius and Réunion, 1770–1820: Expanding the History of Mascarene Slavery." In *History, Memory and Identity*, edited by Vijayalakshmi Teelock and Edward A. Alpers, 195–236. Port Louis: Nelson Mandela Centre for African Culture/University of Mauritius, 2001.

Lau, Brigitte. "Conflict and Power in Nineteenth-Century Namibia." *The Journal of African History* 27 (1986): 29–39.

Lau, Brigitte. *Southern and Central Namibia in Jonker Afrikaner's Time.* Second Edition. Windhoek: National Archives of Namibia, 1994.

Lau, Brigitte. "'Thank God the Germans Came', Vedder and Namibian Historiography." In *History and Historiography: 4 Essays in Reprint*, edited by Annemarie Heywood, 1–16. Windhoek: Discourse/ MSORP, 1995.

Laurel, Juan Tomás Ávila. "El cristianismo en la tradición oral de Annobón." In *De Boca en Boca: Estudios de literatura oral de Guinea Ecuatorial*, edited by Jacint Creus, 8–16. Vic: CEIBA, 2004.
Lebo, Susan. "Hawaii's 19th-Century Whaling Economy: Whale Traditions and Government Regulation of Hawaii's Native Seamen and Whale Fishery." In *Whaling and History III*, edited by Jan Erik Ringstad, 103–14. Sandefjord: Vestfoldmuseene IKS/Hvalfangstmuseet, 2010.
Le Comte, Christian C. G. *Mauritius from its Origin*. Mauritius: Christian Le Comte, 2005.
Lefkowicz, Edward J. "Whaling Narratives." In *Encyclopedia of American Literature of the Sea and Great Lakes*, edited by Jill B. Gidmark, 468–70. Westport: Greenwood Press, 2001.
Lemisch, Jesse. "Jack Tar in the Streets: Merchant Seamen in the Politics of Revolutionary America." *The William and Mary Quarterly* 25, no. 3 (1968): 371–407.
Leven, Karl-Heinz. "Krankheiten: Historische Deutung vs. retrospektive Diagnose." In *Medizingeschichte: Aufgaben – Probleme – Perspektiven*, edited by Norbert Paul and Thomas Schlich, 153–85. Frankfurt a. M., New York: Campus 1998.
Liesegang, Gerhard. "Dingane's Attack on Lourenco Marques in 1833." *The Journal of African History* 10, no. 4 (1969): 565–79.
Liesegang, Gerhard. "Die Guanogewinnung auf den Inseln und an der Küste Südwestafrikas." *Erdkunde* 4, no. 1/2 (1950): 35–43.
Liesegang, Gerhard. "Mozambique: Nguni/Ngoni Incursions from the South." In *Encyclopedia of African History*, edited by Kevin Shillington, 1033–4. New York: Fitzroy Dearborn, 2005.
Liesegang, Gerhard. "Mozambique: Nineteenth Century, Early." In *Encyclopedia of African History*, edited by Kevin Shillington, 1032–3. New York: Fitzroy Dearborn, 2005.
Liesegang, Gerhard. "Nguni Migrations between Delagoa Bay and the Zambezi, 1821–1839." *African Historical Studies* 3, no. 2 (1970): 317–37.
Lindgren, James M. "'Let Us Idealize Old Types of Manhood': The New Bedford Whaling Museum, 1903–1941." *The New England Quarterly* 72, no. 2 (1999): 163–206.
Linebaugh, Peter, and Marcus Rediker. *The Many-Headed Hydra: Sailors, Slaves, Commoners, and the Hidden History of the Revolutionary Atlantic*. Boston: Beacon, 2000.
Liniger-Goumaz, Max. *Äquatorialguinea: 30 Jahre nguemistischer Verbrecherstaat*. University of Leipzig Papers on Africa, Politics and Economics 21. Leipzig: Institut für Afrikanistik, 1999.
Liniger-Goumaz, Max. *Small Is Not Always Beautiful: The Story of Equatorial Guinea*. London: Hurst, 1988.
Lipski, John. "The Spanish Language of Equatorial Guinea." *Arizona Journal of Hispanic Cultural Studies* 8 (2004): 115–30.
Lobban, Richard A., jr. *Cape Verde: Crioulo Colony to Independent Nation*. Boulder, San Francisco, Oxford: Westview Press, 1995.
Lobban, Richard A., jr., and Paul Khalil Saucier. "Whaling." In *Historical Dictionary of the Republic of Cape Verde*. Vol. 4. Edited by Richard A. Lobban jr. and Paul Khalil Saucier. Lanham: Scarecrow, 2007: 241.
Loth, Heinrich. *Die christliche Mission in Südwestafrika: Zur destruktiven Rolle der Rheinischen Missionsgesellschaft beim Prozeß der Staatsbildung in Südwestafrika (1842–1893)*. Berlin: Akad.-Verl., 1963.
Lüdtke, Alf. "Alltagsgeschichte, Mikro-Historie, historische Anthropologie." In *Geschichte: Ein Grundkurs*. Third Edition. Edited by Hans-Jürgen Goertz, 628–49. Reinbek: Rowohlt, 2007.

Lüdtke, Alf."Herrschaft als soziale Praxis." In *Herrschaft als soziale Praxis. Historische und sozialanthropologische Studien*, edited by Alf Lüdtke, 9–63. Göttingen: Vandenhoeck & Ruprecht, 1991.

Lüttge, Felix. "Datenmeere. Ozeanographie im Archiv." *Jenseits des Terrazentrismus. Kartographien der Meere und die Herausbildung der globalen Welt*, edited by Wolfgang Struck, Iris Schröder & Felix Schürmann, 57–86. Göttingen: Wallstein, 2022.

Luutz, Wolfgang. "Vom ‚Containerraum' zur ‚entgrenzten' Welt: Raumbilder als sozialwissenschaftliche Leitbilder." *Social Geography* 2, no. 2 (2007): 29–45.

Ly-Tio-Fane Pineo, Huguette. *In the Grips of the Eagle: Matthew Flinders at Ile de France, 1803–1810*. Moka: Mahatma Gandhi Institute, 1988.

Ly-Tio-Fane Pineo, Huguette, and Edouard Lim Fat. *From Alien to Citizen: The Integration of the Chinese in Mauritius*. Rose-Hill: Éditions de l'océan Indien, 2008.

Macdonald, Barrie. *Cinderellas of Empire. Towards a History of Kiribati and Tuvalu*. Canberra et al.: Australian National UP, 1982.

MacGaffey, Wyatt. "Dialogues of the Deaf: Europeans on the Atlantic Coast of Africa." In *Implicit Understandings: Observing, Reporting, and Reflecting on the Encounters between Europeans and other Peoples in the Early Modern Era*, edited by Stuart B. Schwartz, 249–67. Cambridge: Cambridge UP, 1996.

MacGaffey, Wyatt. *Religion and Society in Central Africa: The Bakongo of Lower Zaire*. Chicago: U of Chicago P, 1986.

MacGaffey, Wyatt. "The West in Congolese Experience." In *Africa/the West: Intellectual Responses to European Culture*, edited by Philip D. Curtin and James W. Fernandez, 49–74. Madison: U of Wisconsin P, 1972.

Mackay, David. *In the Wake of Cook: Exploration, Science & Empire, 1780–1801*. London: Croom Helm, 1985.

Macy, Obed. *The History of Nantucket: Being a Compendious Account of the First Settlement of the Island by the English, together with Rise and Progress of the Whale Fishery, and other Historical Facts Relative to Said Island and its Inhabitants*. Boston: Hilliard, Gray & Co., 1835.

Malloy, Mary, "Journals and Logbooks." In *Encyclopedia of American Literature of the Sea and Great Lakes*, edited by Jill B. Gidmark, 220–22. Westport: Greenwood Press, 2001.

Manjakahery, Barthélémy R. L., and Marie C. Radimilahy. "Archaeology of St Augustine's Bay, Lower and Middle Onilahy Valley, South-western Madagascar." *Studies in the African Past* 5 (2006): 60–94.

Marcus, George E. "Ethnography in/of the World System: The Emergence of Multi-Sited Ethnography." *Annual Review of Anthropology* 24 (1995): 95–117.

Marikandia, Mansaré. "The Vezo of the Fihereña Coast, Southwest Madagascar: Yesterday and Today." *Ethnohistory* 48, no. 1–2 (2001): 157–70.

Maris-Wolf, Edward D. "Annobon." In *Encyclopedia of the Middle Passage*, edited by Toyin Falola and Amanda Warnock, 39–40. Westport, London: Greenwood P, 2007.

Martin, Phyllis M. "Cabinda and Cabindans: Some Aspects of an African Maritime Society." In *Africa and the Sea*, edited by Jeffrey C. Stone, 80–96. Aberdeen: Aberdeen University African Studies Group, 1985.

Martin, Phyllis M. "The Cabinda Connection: An Historical Perspective." *African Affairs* 76, no. 302 (1977): 47–59.

Martin, Phyllis M. *The External Trade of the Loango Coast, 1576–1870: The Effects of Changing Commercial Relations on the Vili Kingdom of Loango*. Oxford: Clarendon Press, 1972.

Martin, Phyllis M. "Family Strategies in Nineteenth-Century Cabinda." *The Journal of African History* 28, no. 1 (1987): 65–86.

Martin, Phyllis M. "Power, Cloth and Currency on the Loango Coast." *African Economic History* 15 (1986): 1–12.

Matos, Raimundo José da Cunha. *Corografia historica das ilhas de S. Tomè, Principe, Anno Bom, e Fernando Po*. São Tomé: Imprenza Nacional, 1916.

Mbembe, Achille. *On the Postcolony*. Berkeley/Los Angeles/London: U of California P, 2001.

McClintock, Anne. "The Angel of Progress: Pitfalls of the Term 'Post-Colo nialism'." *Social Text* 31/32 (1992): 84–98.

McCormick, Peter H. *Two New Bedford Whalemen, 1833–1895*. Mattapoisett: Vining Press, 2007.

McNeill, William H. "Comment on Miller." In *Recent Themes in the History of Africa and the Atlantic World: Historians in Conversation*, edited by Donald A. Yerxa, 29–32. Columbia: U of South Carolina P, 2008.

McPherson, Kenneth. *The Indian Ocean: A History of People and the Sea*. Delhi/New York: Oxford UP, 1993.

Medick, Hans. "Mikro-Historie." In *Sozialgeschichte, Alltagsgeschichte, Mikro-Historie: Eine Diskussion*, edited by Winfried Schulze, 40–53. Göttingen: Vandenhoeck & Ruprecht, 1994.

Meintel, Deirdre A. "Cape Verdean Transnationalism, Old and New." *Anthropologica* 44, no. 1 (2002): 25–42.

Meintel, Deirdre A. "The Creole Dialect of the Island of Brava." In *Miscelânea Luso-Africana*, edited by Marius Volkhoff et al., 205–56. Lisboa: Junta de Investigações Científicas do Ultramar, 1975.

Meintel, Deirdre A. *Race, Culture, and Portuguese Colonialism in Cabo Verde*. Syracuse: Syracuse University, 1984.

Melo, António B., de. *The Delagoa Bay World*. 2010–2014. Accessed September 15, 2022. https://delagoabayworld.wordpress.com.

Metzkes, Johann. *Otjimbingwe: Aus alten Tagen einer Rheinischen Missionsstation im Hererolande, Südwestafrika 1849–1890*. Windhoek: S.W.A. Wissenschaftliche Gesellschaft, 1962.

Miller, Joseph C. *Way of Death: Merchant Capitalism and the Angolan Slave Trade, 1730–1830*. Madison: U of Wisconsin P, 1988.

Miller, Pamela A. *And the Whale is Ours: Creative Writing of American Whalemen*. Boston; Sharon: D.R. Godine; Kendall Whaling Museum, 1979.

Moree, Perry J. *A Concise History of Dutch Mauritius, 1598–1711: A Fruitful and Healthy Land*. London, New York et al.: Kegan Paul, 1998.

Moran, Emilio F. "The Evolution of Cape Verde's Agriculture." *African Economic History* 11 (1982): 63–86.

Morison, Samuel E. *The Maritime History of Massachusetts, 1783–1860*. Boston/New York: Houghton Mifflin, 1921.

Morison, Samuel E. "The United States Africa Squadron at the Cape Verde Islands." In *Portugal and Brazil in Transition*, edited by Raymond S. Sayers, 145–8. Minneapolis: U of Minnesota P, 1968.

Moritz, Walter. *Die Nara, das Brot in der Wüste*. Windhoek: Meinert, 1992.

Mossolow, Nicolai. *Die Geschichte von Rooibank-Scheppmannsdorf*. Spenge: Eigenverlag Walter Moritz, 1969.

Mossolow, Nicolai. "Franz Heinrich Kleinschmidt 1812–1864, biographische Skizze." *Afrikanischer Heimatkalender* (1971): 37–48.
Mrantz, Maxine. *Whaling Days in Old Hawaii*. Honolulu: Aloha Graphics, 1976.
Mühleisen, Susanne. "'I've Crossed an Ocean / I've Lost my Tongue': Von Sprachbanden und Sprachbrüchen auf hoher See." In *Das Meer als kulturelle Kontaktzone: Räume, Reisende, Repräsentationen*, edited by Bernhard Klein and Gesa Mackenthun, 301–17. Konstanz: UVK, 2003.
Nehusi, Kimani S. K. "Water." In *Encyclopedia of African Religion*. Vol 1. Edited by Molefi Kete Asante and Ama Mazama, 705–9. Los Angeles et al.: SAGE, 2009.
Newitt, Malyn D. D. "Angola in Historical Context." In *Angola: The Weight of History*, edited by Patrick Chabal and Nuno Vidal, 19–92. New York: Columbia UP, 2008.
Newitt, Malyn D. D. *The Comoro Islands: Struggle Against Dependency in the Indian Ocean*. Boulder, London: Westview/Gower, 1984.
Newitt, Malyn D. D. "The Comoro Islands in Indian Ocean Trade before the 19th Century." *Cahiers d'Etudes Africaines* 23, no. 89/90 (1983): 139–65.
Newitt, Malyn D. D. "Drought in Mozambique, 1823–1831." *Journal of Southern African Studies* 15 (1988): 14–35.
Newitt, Malyn D. D. *A History of Mozambique*. London: Hurst, 1995.
Newitt, Malyn D. D. "The Portuguese on the Zambezi: An Historical Interpretation of the Prazo System." *The Journal of African History* 10, no. 1 (1969): 67–85.
Ndongo Bidyogo, Donato F. *Historia y tragedia de Guinea Ecuatorial*. Madrid: Ed. Cambio, 1977.
Nöel, Karl. *L'Esclavage à l'Isle de France (Ile Maurice) de 1715 à 1810*. Paris: Editions Two Cities, 1991.
Noli, Dieter, and Graham Avery. "Stone Circles in the Cape Fria Area, Northern Namibia." *The South African Archaeological Bulletin* 42, no. 145 (1987): 59–63.
Norling, Lisa. "The Sentimentalization of American Seafaring: The Case of the New England Whalefishery, 1790–1870." In *Jack Tar in History: Essays in the History of Maritime Life and Labour*, edited by Colin D. Howell and Richard J. Twomey, 164–78. Fredericton: Acadiensis Press, 1991.
Northrup, David. *Africa's Discovery of Europe, 1450–1850*. New York: Oxford UP, 2002.
Nunes, Maria L. *A Portuguese Colonial in America, Belmira Nunes Lopes: The Autobiography of a Cape Verdean American*. Pittsburgh: Latin American Literary Review Press, 1982.
Nwulia, Moses D. E. *The History of Slavery in Mauritius and the Seychelles, 1810–1875*. Rutherford et al.: Fairleigh Dickinson University Press, 1981.
O'Dea, William T. *The Social History of Lighting*. London: Routledge & Paul, 1958.
Oesau, Wanda. *Die deutsche Südseefischerei auf Wale im 19. Jahrhundert*. Glückstadt, Hamburg, New York: J. J. Augustin, 1939.
O'Keefe, Phil. "Toxic Terrorism." *Review of African Political Economy* 42 (1988): 84–90.
Ortega, Ángel Antonio López. "La voz, el ritmo y la memoria: la oralidad lírica de Guinea Ecuatorial." In *De Boca en Boca: Estudios de literatura oral de Guinea Ecuatorial*, edited by Jacint Creus, 145–71. Vic: CEIBA, 2004.
Pastene, Luis A., and Daniel Quiroz. "An Outline of the History of Whaling in Chile." In *Human Culture from the Perspective of Traditional Maritime Communities*, edited by International Center for Folk Culture Studies, 73–98. Kanagawa: Kanagawa Shimbun Press, 2010.
Patterson, K. David. "Epidemics, Famines, and Population in the Cape Verde Islands, 1580–1900." *International Journal of African Historical Studies* 21, no. 2 (1988): 291–313.

Pearce, Francis B. *Zanzibar: The Island Metropolis of Eastern Africa*. London: T. Fisher, 1920.
Pearson, Mike P. "Close Encounters of the Worst Kind: Malagasy Resistance and Colonial Disasters in Southern Madagascar." *World Archaeology* 28, no. 3 (1997): 393–417.
Pearson, Mike P., and Karen Godden. *In Search of the Red Slave: Shipwreck and Captivity in Madagascar*. Stroud: Sutton, 2002.
Peerthum, Satteeanund, and Satyendra Peerthum. "'Shattering the Shackles of Slavery': Rural Maroons in Port Louis with some Comparisons with Cape Town, 1811–1835." In *Maroonage and the Maroon Heritage in Mauritius*, edited by Vijayalakshmi Teelock, 77–86. Réduit: U of Mauritius, 2005.
Pereira, Clifford. "Black Liberators: The Role of Africans & Arabs sailors in the Royal Navy within the Indian Ocean 1841–1941" *The Slave Route*. Accessed December 16, 2014. http://portal.unesco.org/culture/en/files/38503/124697397957._Black_Liberators.pdf/7.%2BBlack%2BLiberators.pdf.
Pesek, Michael. "Die Kunst des Reisens: Die Begegnung von europäischen Forschungsreisenden und Ostafrikanern in den Kontaktzonen des 19. Jahrhunderts." In *Kommunikationsräume – Erinnerungsräume: Beiträge zur transkulturellen Begegnung in Afrika*, edited Winfried Speitkamp, 65–99. München: Meidenbauer, 2005.
Philbrick, Nathaniel. *In the Heart of the Sea: The Tragedy of the Whaleship Essex*. New York: Viking, 2000.
Piat, Denis. *Pirates and Corsairs in Mauritius*. Pereybere: Christian le Comte, 2007.
Pinto, Alberto O. *Cabinda e as construções da sua história (1783–1887)*. Lissabon: Dinalivro/Fundação Eng. António de Almeida, 2006.
Pool, Gerhard. *Samuel Maharero*. Windhoek: Gamsberg Macmillan, 1991.
Pope, Peter. Review of: *Between the Devil and the Deep Blue Sea: Merchant Seamen, Pirates and the Anglo-American Maritime World, 1700–1750*, by Marcus Rediker. *International Journal of Maritime History* 1 (1989): 330–4.
Popitz, Heinrich. *Prozesse der Machtbildung*. Third Edition. Tübingen: Mohr, 1976.
Post, Marike. "Fa d'Ambu." In *Pidgins and Creoles: An Introduction*, edited by Jacques Arends, Pieter Muysken, and Norval Smith, 191–204. Amsterdam: Benjamins, 1995.
Pratt, Mary L. *Imperial Eyes: Travel Writing and Transculturation*. London, New York: Routledge, 1992.
Prestholdt, Jeremy. *Domesticating the World: African Consumerism and the Genealogies of Globalization*. Berkeley: U of California P, 2008.
Putney, Martha S. "Black Merchant Seamen of Newport, 1803–1865: A Case Study in Foreign Commerce." *The Journal of Negro History* 57, no. 2 (1972): 156–68.
Pybus, Cassandra. *Epic Journeys of Freedom: Runaway Slaves of the American Revolution and Their Global Quest for Liberty*. Boston: Beacon, 2006.
Randeria, Shalini. "Geteilte Geschichte und verwobene Moderne." In *Zukunftsentwürfe: Ideen für eine Kultur der Veränderung*, edited by Jörn Rüsen, Hanna Leitgeb, and Norbert Jegelka, 87–95. Frankfurt a. M., New York: Campus, 1999.
Reddi, Sadasivam. "Aspects of Indian Culture in Ile de France during the Period 1803–1810." In *History, Memory and Identity*, edited by Vijayalakshmi Teelock and Edward A. Alpers, 33–9. Port Louis: Nelson Mandela Centre for African Culture/University of Mauritius, 2001.
Rediker, Marcus. *Between the Devil and the Deep Blue Sea: Merchant Seamen, Pirates, and the Anglo-American Maritime World, 1700–1750*. Cambridge: Cambridge UP, 1993.
Rediker, Marcus. "The Common Seaman in the Histories of Capitalism and the Working Class." *International Journal of Maritime History* 1 (1989): 337–57.

Rediker, Marcus. "Der rote Atlantik: oder: 'a terrible blast swept over the heaving sea'. " In *Das Meer als kulturelle Kontaktzone: Räume, Reisende, Repräsentationen*, edited by Bernhard Klein and Gesa Mackenthun, 143–73. Konstanz: UVK, 2003.

Reeves, Randall R. "The Origins and Character of 'Aboriginal Subsistence' Whaling: A Global Review." *Mammal Review* 32, no. 2 (2002): 71–106.

Reeves, Randall R., and Tim D. Smith. "A Taxonomy of World Whaling: Operations and Eras." In *Whales, Whaling, and Ocean Ecosystems*, edited by James A. Estes, Douglas P. Demaster, Daniel F. Doak, Terrie M. Williams, and Robert L. Brownell jr., 82–101. Berkeley: Univ. of California P, 2006.

Reid, Richard. "Past and Presentism: The 'pre-colonial' and the Foreshortening of African History." *Journal of African History* 52, no. 2 (2011): 135–55.

Reilly, Kevin S. "Slavers in Disguise: American Whaling and the African Slave Trade, 1845–1862." *American Neptune* 53.3 (1993): 177–89.

Reinhard, Wolfgang. "Kolonialgeschichtliche Probleme und kolonialhistorische Konzepte." In *Kolonialgeschichten: Regionale Perspektiven auf ein globales Phänomen*, edited by Claudia Kraft, Alf Lüdtke, and Jürgen Martschukat, 67–91. Frankfurt a. M., New York: Campus, 2010.

Rice, Alan J. *Radical Narratives of the Black Atlantic*. London: Continuum, 2003.

Richards, Rhys. *Pakehas around Porirua before 1840: Sealers, Whalers, Flax Traders and Pakeha Visitors before the Arrival of the New Zealand Company Settlers at Port Nicholson in 1840*. Wellington: Paremata Press, 2002.

Richards, Rhys. *Whaling and Sealing at the Chatham Islands*. Canberra: Roebuck Society, 1982.

Richards, Rhys, and Thierry Du Pasquier. "Bay Whaling off Southern Africa, c. 1785–1805." *South African Journal of Marine Science* 8 (1989): 231–50.

Richter, Roland. "Giftmüllexporte nach Afrika: Bestandsaufnahme eines Beispiels der Zusammenhänge zwischen Ökosystem, Ökonomie und Politik im Rahmen der Nord-Süd-Beziehungen." *Africa Spectrum* 23, no. 3 (1988): 315–50.

Rivière, Marc Serge. *"No Man Is an Island": The Irish Presence in Isle de France/Mauritius (1715–2007)*. Stanley, Rose-Hill: Editions de l'ocean Indien, 2008.

Rogers, Francis M. "Cape Verdeans." In *Harvard Encyclopedia of American Ethnic Groups*, edited by Stephan Thernstrom, 197–200. Cambridge: Belknap Press of Harvard UP. 1980.

Rosenstone, Robert A. *The Man Who Swam Into History: The (Mostly) True Story of my Jewish Family*. Austin: U of Texas P, 2005.

Rosunee, Pritilah. "Manumission and Maroonage: Resistance Strategies of Slave Women in 18th Century Isle de France." In *Maroonage and the Maroon Heritage in Mauritius*, edited by Vijayalakshmi Teelock, 59–75. Réduit: U of Mauritius, 2005.

Russell, Lynette. *Roving Mariners: Australian Aboriginal Whalers and Sealers in the Southern Oceans, 1790–1870*. Albany: State U of New York P, 2012.

Sahlins, Marshall D. *Historical Metaphors and Mythical Realities: Structure in the Early History of the Sandwich Islands Kingdom*. Ann Arbor: The Association for Social Anthropology in Oceania/U of Michigan P, 1981.

Sahlins, Marshall D. *How "Natives" Think: about Captain Cook, for Example*. Chicago: U of Chicago P, 1995.

Saint, Chandler B., and George A. Krimsky. *Making Freedom: The Extraordinary Life of Venture Smith*. Middletown: Wesleyan UP, 2009.

Salau, Mohammed Bashir. "Illegal Slave Trade, Brazil." In *Encyclopedia of the Middle Passage*, edited by Toyin Falola and Amanda Warnock, 223–4. Westport/London: Greenwood Press, 2007.

Sandelowsky, B. H. "Mirabib: An Archaeological Study in the Namib." *Madoqua* 10, no. 4 (1977): 221–80.

Sanderson, Ivan T. *Follow the Whale*. Boston, Toronto: Little, Brown & Co., 1956.

Schivelbusch, Wolfgang. "The Policing of Street Lighting." *Yale French Studies* 73 (1987): 61–74.

Schlögel, Karl. *In Space We Read Time: On the History of Civilization and Geopolitics*. New York City: Bard Graduate Center, 2016.

Schmitt, Frederick P. *Mark Well the Whale! Long Island Ships to Distant Seas*. Port Washington, London: Ira J. Friedman Division, Kennikat Press, 1971.

Schokkenbroek, Joost C. A. *Trying-out: An Anatomy of Dutch Whaling and Sealing in the Nineteenth Century, 1815–1885*. Amsterdam: Aksant, 2008.

Schultze, Arnold. "Die Insel Annobon im Golf von Guinea." *Dr. A. Petermanns Mitteilungen aus Justus Perthes' Geographischer Anstalt* 59, no. 1 (1913): 131–3.

Schultze, Leonhard S. *Aus Namaland und Kalahari: Bericht an die Kgl. preuss. Akademie der Wissenschaften zu Berlin über eine Forschungsreise im westlichen und zentralen Südafrika, ausgeführt in den Jahren 1903–1905*. Jena: G. Fischer, 1907.

Schumann, Gunter E. von. "Schiffe und ihre Mannschaften vor Namibias Küste: Ein Rückblick in die Geschichte der Seefahrt." *Afrikanischer Heimatkalender* (1995): 101–10.

Schürmann, Felix. "Neue Hilfsmittel zur amerikanischen Walfanggeschichte." *Deutsches Schiffahrtsarchiv* 34 (2011): 256–8.

Schürmann, Felix. Review of: *A Narrative of the Life, Travels, and Sufferings of Thomas W. Smith . . .*, by Thomas W. Smith, edited by Damien Sanders (2009). *geschichte. transnational*, 30.07.2010. Accessed Septmber 15, 2022. http://geschichte-transnational.clio-online.net/rezensionen/id=14802.

Schürmann, Felix. "Die Wale, ihre Jäger und der Strand von Annobón." In *Afrikanische Tierräume: Historische Verortungen*, edited by Winfried Speitkamp and Stephanie Zehnle, 43–76. Köln: Köppe, 2014.

Schwartz, Stuart B. "Introduction." In *Implicit Understandings: Observing, Reporting, and Reflecting on the Encounters between Europeans and other Peoples in the Early Modern Era*, edited by Stuart B. Schwartz, 1–19. Cambridge: Cambridge UP, 1996.

Scott, Julius S. *The Common Wind: Afro-American Currents in the Age of the Haitian Revolution*. London/New York: Verso, 2018.

Shell, Robert C.-H. "The Twinning of Maputo and Cape Town: The Early Mozambican Slave Trade to the Slave Lodge, 1677–1731." In *History, Memory and Identity*, edited by Vijayalakshmi Teelock and Edward A. Alpers, 178–88. Port Louis: Nelson Mandela Centre for African Culture/University of Mauritius, 2001.

Shepherd, Gill. "The Comorians and the East African Slave Trade." In *Asian and African Systems of Slavery*, edited by James L. Watson, 73–99. Berkeley: U of California P, 1980.

Sherman, Stuart C. "The Nature, Possibilities and Limitations of Whaling Logbook Data." In *Historical Whaling Records*, edited by Michael F. Tillman and Gregory P. Donovan, 35–9. Reports of the International Whaling Commission, Special Issue 5. Cambridge: International Whaling Commission, 1983.

Sherman, Stuart C. *The Voice of the Whaleman: With an Account of the Nicholson Whaling Collection*. Providence: Providence Public Library, 1965.

Sherman, Stuart C. *Whaling Logbooks and Journals, 1613–1927: An Inventory of Manuscript Records in Public Collections*. New York/London: Garland, 1986.
Shillington, Kevin. *History of Africa*. Oxford, New York: Palgrave Macmillan, 2005.
Silva, Filipa R., da. *Dutch and Portuguese in Western Africa: Empires, Merchants and the Atlantic System, 1580–1674*. Leiden, Boston: Brill, 2011.
Simons, Ben. "Christopher Hussey Blown Out (Up) to Sea." *Historic Nantucket* 53, no. 3 (2004): 9–10.
Sittert, Lance, van, and Rob Crawford. "Historical Reconstruction of Guano Production on the Namibian Islands 1843–1895." *South African Journal of Science* 99 (2003): 13–6.
Smith, Alan K. "The Indian Ocean Zone." In *History of Central Africa*, edited by David Birmingham and Phyllis M. Martin, 233–6. London, New York: Longman, 1983.
Smith, Alan K. "The Peoples of Southern Mozambique: An Historical Survey." *The Journal of African History* 14, no. 4 (1973): 565–80.
Smith, Alan K. "The Trade of Delagoa Bay as a Factor in Nguni Politics, 1750–1835." In *African Societies in Southern Africa*, edited by Leonard Thompson, 171–90. London, Ibadan, Nairobi: Heinemann, 1969.
Smith, Andrew B., and John Kinahan. "The Invisible Whale." *World Archaeology* 16, no. 1 (1984): 89–97.
Smith, Tim D., Randall R. Reeves, Elizabeth A. Josephson, and Judith N. Lund. "Spatial and Seasonal Distribution of American Whaling and Whales in the Age of Sail." *PLoS ONE* 7(4): e34905. doi:10.1371/journal.pone.0034905, 2014. Accessed September 15, 2022. http://www.plosone.org/article/info%3Adoi%2F10.1371%2Fjournal.pone.0034905
Smoltczyk, Alexander. "Volltanken in Malabo." *Der Spiegel* 35 (2006): 82–101.
Solow, Barbara L. "Capitalism and Slavery in the Exceedingly Long Run." *Journal of Interdisciplinary History* 17, no. 4 (1987): 711–37.
Sorge-English, Lynn. "'9 Doz and 11 Best Cutt Bone': The Trade in Whalebone and Stays in Eighteenth-Century London." *Textile History* 36, no. 1 (2005): 20–45.
Spence, Bill. *Harpooned: The Story of Whaling*. Greenwich: Conway Maritime Press, 1980.
Spivak, Gayatri C. *Can the Subaltern Speak? Postkolonialität und subalterne Artikulation*. Wien: Turia + Kant, 2008.
Stackpole, Edouard A. *The Sea-Hunters: The New England Whalemen During Two Centuries, 1635–1835*. Philadelphia et al.: Lippincott, 1953.
Stackpole, Edouard A. *Whales & Destiny: The Rivalry between America, France, and Britain for Control of the Southern Whale Fishery, 1785–1825*. Amherst: U. of Massachusetts Press, 1972.
Starbuck, Alexander. *History of the American Whale Fishery*. Secaucus: Castle Books, 1989.
Starbuck, Alexander. *The History of Nantucket: County, Island and Town, Including Genealogies of the First Settlers*. Rutland: Charles E. Tuttle, 1969.
Stern, Jonathan. "Migration and Movement Patterns." In *Encyclopedia of Marine Mammals*, edited by William F. Perrin, Bernd Wursig, and J. G. M. Thewissen, 726–730. San Diego: Academic Press, 2004.
Stolberg, Michael. "Der gesunde Leib: Zur Geschichtlichkeit frühneuzeitlicher Körpererfahrung." *Historische Zeitschrift*, Beiheft 31 (2001): 37–57.
Stone, Thomas. "Whalers and Missionaries at Herschel Island." *Ethnohistory* 28, no. 2 (1981): 101–24.
Storey, William K. *Science and Power in Colonial Mauritius*. Rochester: U of Rochester P, 1997.

Strickrodt, Silke. "Die brasilianische Diaspora in Westafrika im 19. Jahrhundert." In *Afrika 1500–1900: Geschichte und Gesellschaft*, edited by Andreas Eckert, Ingeborg Grau, and Arno Sonderegger, 194–217. Wien: Promedia-Verl., 2010.

Stubbs, Tristan. "Abolition of the Slave Trade, Brazil." In *Encyclopedia of the Middle Passage*, edited by Toyin Falola and Amanda Warnock, 3–5. Westport, London: Greenwood Press, 2007.

Subrahmanyam, Sanjay. "Connected Histories: Notes towards a Reconfiguration of Early Modern Eurasia." *Modern Asian Studies* 31, no. 3 (1997): 735–62.

Sundiata, Ibrahim K. *Equatorial Guinea: Colonialism, State Terror, and the Search for Stability*. Boulder, Colorado: Westview, 1990.

Sundiata, Ibrahim K. *From Slaving to Neoslavery: The Bight of Biafra and Fernando Po in the Era of Abolition, 1827–1930*. Madison, London: U of Wisconsin P, 1996.

Sydow, Wolfgang. "Contributions to the History and Protohistory of the Topnaar Strandloper Settlement at the Kuiseb River Mouth near Walvis Bay." *The South African Archaeological Bulletin* 28 (1973): 73–7.

Teelock, Vijaya. *Bitter Sugar: Sugar and Slavery in 19th Century Mauritius*. Moka: Mahatma Gandhi Institute, 1998.

Teelock, Vijaya. *Mauritian History: From its Beginnings to Modern Times*. Moka: Mahatma Gandhi Institute, 2009.

Teelock, Vijaya. "From Mozambique to Le Morne Brabant Mountain: Being Young, Male and Mozambican in Colonial Mauritius." In *Slave Routes and Oral Tradition in Southeastern Africa*, edited by Benigna Zimba, Edward A. Alpers, and Allen Isaacman, 279–94. Maputo: Filsom Entertainment, 2005.

Teller, Walter M. *Twelve Works of Naive Genius*. New York: Harcourt Brace Jovanovich, 1972.

Theal, George M. *History of South Africa, 1795–1834*. London: Swan Sonnenschein, 1891.

Theal, George M. *History of South Africa under the Administration of the Dutch East India Company, 1652 to 1795*. Vol. 2. London: Swan Sonnenschein, 1897.

Thornton, John K. *Africa and Africans in the Making of the Atlantic World, 1400–1800*. Second Edition. Cambridge: Cambridge UP, 1998.

Tonkin, Elizabeth. "Creating Kroomen: Ethnic Diversity, Economic Specialism and Changing Demand." In *Africa and the Sea*, edited by Jeffrey C. Stone, 27–47. Aberdeen: Aberdeen University African Studies Group, 1985.

Tønnessen, Johan N., and Arne O. Johnsen. *The History of Modern Whaling*. Berkeley: U of California P, 1982.

Toorawa, Shawkat M. "The Medieval Waqwaq Islands and the Mascarenes." In *The Western Indian Ocean: Essays on Islands and Islanders*, edited by Shawkat M. Toorawa, 49–65. Port Louis: Hassam Toorawa Trust, 2007.

Toussaint, Auguste. *Early American Trade with Mauritius*. Port Louis, Mauritius: Esclapon, 1954.

Toussaint, Auguste. *History of the Indian Ocean*. London: Routledge and Kegan Paul, 1966.

Toussaint, Auguste. *Port Louis: A Tropical City*. London: Allen & Unwin, 1973.

Toussaint, Auguste. "The Role of Trade in the Settlement of Mauritius." In *Historical Relations Across the Indian Ocean: Report and Papers of the Meeting of Experts Organized by UNESCO at Port Louis, Mauritius, from 15 to 19 July 1974*, edited by UNESCO, 117–24. Paris: UNESCO, 1980.

Townsend, Charles H. "Where the Nineteenth Century Whaler Made His Catch." *New York Zoological Society Bulletin* 34, no. 6 (1931): 173–9.

Treinen, Heiner. "Parasitäre Anarchie: Die karibische Piraterie im 17. Jahrhundert." *Kölner Zeitschrift für Soziologie und Sozialpsychologie* 33 (1981): 50–72.
Trüper, Ursula. *The Invisible Woman: Zara Schmelen, African Mission Assistant at the Cape and in Namaland*. Basel: Basler Afrika Bibliographien, 2006.
Ulrich, Nicole. "Dr Anders Sparrman: Travelling with the Labouring Poor in the Late-Eighteenth-Century Cape." *South African Historical Journal* 61, no. 4 (2009): 731–49.
Unzueta y Yuste, Abelardo, de. *Islas del Golfo de Guinea (Elobeyes, Corisco, Annobon, Principe y Santo Tome)*. Madrid: Inst. de Estudios Políticos, 1945.
Uys, Cornelis J. *In the Era of Shepstone: Being A Study of British Expansion in South Africa (1842–1877)*. Lovedale: Lovedale Press, 1933.
Vail, Leroy, and Landeg White. *Capitalism and Colonialism in Mozambique: A Study of Quelimane District*. London: Heinemann, 1980.
Van den Boogaerde, Pierre. *Shipwrecks of Madagascar*. New York: Eloquent Books, 2009.
Vansina, Jan. *Paths in the Rainforests: Toward a History of Political Tradition in Equatorial Africa*. London: Currey, 1990.
Varma, Moonindra N. *The Making of Mauritius*. Vacoas: Éditions Le Printemps, 2008.
Vaughan, Megan. *Creating the Creole Island: Slavery in Eighteenth-century Mauritius*. Durham: Duke University Press, 2005.
Vaughan, Megan. "Slavery and Colonial Identity in Eighteenth Century Mauritius." In *History, Memory and Identity*, edited by Vijayalakshmi Teelock and Edward A. Alpers, 41–80. Port Louis: Nelson Mandela Centre for African Culture/University of Mauritius, 2001.
Vedder, Heinrich. *Das alte Südwestafrika: Südwestafrikas Geschichte bis zum Tode Mahareros 1890, nach den besten schriftlichen und mündlichen Quellen erzählt*. Berlin: M. Warneck, 1934.
Velde, Paul van der. "Jacob Haafner in Mauritius, 1786–87." In *The Western Indian Ocean: Essays on Islands and Islanders*, edited by Shawkat M. Toorawa, 67–90. Port Louis: Hassam Toorawa Trust, 2007.
Venables, Bernard. *Baleia! Baleia! Whale hunters of the Azores*. New York: Knopf, 1969.
Vickers, Daniel F. Review of: *Between the Devil and the Deep Blue Sea: Merchant Seamen, Pirates and the Anglo-American Maritime World, 1700–1750*, by Marcus Rediker. *International Journal of Maritime History* 1 (1989): 311–3.
Vieira, Alberto. "The Fortunate of the Fortunates: The Islands and the Atlantic System." In *Atlantic History: History of the Atlantic System, 1580–1830*, edited by Horst Pietschmann, 199–248. Göttingen: Vandenhoeck & Ruprecht, 2002.
Vieira, Nina, Cristina Brito, Ana Catarina Garcia, Hilarino da Luz, Hermano Noronha & Dúnia Pereira. "The Whale in the Cape Verde Islands: Seascapes as a Cultural Construction from the Viewpoint of History, Literature, Local Art and Heritage." *Humanities* 9.3 (2020): 90, https://doi.org/10.3390/h9030090.
Vigne, Randolph. "The Hard Road to Colonization: The Topnaar [[]Aonin] of Namibia, 1670–1878." *Journal of Colonialism and Colonial History* 1, no. 2 (2000).
Vink, Markus. "'The World's Oldest Trade': Dutch Slavery and Slave Trade in the Indian Ocean in the Seventeenth Century." *Journal of World History* 14, no. 2 (2003): 131–77.
Volavka, Zdenka. *Crown and Ritual: The Royal Insignia of Ngoyo*. Toronto, Buffalo, London: U. of Toronto P., 1998.
Waerebeek, K., van, P.K. Ofori-Danson, and J. Debrah. "The Cetaceans of Ghana, a Validated Faunal Checklist." *West African Journal of Applied Ecology* 15, no. 1 (2009). Accessed September 15, 2022. http://www.ajol.info/index.php/wajae/article/view/49428/35762.

Walcott, Derek. *Selected Poems*. Edited by Edward Baugh. New York: Farrar, Straus and Giroux, 2007.
Walker, Barbara. "African Fisheries." In *Africana: The Encyclopedia of the African & African American Experience*. Vol. 2. Edited by Kwame Anthony Appiah and Henry Louis Gates, jr., 655–7. Oxford: Oxford Univ. Press, 2005.
Wallace, Frederick W. *Wooden Ships and Iron Men: The Story of the Square-rigged Merchant Marine of British North America, the Ships, their Builders and Owners and the Men who Sailed them*. London: Hodder & Stoughton, 1924.
Wallace, Marion. *History of Namibia: From the Earliest Times to 1990*. London: Hurst, 2011.
Warrin, Donald. *So Ends This Day: The Portuguese in American Whaling, 1765–1927*. North Dartmouth: University of Massachusetts Dartmouth, Center for Portuguese Studies and Culture, 2010.
Watson, Arthur C. "The Guano Islands of Southwestern Africa." *Geographical Review* 20, no. 4 (1930): 631–41.
Webb, Robert L. *On the Northwest: Commercial Whaling in the Pacific Northwest, 1790–1967*. Vancouver: U of British Columbia P, 1988.
Weber, Max. *Wirtschaft und Gesellschaft: Grundriss der verstehenden Soziologie*. Frankfurt a. M.: Zweitausendeins, 2005.
Weibust, Knut. *Deep Sea Sailors: A Study in Maritime Ethnology*. Stockholm: Nordiska museet, 1969.
Weir, Caroline R. "Occurrence and Distribution of Cetaceans off Northern Angola, 2004/05." *Journal of Cetacean Research and Management* 9, no. 3 (2007): 225–39.
Weir, Caroline R. "A Review of Cetacean Occurrence in West African Waters from the Gulf of Guinea to Angola." *Mammal Review* 40, no. 1 (2010): 2–39.
Werner, Michael, and Bénédicte Zimmermann. "Vergleich, Transfer, Verflechtung: Der Ansatz der Histoire croisée und die Herausforderung des Transnationalen." *Geschichte und Gesellschaft* 28 (2002): 607–36.
Werz, Bruno E. J. S. "The 'Vlissingen': A Dutch East India Company Ship that Perished along the Namibian Shore in 1747." In *Namibia and The Netherlands: 350 Years of Relations*, edited by Huub Hendrix, 21–9. Windhoek: Ambassade van het koninkrijk der Nederlanden, 2006.
"Whaling." In *The Oxford Companion to Ships and the Sea*, edited by Peter Kemp, 933–6. London, New York, Melbourne: Oxford UP, 1976.
Whitehead, Hal. "Sperm Whale." In *Encyclopedia of Marine Mammals*, edited by William F. Perrin, Bernd Wursig, and J. G. M. Thewissen, 1091–7. San Diego: Academic Press, 2004.
Widlok, Thomas. "Dealing with Institutional Changes in Property Regimes: An African Case Study." Max Planck Institute for Social Anthropology Working Papers 12. Halle/Saale: Max Planck Institute for Social Anthropology, 2000.
Wigen, Kären. "Introduction." In *Seascapes: Maritime Histories, Littoral Cultures, and Transoceanic Exchanges*, edited by Jerry H. Bentley, Renate Bidenthal, and Kären Wigen, 1–20. Honolulu: U of Hawai P, 2007.
Wilken, J. J. J., and G. J. Fox. *The History of the Port and Settlement of Walvis Bay, 1878–1978*. Johannesburg: Perskor, 1978.
Williams, Dwayne E. "Rethinking the African Diaspora: A Comparative Look at Race and Identity in a Transatlantic Community, 1878–1921." In *Crossing Boundaries: Comparative*

History of Black People in Diaspora, edited by Darlene C. Hine and Jacqueline MacLeod, 105–20. Bloomington: Indiana UP, 1999.
Wilmsen, Edwin N. *Land Filled with Flies: A Political Economy of the Kalahari*. Chicago: U of Chicago P, 1992.
Williams, J. R. "The Whale Fishery." *North American Review* 38, no. 82 (1834): 84–116.
Worden, Nigel. "Cape Town and Port Louis in the Eighteenth Century." In *The Indian Ocean Rim: Southern Africa and Regional Cooperation*, edited by Gwyn Campbell, 42–53. London: RoutledgeCurzon, 2003.
Wray, Phoebe, and Kenneth R. Martin. "Historical Whaling Records from the Western Indian Ocean." In *Historical Whaling Records*, edited by Michael F. Tillman and Gregory P. Donovan, 213–41. Reports of the International Whaling Commission, Special Issue 5, Cambridge: International Whaling Commission, 1983.
Wright, Carol. *Mauritius*. Newton Abbot: David Charles, 1974.
Wyatt, T. "Morrell's Seals." *Journal du Conseil International pour l'Exploration de la Mer* 39, no. 1 (1980): 1–6.
Young, Eric. "Angola." In *Africana: The Encyclopedia of the African & African American Experience*. Vol. 2. Edited by Kwame Anthony Appiah and Henry Louis Gates, Jr., 207–12. New York: Basic Civitas Books, 1999.
Young, Sherilynn. "Fertility and Famine: Women's Agricultural History in Southern Mozambique." In *The Roots of Rural Poverty in Central and Southern Africa*, edited by Robin Palmer and Neil Parsons, 66–81. London, Ibadan, Nairobi: Heinemann, 1977.
Zamora Loboch, Francisco. "Los Paraisos Imposibles." Paper presented at Hofstra Cultural Center. *Between Three Continents: Rethinking Equatorial Guinea on the Fortieth Anniversary of its Independence from Spain*, Hempstead, 02.–04.04.2009. Accessed December 16, 2014. http://www.hofstra.edu/pdf/Community/culctr/culctr_guinea040209_VIIIBloboch.pdf.
Zamora Loboch, Miguel. *Notícia de Annobón: Su Geografía, Historia y Costumbres*. Madrid: Papelería Madrilena, 1962.
Zeuske, Michael. "Mongos und Negreros: Atlantische Sklavenhändler im 19. Jahrhundert und der iberische Sklavenhandel 1808/1820–1873." In *Sklaverei und Postemanzipationsgesellschaften in Afrika und der Karibik*. Periplus – Jahrbuch für außereuropäische Geschichte 20. Edited by Christine Hatzky and Ulrike Schmieder, 57–115. Berlin: Lit, 2010.

University Publications

Berat, Lynn. "Walvis Bay and the Decolonization of International Law." PhD diss., Yale University, 1988.
Booth, Alan R. "Americans in South Africa, 1784–1870." PhD diss., Boston University Graduate School, 1964.
Cantús, Dolores G. "Fernando Poo: Una aventura colonial Española en el África occiental (1778–1900)." PhD diss., Universitat de Valencia, 2004.
Carr, James R. "In the Wake of John Kanaka: Musical Interactions Between Euro-American Sailors and Pacific Islanders, 1600–1900." PhD diss., University of California, Santa Barbara 2007.

Chappell, David A. "Beyond the Beach: Periplean Frontiers of Pacific Islanders aboard Euroamerican Ships, 1768–1887." PhD diss., University of Hawai'i, 1991.
Chatwin, Dale. "'A Trade so Uncontrollably Uncertain': A Study of the English Southern Whale Fishery from 1815 to 1860." M. A. Thesis, Australian National University, 1997.
Dillard, Jessica. "A Whale of a Man: Manhood, Homoeroticism, and Herman Melville's 'Moby-Dick'." PhD diss., Sarah Lawrence College, 2006.
Dubins, Barbara D. "A Political History of the Comoro Islands, 1795–1886." PhD diss., Boston University, 1974.
Gatlin, Darryle J. "A Socioeconomic History of São Vicente de Cabo Verde, 1830–1970." PhD diss., University of California, Los Angeles, 1990.
Haywood, Carl N. "American Whalers and Africa." PhD diss., Boston University, 1967.
Hedges, David W. "Trade and Politics in Southern Mozambique and Zululand in the Eighteenth and Early Nineteenth Centuries." PhD diss., University of London, 1978.
Hilt, Eric D. "Contracts, Risk Taking and Diversification in the American Whaling Industry." PhD diss., Columbia University, 2002.
Hooper, Jane L. "An Empire in the Indian Ocean: The Sakalava Empire of Madagascar." PhD diss., Emory University, 2010.
LaPorte, Laurie L. "The Continuities of Modernity: Cape Verdean Identity and Emigration." PhD diss., Boston University, 2007.
Liesegang, Gerhard J. "Beiträge zur Geschichte des Reiches des Gaza Nguni im südlichen Moçambique, 1820–1895." PhD diss., Universität zu Köln, 1967.
Mc Devitt, Joseph L. "The House of Rotch: Whaling Merchants of Massachusetts, 1734–1828." PhD diss., The American University, 1978.
Meintel, Deirdre A. "Cape Verdean-Americans: Their Cultural and Historical Background." PhD diss., Brown University, 1978.
Pilgrim, Aminah N. "'Free Men Name Themselves': Cape Verdeans in Massachusetts Negotiate Race, 1900–1980." PhD diss., Rutgers University, 2009.
Schürmann, Felix. "Land zu Territorium? Zur Territorialisierung von Herrschaftsstrategien im südwestlichen Afrika, ca. 1790–1890." M. A. Thesis, Leibniz-Universität Hannover, 2007.
Smith, Alan K. "The Struggle for Control of Southern Moçambique, 1720–1835." PhD diss., University of California, Los Angeles, 1971.
Vaz, Neil. "The Trans-Atlantic Slave Trade and the African Origins of the Peoples of Grenada, 1709–1837." M. A. Thesis, Howard University, 2011.
Vickers, Daniel F. "Maritime Labor in Colonial Massachusetts: A Case Study of the Essex County Cod Fishery and the Whaling Industry of Nantucket, 1630–1775." PhD diss., Princeton University, 1981.

Encyclopedias, Bibliographies and Databases

Appiah, Kwame A., and Henry Louis Gates Jr., eds. *Africana: The Encyclopedia of the African & African American Experience*. Oxford: Oxford UP, 2005.
Asante, Molefi K., and Ama Mazama, eds. *Encyclopedia of African Religion*. Los Angeles et al.: SAGE, 2009.
Burton, Maurice, and Robert Burton, eds. *International Wildlife Encyclopedia*. Third Volume. Tarrytown: Marshall Cavendish Corp., 2002.

Falola, Toyin, and Amanda Warnock, eds. *Encyclopedia of the Middle Passage*. Westport, London: Greenwood Press, 2007.
Fegley, Randall. *Equatorial Guinea*. World Bibliographical Series 136. Oxford: Clio, 1991
Gidmark, Jill B., ed. *Encyclopedia of American Literature of the Sea and Great Lakes*. Westport: Greenwood, 2001.
Jones, A. G. E. *Ships Employed in the South Seas Trade, 1775–1861 (Parts I and II) and, Registrar General of Shipping and Seaman: Transcripts of Registers of Shipping, 1787–1862 (Part III)*. Canberra: Roebuck Society, 1986.
Kemp, Peter, ed. *The Oxford Companion to Ships and the Sea*. London, New York, Meulbourne: Oxford UP, 1976.
Lau, Brigitte. *Carl Hugo Hahn 1837–1860: A Missionary in Nama- and Damaraland – Register and Indexes*. Carl Hugo Hahn Papers 5. Windhoek: Dep. of National, 1985.
Liniger-Goumaz, Max. *Historical Dictionary of Equatorial Guinea*. Third Edition. African Historical Dictionaries 21. Lanham: Scarecrow, 2000.
Lobban, Richard, and Marlene Lopes. *Historical Dictionary of the Republic of Cape Verde*. Third Edition. African Historical Dictionaries 62. Metuchen: Scarecrow, 1995.
Lund, Judith N., Elizabeth A. Josephson, Randall R. Reeves and Tim D. Smith. *American Offshore Whaling Voyages: A Database*. National Maritime Digital Library, 2008. Accessed September 15, 2022. http://www.nmdl.org.
Lund, Judith N. et al. *Whaling Crew List Database*. New Bedford Whaling Museum, 2011. Accessed September 15, 2022. http://www.whalingmuseum.org/online_exhibits/crewlist.
Lobban, Richard A., jr., and Paul Khalil Saucier, eds. *Historical Dictionary of the Republic of Cape Verde*. Fourth Edition. Lanham: Scarecrow, 2007.
Middleton, John, ed. *Encyclopedia of Africa South of the Sahara*. New York: C. Scribner's Sons, 1997.
Núñez, Benjamin. *Dictionary of Portuguese-African Civilization: Vol. 1: From Discovery to Independence*. London et al.: Zell, 1995.
Overbeek, Jaap, van. *De VOC Site*. 2002–2012. Accessed September 15, 2022. http://www.vocsite.nl.
Perrin, William F., Bernd Wursig, and J. G. M. Thewissen, eds. *Encyclopedia of Marine Mammals*. San Diego: Academic Press, 2004.
Shillington, Kevin, ed. *Encyclopedia of African History*. New York: Fitzroy Dearborn, 2005.
Tabler, Edward C. *Pioneers of South West Africa and Ngamiland, 1738–1880*. Kapstadt: Balkema, 1973.
Thernstrom, Stephan, ed. *Harvard Encyclopedia of American Ethnic Groups*. Cambridge: Belknap Press of Harvard UP, 1980.
Voyages Database. *Voyages: The Trans-Atlantic Slave Trade Database*. 2009. Accessed September 15, 2022 http://www.slavevoyages.org.
Yamamoto, S., ed. *Sailing Navies*. 2002. Accessed December 16, 2014 http://www.sailingnavies.com.

Vessels Index

Unless otherwise stated, the vessels listed below are whalers.

A. E. Whyland 485
A. M. Nicholson 485, 494
A. R. Tucker 216, 351, 356
Abigail 311
Acredam 42 f., 366
Acushnet 195, 443
Adelia Chase 485
Adeline 228, 236
Adeline Gibbs 384, 433, 436
Admiral Blake 327, 400, 403, 429, 430, 433, 462
Adventure 447
Alabama (privateer) 283
Albert (expedition vessel) 404
Alcyone 165, 312, 320
Alexander 162
Alexander Barclay 344
Alliance 5, 6, 48, 122, 146, 147, 194, 213, 301, 303, 310, 319, 320, 471
Alto 262–63
Amelia 437
Ann (guano transport vessel) 105
Ann 68, 89
Ann Alexander 195, 207
Ann Maria 149, 243
Ann Parry 232, 311, 314, 315, 318, 331, 324, 336
Annie Ann 315
Antarctic (sealing vessel) 93
Arab 54
Arcturus (packet vessel) 501
Argo 18
Arthur V. S. Woodruff 478
Asia 5–7, 48, 213, 303
Atlantic 65, 225, 283, 312, 321
Aurelia 270
Aurora 437
Averick 236
Avola 268, 311

Baltic 485
Barracouta (expedition vessel) 373, 382

Bellisle 45
Benjamin 123
Bertha 170, 195n185, 367, 385, 387, 432 f., 437, 480, 485, 494
Betsey 65, 89
Boode (expedition vessel) 78, 79, 85, 92, 97
Boston 243
Boston Packet 68
Braganza 436
Bramin 147
Brewster 177, 319
Britannia 48
Brookline (guano transport vessel) 106
Bruce 21, 22n66, 172 f., 207, 235, 241, 242, 265, 330, 347, 349, 355 f., 358, 448, 468

Caleb Eaton 437
Cameo 485
Canton 121
Canton II 420, 485
Carleton Bell 485, 494
Cassandra (merchant vessel) 248
Ceres 24, 337, 269n118, 307, 322, 461n55
Charles and Henry 443
Charles Carroll 193, 212
Charles Colgate 141n91, 467, 477
Charles Henry 476
Charles W. Morgan 165, 170, 284, 432, 444, 483–85
Charles W. Morse 394
Charming Susanna (slave ship) 4
Chili 475, 484
Cicero 379
Clara Bell 202n223, 211, 213, 226, 229, 234, 259, 266, 355
Clara L. Sparks 352
Clarice 392, 433, 477n150
Clarkson 196
Claudia 485
Cleopatra (warship) 232, 234, 305
Cohannet 436
Colonel Crocket (merchant vessel) 148

Columbia 167n49, 461
Commodore Perry 71, 90, 98
Condor 487
Coquette 271
Coral 487
Coriolanus (packet vessel) 494, 496, 501
Cornelia 436
Cyrus 124

Dale (warship) 275 f., 505
Dauphin 123
Delta 156
Desdemona 216, 385, 388, 437
Dimon 243

Eagle (merchant vessel) 108
Edward 122, 237
Eleanor B. Conwell 485
Eliza 67n10, 120, 148n135, 280 f., 311
Eliza Adams 437
Eliza Grant 473
Elligood 213
Emerald 17, 55, 174, 212, 344
Emigrant 24, 38n2, 175, 193n164, 199, 300, 313, 333, 445
Emilia 48
Emma (merchant vessel) 112
Enterprise 487
Era 483
Ernestina (packet vessel) 501
Esquimaux 165
Essex (warship) 51
Essex 20, 195 f.
Eugenia 311
Eunice H. Adams 485
Eureka 140
Europa 485

Falcon 17n49, 216, 237, 393, 397, 433, 436 f.
Fannie Byrnes 485
Flora (merchant vessel) 76
Florida (privateer) 283
Foam (merchant vessel) 107n245, 112
Foster 193
Foxhound 244

Frances A. Barstow 334
Francis Allyn 477
Franklin 70, 91
Friendship 101
Funchal (merchant vessel) 473

Gazelle 436
General Pike 235
George 148
George and Mary 388
George and Susan 335, 436, 437
George Howland 436
Georgia 149, 243
Gertrude Howes (merchant vessel) 113 f.
Globe 10, 20, 53, 177, 336 f., 364, 366, 379, 384, 391, 402, 414, 416 f., 429–431
Golconda II 236
Golden City 485
Good Intent 120, 122
Gorgon (warship) 117 f., 146
Governor Carver 379
Grand Turk 231, 235, 309
Greyhound 123, 351, 434, 437, 494
Grundel (expedition vessel) 78

Hadley 436, 437
Harmony 195
Harrison 335, 337n59
Hecla 193
Helenmar (merchant vessel) 102
Henrietta 244
Herald II 265, 327, 340, 352, 462, 468
Hercules 56
Hercules II 34n112, 71n35, 76n60, 148, 213n17
Hibernia 462
Hope 73n49, 95, 96n180, 101n218
Houqua 232
Hudson 202, 229, 231
Hunter (merchant vessel) 319

Intrepid 447
Isabella 437
Islander 326

Israel 145, 147, 149, 176n94
Izette 230

J. H. Duvall 312
James Allen II 437
James Edward 315
James Maury 163
Janet 196, 429
Janus 56, 228, 353, 423 f., 427
Jasper (merchant vessel) 209
Java 287, 289, 300, 308, 316
John and Edward 237, 243, 378, 380, 385–87
John Dawson 268, 308
John Howland 437
John and Winthrop 436
Joseph 122
Josephine 61, 245, 283, 288, 321
Judith 50, 101
Junius 118, 212

Kathleen 39n5, 74, 194 f., 196n191, 198n205, 241, 244 f., 264, 267 f., 333, 363, 366, 378, 380, 382, 384, 386, 391, 396 f., 472, 480, 485, 490
Kent 447
Keoka 71n38, 379
Kingston 48, 74n56, 213, 463, 468

l'Héroïne (warship) 71, 80n83, 93, 98, 102
La Circé (warship) 71
La Vénus (warship) 78
La Zélée (warship) 276
Leonidas 236, 382, 414, 429, 436
Leven (expedition vessel) 89, 92, 98, 113, 224, 373, 382
Leviathan 45, 69, 159n16
Lion (merchant vessel) 118n7
Liverpool (privateer) 50, 69, 101
London 68, 73, 89, 99, 161
Lottie Beard (tender ship) 388–90, 392, 395, 397
Lottie E. Cook 146
Louisa Sears 200, 378
Lucas 212
Lucy Ann 443

Magnolia 485
Malay 212
Marcella 163, 178, 244, 256, 268
Margaret Scott 311
Margarett 485, 494
Maria 124, 274 f., 277
Mars 226, 233, 237, 397
Martha 120, 147 f.
Martha II 301
Mattapoisett 437, 468, 470
Mechanic 287
Medusa (warship) 471
Meermin (expedition vessel) 76, 92 f., 95, 98, 100 f.
Mercury 287, 311, 337, 348, 431, 433, 436
Merlin 273, 301, 305n80
Mermaid 339, 392, 437
Milton 397
Milwood 160, 237
Minerva 225, 402, 413
Minnesota 436, 437
Modeste (privateer) 124
Monmouth 326
Montgomery 212n8, 237
Montreal 348
Morning Star 389, 485

Nathaniel S. Perkins 462
Nautilus (expedition vessel) 67, 78, 91, 101
Nautilus 92, 212, 193, 362, 386, 417, 421, 423, 432
Nellie May (merchant vessel) 493
Nelson 470
Nemesis (warship) 148
Nereid 134
New Hope 120
Niagara 397
Niger 437
Nisus (warship) 118, 124, 212, 256
North America 68, 91
North West 311, 315
Nye 378n63, 379, 382–84

Obed Mitchell 189, 206
Ocean 436, 437

Octavia 226
Osceola II 193, 312

Pacific 148, 202, 212, 301f., 309, 317, 320, 326, 339f., 348, 486
Palestine 260f., 265
Para 320
Pavilion 178n103, 360, 392
Pedro Varela 178, 356, 382–85, 406, 422, 424, 431, 437, 463, 485
Pembroke 45
Pénélope 121
Penobscot 235
Peru (merchant vessel) 270
Petrel (merchant vessel) 378
Petrel 270, 397, 436
Phebe 50, 69, 101
Phoenix 273f.
Pioneer 315, 397, 437
Platina 216, 394
Pocahontas 71, 98
Polly 45, 446, 460
Port de Paix
President 436
President II 387
Prince Edward (merchant vessel) 67, 112
Prince Town 69
Princess 124
Princess of Wales (sealing vessel) 89n127, 90, 95, 99n205, 461

Queen of the West (merchant vessel) 234

Rainbow 436
Rambler 212, 234
Ranger 66
Reaper 17, 235n124, 345
Regent Packet (merchant vessel) 111
Renomee 447
Rhine 256
Richmond II 468
Rising Sun 485
Robert Morrison 436
Rochester 45
Roscoe 231, 321
Roswell King 436

S. R. Soper 339
Sally Ann 198
Sally Anne 256
Salomon 280
Samuel and Thomas 425 Fig. 36, 426, 428 Fig. 37, 430, 487
Sandwich 66, 77
Santa Teresa (merchant vessel) 411
São Cristóvão (expedition vessel) 78
Sarah 120, 143, 145–47, 434
Sarah Louisa 466
Savoia (packet vessel) 497 Fig. 42, 501
Scorpion (warship) 124
Scorpion 471
Sea Eagle (merchant vessel) 378
Sea Flower 447
Sea Fox 276, 357, 419, 423, 476, 482
Sea Ranger 397
Seine 437
Sir James Ross 244
Slacombe
Smyrna 316
Soleil (slave ship) 224
Sonnesteijn 43
South America 467
South Carolina 120, 235
Splendid 319
St. Peter 264
Stafford 146, 397, 437
Star (expedition vessel) 69, 83, 101
Stephania 74, 91, 94n171, 433, 436
Sullivan 61, 403
Sunbeam 40, 61, 72, 73, 94, 187, 195, 343, 368, 389, 391, 394, 396, 437, 449, 451, 465 Fig. 40, 494
Superior 56
Surprise 244
Susan (merchant vessel) 107
Swallow 244
Swan 53

T. Towner 485
Thomas Pope 244, 279f., 311, 353
Thriver 485
Triumph 101
Trois Amis 69

Tropic Bird 431, 437
Two Brothers 474

U. D. 436
Union 68, 73, 95n173
United States 261, 280
USS Dale (warship) 275, 276 Fig. 29, 505
USS Jamestown 466
USS Portsmouth (warship) 487

Valkyria 494
Varnum H. Hill 436
Vesta 399 f.
Vigilant 327
Vrijheijt 43

Wanderer 59–62, 64 Fig. 4, 178, 188, 363, 390, 483
Washington Freeman 436
Wave 233
William 122
William A. Graber 485, 494
William and Ann 48
William Badger 266
William Penn 123
Willis 436

Yarmouth 45
Young Phenix 311, 436

Zone 486

Places Index

|Awa-!haos 88, 104, 105, 110–112
ǂKhîsa-ǁgubus 83, 86, 92, 93, 96, 98, 107

Ambriz 366, 394
Ana de Chaves 399
Angola 16, 34, 40, 45, 49, 58–61, 71, 84, 114, 194, 195n185, 196n191, 335, 353, 363 f., 366, 379, 387, 389, 392n142, 394 f., 402, 408
Angra Pequeña 69 f., 71n35, 78n70, 96n181, 100–02, 105, 150
Anjouan 13, 34, 54, 117, 198, 223, *239–278*, 326, 330, 339
Annobón 34, 59, 179, 367, 395, 398, *399–442*, 463, 504, 506 f.
Anomabu 4

Baía de Lagoa see Delagoa Bay
Baía dos Tigres 49, 59, 114, 366 f.
Bassas da India 190
Bayonne 42
Benguela 366, 373, 393
Bight of Sofala 49, 125
Boa Vista 444, 447, 447n18, 449, 460, 469–471, 483
Bourbon 221, 226, 262, 280, 319
Brava 34, 60, *443–502*

Cabinda 34, 360, *362–398*, 433, 463, 504 f.
Cameroon 45, 412, 438
Cape Lopez 404, 442
Cape of Good Hope 6, 41, 42, 48, 51, 58, 78, 150 f., 211, 290 f.
Cape Town 6, 25n81, 26, 35, 67, 76, 94n168, 101, 101n218, 103, 105–113, 116, 118, 134, 140, 146, 151, 155, 199, 215, 237, 249 f., 256, 299, 303, 320, 326, 328, 330n27, 344, 352
Cape Verde 6, 26, 45, 62, *443–502*, 504
Chioua 371 f., 381
Comoros (Comoro Islands) 34, 53 f., *239–278*, 291, 297

Delagoa Bay 34, 48–50, 62, 102, *117–155*, 238, 280 f., 505
Domoni (Anjouan) 245–248, 250, 252
Durban 484

Equatorial Guinea 408, 408n33, 422
Equimina 366
Europa Island 190

False Bay 49
Fernando Póo 409–412, 438, 441, 449
Fogo 344, 403, 444 f., 448–50, 452, 454, 463, 469, 473 f., 488, 498 f.
Fort Dauphin see Tôlanaro
Furna (Brava) *443–502*, 504, 506

Gabon 43, 49, 58, 343, 366, 402, 404
Ghana 4, 25n81, 339
Gulf of Guinea 44 f., 48 f., 58 f., 62, 367, 370, 399 f., 403 f., 407, 410–414, 420 f., 438, 440–442
Grande Comore 248
Guinea 45, 339, 453
Guinea-Bissau 453, 460

Ichaboe 65n1, 105 f.
Île Bonaparte see Réunion
Île Bourbon 221, 226, 262, 280, 319
Île de France see Mauritius
Île Sainte-Marie 6 f., 212, 280
Îles de Los 339
Ilha de Moçambique 126, 245, 249, 253
Inhaca 119, 126–128, 130 f.

Jamestown (St. Helena) 17n49, 25n81, 106, 327, 389 f., 399 f., 487
Johanna see Anjouan

La Réunion 25n81, 54, 224–226, 249, 262, 280, 285
Le Havre 53, 71n37

Liberia 25n81, 394, 476
Loango 370, 373
Lourenço Marques 25, 25n81, 121n20, 126, 132–137, 139, 143, 146, 150, 153, 155
Luanda 25, 25n81, 364, 366, 372 f., 379, 381, 388, 392–398, 430

Mábana (Annobón) 439
Madagascar 6, 13, 25n81, 26, 34, 39n5, 40, 48 f., 53 f., 58, 176n94, 198n206, 204, *211–238*, 239, 244–252, 254, 276, 280, 282, 290–292, 297, 320, 329, 337, 340, 343, 348, 503
Mahajanga 223 f., 253
Mahé 251n81, 53, 331, 334f, 337n59, 340, 349, 353
Maio 446n10, 447, 449, 460, 464, 469, 472 f.
Majunga 212
Malemba 370
Maputo see Delagoa Bay
Mauritius 6, 25n81, 26, 34, 54, 106, 108, 138 f., 195n186, 221, 224, 249, 252, 255, 262, 268, *279–323*, 327, 506
Mayotte 247–249, 252, 256
Mayumba 366
Mbanza Ngoyo 369, 371
Mindelo 463, 463n70, 465, 469 f., 475, 487
Moçâmedes 113, 113n271, 335 f., 353, 366, 379, 392n142, 394
Mohéli 247–249, 252
Mozambique 25n81, 26, 48 f., *117–155*, 239, 252 f., 262, 290 f.
Mutsamudu (Anjouan) *239–278*, 505

Ndame 412, 438
Nosy Be 212, 224
Nova Sintra 445, 452, 493
Nzwani see Anjouan

Otjikango 110
Otjimbingwe 94, 112

Port Dauphin (Tôlanaro) 212, 340, 345
Port Louis (Mauritius) 6, 25, 25n81, 26, 34, 54, 237, 250, 257, 268, *279–323*, 337, 341, 351, 354, 506
Port Natal 136, 152
Porto Rico see Chioua
Portsmouth 71, 102, 232, 243, 311, 314, 315, 318, 331, 336
Possession Island 65, 105n234
Praia 447, 453, 463 f., 468–473, 475, 487
Príncipe 58, 398, 400, 408 f., 412, 460

Quelimane 139 f.

Ribeira Grande 452 f., 464

Saint Augustin 34, 176n94, *211–238*, 504 f., 507
Saint-Denis 25n81, 250
Sainte-Marie see Île Sainte-Marie
Sal Rei 470
Saldanha Bay 6, 49
San Antonio de Palé (Annobón) *399–442*, 505
Sandwich Harbor 97
Santiago 25, 25n81, 445, 447–450, 452 f., 456, 461, 462n59, 463, 467–469, 471 f.
Santo Antão 444, 467n87, 474 f., 483 f.
Santo António 399, 405n21
São Nicolau 446n10, 449, 464, 479, 482, 487
São Tomé 58, 399 f., 404, 408 f., 412, 442, 460, 460n52
São Vicente 443, 448 f., 463, 468, 472, 478
Senegal 25n81, 45, 346, 453
Seychelles 25n81, 53 f., 117, 193, 215, 243, 246, 248, 257, 262, 281, 331, 349, 354–360
Sierra Leone 25n81, 453
Simulambuco 371, 375n52, 381
Skeleton Coast 74, 193

South Africa 13, 25n81, 35, 41, 64, 78, 85n107, 115, 130, 132, 152
St. Helena 60, 103, 390, 396
St. Helena Bay 49

Table Bay 42, 49
Taffe 165n38, 371, 376, 380 f.
Tôlanaro (Port Dauphin) 212
Tulear 221 f., 228

Victoria (Mahé) 331, 335, 352

Walvis Bay 14, 34, 41, 43, 46, 48–50, 62, *65–116*, 121, 125, 150, 238, 281, 366 f., 398, 504 f.
Windhoek 103f.

Xefina 126, 136

Zanzibar 25n81, 26, 35, 53, 117, 152, 198n205, 198n206, 215, 243, 253, 256 f., 262, 268–270, 282, 291, 327 f., 335 f., 337n59, 349, 351, 353, 355 f., 358, 404

www.ingramcontent.com/pod-product-compliance
Lightning Source LLC
Chambersburg PA
CBHW051532230426
43669CB00015B/2570